Ate the Dog Yeste

# Ate the Dog Yesterday

Maritime Casualties, Calamities and Catastrophes

by Graham Faiella

Whittles Publishing

Published by
**Whittles Publishing Ltd.,**
Dunbeath,
Caithness, KW6 6EG,
Scotland, UK

**www.whittlespublishing.com**

ISBN 978-184995-089-3

Printed by Charlesworth Press, Wakefield

# CONTENTS

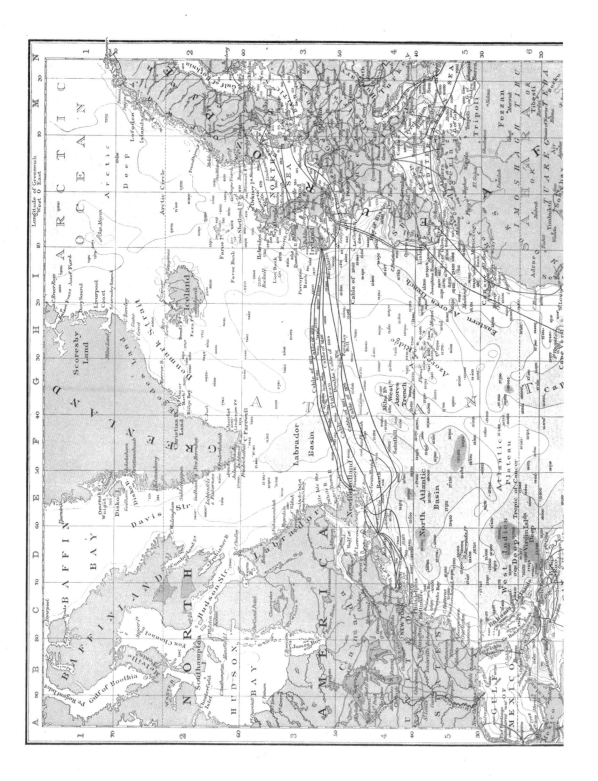

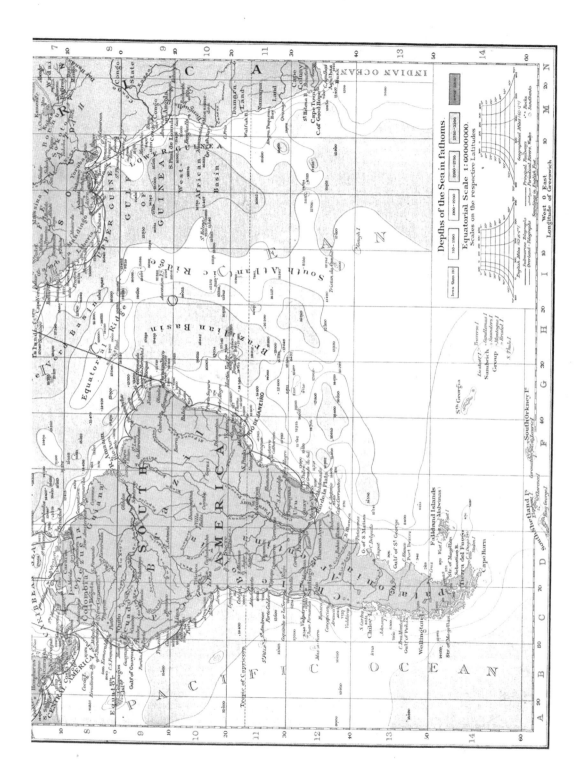

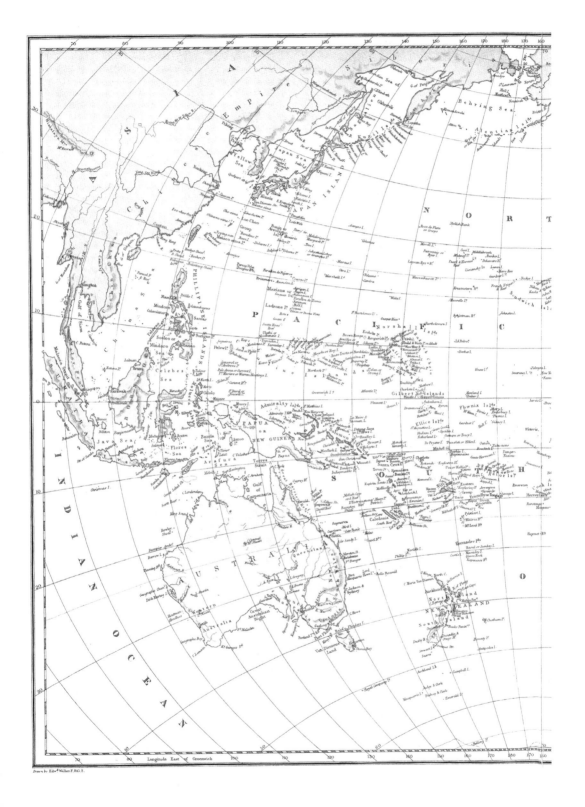

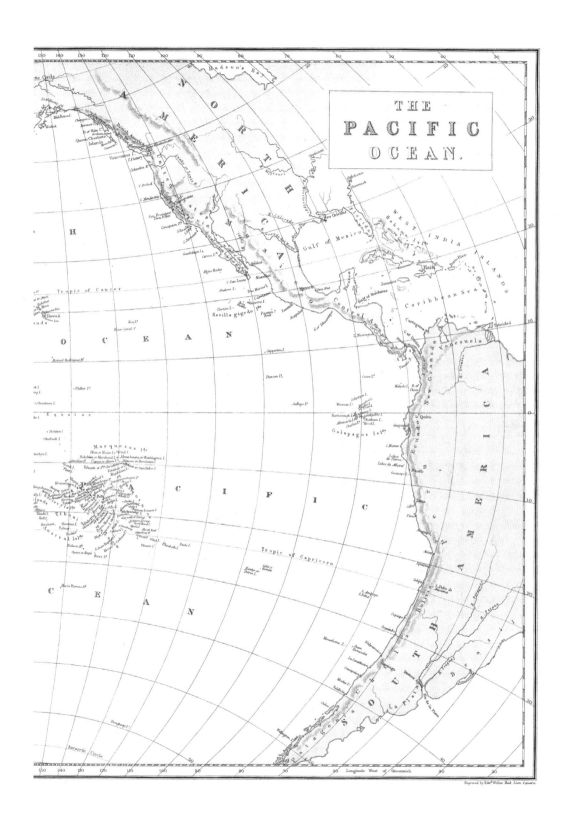

# THE PACIFIC OCEAN.

Engraved by Edw.d Weller Red. Lion Square.

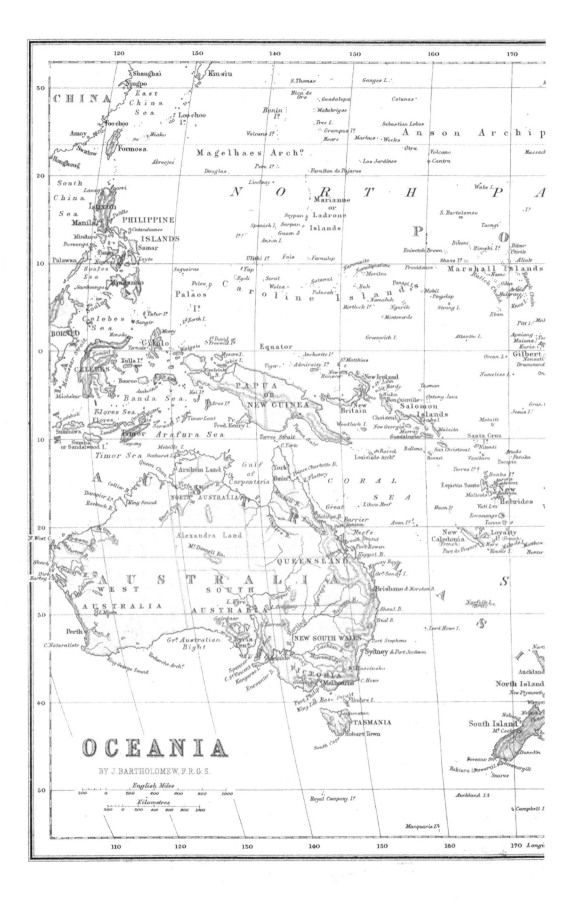

# OCEANIA

BY J. BARTHOLOMEW, F.R.G.S.

English Miles

Kilometres

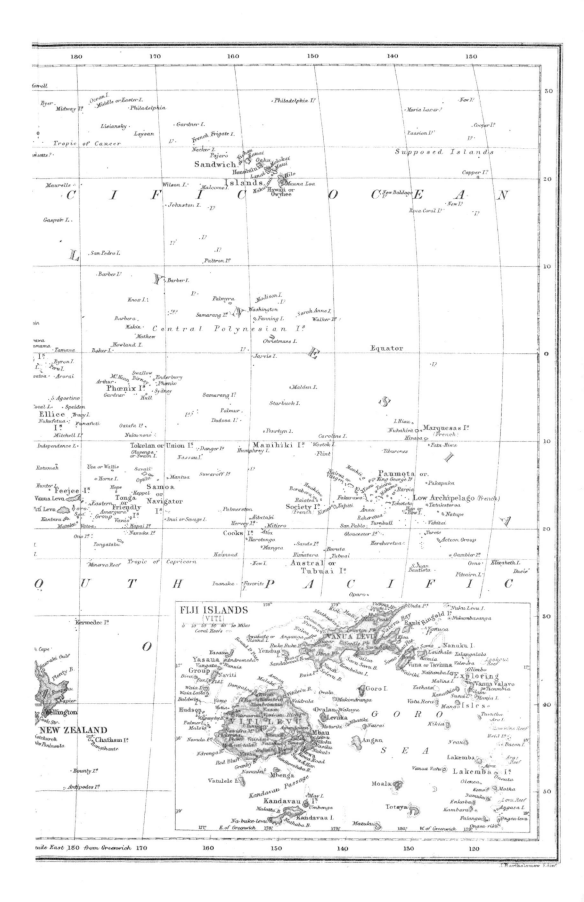

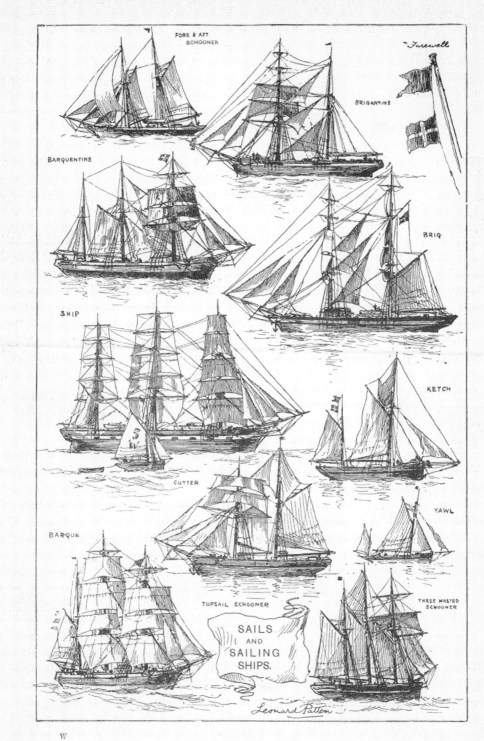

FORE & AFT SCHOONER

"Farewell

BRIGANTINE

BARQUENTINE

BRIG

SHIP

KETCH

CUTTER

YAWL

BARQUE

TOPSAIL SCHOONER

SAILS AND SAILING SHIPS.

THREE MASTED SCHOONER

Leonard Patten

W

# PREFACE

This is the story of the true-life dramas and chronicles of the perils and misfortunes of numerous deep-sea sailing ships and sailors of the late 19th and early 20th centuries; of the constant dangers they faced; and of the battles they waged, and all too often lost, against the hazards of the sea.

Shortly before a visit to Bermuda by Edward, Prince of Wales in October 1920, the hulks of two deep-sea sailing ships, the British *Emily A Davies* and the Norwegian-flagged *Norrköping*, were beached together at a small cove known as Black Bay in the parish of Southampton of that mid-Atlantic island. The rusting hulks were considered unsightly in the harbour at St. George's, at the east end of Bermuda, where they had lain for more than a decade. Better, it was thought, to hide them away and out of sight of royal sensibilities at the inconspicuous little Black Bay.

Both vessels had been brought into Bermuda as casualties of heavy winter weather in the North Atlantic: the *Emily A Davies* in the winter of 1901–02, and the *Norrköping* in February 1908. Both had been three-masted iron barques. Both were built in the great shipbuilding centre of Sunderland, on the northeast coast of England: the *Norrköping* (launched as *Runnymede*) in 1869, the *Emily A Davies* in 1876.

Both ships hauled their common, often dirty and sometimes dangerous freight across all the oceans of the world for the best part of three decades. Thousands of other deep-sea commercial sailing ships of that era did the same.

Life was tough for 19th century sailors in sail. Shipboard work was hard. It was often and routinely dangerous. Crew members could be and frequently were maimed or even killed by the sea, or by any number of routine dangers they faced while working their ships. And it was the same for crews in all merchant sailing ships of that time: nothing out of the ordinary, except for the extraordinary hardships that sailors bore as nothing more nor less than their duty to obey their captains and drive their ships to a safe port to discharge or take on cargoes.

The Bermudian historian William Zuill wrote in his 1946 guidebook *Bermuda Journey* that Black Bay was hideously marred by two disintegrating iron hulks.

But the *Emily A Davies* and the *Norrköping*, like countless other sailing ships – and sailing men (and some women) – of their time, had lives much like the rest of us: mostly routine, highlighted occasionally by incidents of tragedy or coincidence, but generally unacknowledged, unremarked and, to the rest of the world, unremarkable.

These, amongst untold many others, are their stories.

# NOTE

All the extract narratives that follow are from the **Casualties** columns and pages of the daily shipping newspaper *Lloyd's List*. All date from within the lifespan of the two Black Bay ships, from 1869 up to the early years of the 20th century – the heyday of deep-sea commercial sail, transitioning into the steamship era.

The dated extracts are for the issue of *Lloyd's List* in which they appeared. Any other supplementary material is dated and by-lined according to its source.

PLATE CLXX.

SHIP,
TO ILLUSTRATE TERMS APPLIED TO THE
SAILS, AND RUNNING RIGGING.

BLACKIE & SON, GLASGOW EDINBURGH & LONDON

# PART I

Of Sailors, Ships and the Sea

# 1  Lloyd's and Lloyd's List

The daily shipping newspaper *Lloyd's List* has recorded news of ships and shipping, and the worldwide port movements of merchant ships, since the late-1600s. The title *Lloyd's List* derives from Edward Lloyd's coffee house in London that he opened in 1691 and which became a meeting place for shipping merchants and insurance underwriters.

In 1692 Lloyd began to publish a weekly report of shipping news with the rather ungainly title of "Ships Arrived at and Departed from several Ports of England, as I have Account of them in London...[and] An Account of What English Shipping and Foreign Ships for England, I hear of in Foreign Ports".

From the 1770s this weekly report became abbreviated as *Lloyd's List*. From 1 July 1837 it began to be published six days a week, which it has continued to do to this day. In July 1884 it was merged with the *Shipping and Mercantile Gazette* (published since 1838), becoming the *Shipping Gazette and Lloyd's List*. (In reports, this was commonly cited by abbreviation to the *Shipping Gazette*.)

(The association of marine insurance underwriters who met at Mr. Lloyd's coffee house was incorporated as the Corporation of Lloyd's, or Lloyd's of London, in 1871. From June 1914 the Corporation took over the publication of *Lloyd's List* until 1973, after which it was published by Lloyd's of London Press Ltd.)

The voyage passages of the two Black Bay ships, along with thousands of other vessels, were recorded in *Lloyd's List* as a series of their movements from port to port: vessels were reported arrived at a particular port, on a particular date, from another port; or departed from a port, on a certain date, to sail to the next port as named. (A *passage* was a run from one port to another. A *voyage* was, technically, a complete run of passages from and back to her start port or nearby, which might take three years or more. In practice, however, the terms were used interchangeably to mean any run from one port to another – although a passage could never be a round-trip or multi-port voyage.)

Each recorded movement of a vessel was listed under a particular port of arrival or departure, or sometimes a waypoint along the coast of Britain or Ireland (Gravesend, for example, at the entrance of the Thames estuary for ships coming from and going to London) or elsewhere (the island of St Helena in the South Atlantic was a busy mid-ocean waypoint for ships passing by to report themselves there).

The information on a vessel included all or some of the following: her name; the type of vessel she was, in brackets (for example, a *barque*, abbreviated as "barq." or "bq."; *schooner*, abbreviated as "schr"; "brigant." for *brigantine* (and "brig", kept as is for *brig*); or "ship", which meant *full-rigged ship*). This was preceded sometimes by her nationality or port of registry, most commonly abbreviated, such as "Br." or "Brit." for British, "Ital." for Italian, "Fr." For French, "Ger." for German, "Aus." for Austrian – because Austria-Hungary was then a sea power - or "Amer." for American; and usually the surname of her master (captain), such as:

*Emily A. Davies* (Br. barq.), Mendus

Most reports included the port from which the vessel's voyage had begun, and the port for which she was bound. A further notation might occasionally specify the cargo the vessel carried, such as "(timber)", "(wheat)", "(rice)" or "(logwood)".

Steamships

Steamships, or "steamers", were identified with the notation "(s)" or "(ss)" after their name. Towards the end of the 19th century steam took over from sail as a more competitive and reliable form of sea transport. By that time steamships had increasingly predominated amongst the shipping reports in *Lloyd's List*.

For the year 1869 *Lloyd's List* reported 10,359 casualties for sailing vessels and just 1,247 for steamers. On the threshold of the 20th century, in 1898 there were 218,016 men employed in British-registered merchant ships. Of that total, 168,158 (77%) were in steamships; just under 50,000 (23%) were in sail.

A tabulation of all merchant shipping in the years 1870–1874 showed both the domination of British shipping and the predominance of sailing vessels around that time, summarised as follows:

**Mercantile Navies of the World 1870–1874**

|  | 1870 | (Avg. tons*) | 1874 | (Avg. tons*) |
|---|---|---|---|---|
| *Sailing Vessels* |  |  |  |  |
| **Number** | 59,518 | (270) | 56,289 | (258) |
| *Of which:* |  |  |  |  |
| British | 23,165 | (302) | 20,538 | (262) |
| American | 7,025 | (341) | 6,869 | (318) |
| French | 4,968 | (180) | 3,780 | (195) |
| German | 4,320 | (242) | 3,483 | (246) |
| Norwegian | 3,652 | (271) | 4,464 | (302) |
| Italian | 3,395 | (267) | 4,343 | (283) |

| Tonnage: | | | | |
|---|---|---|---|---|
| British | 6,993,153 | | 5,383,763 | |
| American | 2,400,607 | | 2,181,659 | |
| | **1870** | (**Avg. tons\***) | **1874** | (**Avg. tons\***) |
| German | 1,046,044 | | 852,789 | |
| Norwegian | 989,882 | | 1,349,138 | |
| Italian | 907,570 | | 1,227,816 | |

*Steamships*

| **Number** | 4,132 | 5,365 |
|---|---|---|
| *Of which:* | | |
| British | 2,426 | 3,002 |
| American | 597 | 613 |
| French | 288 | 315 |
| **Tonnage:** | | |
| British | 1,651,767 | 3,015,773 |
| American | 513,792 | 768,724 |
| French | 212,976 | 318,757 |

\* tons per vessel, average

**Source:** *Lloyd's List*, 4th and 13th February 1875

By the end of the 19th century very few commercial sailing ships were being built by British yards, compared with the number of new steamships. In 1900 just 28 sea-going commercial sailing vessels were launched by British shipyards compared with 664 steamships. A brief analysis of the world's merchant shipping fleet by *Lloyd's List* in July 1901 noted that, in the three years from 1898 to 1901 "there has been an average annual increase of, roughly speaking, 1,500,000 tons of steam, and this against an average annual decrease in sailing ships of about 150,000 tons". It goes on to remark that "To suggest…that we have merely substituted steam for sail is absurd". The increase in steam shipping reflected, it noted, "the provision of much more efficient instruments of ocean navigation than would have been the case ten or twenty years back". Steamships were clearly the more "efficient instruments of ocean navigation". Sail could never compete on those terms.

The Black Bay ships sailed through the heyday of merchant sail and into the transition era of steamship transport. Their demise in the early 1900s coincided with the final flickering years of merchant sailing fleets worldwide. By the time both ships were beached to rest, and rust, forever in Black Bay in Bermuda, big commercial sailing ships were rare on the oceans of the world; steam by then had become queen of the seas.

## REPORTING TO LLOYD'S

Lloyd's agents reported on the arrival and departure of vessels, and any other information relating to such vessels, at all the main ports of the world. There was plenty of room for error in those early days of telegraphic communication, and at such far-flung locations. The names

THE LATE STORMS: THE "LOSS-BOOK," A SKETCH AT LLOYD'S.

of masters of vessels could be misspelled variously and for a variety of reasons. At foreign ports a busy port agent whose mother tongue was often not English might easily take down a name incorrectly. The name of a non-English master might be difficult to spell. The name might become misspelled when it was transmitted to *Lloyd's List* by telegraph, or recorded incorrectly by the clerk writing up the reports. Everything was done by hand. There was always plenty of room for error.

(Radiotelegraphy was invented and developed by Guglielmo Marconi [1874–1937] in the late 19th century. The first Marconi radiotelegraph equipment was installed on merchant ships from the early 1900s.)

Where a ship was reported "by tel." it meant by telegraph (or "cable"), which was the most efficient means of reporting back to London. In many cases the date of a report in *Lloyd's List* might be several weeks or even months after the actual event was recorded: if the report was sent by mail, it had to go by ship. Depending on where the port was, it could take several months or more to arrive at London. By that time, too, the vessel might have already been reported elsewhere more quickly (by telegraph, for example), so that, in some cases, the chronology of a vessel's movements appeared to be inconsistent.

There were also gaps in the record of port movements of ships identified in *Lloyd's List*. In some cases a vessel would be reported to have sailed for a certain port, and there would be no later report of her arrival at or departure from that port. This was because some small ports would not have had a Lloyd's agent to report arrivals and sailings. The next listing for the vessel would therefore be from the next port at which her arrival was reported there by the Lloyd's agent.

When a ship departed from the Port of London her movement was recorded under "London Customs" (or "Custom-House") Entries", with the note "Cleared Outwards" on a certain date, followed by her port of destination, the ship's name, her master, the berth she was leaving from, and the name of the shipping agent. The ship *Runnymede*, for example, made many voyages from London to Australia from "B700 Sth WID", which meant Berth 700 South in the West India Docks ("WID"). The final notation (if included) was the name of the ship's agent.

Ships were regularly reported by certain shore stations, especially at English Channel ports such as Plymouth, Deal or Dover. They recorded the vessel as "passed", or "passed west", or "passed east", or "arrived off" the port, to indicate where the ship was in relation to her outward or inward voyage. If the vessel was coming from London, she was reported as "from the river". "The river" was the name for the part of the River Thames around the London docks in the East End from or to which most merchant ships sailed. Sailoring people used to call this part of the Thames "the London River", which *Lloyd's List* reports abbreviated to "the river" or "the River".

Ships sometimes anchored for a day or so at Channel ports such as Deal in Kent or Falmouth in Cornwall, to wait for a favourable tide or winds, or, more unusually, to take shelter from stormy weather. Gravesend on the Kent coast at the Thames Estuary was the first port most often cited for ships going to or from London. Vessels from "the river" entered the North Sea at Gravesend which was the true start of their ocean-going passage, especially for sailing vessels which were towed down river by a tug.

# 2  Voyages and Voyagings

The voyage from England to Australia or New Zealand was one of the most common routes followed by British 19th century sailing ships, taking British emigrants to the new colonies. These voyages down the North and South Atlantic, around (but well to the south of) the Cape of Good Hope and across the southern Indian Ocean usually took around three months. Anything less than 90 days was considered fast. If a vessel took a long time to get through the calms of the doldrums around the equator in the Atlantic, the voyage could be, and frequently was prolonged to well over 100 days.

Sailing ships made good time in the strong westerly winds from the South Atlantic and across the Indian and Southern Oceans. There they achieved their best speeds "running their easting down" through the Roaring Forties, between 40° and 50° south latitude. The return voyage from Australia back to England was usually eastward around Cape Horn, a longer passage which therefore generally took somewhat longer than the outward passage. (Vessels heading back to European waters from the Far East took the Cape of Good Hope route, across the Indian Ocean, which was the shortest passage for them but with the danger of being struck by cyclones at certain times of the year.)

The return voyage from Australia and New Zealand was usually, though not invariably across the desolate wastes of the far southern reaches of the Pacific and around Cape Horn. Westerly gales and hurricane force storms of the Furious Fifties, between 50° and 60° south latitude, drove them on to round Cape Horn (at lat. 56° S) into the Atlantic. It was a typically boisterous route but with the advantage of reliable and usually strong following winds from the west, an important consideration for square-riggers which did not sail well into the wind. For many ships sailing in the Australia and New Zealand trade a full return voyage was a complete circumnavigation of the globe.

Passenger ships in particular, however, often returned to the United Kingdom the same way they had come out, via the Cape of Good Hope and up the South and North Atlantic. This was a somewhat more benign "trade winds" route. Short stops were often made at Cape Town, the islands of St Helena, Ascension or Madeira, for the benefit and enjoyment of the passengers. Sailing ships that took this route headed north into the Indian Ocean monsoon winds regions to get around the Cape of Good Hope, rather than beat back against the westerlies, storms and cyclones of the southern Indian Ocean.

The *Torrens* was a famously fast three-masted composite-built ship of 1,276 tons, constructed by James Laing, at Sunderland, in 1875, for Capt. H.R. Angel, her principal owner. On his return voyages from Adelaide to London, Capt. Angel usually called at Cape Town, St. Helena and Ascension, for the pleasure of the *Torrens'* passengers. Capt. Angel retired from the sea in 1890 and died, aged 93, in 1923. One of his sons, Capt. Falkland Angel, took over command of the *Torrens* in 1896. Under him the ship recorded her greatest ever day's run of 370 miles (in 1897).

## 10 July 1885

**Maritime Intelligence**

Weather and Navigation

London, July 9.- The Torrens, Angel, from Adelaide, arrived in the river, reports:-

"Sailed from Adelaide on March 21, with a full cargo and passengers to the number of 70. Fine weather prevailed along the Australian coast to rounding Cape Leuwin [southwest corner of Australia], across the Indian Ocean, and into Table Bay [Cape Town], where we arrived on May 14. Sailed again on the 16th, fine weather prevailing, and anchored at St. Helena on the 27th, where we remained three days, giving the passengers plenty of time to enjoy the scenery of that beautiful island.

Starting from there on the 30th we reached the Island of Ascension on June 6, and remained 24 hours, bringing with us some delicious turtle, which proved a great treat to our passengers, particularly the invalids. Crossed the line [equator] on June 11, and quickly picked up the NE trades in lat. 7 N. These trades proved good and carried us up to lat. 32 N, and the easterly wind still continuing, carried us up to lat. 45 N and long. 32 W.

On June 30 passed a large fleet of ships, homeward bound, between lat. 40 N and 45 N, and long. 35 W, and again in lat. 47 N, long. 29 W, July 2, reporting variable winds and calms for many days. The barometer for the past week has been standing at 30 70 (the highest I have ever seen). On July 5, in lat. 48 N, long. 20 W, strong south wind, going 14 knots an hour, and on one day made 332 knots [nautical miles]. Signalised the Lizard at 3 p.m. on the 7th, and came up channel with a fair south wind, and reached the London Docks at noon on July 9, after a most pleasant and successful voyage."

(For the narrative of the *Torrens'* collision with an iceberg in the southern Indian Ocean, see **Ice!, 11 March 1899**)

## CAPE HORN PASSAGES

The Cape Horn route tended to be a rather livelier passage, especially in the southern hemisphere winter (June – September).

## 28 Sept 1895

**Maritime Intelligence**

Ballachulish.- London, Sept. 28.- A letter from the captain of the Ballachulish, from Caleta Buena [nitrate port just north of Iquique, Chile], at Plymouth, states:-

"Ballachulish had a fearful time; 45 days out was in lat. 59 20 S, long. 67 W [ie., due south of Cape Horn], frozen up fore and aft. This was about 27th – 28th June. Crew mostly all frozen. Had only 8 to 10 or 12 people, all told, to work the ship with. One day mercury 24 deg below zero. This was 7th July. Had frightfully hard weather off Cape Horn."

## 3 May 1881

Report of the Wagoola, Hurburgh, from Hobart Town, arrived at Gravesend May 1:

"Left Hobart Jan. 20, with a gale at WSW, and a heavy confused sea running. Carried the wind from the SW quarter for 12 days after sailing, and it terminated in a whole gale at S by E, and from thence to the Horn had dirty, unsettled weather from NW and NE, with a low glass [barometer]; and on Feb 15, in lat. 56 44 S, and long. 81 4 W, the wind shifted quickly from N into S, and blew furiously for 12 hours, the glass rising nearly 1 ½ inch during the gale. On Feb. 17 sighted the Island of Diego Ramirez [near Cape Horn].

Had moderate NW weather to 31 S, when the wind settled into N and NNW, and blew hard for some 10 days prior to getting the SE trades, and during the first four days with heavy thunder and lightning, and vicious squalls. Both the SE and NE trades proved fine and fresh, and carried an E wind between the trades. Crossed the Equator in long. 25 W on March 22. Had nine days very light winds after parting with NE trades.

Passed between Flores and Fayal [Azores] on April 14, and on the 16th a heavy gale set in from the north, and since that date up to April 25 had gales and strong winds from N to ENE, attended with a heavy ENE sea. Sighted Cape Finisterre on April 25, when the wind came in westerly. Sighted Ushant on the 29th, and the Wight [Isle of Wight] on the 30th, wind westerly and very unsteady.

On April 11 the steward, George Marchant, died, apparently from sunstroke."

## 6 May 1881

Report of the barque Scottish Lassie, of London, Le Couteur, from San Francisco, arrived at Falmouth May 3:-

"Sailed Dec 11 [1880], pilot leaving ship at 1 PM, barques Snowdon and West Glen in company. Light NW winds and thick fog (at times quite dense) to the 14th. Favourable trades took us to lat. 8 N, long. 124 W, when a sudden and heavy gale from the east set in with thunder and lightning, which lasted six hours, during which several sails were split. SE trades set in Dec. 16, in lat. 6 N, long. 123 39 W, and proved very favourable.

Crossed Equator in long. 128 W on Dec. 31. To Jan. 6, in lat. 16 S, long. 128 W, pleasant and moderate trades; light northerly to NE winds set in, followed by light airs and calms, with much rain, lasting to the 15th (having only sailed 569 miles in past nine days), which continued to the 30th, in lat. 45 S, long. 122 W, with fair weather. NW to SW winds then prevailed variously to and around the Cape [Horn] until Feb. 27, in lat. 30 S, long. 32 W. Experienced a very heavy gale on Feb. 17, in lat. 52 S, long. 56 W, with a very high and dangerous sea running; ship's decks frequently filled to the top of topgallant rails, but ship behaving well throughout.

From Feb. 27 light northerly breezes set in, lasting until the SE trades were met, March 16, in lat. 14 S, long 25 ½ W. A very great number of ships were seen in company, also several bound southwards. The Equator was passed March 23, in long. 27 W, we being 102 days out [from San Francisco]. Lost the SE trades in lat. 3 28 N, long. 27 W, March 25, encountering NE trades same time. They proved of moderate strength, with fine weather, and carried ship to lat. 21 44 N, long. 38 45 W, by the 5th April. From this date to the 12th calms and very light airs prevailed, with fine weather, total absence of squalls. A great many ships seen in company; also others bound west. In these nine days we only logged 394 miles, about 44 per day.

Light winds from NW were then met, except 15th to 18th, when they blew a fresh gale, again falling light to the 20th, when we sighted the island of St. Michael's [Sao Miguel, Azores]; the wind still kept very light, and hauled more northerly still, with an exceedingly high barometer. On the 26th the marine bar. [barometer] stood at 30 650 [30.65 inches]. A fall in the bar. brought moderate W to SW winds, and we reached the edge of soundings, 200 miles west of Cape Clear, when the wind shifted to NE, and drove us towards the English Channel. I deem it worthy of remark that during our passage (up to soundings) we have sighted no less than 107 ships."

## 21 Feb 1883

Liverpool, Feb. 17.- The Sarah Bell, from Portland (Oregon), arrived here, reports:-

"On Oct. 17 [1882], at noon, sailed from Astoria [Oregon]. At 3 p.m., tug and pilot left the ship, wind southerly, and increasing; midnight, hard gale, with heavy rain. 18th, at 7 a.m., wind shifted to the northward, and continued light from that quarter until Nov. 7, lat. 7 30 N, long. 119 W, when we got the SE trades, which proved strong all through, and were lost Nov. 21, lat. 30 S, long. 126 40 W.

The wind then set in to the northward, and continued from that quarter principally until Nov. 30, lat 46 35 S, long. 107 W, when we got the beginning of a hurricane commencing at N and ending at W, the most violent part lasting 18 hours; the barometer fell from 30 70 to 29 [inches]. The wind after this blow took a more westerly direction, and continued so. Dec. 9, at 6 p.m., we passed close to Diego Ramirez, and saw a schooner anchored on the NE side of the island, which would probably be a sealer.

The next morning we passed close to Cape Horn, wind northerly and light. 11th, at noon, passed Staten Island. 13th, wind W (true), hard gale, with violent squalls and high seas, ship running under lowertopsails and foresails. At 11 45 p.m. Albert Tamblad, A.B., fell from the maintopgallantyard; he struck the lee topgallant rail when he fell and then dropped overboard, and as the ship was running in a heavy gale with mountainous sea we were unable to render him any assistance.

The wind now set in to the S.W., and continued strong from that quarter until 19th, lat. 38 S, long. 36 W. 21st, lat. 34 02 S, long. 35 26 W, had a fresh gale from the eastward, lasting 12 hours, then light variable northerly until the 25th, lat. 29 53 S, long. 32 09 W, when we had a hard gale from NW by N, with incessant rain and very high sea, last 10 hours very heavy. Then the wind shifted to the southward with fine clear weather, and veered into the northward, and continued from that quarter until Jan. 3, lat 21 28 S, long. 25 23 W, when we got the SE trades.

On the 9th, at 5 p.m., we passed in sight of Fernando Noronha [island off northeast Brazil], and on the 11th crossed the Equator in long. 31 55 W, and lost the SE trades the same day. Across the variables we had the wind mostly from the NE. Jan. 14, in lat. 3 N, long. 33 45 W, got the NE trades, which proved very northerly and very strong all through, at times amounting to a fresh gale, with violent squalls, and high sea. On the 27th, in lat. 20 30 N, long. 53 50 W, lost the NE trades, and then we had a few days variable wind, and then got the beginning of a course of most unsettled and stormy weather, which continued with us until arriving in port. The wind was from NW to SW, at times blowing with hurricane force with mountainous high cross sea.

On the 11th February at 5 30 p.m., wind SW, blowing a hurricane, rounded to under the lee clew of the lower maintopsail, and continued hove to for 30 hours, the wind and sea both so heavy that we were unable to run; after which it abated for a little time, and we were able to run for a few hours, when the wind again increased with renewed violence from SW, and we again had to heave to for 30 hours; the last time we hove to our position was SW by W (true), off Cape Clear [southern Ireland] 150 miles. 14th, we sighted Cape Clear, and had fair winds up channel. Arrived in Liverpool Feb. 16. Passage from Portland to Liverpool 122 days."

## 21 Feb 1889

Sharpness [on the River Severn], Feb. 19.- The Eaton Hall, from San Francisco, [sailed] Oct. 8, arrived here, reports:-

"Had light airs and fog for 36 hours before clearing Farallones [Farallon Islands, 43 km off San Francisco Bay]. Had moderate to light NE trades from lat. 30 N to lat. 10 N, where we lost them. Took SE trades in lat. 5 N and carried them without a break to lat. 40 S, long. 124 W, crossing the equator in long. 123 W, 28 days out. Thence to Cape Horn had moderate and fine weather. Had eight days of steady easterly winds and fine weather W of Cape Horn, which was passed on Dec. 10, 64 days from port.

Passed Cape St. John 11th. On the 12th, 13th, and 14th had heavy westerly and south-westerly gales, with very high cross sea, barometer down to 28 400. On the 14th, at 6 p.m., whilst running before a heavy gale, the ship was pooped by a heavy sea, breaking right over the taffrail*, carrying away the wheel, skylight, binnacle, etc., the weather helmsman, Charles Radford, receiving such terrible injuries that he died in two hours. The lee helmsman and master were carried forward on main deck and severely bruised. The ship was then hove to.

On the 15th, after burying the deceased and repairing damages, kept our course before a decreasing gale, and with fine weather. Had moderate weather and light winds to lat. 24 S, long. 27 W, where we took the SE trades, which were light and very easterly. Crossed the equator on Jan. 15, 100 days out, in long. 27 W. Carried SE trades to lat. 6 20 N, and had light SE and ESE winds and rain to lat. 17 N, long. 32 W. Thence to Azores had brisk ENE to ESE winds, without a break in the calm belt of Cancer [the Tropic of Cancer – from the equator to lat. 23.5 N]. Rounded the Azores on Feb. 4 with brisk SE winds and fine weather and high barometer.

On the 7th, in lat. 45 13 N, long. 27 W, the barometer touched the highest point of the voyage, viz. 30 896. Thence to port had fresh to heavy gales from NW to NE. Received orders off Queenstown night of 14th inst., and had heavy gale in Channel from W, and thick weather. Arrived at Kingroad 15th, and docked at Sharpness 16th."

\* The *poop deck* was the raised deck at the furthest after (stern) end of a sailing vessel. In stormy weather, with the ship sailing downwind (the wind coming from directly behind), a big following sea might rise up and come aboard over the stern of the ship. It would wash over the *taffrail* (the rail running around the stern of the vessel) onto the poop deck where the wheel and helmsman, and steering compass were located, and where the officers of the ship stood to keep their watch. A ship "pooped" by such a sea could be severely damaged by the immense force of the water coming on board. This might include injuring the helmsmen – there would usually be at least two men at the wheel during very stormy weather – and any officers on watch on the poop deck. The possibility of them being washed overboard and drowned was very real.

## Turning East About

The westerly gales of the Southern Ocean, and around Cape Horn, sometimes made it impossible for square-rigged sailing vessels heading west to make any headway. Occasionally captains turned their ships around to run east, with a following west wind better suited to square-rigged ships, to reach their destination.

## 18 Dec 1885

### Maritime Intelligence

> Mountaineer.- San Francisco, Dec. 1.- The Mountaineer, which arrived here yesterday from Hull, is reported to have had very bad weather off Cape Horn, during which wheel was smashed, sails carried away, and other damage sustained. Being driven back by storms the captain, after repairing damages as well as possible, shaped his course for the Cape of Good Hope, reaching port by that route.

The *Mountaineer* left Hull around mid-April 1885. She would have sailed the usual way towards San Francisco, down the North and South Atlantic and around the southern tip of South America, Cape Horn. Unable to proceed around Cape Horn, in the teeth of the usual westerly gales thereabouts, the captain took the option of turning his vessel around to sail with the great and reliably steady westerly winds of the Southern Ocean behind him, south of Africa and the Cape of Good Hope, across the southern Indian Ocean and the Pacific, to reach San Francisco by that much longer route. A voyage of four or five months by way of Cape Horn thereby became one of around nine months by sailing almost right round the world, but preferable to struggling against the storming westerly gales of those latitudes.

An old Cape Horner, Capt. A.G. Course, in his 1969 book *Windjammers of the Horn*, told how the three-masted steel barque *Inverneill* (1,340 tons) attempted to sail the 2,000 miles across the Great Australian Bight from Sydney on the east coast of Australia to Bunbury, near Perth in Western Australia, against unceasing westerly gales, in 1919. In the face of such persistent adverse winds, the barque's master, Capt. J.H. Shippen, turned the *Inverneill* around "to make the passage to the eastward, right round the world, with the fair westerly winds of the Roaring Forties and Howling Fifties (between 40° and 50° south latitude)".

The *Inverneill* sailed around the northern tip of New Zealand, across the South Pacific to Cape Horn, to the south of the Cape of Good Hope and across the South Indian Ocean. She reached Bunbury after a very creditable passage of 76 days from Sydney, considering that she had sailed a total of 14,563 miles in the opposite direction to the 2,000 miles direct route, but with favourable if boisterous winds preferred to the battering gale force headwinds of the Great Australian Bight that year.

## "SPEAKINGS"

During sailing ship voyages vessels sometimes "spoke" each other when they coincidentally met at sea and communicated briefly with each other by signal flags. These were recorded in *Lloyd's List* as "Ships Spoken" or "Vessels spoken with" or just "Speakings". The meeting was recorded in the homeward bound ship's log and reported upon arrival at her destination port. The report typically included the name of the ship "spoken", the date of the meeting, where they met (the ship's position in latitude and longitude), sometimes the direction in which the "spoken" ship was bound, and finally the name of the reporting vessel and the port at which the report was made which was very often Queenstown in Ireland (now called Cobh, the main port of Cork in the Republic of Ireland), or English Channel ports such as Falmouth or Portsmouth, or Liverpool.

The following shows that the **Emily A Davies**, a **barque**, registered at **Swansea**, heading **south**, was spoken on **Feb. 14 (1887)**, at **lat. 5° S, long. 32° W**, by the steamship *Corean* which reported the details of their encounter when the *Corean* reached port (**Dunkirk**). The "speaking" appeared in the **12 March 1887** issue of *Lloyd's List*.

## 12 March 1887

### Ships Spoken

*Emily A Davies, barque, of Swansea, bound south, Feb. 14, lat. 5 S, long. 32 W, by the Corean (s), at Dunkirk*

## CREW'S ARTICLES AND CONDITIONS

Crews signed on ships for specific voyages. Sailors had to sign a document titled Agreement and Account of Crew, more commonly known simply as the ship's Articles. This document outlined all the terms and conditions by which the seamen agreed to abide for the duration of the voyage for which they were engaged. All crew members who signed Articles included their year and place of birth, the ship in which they last served (if any), the date and place of joining the present ship, the capacity in which they were engaged (Able Seaman [AB], first or second mate, boatswain [bosun], steward-cook, sailmaker, apprentice), and their respective wages for the voyage. Wages were indicated either by week, month, share of profits (mainly in whaling ships), or, uncommonly, for the entire voyage. (Apprentices were not paid; their parents or guardians paid the shipowner for taking them on for a specified period of indenture, usually three or four years. During that time they would make as many voyages as the period of their apprenticeship dictated, when they would learn the essential skills of their sailoring trade.)

By and large the general terms of Articles on British ships were standard, as established by the Board of Trade at the time. These included the crew's daily food and drink allowances, geographical limits of the voyage, and the crew's wages. If a crew member was illiterate, he put his mark (usually a cross) which was confirmed by his name written above it by the master and the notation 'his mark'.

## A Typical Voyage

The voyage undertaken by the *Emily A Davies* from 16 April 1881 to 21 July 1882 was typical of her day. The ship's Articles defined the scope of the crew's engagement as "from Liverpool to Port Natal & any ports & places within the limits of 72 Degrees North Latitude & 65 Degrees South Latitude to & from & calling for orders if required & back to final port of discharge in the United Kingdom or Continental Europe term not to exceed 3 years".

Daily provisions allowed for the crew were outlined in a table titled "Scale of Provisions to be allowed and served out to the Crew during the Voyage, in addition to the daily issue of Lime and Lemon Juice and Sugar, or other antiscorbutics [to prevent scurvy] in any case required by Law". The table for this voyage was typical and specified the following allowances:

| | Bread | Beef | Pork | Flour | Peas | Tea | Coffee | Sugar | Water |
|---|---|---|---|---|---|---|---|---|---|
| | lb | lb | lb | lb | pint | oz | oz | oz | qts |
| **Sunday** | 1 | 1½ | ½ | | 1/8 | ½ | 2 | 3 | |
| **Monday** | 1 | 1¼ | 1/3 | | | Daily | | | |
| **Tuesday** | 1 | 1½ | ½ | | | | | | |
| **Wednesday** | 1 | 1¼ | 1/3 | | | | | | |
| **Thursday** | 1 | 1½ | ½ | | | | | | |
| **Friday** | 1 | 1¼ | 1/3 | | | | | | |
| **Saturday** | 1 | 1½ | | | | | | | |

A Note below the table added that "In any case an equal quantity of Fresh Meat or Fresh Vegetables may, at the option of the Master, be served out in lieu of the Salted or Tinned Meats or Preserved or Compressed Vegetables named in the above scale". Additionally, "SUBSTITUTES" for the above could be served as "Equivalent at Master's option". The beef and pork was salted and carried in barrels. "Bread" might be baked daily by the cook, but usually only for the ship's officers; more usually for the deckhands it was in the form of hard ships' biscuits, commonly infested with weevils and the like. The crew's coffee was black, and if sweetened, with molasses (sugar was reserved for the captain). Fresh provisions could be obtained at origin and destination ports. Some livestock, such as chickens or a few pigs, might be carried on deck, in pens, to be used from time to time for fresh meat. It was not uncommon for those to be washed overboard, pens and all, in particularly stormy weather.

The *Emily A Davies* had certified accommodation for 13 seamen. For this voyage, the master of the vessel noted in a space allocated for "any other stipulations [that] may be inserted to which the parties agree, and which are not contrary to Law", that "The Crew shall consist of a Mate, Bsn [bosun], Std. [steward] & Cook, 3 seamen & 3 apps. [apprentices]". The other "stipulation" added in that space was "No grog allowed".

The crew that actually signed on for this voyage in Liverpool comprised: the master, Capt. Morris Morgan; a first and second mate; a steward/cook; six ABs; and three apprentices.

Another first mate and steward were signed on at Rangoon to replace the original ones who were discharged there during the voyage. Another crew member who was signed on at Rangoon as a steward deserted the ship at Callao (the port for Lima, in Peru).

The apprenticeship time of two of the three apprentices on board expired during the voyage, so they were upgraded to ABs by the end of the voyage. The term of their indenture was four years, from 20 June 1878 to 19 June 1882. At the time their indenture expired the vessel was on her homeward passage from Pisco, on the west coast of South America, to Liverpool, somewhere around mid-Atlantic and about a month away from Liverpool. Both apprentices were aged 20 when their apprenticeship finished. The third was only 16 when he joined the ship and so was just beginning his four year term of apprenticeship.

The monthly wages of the crew were as follows:

| Position | Wage (£ s d) |
|---|---|
| First Mate | £6/0/0 |
| Second Mate | £3/10/0 |
| Steward/cook | £3/10/0 |
| Able Bodied seaman (AB) | £2/10/0 |

This voyage of the *Emily A Davies* started with her departure from Liverpool on 16th April 1881. She arrived at Port Natal (Durban), in South Africa, a little over three months later on 25th July and sailed for Rangoon two months later on 20th September. From Rangoon she sailed to the west coast of South America, arriving at Callao on 19th January 1882. She carried on to Pisco, a little further down the coast, before commencing her return voyage around Cape Horn to Liverpool where she arrived on 21 July 1882 and where her 15-month voyage officially terminated. (A *voyage* meant a full voyage from her original departure port back to that or a nearby port; a *passage* meant any leg of the voyage.)

This was an absolutely typical voyage of a typical commercial deep-sea sailing ship of the time. The *Emily A Davies*' next voyage was similar, except that she returned to Gravesend and London from Rangoon (with a cargo of rice), rather than going to the west coast of South America. The composition of her crew was virtually the same except that she only carried two apprentices, and there were no changes to it throughout the voyage. The duration of the voyage – a little over a year, from 25 September 1882 to 8 October 1883 – was a few months less than her previous one, in part because she did not go to South America.

# 3 Tonnage and Ships' Measurements

In the 19th century different countries measured ships by slightly different criteria. The definitions below were used by the British Board of Trade for British-registered vessels. Ships registered elsewhere, in Germany, Finland, France or the United States for example, were measured by the practices of those respective countries. A ship that transferred ownership and registration from the flag of one country to another had to be re-measured by the method used in that other country. This is why the measurements of some ships, such as *Runnymede*, changed slightly over the course of their lives, even though the ships themselves did not.

Ships of the 19th century – and into the 20th century – were measured by various means. Tonnage was actually a measurement of a ship's internal volume rather than a weight measurement. The unit of volume measurement was (and continues to be to this day) a *ton of 100 cubic feet*. The three kinds of volume tonnage measurement were *gross registered tonnage (grt)*, *under deck tonnage*, and *net or registered tonnage* (or *net registered tonnage*).

**Gross registered tonnage (grt)** is the volume measure of a ship's entire interior space, including holds, cabins, stores and any other space contained within the hull of the vessel. GRT is the usual method of determining the size of merchant ships.

**Under deck tonnage** is grt minus any enclosed spaces situated above the upper deck (when less than three decks).

**Net** or **registered tonnage** (or **net registered tonnage**) is the volume measure of a ship's cargo and passenger carrying capacity. In commercial sailing ships that meant her hold (and so her earning capacity as a measure of how much freight she could carry) and passenger accommodation. Specifically, it is grt minus various deductions for crew space, navigating space, stores and so on. In the case of a steamship it excludes propulsion space (the engine room).

A fourth tonnage measurement, not often used for merchant sailing ships of the 19th century, is **deadweight tonnage**. This is the vessel's carrying capacity (in tons) when floating at her *loaded draught*.

## PLIMSOLL MARKS AND LINES

The loaded draught – or loadline – of any ship, to this day is shown by a series of lines and marks on the vessel's side known as Plimsoll lines and marks. They show the lowest level that the vessel can legally sit in the water when fully loaded, measured from the main deck, and therefore the maximum cargo she can load depending on what conditions the vessel will be trading in, namely, tropical waters, fresh waters (lakes, rivers), tropical fresh or salt waters, summer or winter salt water, or winter North Atlantic. Since the density of water in each of these conditions is different, the draught of a vessel – how deeply it sits in the water – changes accordingly. The lines are accompanied by a circle through which a line is drawn that marks the minimum allowable freeboard – the distance from the waterline to the deck when the vessel is fully loaded, in salt water, in summer – together with the initials of the registration society with which the ship is registered (for example, L and R for Lloyd's Registry).

The concept of loadlines for British ships was introduced by Samuel Plimsoll (10 February 1824 – 3 June 1898) – hence the name Plimsoll lines and marks – in the 19th century in order to ensure that vessels were not too heavily loaded and thus sitting too low in the water for their safety and the safety of their crews. Plimsoll was born in Bristol but spent most of his boyhood and adolescence in the north of England. After moving to Sheffield he became a Liberal Member of Parliament for Derby in 1868.

Plimsoll initiated the process that resulted in legislation known as The Unseaworthy Ships Bill to prohibit the overloading of ships, thus making them safer. The law was passed by Parliament on 10 August 1875 and came into force for every British vessel registered after 1 January 1876. Before that unscrupulous shipowners commonly overloaded (and undermanned) their vessels – colloquially called coffin ships – to collect on the insurance when the vessels foundered or otherwise came to grief. However, according to The Unseaworthy Ships Bill, the responsibility of determining the loadline still lay with shipowners. It took another Act of 1890 to legislate that the loadline had to be officially determined by a neutral agency, the Board of Trade, which was responsible for overseeing British merchant shipping.

## LINEAR MEASUREMENTS

Linear measurements were used to describe the *length*, *breadth* and *depth* of a vessel. The length of a sailing vessel was that of her hull, not including her bowsprit. The British method of measuring a ship's length only went up to her sternpost and excluded the length of overhang of a ship's counter stern if she had one (and most did). The counter stern curved back under the furthest after part of the stern – the point along the deck at its furthest extremity aft – towards the sternpost along the hull from which the rudder was hung. A British vessel's official length excluded that length of overhang of the ship's stern from the furthest point aft to the sternpost. (Today, a ship's *overall length* would go from her two furthest extremities, such as the end of her stem, or if she had one, bowsprit, to the furthest point aft of her stern.)

The *length* of a vessel was therefore measured from the fore-side (front) of the vessel's stem to the after-side (back) of her sternpost, along the upper deck beams. (Today it would be measured at the level of her registered loadline.) Her *breadth* (or *width*, or *beam*) was measured from one side of the hull to the other at its widest point. *Depth* was measured in two ways: first, as the depth of a vessel's hold; and second, the whole depth of a ship's hull from her keel to her deck, which was called *moulded depth*. The *depth of the hold* was the greatest vertical distance from the bottom of the hold to the top, measured from the centre of the bottom of the hold (the centre-line of the ship's length).

SAMUEL PLIMSOLL, ESQ., M.P.

# Part II

## Casualties, Calamities, Catastrophes and Curiosities

In the days of merchant sail ships regularly incurred problems varying from slight mishaps such as a temporary grounding in a harbour or a bump in the dark against another vessel, to the total loss of a vessel and part or all of her crew. Casualties were written up in *Lloyd's List* in columns titled "Casualties – Home" or "Casualties – Foreign", "Maritime Intelligence", and sometimes under "Weather & Navigation", "Miscellaneous" or "Derelicts and Wreckage". There was a regular section for "Missing Vessels", reports of which always ended with "…and has not since been heard of".

(*Lloyd's List* was revamped from 1 February 1870 with a much clearer layout of reports of casualties under "Home" and "Foreign", according to whether the reports were from ports in the British Isles ("Home"), or from elsewhere in the world ("Foreign"). Before that the reports were simply organised by the ports from which the reports were received, and by date. Later on the casualties columns were re-titled overall as "Maritime Intelligence").

Lloyd's kept track of casualties by British-flagged vessels on its *Loss Book*. *Lloyd's List* sometimes published observations on the incidence of casualties for a particular year based on those records.

## 1 March 1878

### Casualties Posted on Lloyd's Loss Book During The Year 1877

Referring to the table published in yesterday's *Lloyd's List*, it may be interesting to give the following percentages of casualties posted on Lloyd's Loss Book upon the mercantile [merchant] navies of the world, taking the figures given in the Répertoire Général, published by the Bureau Veritas, as the basis of comparison.

In 1874 these sailing vessels numbered 56,289, while in 1877 they had decreased to 51,912, or by 4,377. Taking the mean of these figures, we have 54,100 vessels.

The average of casualties to sailing vessels posted in the 3 years 1875-77 inclusive, was 2,175, or equal to 4.02 per cent. upon the mean as given above. The mean number of steamers so given was 5,368, and the average casualties to steamers posted during the above period [1875-1877] was 332, or 6.18 per cent., while the percentage for sailing vessels and steamers together was 4.22 per cent.

In 1877 the number of sailing vessels is given as 51,912, and the casualties to sailing vessels posted were 2,123, or 4.09 per cent.

The steamers in 1877 were 5,471, and casualties posted thereto were 305, or 5.57 per cent., while the percentage of casualties to [sailing] ships and steamers together was 4.23 per cent.

It would therefore result, apparently, that the percentage of casualty relatively is slightly higher to sailing vessels – rather lower to steamers; while it only varies by a single hundredth per cent. upon the two combined."

## COMMUNICATION

It might be many months before a casualty was reported to Lloyd's, especially if the vessel was at a rather out of the way place. If it had foundered and the crew was taken aboard another vessel, it might take three or more months for the ship to reach her destination and make a report of the incident. The rescue of any crew members picked up would only be known when they were landed, sometimes in a port on the other side of the world from where they were rescued. Until then they were presumed to be missing and probably dead.

Not all "casualties" reported by Lloyd's were entirely accurate. There was considerable scope for error in those years when most reports were recorded by hand, and when telegraphy was in its infancy. As a single example, the America's Cup yacht *Valkyrie* was variously reported sunk with loss of life, and the report subsequently denied, according to the following sequence:

### 11 May 1894

**Maritime Intelligence**

*Valkyrie* (yacht).- Mentone, May 8.- A rumour is current here, which though it has not yet received trustworthy confirmation, seems to be generally credited [believed], that the yacht *Valkyrie*, owned by Commendatore Florio, has been lost off Civita Vecchia [Rome]. According to the report, only the captain and two of the crew have been saved.

### *17 May 1894*
**Maritime Intelligence**

*Valkyrie* (yacht).- Cowes, May 16.- Intelligence reached the Royal Yacht Squadron Castle at Cowes to-day that the *Valkyrie* cutter, formerly belonging to Lord Dunraven, and sold by him to an Italian gentleman, has foundered off the coast of Africa with the loss of all hands.

### *19 May 1894*
**Maritime Intelligence**

*Valkyrie* (yacht).- Liverpool, May 19.- It is stated that there is no truth in the statement that the *Valkyrie*, owned by Mr. Ignacio Horio, of Palermo [Sicily], has been wrecked, and that all hands were lost.

The "intelligence" referred to in such reports was news-based sometimes on no more than rumour, hearsay or half-truths. The details relating to the *Valkyrie* above were as variable as they were unreliable. Few reports, however, were quite so consistently inaccurate in so many ways. The irony was that the *Valkyrie* did actually sink a few months later, on 5 July 1894, during races of the Mudhook Regatta on the Firth of Clyde, Scotland. She was rammed by another contestant, the yacht *Satanita*. Lord Dunraven and the crew were saved as the *Valkyrie* sank in about 20 fathoms (she was refloated a week later).

A vessel taking a long time on a passage might also generate unfounded assumptions that she was lost. In 1881 the *Wandering Minstrel* should have taken around six weeks to make her passage from Cape Town to Calcutta. After a period of twice that time she was feared to have been lost in an Indian Ocean cyclone. A few days later, however, she turned up at Calcutta.

## 9 March 1881

**Casualties – Foreign**

Wandering Minstrel, from Table Bay [Cape Town] for Calcutta. – Messrs Wm Dunn & Co write as follows:- "Under date 4ᵗʰ inst. [March] our Calcutta friends telegraph as follows:- 'Fear Wandering Minstrel lost Mauritius in a cyclone.' You will observe that this information is not positive, but as this vessel is now 82 days out from Table Bay, bound for Calcutta (in ballast), we are afraid it is likely to be true."

### *14 March 1881*

Wandering Minstrel – Messrs Wm Dunn and Co advise that their Calcutta friends have telegraphed the arrival there of the Wandering Minstrel [arrived Mar 12, 7 PM].

The vagaries of erratic communication could also produce inaccurate reports even between places relatively near to each other.

## 22 Dec 1883

**Casualties, Etc.**

Regina.- Liverpool, Dec. 21, 3 32 p.m.- The Regina, Bain master, from Philadelphia for London, cargo petroleum (6,650 barrels), on 1ˢᵗ inst., when in about lat. 39 N, long. 58 W, encountered a gale, ship labouring very heavily and seas breaking over her. At midnight a heavy sea broke over the vessel, bursting tarpaulins over hatches and letting down water. She also had bulwarks [the sides of a ship around the deck] and stanchions carried away from fore rigging to poop, and vessel took a heavy lurch. She righted upon the main and mizen masts being cut away, and subsequently became full of water, which burst the main hatch and let the cargo out.

Crew left the vessel in the boats, but boarded her again the next day. They began to construct a raft. The vessel was then beginning to break up. A raft was launched on the 4ᵗʰ, vessel being then completely over on beam ends. Captain and eight hands got into a boat, five hands remained on the vessel, and some of the crew got on a raft. Two men died from exposure, and one man was drowned. The chief officer got on portion of poop, which was detached from vessel, and on 5ᵗʰ he was rescued by the Boroma, from Savannah, and landed at Liverpool this day. Nothing was afterwards seen of the ship, boat or raft.

### *26 Dec 1883*
**Casualties, Etc.**

Regina.- Queenstown, Dec. 23\*, 7 20 p.m.- The master of the Henry Finlayson reports that on the 6ᵗʰ inst., in lat. 39 N, long. 51 W, rescued off a raft the master and five men, part of the crew of the ship Regina, of Nova Scotia, from Philadelphia for London, with oil, which vessel was abandoned in a sinking condition on Dec. 1, in lat. 38 N, long. 52 W. The fate of the remainder of the crew – part in a boat and part on board the ship – is unknown [*sic*]. The six men when picked up were in a very exhausted condition, having been without food or water during the time they were on the raft [two days]. They have been landed at this port.

In fact, the fate of at least one other crew member of the *Regina*, the chief officer (mate), was known by this time: he was rescued by the ship *Boroma* and landed at Liverpool on 21 December. This was apparently not known at Queenstown, Ireland (above), where the master and five of the crew of the *Regina* were landed by the *Henry Finlayson* a few days later on 23 December. Moreover, the first report, which must have derived from the recollections of the mate who was saved by the *Boroma*, said that the master and eight men got into a boat and "some of the crew got on a raft". The second report said that the captain and five men were "rescued off a raft". The only certainty is that just seven of the *Regina*'s crew were rescued. The others, number unknown but probably about ten, must have perished.

Such inconsistencies in reports of casualties were a consequence of the confused and extreme conditions prevailing at the time of such incidents, combined with not wholly reliable means of communication in the early days of telegraphy.

Not all ships met disaster on the high seas. One, the small coastal steamship *Daphne* capsized and sunk on the day she was launched at Govan on the Clyde, on 3 July 1883. On that day when she went down the slipway for the first time the little ship had almost 200 workers and boys on board, to finish fitting her out. Her anchors and cables were supposed to take the speed off her as she entered the water, but one anchor dragged and the current of the river flipped her on her side. She sank in deep water. One hundred and twenty-four workmen and boys drowned.

## Leaky Ships

Probably the most common casualty amongst sailing ships of those years (especially wooden-hull ships) was that they were "leaky", reported as such when they put into a port with several feet or more of seawater sloshing around their hold. A ship that leaked badly had to be pumped more or less constantly by the crew until they could reach a port to effect repairs. The more pumping a leaky ship required, the more it tired the crew; some leaky ships put into port with crews exhausted virtually to the point of incapacity. Most ships, however, were reported as just "leaky" – not severely, not fatally or catastrophically so, but an inconvenience that nevertheless required attention and merited reporting.

Leaks were often caused by the refusal of stingy shipowners to invest enough in repairs and maintenance when profits were tight, as they usually were. Also, a wooden ship's seams could open up simply because its hull was old and hard-worked by the accumulation of hundreds of thousands of sea miles voyaging.

And then there were shipworms, commonly called teredo worms, or "termites of the sea", which were actually bivalves (not worms at all) that bored into and digested the wood of a wooden ship's hull. There was little protection in those days from the teredo worm's attraction to wooden hulls, especially in warm tropical waters. Their borings could fatally compromise a ship's seaworthiness under the stresses and strains of long ocean passages. Copper sheathing

THE GREAT DISASTER AT A SHIP LAUNCH ON THE CLYDE: SINKING OF THE DAPHNE, WITH TWO HUNDRED MEN.

# THE ILLUSTRATED LONDON NEWS

REGISTERED AT THE GENERAL POST-OFFICE FOR TRANSMISSION ABROAD.

No. 2308.—VOL. LXXXIII.     SATURDAY, JULY 14, 1883.     WITH TWO SUPPLEMENTS SIXPENCE. By Post, 6½d.

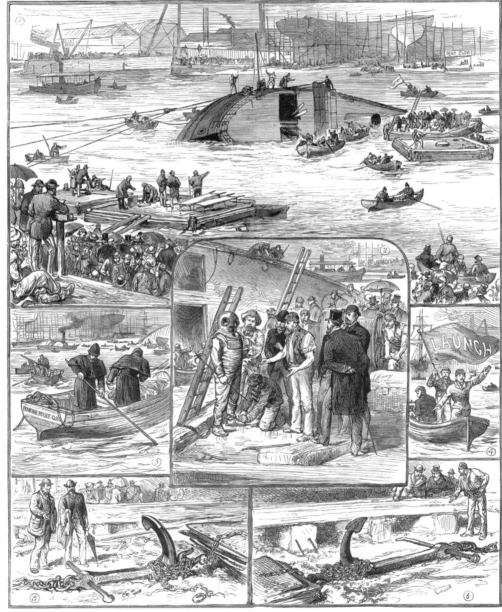

1. Hull of the Daphne as it appeared at low tide, sketched from Messrs. Stephen's yard, Linthouse, with Messrs. Barclay and Curles' yard on the opposite (north) shore.
2. The diver preparing for his descent alongside the hull of the Daphne.     3. River police assisting to remove the dead.     4. Boat with flag, usually employed at launches to warn passing vessels.
5. The starboard anchor, to which the chains were attached to guide the Daphne in the launch.     6. The port side anchor for the chains at the launch.

SKETCHES OF THE SHIP-LAUNCH DISASTER AT GLASGOW.

was sometimes fastened to the hull, to protect it against shipworms, but it was an expensive preventative remedy.

## DERELICTS

Ships often reported seeing abandoned vessels or the wreckage of a vessel on the high seas (though not often with a large black dog on deck), which might take weeks or months to report until the ship had reached port.

## 2 March 1885

### Maritime Intelligence

Observant, Queenstown, Feb. 28, 5 27 p.m.- The Salus, at Queenstown, reports having sighted, on Feb. 3, in lat. 45 N, long. 42 W, a disabled vessel with lower masts standing. Bore down on her and went close under her stern, and found her to be the Observer [*sic - Observant*], of Christiansund. The only living thing to be seen about her decks was a large black dog. The foreyard was lying across the forehouse. She had poop and house aft, and was painted white inside and black outside. The copper [copper sheathing fitted along the underside of her hull] looked to be nearly new and coppered high. By her lower masts, schooner or brigantine rigged.

Observant – London, March 2.- The Observant, derelict vessel, was passed Feb. 13, in lat. 45 N, long. 32 35 W. A large black dog was seen on the poop.

The North Atlantic in particular was littered with such wreckage in the second half of the 19 century: dismasted, waterlogged, capsized and otherwise derelict vessels, usually (but not always) with no persons aboard; spars and rigging ripped from foundering or storm-battered ships; and casks, small boats, planks, and bits of cargo jettisoned or washed overboard. Waterlogged derelicts of wooden ships, or parts of them, also drifted just below the surface of the ocean. There were various reports of ships striking unknown objects which were presumed to be drifting and unseen derelicts of this kind. Besides ships and parts of them, drifting navigation buoys were the most common kind of flotsam reported by vessels from the North Atlantic in particular.

The North Atlantic basin is a big gyre of surface water spinning slowly around in a clockwise direction. Wreckage of any kind might circulate around the ocean for many months or even years before it sank or was washed ashore. Ships reported any sighting of such flotsam or jetsam in a dedicated column of *Lloyd's List*, to warn other vessels that they were a hazard to navigation. Derelict and abandoned vessels were also commonly reported off Cape Horn and in the wastes of the southern Indian Ocean, which, in the 19th century, were criss-crossed by busy trade routes for merchant sailing ships. They were also places of hurricane force storms and cyclones that routinely battered ships, and crews, into terrible submission.

In the early months of 1883 many vessels reported sighting a derelict Norwegian barque, the *Carl*, drifting around the North Sea. The ship was often reported as a danger to navigation amongst the busy shipping areas then off the east coast of England in particular. It is somewhat surprising that none thought to set the vessel on fire and sink it, a common practice in other deep-sea waters. From March to May 1895 numerous vessels arriving at British ports reported sighting the derelict wreck of the Norwegian barque *Birgitte* drifting around just at the western approaches to the English Channel, to the south of the Isles of Scilly. In April that year a steamship, the *Slavonia*, tried to set it on fire, to sink it, but without success. The *Birgitte* was eventually towed into Queenstown (now Cobh, Ireland) on 7 May by the tug *Gamecock*, from 90 miles southwest of the Old Head of Kinsale.

An American three-masted schooner, the *Fannie E. Wolston*, was dismasted in a hurricane and abandoned by her crew north of Cape Hatteras in October 1891. The timber-laden and waterlogged derelict drifted back and forth across the Atlantic three times over three years – and more than 10,000 miles – before finally wrecking, apparently, on the west coast of Scotland late in 1894.

## LATITUDE & LONGITUDE

The location of casualties, speakings and anything else to do with nautical positions was given in degrees and minutes of latitude (abbreviated as "lat.") North (N) or South (S) of the equator, and degrees and minutes of longitude (abbreviated either as "lon." or "long.") East (E) or West (W) of the Greenwich meridian (0 degrees). In fact, positions were often given only in whole degrees, omitting the minutes (a degree of longitude or latitude is divided into 60 minutes, one minute equalling a nautical mile), either because a position could not be determined to the precision of minutes, or because it was not considered necessary to do so.

Inaccuracies in communication sometimes made for interesting errors.

## 18 Oct 1894

**Maritime Intelligence**

Ainsdale.- Queenstown, Oct. 17, 7 32 p.m.- Ainsdale, Owens, from Portland (Or.), wheat, arrived here to-day, reports that on July 10, in lat. 42 N, long. 114 W\*, a very heavy sea struck ship on port side with terrific force, which caused her to tremble heavily, and washed overboard and drowned two able seamen named Classen, of Stockholm, and Thompsen, of Denmark, and two apprentices, Flinton and Rendall, both of Scarborough; they were at the time of the unfortunate occurrence employed in hauling in the fore braces. Three other members of the crew were knocked down and injured, but not seriously, with the exception of one able seaman, William Breen, of Portaferry, who is suffering from injuries to the legs, and will be removed to the hospital here for medical treatment.

\* This location of the incident reported here - "lat. 42° N, long. 114° W" – is on the western slopes of the Rocky Mountains somewhere in southern Idaho! It is most likely to be, in fact, long. 141 W, which, at lat. 42 N, is about 600 miles off the west coast of the United States in the Pacific, between the ship's port of departure, Portland, Oregon, and San Francisco.

# 1  Message in a Bottle

## "ATE THE DOG YESTERDAY"

## 29 June 1875

*Galveston, 2nd June.- A bottle containing a paper on which is written the following, has been picked up on the beach east of this port:- "May 19, 1873.- Ate the dog yesterday, schooner James, from Liverpool to Jamaica, foundered on a reef of rocks about 1000 miles from land. Any one finding this will please publish in the papers and oblige your humble servant, James Jones, 23 Scotland Road, Liverpool, England. Thirty-two men on board and no water. God save us."*

Messages found in bottles set adrift at sea in the late-19th and early-20th centuries were one of the most poignant and often only indications of a casualty at sea. Messages were usually written by sailors in the most extreme circumstances, when their vessel was about to sink as they faced almost certain death – and they knew it. Bottle messages picked up on beaches and shores, mainly around North Atlantic and Baltic coasts, were handed to a Lloyd's agent and reported in *Lloyd's List* as "Bottle (or sometimes Bottles, if more than one) Picked Up" or "Bottle Report". They might also have been included under "Miscellaneous" in the "Maritime Intelligence" columns.

Messages written by sailors *in extremis* were usually brief: their vessel was on the verge of sinking; they were on the verge of death by drowning; time was of the essence; a simple farewell was all they had the time (or inclination) to express.

## 15 Dec 1893

**Bottle Picked Up**

*Dundee, Dec. 14.- A bottle, containing a piece of pencilled paper, has been picked up on the beach at Kircaldy [Firth of Forth coast, north of Edinburgh]. The following is the writing:- "Sinking Yaikam, Weil, with coal Denmark 8/12/93. Good-bye."*

On occasions there was time to express a bit more of their personal feelings, or a few details of their circumstances. Quite often they included a plaintive appeal to the Almighty as they stared at death in the face of a watery grave.

## 28 Aug 1872

**Bottle Picked Up**

*A bottle has been picked up at Wicklow [Ireland], containing a paper on which the following was written:- "Newfoundland, 18ᵗʰ June 1872. (The outward bound) N.S., sprung a leak on the night of the 18ᵗʰ June, and went down with all hands on board. J. Folge. Master and two hands on a raft.- God help us."*

## 30 Aug 1876

**Bottle Picked Up**

*Elsinore, 23 Aug.- The master, Karnowsky, of the Ariadne (barq.), which passed here to-day, from Sunderland, reports having picked up 16ᵗʰ Aug., the Scaw\* bearing SSE 20 miles, a bottle containing a piece of the 'Scotsman' newspaper, on which was written in pencil: "S.S. 'Midlehans' cargo shifted, small hopes, one man washed overboard. I trust to God. W. Wilson."*

\* Scaw (or Skaw) is the anglicised version of Skägen, the town at the northern tip of Denmark. The Skaw was well known to sailors passing to and from the Baltic and North Sea, via the Kattegat channel between Denmark and Sweden, and the Skagerrak between Denmark, Sweden and Norway, as they rounded the northernmost tip of Denmark.

## 19 Sept 1879

*Ymuiden [Ijmuiden, Netherlands], Sept. 16.- A bottle was found yesterday in the outer harbour containing a piece of paper apparently torn out of a pocket-book, on which was written, in Dutch:- "14ᵗʰ September – The barque Margareta lost on the English coast, Captain Graad (Graat), Hollander; God be merciful to us."*

## 2 April 1903

**Bottle Picked Up**

*Tromso [Norway], March 20.- On March 13 a bottle, containing a paper on which the following was written in Norwegian, was picked up near Tromso:- "Our fate is sealed. All erections destroyed by a sea. No saving. Steamer Colibri. 28/5, 1902. God help us. Greet all. We have prayed. H. Worsoe."*

Occasionally a message that implied some degree of distress turned out otherwise, as with the following German steamship trapped in the Arctic ice but later freed.

## 7 Sept 1889

**Bottle Picked Up**

*Christiania, Sept. 5.- At Besaker\*, between Drontheim\* and Namsos, a bottle has been found containing a slip of paper, on which was written in pencil:- 'S.S. Mimi, of Kiel, owner Dietrichsen, stranded in the Arctic Sea."*

### *16 Sept 1889*
**Miscellaneous**

*Rotterdam, Sept. 12.- The Mimi (s), of Kiel, Voge, arrived in the New Waterway this evening from Archangel [White Sea port, northwest Russia].*

\* Drontheim is Trondheim, the port city on the mid-southwest coast of Norway. Besaker is a coastal town about 55 miles north of Trondheim. The *Mimi* was probably "stranded in the Arctic sea" by being caught in ice, on her voyage from Archangel, on the White Sea of northwest Russia, round the north of Norway and down to Rotterdam where she eventually arrived safely.

Whilst some messages included a few brief words to loved ones they were about to leave behind, others were brief notes with simple and straightforward details of a tragedy at sea.

## 23 Aug 1871

**Bottle Picked Up**

*St. Malo, 21st Aug.- A bottle containing a paper, on which the following is written in pencil, was picked up a few days ago on a sand bank about three miles North of this port:- "The Lilly Black, Captain Smithers, off Jersey, 24th July, 1871. Ten feet of water in the hold, both boats stove in, commencing to sink. Two men washed overboard. John Smithers, master."*

## 26 June 1897

*Deal, June 26, 8 58 a.m.- A bottle was picked up on Deal beach this morning, containing a paper on which is written:- "This, if ever found, is to certify that the brig Martin foundered with all hands on April 19, 1895. H.G. Floyd, first mate."*

## 22 Aug 1872

*Dunbar [east coast Scotland], 20th Aug.- A bottle has been picked up near this place containing a paper, on which the following is written:- "The ship the Carrondelet, middle of the German Ocean [North Sea], Aug. 2nd, 1872. The ship is sinking fast; if ever this gets to shore, whoever finds it will please to let it be known this ship sunk with 21 hands on board. She is going now.- Herr Inglan, a native of Hamburg."*

## 19 Aug 1889

**Maritime Intelligence**

Bottle Report

*Leba [Baltic coast of Poland], Aug. 14.- A bottle was found yesterday afternoon near the mouth of the [River] Leba containing a slip of paper, on which was written, in German:- "We are going down, Elizabeth, Captain Orloff."*

## 27 Sept 1901

*Christiansand [Kristiansand, southern Norway], Sept. 23.- On Sept. 14 some pilots picked up near Ramsoen [island near Kristiansand] a bottle containing a piece of paper, on which was written:- "45 23 N, 37 29 W, barque Hercules, Sunderland. We are in great distress, and have no hope of being saved.- George Smith captain, 24.3.1901"*

In February 1900 the master of the German ship *Washington* used a message in a bottle as a postal device to report his attempt to take a derelict schooner in tow.

## 17 Feb 1900

**Bottle Picked Up**

*Falmouth, Feb. 16.- A bottle containing the following message has been picked up by the Brixham trawler Osprey, and landed here:- "German steamship Washington, Feb. 14, 1900. This morning, 11 o'clock, I did meet the British schooner Tilby or Guilby, of Heinmouth or Teignmouth. British flag was flying union down [ie., distress signal]; no men were on board; schooner seemed to be new. Tried to get her in tow; as soon as hawser was connected with the vessel ship went down and I had to cut the tow-rope. We met the schooner about 30 miles ESE of Start Point. The schooner had the lower topsail, forestaysail, jib and mainsail set. C. Dinekgage, master German s.s. Washington."*

The following message communicated more than just the distress of a ship in danger of wrecking.

## 23 Nov 1876

### Bottle Picked Up

*Rotterdam, 21ˢᵗ Nov.- Advices from Oostzaan [northern Holland], of yesterday's date, state that there had been picked up in the river a bottle, containing a piece of paper, on which was written:- "On board the Louise – the master has been murdered by the mate; rudder lost; ship a wreck; help. Lat. 52 N, lon. 20. W."*

The final words of some desperate seamen were committed not to messages in bottles but to whatever material to hand that they could write on – such as a piece of wood or other flotsam.

## 12 Dec 1899

*Kirkwall [Orkney Islands], Dec. 11.- A piece of wood has been found at Rothiesholm, Stronsay [Island], with the following message written on it in pencil. The writing is perfectly legible with the exception of a few words:- "North Sea, Oct. 28, 1899, Star, of Grimsby, in a sinking condition, working hard at the pump, but all of no use. Water gaining hard on us. Only chance of a steamer passing, which is not likely. Our boat could not live in such a sea. (Signed) J.D. Beresford." "Off Cape Wrath" appears to have been put on the top corner of the message after the rest of it was written.*

## 24 Nov 1896

### Maritime Intelligence

Derelicts and Wreckage

*Saeby [northeast coast of Denmark], Nov. 19.- A small cask has washed ashore on the north beach here, on which the following message is written in pencil:- "Schooner Nautilen, Navarra; farewell. Sinking on Scaw Reef\* on 2/10/96. Two men drowned, four still left."*

   \* Scaw Reef is off the north coast of Jutland, the northernmost point of Denmark. On 13ᵗʰ February 1811 HMS *Pandora* ran aground there with the loss of 29 men.

## 27 Dec 1890

### Maritime Intelligence

Wreckage

*London, Dec. 27.- A piece of wood, burnt at the end, square, 6 inches by 4 inches, with a hole in the centre, has been washed ashore at the island of Veira [Wyre], Orkney [Islands], with the following message written in pencil:- "Off Cape Finisterre [northwest Spain] Nov. 4, 1890. Golden Cloud burnt at sea; all hands lost except the captain and three others, who went off from the ship in the cuddy [small boat]. The ship belongs to Boston, North America. Signed Robert Showell."*

The direct sea distance from Cape Finisterre to the Orkney Islands is around 1,200 miles. The piece of wood had six or seven weeks to drift that distance (at a rate of about 1 knot). However, it was more probably carried on the North Atlantic Drift extension of the Gulf Stream which flows northeast up between Iceland and Scotland. The piece of wood must have been carried into the mid-Atlantic to catch the northeast flowing current of the Gulf Stream, making its drift distance – and speed – around twice as great as the direct distance between Cape Finisterre and northern Scotland. (The island of Wyre, sometimes previously called Veira, is just off the bigger island of Rousay.)

## 24 March 1903

### Maritime Intelligence

Miscellaneous

*Castletown [Isle of Man?], March 23, 2 50 p.m.- Board picked up on shore as follows:- "I have left a few more minutes before I die. J. Kelly of smack Seagull No. 62 sinking off Point of Ayre [Isle of Man?] if found let owners known no powder. R. Kelly."*

Most bottles were found on a beach. One, however, was ostensibly if implausibly reported to have been recovered by fishermen from inside a skate they had caught.

## 18 April 1882

*A small bottle, containing a paper with some writing, of which the following is a copy, is stated to have been found by fishermen, inside a skate:- "Apl. 2/82. Ship Marry Port Dundee Watter Log foundering lat. 22 long. 15. Pleas forward to Mrs. Mary Smith. Captain Smith. God help us. All ill with scurvy."*

This is clearly a hoax: the position of the supposedly foundering ship is stated to be "lat. 22°, long. 15°". Lat. 22° N, long. 15° W is in the Western Sahara desert. Lat. 22° S, long. 15° W is in the South Atlantic, but in far too isolated a position for the note to be written just a few weeks before it was found and reported. And long. 15° E, either north or south of the equator…is on dry land! Skate, moreover, live on the seafloor. For a bottle to sink to that depth it must have filled with water and thereby destroyed the message (if any) inside. Or perhaps the fishermen did find a bottle inside a skate and inserted their own hoax message in it, for their amusement. Whatever the source of the message, it was distinctly fishy.

Many messages included the date they were written and the position of the vessel (or, at least, the author of the message) at the time. The date they were reported found, however, did not necessarily indicate how long bottles drifted: a bottle might have stranded on a shore some considerable time before it was found. You could hazard a guess at the rate of drift of a bottle by comparing the location and date a bottle message was set adrift with the date and location it was found – by dividing the distance between the two places by the number of days between the two dates, taking account of known currents and winds – but the result could only be speculative.

This bottle was picked up at Southport, near Liverpool.

## 2 April 1870

*A bottle was picked up, on the 23rd March, at Southport, containing a paper, much discoloured, with the following words:- "We were wrecked off the Canary Isles, and now I, the first mate, and three of the crew are in the jollyboat, with three weeks provisions, and the rest of the crew of the brig Dolphin are all drowned. (Signed) Will. Cox, Jim Rooks, Jacob Jones, Phil. Owen."*

It is difficult to see how the bottle could have drifted directly north-northeast approximately 1,500 miles from the vicinity of the Canary Islands to the northwest coast of England: the current near the Canary Islands flows to the southwest across the Atlantic towards the Gulf of Mexico. A bottle dropped off the Canary Islands would most probably have drifted westwards across the Atlantic, been picked up by an eastern offshoot of the Gulf Stream and eventually deposited where it was picked up, after a round-the-Atlantic journey of 5,000 miles or so. As such it had probably been in the water for some considerable time since the castaways wrote the message in it.

In 1870 the ship *Dunkeld* became overdue on a voyage from Newcastle, New South Wales to Melbourne. It was assumed that she was wrecked on the Australian coast. Nine months later a message in a bottle found at Addis Bay, near Cape Otway in Victoria State, confirmed her fate (although, since the message was dated 17 August, she seems to have been at sea a very long time before foundering, considering the relatively short coastal passage she was making).

## 9 Sept 1870

**Casualties – Foreign**

*Adelaide, 14th Aug.- The ships Harlech Castle and Dunkeld have been lost on the Australian coast.*

*28 Sept 1870*
**Casualties – Foreign**

*Newcastle, N.S.W., 29th July.- The Dunkeld, Hook, which sailed hence, 6th June, for Melbourne, has not arrived at her destination. The Ceres, Bell, arrived at Melbourne, reports having been in company with a barque, supposed [believed] to be the Dunkeld, on the night of 27th June, during a strong gale. When last seen she was running back to the NE, with sails split or lost.*

*1 June 1871*
**Bottle Picked Up**

*Wellington, N.Z., 3rd Apl.- A vinegar bottle was lately picked up in Addis bay, amongst other things, and was found to contain a piece of paper, on which was written:- "Aug. 17th. 7. – Ship Dunkeld. We are foundering; the ship is sinking fast; there is no chance of saving her. Captain Hook."*

## 22 April 1871

*Hull, 20th Apl.- The following is a translation of a memorandum [message] in the German language, found in a bottle picked up by the coastguard at Holmpton, near Hornsea [Essex coast]:- "Ernst Froebe, Theodor Speil, Gustav Holtkotter, on the voyage from Hamburg to Hull, before the vessel founders, send their last farewell to the world, and request the finder of the same to report their last words to the province of Saxony, their home." On the paper is a drawing resembling a shamrock leaf.*

## 21 Sept 1871

*New York, 6th Sept.- A memorandum [message], written in pencil, of which the following is a copy, was picked up in the Gulf of Mexico and taken to Pensacola [Florida]:- "Off East Coast of Brazil, January 21, 1871.- This is to certify that we three are the only survivors of the English ship Lilian, lost on the night of the 15th of this month. We have now been drifting in an open boat for six days, suffering hunger, thirst and hardships which none but those that has experienced can illustrate. We have been looking out for a sail since the ship went down: what became of the captain and rest of the men God can only tell. (Signed) Jno. Thomas, second mate; Michael Dooley, seaman; Jno. Duger, seaman."*

## 17 Jan 1872

### Bottle Picked Up

*Hull, 16th Jan.- The following has been found in a bottle picked up at Sunk island, River Humber, 14th Jan.- "The finder of this will get to know that I Thomas Martin and crew 27 lives, captain of the Tiger (s), from Quebec, have no hope being saved; no time to say more. Good bye."*

## 27 Jan 1872

*Rio Grande [southern Brazil], 11th Dec. [1871].- On the 24th Nov. [1871], a sealed bottle containing a slip of paper, was found at St. Simon's beach, near Mostardas, about 160 miles north of this place. The following is a translation of the manuscript:- "Portuguese barque Saudade stranded on the Abrolhos, at 11 on the night of the 4th November 1871. There is no hope. God have mercy on us."*

The Abrolhos Islands – Ilhas Abrolhos – are located near Bahia off the northeast coast of Brazil and are a National Marine Park. The warm Brazil Current, flowing from north to south along the Brazilian coast, would have carried the bottle southward from the Abrolhos to the place it was picked up near Rio Grande, a distance of about 1,150 miles. Over 20 days, from the time the message was written till the date it was picked up, the bottled drifted at an apparent average speed of just over 2 knots (apparent, because it is not known, of course, how long the bottle was stranded at St. Simon's beach before it was found).

## 23 July 1872

### Bottle Picked Up

*Gothenburg, 19th July.- A bottle has been found in the neighbourhood [ie., near Gothenburg, Sweden], containing a piece of paper on which the following was written in Swedish:- "Skaggerack, 3/3 1872 – Vessel Blixt, Bimdsin, heavy storm, 2 men overboard, thick fog; almost everything lost; thus without hope, send greetings home."*

## 24 July 1872

### Bottle Picked Up

*Glasgow, 22nd July.- The following communication was found in a bottle by a fisherman on the*

*19th inst., off Portpatrick [southwest coast of Scotland]:- "Elite, New York off the Fastnets [Fastnet rocks, southern Ireland], ship making water; no life expected. May 21st, John Breaken, master."*

## 3 Oct 1872

*Rotterdam, 30th Sept.- A bottle has been picked up between Worcum and Hindelopen, Friesland [on the Zuider Zee, Netherlands], containing a piece of paper on which was written:- "To Johanna, lost on 29th Aug., good-bye to all his friends and his mother, No. 26 Alfred Place, Bedford St., London."*

## 15 Nov 1872

**Bottle Picked Up**

*A bottle has been picked up by the coastguard at – [place name omitted]; it contained a paper, with writing upon it in the French language, of which the following is a translation:- "The three-masted Ville de Geneve has been lost in lat. 20, lon 14\*; we are four, Pisanelli, Antonelli, Landini, and Sampierre, in a boat at the mercy of God – inform our families."*

\* It must be assumed that the vessel was lost in 20° **South** latitude, at 14° **West** longitude, in the middle of the South Atlantic: 20° North latitude, at 14° either West or East longitude, is in the Sahara Desert; and 20° South latitude, at 14° **East** longitude, is also on land, on the coast of Namibia.

## 26 Feb 1873

*Rotterdam, 25th Feb., 9.55 a.m.- A bottle has been picked up containing a paper on which the following is written in the Dutch language:- "Anna Elisabeth – we perish – God have mercy – near the Wight [Isle of Wight] – Kolk, sailor."*

## 8 July 1873

*Casablanca [Morocco], 20th June.- A bottle has been found on shore 20 miles S of this port, containing a slip of paper on which was written, in Dutch, as follows:- "Cape St. Vincent, 4th May.- Ship Carl Peter full of water and sinking, nothing, no hope of being saved; boats carried away. We go into the deep. Farewell."*

Cape St Vincent is a headland of southern Portugal on the southwest tip of the Algarve region. The bottle message, above, was found near the port of Casablanca about 200 miles south of Cape St Vincent, carried there by the south-setting current in that area.

## 10 July 1873

**[Le] Havre, 8th July**

*A letter from Chanco, published by the 'Idea', of Linares, Chili [Chile], states that a bottle had been picked up at sea, by a fisherman, which contained a piece of paper with a statement to the following effect written on it, in French:- "On board the Philomene, about 200 miles off Tierra del Fuego. I, Bertrand Duguesclin, master of the above vessel, after a violent gale, during which she sustained damage to masts and hull, saw her founder from under my feet, drawing down with her the greater part of the crew. I, the mate, and two men escaped, but having no provisions, we have suffered cruelly from hunger, and by tomorrow we shall undoubtedly have ceased to live. The vessel belonged to Messrs. Lamenais Dubreuil and Co., of Toulon. The finder of this writing is requested to have it published, in order that M. Lamenais may communicate the news to my dear M---, Rue Dernicur, No. 328, Toulon."*

## 17 July 1873

**Bottle Picked Up**

*Leigh [Leigh on Sea, south Essex coast], 15th July.- A bottle containing a piece of paper on which the following is written in pencil, has been picked up here:- "Lost on the 13th July, on the Goodwin sands, the Alexander steamship; dreadful weather. W.S. Shuth. Good bye all. God bless you."** 

*The Goodwin Sands (or "the Goodwins") are a series of sandbanks and shoals in the eastern English Channel, just off the coast of Kent. At least 1,000 ships have been recorded as wrecked on the Sands; the actual number is probably 2,000 to 3,000. The first recorded shipwreck there was an un-named vessel from Flanders wrecked in the year 1298. The Goodwins dry out at low tides. A long-standing annual cricket match used to be played on them until 2003 when the event was discontinued.

## 5 Nov 1873

*Gothenburg [Sweden], 31st Oct.- A fisherman at Grundsund has picked up a bottle, containing a paper, on which the following was written in pencil:- "All hope gone. Ship sinking rapidly as leak gaining. God save you, Sarah, and the little ones. 13th December, 1872. Ship Friendship."*

## 18 Feb 1874

**Bottle Picked Up**

*Napier, N.Z., 16th Dec.[1873] - The following [message] was picked up at the Waikato heads* on the 23rd Nov. [1873]. It is written in a small piece of paper, and was enclosed in a bottle:- "Ship Masconomo lat. 49 S lon. 130 E. Ship sinking, Jan. 14, 1872."*

* Waikato Heads is on the west coast of the North Island of New Zealand, around 50 km southwest of Auckland. The bottle found there with the message inside was written almost two years before it was picked up. It was set adrift around 1,200 miles due south of Australia in the Southern Ocean. From there it was carried by the eastward-setting current between Australia and New Zealand before coming to rest on New Zealand's North Island – a drift distance of around 2,000 miles at an average drift speed of around 2.5 knots.

## 15 May 1874

*Glasgow, 13th May:- A bottle has been washed ashore at Nairn [on the Moray Firth, northeast Scotland] containing a slip of paper on which the following was written: 'Mid-sea, off Cape Wrath [northwest coast of Scotland], schooner Ocean Bride, of Liverpool, in storm for four days. Masts gone, ship rapidly filling, complete wreck. Captain Hendrie's two legs broken by fall of mast. Hopeless. Signed Wm. Massey, Burghead'.*

## 29 Sept 1874

*Aalborg [Denmark], 24th Sept.- A bottle was picked up at Hals [northeast coast Denmark], containing a paper on which was written in pencil, in the German language:- "26th Aug., 1874, brig Aurora, of Calmar, Capt. Steensoe; vessel abandoned in the North Sea, waterlogged. One man washed overboard; if we are not picked up soon, shall go the same way."*

## 3 Oct 1874

*A bottle containing a paper on which the following is written in pencil, has been picked up at Cahir [southeast Ireland]:- "On board ship Spring, 22nd Sept., 1874. Off Islands. Boats washed away. Ship sinking. All hope lost. Good-bye to dear Erin. Wm. McAule, mate."*

## 15 April 1875

*A bottle has been found on the coast of Nice, containing the following letter:- "Dear Jane.- Our ship, the Falcon, is a total wreck on the Zaffarin islands. If we reach the shore alive you will hear more of us; if not, perhaps this may give you an account of our death.- Yours, Catherine Thompson. Falcon, 24th Mar., 1875." This letter is enclosed in an envelope, on which is written:- "The finder is begged to forward this to Mrs. J. Blake, 6 Hyde Park Place, London, W."*

These "Zaffarin islands" (or Islas Chafarinas, or Djaferin Islands) are three small islands 5 km off the northeast coast of Morocco and the North African Spanish enclave of Melilla – Isla Isabel II, Isla del Congreso and Isla del Rey – with an aggregate land area of just 0.5 km². A 190-strong Spanish military garrison on Isla Isabel II is the only resident population. The islands have been claimed by Spain as sovereign territory since 1847. The bottle with Catherine Thompson's message in it must have drifted northeast around 750 miles in just three weeks or so from these islands to the south coast of France near Nice, indicating a rate of drift of around 35 miles a day at 1.5 knots.

Clues about the fate of a vessel wrecked at sea are contained in the following reports: the first about pieces of the wreckage from the vessel washed ashore; the second a message in a bottle from a clearly distressed and soon to be drowned victim of the vessel.

## 29 Oct 1875

*Shields, 26th Oct.- The stern of a boat marked "Dorothy Jobson", and the ship's stern, marked, as well as a medicine chest, have washed ashore near Stonehaven.*

***Shields, 26th Oct.***
*A bottle containing the following has been picked up:-*
*"Dorothy Jobson", Oct. 25, 1875*
*"Dear Father.- At 4 p.m., midway between Fifeness and Buchanness [southeast coast of Scotland], trying to keep her off the shore, a heavy sea struck the vessel, carrying away mainmast and wheel, and washing master and mate overboard. The remainder of us got the boat out in the forenoon, but she swamped. We made a raft, but the painter [bow rope] carried away. About 2 p.m. a schooner hove in sight, and answered our signals for assistance, but offered us no assistance.*

*It is 4.30 p.m. now, and we expect to go down in another hour. John Ross, Robert Hope, William Kingston, join me in bidding farewell to our parents and friends. So, therefore, good-bye dear father, and may God prosper you. Charles Charlton, Felix Symon, send their farewell to all friends. Any one who picks this up will do our friends a great favour if he sends it to Mr. W.C. Bergen, 5, Eldon-street, Blyth, Northumberland.*

*I am, your loving son, W.C. Bergen.*
*"Je meurs en regretant ma soeur, Alex. Simon, et ma bien aimée, Annie Rowan." ["I die in sorrow for my sister, Alex. Simon, and my dearly beloved, Annie Rowan."]*

Remnants washed ashore of another wrecked vessel, below, were followed by the discovery of a message written by the mate of the vessel in his (and her) final moments.

## 13 Jan 1894

*Courier.- Dantzic, Jan. 9.- The schooner Courier, of this port, [Capt.] Prohl, has probably been lost on the Swedish coast while on her voyage from Hartlepool for Dantzic. Information has been received here from the German Consulate in Gothenburg, that fragments had been found on the coast there, also a bottle containing a letter addressed by the mate (O. Fisser) to his mother at Dantzic, telling her that the vessel had suffered greatly, and was about to sink. Most of the vessel's crew were Dantzic men, and as no news of her has been received from anyone of them, it is feared that all hands were lost.*

### 16 Jan 1894

*Courier.- Dantzic, Jan. 11.- A despatch from the German Consulate in Gothenburg states:- In a bottle found on the Swedish coast were the following lines:- "Dear Mother,- To-day, at 8 o'clock in the evening, the 17th Nov., the rudder was carried away, and Capt. Prohl and the sailors Zillmer and Halbmann went overboard, and the same fate will shortly be ours. Greet all and comfort thyself. Thy son, true till death.- O. Fisser, mate, ship Courier, Dantzic."*

The next two messages are from two vessels close by each other more or less simultaneously on the verge of oblivion.

## 30 Dec 1876

*Berwick, 27th Dec.- In a tin box picked up by a fisherman on the shore here has been found a letter which contained the following:- "Schooner Regina, of Jersey, 21st December. To whoever may find it.- H.P. Erith Fair View-place, Gorey, Jersey, 4 p.m. Blowing a fearful East gale, sea terrible, hourly expecting to go on shore. Can do nothing for her. Tried to sail several times; she won't bear it. Have told crew what to expect to-night. God grant wind may veer in time to save us.*

*Soundings in 27 fathoms rock, so now there is no chance. Expect to go ashore between Ferns and Coquet. No chance of saving life with this sea. Should like to see something. Weather thick. Have been lying-to two days. Have done all I could to keep her off, but can't carry canvas. Praying the Lord may have mercy on our souls, and take us to heaven. W. McReddy (or McReilly)...Tell my dear sisters I am thinking and praying for them."*

### 8 Jan 1877

*Berwick, 5th Jan.- A bottle, containing a letter, dated 21st Dec., 1876, and on which was written the following, was picked up at Cheswick this morning:- "Barque Rosella (? Borelia), Shields, 60 miles SE of Fern lights, fearful sea; lost captain and my brother overboard an hour ago. A schooner sank beside us; every sea expecting to be our last. Whoever picks up, etc."*

The *Regina* of the first message and the *Rosella* (or *Borelia*) of the second message were in the North Sea off the Northumberland coast, south of Berwick-upon-Tweed. The Fern (Farne) Islands are near Holy Island (Lindisfarne), about 18 miles southeast of Berwick; Coquet Island is some 20 miles further south. Both the *Regina* and the *Rosella* (or *Borelia*) were close by each other on the same day, 21 December 1876, in atrocious weather conditions. The schooner that sank next to the *Rosella* (or *Borelia*) must almost certainly have been the *Regina* of the first message, which itself must have foundered or wrecked on the coast soon thereafter.

## 17 Jan 1877

*London, 16th Jan.- The Hull 'Eastern Morning News' publishes a letter from Messrs. Wells, owners of the Wells (s), and the following letter which was picked up in a bottle washed ashore at Lybster, on the night of the 12th Jan.- "December 21, 1876. My dear wife and son.- We are laid to in the North sea, about 100 miles Westward of the Holman, with our hatch stove in and gangways gone. The sea is fearful. It is washing in and out of the main hatchway, and washing the linseed out of the hold. It happened at 4 a.m. this morning. My dear, we have the boat swung already for lowering, but we dare not for the sea. There is no water in the after-hold, and the engines are going ahead to pump the water out, but I am afraid it is to no purpose. I don't think we shall live the night out. Pray to God to forgive us our sins, for we have many.*

*My dear wife and son.- It is a painful thing to write to you both and say that I expect every moment to be my last. The ship was too deep down to Plimsoll's mark. Ships ought not to be allowed to load so deep. Good day. God bless you both, and I hope he will protect you; and tell John to be a good boy, and keep honest and sober.- Your affectionate husband, John Cook, chief mate, Wells (s), of Hull – 130 Day street, Hull."*

## 9 April 1878

*Rotterdam, 7th Apl.- The following is the translation of a document in French, which has been picked up in a bottle in the harbour of Ymuiden [Ijmuiden, Netherlands]:- "The crew (eight men) of the vessel named the Constantinople are dying of extreme want. The master and his wife are already dead. The chief officer is named Gardieux and the master M. Valois. Adieu, we are without hope. The gale has driven us towards the English coast. We have no more time to lose, being on the point of death. 29th Mar., 1878."*

The next two messages are from two bottles picked up at two locations just about 350 miles apart, from two different vessels of virtually the same name, within about a month of each other being lost in the North Sea, the first vessel (*Mary An*) being wrecked on the coast of Jutland, in Denmark, the second (*Mary Ann*) apparently foundering off the northeast coast of Scotland.

## 22 July 1879

*Warberg [Sweden], July 15.- "Mary An" – Fishermen picked up on July 13, between the fort here and the Skrifvare Rock, a bottle containing a paper, on which was written in Swedish and Danish:- "The ship 'Mary An', from Holmestrand [Norway], is a wreck on the Jutland Coast [Denmark]. There seems no hope of being saved. God be merciful to us all. Give this my last greeting to my parents. (Signed) August Rerg (?) – surname indistinct – from Westervik [Västervik, Sweden], the 7/5 79."*

### 20 Aug 1879

*Fraserburgh [northeast Scotland], Aug. 17.- The enclosed portion of an envelope was picked up on the beach at a place called Pitullia, about four miles to the westward of Fraserburgh. The piece of envelope was in a soda-water bottle, corked and sealed. The seal bore the name of Gratton &*

Co., Belfast. The paper has on it the following words:- "Ship Mary Ann fast sinking off Buchan Ness, 2 men washed overboard. Lord preserve us."

## 20 Sept 1879

A bottle has been picked up, July 16, on the coast of New Zealand, containing a small scrap of blue paper on which the following was written:- "Strathnaver on fire off Polly Beach, 29 Apl. 1876.- W. Waller, chief officer." The Strathnever, of Aberdeen, from Sydney, with wool, was posted as "Missing Vessel" on Nov. 3, 1875. According to the Sydney Morning Herald, Samuel Waller was mate on board the vessel.

This message, above, bears the only information about the fate of the *Strathnaver* and her crew, three and a half years after the vessel burned and was presumed lost with all on board.

## 29 Oct 1881

A bottle containing paper on which the following message was written has been found at the east side of the island of South Ronaldshay, Orkney [Islands], by Mr. Norquay:- "Barque Minner Watson, N.S. (Nova Scotia), latitude 50 10 north; longitude 4 45 west. Oct. 17, three days off, fearful weather, leaking very much, never expect to see home or friends again. God bless all.- Thomas Jackson." On the other side of the paper was written "Our last day. Oh! Such a gale and sea. The poor ship is nearly a complete wreck. Heaven have mercy on us."

The *Minner Watson*, in its and, apparently, the writer's last hours, was just off the eastern side of the Lizard Peninsula, Cornwall. The bottle, however, was picked up on the Orkney Islands to the northeast of Scotland. In the less than two weeks between the date the message was written (17 October) and the date it was found (on or about 28 October), the bottle must have drifted all around the coast of Britain, from almost the farthest southwest to almost the farthest northeast. Given the numerous headlands, bays, islands, rocks and inlets along the west coast of Britain (as well as the not inconsiderable obstacle of Ireland) where the bottle might have stranded, it seems more likely to have drifted the 800 or so miles around the east coast of Britain where such features and obstacles are far fewer.

## 17 April 1882

Amble [Northumberland, northeast coast England], April 15, 11 30 a.m.- A bottle was picked up last night (April 14) on Hauxly beach. It contained the following:- "Ship Jane, lat. 46 [N], long. 56 [W], iceberg struck us under. God help us. M. Anderson, Perth; P. Gray, R. Hunter, High-street."

According to the message inside this bottle, it was thrown off the ship *Jane* at a point just southwest of Cape Race, Newfoundland, after the vessel struck an iceberg. The bottle must have been carried right across the Atlantic and around the north of the British Isles by the Gulf Stream and its northern continuation, the North Atlantic Drift, which flow up the coast of southern Newfoundland to the north of the British Isles between Scotland and Iceland, to end up on the northeast coast of England.

## 26 Aug 1882

Copenhagen, Aug. 23.- Anna.- A bottle has washed ashore at Brako, in Horsens Fjord, containing a slip of paper on which is written:- "On board the brig Anna, Aug. 3, 1882. Terrific gale. Vessel leaky – can no longer keep at the pumps. I shall perhaps never see you more, my Else, my darling *girl. – therefore I write this greeting, which the good finder will bring to you. You will see that you have been loved to the last by, yours faithfully till death, Jens Madsen, mate of the Anna, belonging to Give, near Velle. To Miss Else Marie Mortensen, Kryblly, near Velle."*

Horsens Fjord is on the mid-east coast of Denmark, just north of Vejle Fjord. "Velle" is the town of Vejle which has since incorporated the small adjoining Danish town of Give.

## 14 Nov 1882

*Penzance [Cornwall], Nov. 11.- A corked bottle has been picked up on the beach at Porthleven recently. Some grains of maize were in the bottle, also a piece of paper, having the following written upon it:- "Ship Anna, from America to London, caught fire on the Atlantic, after a gale. I think all hands will be burned or drowned, having no boat. (Signed) T. Williams. Lord have mercy on us."*

## 27 Dec 1882

**Bottle Picked Up**

*A bottle was found below Graemshall Holm, Kirkwall [Orkney Islands], on Thursday last, containing the following message:- "Ship Francesca, December 10, 1882. Waterlogged and sinking in Pentland Firth\*; crew 18. God help us. 12 o'clock.- Carl Wred."*

* The Pentland Firth is a notoriously stormy channel of often boisterous sea, about seven miles wide, between the northeast tip of Scotland (Duncansby Head) and the southernmost point of the Orkney Islands (Brough Ness).

## 11 July 1885

*Stranraer [southwest Scotland], July 9.- A bottle was found in Dumbreddan Bay, containing a note written in pencil, which reads:- "The brig Norseman is going to pieces, and we are in a helpless state, but put ourselves into God's hands; Amen. Peter Johnson, Jose Thomson, Jos. Anderson."*

## 27 July 1885

*Youghal (by Tel. dated Cork, July 27, 10 45 a.m.).- On a card washed ashore at Ballycronane [southwest Ireland] there was written:- "Barque Acadia, timber-laden, sprung leak June 5; three men on raft.- Signed, Brown, mate."*

## 29 July 1885

*Ballycronane (Castlemarty), July 25.- A bottle has been found on the strand here containing a piece of cardboard, on one side of which is written:- "The barque Batavia lost on June 5. We are on a raft, God help us. J. Brown, mate, H. Good and J. Derry;" and on the other side, "barque laden with timber; sprung a leak and here we are. J. Brown, mate."*

The two messages above are clearly from the same castaways, and from a wrecked ship most probably named *Batavia* rather than *Acadia*: the name on the piece of card washed ashore at Ballycronane was probably defaced by the elements and mistakenly read or reported as *Acadia*.

## 1 Dec 1885

*London, Dec. 1.- A bottle was picked up on South Shields beach yesterday containing a piece of paper with the following words written upon it:- "Steamer Derwent, off Boston Deeps, Saturday night, 8 p.m. Fires all out; no hope left for us. Full of water. Good-bye, cannot say any more now. Nothing in sight. Only one other plunge."*

## 2 March 1886

*Sunbeam.- Wexford [Ireland], March 1.- A bottle was picked up on Curracloe Strand yesterday, containing a copy of the National Anthem from the National Temperance Hymnal, published in Ilfracombe, on the back of which the following is written:- "The ship Sunbeam is on fire. I commit myself in hand of the Blessed Saviour. Bay of Biscay, Jan., 1886."*

## 26 April 1886

*Wick [north coast Scotland], April 24, 1 44 p.m.- Bottle found in Sinclair Bay, Wick, containing the following message, written on a piece of grey paper: "Ship Admiral, Pentland Firth, great distress, making water rapidly, sinking fast; good-bye to my dear wife, Annie Anderson, Kircaldy; my last testimony, James Anderson."*

## 29 Jan 1887

*Falke.- Rio [de] Janeiro, Jan. 8.- The commander of the Brazilian gunboat Lomba, employed in the quarantine service, picked up a bottle at sea containing the following statement:- "In the night of Dec. 10, 1886, the Norwegian vessel Falke sank near the coast of the island of San Francisco. The vessel's two boats, on which the crew were going to get, were smashed against the vessel, so that we have no resource except to take refuge in the vessel itself, which will not be able to resist two hours longer the water that is coming in at her bottom. Therefore it was resolved to send off this bottle with the present declaration, in order, if possible, to get some assistance from shore. (Signed) The captain, Johan Gulver."*

*This declaration was enclosed in a champagne bottle, and was picked up on the 19th at the north point of the bar of San Francisco. The commander of the gunboat's instructions did not permit him to lose sight of the bar, but he cruised, although nine days had elapsed, as far as the Gracas Islands, going among them in every direction. He, however, neither found anything nor obtained any information from the vessels which he spoke.- [The Norwegian brigantine Falke sailed from Cardiff on May 10 (1886) for Parana, the master's name then reported was Matthiesen.]*

San Francisco Island – Ilha de São Francisco – named in the message is just off the coast of the State of Santa Catarina, in southeastern Brazil.

## 30 June 1887

*Newport [south Wales], Mon., June 29, 5 15 p.m.- Police sergeant in charge at Newnham, Gloucester, writes Custom House here giving contents of a letter enclosed in a bottle which was picked up there on the 27th. It reads as follows:- "Tusker Rock, 22d June, 1887.- The ship Adelaide has stranded off the above-named rock; help needed at once; filling every minute. The captain, W. Thomas. God save my wife."*

The Tusker Rock in the message above lies off the south coast of Wales; it is not the much larger Tuskar Rock off the southern Irish coast, which has a lighthouse on it. There is another Tusker Rock off the Welsh Pembrokeshire coast, near Skomer Island. The next message concerns Bishop Rock (and its lighthouse), at the Scilly Isles.

## 10 April 1888
### Bottle Report

Pembroke Dock [Wales], April 9.- A bottle was picked up yesterday near Lawrenny, in this harbour, containing a paper on which the following is written:- "Barque St. Vincent sinking off Bishops*; boats all gone.- J. Wilson, March 20, 10 10 p.m."

*Bishop Rock Lighthouse, located four miles west of the Scilly Isles. The dangerous rocks, reefs and ledges of the Scilly Isles had wrecked numerous ships before it was decided to build a new lighthouse there in the mid-1800s. The only one near there at the time was on the island of St. Agnes, which was built in 1680 and considered inadequate for the protection of vessels sailing in the vicinity of the archipelago. (St. Agnes Lighthouse was turned off in 1911, when Peninnis Lighthouse, on the main island of St. Mary, was constructed. The 138-ft high lighthouse tower on St. Agnes is now used as a daymark, for vessels navigating around the islands.)

Construction of the Bishop Rock Lighthouse began in 1847. Two years later it was completed except for installation of the light itself. In February 1850, however, a violent gale destroyed the edifice and work had to begin again. The light of the new Bishop Rock Lighthouse was first lit on 1 September 1858. In the 1880s the structure was reinforced and the elevation of the light increased by 12m. Since 1992 the light has been automated; the last lighthouse keepers left on 21 December 1992. The lighthouse tower is 49m high. The light itself is 44m above the mean high water mark and the range of the light is 24 nautical miles.

## 6 Oct 1888

*Fraserburgh [40 miles north of Aberdeen, Scotland], Oct 5, 8 10 p.m.- Piece of paper picked up in ginger-beer bottle, half-mile east Rosehearty, dated Aug. 12, 1888:- "Schooner Edinburgh Castle, of Newcastle, sinking fast mid-ocean; if no help comes, will soon be in eternity. God help us. Signed Gd. Fellows."*

## 29 Oct 1888

*Ballycotton [Co. Cork, Ireland], Oct. 27, 4 15 p.m.- Bottle picked up in Ballycotton Bay containing scrap of paper, with the following written in ink on it:- "The barque Jane, of Bilbao, going down, all hands on board. God save us all, good-bye to my dear wife Jane Murray, Ganges-street, Newcastle."*

The note written by a crew member on the barque *Cumeria*, below, was prescient. (The name of the vessel reported at first as *Camera* was corrected in a later issue of *Lloyd's List* to *Cumeria*.)

## 14 Nov 1888

*Amble [Northumberland coast], Nov. 13.- Picked up in Druidge Bay, a bottle containing a paper; writing on it:- "Barque Camera, May 9. Should this be picked up please tell all my friends that the treatment I am receiving from the mate is awful, and all the crew say that we will never reach port, the ship making so much water. Westerley, apprentice."*

### *14 Nov 1888*

*The Cumeria, Hilton, of Liverpool, Off. No. 63,195, sailed from the Tyne, for Valparaiso, for orders, with coal, on April 20 last, was spoken on June 12, in lat. 30 S, long. 50 W, and has not since been heard of.*

Apprentice Westerley was correct: the *Cumeria*, after being spoken off the coast of southern Brazil ("in lat. 30 S, long. 50 W") on 12 June 1888, never reached port and "has not since been heard of".

## 23 Nov 1888

*Dunbar [southeast Scotland], Nov. 20.- A bottle was picked up on the shore last night, containing a paper on which the following is written:- "Off coast of Spain, lat. 35 3 [N], long. 16 9 [W], ship sinking fast, cargo of copper ore from Chili [Chile], decks washed bare. Adam Liddle, Captain. II Corinthians, iv., 3. 15 June, 1888."*

This bottle message, above, was set adrift just to the northeast of the island of Madeira, where the ocean currents flow generally southwards. Five months later it was found on the southeast coast of Scotland. To get there, realistically it must have drifted westward across the Atlantic, then been transported back across the North Atlantic in the Gulf Stream and North Atlantic Drift, round the north of Scotland to fetch up on the Scottish coast just south of the Firth of Forth – a distance of some 6,000 miles or so over 150 days at an average rate of drift of 1.5–2 knots. "II Corinthians, iv., 3" is Ch. 4, verse 3 of the Second Epistle of Paul the Apostle to the Corinthians: 'But if our Gospel be hid, it is hid to them that are lost'.

## 28 Aug 1889

**Maritime Intelligence**

**Miscellaneous**

*An unsigned telegram has been received from Lossiemouth [northeast Scotland], dated Aug. 27, 2 35 p.m., which states as follows:- A small tin box containing slip of paper, having the following written on it in pencil, was picked up on strand, east of Lossiemouth, last night:- "Steamship Lady Ann foundering at sea NNE 20 men 100 horses 41 passengers – to my mother at 69 Back St., Findhorn\*, Mrs. Smith."*

\*Findhorn is a small coastal village just to the west of Lossiemouth at the mouth of the Moray Firth, northeast Scotland.

## 20 Sept 1890

*Copenhagen, Sept. 16.- A bottle was picked up Sept. 9 on Starholm Strand [beach] containing a piece of paper, apparently torn off from an account form such as is used by captains. On the paper was written in pencil:- "S. Hansen Jorgensen, Svendborg", and the balance stated was 325 kroner 42 oere, but there was no signature. On the other side was written in Danish:- "Will you greet Klara Bring, Odense. Leaky in the North Sea, and we can no longer keep the ship afloat with the pumps, but we have the prospect of a wide grave in the North Sea. Farewell dear parents in Odense, Funen, Denmark." There was no signature.*

Funen, or Fyn, in Danish, is the third largest island in Denmark. Odense is its main town.

The next two reports concern a Welsh trading schooner that was reported missing four and a half months before a message in a bottle written by the mate of the vessel was found that explained what happened to her.

## 29 April 1891

*Resolute, Jones, of Aberystwith, Off. No. 13,155, sailed from Aberdovey for Weymouth on Feb.*

26, 1891, with a cargo of coal; left Milford Haven on March 7, 1891, and has not since been heard of.

### 14 Sept 1891

London, Sept. 14.- A bottle has been picked up near the harbour at Aberystwith, containing the following communication:- "Schooner Resolute, of Borth, P. [port] of Aberystwith (Wales), 16 miles W of Isle of Wight; great snowstorm; vessel stretched timbers and in sinking condition; no chance of escape from drowning; good bye, mate. If found please communicate with friends of captain and crew; am afraid hope is gone by the way she is tossed about; she has lost maintopmast and sails. Progress has kept head, and we have lost sight of her. Good-bye; vessel nearly gone."

## 22 Sept 1892

Helene.- Rostock, Sept. 17.- A bottle was found yesterday ashore near Dierhagen [on the Baltic coast of northern Germany, northeast of Rostock], in the Baltic, containing a paper on which was written:- "Captain Anderson, ship Helene, try to take care of this. We see death before our eyes, as we find ourselves in great danger." As wreckage has also recently washed ashore near Dierhagen, it is feared that a vessel has been wrecked in the neighbourhood.

## 14 Oct 1892

London, Oct. 14.- A bottle containing the following letter was picked up near Fraserburgh [northeast coast of Scotland]:- "Oct. 7, 1892. At Sea, smack Prince Wales. Dear Mother,- We are lying to in a horaken [hurricane] of wind, of Orknes [off Orkney Islands], and the sea is ofal heavy, hardly possabel to us to live in it. If I never see you anie mor God will provid for you. The two other men is keeping up with a good harth [heart]. Love to all.- From your son, Charles Gilbertson." The bottle and document have been handed to the local Customs' officer, who states that the Prince of Wales is a cutter of 46 tons, and is owned by Mr. Jame Hay, of Limerick.

The following sequence of reports concerns the fate of the steamer Noranside.

## 22 April 1893

Noranside.- Amsterdam, April 21.- A fishing smack, arrived at Ymuiden [Ijmuiden, Netherlands], reports having in lat. 56 25 N, long. 5 20 E, fallen in with a boat bearing the name of "Noranside," with the dead bodies of four sailors tied to the seats; boat painted black and white; high sea prevented approach.

Noranside (s).- London, April 22.- The following telegram has been received from the owners of the Noranside (s), dated Newcastle, April 22, 11 54 a.m.:- Steamer Cameo picked up lifeboat marked "Noranside, Newcastle," containing five dead bodies, off Hanstholm [northern Denmark]. This only information. From Gothenburg.

### 24 April 1893

Noranside (s).- Gothenburg, April 21.- Captain Potter of the steamer Cameo, from Hull, reports that when about 100 miles WSW of Hanstholmen, he picked up a lifeboat belonging to the steamer Noranside, containing the corpses of five men. Everything in the boat pointed to the conclusion that the men had been obliged, unprepared, to jump into the boat to save their lives. The boat was drifting in the general route of steamers.

*11 May 1893*

*London, May 11.- A bottle was picked up at sea off South Shields yesterday, containing a scrap of paper. The message from the sea is as follows:- "Steamship 'Noranside.' In open boat without food or oars.- C.P.L. Harrison."*

*17 May 1893*

**Missing Vessels**

*The Noranside (s), C. Harrison, of Newcastle-on-Tyne, Official No. 72,132, sailed from Blyth for Neufahrwasser [near Gdansk, Poland; then Western Prussia], with a cargo of coal, on April 11, 1893, and has not since been heard of.*

The author of the bottle message, "C.P.L. Harrison", is identified by the Missing Vessel report as the master of the *Noranside*. It seems quite likely that Capt. Harrison was one of the five corpses in the lifeboat found by the *Cameo* 100 miles off the west coast of Denmark in the North Sea. Whether or not that boat was the same one spotted by the Dutch fishing smack, "with the dead bodies of four [*sic*] sailors tied to the seats", is not and almost certainly cannot ever be known.

## 22 Dec 1893

**Bottle Picked Up**

*Madrid, Dec. 21.- The naval authorities at Almeria have telegraphed to the Minister of Marine, stating that some fishermen have found a bottle in the sea, near the harbour, containing the following message:- "Owing to the storm the steamer Carolina, belonging to Bilbao, has foundered off Roquetas [near Almeria]. All hands are lost; I alone am left awaiting the hour of death." The message is signed "captain."*

## 30 Jan 1894

*London, Jan. 30.- An envelope has been found in a bottle floating off the shore at Kilbaha, near Loophead, County Clare [Loophead Peninsula, West Clare, Co. Clare, Ireland], by a man named John O'Neill. The following is the message:- "Friday evening. Dear Louisa.- I am in sight of land off Blaskets [Blasket Islands, off southwest coast of Ireland] this evening. We have lost our deckload of timber, and I am thinking our gallant barque will be lost too. Farewell, dear Louisa, and the children, until I meet you in Heaven.- Your loving husband, Henry Keogh." The message is addressed to Mrs. Captain Keogh, Isle of Wight.*

## 15 Feb 1894

*Campletown, Feb. 14, 7 30 a.m. – 8 p.m. a small bottle was picked up on the shore off Island of Gigha [between Kintyre Peninsula and Island of Islay, west coast Scotland] on Thursday last containing a piece of paper about three inches long by one and a half inch broad, on which the following was written in pencil:- "Sept. 1893, sinking in mid-Atlantic, Horn Head in collision iceberg, mate." (Memo: the Horn Head (s), from Baltimore to Dublin, was posted missing Oct. 25 [1893].)*

## 3 Sept 1894

*Glasgow, Aug. 31.- A sealed bottle has been picked up on the rocks at Bangor, County Down*

*[Ireland], containing a page of small note paper on which was written:- "May Queen off Point of Ayre July 28 1894, sprung leak last night in gale; pumping since, but cannot make any way; mast gone, punt stove in; may float for two hours. God save us. Reginale Mesley, captain, Liverpool; James Arkwright, A.B., Greenock; Michael Kennedy, A.B., Kingston [now Dun Laoghaire]; James Crossley, boy, Greenock."*

God, or Fate, did intervene in the *May Queen*'s deliverance, confirmed by the next report.

### 6 Sept 1894
### Maritime Intelligence

*May Queen (yacht).- London, Sept. 6.- With reference to a report recently published in regard to the washing ashore of a bottle containing a message relating to the yacht May Queen, it is stated that the Waterford [Ireland] steamer Creaden bore down on the helpless yacht, and towed her into Ramsey [Isle of Man].*

### 8 Oct 1894

*Aberdeen, Oct. 8.- A bottle has been found on the sands near Philorth River [Water of Philorth, Aberdeenshire, northeast Scotland], containing the following message:- "Smith s. Brodrick. Ship struck on Monday, June 5, by unknown vessel, all have drowned except myself, who is on a raft about 80 miles east of Newcastle."*

### 22 May 1895

*Dunkirk, May 21.- The following letter was found in a bottle picked up on the shore at Dunkirk:- "Thursday night, May 19 – Barge Cynthia: We are sinking, rudderhead gone, boat, hatches. We are off the Weillingen [De Wielingen, northeast coast of Belgium, southwest coast of Holland]. Have had distress signal flying all day. Farewell to all we love. Captain Gentry, Malden; Carrington, Mistley; Brown, London. Should this be picked up, please send on to 66 Wanty-road, Malden, Essex." It is believed that the vessel must be the barge Cynthia, of Harwich [Essex], registering 74 tons.*

### Maritime Intelligence

*Cynthia.- London, May 22.- The following has been received from the owners with reference to the report of a bottle having been picked up, supposed [believed] to come from the Cynthia (barge):- The vessel left London about the 12th or 13th inst. [May], bound for the Rhine, with a cargo of empty bottles for the Apolinnaris company, and no doubt was caught in the dreadful gale the early part of last week. We received a letter yesterday morning from Mr. De Baecker, of Dunkirk, to say the British Consul had received a letter which had been picked up at sea signed by the captain, mate and sailor, intimating that the Cynthia was in a sinking position. This is the only information we have. From the account we have received of the vessel's dangerous locality we fear the men have been lost.*

The *Cynthia* would have been a sailing barge used to transport cargoes locally around the North Sea and Channel coasts of Britain and to and from nearby northern European ports, particularly in France, Belgium, Holland and Germany. Typically she would have been manned by a crew of three: captain, mate, and deckhand or boy. The owners' fear that all three crew on the *Cynthia* perished when she sunk was confirmed by the fact that nothing more was ever heard from them.

## 9 May 1896

*Nevin [Nefyn, north coast of Lleyn Peninsula, north Wales], May 8.- A bottle was picked up on the 7ᵗʰ inst. on the Nevin Beach containing a slip of paper with following inscription:- "Ship Clare, of Portmadoc, was lost this day, August 8, 1894."*

In 1894 there was a ship named the *Clare*. Her master was Capt. Owen, a common Welsh name, so she probably was the same vessel as above "of Portmadoc", at the eastern extremity of the Lleyn Peninsula in north Wales. Nothing more was heard from her after May 1894 until the discovery of this bottle message two years later.

## 10 June 1896

*Drogheda [east coast of Ireland], June 9.- A bottle has been picked up on Laytown Beach, south of River Boyne, containing a paper stating that the steamer Portia, 30 hands, was foundering off Bermuda on Jan. 5, 1896.*

The 1,156-ton passenger and freight steamship *Portia*, launched in 1884, was operated by the Red Cross Steamship Line on a regular run between New York and St. John's, Newfoundland via Halifax in the 1880s and '90s. She left St. John's on 28 December 1895 for New York via Halifax, which could have put her in the general vicinity of Bermuda on 5 January 1896. Although someone on board might have thought she was sinking, possibly because of bad winter weather, she did not; her voyagings continued throughout 1896 and beyond. She was wrecked on Big Fish Shoal, Newfoundland, in July 1899 on a voyage from New York. The message in the bottle, above, could quite conceivably have drifted the 3,500 miles or so between the Bermuda area and the east coast of Ireland within the six months from when it was written until it was picked up near Drogheda, transported on the northeast flowing warm water conveyor belts of the Gulf Stream and North Atlantic Drift.

## 1 July 1896

*Haverfordwest [Pembrokeshire coast, southwest Wales], July 1, 11 55 a.m.- Picked up at Littlehaven, St. Bride's Bay, yesterday, bottle containing a slip of paper marked "Drummond Castle off Ushant, struck rocks, filling quickly, no boat, Morris, Fort Salisbury."*

The steamship *Drummond Castle* was just over 3,700 tons, 365 ft long, 43.5 ft wide, 31.3 ft deep, and brig-rigged. She was built at Glasgow and launched in 1881 for D. Currie & Co., of London, whose Castle Mail Packets Co. (a forerunner of the Union-Castle Line) operated the vessel on a regular run taking passengers and freight between South Africa and the United Kingdom. On 28 May 1896 she left Cape Town for her voyage to London, via Las Palmas, in the Canary Islands, which she left at 3 p.m. on 12 June with a complement of about 246 persons, comprising 143 passengers and 103 crew. The *Drummond Castle* was under the command of Capt. W.W. Pierce, who had joined the Castle Line as an apprentice in 1868 at the age of 14 and been with the company almost continually since then.

On the night of 16 June 1896 the vessel was off Ushant, the island off the northwest tip of Brittany considered the southern point of the western entrance to the English Channel (the Isles of Scilly being the northern point of the gateway). The weather was foggy and visibility restricted. At around 11 p.m., steaming at around 12 knots, the *Drummond Castle* struck the Pierres Vertes rocks off Ile-Molène near Ile Oessant (the island of Ushant). She sank apparently in less than five minutes. Of the 246 people on board, only three survived: a First Class passenger, Mr. Charles Marquardt, and two members of the crew, the quartermaster named Wood and a seaman named Godbolt, who were all rescued by local fishermen.

Of the 243 who perished in the *Drummond Castle* disaster, only about 70 bodies were eventually recovered. Many of them were buried on Ile-Molène and at Conquet on the mainland.

The *Drummond Castle's* passenger list included a Mrs. Morris "from Natal", meaning that she embarked on the *Drummond Castle* at Port Natal (now Durban, in South Africa). The "Fort Salisbury" in Mrs. Morris's message was in Mashonaland (now Zimbabwe), and was founded by Cecil Rhodes as a fort in 1890. It subsequently became Salisbury, the capital town of Rhodesia in its various manifestations, and, from 1982, Harare, capital of the newly-established (1980) Zimbabwe.

Mrs. Morris apparently disembarked from the vessel at Cape Town where she picked up her two sons from school so that the three of them could travel to England together. Both sons also drowned in the disaster. (Mr. Morris, travelling on another vessel, found out about the loss of the *Drummond Castle*, and the death of his wife and children, some time afterwards when his ship touched at Madeira en route to England.) Mrs. Morris's body was never recovered, or at least never identified. Her last communication, which must have been written in great haste, was committed to the fate of a bottle's drift, and eventual discovery, for posterity.

## 10 July 1896

*Amsterdam, July 9.- There was washed ashore on Texel yesterday a bottle containing a small note, on which the following was written:- "I am flowing along on the ocean in a small boat, without food or water. I will die in a few hours. Notify my wife, 13, Plymouth-street, London.- John Smith." This note has been forwarded to the British Consul at Amsterdam.*

## 21 July 1896

*Haverfordwest, July 20, 6 29 p.m.- Bottle picked up at Broadhaven yesterday, containing paper marked: "We, the survivors of the trawler Mary Ann, of Swansea, are adrift in a boat near St. Bride's Bay, in Pembrokeshire. The trawler was sunk in a collision during the night of July 14. Captain Hendry Thomas. Urgent assistance is needed."*

## 27 Nov 1896

*Buenos Ayres, Nov. 2.- Telegrams from Valparaiso announce that the captain of the steamer which arrived at Port Montt [Puerto Montt, in the south of Chile] on the 28th inst., picked up a bottle in mid-ocean containing a piece of paper with the following words:- "Impossible to save the ship, boat dashed away by the sea. Nothing remains but to die. Barque Stella – Hamburg – Grangler."*

## 7 Dec 1896

*London, Dec. 7.- The Australian steamer Warrimoo, on arrival at Victoria, British Columbia, on Saturday, reported having picked up a bottle at sea containing an unsealed message, yellow with age, and saying the ship Mohawk had sprung a leak and the crew were taking to the boats. The message concluded:- "God help us – John Franklin." The Mohawk was lost 16 years ago [1880] and was never since heard of. She belonged to Troon, Ayrshire, and Franklin was the name of the mate. This message is the first indication of the vessel's fate.*

On 30 April 1880 the *Mohawk* sailed from San Francisco bound for Cork in Ireland, under the command of Capt. Macauly. She should have arrived at Cork towards the end of the summer of 1880. The message found 16 years later, above, confirmed that she foundered somewhere in the Pacific along her route towards Cape Horn, and that all her crew perished either by drowning along with their ship or lost at sea in her boats.

## 25 Jan 1898

*Valparaiso, Dec. 22.- A Serena [La Serena, near Coquimbo] newspaper says that an employee of the San Joaquim Estate picked up on Sunday the 14th inst., on the seashore at the mouth of the River Coquimbo, a sealed bottle which contained a piece of paper on which written the following:- "Hemos naufragado lat. 33 Sur long. 0 73 G. We are shipwrecked lat. 33 S, long. 76 W. Gr. [?] Help! Au secours! Salvadnos! [Save us!] Barca Britanica [British ship] Cleo." The paper is of the ordinary white colour, blue lined, and has some brown spots, perhaps owing to its immersion in water. The paper bears no date.*

The position stated in the message above is in the Pacific about 190 miles due west of Valparaiso, Chile.

## 2 March 1898

### The Loss of the Elbe

### A Message From the Sea

### Paris, March 1

*Some trawlers on the Calvados coast [northern France around Caen, just west of Le Havre] lately dragged up with deep-sea oysters a bottle in which they found a card. The cork had been damaged by sea water, and some writing on the card was greatly blurred in consequence. A fisherman brought the card to M. Aubert, ex-Librarian of the National Library, who was visiting the neighbourhood. He took it to Paris and showed it to a German librarian, who read the blurred writing. It was:- "Wreck of the Elbe. My darling fiancée Mina.- I shall never see you again unless in another world. I beg the person who may find this card to send it to Mina Frankel, at Buchan Federsee, Wurtemburg." On the front of the card was printed "Bernard Ramsporge, of the firm of C. Gomer, stocking manufacturers at Weingarten."*

The *Elbe* was lost in the North Sea in 1985 with 380 out of 400 passengers. Mina Frankel and the firm of C. Gomer have been apprised of this message from the deep.

The Norddeutscher Lloyd liner *Elbe*, of 4,510 tons, was built in 1881 by John Elder & Co. at Govan, Glasgow. She had accommodation for a total of 1,117 passengers (179 first class, 142 second class, and 796 in steerage). On Tuesday, 29 January 1895 she left Bremerhaven for New York via Southampton where she was scheduled to pick up other passengers before heading across the Atlantic. She carried 354 persons, comprising 199 passengers and 155 crew including one German and one English pilot.

Around 5:30 on the morning of 30 January the *Elbe* was just off the Suffolk coast of southern England, driving hard into a heavy sea and blizzard conditions. At the same time a small steamship of 475 tons, the *Crathie*, from Aberdeen in northeast Scotland and bound for Rotterdam, was heading straight for the *Elbe*. The liner was lit up brightly and even firing rockets to warn other vessels of her presence. The *Crathie* should have altered course to keep out of the way of the *Elbe* which had the right of way. Instead, seemingly oblivious of the big liner, she collided with the *Elbe* on her port side. Within half an hour the *Elbe* sank by her stern, taking with her the lives of 334 persons, including her master, Capt. von Gossell. Only one boatload of five passengers and 15 crew from the *Elbe* survived the tragedy, rescued by a fishing smack, the *Wildflower*, from the nearby port of Lowestoft, about five hours after they were cast adrift.

The *Crathie*, meanwhile, which was holed just below the waterline, continued on her course to Rotterdam in the belief that the *Elbe* had suffered no worse than she and would therefore not require assistance. A later Board of Trade court of inquiry found the *Crathie*'s first mate, Mr. Craig, wholly and solely responsible for The Disaster; he had left the bridge so that there was no proper lookout at the critical time just as the two vessels were about to cross paths. His certificate was cancelled. The court found fault with the *Elbe*'s officers only in that they should have taken action to avoid a collision when the danger of it became imminent, notwithstanding the *Elbe*'s right of way over the *Crathie* when both were on a collision course heading towards each other.

## 22 Sept 1898

*Hull, Sept. 21.- A ginger-beer bottle was picked up on the Seaforth Sands yesterday. On being opened it was found to contain the following:- "Brittany, ship sinking. Heaven help us."*

## 3 Oct 1898

*Agger, Jutland [Denmark], Sept. 30.- A piece of paper was found in a bottle on the coast here yesterday, containing the following:- "John Strachan, Capt.; Alexer [probably Alexander] Mitchell, 1st mate; William Gouk, 2nd mate; Charles Galloway, scullery boy. Wrecked on the 2nd July, 1898, all hands is looking for the worst, there is no hope, good bye. J. St., Capt."*

## 17 Nov 1898

*Fremad.- Christiansund [Norway], Nov. 4.- A bottle was found on Sept. 2, in Langsund, south of Sveggen, containing a slip of paper on which was written:- "Schooner Fremad. To each and all, 21/4/1898, we had a hurricane from NNW. Our ship is going down, Captain H. Reiner. Two boats are smashed. God help us. Amen!"*

## 14 Feb 1899

*London, Feb. 14.- A passenger from Dublin to Holyhead related the following incident, which occurred during the passage:- After a very rough voyage, and when within four miles of Holyhead, a bottle was thrown upon the deck [by the sea], which was found to contain a message written in Danish, which was translated as follows:- "Barque Dhjoric: We have sprung a leak and are sinking. Have had fearful weather for some days. Total hands on board 16; three washed overboard to-day. Good-bye. God help us." Signature was faded and indistinct.*

This was certainly one of the most unusual ways a bottle with a message in it was ever found!

## 20 March 1899

**Maritime Intelligence**

*Recepta (s).- Boston [Lincolnshire], March 20, 10 40 a.m.- The steamer Recepta, of London, from Tyne for Pillau\* (coals), foundered in the North Sea; Captain Walsh and 12 men landed here by steam trawler Kirton, of Boston; one boat and four men missing.*

## 26 May 1899

**Bottle Picked Up**

*Whitby, May 25.- A bottle containing the following message, written in pencil, was picked up on the shore at East Row Beck, Sandsend, this morning:- "Boat and four hands Recepta (s) floated two days; don't think we will float much longer, and good-bye."*

* The destination of the *Recepta* was Pillau, the German name for a seaport on the Gulf of Danzig, at the northern entrance to the Vistula Lagoon in what was at the time East Prussia and part of Germany. At the end of World War II, East Prussia was officially annexed to Russia and renamed Kaliningrad. Pillau was renamed Baltiysk. Today Kaliningrad Oblast (a province of the Russian Federation) is the westernmost part of Russia, an isolated exclave with no land connection to Russia and bordered by Poland, Lithuania and the Baltic Sea.

## 7 April 1899

*Kimmeridge [near Poole, on the south Dorset coast], April 6, 1 50 p.m.- The following message was found in a bottle picked up on Kimmeridge beach, dated March 15:- "We are on a raft outside Eddystone Lighthouse; all our efforts to attract the men [in the lighthouse] are in vain; we come from Lowestoft; there are four of us. Anyone finding this get help at once.- H. Oakley and Jackson N. Oldery McDuff."*

## 5 June 1899

**Maritime Intelligence**

*Gessner.- Abo [Swedish name for the city of Turku in southwest Finland], May 27.- The owner, Robert Mattson, of the barque Gessner, of Mariehamn, Janson, which left Antwerp Jan. 26 for Sapelo [presumably Sapelo Island, Georgia, USA], has received, through the Russian Consulate, a communication from the Board of Trade, stating that on April 21 the following bottle message was found near the Bishop Rock [lighthouse near Isles of Scilly]:- "Ship Gessner, of Mariehamn\*, was lost in the Atlantic on Feb 12, 1899. Greetings to Aaland\* and my betrothed; she lives in Saltvik\*, and we shall meet at the gate of Heaven with the Redeemer. Greet my parents and sister, we shall also meet with God in heaven; it is so hard to part, very hard. T.J. Holmberg, second mate." John Theodor Holmberg shipped in the vessel Oct. 8 as second mate.*

* Mariehamn is the main town of the Åland Islands off the southwest coast of Finland, at the mouth of the Gulf of Bothnia between Sweden and Finland. Saltvik is a small village in the northern part of the archipelago. The Åland Islands were renowned for their great seafaring heritage and particularly for the deep-sea sailing ships from Mariehamn. Capt. Gustav Erikson (1872–1947), the most admired Finnish sailing ship owner of the time, was from the Åland Islands.

## 14 June 1899

*San Francisco, June 1.- Letter received at Merchant's Exchange to-day from Kodiak [Alaska] dated May 18, 1899, included a note which was extracted from a bottle and picked up on the 15th May on the beach in Portage Bay, on the Peninsula of Alaska, lat. 57 34 N, long. 155 35 W. It will possibly throw some light on the mystery of a missing vessel, probably Pelican (s). Note reads as follows:- "Steamer Pelican, lat. 50 N, long. 175 W. The ship is sinking. We are leaving her in frail boats. Please report us," and signed M.S. Patterson, chief officer. The above note was written on a Northern Pacific Steamship Company's blank. [Memo: The Pelican was posted as missing on Feb. 9, 1898.]*

## 27 Nov 1899

*London, Nov. 27.- A bottle picked up in the estuary of the Taw, a few miles from Barnstaple [north Devon], contains the following message written in pencil on a leaf torn from a pocket-book:- "Whoever thou art that findest this communicate with the authorities. We are lost on a island in the Atlantic, not far out of the track of steamers near Newfoundland. We are nearly starving. Save us.- Signed James McCoy, Thomas Brown, H. Henry Thornton (his mark), dated Sept. 3, 1899. PC.- Haste or you may be too late." All the message is in one handwriting, except the signature of Thomas Brown.*

The only islands "in the Atlantic, not far out of the track of steamers near Newfoundland" were the inhabited French islands of St. Pierre & Miquelon. Uninhabited Sable Island, the 'graveyard of the Atlantic', lay somewhat further south. Any bottle message set adrift from either place would have been carried across the North Atlantic by the Gulf Stream, a distance of some 2,000 miles to the southeast coast of England where it was found. The maximum rate of drift of about 1.5 knots, or some 35 miles/day (assuming that the bottle was picked up on the Devon coast soon after it washed ashore there, after a drift of about two months), would be about right for the average flow of the Gulf Stream in that part of the Atlantic.

## 1 Feb 1900

*Valentia Island [Ireland], Jan. 31, 7 20 p.m.- Bottle picked up on beach near Valentia, containing following [message]:- "Latitude 52 37 [N], longitude 13 45 [W], dated Jan. 17, 1900, on board barque Farantam (?), left St. John's, Newfoundland, Dec. 14, with cargo timber for Queenstown. On 22nd encountered severe gale, cargo shifted and vessel sprung leak; working pumps two days and nights, and exhausted. We are driving before WSW wind, toward south-west Ireland. Signed Henrie Nicholson, master."*

Although no vessel named *Farantam* (or anything similar) was recorded as having left St. John's, Newfoundland on or around 14 December 1899, and no other information was posted about the vessel for the year 1900, the particulars of the message have a ring of authenticity about it. At the time the message was written the vessel would have been off the west coast of Ireland about 150 miles northwest of Valentia. If the message was genuine, she probably sank soon after or was wrecked on the Irish coast.

## 14 July 1900

**Maritime Intelligence**

**Miscellaneous**

*Orford, Roach River, Foulness [Essex], July 13, 12 10 p.m.- A tin has been picked up on Foulness Island [Essex], containing a paper, a leaf from a pocket-book, with following message thereon:- "S.S. Broderick Castle, ship sinking; struck on Ushant on 24th April, 1900; terrible agony; all drowned bar me; give love to mother.- James Williams, First Mate. Give love to wife, six children."*

## 24 May 1901

*London, May 24.- "Ship sinking fast. No hope. All hands going down. No time. Whoever gets this note send at once to my wife, Mrs. Haggart, Churchill-terrace, Edinburgh. Farewell. Waiting death now." The above message was picked up yesterday morning in a bottle off Granton, in the Firth of Forth, and relates to the vessel Croft, which left Leith in October, 1898, and was never again heard of.*

## 26 June 1901

*London, June 25.- The Press Association's Portsmouth correspondent telegraphs:- A champagne bottle was picked up in Portsmouth dockyard to-day. It was found to contain the following message:- "Steamship Tiger about to sink after collision with steam trawler off Cape Finisterre. Trawler and all hands lost. Captain and mate of Tiger drowned. We have committed ourselves to God.- June 1, 1900.- William Wright, second mate."*

## 22 July 1901

*Boulogne, July 20.- The French ketch Esperance, of Cherbourg, Captain Vitel, arrived here from Cherbourg, found at sea, 18th inst., 12 miles off, between Treport and Dieppe, a bottle, containing, written in English, the following note:- "M. Brown, sailor, June 13/6/1901. We have been wrecked on the Needles rocks in the ship Monarch. All hands lost but three, and we are starving in an open boat."*

The Needles is a formation of three sea stacks of chalk rock off the western extremity of the Isle of Wight. The name derives from a fourth pinnacle, called Lot's Wife, shaped like a needle but which disappeared in a storm in 1764. The name of the formation, however, has remained intact to this day.

## 23 Jan 1902

*Basuto (s).- London, Jan. 22.- The owners of Basuto (s) advise that they hear that the steamer Gibraltar, just returned to London, reports having been in company with Basuto (s) and Franklin (s) on Dec. 13 [1901] when entering the Bay of Biscay. During the night of Dec. 13 the steamer Gibraltar encountered a fearful gale, which the captain described as the worst he has ever experienced. On morning of 14 Dec. the steamer Gibraltar had lost the company of Basuto and Franklin, and neither of these vessels was again seen.*

### 1 Feb 1902

*London, Feb. 1.- Our Ostend correspondent telegraphed last night that a bottle had been washed ashore during the afternoon containing this note:- "S.S. Basuto; ship sinking; Four boats overboard. No time for more. Drowned Captain Drummond."*

Lloyd's posted the *Basuto* missing on 5 February 1902.

## OCEAN CURRENTS

Not all messages in bottles were from doomed seamen about to meet their Maker. More innocent messages found in bottles were dropped off ships to see where and for how long they drifted, if and when they were picked up. These were commonly filed under "Ocean Currents". The Victorian sense of curiosity moved the authors of these missives to drop them overboard to 'ascertain the drift of ocean currents', by comparing the location and time of their discovery with the location and time they were set adrift. Others were dropped by sailors at sea as a kind of amusement on a long voyage, on the chance that someone might find the message and report it, but with no particular scientific interest in ascertaining the drift.

## 28 June 1884

*Casablanca [Morocco], May 4.- This morning native fishermen brought me (Lloyd's Agent) a bottle picked up by them at sea, which contained a slip of paper torn off a log book, on which the following observation is made, viz:- "German barque Anna, Ferd. Lange master, in 42° N, 13° 10 W of Greenwich, the 13th day of September 1883, weather has been for several days fine with light northerly winds – my best respects to him who finds this.- F.L."*

The bottle above was dropped some 200 miles off the northwest coast of Spain. It drifted for eight months, and approximately 650 miles, before it was picked up off the coast of North Africa.

## 7 Jan 1880

*Killorglin (Co. Kerry [Ireland]), Jan. 3.- On the 1st instant, a bottle containing two notes was picked up on Cromane Point beach, on which the following was written:-*

*"Ship Maraval, Nov. 2, 1879.- Had a gale of wind last night passing Plymouth Sound; it did not last more than an hour. Fine breeze this morning; every prospect of making a fair passage to New Zealand; about 250 passengers on board, most of us very sick.- Joseph Herbert Phillips, North Street, Wiveliscombe, Somerset, England."*

*"Ship Maraval, Nov. 2, 1879.- Lovely morning, sea rough, all well; last night experienced a sudden severe gale…many of us were very much terrified. Praise God we are all well.- From John Robinson, of Great Grimsby, Lincolnshire, England, and Charles H. Hinman, Teigh, Oakham, Rutland."*

## 18 June 1889

*London, June 15.- The following copy of a bottle message, stated to have been thrown overboard from the ship Grassendale, of Liverpool, in lat. 10 16 N, long. 40 24 W, on the 24th February last, and picked up on the island of Barbadoes on the 16th ultimo [May] has been received from the Board of Trade:- "24.2.'89.- Ship Grassendale, lat. 10 16 N, long. 40 24 W, all well. The bottle was thrown overboard from the British ship Grassendale, of Liverpool, from San Francisco, bound for Falmouth for orders, 107 days out, all well on board; am now getting very poor trade winds. Crossed the Equator in 27 W long. On the 18th February, in [lat.] 3 N, spoke the Belgian screw steamer Lys, from Pernambuco for Teneriffe, Canary Islands. The master [ie., of the Lys] promised faithfully he would report us all well, which I trust he will do, as we are getting very light winds. Lat. 10 16 N, long. 40 24 W. Any one picking this up will please report us.- Ship Grassendale, Forbes master." [The Grassendale arrived at Fleetwood April 4.]*

The bottle above was thrown overboard in the Atlantic about 1,200 miles to the east of Barbados. It drifted on the westward flowing north equatorial current to be found at Barbados almost three months later. The ship itself took about six weeks to reach its destination of Fleetwood in Lancashire on the northwest coast of England.

## 31 May 1895

*Antigua, May 10.- A bottle was picked up May 6 on the east coast of [the island of] Barbuda, containing a slip of paper on which was written:- "Bark Kronprinds Frederich, of Fano, from Grimsby for Buenos Aires, 15th April 1894, lat. 37 10 N, long. 15 12 W, 15 days at sea. Wind westerly, clear, and fine." NB: This vessel has since been lost.*

The next bottle, above, would have been swept northeast across the North Atlantic by the Gulf Stream and its northerly continuation current, the North Atlantic Drift, which courses up into the Arctic off the west coast of Norway.

## 26 July 1895

*Egersund [southwest Norway], "June 25."- A bottle was found in this neighbourhood last week, containing an envelope with a slip of paper in it, on which was written:- "This letter was thrown into the sea in a Clayton Bros. effervescing lemonade bottle about 300 miles from Newfoundland by C.H. Haydon, S.S. Madura." On the envelope is:- "Please post this, 28 August 1893.- C.H. Haydon, Esq., King-street East, St. John, New Brunswick."*

The S.S. *Madura*, operated by the old colonial British India Line, had quite an illustrious life. In March 1889 she carried Rudyard Kipling on a voyage from Calcutta to Rangoon. A few years earlier she embarked the members of the Emin Pasha Relief Expedition, led by Henry Morton Stanley, from 1887–1890 (the same Stanley who had earlier led an expedition to find Dr Livingstone in central Africa). Emin Pasha was a German Jew born Isaak Eduard Schnitzer. The title of 'pasha' (he was also called Mehmet Emin Pasha) was only conferred on him after he was appointed by General Charles Gordon to be Governor of the Equatorial Province of the Sudan in 1878. By 1883 Emin Pasha had been cut off from the rest of the world at his base near Lake Albert in today's Uganda, after the revolt of the Mahdi against Egypt. Stanley's Emin Pasha Relief Expedition was established in England in 1886 to find Emin Pasha and deliver him to safety out of Africa.

The 1,942 tons *Madura* set out from Zanzibar on 25 February 1887, disembarking the expedition party at Banana Point, at the mouth of the Congo River in West Africa on 21 March that year. After numerous travails and tribulations during their long trek through the jungles and forests into the dark interior of central Africa, Stanley eventually found Emin Pasha, meeting him on 27 April 1888. Emin Pasha, however, was reluctant to leave with Stanley for the east African coast until the following year, 1889. There Pasha joined the German East Africa Company. He was killed by tribesmen in 1892.

## 2 Feb 1898

### Ocean Currents

*Warrnambool [south coast of Victoria state, 250 km west of Melbourne], Dec. 16.- On Dec. 9 [1897] there was picked up at Curdies Inlet a bottle containing a paper purporting to have been* *thrown overboard by the ship Samuel Plimsoll\*, from London to Sydney, on June 8 [1897], in lat. 39 37 S, long. 121 28 E.*

\* The 1,444-ton iron ship *Samuel Plimsoll*, launched in September 1873, was one of the great clipper ships of the Aberdeen White Star Line, taking emigrants from the United Kingdom to Sydney and Melbourne and carrying back wool on the homeward passage. In 1899 she was severely damaged by fire while lying in the Thames. Repaired, she was sold to Walter Savill, a co-founder of one of the two largest shipping companies serving New Zealand in the late 19 century, Shaw, Savill & Co. (the other being the New Zealand Shipping Company). A few years later, however, in 1902 the *Samuel Plimsoll* was dismasted in heavy weather on a passage to Port Chalmers (Dunedin), New Zealand, and later converted as a coal hulk at Fremantle, Western Australia.

The message in a bottle, above, was dropped off the *Samuel Plimsoll* about 200 miles south of the coast of Western Australia as the ship was sailing towards Sydney. (Around this time the *Samuel Plimsoll* was mainly sailing to Melbourne; this voyage to Sydney, her destination for the first 15 voyages of her life, from 1873 until 1887, was somewhat unusual.) The bottle was carried in the easterly setting current to drift ashore and be picked up approximately 1,100 miles away at Curdies Inlet near the Cape Otway peninsula on the south coast of the State of Victoria, some 250 km southwest of Melbourne.

## 4 Feb 1899

*Christiania, Feb. 1.- A bottle was picked up on Jan. 1 at Thykkvaboe Ros (Iceland), containing a postcard on which was written:- "Bottle message thrown out during the second Norwegian polar voyage with the Fram, Captain O. Sverdrup, on July 11, 1898, in lat. 62 33 N, long. 28 47 W." This position is 10 miles SW of Iceland.*

The Second Norwegian Polar Expedition set off from Christiania (Oslo) on 24 June 1898 on the *Fram*, under the command of the experienced Arctic explorer Capt. Otto Sverdrup (1854–1930). The four year voyage of discovery in the Canadian High Arctic centred around Ellesmere Island. The expedition, which had mapped about 115,000 m² of territory in the Canadian High Arctic and brought back thousands of scientific specimens, returned to Christiania on the *Fram* in the late summer of 1902.

In 1914 a survey of the *Fram* found dry rot in her timbers. In 1916 Sverdrup began a campaign to restore the ship, but he died before the *Fram*'s final fate could be decided. In May 1935 the ship was pulled up onto a concrete foundation at a ten acre site near Oslo. A year later it was officially opened by King Haakon as the Fram House. The Fram Museum today, in the Bygdoy district of Oslo, shares the area with the Norwegian Folklore Museum, the Kon-Tiki Museum, the Viking Ship Museum, and the Norwegian Maritime Museum.

## 27 Jan 1876

### Bottle Picked Up

*Berbice [near Georgetown, Guyana], 20ᵗʰ Feb., 1874.- A bottle containing a paper on which was written the following, was picked up, 17ᵗʰ Feb. [1874], on this coast, in lat. 6 N lon. 57 W:- "N.G. barque Johann Heinrich, of Altona [Hamburg, Germany].- To ascertain the set of the current this was thrown overboard at 2 p.m., on the 7ᵗʰ Dec., 1873, in lat 0° 20' S lon. 30° 54' W\*. The person* *into whose hands this falls is requested to publish the date and the place when and where it was picked up. E. Hacke, Master. H. Jansen, passenger."*

\* The bottle was thrown overboard just 20 miles south of the equator near St. Paul Rocks, 550 miles off the northeast coast of Brazil. The westward flowing Equatorial Current must have carried it along the northeast coast of South America approximately 1,700 miles before it was picked up two and a half months later on the coast of Guyana, suggesting a drift speed averaging around 1 knot.

## Hoaxes, Curiosities and Mysteries

A hoax message in a bottle could be exposed as such if the name of the ship in the message was not known to Lloyd's (although that wasn't necessarily conclusive evidence), or if latitude and longitude coordinates scribbled in the message were unrealistic (such as being on land!), or by some other unlikely 'fact' written in (or, indeed, omitted from) the message. Some messages, or just the bottles, or other means of conveyance were interesting for the way they were written or set adrift or picked up. Others hinted at mysteries that provoked speculation but were otherwise ultimately unfathomable as to their provenance, attribution or veracity.

A message purporting to be from the *County of Carnarvon*, which was wrecked on the North Island of New Zealand in 1889, included the names of three sailors who did not appear on the list of the ship's crew.

## 27 Nov 1889

**Maritime Intelligence**

*County of Carnarvon.- Melbourne, Oct. 11.- County of Carnarvon ship, Newcastle [New South Wales] for Valparaiso:- A quantity of wreckage, among which is a figurehead, representing a woman, and a board with gold lettering "County of Carnarvon," has been washed ashore in Spirits Bay, near North Cape, New Zealand. A steamer has been sent to the bay by the New Zealand Government. A number of barrels of tallow, a binnacle stand, and some doors and door panels have come ashore since the first wreckage was seen.*

*28 Nov 1889*

**Missing Vessels**

*County of Carnarvon, [Capt.] Roberts, of Liverpool, Off. No. 76,477, sailed from Newcastle (N.S.W) for Valparaiso, with coal, on the 1ˢᵗ June last, and has not since been heard of.*

***Otago Witness* (New Zealand newspaper)**

*2 January 1890*

**A Message from the Sea,**

*The Missing County of Carnarvon*
*Wanganui, December 27 [1889]*
*Mr Pinagon, a well-known resident here, found on the beach, two miles from the heads, yesterday, a corked bottle containing the following pencilled message:- "Ship County of Carnarvon, September 3, 1889.- Anyone who should find this bottle will earn the dying blessing of three men,*

*who do not expect to live an hour, by letting our friends and relations know our fate. We are sinking fast. All hands but us three were washed overboard last night. We were dismasted, and the binnacles and everything washed away by the sea. Every sea washes over the deck fore and aft. I don't know where we are, but by the skipper's reckoning at midday yesterday we were about 100 miles from New Zealand. We have been sinking fast ever since the squall struck us. May God help us, for we may sink at any minute.- George Wright. The other men with me are Vincent Wallace and James King."*

Although this message sounds convincingly genuine, it was most probably a hoax: the names 'George Wright', 'Vincent Wallace', and 'James King' were not amongst the list of names of the 22-strong crew of the *County of Carnarvon* published by the *Liverpool Post* of 12 October 1889 ("Lost Ship County of Carnarvon – List of the Crew"). Moreover, the statement that "the binnacles and everything" were washed away belies the fact that a ship had only one binnacle (compass) by which the helmsman steered.

The iron-built *County of Carnarvon*, of 1,305 tons, was a full-rigged ship built in 1877 and owned by Wm. Thomas & Co., of Liverpool. On her last voyage she sailed from Barrow-in-Furness on the coast of Cumbria, for Melbourne, and thence to Newcastle, New South Wales to pick up a cargo of coal for Valparaiso, Chile. Her master was a Welshman, Capt. Robert Roberts, and her crew composed of Welsh, English, Scandinavian and other nationalities. She was wrecked in a storm at or near the North Cape of North Island, New Zealand, probably within a week of her departure from Newcastle on 1 June 1889, and her entire crew of 22 lost.

## 26 Sept 1873

*A bottle was picked up, 12ᵗʰ Sept., on the coast of Crotoy, district of St. Valery-sur-Somme [northwest France], containing a paper on which was written in pencil:- "September 18ᵗʰ, 1873.- S.S. Alexandra.- Farewell to all. We are sinking. Never no more shall I behold my darling.- E.R. Smith."*

The date of the message above ("September 18, 1873") was *after* the date it was picked up (12 September 1873). There could hardly be clearer evidence that the message was fictitious – a hoax. A similar though not quite so conclusive clue appeared with the following message.

## 27 June 1903

**Bottle Picked Up**

*Constantinople [Istanbul], June 25.- A Greek fisherman recently found on the island of Carpathos a hermetically-sealed bottle, containing a paper which read as follows:- "2.9.1702. The ship Clown, on board which we were, foundered at the beginning of October, 1702. She foundered so quickly we hardly had time to get off on the raft, on which we now are, without food or drink. Whoever finds this paper is begged, in the name of humanity, to forward it to the Government.- One of the Castaways (Manter)."*

The date of the message in the bottle, 2 September 1702 ("2.9.1702"), was before the ship apparently sank "at the beginning of October, 1702". The supposed castaway, Manter, might easily have confused his months in such a time of distress, or because he might not have been particularly intelligent. If that was the case, this was certainly the oldest message in a bottle ever reported to Lloyd's. Otherwise the message was probably a hoax.

The following, apart from not having a message as such, was just plain interesting for its manner of conveyance as a hit-or-miss postal device and the thoughtful addition of compensation to the finder.

## 27 Dec 1870

*Two bottles, strung together and securely sealed, have been washed on the beach at Hayle [near St. Ives, Cornwall], one of them containing three letters directed to Hamburg and two sixpences to defray the cost of postage. The other bottle contains a pint of rum to recompense the finder for his trouble in posting the letters, which are from the Anne Georgiana (Danish brig), bound to La Guayra. (The Anne Jorgiane, Mathiesen, sailed from Hamburg 8<sup>th</sup> Nov. for La Guayra.)*

## 15 Oct 1875

*Harlingen, 12<sup>th</sup> Oct.- A bottle has been washed ashore at Schiermonnikoog, containing a paper on which the following is written:- "Lost with all hands the Lady McNaughton, lat. 18 S lon 33.24 W. This written by the only – who is on a – hoping to be saved."*

Harlingen is small town on the north coast of the Netherlands in Friesland province. Schiermonnikoog is one of the Frisian Islands off that coast. The message in the bottle was dropped, according to the position given, in the South Atlantic about 350 miles off the central coast of Brazil. If the bottle had drifted directly to the place it was picked up, it would have travelled at least 5,000 miles.

But the currents offshore of the coast of Brazil below the equator, where this bottle was apparently dropped, flow southeasterly, in a circular, counter-clockwise gyre. The bottle therefore would have to have drifted in a circle around the South Atlantic before being picked up and carried by the westward flowing South Equatorial Current up and over the north coast of South America, through the waters of the Caribbean and Gulf of Mexico to join the Gulf Stream, and eventually carried by the Gulf Stream towards northern Europe. This would have entailed a journey many times greater than the 5,000 miles direct distance, and would have probably taken several years to complete, and without the bottle coming ashore anywhere along its long drift – assuming the message was genuine. The greater probability, however, suggests that it was a hoax.

## 24 Nov 1877

*Bognor, 23<sup>rd</sup> Nov., 7.5 p.m.- A bottle was picked up at the Coastguard station at Chichester harbour this morning containing a paper with the following information:- "Ship Mary Jane, of Cardiff, 11<sup>th</sup> Nov., lat. 45.0 N lon. 43.0 W, all starving for want of provisions and water. (Signed) J.H. Smith master."*

This message was set adrift, apparently, in the Atlantic about 450 miles east-southeast of Newfoundland on 11 November. Twelve days later, apparently, it was picked up some 3,000 miles away off Chichester, on the south coast of England – an average rate of drift of 250 miles a day at an average speed of over 10 knots (faster than any sailing ship afloat at the time). Unless the message was actually written the previous year, 1876, or even earlier, it must have been a hoax.

## 15 May 1878

*Flushing [Vlissingen, Netherlands], 12<sup>th</sup> May.- A bottle, containing a paper, on which the following* *is written in pencil, has been picked up to-day on the coast of Walcheren:- [Translation.] "I, with all the crew of my vessel, perished in lon. 70.30 W lat. 30.45 N. Capt. Verschuur."*

A message in a bottle written apparently in Dutch (the surname – Verschuur – is Dutch) by an apparently Dutch sea captain who claims to have "perished" in the Atlantic around 250 miles southwest of Bermuda – over 3,000 miles from the Netherlands – and without giving either a date or the name of the vessel, and that happens to wash up on the relatively small length of Dutch coastline bordering the North Sea, is highly coincidental – and suspiciously like a hoax.

## 21 Sept 1878

*Limerick [west coast Ireland], 20th Sept., 12.37 p.m.- A bottle containing the following message was picked up yesterday at Ballybunion, County Kerry:- "Barque Amy Turner, 29th May, all hands been at the pumps all night; think she will go down; cargo shifted; lat 50.7 N, lon. 10.36 W; no hope; God help us. If this reaches the shore send to owners, New Bedford, Massachusetts, U.S.A." [The new Amer. barq. Amy Turner is reported to have sailed from Boston, U.S., for Honolulu on the 27th May, and therefore could not have been in the locality indicated on the 29th May.]*

This is obviously a hoax message: the location of the ship where the message was purportedly written ("lat 50.7 N, lon. 10.36 W") was less than 100 miles south of Ireland, compared with the actual likely position of the ship just two days out of Boston, Massachusetts, on the other side of the Atlantic.

The 991-ton, 225-ft long, wooden barque *Amy Turner* was built in 1877 in Boston for C. Brewer & Co. She sailed regularly to the Pacific islands in particular on round the world voyages, and was very near Krakatoa during its eruptions of August/September 1883; her master at the time, Capt. Newell, reported that some pumice from the eruption washed on board the ship when they were 270 miles southwest of Krakatoa in mid-September 1883.

In fact, the *Amy Turner* had a long and varied sailing life of 46 years. After she foundered in a typhoon off Guam on 27 March 1923, the four survivors out of the crew of 14 "reached Manila May 3, suffering from a terrible journey of 1,000 miles in an open boat", according to an account recorded in L. Vernon Briggs' book *Around Cape Horn to Honolulu on the Bark 'Amy Turner' (1880)*, published in 1926.

## 10 May 1888

*Guernsey, May 9, 4 36 p.m.- Bottle picked up on West Coast of Guernsey, containing a piece of old envelope, on which is written:- "S.S. Woolerporoo, latitude 41 N, longitude 19 20 E, sixth May, 1888, sinking fast. T. Mucks, captain."*

This is obviously a hoax message. The location of the "sinking fast" ship – "latitude 41 N, longitude 19 20 E" – is in the Adriatic, off the southeast coast (the heel) of Italy. The date of the message, "sixth May, 1888", is just three days before it was picked up on 9 May 1888 – at Guernsey, in the Channel Islands!

## 21 July 1888

*Glenbeigh (Killarney [Ireland]), July 19.- A sealed bottle was found, July 14, ashore in Dingle Bay*

THE LAST RESOURCE: TAKING TO THE RIGGING

DRAWN BY FRANK BRANGWYN

*(Kerry), containing a slip of paper, on which was written:- "Ida wrecked, crew on a raft, lat. and long. unknown. P.S. – Supposed to be on the east of the Mediterranean, March 5, 1888."*

Could a bottle thrown overboard in "the east of the Mediterranean" drift out of that almost land-locked sea and, against the prevailing Atlantic currents, arrive on the shores of Dingle Bay in southwest Ireland – within four months of the message inside being written? It seems highly unlikely, and much more likely to be a hoax.

Messages in bottles were sometimes shown to be hoaxes when the person whose signature appeared on the message was not on the crew or passenger manifest. The following appears to have been just such a hoax.

## 22 Feb 1893

*Melbourne, Jan. 14.- A bottle was picked up on the 8th inst., between South Head and Little Head of Broken Bay (N.S.W.) lightly corked, containing a paper with these words written in pencil:- "Should this be picked up, lost on Queensland Coast, barque Barunga, Frank Lynch, passenger R.I.P." In reference to the above, telegraphic advice has been received from Messrs. John Grice and Co., the agents of the Barunga, at Kingston (S.A. [South Australia]), stating that the vessel left that port for London, via Cape Horn, on Dec. 10 [1892], intending to pass south of Tasmania, and that there were no passengers aboard.*

The 1,030-ton *Barunga*, was built as a three-masted iron ship by J. & W. Dudgeon of London, and launched as the *Apelles* in May 1863. In 1881 she was re-rigged as a barque and renamed *Barunga* when sold to Trinder, Anderson & Co. of London, for employment in the Australian wool trade. The *Barunga* was abandoned at sea in January 1899 when she was struck by a violent storm in the Atlantic and lost most of her rigging in the course of a transatlantic voyage to France.

## 20 July 1895

*Killough [Co. Down, southeast coast Northern Ireland], July 19, 8 5 p.m.- Bottle picked up floating near Killough Harbour, containing a paper with the following message:- "17th May, 1895, struck on a rock at low tide 150 miles from Canary Islands. The ship filling fast, and only 20 minutes to live. Unable to reach the shore, the boats being all washed away. Seven hands on board the ship Sea Swallow, of Cardiff, Captain James Ohagan." [Memo: No vessel can be traced of the above name.]*

The validity of this message in a bottle is difficult to ascertain. First, Lloyd's reported that there was no trace of a vessel named the *Sea Swallow*. Second, although there are some isolated uninhabited islands approximately "150 miles from Canary Islands", the Ilhas Selvagens to the north, a message in a bottle from that location would almost certainly have had to drift at least halfway across the North Atlantic and only then back up towards Ireland, since the currents in that area (the Canary Current in particular) flow towards the southwest as part of the clockwise rotation of the North Atlantic oceanic circulatory system. The bottle would therefore have drifted approximately – and at least – some 3,500 miles in two months, between the date the message in it was written and the date it was picked up on the northeast coast of Ireland, at an average rate of drift of around 2.5 knots. This would be an interesting, and impressive drift for a message in a bottle – if it was not, in fact, a hoax…

A sailing vessel named the *Sea Swallow* did sink at the end of December 1894, but it was at lat. 24 N, long. 122 E – on the other side of the world, just north of the island of Taiwan (Formosa). Another *Sea Swallow* around this time, a steamship, was at Liverpool in mid-November 1894. There were no reports by *Lloyd's List* of any sailings of any vessel by the name of *Sea Swallow* in 1895.

## 2 Nov 1895

*Malin Head [north coast of Ireland], Nov. 1, 2 15 p.m.- Bottle picked up yesterday one mile east of station with following letter:- "Lat. 29, long. 24, yacht Chieftain on rocks, terrible seas; captain drowned, signed John M.B."*

Either the writer of this message had no idea where he was – "lat. 29 [presumably N], long. 24 [presumably W]" is 400 miles west of the Canary Islands, where not only are there no rocks but the Atlantic Ocean thereabouts is some 17,000 ft deep – or, more likely, it was a hoax. The "station" a mile away from where the bottle was picked up was the Lloyd's coastal signal station, which reported on weather conditions at Malin Head from about 1885.

## 29 Nov 1895

*South Shields, Nov. 29, 11 38 a.m.- Bottle picked up at the mouth of the Tyne, containing a leaf of note-book rolled in canvas:- "On board the schooner Joseph and Mary, Nov. 22. We are sinking fast, and I enclose this note to say that all hands are calmly waiting their fate. Hoping this will reach our friends, we remain, trusting in the Lord, yours, Richard Williams, 40, King-street, North Shields, Durham. 'Lat. 29, long. 61' "*

The main part of this message has the ring of truth about it. The final part – the position of "lat. 29 [presumably N], long. 61 [presumably W]", and the location it was picked up near South Shields so close to the home town of its author – renders it more dubious. First, the position was on the other side of the Atlantic, to the southeast of the island of Bermuda, a long way from its final resting place on the northeast coast of England. Secondly, the bottle supposedly drifted all the way across the Atlantic to more or less precisely the same place the author of the message was from ("North Shields, Durham"). And thirdly, the date the message was picked up (29 November) was highly coincidental with the date it was written ("Nov. 22"), despite the latter having no year attached. All those clues suggest a hoax.

## 27 July 1896

*London, July 27.- Yesterday the following message was picked up on the beach at Hayling Island [near Portsmouth, south coast of England] in a small phial:- "May 6.- Steamship St. Agnes, from Pernambuco to Liverpool, with cargo of cotton, coffee, sugar, etc., run into and sunk by an unknown ship in a gale. Ship sank in 10 minutes. Only one boat launched with seven men, including captain and his wife. We are trying to make for the Canaries, about 500 miles distant. We have no provisions. God help us. Thomas Goodman, passenger."*

*Lloyd's List* mentions no steamship named *St. Agnes* between 1893 and 1896, other than from this message in a bottle. It is possible, however, that the vessel was not registered with Lloyd's – the message does have a tone of authentic distress – or, equally, that the message was a hoax.

## 18 Nov 1896

*Surprise.- Amsterdam, Nov. 17.- A bottle has washed ashore on Terschelling [one of the West Frisian Islands off the north coast of Holland], containing a paper on which the following is written:- "North Cape, Oct. 19, 1896 – Whaler Surprise: Have been drifting about for eight days, through being dismasted. Captain having been drowned on the passage out, the first mate shot himself. Rest of crew have been washed overboard and drowned. I am the only survivor. My name is James Markham, 16, Rosherville-road, Liverpool. Wind is blowing a gale from SE; heavy seas washing over the deck. God send me help."*

Assuming that this message was written by James Markham on the supposedly disabled whaling ship *Surprise* off the North Cape, at the northern tip of Norway, it must have drifted some 1,500 miles in less than a month before it was found off the Dutch coast. The currents around the North Cape flow predominantly northeastwards into the Barents Sea. This message must therefore somehow have got into a southwesterly flowing current to end up where it did – unless it was, in fact, a hoax.

There was no "Rosherville-road" in Liverpool, but the Rosherville Gardens, at Gravesend in Kent, were quite famous at the time. A bottle set adrift from Gravesend could quite believably drift with the current into the North Sea and onto the Dutch island of Terschelling within a few weeks.

## 2 Sept 1897

**Bottle Picked Up**

*Morthoe, Sept. 1, 2 17 p.m.- Picked up bottle with paper "the Rifleman wrecked off Good Hope goodbye all." Cannot understand date.*

If this really was a message from a vessel named the *Rifleman* wrecked off "Good Hope" (the Cape of Good Hope), it would have had to drift up the South and North Atlantic some 5,500 miles to reach the north Devon coast where it was ostensibly discovered – which it was highly unlikely to have done, and much more likely to have been a hoax.

## 23 Sept 1897

*Liverpool, Sept. 23.- Yesterday a bottle was picked up on the shore at Garston, inside of which was a paper, on which was written the following:- "Wrecked during a terrible storm off the Cape of Good Hope. W.H. Phillips, January 21ˢᵗ, 1897, S.S. Sophie."*

Since this message, above, was picked up on the shore at Garston on the River Mersey, near Liverpool, it seems highly unlikely (indeed, impossible) to have drifted there from the Cape of Good Hope. Unless it was carried there by the allegedly shipwrecked "W.H. Phillips", it was almost certainly another hoax-in-a-bottle message.

If the message below was written by a midshipman (a naval cadet rank), he must have been on a navy ship, and most likely of the Royal Navy. However, the only HMS *Invincible* at that time was an armoured battleship that sunk in 1914. The message by "Thomas Fitzpatrick, midshipman" must have been a hoax.

## 2 Feb 1898

*London, Feb. 2.- A Dalziel's telegram\* from Perth [Western Australia], Feb. 1, states:- A message,* which is supposed [believed] to have been washed up from the sea, has been found on the beach near Fremantle. The writing, which is undated, is as follows:- "Ship Invincible, wrecked South Sea Islands. No help available. All lost. Thomas Fitzpatrick, midshipman."

* The Dalziel News Agency, the source of "Dalziel's telegrams", was set up by Davison Alexander Dalziel (1852–1928), 1st and last Baron Dalziel of Wooler in the County of Northumberland. Dalziel moved from England to Sydney, Australia in the 1880s to work as a journalist on the *Sydney Echo*, and then to the United States to work in newspaper management. He founded the Dalziel News Agency when he returned to England in 1890. Dalziel was a Member of Parliament for Brixton, south London, from 1910 to 1923, and again from 1924 until he resigned from the House of Commons in 1927 (because he was raised to the baronetcy, and went thenceforth into the House of Lords, on 4 July 1927).

The topsail schooner *Marmion* was wrecked and lost with all hands probably quite soon after she left Napier bound for Tairua on the Coromandel Peninsula across the Bay of Plenty on North Island, New Zealand, in March 1899. She was most likely wrecked off East Cape, the easternmost point of North Island around which the *Marmion* would have had to turn to cross the Bay of Plenty westwards to reach Tairua. The reported sighting of wreckage "on the beach at Whangaroa", well to the north of Auckland, is in fact unlikely to have been that of the *Marmion*, being nowhere near the vessel's route to Tairua (unless she was blown far off course by tempestuous weather).

## 23 May 1899

*Marmion.- Melbourne, April 14.- Marmion, schooner, bound from Napier for Tairua [both on North Island, New Zealand], is a month out, and fears are entertained for her safety.*

### 28 June 1899

*Melbourne, June 20.- A bottle has been picked up at Auckland, containing the following message:- "April 10, 1899.- Schooner Marmion in terrible gales since Saturday last. We had two men washed overboard. The schooner is breaking on a reef. Help us if this found. (Signed) J. Simonson, able seaman." The collector of customs, to whom the matter was reported, considered the message a hoax, and wired to the Napier collector, asking if Simonson was one of the crew. The reply stated that no able seaman of that name was in the Marmion's list. The schooner Marmion left Napier 63 days ago, and has not since been reported.*

### 6 July 1899

*Melbourne, May 27.- A ship's mast and other wreckage have been found on the beach at Whangaroa, near Auckland. They are supposed [believed] to be the remains of the schooner Marmion.*

The bottle message was apparently written on 10 April, six weeks after the *Marmion* left Napier, which seems a very long time for the vessel to have been at sea, even if impeded by bad weather. So that message seems likely to have been a hoax, especially if there was no one named "J. Simonson, able seaman" on her crew list. A *Hawke's Bay Herald* newspaper article dated 15 April reported that the *Marmion* was overdue and that the government steamer *Tutanekai* was going to search for her, so she was in the news, which might have suggested to a hoaxer to write the bottle message.

## 26 Aug 1901

*Appledore [north Devon coast], Aug. 26, 11 35 a.m.- Following found in bottle at Westward Ho:- "Steamship Caledonian, from Aberdeen. Help, help, we have to abandon ship, lat. 40 N, long 80 W. Sprung leak, sinking fast, taken to boats, but have little hope of reaching land. D. Watkins, captains, July 7, 1901."*

The position where the message was supposedly written – "lat. 40 N, long. 80 W" – was near Pittsburgh, Pennsylvania – several hundred miles from the nearest ocean and a significant clue in determining that it was a hoax.

The next report is a curiosity concerning an albatross, a shipwrecked crew and the sailors' last words communicated via that bird to the outside world.

## 18 Oct 1887

*Tamaris.- London, Oct. 18.- According to a telegram received from the Governor of South Australia, dated 22d ult. [ie., September], a dead albatross has been found on the shore at Fremantle [near Perth, Western Australia], and attached to its neck was a piece of tin, on which the following was written in French:- "Thirteen shipwrecked persons on the Crozet Islands, Aug. 4, 1887." The vessel to which these shipwrecked persons belonged, according to the Journal du Havre of Oct. 15, is supposed [believed] to be the Tamaris, bound from Bordeaux for Noumea [New Caledonia], which vessel was posted as missing on Aug. 31, and the crew of which was composed of 13 men.*

The isolated and rocky Crozet Islands, 1,200 miles southeast of South Africa, in the Southern Indian Ocean, lay directly in the path of sailing vessels running their easting down in the Roaring Forties, as the *Tamaris* was doing on her passage from Bordeaux towards Noumea on the French island of New Caledonia in the western Pacific.

*Tamaris* was a 463-ton (grt) three-masted iron French barque owned by the famous French shipping firm of Bordes, of Bordeaux. On 28 November 1886 she left Bordeaux for New Caledonia, commanded by Capt. P. Majou. On 9 March 1887 *Tamaris* wrecked on a reef off Ile des Pengouins in the Crozets. Two days later the 13-man crew of the *Tamaris* made it ashore onto Ile aux Cochons. There, on 4 August 1887 they attached their message around the neck of an albatross. It was found on the dead bird at Fremantle, Western Australia – 3,000 miles away – six weeks later around 21 September.

In November 1887 the French ship *Meurthe* was despatched from Madagascar to look for the castaways. Reaching Ile aux Cochons on 1 December 1887, the *Meurthe* crew found a shelter set up by the *Tamaris* castaways, as well as a diary written by Capt. Majou. Despite searching all the other islands in the archipelago, they never found any of the *Tamaris* castaways or their remains. The incident was the basis for a book by Yves Le Scal titled *Le novice du "Tamaris"*.

## 14 Nov 1888

*Queenstown, Nov. 13, 3 17 p.m.- A bottle was this morning washed ashore at the entrance of Kinsale Harbour [Ireland], containing the following letter:- "Nov. 10, 1888. Norwegian barque Nor, of Tonsberg, disabled off Old Head of Kinsale; crew taken off by steamboat; expecting to strand at Kinsale Bay; cargo timber, St. John (N.B.) Queenstown for orders. (Signed) W. McKenzie."*

This message in a bottle is mysterious, because the Norwegian barque *Nor* was actually already wrecked by the time it was written (10 November 1888). She had collided with a steamship in the English Channel and was eventually wrecked, not at Kinsale on the southern coast of Ireland but in the English Channel off the south coast of the Isle of Wight, around a week before the above message was written.

The *Nor* was the only vessel of that name and from Tonsberg, southeast Norway, at that time. She was carrying a cargo of case oil (petroleum in casks), not timber, from New York to the Polish port of Stettin (Szczecin), not from St. John, New Brunswick, to Queenstown for orders, when she collided with the steamship *Saxmundham*, with coal and coke, from Newcastle, northeast England, for Ancona, Italy, early on the morning of 4 November 1888, just south of the Isle of Wight. The *Nor* was commanded by Capt. Bjonness on her return voyage from New York to Europe when she collided with the *Saxmundham*.

The crews of both vessels were rescued. The *Nor* was abandoned, waterlogged, and eventually stranded on the Shingles, a notorious shoal of water off the Needles, Isle of Wight. Casks of her cargo were washed ashore and salvaged over the following weeks. The Scottish poet William Topaz McGonagall (1830–1902) wrote a poem, *The Collision in the English Channel*, to commemorate the incident. The contents and source of the message in the bottle remain a mystery.

## 24 June 1895

*Bessel (s).- Dover, June 23, 9 47 a.m.- Captain Alcot and 28 others, forming the crew of the screw steamer Bessel, of Liverpool, from London for Lisbon and Brazil, general cargo, were landed here at 11 last night from screw steamer Hero, of and for Hull from Jersey, with which vessel the Bessel had collided at 2 yesterday afternoon, west of Royal Sovereign Lightship, and sunk in seven minutes. All hands saved. Hero has proceeded to Hull seriously damaged.*

### 1 July 1895

*Bessel (s).- Brixham, June 29.- The trawler Vine has landed here from the ship Thor, which was off the Start yesterday, a Norwegian made boot, on the sole of which the following is written:- "Deliver this to the newspaper. Was picked up by the Norwegian ship Thor ten miles south of Beachy Head. A lot of things were drifting on the water – hatches, brooms, barrels, and a broken boat. I picked up a cork fender and a bucket marked 'Bessel.' Looks to have belonged to a steamship that has been run down. Thick fog to-day and last night. Ship Thor, June 25, 1895. H. Andresen, master, bound to Savannah."*

What happened here was that the steamship *Bessel* sank after colliding with another steamship, the *Hero*, at 2 p.m. on 22 June 1895 in the English Channel. The *Hero* picked up the 29 crew of the *Bessel* and landed them at Dover later the same day. A few days later Capt. H. Andresen, master of the full-rigged Norwegian ship *Thor*, coming down-Channel en route to Savannah sailed through the wreckage of the collision. He picked up a variety of items, including a boot which he used to write his message on. He passed the boot on to the trawler *Vine* which landed it at Brixham. Why Capt. Andresen didn't just write a note on a piece of paper and attach it to the flotsam he picked up is something of a mystery.

## 2 April 1896

*Liverpool, April 2, 9 42 a.m.- The following, written on a piece of paper in a bottle, was found off the Red Noses [promontory at mouth of River Mersey] yesterday:- "Steamer Sunflower wrecked in the Irish Channel; send assistance at once, master."*

## 22 May 1896

*Sunflower (s).- Carrickfergus [mouth of Belfast Lough], May 22, 9 47 a.m.- Steamer Sunflower, of and bound for Belfast from Glenarm, with cargo of whiting [fish], struck on rock in Whitehead Bay [just northeast of Carrickfergus], began to make water, steamed for Carrickfergus Harbour and sunk at entrance. No lives lost.*

The captain of the *Sunflower* must have written the message in a bottle some time well before it had drifted and been found off the mouth of the River Mersey on 1 April 1896. Seven weeks later the vessel sank at Carrickfergus at the mouth of Belfast Lough leading up to Belfast. The message in a bottle therefore must have referred to an incident earlier in the year, possibly even many months before it was found, completely unrelated to the vessel sinking at Carrickfergus. Either way the *Sunflower* lived to sail another day; at Carrickfergus she was refloated and repaired.

## MESSAGE IN A SHARK

Ernest Richards recounts a curious incident of a message in a bottle in his 1907 narrative as an apprentice in a British sailing ship in the late-1800s, *In A Deep-Water Ship*:

"On the poop that night the second mate told me a yarn about a shark which I will leave the reader to accept as true or otherwise according to his own notions.

'When I was serving my time,' said the second mate, waking me up for the third time, as I leaned against the mizzen-mast, 'we were becalmed on the line, and a big lump of a shark which had followed us for days hung around. We didn't bless him I can tell you, because he stopped us bathing. But do what we would we couldn't catch him.

'Now, the very funniest thing happened I ever heard tell of. One of our men, a Russian Finn, had a dream, and he dreamt there was a ship in distress to the nor'-west of us. Well, they laughed at the man, but on the second night the skipper dreamt the same thing. He said he saw the men leaving the ship in a boat, and they had been drifting about for some days helpless and starving. The Finn had this in his dream also. On the third night all the hands dreamt the same thing, and everybody especially remembered how twelve men in a boat had seemed to plead for help and yet were speechless through suffering. In the morning we had a breeze – the S.E. Trades – and the "old man" mustered the hands aft and asked them what they thought. Some were for going back and some were for going ahead. But the old Finn and the nigger cook refused to work unless we ran down a nor'-west course for twenty-four hours, and at last the old man, thinking of his own dream as well, decided to do so.

'Accordingly we went nor'-west, with a wind dead aft, and though it was miles out of our course.

'Meanwhile the nigger cook said, "Dat shark got sumfin to do with dis dream. I don't tink." And he and I got the fishhook out and had another try, because the nigger said, "It's p'r'aps we catch him now, sonny, now we alter our course." Well, sure enough, we did catch him and cut him open, and inside what do you think we found, sonny?' 'I don't know,' I replied. 'Well, we found a bottle, with a note inside, which the shark had swallowed, and on the note we read: "The barque *Petrel* is sinking. Lat. 1 degree N.; long. 26 degrees W. Crew in pinnace just casting off from ship. Shall try to reach Brazil. James Williams, Master." This seemed to make our dream true.

'Well, sonny, the shark's message and our dream *was true*. We told the skipper of the shark, and found that it was about one hundred and fifty miles to the spot, and, sure enough, next day we saw the boat, in which the fellows had been lying for six days, becalmed, until within a few hours of seeing us. They had had no food and but little water in that time, having left the ship in a hurry, for she foundered in an explosion. Two days after it was Christmas, and by this time they had recovered, and ate a good Christmas dinner.

'You don't believe it?' said the second mate. 'All right, sonny, go aloft and overhaul the buntlines for looking at me as though I was a liar.' "

The story might have been true; stranger things have happened at sea than a postal delivery shark. Sharks do certainly swallow almost anything. *The New York Times* reported on 21 June 1902 that a New Jersey woman, Mrs. George Cummings, had received a letter from the commander of a British warship, the *Thunder*, after the vessel's crew caught a shark off the coast of Portugal. Inside the shark they found a bottle with a message in it. The message had been written by Mrs. Cummings a year before. She set it adrift in Delaware Bay inside a 'rubber-corked beer bottle', with a request that the finder of the message write back to her. This the commander of the *Thunder* duly did after recovering it from the stomach of the shark that ate it.

On the other hand it might just have been a good sailor's yarn amongst many to while away a quiet night watch on a sailing ship in the tropics, becalmed on the 'line', with a captive young apprentice as audience to the older salt.

## JOHN SANDS AND THE ST KILDA MAILBOAT

The islands of St Kilda lie some 40 miles away from the Outer Hebrides off the west coast of mainland Scotland. The biggest island, St Kilda (or *Hiort* in the native Scottish Gaelic), is a high scrubby rock of 670 hectares (1,656 acres). The highest point on the island, Conachair, at 430 metres (1,411 ft), falls sheer to the sea along its north face and is the highest sea cliff in the United Kingdom. St Kilda was inhabited for thousands of years before the entire population of 36 St Kildans was evacuated to the Scottish mainland in 1930 as a consequence of depopulation, crop failures, disease and the increasingly adverse effects of extreme isolation.

### 13 Feb 1877

**Casualties – Home**

*Stromness [Orkney Islands], 12th Feb., 10 a.m.- The following message was picked up on the 8th, in the parish of Birsay [ancient capital of Orkney], in a bottle secured to a lifebuoy, and was handed to me (Lloyd's Agent) last night:- "St. Kilda, 22nd Jan., 1877.- The Pete [sic] Mubrovacki, of Austria, 886 tons, was lost near this island on the 17th inst.; the captain and eight of the crew are in St. Kilda, and have no means of getting off; provisions are scarce. The finder of this will much oblige by forwarding this letter to the Austrian consul in Glasgow. Written by J. Sands, who*

HILL TOP

A ST. KILDIAN WOMAN

A ST. KILDIAN MAN

A FREE CHURCH MINISTER

ST. KILDIAN BOY WITH YOUNG SOLAN GOOSE

A ST. KILDIAN WOMAN

FINLAY GILLIES, NATIVE OF ST. KILDA

VILLAGE AND BAY—THE ONLY PLACE WHERE SHIPS CAN ANCHOR OR BOATS LAND

THE MOST REMOTÉ SPOT IN THE UNITED KINGDOM—NOTES IN THE ISLAND OF ST. KILDA

*came to the island in summer, and cannot get away." [The Peti Dubrovacki sailed from Glasgow, for New York, 11th Jan.]*

## 26 Feb 1877

**Casualties – Home**

*London, 24th Feb.- The following telegram was received yesterday at the Admiralty from Lieutenant Digby, of HMS Jackal, dated Portree, 23rd Feb.:- "Succeeded reaching St. Kilda yesterday; took off Sands, of Edinburgh, Captain Chersanaz and son; Feuke, mate; Pavlovitch, boatswain; Dorcash, Sateueach, Franks, Pavetich, Calagham, seamen; ship Peti Dubrovacki abandoned; seven crew supposed [believed] drowned; am proceeding to Greenock [near Glasgow] then Rothsay [Rothesay, Isle of Bute, in the Firth of Clyde]."*

John Sands (1826–1900), who wrote the message above that led to the rescue of himself and the surviving crew members of the *Peti Dubrovacki*, was a Scottish freelance journalist and artist. His interest in archaeology and folk customs led him to visit St Kilda twice, in 1875 and 1876–77. On his second visit he arrived on St Kilda on 22 June 1876. He became stranded on the island into the early months of 1877 because the owner of St Kilda, Sir John MacLeod, did not send a boat to the island with provisions for the St Kildans, which he had promised to do. (MacLeod was supposed to send a small boat to St Kilda twice a year, in summer and autumn, to collect rents, take supplies, and carry away the islanders' produce.) The result of MacLeod's negligence, according to Sands, 'was little short of culpable homicide', because the islanders suffered terribly from hunger that winter.

The *Peti Dubrovacki* left Glasgow in ballast for New York on 11 January 1877 and foundered, as a result of bad weather, some eight miles off St Kilda on 17 January. Eight men and the captain left the ship in a small boat and landed on St Kilda; the other seven crew members stayed with the ship and perished. On 22 January Sands inserted his letter about the castaways into a bottle and attached it to a lifebuoy which he set adrift in the hope that whoever found the message would eventually alert the authorities to undertake a rescue mission.

The lifebuoy, and message, drifted ashore on the Orkney Islands off the north coast of Scotland. It was picked up by someone on 8 February and handed to the local Lloyd's agent at Stromness. The Admiralty, subsequently informed of the plight of the castaways on St Kilda, ordered HMS *Jackal* to proceed to the island to take the men off, which it did on 22 February 1877, about a month after Sands had launched his lifebuoy message and eight months after he had arrived the previous summer.

Based on Sands' novel method of communicating news of the castaways, the St Kildans adopted his idea as a regular, if rather hit-or-miss means of communicating generally with the outside world. They would carve a piece of wood in the shape of a boat which they attached to an inflated sheepskin bladder. Inside the bladder they placed a small bottle or tin case which contained whatever message they wanted to send. The bladder and wooden boat was set adrift when the wind blew from the west. A westerly wind would, they hoped, blow their message to one of the Scottish islands or onto the west coast of the mainland. Around two-thirds of the messages were picked up, though some, apparently, drifted on to Norway! Sands' invention as used by the St Kildans came to be known as the 'St Kilda mailboat'.

## The *Vermont*

The master of the full-rigged ship *Vermont*, Capt. J.M. Richardson, believed his vessel was in such danger of being shipwrecked in stormy weather off the coast of Burma in 1877 that he wrote a message to that effect in the expectation of their certain demise – a fate which in fact turned out not to be.

### 28 Sept 1877

*Maulmain [Burma], 27ᵗʰ Aug.- A sealed bottle was picked up opposite the Southern Moocas islands, on the 17ᵗʰ Aug., and taken to the Deputy Commission Tavoy, with the following writing on it:- "Ship Vermont went ashore night of 8ᵗʰ Aug., on Tenasserim coast – written in sight of death, J.M. Richardson master."*

The "Moocas islands" are probably the Maungmagan Islands off the southwest coast of Burma (Myanmar). Tavoy is the main town along that coast. The Tenasserim coast is further south, with dozens of islands scattered along it.

### 21 Dec 1877

*St. Helena, 30ᵗʰ Nov.- The Vermont, Richardson, from Maulmain to Falmouth, put in here, 21ˢᵗ Nov., and proceeded the same evening. With reference to the paper picked up in a bottle, stating that the vessel went ashore, 8ᵗʰ Aug., on the Tenasserim coast, the master reported that he threw overboard the bottle in question. He added that at the time the ship was on the verge of breakers and in imminent peril, but that subsequently she was got out of danger and proceeded on her voyage. He further stated that when 40 days out he signalled a French steamer bound to Ceylon, and requested to be reported [ie., to Lloyd's].*

When the *Vermont* finally arrived at Falmouth, Capt. Richardson explained the nature of their perilous dilemma off the Burmese coast.

### 17 Jan 1878

*Falmouth, 15ᵗʰ Jan.- The Vermont, Richardson, arrived here from Maulmain, reports:- "Left Maulmain July 29 [1877]. From Aug. 3 till 12ᵗʰ had a succession of terrific gales, at times a hurricane, and tremendous sea, and had hard pressing to hold to windward, especially on the night of the 5ᵗʰ. When about 20 miles off the Moocas isles, a terrific squall broke on us from WSW. Had to furl all lowertopsails, ship drifting fast toward the land with both wind and current.*

*At about midnight, still blowing hard, wind veered W and WNW, the water suddenly shoaled from 20 to 15 and 13 fathoms, mixed ground [ie., sand and shells, etc., picked up by the sounding lead], a tremendous sea running; thought we saw the breakers to leeward. About this time I threw over the bottle which was picked up. Cannot remember what I wrote on the paper, but we all thought it was our last night.*

*About 1.30 a.m., wind WNW, still in 15 fathoms, mixed bottom, I concluded it would be prudent to press on canvas, even if we carried something away, and try to keep along the shore as long as possible; so set everything we possibly could. Ship diving and pitching fearfully and lying over, but heading SW by S and making little lee way, expecting every moment something to give way, but all held well. At 4 a.m. deepened to 18 fathoms, mixed bottom. At 6.30 in 20 fathoms, shells\*, and less wind, but still dark and rainy. At 7 wind veered to SSW and moderated; wore* *ship to westward off shore. A French steamer, the Iraouaddy, passed close to us, in lat. 5 N lon. 92 E; asked her to report us."*

After Capt. Richardson's message was picked up, ships looked for the wrecked *Vermont* along the Burmese coast for several months. Until she stopped at St Helena for a few hours in late November on her way to Falmouth, three months after the message in the bottle was found, the *Vermont* was assumed to have been lost with all hands. On her very next voyage, however, from Cardiff to Rio de Janeiro, under a different master (Capt. Southern), she ran out of luck: the ship was abandoned and sank off the coast of Ushant, northwest France, in April 1878, with the loss of one man drowned and the rest of the crew rescued by another vessel.

## THE MYSTERY OF THE *NARONIC*

The case of the SS *Naronic's* disappearance in 1893, and the messages in bottles purported to have come from the vessel, were and to this day remain a true mystery.

## 30 March 1893

*New York, March 30.- The Sun's Norfolk correspondent telegraphs that a champagne bottle has been found on the beach at Ocean View, Virginia, containing a letter alleged to have been written by John Olsen, a cattleman on board the White Star steamer Naronic. It is dated Feb. 19, and runs as follows:- "The ship is fast sinking. It is such a storm that we can never live in the small boats. One boat with its human cargo has already sunk. We have been struck by an iceberg in the blinding snow. The ship has floated for two hours. It is now 3 20 in the morning, and the deck is level with the sea." In conclusion the writer asks the finder of the letter to report to Messrs. Kerseys, the New York agent of the line. [The conclusion actually reads: "Report to the agents at Broadway, New York, M. Kersey & Company. Goodby all."]*

### 4 April 1893

*London, April 4.- A Dalziel telegram from New York, dated yesterday, states:- To-day's evening papers state that William Clare, of Bay Ridge, an inlet of New York Bay, about seven miles from the city, found a bottle on the beach yesterday containing the following note:- "March 1, 1893.- The Naronic is sinking with all hands. We are praying to God to have mercy on us.- L. Winsel." The bottle bore the stamp of John Hogg, New York.*

### 26 Oct 1893

*Naronic (s).- London, Oct. 26.- The master of the Norwegian barque Emblem, arrived at Buenos Ayres from Saguenay [Quebec], writing from the former port, under date Sept. 20, reports that on July 21, in lat. 36 N, long. 33 W, he picked up a boat with name on stern ""SS Naronic, Liverpool." The boat was lying bottom up, was covered with a thick layer of barnacles, and had a big hole in the bottom. There was nothing in the boat. The lashings of the boat seem to have been cut in a great hurry and with force, so that, particularly in one place, the boat's rail underneath the lashings was cut right through, and the patent unhooking apparatus in the boat had not been used.*

The White Star cargo steamship *Naronic* departed Liverpool on 11 February 1893, bound for New York. She was carrying 74 persons: 14 cattlemen and 10 horse tenders (to care for

# SKETCHES AT ST. HELENA.

JAMES TOWN AND THE LADDER, FROM MUNDEN'S BATTERY.

LOT AND LOT'S WIFE.

her cargo of livestock), and 50 crew. By 3 March *Naronic* was being reported overdue. Ships on transatlantic voyages had been looking out for the vessel for weeks. She was never sighted.

The mystery of her whereabouts deepened with the discovery of the messages found in the bottles picked up not only on beaches in New York and Virginia but also on the other side of the Atlantic, in the English Channel and in the River Mersey, near Liverpool. All the messages purported to be from persons on board the vessel which they claimed was sinking. None of the names of those persons, however, were listed on the manifest of persons on board the *Naronic* (although crew and passenger manifest lists at the time were not always wholly accurate).

The only other 'evidence' of the fate of the *Naronic* were two lifeboats, with the name *Naronic* on them, encountered by the steamship *Coventry* on 4th March during a voyage from Newport News, Virginia to the United Kingdom. The first, overturned, was encountered in the early hours of the morning, at lat. 40 N, long. 47 37 W. The second lifeboat, encountered later the same day, was upright; its sails and masts were floating in the water, attached to the boat by a line. The *Emblem*, at Buenos Aires, seems to have picked up the first overturned boat. If so, the boat had drifted approximately 800 miles to the east-southeast, from about 450 miles southeast of Cape Race, Newfoundland, to very near the Azores, in four and a half months.

The subsequent Board of Trade Inquiry into the loss of the *Naronic* dismissed the messages in bottles as unreliable evidence, because the signatures did not match anyone on the crew manifest. The Board also doubted that the vessel had been sunk by an iceberg, because they did not think icebergs could be in that area at that time of year. (The *Titanic*, of the same White Star Line, however, was sunk by an iceberg, on 15 April 1912, at lat. 41 43 N, long. 50 W, around 375 miles south-southeast of Cape Race, Newfoundland in the approximate vicinity of the position of the *Naronic* lifeboats encountered by the *Coventry*.)

What actually happened to the 6,594-ton, 470-ft long *Naronic* will probably forever remain yet another mystery of the sea. The captain of a vessel in similar atrocious weather and sea conditions, sailing in the vicinity of the *Naronic's* position at around the same time, offered his own opinion in a letter to the Editor of *Lloyd's List* a few months later:

*8 April 1893*

**Correspondence**

**The Loss of the Naronic**

**To the editor**

Sir,- The loss of this fine steamer is still a mystery. If the report is true about the bottle being washed on shore on the American coast containing a written statement by one of the cattleman, I have every reason to believe the *Naronic* was lost in ice on the night of the 18th February, during the terrible blizzard that was prevailing on this date to the eastward of Newfoundland. I was on my passage from Hamburg to Philadelphia at the time, and had the full force of the blizzard. I will give you the following extract from the ship's log-book:-

Feb. 17, long. 44 W., lat. 48 50 N., wind N.N.W., strong gale, and very heavy sea, with blinding snow and intense frost. Feb. 18, long. 46 50 W., lat. 47 35 N., wind N.N.W., heavy gale, terrible blizzard and intense frost. Feb. 19, long. 49 50 W., lat. 45 50 N., wind easterly, moderate, weather quite clear, heavy sea still running.

At midnight of the 18th, in about long. 48 30 W. and lat. 47 N., we fell in with floating ice. How much there was we could not say; it was so dark with heavy snow that we could not see 50 yards. I at once ran the ship off to the south till daylight, and then hauled to the westward. I ran south about 60 miles, and we saw no more ice.

Reports say the *Naronic* sailed from Liverpool on 11th February. Supposing her average speed to be from the time of sailing 240 per day (10 knots), which would be as much as she would average against the heavy westerly gales that were blowing at the time, it would put her on the meridian [ie., her longitude position] at midnight of the 18th of February about 47 40 W. She would have the full force of the blizzard, and there is no doubt she came in contact with the ice that was floating about in the vicinity.

I have every reason to believe she met her fate that night, and, if the bottle report is true, it confirms my belief, although I must say it is impossible for a bottle to drift so far to the westward in so short a time. Reports say that the *Coventry* (s) passed her lifeboats in long. 46 W. If this is the case, it also goes to prove that my opinion is correct.

Yours, etc.,

J.P. Crosby, Master of *Westhall* (s)

Rotterdam, April 5, 1893

## The *Upupa* Messages in Bottles off Southern Ireland

## 19 Jan 1903

### Maritime Intelligence

Upupa (s).- London, Jan. 16.- The Press Association's Cork correspondent telegraphs:- The City of Cork Steam Packet Company's steamer Upupa, Captain Kearney, from Cardiff for Cork, with coal, is reported missing since Friday morning (Jan. 16). She left Cardiff early on Thursday morning (Jan. 15), and must have encountered the full force of that night's gale. This afternoon some wreckage, consisting of deck, cabin boats and spars, bearing the name "Upupa," were washed ashore at Garryvoe Strand, near Ballycotton Bay, on the Cork coast. The Upupa carried a crew of about 20 and some steerage passengers.

### *27 Jan 1903*

### Maritime Intelligence

Upupa (s).- London, Jan. 27.- A report was received at Queenstown last evening that a bottle, to which pieces of cork were attached by wire, has been picked up on the coast at Ballyandreen, near Ballycotton, and that when opened it contained a piece of paper, having a message on it from a member of the crew of the lost Cork steamer Upupa, addressed to Mrs. Murphy, of Ballintemple, near Cork. The message stated that the steamer was fast sinking, and that the signals of distress which the crew made to another steamer were left unheeded. Part of the message is of a private nature.*

* The Board of Trade Inquiry into the loss of the *Upupa* was held in April 1903. It revealed that three bottle messages supposedly from the *Upupa* had been picked up, but it "did not

attach much importance" to two of them which were reported found near Queenstown. The third message, cited above, was picked up by a young boy, Patrick Walsh, at Ballylandreen near Ballycotton. The message, as follows, was from Michael Murphy but apparently written by his son, John Murphy, another member of the crew, because his father "could not write":

*"Friday, Jan. 16, 1903.- To my dear Wife and Family.- We are in distress not far from home, and no chance of launching a boat. God help us, we are looking out for help, and we see a boat coming. Our hearts stop beating with joy, and we are sending up signals of distress, but to our horror she passes us. We think it is the Innisfallen. Our dying curse on them, so I have not much time to finish this letter, as we may go any minute. Merciful heavens, to think of it! So whoever finds this, no matter if in 20 years, report it, and the Innisfallen, to the Board of Trade – to think they would see us drowning. God's curse on them! What's that – a heavy sea, and an explosion. We are done again. All on board are cursing the Innisfallen. It is wicked to see and hear all hands crying and shouting. All is excitement on board with us. Give my dying love to yourself and family, friends and neighbours, and pray for us, as there is no possible chance of escape. Good-bye; God bless you all. Good-bye! ++ May Heaven punish the Innisfallen for seeing us go to a watery grave when they would be in time to save us. Don't forget to report this to the Board of Trade. To Mrs. Murphy, Ballintemple, Co. Cork, Ireland."*

The master and first mate of the *Innisfallen*, Capt. Hoare and John Martin Quinlan, respectively, both gave evidence at the Inquiry that they saw no signals of distress on the night of 16 January, being in the vicinity of the *Upupa's* position on their voyage from Milford, south Wales, to Cork. Chief Officer Quinlan saw the lights of a vessel that he took to be a trawler but which he conceded later at Cork might have been the *Upupa*.

Mrs. Norah Murphy deposed at the Inquiry that: "Her husband [Michael Murphy] could not write, but her son [John], who had spent nine years in the Royal Artillery in Bermuda, prior to entering the service of the Packet Company, could write". Other members of the family confirmed that the writing on the bottle message was John Murphy's, "although the name of his father, Michael Murphy, was placed to it". The Inquiry nevertheless was "unable to come to any definite conclusion as to whether the bottle message picked up by the boy Patrick Walsh…[was] a genuine document or otherwise", because they had no other writing by John Murphy to compare it with.

The indignation and distress of the message, together with the family's testimony, indicate that the message almost certainly came from the father and son, sailors on the *Upupa* in their final moments before perishing with all their other shipmates (and several others unknown, possibly stowaways) on that bleak and stormy winter morning off the southeast coast of Ireland in January 1903.

# 2  Corpses

Bottle messages were not the only attestation of a disaster at sea. Dead bodies, whether drifting, washed ashore or found on ships or boats at sea, were quite literally bodies of evidence of a catastrophic event to which they had borne living witness but silent testimony in death. Shipwrecks could be prolific sources of corpses along a stretch of coast. Derelict vessels and boats and rafts at sea were also encountered with corpses on them.

Bodies that had been in the water a long time and washed ashore were often described as "much decomposed" or otherwise mutilated by the elements – or both. Sometimes, though, bodies could provide clues about the identity of the disaster that befell their living souls. It might be a name on their clothing or on some article about their person which could be linked to the name of the vessel that wrecked or sank or was otherwise disabled, bits of which might have washed ashore near the bodies.

## 26 April 1895

**Maritime Intelligence**

**Derelicts and Wreckage**

London, April 26.- On Tuesday a boat with the name "s.s. Marie" on her stern washed ashore in Bigbury Bay [near Plymouth, Devon], and subsequently a ship's lifeboat came ashore. The body of a seaman was also washed up on Tuesday, and on Wednesday four more bodies were found along the shore. On several of the bodies were lifebelts without the name of a vessel. One was picked up near the breakwater at the entrance to Plymouth Sound, and the others at different points of the coast immediately to the eastward.

An oar, 18 feet long, part of a set of drawers with handles, and a door marked "boatswain's stores" were also picked up yesterday. So far there does not appear to be evidence leading to the identification of the men and no clue to the cause of the loss of the Marie. Dense fogs have prevailed in the [English] Channel this week, and it is thought that the steamer has foundered as the result of a collision.

## *27 April 1895*
**Maritime Intelligence**

**Derelicts and Wreckage**

London, April, 27.- A Plymouth correspondent of the Morning Advertiser telegraphs that one of the bodies washed ashore on the coast of south Devon, along with some wreckage marked "S.S. Marie," is believed to be that of a Frenchman from the fact that the coins found upon it are French. Another of the bodies washed ashore is that of a young man having the appearance of an assistant engineer. On the body of the latter was a rosary and a talisman of a kind worn by Roman Catholics. Both bodies had on lifebelts.

*29 April 1895*
**Maritime Intelligence**

Marie (s).- London, April 29.- It has now been definitely ascertained that the vessel which foundered with all hands last week off the south coast of Devon was the three-masted steamship Marie, of London, bound from Dunkirk. Mr. Henderson, one of the owners of the vessel, arrived in the neighbourhood on Saturday, and recognised portions of the wreckage and the bodies of some of the crew that had been washed ashore, including that of Mr. Riley, the second engineer. From the fact that the men whose bodies have been found were fully attired it is supposed [believed] that the vessel ran on a rock during the gale of last Tuesday, and that slipping off into deep warder she foundered. There is no doubt that all the crew have perished.

One survivor of a wreck off the English coast gave evidence as he was found and brought ashore. They were his final words, however; he expired immediately thereafter.

## 3 Oct 1895

**Maritime Intelligence**

Lanisley.- Ilfracombe [north Devon coast], Oct. 3, 1 42 p.m.- Schooner Lanisley, of Penzance, bound for Penzance, with coals, foundered in Bristol Channel off Bull Point yesterday morning. All hands lost.

**Miscellaneous**

London, Oct. 3.- Off Lee Bay, a short distance to the west of Ilfracombe, a man was seen yesterday morning floating about on a lifebuoy. He was subsequently washed in by the tide, but died a few minutes after being brought to shore. Before he died he furnished the information that he was the captain of a Penzance schooner which foundered off Bull Point at 1 o'clock in the morning with the loss of five hands. Another report states that he is understood to have given the name of McKellick.

Mainly, though, dead bodies were the human flotsam of a disaster with no in the main, articulated narrative, no details of how it happened, nothing to say about it except that something terrible did happen. Dead bodies revealed that, and whatever the disaster was, it involved human beings and a human story that for the most part would remain unwritten, untold and, in most respects, unknown.

## 7 March 1872

**Casualties – Home**

Dover, 5th Mar.- The Caesar Kroger, from Norway to Liverpool, arrived off here, reports having, on 3rd Mar., passed a boat with the dead body of a man in it, about 22 miles West of the West Hinder lightvessel.

The *Poonah*, below, experienced more than just an encounter with floating corpses on her voyage home from Calcutta.

## 19 June 1872

**Casualties – Foreign**

St. Helena, 18th May.- The *Poonah*, Rickaby, from Calcutta, which arrived here to-day, reports having passed, 16th May, about 90 miles from this island, the dead body of a white person, and, after twenty miles had been run, two more dead bodies, also white. All three were apparently naked. Yesterday, when close to St. Helena, in the same direction as the bodies, she passed a spar with a cask attached to each end, which appeared to have been used as a raft.

"  –  " 27th May.- The *Poonah* also reports that on the 6th Mar., while in the Bay of Bengal, cholera broke out on board and lasted twenty-two days, causing the death of seventeen coolies and one seaman.

## 8 Oct 1872

**Casualties – Foreign**

Amsterdam, 5th Oct.- Accounts from Vlieland state that there had been washed ashore, on the Vliehors, on a plank, the body of a seaman having on breeches of English leather, white woollen stockings, white woollen drawers, blue striped under waistcoat, blue woollen shirt and striped waistcoat; gold rings in his ears; a copper match box in one of the pockets; all things unmarked.

## 14 May 1873

**Casualties – Foreign**

Santander [northern Spain], 8th May.- A letter from Gijon announces that some fishermen belonging to Candas had found, the previous week, two rafts, on one of which was attached the body of a man and a United States flag, and on the other five corpses in an advanced state of decomposition.

## 28 March 1874

**Casualties – Foreign**

Copenhagen, 23rd Mar.- The master, Laverick, of the Baron Hambro (s), from Cardiff to Stockholm, reports:- "On the 21st Mar., in lat. 56 N lon. 5 E, sighted the Nina Maria (ship), with bulwarks and topmasts gone, and full of water. Sent a boat to the wreck, as we saw some men in the mizen rigging. When our boats got close to the vessel, it was found impossible to board her on account of the heavy sea and the quantity of wreckage floating about, but it was seen that the men we had noticed were the corpses of four men who were lashed to the shrouds…"

## 30 Nov 1874

**Casualties – Foreign**

Boulogne, 19th Nov.- The dead body of a female, supposed of English or American nationality, washed ashore, 17th Nov., opposite the semaphore at Portel; height about 5 ft. 6 in.; thick brown hair, grey eyes, long face, a broken tooth on the left side, three warts on the left shoulder, and one on the left breast; apparently about 28 or 30 years of age; dressed in a brown dress and a man's overcoat, and having on a gold wedding ring, marked 'H.A.M.' Five dead pigs and a plank were also picked up on the beach on the same day. On the plank there were letters, deciphered with great difficulty, and apparently forming the words: John SEA LARK Rigden down'.*

* This was probably a message written on the plank and meaning: "John": the writer of the message; "SEA LARK": the name of the vessel; "Rigden": the captain's name; "down": sunk.

## 13 Aug 1878

**Casualties – Foreign**

Nicolaiefsk, 24th May.- At the commencement of this month, the *Tungus* (sealing schr.) discovered a small schnr. [schooner] with the name 'Nelly' abandoned, and in a very bad state, in a bay on the East side of Great Schantar island, sea of Ochotsk [Sea of Okhotsk, northeast Pacific coast of Russia], about 120 miles from the Amoor [Amur River]. Later on, the bodies of three Europeans and two Chinese were found ashore. On one of the bodies, presumably that of the master, there was a pocket book, containing the following information:-

"On the 17th Sept., 1876, Captain Thos. Thompson and his crew erected a hut, in which to pass the winter on Great Schantar island. On the 18th Oct., one of the crew, named Brown, fell sick, and died on the 8th Apl., of scurvy, which had also attacked the others, viz., Captain Thompson and two Chinese."

## 16 Sept 1879

**Casualties – Home**

Ventnor (I.W.), Sept. 14.- Captain Beecham of the Deal lugger Walmer Castle, reports having picked up on the 13th inst., five miles south of St. Catherine's, the body of a boy, apparently about 11 years of age, having on a dark jacket and trousers, red handkerchief with white diamond-shaped spots, black and white check Garibaldi shirt, grey worsted stockings, leather strapped carpet slippers. The body, which was too much decomposed to bring ashore, was buried at sea. The handkerchief was brought ashore here.

## 15 Oct 1879

**Casualties – Home**

Wexford [Ireland], Oct. 12.- The body of a child, about six years old, was found to-day amongst the rocks, near Carsnore Point, greatly decomposed; supposed [believed] to be one of the three children lost by the capsizing of a boat from the Langdale lately wrecked there.

## 3 April 1880

**Casualties – Home**

Rochester [Kent], March 31.- The Swedish screw-steamer Trafik, from Stockholm for Rochester, picked up in the North Sea a boat with three dead men in it. The bodies were so far decomposed that the master ordered them to be buried in the sea. There were no marks on the boat to identify to what ship she belonged.

## 2 June 1880

**Casualties – Home**

Queenstown, June 1, 2 22 p.m.- Captain Sturrock of the Scotia Queen, from Demerara, reports that on April 30, in about lat. 30 N, long. 60 W, a raft was passed, and two days after, two dead bodies.

2 40 p.m.- Captain Sturrock of the Scotia Queen further states that the raft passed was apparently made on board a man-of-war or first-class steamer, as it was bolted together and not lashed with chain. Passed two days after several dead bodies with white jumpers on, bodies much swollen.

## 28 Nov 1882

**Casualties, Etc.**

**Miscellaneous**

A body washed ashore in Freshwater West Bay [southwest Welsh/Pembrokeshire coast] last night. It was picked up by a Coastguard, and without clothes. The face was eaten away, and the body was that of a very large man, probably belonging to the Petroslava, wrecked on Skokham Island on Nov. 1. – (*Angle, near Pembroke [Wales], Nov. 25*)

## 11 Aug 1885

**Maritime Intelligence**

**Wreckage**

Paris, July 26.- A clinker built whaleboat, painted white, and marked on the stern "Sichard – Laurvig" [sic - the *Sichar*, from Larvik, Norway], was picked up at sea at the beginning of June, in lat. 47 50 N, long. 24 W, half full of water, and containing the bodies of three men, who appeared to have been dead several days. [The Norwegian ship Sichar, Steen, sailed from Hull, April 10, for Quebec.]

Not all corpses were anatomically complete when they were found...

## 29 Aug 1887

**Body Picked Up**

Porthleven [Mount's Bay, Cornwall], Aug. 27.- The body of a lad, without head, about six years old, was picked up off the harbour this morning and brought in here; supposed [believed] to be the son of – Keene, Esq., barrister, of London. The boy was drowned off the Lizard some weeks ago.

## 23 Jan 1893

**Miscellaneous**

North Foreland [northeast Kent coast], Jan. 21.- The fishing vessel Reindeer, R62, arrived at Ramsgate, and the master reports having picked up at sea a headless body, very much decomposed and supported in a lifebelt marked "M. Symon Potter, 26, Clyde-street, Glasgow."

The only confirmation of the wreck of the English barque *Donegal* at the Azores late in December 1887 was from the identification of one of the corpses washed ashore on the island of Sao Jorge.

## 11 Feb 1888

### Bodies Picked Up at the Azores

We read in the Echo, a newspaper published at St. George's [Sao Jorge], Azores, that during the night of Dec. 27 last [1887], there was wrecked on the south coast of Rosais of the Island of St. George, between Ponta Gorda and Nateiro, a vessel thought to be English, of 2,155 tons register, and built in 1871. It is presumed that the ship drifted to the west by the great storm which arose on the 26th, and six corpses were washed ashore…One of the officers of the ship was David Deans, as appears from the certificate which had been given him by different captains of English ships whom he had served, and which were washed ashore in a small tin…

### *16 Feb 1888*

### Maritime Intelligence

Donegal.- London, Feb. 15.- It has been ascertained that David Deans, referred to in the paragraph published in issue of Feb. 11, page 3, under heading "Bodies Picked Up at the Azores," belonged formerly to the [ships] Leading Chief and Euromia. He subsequently joined the Donegal, Off. No. 88,872, in the capacity of first mate at Grangemouth, in the latter end of April last, that vessel being then bound for South America. The Donegal is a barque of 693 tons, and was built in 1869; she sailed from Savannah on the 6th December [1887], bound for Trieste.

Donegal.- London, Feb. 16.- With reference to the Donegal, the following telegram has been received this morning from the owner in answer to an inquiry:- "David Deans was mate [of the] barque Donegal, Savannah for Trieste. Cannot doubt but that this vessel wrecked there (Azores)."

The fate of the small snow brig *Hannah* in 1891 was deduced from the washed up body of the vessel's master.

## 14 Jan 1891

### Miscellaneous

Newcastle, Jan. 14.- Considerable anxiety is felt for the safety of the brig Hannah, 214 tons register, belonging to South Shields, which sailed from Sunderland for Southampton on Dec. 3 [1890]. She was spoken in Grimsby roads on the 11th of the same month, but since that time nothing further has been heard of her.

### *28 Jan 1891*

### Miscellaneous

Guernsey, Jan. 26.- The body of an elderly sailor was found yesterday on the coast of the Island of Sark [Channel Islands]; it was in a state of decomposition, having been some time in the water. From papers found in the clothes it would appear to be that of a man named J. Reed, and from another (a towage bill dated at Sunderland, Dec. 3, 1890) it is inferred that he was master of the snow* Hannah, of Aberystwith [Wales], but owned in South Shields.

* A *snow* was a slightly modified brig, a two-masted vessel square-rigged on both the foremast and mainmast, and with a fore-and-aft *spanker* sail set on the lower mainmast. On a snow, the spanker was set on its own mast which was attached to the after-side of the lower

mainmast. After about 1830 the term snow gradually declined and the more generic term *brig* became most commonly used for both rigs.

The German schooner *Sara* was confirmed wrecked after the dead bodies of the master and mate of that vessel washed ashore on the German coast in December 1891.

## 29 Dec 1891

**Miscellaneous**

Amrum [one of the North Frisian Islands on the German North Sea coast], Dec. 15.- The dead body of a man, apparently a German, was found yesterday afternoon on the beach at Norddorf. It was dressed in a yellow cork jacket, yellow oilskins, etc. The maker's name, "O.H. Svendsen, Regnklaede Fabrik, Frederikstadt," was on the oilskin jacket, and on the stockings was a linen label marked "Hemken." On the ring finger was a gold betrothal ring marked "G. Meyer, 1890." The body seemed not to have been floating about long. The description is as follows:- Medium stature; forehead high; teeth sound; eyes blue; hair fair; beard, moustache, and whiskers reddish.

*31 Dec 1891*

Sara.- Geestemunde, Dec. 28.- The dead body of a man which came ashore Dec. 14 on Amrum has been identified as that of Mr. Hemken, the mate of the schooner Sara, Greiff, which left Bo'ness [on the Firth of Forth, Scotland] Dec. 4 for the Weser.

*9 Jan [1892]*

Sara.- Wyk-on-Fohr [on the North Frisian Island of Föhr], Jan. 3.- The body of a sailor, having on a cork jacket, came ashore yesterday on the west coast of this island. On one finger of the right hand was found a seal ring, with the name "Greiff" upon it. The body is probably that of Captain Greiff, of the Sara, of Geestemunde, which sailed from Bo'ness Dec. 4 for Bremerhaven. The body of the mate of this vessel had previously washed ashore at Amrum.

## 26 March 1889

**Maritime Intelligence**

**Wreckage**

New York, March 25.- The captain of a steamer which has arrived here reports that on the 23rd inst., in lat. 37 N, long. 74 W, he saw a life-raft on which were two dead bodies. The raft bore the inscription "Captain Jonathan Cone, builder, Wilmington, Delaware." A quantity of wreckage was also observed. In the pocket of one of the dead men was a card bearing the name of a grocer at Havre [Le Havre, France].*

* Several other ships reported having passed wreckage and a floating dead body in the same location. It was generally surmised in New York shipping circles that they were from a small 248-ton steamship, the *Nanticoke*, deep laden and recently departed from Newport News, Virginia, bound for Central America, which probably foundered in a northeasterly gale just off the coast.

## 5 Dec 1892

**Maritime Intelligence**

Greystoke (s).- Busum [on North Sea coast of Germany], Dec. 1.- This morning several fragments of a vessel were picked up on a beach here, probably coming from the steamer (supposed Greystoke) ashore on the Gross Vogelsund, amongst them are hatches and several portions of ship's boats. Two bodies have just been picked up near the beach here, both of which were provided with cork jackets [lifejackets].

Greystoke (s).- Ganding, Dec. 1.- A boat washed ashore here yesterday about 10 a.m. at Vollerwick, Eiderstedt district, containing three male corpses and a large dead dog. One of the bodies, that of a large powerful man, about 30 years old, with long light hair and full beard and wearing a lifebelt, marked "R. Ropner & Co., Warranted Solid Cork, J. & A.W. Birt, Mark Tower Works, London."

The second corpse, middle height, age about 30, brown hair, full beard; under clothing marked "D.C.E." The third corpse, medium height, age about 20, light hair, no beard; under clothing marked "D.C." The boat had on it "West Hartlepool – S.S. Greystoke." According to medical opinion the unfortunate men had frozen to death.

## 22 April 1893

**Maritime Intelligence**

Noranside.- Amsterdam, April 21.- A fishing smack, arrived at Ymuiden [Ijmuiden, Netherlands], reports having in lat. 56 25 N, long. 5 20 E, fallen in with a boat bearing the name of "Noranside," with the dead bodies of four sailors tied to the seats; boat painted black and white; high sea prevented approach.

Noranside (s).- London, April 22.- The following telegram has been received from the owners of the Noranside (s), dated Newcastle, April 22, 11 54 a.m.:- Steamer Cameo picked up lifeboat marked "Noranside, Newcastle," containing five dead bodies, off Hanstholm [northern Denmark]. This only information. From Gothenburg.

### 24 April 1893
**Maritime Intelligence**

Noranside (s).- Gothenburg, April 21.- Captain Potter of the steamer Cameo, from Hull, reports that when about 100 miles WSW of Hanstholmen, he picked up a lifeboat belonging to the steamer Noranside, containing the corpses of five men. Everything in the boat pointed to the conclusion that the men had been obliged, unprepared, to jump into the boat to save their lives. The boat was drifting in the general route of steamers.

### 11 May 1893
**Bottle Picked Up**

London, May 11.- A bottle was picked up at sea off South Shields yesterday, containing a scrap of paper. The message from the sea is as follows:- "Steamship 'Noranside.' In open boat without food or oars.- C.P.L. Harrison."*

### 17 May 1893
**Missing Vessels**

The Noranside (s), C. Harrison, of Newcastle-on-Tyne, Official No. 72,132, sailed from Blyth for Neufahrwasser [near Gdansk, Poland; then Western Prussia], with a cargo of coal, on April 11, 1893, and has not since been heard of.

* The author of the bottle message, "C.P.L. Harrison", is identified by the Missing Vessel report as the master of the *Noranside*. It seems likely that Capt. Harrison was one of the five corpses in the lifeboat found by the *Cameo* 100 miles off the west coast of Denmark in the North Sea. Whether or not that boat was the same one spotted by the Dutch fishing smack, "with the dead bodies of four [sic] sailors tied to the seats", is not and almost certainly cannot ever be known.

## 30 April 1894

**Miscellaneous**

London, April 30.- Intelligence has just reached Skibbereen [south coast Ireland, Co. Cork] of the washing ashore of six bodies on Rosscarbery strand on Saturday morning. During the storm of Tuesday a fishing smack was said to have foundered off that part of the coast.

## 2 Jan 1895

**Maritime Intelligence**

**Miscellaneous**

Whitby, Jan. 1.- The body of a man, much decomposed, face eaten away, washed ashore near Spa ladder at 10 a.m. to-day. Height, 5 feet 6 inches, or thereabouts. Thick set. Had on pair shoes, elastic sides, four Blakey boot protectors on each sole; no nails [no hobnails on his boot soles, that is – not fingernails or toenails!]. No clothes. Must have been in water some months. Age, doubtful.

## 20 Sept 1895

**Maritime Intelligence**

Clodian.- Nordmaling [mid-coast of Sweden on Gulf of Bothnia], Sept. 15.- A ship's boat, having in it the dead bodies of two young men, has driven ashore at Tjornskar, near Jernas. The boat is marked "Clodian, London." A shipwreck is feared, as much wreckage is drifting near Jernas, and it is thought that the wrecked ship belonged to Fredrikstad [south of Oslo, Norway].

Clodian.- Nordmaling, Sept. 16.- The barque Clodian, of Fredrikstad, stranded during the night of Sept. 11 on Lordagshallan [a rocky shoal off the coast] and became a wreck. The crew, 10 in number, are supposed [believed] to be lost. Of the two bodies found in a boat one appears to be that of the mate. On one of its fingers is a gold ring, marked "Din Inga 11/11/94." On one hand of the other body the letters "O.K." are tattooed. Both men seem as if they had died of cold and hunger.

## 16 Dec 1895

**Maritime Intelligence**

**Miscellaneous**

Flushing [southern Netherlands], Dec. 15.- A ketch, probably British, name unknown, has foundered in the Roompot [Zeeland, southern Netherlands]. Only part of the rigging is above water; two dead bodies are hanging in it.

## 14 March 1896

**Maritime Intelligence**

Pickwick.- Bridgwater [Somerset], March 12.- The ketch Pickwick, of Bridgwater, is lying sunk two miles SW of the East Culver buoy, with her two masts showing at low water. The dead body of the mate (Hoyal) was found lashed to the rigging.

## 27 Dec 1895

**Maritime Intelligence**

Fanny Scott.- Rome, Dec. 26.- A private message from Palermo [Sicily] states that a boat, containing the dead body of a seaman, has been found on the shore near Terrasini. The boat bore the name of the Fanny Scott, which is that of a sailing vessel of 200 tons belonging to London. There was no clue to the man's identity, and death appeared to have been due to starvation and exposure. It is feared that the Fanny Scott has foundered at sea. A boat, believed to be that picked up near Terrasini, is reported to have been seen recently with five or six dead bodies in it five miles from the shore.

## 20 July 1900

**Maritime Intelligence**

**Derelicts and Wreckage**

Boston, July 7.- Captain Larsen, of the Norwegian barque Coronae, at Charlottetown (P.E.I. [Prince Edward Island]), from Liverpool, states:- When crossing Newfoundland banks sighted an open boat with a handkerchief tied to an oar as a signal of distress. The body of a man was lying in the bottom of the boat.

# 3 Hard Weather Voyages: Gales, Storms and Hurricanes

**W**eather was often a contributory factor in casualties. A voyage around Cape Horn in the southern hemisphere winter (June–September) was usually a hard-weather voyage. Many sailing ships foundered amongst the stormy mountains of waves ('greybearders') around Cape Horn, at the southern tip of the South American continent, pummelled for days or weeks on end by hurricane force winds that might eventually overwhelm vessels with the loss of their entire crew. In truth, though, a vessel could be overwhelmed by storm, wind and sea almost anywhere on the oceans and seas of the world (the main exception being the doldrums regions of calm along the equator). Many losses, however, were not reported, because there was no trace of their demise.

The master of the *Plantagenet* reported the details of his vessel's fairly typical passage from the west coast of South America round Cape Horn to Falmouth, in 1878–79.

## 2 Jan 1879

Report of the Plantagenet, from Huanillos [a Chilean nitrate port], at Falmouth:-

Sailed from Huanillos Aug. 19. Had very good SE trades from there to lat. 31 S, long. 79 W. From that to lat. 54 S, long. 78 W, had moderate W and WSW winds, smooth water, and fine weather. Sept. 10 experienced a strong E gale from SSE to ESE, with a very heavy cross sea running. From lat. 56 S, long. 81 W, to the Falkland Islands had light variable winds, fine weather, and smooth water. Sept. 26, lat 51 40 S, long. 51 20 W, passed a small iceberg. Next morning saw very large icebergs, and for four days we were passing ice, some very large, and some awash. We saw over 100 icebergs.

Had light variable winds from WNW to SW for 10 days; from lat. 34 S, long. 21 W, to lat. 15 S, long. 35 W, light N and NE winds. From that to the Line [equator] had E to ENE winds; no SE Trades whatever. Crossed the Line Nov. 8, long 29 30 W, 81 days out. Got the NE trades [in] lat. 7 N; had them very light all through, and lost them in lat. 24 N, long. 34 W.

From that to the Western Islands [the Azores] had light variable winds and a deal of calms, with a heavy east swell at times. Dec 5, off the Western Islands, lat. 39 N, long. 30

A GALE AT SEA: "POOPED"

DRAWN BY FRANK BRANGWYN

20 W, experienced a very heavy easterly gale for four days, with a high sea running, the ship labouring very much. Dec. 6 shipped a heavy sea on the starboard side, stove two boats, smashed the after hatch-house to pieces, washed away a quantity of port bulwarks, started the knee on the forward end of the poop, filling the cabin with water, and doing other considerable damage about decks. In the afternoon shipped another heavy sea, which smashed the doors and windows of the forward house.

From Dec. 9 to 24th had easterly winds, ENE to SE, blowing strong at times, and a very unsettled appearance in the weather. Dec. 24, lat. 47 40 N, long. 15 30 W, encountered a terrific gale from E to ESE, with a very high sea running, ship labouring very heavily and shipping large quantities over all. 8 A.M., gale increased to a hurricane.

I deemed it prudent to run the ship to clear the storm, so squared the yards and kept before the wind, running under two lower topsails. At noon, blowing with increased violence, a tremendous sea stove all the doors and windows of forward house. At 6 30 P.M. the gale suddenly lulled and hauled to SSE, during which a heavy sea broke aboard and started the pilot-house stairing, windows, and doors, also starting the cabin skylight and breaking the glass, and doing other damage about the ship. At 8 P.M. hauled the ship to the wind on the starboard tack.

From that to the Channel had variable winds and very unsettled weather. Arrived Falmouth Dec 29 at 9 P.M. Passage 132 days.

## Winds, Weather and Seas

Ships often reported "hurricane" winds. Most of the time these conditions, especially around Cape Horn or in the North Atlantic, indicated storms of hurricane *force* winds of a particularly violent nature, rather than actual revolving storms called hurricanes which occurred only during the hurricane season. (Revolving subtropical storms called *hurricanes* in the Caribbean, Atlantic and eastern Pacific, *typhoons* in the western Pacific, and *cyclones* in the Indian Ocean are all the same kind of revolving storm.)

A captain who reported "baffling winds" did not mean he was baffled, or mystified by such winds but rather that they came from many different directions. They contrasted with "steady" winds predominantly from one direction, such as trade winds.

Casualty reports very often described "terrific weather". In the English language usage of those times, "terrific weather" meant terrifically *bad* weather, as can be inferred from the nature of the report, rather than *very pleasant* as terrific tends to mean today!

Equally, "terrific seas" meant phenomenally high seas of 30 or even 50 feet in height – or more! In the vast expanses of the open ocean, and particularly in the Southern Ocean such seas could be half a mile or more long. Ships could ride over them if they were sailed with skill and experience. Big seas could also, however, break with tremendous violence and easily overwhelm a vessel by "pooping" her (coming over the poop, or stern deck, of the ship and washing her main decks fore and aft), or by coming over her side if the vessel lay broadside to the seas, throwing her on her beam ends (that is, on her side). A vessel on her beam ends might roll over completely if she became flooded; or she could roll upright, eventually, but often with considerable damage to her masts and rigging.

In the shallower depths around the continental shelf (off Cape Horn or the Cape of Good Hope, for example), and especially against a counter-current, seas could pile up in a steep and dangerous turmoil that might swallow up a ship without warning, taking her to the bottom and leaving no trace of her or her crew. The North Atlantic was just as dangerous a place in winter or during the Northern Hemisphere hurricane season (June to November).

## NARRATIVES

## 14 Sept 1869

### Liverpool, 13th Sept.

The *Lake Constance*, from Swansea to Valparaiso, running for the Falkland Islands, short of water, having been 56 days trying to get round Cape Horn, was spoken, 15th June, in lat. 56 S, lon. 61 W, by the *Gamma*, Johnson, arrived at Queenstown. The *Gamma*, Johnson, from Junin* to Altona*, which arrived at Queenstown 9th Sept., had lost jibboom and cutwater, and thrown overboard a quantity of cargo during a very violent gale off Cape Horn.

* Junín was a nitrate port, between Iquique and Arica in northern Chile; Altona is at Hamburg, Germany. Almost two months trying to get round Cape Horn in the Southern Hemisphere winter, as the *Lake Constance* experienced, was by no means uncommon for sailing ships hammered by the violent weather and mountainous seas of that region.

## 5 Oct 1869

The Susan N. Smart (whaling schr.), of Boston, U.S., has capsized during a hurricane in the Atlantic. 19 of the crew, with the master's wife and two children, were drowned, and four seamen were taken off the wreck by the *Flatworth*, Oxley, from Penang, arrived in the River.

## 12 Oct 1869

### Milford [Milford Haven, Wales], 8th Oct.

The mate of the Doctor, from Philadelphia to Plymouth, which vessel was towed in here, 6th Oct., reports that she encountered heavy gales, 2nd, 13th, 16th, and 17th Sept. On the last mentioned day, when in about lat. 47 N, lon. 29 W, a very heavy sea broke over the vessel, hove her on her beam ends, carried away the wheel, washed three men overboard, and drowned the master in the cabin. Was obliged to cut away fore and main masts. Fell in with the *Squire*, for Gibraltar, on the 4th Oct., 40 miles W of Scilly.

## 12 Oct 1869

### Gibraltar, 6th Oct 1869

The Rush, Hardest, late Patty, from New York, arrived here, 2nd Oct., with loss of sails, a boat, etc., and her late master, Patty, mate, and 1 seaman washed overboard and drowned in a hurricane, 15th Sept. On the 17th, in lat. 43 N, lon. 35 W, she spoke the *Golden Rule*, Hall, of and for Boston, from Liverpool, which vessel supplied her with her present temporary master.

## 14 April 1870

### Casualties – Foreign

New York, 31st March.- The Two Brothers (Brit. brig), Dickson, hence to Marseilles, with petroleum, reported 30 Mar. as at Bermuda, leaky, had experienced a hurricane on 21st Feb., and lost deckload, sails, etc., stove water casks, sprung foremast, and made so much water that all available hands (several of the seamen being frozen) were constantly at the pumps. She ran towards the Gulf [of Mexico], but was driven 340 miles East of Bermuda, and, as she continued to leak, was taken into St. George's [Bermuda] on the 15th Mar., with officers and crew completely exhausted, and with several feet of water in her hold. She would repair at Bermuda.

## 22 April 1870

### Casualties – Foreign

Reykjavik, Iceland, 5th Apl.- The winter has been very mild, but stormy. There were heavy gales last month, and 35 fishermen were lost in their boats off the coasts in about a week.

## 3 Feb 1872

### Casualties – Foreign

Rotterdam, 1st Feb.- The Baron v. Pallandt v. Rozendaal (Dut.), from Cardiff to Singapore, with coals, which was towed into Bahia [northeastern Brazil], 6th Jan., dismasted, encountered a rain squall, 25th Dec., in lat. 6 S, lon. 25 W, during which a waterspout went right over the vessel, breaking main and fore masts; the topmasts and topgallantmasts hanging caused much damage to other spars and gear.

## 23 March 1874

### Casualties, Etc.

The Herzog Ernst, Schluter, from Baltimore to Rotterdam, arrived off the Wight [Isle of Wight], reports:- "On 26th and 27th Feb., in about lat. 42 N lon. 46 W, experienced a hurricane with a heavy sea, which strained ship, broke bulwarks and stanchions, started and split covering boards, washed boat and water casks overboard, and caused vessel to make water.

On 28th Feb. spoke the Sultan (brig), of Shoreham [West Sussex], dismasted, and with heavy list to port. Bulwarks and stanchions damaged. Asked if she required assistance, was answered in the negative, but the sea being high and the weather bad, lay by the brig. In about an hour, the gale from south and sea increasing, the brig made signal of distress, when we wore ship* and picked up the crew (who had left in their boat).

Also, on the 1st Mar., in lat. 44 N lon. 30 W, spoke a brigantine, name on stern 'Laura', painted green, with bulwarks and stanchions on starboard side all gone, foresail and lower topsail flying in ribbons. Reported master below with leg broken. Asked if they wanted assistance, but could not get any satisfactory answer. They launched their boat and towed her astern, wore their ship round and lost the boat. We lay by her four hours. If they had made signals of distress, would have sent boat to their assistance."

* "Wore ship": the most usual way for any sailing ship of any size to change course is by tacking. This involves steering the ship's head up into the wind and hauling the sails around to catch the wind from the other side of the ship. The sails then swing the ship's head around into the wind, then further so the wind comes onto the other side of the ship. This brings the vessel onto her new course, with sails reset accordingly.

To tack in the conventional way a big sailing ship needs considerable sea room ahead of her, often as much as a mile, to swing around in the arc described above as she continues to sail on. If land is close by, there might not be enough room ahead to tack. The weather might also make it dangerous to come about by trying to tack into a strong wind and high sea. In those circumstances a master might decide to *wear ship*.

In order to wear ship, instead of tacking by bringing the ship's head up *into* the wind and swinging it around that way onto a new course, the master goes in the opposite direction: he turns the ship *away* from the direction the wind is blowing and swings the ship around until the wind is coming from directly behind. The sails are then hauled around, the ship's head continues to swing round onto its new course – and off she goes. Wearing ship needed more sea room than tacking, but it was often safer to do in very bad weather in mid-ocean. In small boat and yacht sailing, *gybing* is the manoeuvre approximately equivalent to wearing ship, though not usually done for the same reason as a big square-rigger.

## 9 Feb 1875

### Casualties – Home

Poole, 5th Feb.- The Heroine (schr.), McCarthy, which arrived here, to-day, from Newfoundland*, reports:- "Sailed from Twillingate, Nfld., 23rd Dec. [1874], for St. John's, Nfld., with salted codfish in bulk. On the 30th, when off Cape Bonavista, was struck by a sea, and had part of bulwark, mainrail, water casks and lower gear from the decks carried away. Vessel barricaded up with ice on bow and sides. On the 31st, was hove nearly on her beam ends, and had to throw some cargo overboard to right the vessel.

On the 1st Jan., terrific gale and high sea, at 7 p.m., carried away figurehead and bowsprit. Lay to until the 4th, when, finding there was no chance of making St. John's, the vessel bore up for England. On the 7th, heavy gale, schooner hove to, had more bulwarks and stanchions washed away. Vessel lay to until the 12th, when a terrific gale was experienced. Gale continued, and on the 18th a heavy sea carried away galley and bulwarks, stripped side battens of main hatch, and ripped up coat of mainmast, water thereby getting into the hold. Again hove a portion of cargo overboard. On the 24th gale continued, ship hove to, had tiller broken off at rudderhead. Repaired damages. On the 3rd Feb., weather more moderate."

\* The winter North Atlantic gales blew the schooner *Heroine* all the way from Newfoundland, where she was making a relatively short coastal passage, across the other side of the Atlantic to Poole on the south coast of England.

## 29 March 1875

### Casualties, Etc.

The *Pauline*, arrived at Queenstown, from Mexillones [Peru], reports:- "Left Mexillones on 26th Nov. [1874]. Rounded Cape Horn on 25th Dec. Had the wind NE through the SE trades district, which brought us in sight of Pernambuco [Recife, Brazil]. Crossed the equator on 5th Jan., in lon. 34 W. Had no calms or variables between the trades north of the line [ie., the equator]. Had fresh NE trades, with squalls, and lost them in lat. 24 N lon. 45 W.

We then encountered furious gales, with high sea, and heavy squalls from E to N, lasting about a week. Passed Corvo [Azores], on 9th Mar., with the first wind that had any westerly in it since we left Cape Horn.

During the whole passage from Peru there was not above a dozen days that the vessel could lay her course, or come within a couple of points* of it.

* A compass (360°) has 32 directional points. One point of a compass is therefore 360° divided by 32, or 11.25°. So the *Pauline*, on her entire four-month voyage from Peru to Queenstown, Ireland, because of adverse winds, could only sail on 'a dozen' or so days within about 20° either side of the course she would have wanted to steer. Although the *Pauline's* passage was not particularly stormy, it was unusually arduous for the persistence of contrary winds throughout.

## 4 Oct 1877

**Casualties, Etc.**

The Seatoller, Thorburn, arrived at Falmouth, from Iquique, reports:- "Left Iquique 14th June. The first four days had light airs from SSE and calms, and then got moderate winds from SSE to N up to 8th July. In lat. 55 S lon. 83 W, encountered violent gales from S to E, with heavy frost and snow; ship one mass of ice*, which had to be broken off the ropes with capstan bars** in order to get the yards round, a terrific confused sea at the time filling decks, breaking spars adrift, and staving in forecastle companion, smashing wheel box, washing the men away from the wheel several times, and disabling some of them. Four of the hands were laid up through cold and wet. 15th July, passed Cape Horn, and had a continuation of gales from ENE to WSW and high seas, shipping heavy water until 29th July."

* This was mid-winter weather in the deep southern hemisphere latitudes of Cape Horn.

** Capstan bars were iron or hardwood bars fitted into slots around the drum of the capstan on the forecastle head. Each crew member took hold of a bar to push the drum round to heave up the anchor, a laborious task at the best of times but particularly so if a lot of chain was out.

## 27 Nov 1878

**Casualties – Home**

Newry, 24th Nov.- The Galera (barq.), Stewart, from New York, arrived here 22nd Nov, reports that nearly all her voyage was stormy. On 15th Nov., when off the banks of Newfoundland, the mate, carpenter, and steward were washed overboard and drowned, the vessel receiving considerable damage at the same time.

## 13 Feb 1879

**Casualties, Etc.**

Report of the barque Flying Fish, of London, Le Messurier:- "Left Demerara Lightship [Guyana] Dec. 23, 6 p.m., with a general West India cargo, and proceeded with the usual trade winds. On Jan. 10, 7 p.m., in lat. 25 N, long. 52 W, wind NE on starboard tack, sighted unusual lights bearing E by N, about five miles, which seemed to be like a vessel showing signs of distress. Immediately tacked ship and proceeded towards the place, and afterwards found it to be the brigantine Maid of Llangollen*, of St. John (N.B.), from London to that port, being 82 days out, and destitute of all provisions, having been for the last three days without anything to eat, and for 10 days previous to that on less than half allowance.

Supplied them with as much provisions as could be spared, and found by the mate's account that the vessel was strained from successive gales. Had tried to get into Bermuda, but was obliged to run before the wind, as the vessel could not bear it, having the rigging, sails, and spars very deficient. It was the captain's intention to try and reach St. Thomas [Virgin Islands]. At 11 p.m. proceeded northwards, and saw the said vessel set sail and proceed southwards. During the passage they also lost a man overboard from the jibboom.

* The *Maid of Llangollen* left London 30 October 1878 for St. John, New Brunswick. After her encounter with the *Flying Fish* (above) on 10 January 1879, she arrived at St. Thomas, in the Caribbean on 15th January.

## 20 Oct 1880

**Casualties – Foreign**

St. Helena, Oct 2:- Cumbrian*, Edkins, from Akyab for London, arrived here, experienced dreadful weather, on Aug 22, in lat. 31 S, long. 31 E, during which lost lower maintopsail, two boats and skids, and everything movable from decks, also lost one man overboard...

Nagpore*, ship, Robertson, from Calcutta for Liverpool, arrived off the port without anchoring on Sept 19, and reports:- "On Aug 22, in lat. 31 S, long. 32 E, experienced hurricane weather, which heeled ship over to such a degree as to cause cargo to shift, and putting all hatches under water. Had to cut away foretopmast, which carried away jib-boom and sprung maintopgallant and lost bulwarks, a boat, everything movable from decks, and cabin was gutted on starboard side, damaging stores."

* These two vessels were in virtually the same position – just off the east coast of South Africa - on the same date when they experienced the same atrocious weather, probably an Indian Ocean cyclone.

## 28 Nov 1881

**Casualties – Home**

Cardiff, Nov. 25.- The survivors of the barque Adept, of Glasgow, landed here. It appears from their statement that the Adept, commanded by Captain Morrison, left St. John (N.B.) on the 26th Oct. (deals [ie., with a cargo of deals - wood planks) for London. She was a vessel of 1,100 tons register, and owned by Mr. Robert Rankin, Liverpool. On the 10th inst. a fearfully heavy sea was encountered in the Atlantic and the ship became waterlogged. An attempt was made to throw the deck load [ie., the deals] over, when one of the hands was washed overboard, but was thrown on board again by a wave and was saved.

The pumps were kept going, and for 48 hours the men had no water or bread. One-third of the deck cargo had been flung over when a tremendous sea broke on to the vessel and swept the remainder away. A great crash took place, and the bulwarks, the cabin house forward, four large tanks of water, the boats, mizentopmast and maintopgallant, and pumps were carried away.

A fearful scene of confusion ensued, men being jammed among the timber under the surface of the water. At this time 12 men out of the crew of 22 were actually carried away from the vessel and drowned. These included Mr. Donaldson, chief officer; Mr. Swanson, second mate; Alfred Lee, of London; William Brown, a German; and the captain's son, the carpenter's mate. The captain himself was fearfully crushed aft in among the timber, and men who had been in the cabin at the time the vessel was swept went to him at great risk, and eventually extricated him.

The crew remained with the vessel all night, and the next morning their signals were seen by the Memel, of Mel, from Miramichi [New Brunswick], which took them on board. The Memel then came on to Cardiff, where she landed the survivors, excepting the captain, whose injuries prevent him from being brought on shore. On Thursday one of his eyes was extracted, and it is feared that he will lose the sight of the other. The men remain at present at the Sailors' Home.

## 19 Aug 1882

### Weather and Navigation

Queenstown, Aug. 16.- The Otter, barque, Wylie, arrived here from Iquique, reports that she encountered a heavy gale to the westward of Cape Horn, and a succession of strong easterly breezes and gales after passing it up to lat. 40 S. In lat. 40 S, long. 32 W, she experienced a terrific gale, veering from NE by E (blowing hardest from West) round by N to SW; lost almost all the topgallant bulwarks. The sea ran very high and caused the vessel to roll heavily. The decks were continually full of water, and the sea broke on board on all sides, the vessel lying to under a mizen staysail and labouring very much.

On June 16, lat. 21 57 S, long. 25 W, the Otter spoke the Jorsalfarer, Norwegian barque, from Astoria for Queenstown, which vessel had encountered the same gale during which her master was killed, the first mate's leg broken, and a seaman injured. Supplied her with bread. (Mem.: The Jorsalfarer has arrived at Queenstown.)

## 7 Sept 1883

### Hurricane in the Atlantic

New York, Wednesday [Sept 5]. – All incoming vessels report heavy weather at sea. The British ship Macedonia brought yesterday twelve survivors from the wreck of the Swedish barque David, abandoned Aug. 31. She encountered a terrific hurricane off Cape Hatteras on Aug. 28, when a succession of mountainous seas swept over her, carrying away everything above deck, together with the captain, the second mate, and five seamen.

The barque Lady Dafferin reports encountering a similar hurricane when she lost everything movable from the decks. Despatches from Newfoundland report great disasters among the fishing fleets on the banks, where the storm on the 28th and 29th was the severest ever known. Over thirty vessels are missing, and there are grave fears for their safety.

## 19 Sept 1883

### Casualties, Etc.

Lennie.- London, Sept. 18.- The barque Lennie*, Harris, of and from Yarmouth, N.S. [Nova Scotia], for Dover, with timber, which was towed into Dover from the Downs yesterday with loss of foretopmast and bulwarks, reports having encountered extraordinary weather in the Atlantic. The Lennie left Yarmouth, N.S., June 28, and all went well until Aug. 31, when she was overtaken by a heavy WSW gale. Towards evening the lower topsails and foretopsails were carried away, and by midnight the gale had increased to a hurricane. The sea rose to an extraordinary height, the vessel being at times quite engulphed, as it were, between the huge waves. At this time the barometer had fallen to 28.34 deg. [*sic* - inches]; the ship scudding along under bare poles [ie., with no sails set], labouring and straining heavily, and constantly shipping great quantities of water.

Shortly after midnight, a tremendous sea swept over the poop, and it was some time before the ship recovered herself. The binnacle, compass, and ventilators were smashed, the cabins flooded with water, and the whole of the provisions on board destroyed. The ship was then brought to on the starboard tack. An hour later, the sea washed a large portion of the deckload overboard. The poop rail was torn away on the port side, and a part of the planking started [became loose] from the main to the mizen rigging, some being started on the starboard [side] also. The boats were smashed, a clean sweep was made of the bulwarks, and the doors of the forward deckhouse and a part of the structure carried away, the deckload washing from side to side in the greatest confusion, drawing ring-bolts out of the deck in all directions, besides chafing the water-ways, and starting the bitts.

In the course of the morning the gale freshened, and a fearfully high sea continued to run, the ship's lee rail being seldom above water. The fury of the gale continued throughout the morning, and at 2 P.M. it was found that the water had risen to within a foot below the between-deck beams, the ship getting very low in the water. The vessel was then got round on the other tack, and in doing so her jib, flying jib, staysails, etc., were carried away. The foretopmast was then cut away, and the yards on the foremast with the jibboom [jib-boom], were carried away, with all gear attached. Next morning the vessel had 13 feet of water in hold. Provisions were obtained from a passing vessel, and the hurricane abating, the water reduced by the pumps, and the Lennie proceeded.

* Eight years earlier, on 31 October 1875, there had been a vicious mutiny on the *Lennie*: see **Mutiny, Murder and Mayhem**: **The *Lennie* Mutiny**.

## 8 May 1885

### Maritime Intelligence

Northbrook*.- Montevideo, May 7, 12 40 p.m.- The Northbrook, from San Francisco for Cork, was spoken on April 11, in lat. 19 S, long. 32 W, with loss of main and mizen masts.

### *19 June 1885*
### Maritime Intelligence

Northbrook. Lizard, June 18, 6 40 p.m.- The ship Northbrook, of London, from San Francisco, is passing with loss of main and mizen masts by the board, also head foretopgallantmast, in tow of Falmouth tug Victor, and making for that port. She has a jury mizenmast rigged, and does not appear to have suffered in her hull.

Northbrook.- Falmouth, June 19, 10 17 a.m.- The Northbrook, from San Francisco, wheat, reported last evening with loss of main and mizen masts, has also lost two boats, boats' skids, main rail and bulwarks on starboard side and bridge, and had part of poop deck ripped up, etc., during heavy gale on 3rd March, in lat. 57 S, long. 76 W.

* Any well-found vessel, with all rigging intact, would consider approximately 150 days as an average length voyage from San Francisco to the English Channel. The marvel of the

# THE GRAPHIC

## AN ILLUSTRATED WEEKLY NEWSPAPER

No. 820.—Vol. XXXII.
Registered as a Newspaper

SATURDAY, AUGUST 15, 1885

ENLARGED TO
TWO SHEETS

PRICE SIXPENCE
By Post Sixpence Halfpenny

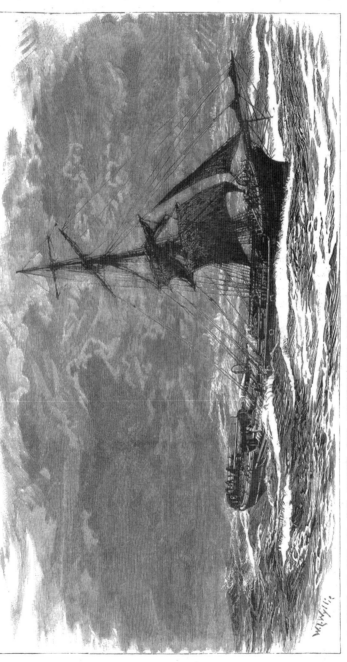

A STORY OF THE SEA—THE BRITISH SHIP "NORTHBROOK," THE DAY AFTER A GALE, MARCH 4, 1885, NEAR CAPE HORN

(THIS VESSEL WAS NAVIGATED NEARLY 9,000 MILES UNDER THE ONE MAST AND A SMALL JURY STUMP AFT)

*Northbrook*'s voyage of 150 days was that she did it with the loss of two of her three masts, and having suffered multiple other damages in fearsome weather just as she was coming up to round Cape Horn on her passage from the Pacific to the Atlantic Ocean. She was therefore obliged to sail the remaining 9,000 miles of the voyage under her single remaining foremast and "a small jury stump aft".

The *Northbrook*, under the command of Capt. Timothy, left San Francisco on 19 January 1885 for Queenstown, Ireland with a cargo of wheat. She was dismasted in stormy weather just before reaching Cape Horn, on 3–4 March, and arrived at Falmouth on 18 June 1885, 106 days after her dismasting and averaging around 85 miles a day (3.5 knots) under jury rig.

## 1 June 1886

### Maritime Intelligence

Erminia dall'Orso.- Mauritius, April 30.- The barque Erminia dall'Orso, of Genoa, Raffo, from Rangoon for Falmouth (rice), which put in here for repairs April 24, reports having experienced a terrific cyclone* on April 17 and 18, in lat. 22 28 S, long. 67 40E, with heavy confused sea, during which the vessel was thrown on her beam ends, and in order to right her had to cut away the main and mizen masts, which were lost with all belonging to them;...

Europa.- Mauritius, April 30.- The barque Europa, of Hamburg, Bruel, from Bassein [Burma] for Falmouth (rice), which put in here April 22 in distress, had sustained loss of starboard bulwarks, stanchions, sails, and everything movable about the decks, and had a heavy list to starboard, the cargo having shifted. The master reports having encountered a severe cyclone* on April 18, in lat. 24 37 S, long. 64 30 E, with tremendous sea, wind veering from ENE to WSW...

Hilston.- Mauritius, April 30.- The ship Hilston, of London, Tidmarsh, from Rangoon for Liverpool (rice), which put in here April 24 with hatches stove in, deck cabins and decks damaged, loss of cabin stores, etc.; three boats and two seamen washed overboard and drowned; had encountered a severe cyclone* on April 17, in lat. 22 26 S, long. 68 43 E, barometer (lowest) 29.30...

Royal Sovereign.- Mauritius, April 30.- The ship Royal Sovereign, of Liverpool, Buntel, from Calcutta for Barrow-in-Furness (jute), which put in here dismasted April 27, the mizen and fore masts alone standing, reports having experienced a terrific cyclone* on April 17 and 18, in lat. 23 09 S, long. 68 04 E, with mountainous sea, wind veering from ENE to N, during which the vessel was thrown on her starboard beam-ends; had starboard bulwarks and stanchions from forerigging to break of poop and mainchain plates carried away; mainmast went by the deck, carrying with it mizentopmast and all belonging to it; foretopmast carried away, taking jibboom with it; lost four boats, pump-wheels and all gear attached, and ventilators; cabin, galley, and starboard forecastle gutted, stores lost and damaged. Relieving tackles and wheel-chains broke adrift, wheel getting broken and injuring the captain and two of the crew...

Urania.- Mauritius, April 30.- The ship Urania, of Hamburg, Inechtenicht, from Rangoon for Falmouth (rice), which put in here April 24 for repairs, reports having encountered a severe cyclone* on April 17, in lat. 22 14 S, long. 67 27 E, wind veering from NE to NNW and W…Vessel was thrown on her beam ends, and had to cut away foretopmast to right her, which, in falling, carried away jibboom and mizentopgallantmast, with all attached; had starboard bulwarks and stanchions from break of poop to forerigging carried away, cabin gutted, stores damaged, and everything movable about the decks washed overboard and lost; crew lost most of their clothes…

Wega.- Mauritius, April 30.- The ship Wega, of Bremen, Leopold, from Bassein for Falmouth, rice, reports that on April 17th and 18th, in lat. 21 58 S, long. 65 04 E, the vessel encountered a terrific cyclone*, the centre passing over her, wind veering from NE to SW…

## 23 June 1886
### Maritime Intelligence

St. Patrick.- St. Helena, June 7.- The St. Patrick, Campbell, from Calcutta for New York, reports:- "On the 18th April, in lat. 23 53 S, long. 65 E, experienced a very heavy cyclone*, with tremendous high seas; had decks swept of all movables, maintopgallantmast sprung, and foretopgallantmast badly damaged, a spare spar and two studding sail booms washed overboard, three boats damaged, several sails blown out of gaskets, and some stores washed away."

* All these vessels and others sustained damage by the same cyclone, in approximately the same location in the Indian Ocean (550–600 miles east and southeast of Mauritius), and on the same days 17 and 18 April. The southwest Indian Ocean cyclone season starts around mid-November and lasts to the following April, though tropical storms and even cyclones in that region do form outside that period. Mauritius was the most convenient sanctuary for sailing vessels damaged by Indian Ocean cyclones, where they could carry out repairs. Many vessels also put in at St. Helena, in the South Atlantic, but the roadstead at Jamestown, is very open and exposed to the sea, as well as being quite deep.

## 2 Aug 1887
### Weather and Navigation

London, July 30.- The Jerusalem, Breach, from Sydney, arrived here, reports:- Left Sydney April 20, with fair wind and fine weather. On the 21st wind backed to SSE and freshened to a gale, which lasted until 29th, during which time we encountered a tremendous sea, which kept the decks continually flooded. Then fine weather set in, and we passed the north end of New Zealand on May 1. On the 2nd wind increased to moderate gale from NNE, which backed to NW, and blew with hurricane force. The whole of the time the decks were continually flooded. On the 6th wind backed to SW, and until June 6 we encountered a continuation of heavy gales.

On May 9, in lat. 49 S, long. 146 W, the fore sheet was carried away in a very heavy squall, at which time a tremendous sea was running, and one was shipped over the starboard side, smashing the starboard boat and doing other damage. On the 10th, at 3 30 a.m., ship running under reefed topsails and reefed foresail, a tremendous sea struck her, carrying away eight stanchions and bulwarks on the starboard side, smashing the stockhouses and washing overboard the starboard water and harness casks, and nearly the whole of the port bulwarks. Sounded the pumps and found ship making large quantities of water. Kept her before the wind, and cleared away the wreck.

Finding ship still making water, ran to the northward for two days, into finer weather, and found that she was making water at the broken stanchion heads, which I had battened over with two parts of canvas. Found the leaks stopped, and proceeded on our course, after securing the bulwarks as best we could with spare spars and studdingsail booms, seas continually making clean breaches over the ship all the time.

After 27 years experience never saw such a continuation of heavy weather.

Rounded the Horn on the 24th, in a terrific gale of wind from the NW, accompanied with lightning and thunder, hail, and snow. From June 6 until our arrival fine weather, with light airs and calms, was experienced. Crossed the Equator on June 20, and had 17 days calm.

Entered the Channel on the 28th July, and made the Start [Start Point, Devon] at 8 p.m. Proceeded up Channel, with light southerly winds, and were taken in tow, off Brighton, at noon on the 29th, by the steamtug Enterprise. Pilot came on board off Dungeness, at 7 30 p.m., and vessel arrived at Gravesend at 8 a.m. to-day.

## 22 Nov 1887

### Maritime Intelligence

Augusta.- New York, Nov. 11.- The Union, from Pernambuco, arrived here yesterday, reports that on Oct. 24, in lat. 20 N, long. 55 W, she sighted a ship's boat; bore down to her and found her to contain six seamen in an exhausted condition. When brought on board they were found to be the second mate and five seamen of the barque Augusta, of Stockholm, Captain Meyer, from Swansea for Aspinwall, who reported that on Oct. 14, lat. 16 N, long. 48 W, had a hurricane* from the east for 48 hours, with high seas, one of which came aboard, making the vessel a complete wreck. Scudded under two topsails and foresail, but the sails were blown to pieces. Hove to and endeavoured to wear ship, but could not. A wave washed away the captain, mate, and one seaman. An effort was made to launch the two boats, but one had her bows stove in the attempt, so that three men had to work continually to keep her afloat, and there is not the slightest doubt but that she sank with her crew of six men in a very short time.**

### *28 Nov 1887*

### Maritime Intelligence

Augusta.- St. Thomas [Virgin Islands], Nov. 10.- The Swedish barque Augusta, of Stockholm, from Swansea for Colon [Panama], with coal, has foundered at sea. The Danish barque Gerson, arrived here from Copenhagen, reports having picked up on Oct. 17, in lat. 18 N, long. 48 W, five of her crew; these men report that the captain was drowned.

* The 1887 Atlantic hurricane season was one of the most active and prolonged in the recorded history of Atlantic hurricanes: hurricane No. 1 (a tropical storm) emerged south of Bermuda in mid-May, while the last storm of the year, No. 19, formed in early December. The *Augusta* was just north of hurricane No. 15, a Category 2 storm when its position was first recorded in mid-October off the northeast coast of South America at around lat. 14 N, long. 48 W.

** With the exception of the captain, the first mate and a seaman washed overboard and drowned, the crew of the *Augusta* all seem to have been rescued, despite the assertion by the first boat's crew that the second boat, whose bow was stove when she was launched, must without "the slightest doubt" have sunk and her six crew drowned. The second boat survived, however, and was picked up by the Danish barque *Gerson* on her voyage from Copenhagen to Panama. The five rescued men were landed at St. Thomas in the Virgin Islands. The first boatload of six survivors was picked up by the *Union*, bound from Pernambuco (Recife) and taken to New York.

## 17 Jan 1888

### Maritime Intelligence

Henry & Richard.- Liverpool, Jan. 17, 10 46 a.m.- Timor, steamer, from Savannah, reports on Dec. 31, in lat. 32 46 N, long. 77 34 W, rescued 10 persons of the American schooner Henry & Richard, of Boston, with cargo of lumber for Martinique, dismasted and waterlogged. Lowered boat and took off master, wife, two daughters, and crew; their suffering had been dreadful; the females had been badly injured, having been carried overboard by falling masts and crushed in water by floating deck cargo, and all had been exposed to bitter cold weather and drenching seas for three days, and were without water.

The Timor experienced a hurricane on that date, with mountainous sea, and weather continued, day after day, with blinding sleet and snow, cold being very severe until 11th January, when wind and sea moderated. Had starboard lifeboat and gig smashed, cabin and officers' berths flooded, and other damage to ship.

## 2 Oct 1888

### Weather and Navigation

Liverpool, Oct. 1, 7 17 p.m.- The master of the Cressington, from Melbourne, at Queenstown, reports that he never experienced such a continuance of heavy weather during 20 years at sea as on the passage here, and that he was afraid the ship would have foundered during one gale; the barometer was down as low as it could fall, and the ship from the poop forward was not visible as she lay buried under the water. The passage from Port Philip [Melbourne] to Cape Horn, which ought to have occupied 30 to 35 days, took 77 days, with a succession of NNE, E and S gales and mountainous seas. It appeared as if there were a hurricane travelling from New Zealand to Cape Horn, and that the ship got into it every now and then*. Captain Bromleys never went to bed or took his clothes off, only to change, for two and a half months.

* This "hurricane" that seemed to accompany the *Cressington* was either a single powerful and deep depression tracking eastwards or, far more likely, a series of closely-spaced depressions commonly encountered in those Southern Ocean latitudes by vessels heading eastwards from Australia and New Zealand towards the Horn.

## 12 Nov 1889

### Maritime Intelligence

Letterewe.- Liverpool, Nov. 11.- The master of the Letterewe writes from Adelaide, on Oct. 7, that he had never before experienced such bad weather as on this voyage from Liverpool. On Sept. 20, in lat. 45 S, long. 88 E, the vessel shipped a heavy sea which smashed the cabin skylight and took a man overboard. The compasses were washed away, and boats and after binnacle smashed. Most of the ship's oil* was used when running on several occasions.

\* Ships trailed oil on the sea in small amounts (a few gallons an hour) from oil bags slung off the sides, to prevent waves breaking and to dampen the effect of the wind in whipping up the waves into sharp crests. Although oil would not reduce a swell, it lessened the probability of big seas breaking onto a ship, especially seas coming up from behind a ship running before the wind (as above). A ship was vulnerable to being 'pooped' by such a heavy following sea which could sweep away the man, or men, at the wheel, and do considerable damage about the decks.

## 16 Oct 1890

### Maritime Intelligence

Yorktown.- San Francisco, Oct. 2.- Captain Delap, of ship Yorktown, which arrived yesterday from New York, reports:- From lat. 25 S to 43 S, had a continuous gale from SW and a head sea, making it impossible to carry sail. During a gale July 1 from NW the boatswain was lost overboard. A boat was sent to his rescue, but in returning the boat was also lost. After several unsuccessful attempts to get the ship before the wind, something was found to be wrong with the rudder, and on looking over the stern it was seen to be swinging from side to side. A hole was cut in the rudder trunk, and the rudder-head was found to be completely twisted off.

When the weather moderated a spare yard was got across the stern and some heavy tackles hooked on to the tiller under water, but another NW blizzard was encountered, which smashed up the whole business and carried away spar tackle and everything connected. The rudder then had full swing until the gale moderated, when it was rigged up again, with two spars and masthead tackles for supporters.

When within about 200 miles of Valparaiso, during a hurricane, with a tremendous sea, the new lower topsails were blown away. In lat. 15 N, long. 118 W, a hurricane was encountered from the SW, blowing away almost an entire suit of sails, and broke foretopgallantmast, all sail being set at the time.

## 22 Dec 1892

### Maritime Intelligence

Dundonald.- Queenstown, Dec. 22.- The Dundonald, ship, arrived at Queenstown yesterday from San Francisco after a protracted voyage of 134 days. She is in a battered state, having encountered a fearful cyclone during the voyage. Her master, Hawthorne, was washed overboard and drowned. The chief officer, Mr. Percy, who has navigated the vessel to Queenstown since the loss of the captain, says the cyclone was the worst he had ever encountered.

It burst on the ship on Aug. 12, 17 days after sailing from San Francisco. The wind was blowing from the north-west, and immediately afterwards the sea ran mountains high from the south-west. The vessel broached to on the starboard tack, and was thrown completely over on her beam ends. Volumes of water rushed down below. The cabin and forecastle became flooded and were gutted. A heavy sea dashed against the port lifeboat and wrecked it, while the force of the wind tore the sails to atoms. One wave caught the captain and carried him overboard. Fortunately the cyclone spent itself and the ship was got upright. Subsequently, when off the Horn, another cyclone struck them but they escaped damage, getting only the steering gear strained.

## 1 Feb 1893
**Weather and Navigation**

San Francisco, Jan. 14.- Lord Templemore, arrived here from Liverpool, reports that when off the River Plate on Aug. 24, experienced a *pampero** with a tremendous sea, which was the beginning of fearful weather, lasting on and off for 70 days. On the 15th of September a steam launch (cargo) was swept away, and various damage done about decks, and steam pipe covers washed away.

Gale after gale followed one another with terrific seas. Sept. 16 port lifeboat was lifted out of the chocks and side port broken. Sept. 24 starboard lifeboat was lifted bodily out of the chocks, lashings, etc., and thrown bottom up on top of the deck house and smashed up. Oct. 10, irons of mizentopmastay snapped close to deck on standing port; nearly lost mast, it being almost impossible to get about decks, which were flooded fore and aft. Oct. 16 it blew a fearful hurricane from SW, lowest reading of barometer 27 97; terrific sea running. At 11 p.m. a tremendous sea hit the ship on the port side, smashing in bulwarks for 40 feet, snapping stanchions and rivets, and bending down screws of forerigging, besides breaking up hog pens, sheep pens, etc., and taking all stock [livestock] overboard. The forepeak was found leaking in the morning.

It was a hard beat all the way around the Cape [Horn], the ship taking 60 days getting 600 miles, and not being fairly round till the 135th day from Liverpool. Had fearful weather all round. Barometer seldom above 28 40.

* A *pampero* is essentially a line squall from a cold front passing over the flat grasslands of Argentina and Uruguay, the pampas, that produces a rapid and violent blast of wind and sometimes even spins off tornadoes. These vicious sudden squalls often struck sailing ships off the River Plate and Argentine coast generally in a cloudless sky that gave no warning of their arrival. If they caught a ship unawares, with, for example, all or most of her sails set, they could cause great damage, including even sinking the ship. An experienced captain or mate, however, could see a pampero coming as a line of churned up frothy sea approaching and get the vessel's sails in before it struck.

## DEVASTATING ATLANTIC HURRICANES

## 6 Sept 1893
**Maritime Intelligence**

Alf.- New York, Aug. 26.- Propheta, arrived here from Demerara, reports:- Fell in with Norwegian barque Alf, from Bahia [Brazil] for New York, with sugar, in a sinking condition. Took off captain and crew of 12 men, and brought them to this port. Captain Petersen, of the Alf, reports:- Aug. 22 had a hurricane* from S to SSW, lasting four hours, during which lost several sails. On the 23rd, 80 miles SE of Highlands [town on New Jersey shore, at entrance to Sandy Hook Bay for New York City harbour], had another hurricane from E to ESE, lasting 10 hours, during which sprung a leak, having eight feet water in hold. Vessel hove down on her beam ends, and on the 24th crew took to the boats and boarded the Propheta.

Orealla.- New York, Aug. 26.- Orealla, arrived here from Calcutta, reports:- Aug. 21, in lat. 33 56 N, long. 72 44 W [off Cape Hatteras, North Carolina], experienced a heavy hurricane* from ESE, decks being continually flooded. The captain was knocked down and had several ribs fractured; broke fore and main braces and lifts. On the 23rd had a very heavy gale from ESE, suddenly shifting to S, decks being continually flooded and everything movable washed away; smashed wheelbox, hen coop, and side-lights.

Propheta.- New York, Aug. 26. Propheta, arrived here from Demerara, reports:- Aug. 21 to 23 experienced a hurricane from ESE, which carried away mainmast 20 feet from the deck with all attached, foretopgallantmast and mizentopmast; also lost and split sails and had everything movable washed off deck.

* Three exceptionally strong Category 2 and Category 3 hurricanes swept up the east coast of the United States and Canada in August 1893. The three reports by ships above almost certainly corresponded to hurricanes No. 3 and No. 4. Both were Category 3 storms, with winds exceeding 100 knots. As hurricane No. 2 rumbled up the US east coast during the second half of August, it was closely followed by hurricane No. 3. Many ships other than the three above reported similar hurricane conditions at sea around the same time (21–24 August), with considerable storm damage and some loss of life and sunken vessels. The track of hurricane No. 5, a Category 2 storm, kept further out to sea causing serious damage to shipping off the North American Atlantic coast.

Meanwhile, just a week or so later, hurricane No. 6 (Category 3) made landfall at the city of Savannah, Georgia, with winds reported to exceed 120 mph. That hurricane generated a storm surge of 16 ft along the coast and offshore Sea Islands of Georgia, causing an estimated death toll of up to 2,000 people, mostly by drowning. As many as 30,000 people were estimated to have been made homeless. The severity of the storm earned it the name of the 1893 Sea Islands Hurricane. It seems likely that the following human casualty was a result of this hurricane:

## 9 Sept 1893

### Wreckage

Charleston, S.C., Aug. 30.- Schooner Morris W. Child, from Brunswick [Georgia, south of Savannah] for Boston, arrived here, reports passing through wreckage, and seeing six men in the water with life preservers on. They were barely alive. No assistance could be given them.

## 12 Aug 1893

### Weather and Navigation

Fayal [Azores], Aug. 28.- A great hurricane* swept over this island to-day between 8 and 10 a.m., and the only two vessels moored at the breakwater – the American barquentine Tremont, and the Italian barque Giuseppe Emmanuele – were driven ashore and totally lost. The Tremont had half her cargo of red pine still on board, the Giuseppe Emmanuele nearly all her cargo of cement. Both vessels went to pieces in less than hour. The remains of the wrecks will be sold to-morrow. The hurricane was the greatest ever known about here. It swept away a great many fishing vessels and five whaling boats, destroyed all craft, blew down some farm-houses, and unroofed others. At one village the sea swept away 21 dwelling houses. Fortunately no lives were lost, but the distress is great.

*10 Oct 1893*
## Weather and Navigation

Fayal, Sept. 18.- The American whaling barque George and Mary, which came in here Sept. 12 to land the season's [whale] oil, reports having experienced a cyclone on Aug. 27, in lat. 33 35 N, long. 34 25 W [just southwest of Azores], before which she had to run three hours under bare poles [ie., no sails set], losing two boats.*

* This hurricane (No. 7 of the 1893 hurricane season) swept up the middle of the Atlantic from the vicinity of the Cape Verde Islands before striking a direct hit on the Azores on 28 August. At that time it was a Category 2 storm, with winds of around 85–90 mph. That was the only land it hit; shortly afterwards it diminished and died out to the northeast of the Azores.

## 24 Jan 1894

### Maritime Intelligence

Normannia (s).- London, Jan. 24.- A Dalziel's telegram, dated New York, Jan. 23, states that the steamer Normannia, which left on Thursday for Naples, etc., has returned disabled. She was on Sunday morning struck by a tidal wave*, which swept away her deck rooms and part of her promenade deck. Seven men and the second officer were severely injured. On Saturday she was steaming half speed in the teeth of a terrific gale. About midnight the gale moderated, the sea quieted somewhat and full speed was ordered.

Suddenly a tremendous sea running mast high appeared on the port bow, burying the forepart of the vessel up to the bridge. The front house on the promenade deck was smashed by the force of the blow, and the first and second officers' rooms were completely wrecked. The music room, the ladies' room, the main saloon, and lower saloon were greatly damaged. The starboard bulwarks and railings were shattered and 14 ventilators were carried away. The water to the depth of 6 feet deluged the steerage quarters, and the cabins on the main deck were flooded to a depth of 3 feet.

* The 500-ft long, 8,242-ton SS *Normannia* was built at Glasgow in 1890 for the Hamburg-America Line. She sailed regularly across the North Atlantic between Hamburg and New York. The damage she incurred here was not the result of a "tidal wave", or *tsunami*, as we understand the term today, but rather more likely from a rogue or freak wave generated by the gale force conditions prevailing at the time.

In the early hours of Sunday, 21 January, the ship was just south of Newfoundland, around 760 miles from New York, having departed from that port on Thursday, 18 January. *The New York Times* published an account of the incident in its 24 January 1894 issue, including the information that, as the wave swept over the ship, 'The screams of women and children were heard above the fury of the gale. Strong men trembled with terror or rushed madly about the decks'.

## 6 Dec 1895

### Maritime Intelligence

Royal Alice.- Queenstown, Dec. 6, 10 55 a.m.- Royal Alice reports on Nov. 21, lat. 45 25 N, long. 23 10 W, encountered fearful weather. The wind blew from NNE, backing round to

SE and S, and backing against the sun [ie., counter-clockwise] to NE, increasing in force to a hurricane. For three days the hurricane raged without abating, and did not cease until the barometer commenced to rise. The seas ran mountains high, whilst the wind blew with terrific force, high seas tumbling on board and flooding the decks. The forecastle and cabin were filled with water and completely gutted. The houses on deck were damaged, and all loose articles washed away.

The vessel was thrown on her beam ends and to release her it was found necessary to cut away the maintopmast, which eased her somewhat. Gigantic waves rolled over the vessel, washed away the starboard jollyboat, carried away the starboard topgallant bulwark, and gutted the forecastle. Water also rushed into the galley. The deck was strewn with wreckage, and when the main topmast fell it carried away the topgallant bulwarks and the starboard light screens. It was also found necessary to jettison over 900 bags of rice, after which the vessel righted herself.

## 4 Nov 1898

### Disaster At Sea - Fatal Effects Of A Great Wave

A Liverpool correspondent sends the following:-

"An extraordinary accident occurred early yesterday morning on board the Ararat, one of the steamers of Messrs. Papayanni & Co., of Rumford-street, Liverpool. The Ararat, which is a regular trader between Liverpool and the Mediterranean ports, made her customary voyage without mishap, and entered the [English] Channel on Wednesday. She was then off the Tuskar Light, a gale blowing and a tremendous sea running. The captain (William Draper) decided to heave to for the night, in the hope that the weather would moderate.

When the morning broke the sea was still running very high, and a strong wind prevailed, but it was believed perfectly safe to proceed, and the master gave the order for the watch, consisting of about half a dozen men, to heave the lead, in order to proceed to port. The men were gathered in a cluster, and the orders were being carried out, when a tremendous sea leaped, as it were, out of the Channel with tremendous suddenness and swiftness, and immense force. It broke over the ship with a fearful noise, scattering the group of seamen in all directions. So sudden and unexpected was the blow that the men were stunned and injured; one, John McCourt, able seaman, was washed overboard.

The utmost consternation prevailed for a while, and it was impossible just then to give effective assistance. The captain was on the bridge when the wave struck, and fortunately was not touched. No one exactly knew what had happened, or what the result had been, but Captain Draper was very cool-headed, and, looking about, he noticed the poor seaman McCourt swept away with the rushing waves. He immediately picked up a lifebuoy and, throwing it into the water, shouted to McCourt to seize it. The struggling seaman was now exerting himself to the utmost to swim back to the ship, and he was fortunate enough to secure the lifebuoy. It was evident, however, that the struggle with the waves was too much for him, and his strength was quickly going. He was too exhausted to make use of the buoy, and in view of the captain he sank and was seen no more.

It was quite impossible, owing to the wild state of the sea and the circumstances on board to launch a boat. Meantime, the scene on deck was pitiable. The mate had been knocked against the wheelhouse, and was severely bruised, while other men also received injuries more or less severe. The worst case was that of John Macris, able seaman, who was totally disabled for the time being. His spine was injured, and he was also suffering from terrible shock.

After these events, the captain, seeing he could be of no assistance to the man overboard, made all haste to port, and the steamer came up the river flying her flag at half-mast, and signaling "Doctor Wanted." Every assistance was promptly given, and when the steamer was boarded it appeared that still another distressful occurrence had taken place, the third steward, named James Close, had just died. He had been ill during the voyage, and was hoping to reach his home when death took place, the knocking about which the seaman received in the Channel doubtless hastening his end. The sad affair cast quite a gloom over the ship, and the owners were much grieved, and extended their sympathetic condolences to all concerned."

## 17 Jan 1899

**Maritime Intelligence**

Dione.- London, Jan. 17.- The schooner Dione arrived at Plymouth yesterday. She left Trapani [Sicily] on Nov. 6 [1898] for Newfoundland. Fifteen days later she passed through the Straits of Gibraltar. Ever since then she has been beating about in the Atlantic in heavy gales. She reached as far as the banks of Newfoundland [the Grand Banks] within about 20 miles of her destination when the weather became violent and the crew being worn out the captain put his vessel before the gale and was driven back across the Atlantic.

## 11 Feb 1899

**Maritime Intelligence**

Martello (s).- London, Feb. 10.- The Martello (s), from New York, arrived at Hull this morning, her rails and bulwarks being bent and broken and three lifeboats missing. On the morning of Jan. 30, the ship was laid to in a hurricane and enveloped in fog. The mate, the boatswain and a seaman were sent to look after the fore hatch, when a wave fell on the deck killing the first two and washing the seaman overboard. The sea also wrecked the crow's nest and carried away a seaman from there.* Another heavy sea hurled the second officer into the winch, where his leg was broken, while the captain was driven to one side of the bridge and rendered unconscious.

* For a sea to reach the lookout post of the crow's nest high up on the foremast of the *Martello*, it must have been in the region of 40 to 50 feet high – and possibly even higher.

## 18 Feb 1899

**Maritime Intelligence**

British Trader (s).- Liverpool, Feb. 17, 2 49 p.m.- Captain Hagan, of steamer British Trader, arrived Antwerp, Feb. 15, from New York, writes as follows:- "On Feb. 2, in lat. 45 N, long 40 W, we were overtaken by a terrific hurricane, which raged with unabated fury for three days. The steam steering gear smashed, and we shipped the hand gear. We shipped one sea which stove in the fore bulwarks, and burst in saloon and engineer's room doors, and mountainous sea broke on board and completely gutted out all rooms, breaking chart-room down and taking the lifeboat with it. It also started saloon house and fidley bunker hatches, and allowing considerable water to run into bunkers.

This sea also washed the second officer (Thomas Eyson) overboard. The third officer was so seriously injured that he is not fit for duty yet. My thumb is broken and my shoulder dislocated, however, I have been able to keep up.

Mr. Pattinson (chief officer) and I have kept watch and watch [ie, alternating watches] ever since. Chronometers and charts were destroyed. I have lost everything. All the ship's papers, my own [master's] certificate, [ship's] articles, and official log-book have been washed overboard. Several others of the crew were more or less injured during the bad weather. Again on Feb. 12 a heavy WSW gale sprang up with a mountainous sea."

# 19 Dec 1899

## Maritime Intelligence

Duntrune.- Montevideo, Nov. 20.- The following is extracted from a document handed by one of the crew of the ship Duntrune to the captain of the steamer Magellan, who gave it to the captain of the steamer Oropesa, and which was received by the Lloyd's Agent here on Nov. 20:-

The ship Duntrune left Barry Dock [south Wales] on 17 June for Junin. When off the [River] Plate we were under short sail for 14 days, having very heavy pampero squalls. On Sept. 2 Mr. Horan, of Birkenhead, was washed off the boom [ie., jibboom] and drowned. On the night of Oct. 3, 150 miles west of Cambridge Island, lost main and mizen masts, the mainmast going four feet below deck, and mizen mast carrying away fore part of poop [deck]. The lifeboat and dinghy were completely destroyed, and the third boat (pinnace) was badly damaged, and the fore lowermast was carried out of her 3 feet below deck.

On the night of Oct. 3, after mainmast going, we spread sails over damaged part of deck and nailed battens round edges, but in spite of this four feet of water got into lower hold, besides what was in 'tween decks. The mainmast going completely destroyed the main pumps. At daylight we started cutting away rigging, which was alongside all night, the ship labouring heavily.

Captain Winterton was forward in afternoon, and after going round ship went and lay down and died in his sleep.

We rigged sea anchors, one out of hawsepipe and another over her bow but could not keep her head to wind. On Oct 5 Patrick Noonan, of Cork [Ireland], died. The weather moderating slightly, we started discharging cargo through the lazarette, and afterwards opening the after hatch. We managed to get five inches of water out by leading force pump hose through main pump hole. Could not rig jurymast on account of heavy weather, but fixed boat-sails and small canvas in different parts of the ship and she drifted into 45 fathoms [depth of water] off Cambridge Island (Oct. 13), where we let go both anchors with 120 fathoms cable on each.

On Oct. 17 boat's crew volunteered to go and look for assistance. Before leaving the ship we launched a raft which we had made, and left it floating astern. We left the ship at midday. On Nov. 9 Vincent Berkeley died from hunger and exposure, and next day we were taken off by the sealing schooner Azores, which transferred us to the steamer Magellan, and we were brought to Sandy Point on Nov. 11, all more or less frostbitten. The Consul sent the second mate back in the Chilian man-of-war Erasaous to look for our shipmates. The following were left on board the ship:- The captain's wife and child, chief officer, boatswain, sailmaker, cook, seven sailors and a boy.*

* This account starts with the *Duntrune's* difficulties in a *pampero* (sudden and vicious squall) off the River Plate, the estuary leading up to Buenos Aires, and continues after the vessel has rounded Cape Horn off the southern Patagonian coast of Chile. By early October the *Duntrune* is "150 miles west of Cambridge Island", a 30-mile long by 5-mile wide island now called Diego de Almagro Island and located at the northwest entrance to Nelson Strait which leads into the Magellan Strait on the southern coast of Chile. "Sandy Point" is the original name and English translation for the city of Punta Arenas on the north shore of the Magellan Strait, Chile's main settlement in the Magallanes (Magellan) region of Patagonia.

## 5 Oct 1900

**Maritime Intelligence**

Gertrude.- Hull, Oct. 5.- A terrible account of the sufferings and hardships endured by a ship's crew has just been received from New Orleans. It appears that the barque Gertrude, bound from Galveston for Rio Janeiro, had weathered the heavy storm* and the crew were getting the vessel in order when she was struck by lightning and set on fire. Captain Oliviera jumped overboard and was drowned, the remainder of the crew taking to the boats, two men in a small one, and ten in a larger. One of the two died on the high seas from starvation, and the other sailor landed on the coast in an emaciated condition. The other boat with ten men has not been heard of, and it is feared they have all perished.

* A powerful Category 4 hurricane that devastated Galveston, Texas in September 1900.

## 21 March 1903

**Maritime Intelligence**

**Weather and Navigation**

London, March 19.- The Dunearn had met with such heavy weather off Cape Horn, in September last [1902], that after buffeting against westerly gales, snowstorms, floating ice, and severe cold for three weeks, the captain was compelled to bear up for Australia and the Pacific, with some men laid up frost bitten.*

* In September 1902 the British barque *Dunearn* turned about after battling Cape Horn storms to run with the prevailing westerly winds of the Southern Ocean to reach her destination of Sitka Bay in southeastern Alaska on 19 February 1903. She arrived apparently "without damage, and with crew all well on arrival", the men evidently having thawed out during that six month passage as she came up through the tropics of the Pacific Ocean.

### LIFEBOAT SERVICE RESCUES

The Royal National Lifeboat Institution (RNLI) in the United Kingdom was established on 4 March 1824 by Sir William Hillary (4 January 1771–5 January 1847). Its original name, the National Institution for the Preservation of Life from Shipwreck, was changed to its current name in 1854. During its long history it has saved almost 150,000 lives from vessels in distress around British and English Channel waters.

## NARRATIVES

## 4 Feb 1873

### Lifeboat Services

### The Heavy Gale

Penzance, Sunday afternoon.- [By telegraph] – We have had (says Mr. Downing, banker, at Penzance), a fearful day here. The shores of Mount's Bay are strewn with wrecks, in the midst of seas the like of which I have not seen during the past 30 years. I am happy to say that our lifeboat, the *Richard Lewis*, has again done some noble work this morning. When the seas were running mountains high a French vessel, La Marie Emalie, of Lorient, was seen to go ashore, and the seas to roll over her. At once the *Richard Lewis* lifeboat proceeded to the wreck, but she was twice driven back by the heavy rollers.

The dangerous position of the boat was now really fearful and unparalleled, having had seven of her oars broken. Still her noble crew persevered, notwithstanding that the boat was actually hurled by the rollers twice on the wreck itself. Nevertheless, the foreigners were not to perish, if Cornish men themselves had to perish in the effort. On the third attempt, thank God, the *Richard Lewis* succeeded, amidst the greatest danger, in saving the whole of the shipwrecked Frenchmen. Mr. Blackmore, the chief officer of coastguard, particularly distinguished himself on board the lifeboat.

Skerries, C. Dublin, 3rd Feb.- A terrible disaster has overtaken the lifeboat on this station. On Saturday night, when it was blowing a strong gale from the East, with a bad broken sea, a vessel was seen on the rocks near Balbriggan. The lifeboat at once put off to the rescue, although she was short-handed, other men, in the face of the awful storm, refusing to go off in the boat. When near the wreck, and after letting go the anchor, the boat was unfortunately upset, when six of her crew were drowned and one died this morning from exhaustion. The crew of the vessel, which was the schooner Sarah, of Runcorn, also unhappily perished on the disastrous occasion.

This is the first fatal accident that has overtaken any of the lifeboats of the National Institution during the past four years, notwithstanding the fearful risks and exposure they constantly incur in saving life. On most occasions the boats are fully manned and admirably handled. The Institution has expressed its deepest sympathy with the families of the drowned men and the survivors, and has promised to subscribe very liberally in aid of the support of the bereaved.

## 19 Nov 1873

### Lifeboat Service

### Wreck of a Large Barque – Gallant Lifeboat Service

Caister, near Great Yarmouth, Monday.- About four o'clock yesterday morning a new Italian barque, the Filatore, of Genoa, 650 tons, bound from Bremerhaven to Cardiff, in ballast, ran on the Cross sand off this coast in the midst of the breakers, the wind blowing in squalls at the time from NNE. She had all sail set at the time. In response to her signals of distress, the Caister large sailing lifeboat, belonging to the National Institution [now the Royal National Lifeboat Institution], proceeded out, and found that the sea was breaking heavily over the stranded vessel, and that prior to her arrival the ship's boat had broken away with four men in it, who had been picked up by a steamer.

At the request of the master, eleven of the crew of the lifeboat went on board to try to save the ship, and the services of two steamers were also engaged, but all efforts in that direction were unavailing, and at last, after some hours had elapsed, she began to break up and fill with water as the tide flowed.

The attention of those in the lifeboat had therefore to be wholly directed to the rescue of the barque's crew and the beachmen who had boarded her. This was hard and dangerous work, for the sea was even heavier than it had been previously, and came down on the lifeboat thundering and foaming and well nigh crushing the crew with its weight, and threatening at any minute to sweep them out of the boat. The men from the ship had to drop some 20 or 25 feet into the lifeboat by means of ropes, and the boat was repeatedly dashed against the vessel's bow, till the stem of the lifeboat was knocked out.

The foreigners seeing this were in great consternation, but, thanks to the valuable properties of the boat, she was still able to continue her work, and in about three quarters of an hour she was instrumental in saving all from the wreck, consisting of ten men, besides the beachmen, all of whom, about 8 o'clock last night, were safely landed at Yarmouth, where the lifeboat has been left for repairs. The coxswain reports that in all his experience he never met with a worse sea, and certainly none but courageous and resolute men could have gone through what the lifeboat men encountered. They speak of the boat as having behaved most admirably.

## 10 Dec 1874

### Gallant Rescue Of A Shipwrecked Crew

On Sunday last just as people had returned from church, intelligence was conveyed to Bude on the North Coast of Cornwall, that the Sarah Charlotte, of Padstow, May, master, had been driven ashore in Widemouth bay, three or four miles to the westward of that place. All who are acquainted with the locality are aware of the terrible sea which breaks on that rocky coast and of the often insuperable difficulties which prevent succour being afforded to the unfortunate mariners who are cast away on it.

The bar in front of the small haven being nearly dry, it was impossible to launch the lifeboat there, and the hilly nature of the country making its conveyance by land a matter of much labour and difficulty, it was decided that the only probable means of rendering timely assistance to the shipwrecked men was by the rocket apparatus, which was quickly taken from Bude to the spot, in [the] charge of Mr. Tickle, chief boatman in charge of the coastguard, accompanied by Captain Charles Gray Jones, R.N., the Junior Assistant Inspector of the National Lifeboat Institution, who happened to be at Bude on the periodical tour of inspection.

For about fifty minutes the efforts to throw a rocket line over the ill-fated vessel were continued, and at last with success, but it was then a long time before the crew could be got to understand how to avail themselves of it, and at last the double line became hopelessly entangled, and as the vessel was fast breaking up the loss of the unfortunate men seemed inevitable. The master, however, with true British pluck and devotion to duty one by one secured each of his men to the lifebuoy of the apparatus, and veered them safely through the surf, whence they were rescued by the bystanders on shore.

When, however, it came to the brave fellow's turn to think of himself, his vital power had well nigh left him, and he had not remaining strength to help himself. In despair he was in the act of leaping into the sea with only a line around him to his certain death, but was dissuaded by the cries and shrieks from the shore, when with a final effort he contrived to get into the buoy and was hauled half way to the beach, when the line again fouling he remained suspended above the fearful breakers until from exhaustion he let go his hold and fell into the sea.

It then became the turn of others to render, at great personal risk to themselves, the same help to him which he had nobly given to his own crew. At once a devoted party from the shore, coastguard and landsmen, headed by the chief officer and Captain Jones, threw themselves into the waves, holding by the line from the wreck, which prevented their being carried seaward by them, and just as a huge surf had broken and retreated they succeeded in seizing the drowning man. All together were hurled on the beach by another wave, and the sea was mulct [deprived] of its prey.

The lifeboat transported by land arrived at the spot just as the work was done, and the vessel was broken into a thousand pieces. Here was noble work from beginning to end, such work as with each recurring winter adds to the laurels of our life saving heroes on the coast, and does honour to the country which claims them as its sons.

# 4   Remarkable Voyages

**M**ost voyages by 19th century sailing ships were routine, even if they included stormy weather, long calms and any number of hardships endured by their crews as just part of the seaman's lot. Others were unusual for being exceedingly prolonged by hard weather, damage to rigging, or even particularly kindly weather in areas of the world where storms would be much more likely to be encountered – off Cape Horn, for example.

Very long passages were recorded for vessels trying to beat into persistent westerly gales around Cape Horn that forced the vessel's master to turn around and make for their destination on the west coast of North or South America by heading east around the globe, running before the strong westerly winds of those southern latitudes. Not only around Cape Horn but wherever a ship had to beat into strong headwinds day after day, even for weeks, might make an otherwise normal passage remarkable.

## NARRATIVES

## 19 Jan 1871

**Casualties – Home**

Liverpool, 18ᵗʰ Jan.- The Weathersfield, arrived here, from San Francisco, did not take in her royals* until after passing Cape Horn; on the 13ᵗʰ Nov. [1870], during a heavy S to SE gale, in lat. 48 S, lon. 52 W, she was struck by a sea, which rose 15 feet up the mainmast, carried away bulwarks, stanchions, and a boat, broke in the port side of poop [deck], destroyed the cabin furniture, partly destroyed the starboard side of cabin, shook deckhouse, etc.

* The royal sails are the highest ones usually carried on square-rigged sailing ships, and the first to be taken in when an increase in wind calls for a reduction in sail. (Skysails are carried above royals, but not so commonly.) The fact that the *Weathersfield* did not take in her royals during her passage from San Francisco until past Cape Horn signifies that she had consistently fair winds, allowing her to keep all sail set, even off the Horn itself. The *Weathersfield* encountered the gale reported above some 300 miles northeast of the Falkland Islands, 800 miles past Cape Horn.

## THE LONE VOYAGE OF ELIZABETH MOUAT AND THE *COLUMBINE*

Elizabeth (Betty) Mouat was born in 1825 into a crofting family in the village of Levenwick at Scat Ness, near Sumburgh Head on the southern tip of Mainland in the Shetland Islands. Her father was a shoemaker. (He died on a whaling voyage to Greenland six months after his daughter was born.) Like many Shetland crofters, she became a skilled knitter.

In February 1886, aged 60, Betty Mouat decided to take her knitwear and similar items from other crofters nearby, to sell in Lerwick. She also wanted to see a doctor there about her poor health, occasioned by a stroke in the summer of 1885. Lerwick was only 24 miles away by sail but the North Sea in winter, no matter how short the voyage, could be perilous if stormy weather suddenly blew up. And this it did shortly after the *Columbine* and her crew – Capt. James Jamieson, mate Jerry Smith and deckhand Oliver Smith – and 60-year-old passenger Betty Mouat set out from Grutness.

## 3 Feb 1886

### Maritime Intelligence

Columbine, Lerwick [Shetland Islands], Feb. 2, 3 40 p.m.- On Saturday forenoon smack Columbine left Gruitness [Grutness], near Sumburgh Head [southernmost point of mainland Shetland], for Lerwick, with crew of three men and one female passenger. Shortly afterwards, with heavy sea, master was taken overboard; when the other men put out boat, and while they attempted ineffectually to rescue him, vessel sailed away seaward beyond their reach and has not since been heard of. The men reached the shore and landed with difficulty. Two steamers have been out searching, but have returned without success.

## 4 Feb 1886

### The Missing Smack Columbine

No further information has been obtained as to the fate of the smack Columbine and the unfortunate woman on board. A Lerwick schooner has just left Lerwick for Norway, and it is thought that the course of this vessel will be nearly that which the ill-fated smack was presumed to have taken. The owner of the smack is making efforts to secure the services of a steamer to proceed as far as Norway in further search of the missing vessel. The prevailing opinion in Shetland is that the vessel has foundered.

## 18 Feb 1886

### The Smack Columbine

[By Telegraph]

Stavanger [Norway], Feb. 17.

Elizabeth Mouat, the woman who was blown across from Shetland in the Columbine, has arrived at Aalesund [Ålesund, on the Norwegian coast, approximately 250 miles northeast of Shetland]. Yesterday she made a statement to the District Judge, which, so far as it was understood, her Scottish dialect being difficult to make out, was to the following effect:-

She said that she was sixty years old, unmarried, and a poor woman. She embarked in the Columbine, intending to visit a niece who lives at Lerwick. They had not got far when, at noon, the vessel struck on a sunken rock off the coast of Shetland. Being very ill, she was

THE CASTAWAY SMACK COLUMBINE: ELIZABETH MOUAT LASHED TO THE DECK.

below at the time, but she felt the shock, and heard the captain and the two sailors running about on deck, and heard the captain give orders for the boat to be lowered. Although very seasick, she at once got up and tried to come on deck, but the steps or ladder fell, and she was unable to replace it.

She heard the boat row off and was terribly alarmed, for the wind was blowing very hard and the sea was high. Still she hoped that the crew would return with assistance. She attempted many times to replace the ladder so as to get on deck, but could not do so, though she could look out of the open hatchway of the cabin.

At night the vessel floated off the rock, and drove along under the double-reefed mainsail, which was set. The only food which she had brought with her was a bottle of milk and two biscuits. There were provisions in the forecastle, but she was unable to reach them. The first night was a terrible one, the vessel rolled heavily, she was in darkness, and seas often washed down the hatchway, keeping her drenched to the skin. Every moment she expected the boat would go to the bottom. When morning broke no land was in sight, nor was there a sail to be seen. The sea was still very rough, but, as the Columbine had lived through the night, Elizabeth now began to hope that she might be saved. From this time, indeed, she says that she never quite despaired, but put her trust in God, and believed that He would send rescue.

During the whole of the seven days and nights she never slept, but at intervals stood up and looked above the hatchway to see if aid was in sight. She saw no sail, but asserts that once in the night she distinctly perceived the red light of a ship. She made the biscuits last as long as possible, but for the last four days she was altogether without food. She suffered more from the wet and from thirst than from hunger, and quenched her thirst so far as she could by licking the drops which condensed on the windows. Gradually she became very weak, her legs swelled, and she could scarcely stand up to look out; she, therefore, lashed herself close to the hatchway, fearing that she might roll away and be unable to get back so as to look out.

The Columbine grounded near Lepso [just north of Ålesund and south of Bergen], but it was some hours before the smack was noticed by any of the inhabitants.

Her account of the manner in which she came to be left alone on board the smack differs from that which was given by the crew, but no doubt the jerking of the boom which knocked the captain overboard so shook the boat that she thought it had struck on a rock, and she mistook one of the men's voices calling upon the other to lower the boat for that of the captain. The change in motion consequent upon the wind taking the drifting boat in some fresh quarter must have made her think that it had got off the rock.

The weather was stormy and the sea high when the Columbine went ashore near Lepso, and when she was first perceived it was supposed that her crew had abandoned her, or had been washed overboard. But suddenly a violent gust blew away the sail and rigging, and then a woman's head was seen to appear above the hatchway. There was no boat near which could be launched, but a young man volunteered to swim out to her. He succeeded in getting on board, and found the woman almost insensible, and tied up against the ladder hooks.

He passed a rope ashore, and fastening the woman to this, she was got to land. She was at once carried to a farmhouse, where she was most kindly treated and nursed, and has since been assisted by Messrs. Bully and Spindler, two English gentlemen. She is still unwell, and complains of pains in her chest and in her swollen legs. The physician who has been attending her considers that there is no longer any fear for her life, and that she will be able to start on her homeward journey in a few days.

*19 March 1886*
**House of Commons**

**Thursday, March 18**

**Elizabeth Mowatt**

Mr. Bryce said: Her Majesty's Minister accredited to Sweden and Norway was instructed, on the 10th inst., to express the gratitude of Her Majesty's Government for the services so humanely rendered to Elizabeth Mowatt on the occasion in question, and the Board of Trade has been consulted as to what steps can be taken to reward these services either by an acknowledgement in the shape of some benefit of a permanent nature to the community of Lepsoe or by gifts to those concerned in the rescue.

Betty Mouat became a sort of celebrity in Shetland for having survived her epic crossing of the North Sea alone on just a bottle of milk and a few biscuits. She was brought back from Norway first to Edinburgh, to recuperate for three weeks, and then to Shetland in late March. Donations totalling almost £400 were raised for her through *The Scotsman* newspaper. Six men who rescued Betty Mouat at her lucky landfall on the southwest coast of Norway received medals and reward money of £2 per man for their efforts from the Board of Trade, plus £10 divided amongst them offered by a private contributor, Mr. John Bruce. The bay where the *Columbine* went ashore there at Lepsoe is now known as Columbine Bukta (Columbine Bay).

Betty Mouat died on 6 February 1918 aged 93, exactly 32 years after her ordeal adrift and at the mercy of the elements across the North Sea.

## THE TEMPESTUOUS ODYSSEY OF THE *BROOMHALL*

5 March 1894

**Maritime Intelligence**

Broomhall.- New York, March 4.- The British barque Broomhall, which was towed in here yesterday in a disabled condition, reports having had a terrible voyage of 108 days from Hamburg. She was in a hurricane* for 90 days and was blown to Iceland. Salt water entered the fresh water tanks, and the men were forced to rely on rain and snow for drinking purposes.

* The *Broomhall* could not have been "in a hurricane for 90 days" which would have been virtually impossible for the time of year and duration of the hurricane; she would have experienced *storm* or *hurricane force winds* for that period from a succession of westerly gales. Note that the vessel would have been sailing from Hamburg on a course taking her up the North Sea and around the north of Scotland, not down the English Channel, to cross the Atlantic.

*7 March 1894*
**Maritime Intelligence**

Broomhall.- Dundee, March 6.- A telegram from New York, dated March 6, states that the barque Broomhall, from Hamburg, was towed into that port in a disabled state on Saturday, and reports having passed through some terrible experiences during her voyage of 113 days. Scarcely had the vessel left port before she encountered a hurricane [sic]. A furious gale blew from the NE, which tore her lowertopsails and ripped the upper ones from the gaskets. Tremendous seas swept her decks from stem to stern. Her hatches were under water. The water penetrated the hold, and the cargo, which consisted of salt, had to be shifted. New topsails were made, but these, too, were carried away.

The wind and current drove the barque from her course, carrying her far to the northeast. She endeavoured to effect a passage between the Shetland and Faroe Islands, but the tempest forced her further to the north-east. Finally she reached lat. 64 deg. N, between Iceland and Greenland, and there had to remain a fortnight. On Jan. 4 she was able to work down to a more southern position, reaching a point about 300 miles NW of Scotland. On the day named, the sea raged with a terrible fury, and a wave passed over the barque, twisting the iron rails and stanchions, tearing the roof from the deckhouse and smashing the doors of the cabin. Charles Mark, a German sailor, was lost overboard.

Until the 15th [January] the hurricane increased in violence. Two new sails were carried away as well as the maintopmaststaysail and mizenstaysail. The sea-water entered the fresh-water tank and rendered its contents undrinkable. Tubs and barrels were then fixed on deck in order to catch rainwater and falling snow.

In addition to sustaining the damage already mentioned, the vessel lost her jib and three mizenstaysails, her starboard cathead was broken, her side-light screens smashed, her capstan bar lost, and 36 feet of her bulwarks were carried away. Four main bulwark ports were destroyed on the starboard side, and 120 feet of her bulwarks were wrenched away on the port side. The pumps were seriously damaged and the lifeboats were smashed, saloon skylight was shattered, and companion stairway wrecked.*

* *The New York Times* reported the *Broomhall* overdue, as follows: "…The British ship *Broomhall* left Hamburg Nov. 11 [1893], bound for this port. She was sighted Jan. 19, sixty-four days out, about 650 miles west of the Irish coast. Since then she has not been heard from. Forty days is the average time consumed in this voyage. The *Broomhall* is an iron ship, owned by W.S. Croudace of Dundee, and is commanded by Capt. Taylor." (*The New York Times*, 28 February 1894)

Probably the most remarkable feature of this horrendous voyage was that, in continuously tempestuous conditions for over three and a half months in the North Atlantic in winter, and considering all the other damage done to the vessel, the *Broomhall* apparently lost only one man.

## *RED ROCK*: "POSTED MISSING" – THEN ARRIVED

# 18 April 1899

**Maritime Intelligence**

**Miscellaneous**

London, April 18.- Red Rock*, Townsville for New Caledonia: The owners of the above vessel write as follows:- "We have a letter from Captain Porter, of the ship Red Rock, under date Feb. 27, stating that he was then west of Magnetic Island, with a breeze from the ESE, which was dead ahead. We are afraid that the ship has gone to leeward of her destination, and being light will probably take some time to beat up to Muco again. (?)"

*8 June 1899*

**Maritime Intelligence**

**Missing Vessels**

> Red Rock, of Glasgow, official number 102,670, Porter master, sailed from Townsville for New Caledonia, in ballast, on the 20th February, 1899, was off Magnetic Island on the 27th of February, 1899, and has not since been heard of.

*13 June*

**Maritime Intelligence**

**Miscellaneous**

> London, June 13.- Red Rock: The owners have received the following telegram from Noumea [New Caledonia], dated June 12, 5 p.m.:- "Put back from stress of weather, all well. Had strong head winds and high seas.- Porter (Captain)."

* Lloyd's advised a "posted missing" notice for vessels that had not reached their intended destination within a reasonable period of time and only after making all possible enquiries about the whereabouts of such overdue vessels. The *Red Rock's* voyage was from Townsville, on the Queensland coast of Australia, to Noumea, New Caledonia, a distance of about 1,200 miles across the Coral Sea. The ship would have been expected to cover that in ten or 12 days.

The *Red Rock* sailed from Townsville on 20 February 1899. A week later her master, Capt. Porter, informed her owners that he was off Magnetic Island, still just a handful of miles from Townsville. Capt. Porter's problem was that his course towards New Caledonia – east-southeast – was the same general direction from which the southeast trade winds blew in that part of the western Pacific. A virtually constant direct headwind like the strong southeast trades made it very difficult for a square-rigged ship such as *Red Rock* to make distance over the ground towards her destination.

Her task was made more difficult by being light in ballast (that is, with no cargo; the 1,600-ton *Red Rock* was going to New Caledonia to pick up a cargo of nickel ore), and therefore riding relatively high out of the water. This exposed more of her hull to the wind, making it easier for the wind to blow her off course.

It was completely understandable for Lloyd's to issue a "posted missing" notice for the *Red Rock* on 8 June 1899 after three months with no word of her whereabouts since her report from near Magnetic Island. Just five days later, however, Capt. Porter notified the ship's owners of his arrival at Noumea, 112 days out from Townsville, having struggled against "strong head winds and high seas".

## Post Script

On her return voyage from New Caledonia to Glasgow, in the first few days of January 1900 *Red Rock* was forced to put in at St. Vincent, in the Cape Verde Islands, short of provisions, indicating that she was making yet another slower than expected passage.

Alan Villiers noted in his book *Posted Missing* that, in the time since Lloyd's first kept records of missing vessels, 29 October 1873, until the time he was writing, 1956, *Red Rock* was the only vessel ever "posted missing" by Lloyd's that eventually reached her destination. That assertion emphasised the truly unusual tardiness of *Red Rock's* voyage, but it was not accurate. For example, in 1906 the little three-masted barque *Peru* (683 tons), took 192 days to sail with a cargo of Australian wheat from Streaky Bay on the Australian Bight to Falmouth (because of adverse winds, mainly calms and light airs). Since vessels might have been expected to average anywhere between 120 to 150 days on that passage, the *Peru* was posted missing before she arrived at Falmouth. There were probably others, although not many.

## The Extraordinary and Eventful Voyage of the *Claverdon*

### 30 Sept 1902

**Maritime Intelligence**

Claverdon*.- San Francisco (by Cable received Sept 30).- Claverdon encountered very heavy weather off Cape Horn for 19 days from May 1, squared away for [Cape of] Good Hope May 19, crossed Equator Aug. 21 in long. 128 W, passed through a cyclone Aug. 29 in lat 12 N, long 123 W. Five of the crew drowned.

### *15 Oct 1902*

**Maritime Intelligence**

Claverdon.- San Francisco, Sept. 29.- British ship Claverdon, arrived here from Hamburg, reports:-

Was off Cape Horn May 1, 68 days out, was off there for 19 days, with a succession of SW gales, with snow squalls and hail. Got as far as the Diego Ramirez [Islands, about 60 miles southwest of Cape Horn] and was blown back to the same position as we were on May 1. The gale still increasing, decided to go east by Cape of Good Hope. Crossed 180° meridian [now the International Date Line, in the Pacific] 59 days from Cape Horn, or 145 days from Hamburg. Passed lat. 32 S, long. 154 W on July 30. Had N winds to Equator, which we crossed 180 days out, in long. 128 W. Had N winds to lat. 38 N. On Aug 29, lat. 12 N, long. 123 W, had a hurricane from NW to SW, with a very high mountainous sea. The vessel shipped a very heavy sea and washed everything movable on deck overboard, drowning five of the crew and injuring nine others. Blew away the foresail out of the bolt ropes, the maintopgallantsail, the mainsail, the fore and main uppertopsails, the mizenlowertopsail, and the forelowertopsail, leaving the ship with only the lowermaintopsail.

### *San Francisco Call*

### *29 September 1902*

**Ship Claverdon Arrives In Port**

**Five Men Are washed From Her Deck Into the Sea**

**Nearly Complete Circuit of Globe During Her Voyage**

The ship Claverdon arrived in port yesterday at noon, after an eventful voyage from Hamburg, which took 218 days to complete. The Claverdon left Hamburg on February

22 with a crew of 30 men and carrying a cargo of 3,600 tons of cement. She was bound for this port by way of the Horn, but owing to a wind and heavy rain storm, during which five men were washed overboard and lost and many of the sails carried away, she was unable to round the Horn, and was forced to complete her voyage by way of the Cape of Good Hope, in this way covering 22,000 [*sic* – 32,000] miles.

First Mate H.T. Reede, in telling of the voyage, said: "We left Hamburg on February 22 with Captain Robert Thomas in command, myself, Edward Akeman, second mate, and thirty German sailors. We experienced strong winds while in the Channel, and a steady blow during our trip to the Horn. Round the Horn we ran head on into a terrific windstorm, in which we were beaten about for nineteen days, unable to make headway.

On August 29 we found ourselves in the center of the storm, which was blowing from the northwest. The sea was running high and pounding us from all directions. A drizzling rain was falling before the gale. Suddenly the heart of the storm struck us. The fore topsail broke away; then the main topsail, main topgallant sail, mizzen topsail and the mainsail went. The sea swept over the ship, carrying five seamen with it. Those that were not carried overboard were thrown violently to the deck and some received serious injuries.

When the sail blew away, the watch sang out, "Sail overboard!" Then came the sea over the rails, carrying two water casks, a hand rail, a poop ladder, and everything that was loose about the deck. After the first big wave had subsided, the watch sang out, "Men overboard!" and we could see the unfortunate sailors swimming in the sea, but it was impossible to assist them. I asked the men if they would take out a boat to try to save the others, but they said they would not. The five men lost were C. Neilson, G. Guppenberg, Charles Jesterkorn, T.H. Ryelt and August Firks.

We were nineteen days in the storm and were forced to put back and make this port by way of the Cape of Good Hope, covering a distance of 32,000 miles in 218 days. Our supply of food just held out and no more. The cargo is damaged considerably, but just how much is not yet known. That was the worst gale that I was ever in, and I do not care to be in another like it. The ship behaved very well and is not damaged from the effects of the storm."

* The iron full-rigged British ship *Claverdon* was built in 1884 as the *Alexandra*, by Oswald, Mordaunt & Co. at Southampton. She was 2,521 tons (gross), and 304ft 7ins long by 41ft 3ins wide by 25ft 2ins deep. She was renamed *Claverdon* when her original owners, J. Coupland, of London, sold her in 1890 to F&A Nodin, of Liverpool. On her 1902 voyage from Hamburg to San Francisco she spent 19 days being battered by westerly gales off Cape Horn. Her master Capt. Robert Thomas determined they would be better off running eastwards to his destination by way of the Cape of Good Hope and across the Indian and Pacific Oceans. Her 218-day, 32,000-mile voyage from Hamburg to San Francisco was, for that reason, exceptionally long; if she had completed the direct Cape Horn route of about 17,000 miles – half the distance – she might have expected to take 130–150 days.

(Many shipmasters actually took considerably longer to get round the Horn, from about lat. 50° S in the Atlantic to the same latitude in the Pacific, than the 19 days spent there by the *Claverdon*. In the notoriously hard Cape Horn winter of 1905 the three-masted ship *British Isles* took over 70 days. That same year the German full-rigged ship *Susanna* spent from 19 August until 26 November – 99 days: over three months! – rounding the Horn, the longest doubling of Cape Stiff ever recorded.)

The accounts above of the loss of five seamen swept overboard from the *Claverdon* by a single mountainous sea differ in their chronology. Capt. Thomas says the men were swept away in a storm in the Pacific as they were coming up towards San Francisco. First Mate Reede's recollection was that it happened off the Horn before they turned east to run for Good Hope. Since the master of a vessel was responsible for the log of her voyages, Capt. Thomas's account must have been the true one.

## SMALL BOAT VOYAGERS

The first recognised and successful single-handed transatlantic voyage by a small boat was undertaken from 15 June to 12 August 1876, by Alfred Johnson, a Danish-born seaman from Gloucester, Massachusetts who was 29 years old at the time (he died in 1927, aged 82). Johnson sailed his 20ft dory *Centennial* (named in honour of the centennial anniversary of the founding of the United States) single-handed from Gloucester, Massachusetts to Abercastle, Wales, and thence onward to Liverpool, arriving there on 20 August 1876.

After Alfred ('Centennial') Johnson's voyage a number of adventuresome men from both sides of the Atlantic embarked in small boats, including rowing boats, to challenge the open sea. Most were transatlantic voyagers, but Capt. Joshua Slocum's was the most famous of all, the first single-handed circumnavigation of the world lasting just over three years, from 24 April 1895 to 27 June 1898. Some of these adventurers undertook the challenge more than once. Several ended not just in failure but in the fathomless fate of that ominous refrain "...and has not since been heard of".

## CAPT. THOMAS CRAPO: *NEW BEDFORD* ACROSS THE ATLANTIC

Thomas Crapo was a 19th century American adventurer-seafarer. He was born on 27 June 1842 in the dominant American whaling port of the mid-1800s, New Bedford, Massachusetts, just as Yankee whaling was reaching its peak. After whaling and commercial seafaring for some years (and four years fighting in the American Civil War), Capt. Crapo, together with his wife Joanna made a transatlantic voyage of just 49 days in the summer of 1877 in what was at the time the smallest boat ever to be sailed across the Atlantic, a 19ft 7ins long dory named the *New Bedford*.

> "I had for years been thinking about crossing the Atlantic Ocean in a small boat, in fact I was very anxious to outstrip any attempt that had ever been made. Anyone would naturally think that knowing what the ocean was by living on it so many years would banish all thoughts of any such attempt, but not so with me. I was venturesome and daring and I thought if I could manage to eclipse all others I could make considerable money by doing so. I knew it would be a daring feat, had it not been I don't think I would have pondered over it as much as I did. The more I thought of it the more decided and determined I became." (from Thomas Crapo's biography – or autobiography; the author is not named - *Strange But True: Life and Adventures of Captain Thomas Crapo and Wife*)

In 1876 Crapo designed a double-ended whaleboat-style dory in which to undertake the transatlantic voyage he had been thinking about for some years. He commissioned the vessel to be constructed by a boat builder named Samuel Mitchell, who was well known for building whaleboats, on Fish Island, in the Acushnet River between New Bedford and Fairhaven across the river.

## THE *NEW BEDFORD*

The boat was just 19ft 7ins long by 6ft 2ins wide by 30ins deep. Fully loaded she drew 13ins and was rigged like a small schooner, the foremast being 21ft 6ins high and the mainmast 20ft 6ins. Sails were rigged in a leg o' mutton fashion, the mainsail being 15 sq yds of "light duck canvas" and the mainsail 10 sq yds of the same. ("Just twenty-five yards of sail to carry two people [he and his wife] across the Atlantic Ocean!") She measured 1.62 tons, "her actual weight being about five hundred pounds". Decked over, she had two scuttles (cockpits), one forward and one aft in which to steer. Fisher completed construction of the boat about 10th May, 1877. Crapo named her the *New Bedford*.

> "My intentions were, to go from New Bedford, Massachusetts, to England, and the most important feature of the trip was that, owing to the boat being so small, I could not carry a chronometer, so the voyage must be made by dead reckoning, depending on passing vessels to furnish me with my position, as the captains always know what latitude and longitude they are in, and about the distance from port, so my readers can see what a seemingly rash undertaking I was about; yet I was confident of success, and never once for a moment doubted my reaching England in safety."

Provisions for the voyage were: 90 lbs of biscuits, 75 lbs of canned meats, 100 gallons of fresh water, as well as tea, coffee, sugar "and other light articles". A small (one pint capacity) kerosene stove was to be used for re-heating the pre-cooked canned food. Crapo was given a compass by Capt. Humphrey Seabury of New Bedford, as well as two charts and "an old fashioned square lantern…fitted to burn candles in, and he also gave me a quantity of candles to burn in it".

## THE VOYAGE

With his wife installed as his only crew, the now Capt. Thomas Crapo (in his first command position) set out from New Bedford in his whaleboat dory *New Bedford* on 28 May 1877, destination: England. His first port-o'-call, however, turned out to be Vineyard Haven on the island of Martha's Vineyard, across the bay, to make a few alterations to the boat – and because she was leaking. Summoning a local Vineyard carpenter, Capt. Crapo added another 200 lbs or so of ballast to the boat, for better stability. They left the island on 1 June, stayed overnight at Chatham on Cape Cod, and eventually departed the mainland of North America at 2 p.m. on 2 June 1877.

A few days later Capt. Crapo declined the invitation of a local fishing schooner captain amongst a fishing fleet on George's Bank to come aboard for coffee and to stretch their legs. The *New Bedford Standard* newspaper later carried a New York newspaper report that the schooner *A.J. Chapman* had encountered Capt. Crapo and wife "well" at lat. 41.55 N, long. 67.10 W. Newspapers would report the encounters of other vessels with Capt. Crapo throughout the *New Bedford*'s transatlantic voyage. The following was somewhat atypical of such reports for its summary explication of the longitudinal distance of the voyage:

THE BOAT NEW BEDFORD, WHICH HAS CROSSED THE
ATLANTIC.

## "The New Bedford Spoken Five Days Out"

New York, June 10th. The ship Gustave and Oscar, from Bremen, reports that on June 7th, latitude 42.20, longitude 64.22, spoke small two-masted boat from New Bedford for London, having one man and woman on board, undoubtedly Captain Crapo and his wife. Crapo's position when spoken was at a point nearly due south from Liverpool, Nova Scotia, and almost due east from Boston. Chatham, from whence he made his last start, is in longitude 70, consequently he had, up to the time he was spoken, in longitude 64.22, sailed five degrees and thirty-eight minutes, or about 5 [&] 2/3 degrees. Falmouth, England, where Mr. Crapo intends stopping, is in about longitude 5, and the whole distance across in a straight line from Chatham, is about 65 degrees. The length of a degree of longitude in latitude 42 is 51 [&] ¼ miles, consequently the New Bedford had sailed, when spoken, a little over 290 miles from Chatham, out of the 3300 and over which she must sail before reaching Falmouth.

*Lloyd's List* reported that first "speaking" between the *New Bedford* and another vessel:

## 25 June 1877

### Maritime Intelligence

### Speakings

New Bedford (small boat), Crapo, New Bedford to London, 7th June, 42 N, 64 W, by the Gustav & Oscar, [Capt.] Hartmann, [reported] at New York

On 24th June the Cunard steamship *Batavia*, from Liverpool to Boston, spoke the plucky Capt. Crapo, although the *Batavia*'s Capt. John Moreland thought at first sight that the *New Bedford* "was a boat with survivors from some wrecked vessel." Much later, in January 1878, Capt. Moreland and Capt. Crapo met over dinner in New York. At that time the Cunard commander gave the *New Bedford* commander a letter confirming the meeting of his 2,553 ton steamship with the "1 & 62/100 tons" dory:

### New York, Jan., 29th, 1878

I hereby certify that I spoke the boat "New Bedford" in latitude 44.00 N, longitude 48.00 W, bound to England, and manned by a man and woman, at 9 a.m., June 20th [*sic* – actually June 24th], 1877. At that time they reported themselves in good condition and required nothing.

John E. Moreland
Commander Cunard Steamship "Batavia"

A singular event in the Crapos' voyage happened around 9 a.m. on 28 June when the two voyagers sighted the barque *Amphitrite*, from Bristol for Quebec. The captain of the barque's report of the incident appeared in *The New York Times* of 19 July 1877 as follows:

### Capt. Crapo's Atlantic Voyage

Quebec, July 18.- Capt. Geare, of the barque Amphitrite, from Bristol, for this port, reports June 26 [*sic* – actually 28th], in latitude 44° 39' North, longitude 43° West, met the 20-foot schooner-rigged whale-boat New Bedford, 22 days out, with Mr. and Mrs. Crapo on board; hove to, and the two voyagers boarded the Amphitrite. They remained to dinner, and expressed themselves well satisfied so far with their voyage to Europe, and stated that they had enjoyed good health. At parting Capt. Geare provided them with wine, water, and a few small articles they required. When the two vessels separated the New Bedford steered east north-east, and the ship's company gave them three cheers and wished them God speed.

Capt. Crapo's route across the North Atlantic virtually guaranteed that he and his wife would regularly meet vessels sailing that well-worn track between North America and northern Europe. On 3 July they obtained a keg of fresh water from the English barque *Ontario*, of Windsor, Nova Scotia, sailing from Hamburg to New York. On the morning of 6 July the Norwegian barque *Honor*, bound for Cork, Ireland, hove into view at about 10 o'clock. Capt Crapo noted, "The captain gave us the longitude as 29.30. He, like all others, urged us to come on board but we respectfully declined". A week later *Lloyd's List* reported:

### 13 July 1877

Queenstown [Ireland], 12th July, 10 19 a.m.- Captain Olsen, of Norwegian barque *Honor*, reports that on 6th July, in lat. 45 N, lon. 29 W, spoke the American sail boat New Bedford, from New Bedford, with a man and woman on board. The man stated that they were then 34 days from New Bedford and had encountered six gales on the passage, and that they intended to run for Falmouth. They were all right and required nothing; the woman seemed quite contented and in good health.

The next day, 7 July, at just around the mid-point between Ireland and Newfoundland, the Crapos encountered and were given water and fresh provisions by the steamship *Denmark*, from New York to London. The *Denmark's* master, Capt. Robert Williams, even gave Capt. Crapo a letter when they met later in London, to confirm the encounter:

### S.S. Denmark

London, December 1877

Capt. Crapo:

Dear Sir: As you are now about leaving England, and some people have been sceptical as to your crossing the Atlantic in the small boat "New Bedford," you are at perfect liberty to use my testimony as to passing you at sea on your voyage, viz: July 7th, 7.30 p.m., latitude 47.12 n; 27° 33 west.

Robert P. Williams<br>Master National Steamship Co.'s Denmark, of Liverpool

Around 15 July Mrs Crapo began feeling unwell. Her husband surmised that "the change from canned goods to fresh meat and vegetables given to us from the *Denmark* was the cause". Stormy weather, fog, cold, tedium, fatigue and cramped accommodation probably also began to take their toll on her. As the experienced seaman, Capt. Crapo observed: "The Atlantic ocean is a very rough place during the winter months, but is generally quite good during the summer. Yet we were having nearly as rough a passage as if it were winter instead of in the summer".

On 16 July, despite the concern for his wife's welfare, the plucky *New Bedford* captain declined an invitation by a passing German barque, the *Astronom*, to go on board to revive their spirits and physical condition. He determined that "we had stood it thus far, and I thought we could stand it a little longer". What they had stood became quite clear, in Capt. Crapo's words, around this time about halfway across the Atlantic:

"Words cannot express, even to sailors themselves, what we experienced on that passage. Gales that were terrible to encounter, especially in a little boat, when many large vessels have been wrecked in gales of less magnitude. Yet there we were, day and night, and I slept on an average of four hours out of each twenty-four during the passage, and not a ghost of a chance to move about enough to keep one's blood in circulation. At all times, especially in heavy weather, my thoughts would turn to my wife who was bearing up bravely under the ordeal, especially as sick as she was, and as she grew worse instead of better plagued me more, I think, than it did her. Of course all I could do under the circumstances was to cheer her up all I possibly could."

## End of the Voyage

Finally, on the morning of Saturday 21 July, the Isles of Scilly, off Land's End, the southwest point of England, emerged out of a clearing fog, their first sight of land since leaving Chatham 49 days before ("Oh! What a welcome sight!"). At 11 p.m. that same day they arrived at Newlyn, the fishing port near Penzance, and moored up alongside a fishing boat there with no one on board. "Our long, perilous voyage was over, and here we were…made fast to a fishing boat belonging to some inhabitant of the British Isles".

*24 July 1877*

Penzance, 22nd July, 5 50 p.m.- The boat *New Bedford*, of and from New Bedford and Chatham, United States, arrived here to-day with Captain Crapo and wife, all well. The boat is 19 feet keel [length], 6½ feet beam, and measures 1½ tons. She has been 49 days from Chatham, experienced several gales on the voyage, and was obliged to lay to 15 days. She will proceed hence to Falmouth and London.

A local Penzance news correspondent wrote on the day after the Crapos' arrival, Sunday, 22nd July:

"I was startled this morning, just at the commencement of church, to hear that the boat which had left America for England, with only a man and woman on board, had arrived at Penzance [sic]. On glancing along the promenade I saw right away under Newlyn, a little boat with two masts lying at anchor, whilst surrounding her were a cluster of Newlyn boats filled with spectators who had come to see the wonderful little craft. The New Bedford is a boat about twenty feet long, and of the registered tonnage of one and sixty-two one hundredths, a little over one and one-half tons.

She carries two masts, one anchor and a drogue. She is built of cedar and is rigged as what is known as 'leg of mutton rigged schooner'. The name of the owner is Captain Thomas Crapo, aged thirty-five, who, with his wife, has so bravely crossed the Atlantic in so tiny a craft. The voyage was commenced on May 28th, when the little vessel left New Bedford, but by stress of weather she had to put into Chatham, Massachusetts, where she stayed until the second of June, when the sails were again hoisted, and the little pigmy left on her voyage with a fair wind…

Among the many extraordinary things connected with the voyage is that it had to be run by dead reckoning, as the New Bedford was not large enough to carry a chronometer.

Captain and Mrs. Crapo seemed wonderfully well after the hardships they had undergone, though the captain has a bad hand, and when he came ashore it was firmly clenched through being forced to steer for seventy hours without rest…"

A week later Capt. Crapo sailed the *New Bedford* from Newlyn the few miles across Mounts Bay to Penzance where he had her lifted out of the water. Capt. Crapo had always aimed to make some money out of the voyage, and to that end he and Mrs Crapo travelled around England, exhibiting the boat, and themselves, throughout the rest of 1877. Another means of profiting from the voyage was a narrative of the voyage that Capt. Crapo wrote soon afterwards, *Captain & Mrs. Crapo's Feat of Crossing The Atlantic In The Tiny Boat The New Bedford from New Bedford, Massachusetts, to Penzance – The Captain's Yarn, Telling the Chief Events of the Voyage.* Price Five Cents. In 2006 a rare copy of the 'yarn' was sold at live auction for $1,495.

On 4 January 1878 Capt. and Mrs Crapo left London for New York on the steamship *Canada*. "Our boat was brought over free of charge, and a pleasant time we had". About three weeks later the *New York Herald* reported their arrival at New York, with another 'yarn' of the voyage by the *New Bedford*'s master:

**Fifty Days of Danger**

**The Smallest Boat That Ever Crossed The Atlantic**

The steamship *Canada*, of the National Line, arrived at her dock, Pier No. 15 North River, after a long voyage from London, having left that port on 3rd January. Among her passengers were Captain Thos. Crapo and his wife, who made the memorable voyage last summer across the broad Atlantic from New Bedford, Mass., in a whale-boat, schooner-rigged, with leg-of-mutton sails. Captain Crapo appears to be a man of about 35 years of age, is of sturdy build, and wears a brown beard. His face is weather-beaten, but a firm mouth denotes the resolution which enabled him to carry into execution his daring plan. In his speech the quick-witted Yankee is plainly traced and every word has a shrewd, practical meaning.

His wife, perhaps his junior by a year or two, is a healthy, cheerful helpmeet, and talks of her successful voyage with a pardonable pride [Joanna Crapo was, in fact, 23 years old at this time, twelve years younger than her husband; she was just 18 when she married Thomas in November 1872]. The twain were found in the freight agent's office on the steamship deck, surrounded by a group of admirers, who were listening to each detail of the fifty days' voyage with breathless interest. The reporter was taken by Captain Crapo to the smoking-room on the deck of the *Canada*, and there the yarn was spun of the trip of the New Bedford.

"Why did I run such a risk? Well, I'll tell you. My first idea was a Yankee one – that is, to beat everything that has been done before. Useless, was it? As long as Englishmen and their cousins are on earth, you'll hear of their trying their 'spunk' against each other. Had I experience? Listen to me, young man. I sailed seven years in the service of Messrs Ramble and Ramsdall, of Harrington, Me. [Maine], and although I am not a captain in the American marine – I never got beyond first mate – I should like to see the man that knows more about ships than I do. Besides, I'm a captain now – captain of the New Bedford – and I'm prouder of that, and what I've done with her, than if I was commander on the quarter-deck of one of Uncle Sam's men-of-war."

Here the captain paused, and took a few puffs of his cigar.

"When I got the first idea of crossing the ocean in the smallest boat that ever succeeded in the attempt I went right to work to design the craft – remember, I had made twenty-one trips over the Atlantic, and spent a good many years whaling – and when I commenced to build the New Bedford people wondered what on earth I wanted such a craft for. My seafaring friends never doubted her qualities. People said I was a fool, but I didn't care., No sir, I knew the risk and the exposure and all that, but I went right on until the boat was launched. One thing kept bothering me." The captain here became thoughtful, and seemed to take a good deal of comfort in watching the clouds of smoke that were wreathing above his head.

"Well, captain, after the boat was launched?"

"Why," he replied, "one thing kept bothering me, for as the time of my departure drew nigh my wife declared she never would consent to my going without her. Good stock, sir; she's a Scotch woman, a native of Glasgow. Her father is a Swede, and her mother was born in Newcastle-on-Tyne. I married her at Marseilles, in November, 1872, on board of the Myronus, Captain Higgins.

"Well, finally I agreed to take her. When I got ready to start a meeting was held in New Bedford, my native town, to wish us God-speed on our journey. Rev. Mr. Butler presided and friends assembled. Cable, compass, ensign, water-kegs, etc., were given me for the voyage. The New Bedford is schooner-rigged, with two masts carrying leg of mutton sails. She draws only one foot of water; her keel is thirteen feet; her total length barely twenty feet; her tonnage 1 62.100. She is thirty-four inches deep. We carried the American ensign and our own burgee.

"We sailed from New Bedford at half-past twelve, 28th May, amid the cheers of the crowd on Roach's wharf, and all the vessels at anchor fired salutes in our honor. We made our real start, however, from Chatham at two o'clock on the afternoon of 2nd June. As my vessel was too small to have a marine document issued to her, I got a letter from Mr. J.A.P. Allan, Collector of Customs at New Bedford, in which, after describing my boat, he said – 'I therefore desire to make known to all whom it may concern that captain Crapo is well known here, and his purpose is entirely legitimate, and he has the good wishes of this community that his voyage may be successfully accomplished.'

"Once fairly out of sight of land we had enough to do and think about. Our chief diet was canned meats, fish, and fruit. Our bread was rather hardish, you may believe. Our provisions were calculated to last out the voyage, even, if more than ordinarily delayed; but the passage was so bad – more like a stormy, winter one – that if we had not got from passing vessels fresh meat, bread, vegetables, and water we should have perished. On several occasions we found ourselves in a shoal of whales, who spouted a good deal and this frightened my wife. Sometimes for two days at a stretch we experienced such rough weather we had to lay to attached to what we called a drag or buoy [sea anchor]. At such times I could get a little rest and when the winds were favorable had to be at the helm the whole time. Once I kept at my post seventy hours without rest. My wife scarcely got a good night's rest during the whole voyage.

"On 19th June we spoke the English barque America in a heavy sea, latitude 43 deg. 42 min., longitude 50 deg. 10 min. On the 21st we spoke the steamer Batavia bound from Liverpool to Boston. There was a heavy gale blowing, and my notes showed that I tended the drag for eighteen hours at a stretch. On the 23rd a Swansea brig offered to tow us into port, but I did not see it in that light, although the sea was running mountains high. At eleven on the morning of the 25th my wife and I boarded the Amphitrite, a barque bound from Bremen to New York, and here we were received with great kindness, and on leaving the captain gave us provisions and a couple of bottles of wine.

"The officers of a good many other vessels we met between this date and 8th July were also kind. On the latter date we were alongside the English steamer Denmark, from New York to London, and were given provisions and two bottles of brandy. On the 15th, during a gale, the German barque Astronom spoke us, and the captain asked if we wanted assistance. Shortly after our rudder was twisted off, but I rigged a new one.

"On the 21st we sighted Wall [Wolf] Rock Light, off Land's End, and at half-past five p.m. that day we passed the light, anchoring at eleven off Newland [Newlyn], Penzance. At midnight I turned in for a sleep, having been out on duty for seventy hours, and the next morning (Sunday) the 'missus' and I went ashore. And that, sir, is a true history of the trip of the New Bedford."

## Mrs Crapo's Letter

Joanna Crapo offered a more summary and spiritual version of her experience of the *New Bedford* voyage in a letter she wrote at Penzance on 22 July to a 'gentleman in New Bedford' and which was published in *The New York Times* on 12th August 1877:

"Dear Sir:

We have had a very hard time of it coming here. We should have gone into Falmouth, but could not on account of a head tide, heavy sea, and foggy weather. We laid upon a wet bed for 49 days, and I have pains all through my body. I fainted twice on the passage. We had seven gales of wind, the last one being very hard, and the seas running mountains high. It lasted from Saturday afternoon till Tuesday morning, but God was with us, and He calmed the sea so that we were able to make sail. The next morning God spoke to me and said, "I am with thee; don't fear. Trust in me, and I will land thee safe on the shore." The tears dropped down my face like rain.

Thomas could not have stood the hardships 15 days more, he was wet through so much and his hands were sore from steering. He was 70 hours without rest. We would not undertake this voyage again for considerable. [?]…Nothing could make us go. The people here were very glad to see us, and have treated us very kindly. Our arrival has caused great excitement in the town.

Yours most truly,
Johanna Crapo"

Capt. and Mrs Crapo exhibited with the *New Bedford* for six weeks at various venues around New York City before going on the road across America with Howe's Great London Circus. On a railway siding at Moberly, Missouri, the baggage car caught fire, and the Crapos lost many of their clothes and gifts given to them in England. They continued their tour of exhibitions, however, the last of which was at Brooklyn for six months.

## LATER YEARS

After the end of the *New Bedford* roadshow around the United States, Capt. Crapo bought and sold various schooners over the following years to engage in the coastal trade around the east and southeast coast of the United States. In August 1885 he and two other crew members were rescued at sea from his schooner *Gustie Wilson* which sank during a hurricane off Cape Hatteras (the three other crew members drowned). Capt. Crapo's rescuer was Capt. H. Stetson, of the schooner *Emily Northam*, on passage to Savannah, Georgia, "as brave a captain as sails the seas anywhere". One of his saved crew members, a Swede named Charles Wickland, "was so overjoyed at the rescue that his mind was affected almost as soon as he got on board of the Northam and had to be put into an asylum as soon as we arrived in port [Savannah]".

Capt. Thomas Crapo only briefly added to his autobiography, *Strange But True: Life and Adventures of Captain Thomas Crapo and Wife*, shortly after the loss of his *Gustie Wilson*, noting that he "bought another schooner named the *Oriole*, and have followed the coasting business up to the present time". Thomas's wife Joanna, however, contributed more details after her husband's death in a few paragraphs she added to the end of her husband's story, included in later printings of the book.

The most significant item (apart from his actual death) was that in 1898 Capt. Crapo was again rescued from another of his vessels, the brig *Manson* which sank in bad weather off the coast of Delaware. "It may be interesting to note here that I was always considered a fit first officer for the *Manson*, and it gives me all the more regret to speak of the loss of the brig, which occurred January 9th, 1898". She further noted: "I also desire to mention that with the famous Manson perished the still more famous 19-foot boat the *New Bedford*, on which Captain Crapo and myself crossed the Atlantic Ocean in 1877, which accomplishment is still fresh in the memory of the people".

In May 1899 Capt. Crapo was lost at sea while attempting to sail his nine-foot-long boat *Volunteer* from Newport, Rhode Island to Cuba. The boat was found entangled in fishing nets just off the coast of southern Rhode Island, near Charlestown. Capt. Crapo's remains were discovered there on Quonochontaug Beach. His widow Joanna had the last word about their life and her husband's death, falling more or less on the mercy of the reading public to support her apparent destitution:

"He [Capt. Crapo] left Newport [Rhode Island] May 3, 1899, and was never heard of again until his body was found off Charlestown beach, he having been drowned by the capsizing of his boat in a severe gale.

Just previous to the death of my husband he had the misfortune to lose almost his entire estate, on account of the loss of his vessel and other things, and I am now solely depending on the result of the book "Strange But True," published by my late husband and myself. I therefore commend the book to those who are in sympathy with increasing the sale of it, believing that it will be both entertaining and instructive to all who read it.

With my best wishes to all,
Joanna Crapo"

## THE VOYAGE OF *LITTLE WESTERN*

### 9 July 1880

**Casualties, Etc.**

The Bulgarian (s), which arrived at Liverpool July 6 from Boston, reports:- "At noon, June 28, in lat. 42 40 N, long 57 W, spoke the small boat Little Western\*, of New York, from Gloucester (U.S.), for London, which reported herself all well except that their timepiece had broken down the day before. The two men looked in good health and spirits; they would not come on board and did not require anything except a clock; we could not spare one. They reported they had had a good time since leaving, and passed a large number of icebergs, some a mile long and from 300 to 500 feet high. We took a letter from them and gave them our position, and parted company from the tiny craft after exchanging three cheers."

### 29 July 1880

**The "Little Western"**

Cowes (I.W.), July 28, 9 a.m.- The American sail boat, the Little Western, with two hands, Thomas and Norman, from Gloucester (Massachusetts) to London, arrived here at 7 o'clock this morning, all well, having been 43 days from land to land. The men reported that, beyond shipping a sea which nearly capsized the boat, on the 25th inst., the voyage had been passed without accident. The dimensions of the boat are:- length, 16 feet 7 inches; beam, 6 feet 7 inches; depth, 2 feet 6 inches. She is cutter-rigged, and carries one small boat. She will proceed on at once.

*The New York Times*

*29th July 1880*

**The Little Western's Long Voyage**

London, July 28.- The dory Little Western arrived at Cowes to-day. The weather during the voyage was rough, and on June 28 the crew had fears of capsizing. On coming ashore, the two occupants, Capt. George P. Thomas and Fred Norman, could hardly stand, but the stiffness soon wore off. The voyage will be continued to London.

*The New York Times*

*21st August 1880*

**The Little Western's Voyage** (from the *London Standard*)

Among the attractions just now at the Aquarium is the "dory" boat Little Western, in which two young American seamen, named G.P. Thomas and Frederick Norman, have just completed a risky passage across the Atlantic. The Little Western is 16 feet 7 inches long over all, 6 feet 7 inches wide, 2 feet 6 inches deep, with raking stem and stern, sharp at both ends, her flat bottom being 13 feet 6 inches long, and 3 feet wide amidships.

She left Gloucester, Mass, which is about 30 miles north-east of Boston, on the 12th June, carrying 500 pounds of general ballast, 50 gallons of fresh water, 100 pounds of bread, 50 pounds of tinned beef and tongue, 48 tins of canned fruit, 12 tins of condensed coffee, some chocolate, milk, corn-meal, oat-meal, dried fruit, and a few knickknacks pressed on them by sympathizing friends as they were leaving.

They were unfortunate in their weather, for the passage was made against a succession of strong easterly winds, high seas, and what American sailors call "Fall" weather, instead of the pleasant time it was fair to expect in midsummer. They encountered a strong gale on the 21st June, in latitude 42° 30' north, longitude 60° west, had to heave to, and were blown back 70 miles. Two seas were shipped during this anxious time, and baling was the order of the day. When the wind lulled a little they found themselves attended by a party of sharks, which swam round and round, eyeing them in so unpleasantly suggestive a style that they hauled in their *drague* [sea-anchor] and jammed their little craft on the wind, preferring the chance of getting swamped to remaining in such company.

The best day's work was performed when in mid-ocean, a slant of wind enabling them to log 160 miles as the day's run. On this day the Little Western bowled off nine knots an hour for several hours in succession, showing that if she had been favored with westerly winds she could have made a good passage. As it was she was 43 days from Gloucester to Scilly [Isles of Scilly], a distance of about 2,700 miles. This gives a daily average distance made good of nearly 63 miles, which, for so small a boat, against high winds and head seas, is a very creditable performance.

The men had a sextant but no chronometer, and the wet soon stopped the only watch they had. They navigated, therefore, by dead reckoning, checked by meridian altitudes of the sun; and, considering their difficulties, made a wonderfully good landfall, a lift in the haze, about 6 P.M. on July 28, showing them the Bishop's Rock Lighthouse, just when, by calculation, they should have been within sight of the islands.

## *4 Aug 1881*
## Casualties – Home

Southampton, Aug. 3, 1 20 p.m.- Little Western – The Donau (s), arrived here from New York, reports having spoken, in lat. 47 30 N, long. 37 W, the sailing boat Little Western, from London for New York, 46 days out. No assistance wanted. Boat's mainboom had broken, and men on board said she leaked four inches an hour.

* The 16ft 7ins long dory *Little Western* left Gloucester, Massachusetts, on 12 June 1880, bound for England, with a crew of two: Frederick Norman, an ex-US Navy seaman, and his friend George Thomas, of Halifax, Nova Scotia. A crowd of some 30,000 gathered to witness their departure. After a *transatlantic* voyage of just 46 days, Norman and Thomas made their landfall at the Isles of Scilly, off Land's End, on 26 July 1880. They arrived at their final destination, Cowes, the Isle of Wight, two days later on 28 July. At that time their boat was the smallest ever to make the transatlantic voyage.

The two men stayed in England for almost a year, touring and exhibiting the *Little Western*. On 15 June 1881 they departed from London on their return voyage across the Atlantic. (The steamship *Donau*, above, spoke them about two-thirds of the way across.) It proved to be a hard slog against the prevailing westerly winds and rough weather. They arrived at Halifax, Nova Scotia, in mid-August, after 62 days at sea, having sailed at an average speed of just 1.6 knots. From Halifax the men sailed the *Little Western* back to Gloucester, Massachusetts, where they arrived on 16 September 1881.

Two years before *Little Western*'s outward voyage, in the summer of 1878, the Andrews brothers had sailed their 19ft long (15ft along the waterline) boat *Nautilus* from Boston to England in 48 days. Norman and Thomas, in a similar sized boat, took just 46 days. The *Nautilus*, moreover, was shipped back to the United States on board a Cunard steamship, whereas Norman and Thomas sailed *Little Western* home. Norman and Thomas therefore not only broke the record time for a *transatlantic* voyage by a small boat (under 20ft), as well as the record for the smallest boat to make the passage on the first leg, they also became the first to complete a return *transatlantic* voyage in a small boat under sail.

## CITY OF BATH ACROSS THE ATLANTIC

### 23 Aug 1881

**Casualties, Etc.**

New York, Aug. 9.- City of Bath*, dory, was spoken July 28, and supplied with provisions by the Victor and Eugenie, French barque, which arrived at St. John's (N.F.), Aug. 7. The dory had previously capsized and spoiled all the provisions on board.

### *25 Aug 1881*

**Casualties – Home**

Liverpool, Aug. 23.- The master, Hansen, of the Norwegian barque Rogeland, arrived here yesterday from Picton (N.S.), reports:- "In lat. 47 N, long. 35 W, spoke the City of Bath (small boat), 14 x 5 x 1.2, bound to Havre, with two men in her, named John Trynee and Ivee Olsen, who reported having capsized and lost all provisions and instruments. Supplied them with both provisions and compass."

* An Englishman from Bristol, John Traynor, and a Norwegian, Ivar Olsen, crewed the little *City of Bath* dory on her transatlantic voyage in the summer of 1881, bound from America for Le Havre in France via England. The dory was shallow-bottomed (just 7ins of freeboard), almost fully decked over with a small cabin underneath, and cutter-rigged, with a mainsail, foresail, and jib run out to a short bowsprit. They also carried a squaresail for occasional use. In the cabin there was a kerosene lamp for cooking provisions which comprised preserved meats, coffee, tea, bread, and other dry foods. The men slept on wooden boards with just a blanket to cover themselves.

The two men set sail from Bath, Maine, on the Kennebec River, on 7 July 1881. A few days later, the boat suffered damage during bad weather, which forced Traynor and Olsen to put into Trespassey, a small town on the southeast coast of the Avalon Peninsula, Newfoundland, to repair the leak. On (or possibly just before) 27 July they continued their voyage eastwards from Newfoundland. Very soon after they encountered more bad weather which capsized the boat and both men were thrown into the sea. Their provisions were spoiled and they lost their sextant and chart. The French barque *Victor and Eugenie* which spoke them on 28 July resupplied them with fresh provisions.

On 7 August, about 750 miles out from Newfoundland, the two sailors spoke another barque, the Norwegian *Rogeland*, which provided them with more provisions and a compass. Yet more provisions came on 18 August from the barque *John Lefurgy*, spoken when the *City of Bath* was approaching the British Isles. Traynor and Olsen arrived in their dory off the Isles

THE NAUTILUS, AFTER CROSSING THE ATLANTIC ON ITS WAY TO THE PARIS EXHIBITION.

of Scilly on 23 August and reached Falmouth the next day after a transatlantic crossing from Newfoundland of just under a month. Traynor and Olsen sailed from Falmouth on (or about) 27 August and arrived at their final destination, Le Havre, on 29 August.

The *City of Bath* was reported to be 14ft long and therefore would have been the smallest boat to have crossed the Atlantic up until then. Her 'length' of 14ft, however, was actually the length of her keel, an old way of measuring a ship's length. In fact the *City of Bath's* overall length was "about 18-ft", according to a report in the *Falmouth Packet* of 27 August 188 (reproduced by Humphrey Barton in his 1953 book *Atlantic Adventurers*). She was certainly *one of* the smallest boats to cross the Atlantic under sail. However, the *Little Western*, sailed eastward across the Atlantic by Frederick Norman and George Thomas in 1880 (and back across the Atlantic westward in 1881) was, at 16ft 7ins, just a bit smaller than the *City of Bath*.

## THE INDOMITABLE CAPTAIN WILLIAM ANDREWS

Between 1878 and 1901 the American small boat sailor Capt. William Andrews made seven attempts to cross the Atlantic from America to Europe in small craft of under 20ft. He succeeded twice: in 1878, with his brother Asa, in the *Nautilus*, and in 1892, single-handed, in the 14ft 6ins *Sapolio*. His 1892 voyage in *Sapolio* remained the record for the smallest boat to cross the Atlantic until the summer of 1965 when Robert Manry, in the 13½ft *Tinkerbelle*, and John Riding, in his 12-ft-long *Sjo Ag* (*Sea Egg*), both completed the crossing in smaller boats. (The Englishman John Riding, who was 6ft 6ins tall, sailed his egg-shaped boat from east to west across the Atlantic, then by stages across the Pacific. He was lost in the notoriously stormy Tasman Sea in 1973, en route from New Zealand to Sydney, Australia.)

## THE *NAUTILUS* VOYAGE

### 26 July 1878

Queenstown [Ireland], 25th July, 2 p.m.- The *Annotbyle*, arrived here from Rangoon, reports:- "Spoke, 22nd July, boat *Nautilus*, with two men, Boston to Le Havre, 38 days [out], all well, in lat. 48 N, long. 29 W; did not require anything. Said they had been hove to [ie., stopped sailing] for 12 days shortly after leaving, and that they had had several days calm weather. At time of speaking the weather was thick and raining, with moderate breeze from south."

### 31 July 1878

Scilly [Isles of Scilly, off Land's End, England], 30th July, 9.20 a.m.- Pilot cutter *Gem* spoke, 30 miles SW of Scilly, the small boat *Nautilus*, from Boston, U.S., all well, 29th July.

Falmouth [Cornwall, England], 29th July, 8 p.m.- The *S. Pierre*, arrived here to-day, from Monte Video [Montevideo, Uruguay], spoke on 27th inst., in lat. 49.14 N, lon. 8.26 W, the American boat *Nautilus*, from Boston for Le Havre, two men on board, required no assistance; 44 days out.

### 3 Aug 1878

Penzance [Cornwall], 2nd Aug., 8.46 a.m.- The *Nautilus* (boat) has arrived in this port from Boston, U.S., 48 days out, bound Le Havre. The boat is only 19 feet overall, 15 feet bottom [waterline length], 6 feet 7 inches beam, and 2 feet 3 inches deep. She draws about 6 inches water, and is manned by two brothers, William and Walter [*sic* – his name was Asa Walter] Andrews, both young men, who had never been at sea before, except fishing. They had some very rough weather on the voyage, and spoke several vessels. The boat arrived off the Lizard, but owing to the strong Easterly gale could not get up Channel, and anchored off Mullion on Wednesday evening, and the men landed here yesterday. They intend proceeding for Le Havre as soon as the wind changes or moderates.

The crossing of the Atlantic by the Andrews brothers in the 19ft-long *Nautilus* in 48 days was a great media event at the time. It was, in fact, one of the most remarkable transatlantic voyages ever undertaken in a small boat. In the first place, neither of the brothers – William, 35 years old, and Asa, 23 – had ever navigated a boat on the open ocean before. Their watch broke a few days after the start of the voyage, so they could only determine longitude positions by dead reckoning – effectively estimating according to their course and speed – or by asking ships they spoke for their position at the time. Their only chart was second-hand and out-of-date. Their most reliable piece of equipment was a good quality compass, made by Baker's of Boston.

The boat was rigged by a simple, even primitive arrangement of a single mast with a lateen sail, like a cat rig used by dinghy sailboats. The vessel itself had no air- or water-tight compartments or other buoyancy aids in case of capsize. There was no life-saving gear of any kind. The total weight of the boat, including stores and provisions, was just 600lbs. "She weighs less with everything in her than the ballast of the smallest boat that ever crossed before them", according to the story of the voyage, published as *A Daring Voyage Across the Atlantic* (E.P. Dutton & Co., 1880).

Finally, the brothers crossed the North Atlantic which, even in summer, is one of the stormiest and most turbulent 3000 miles of ocean on Earth, in what was essentially an open boat hardly bigger than a dinghy.

After reaching their first English landfall, Mullion Cove in Cornwall, at the end of July 1878, the Andrews sailed the *Nautilus* on to Le Havre, on the Normandy coast of France, which they reached on 8 August "with colours flying". The time from their port of departure – Beverly, Massachusetts, just south of Boston – to Le Havre was 48 days. The vessel was taken on to Paris and exhibited at the 1878 Paris Exposition in Avenue Rapp. (The French advertised the Exposition with a headline reading "L'INCROYABLE Traversée de l'Océan de Boston au Havre en 45 Jours, SUR UNE COQUILLE DE NOIX [IN A NUTSHELL]".)

Afterwards the little *coquille de noix* was put on show in London for a few days, and then in Brighton until the autumn of 1879. A Cunard liner subsequently transported her back to America from Liverpool, and she was then exhibited at Boston. William Andrews went on to attempt six more Atlantic crossings in small boats in the late 1800s, only one of which was successful.

## DARK SECRET

Ten years after the voyage of the *Nautilus*, in the summer of 1888, Capt. Andrews aimed to make a crossing of the Atlantic in the smallest boat ever to achieve that feat, a record held until then by George Thomas and Fred Norman in the *Little Western* in 1880. At Boston he built a 14ft-long boat, lateen-rigged on a 17ft yard (longer than the boat itself), and named it the *Dark Secret*. His project was sponsored by the *New York World* newspaper which supplied Andrews with envelopes for sending back reports of his voyage via passing ships.

There was massive public support for Capt. Andrews' voyage; 30,000 people were reported to have witnessed its start on 17 June 1888. Unfortunately, progress was poor: the *Dark Secret* was not a good sea boat as she was rather unstable and leaked badly. After two months Andrews abandoned his attempt to reach Ireland when he met the Norwegian barque *Nor* which picked up his boat and himself about halfway across the Atlantic (at a latitude of 46° 18' N, not "56 N" as stated in the first report below). The *Nor* landed Andrews and the *Dark Secret* back at New York on 21 September 1888. *Lloyd's List* reported the abandonment of Capt. Andrews' voyage in his small craft as follows:

### 21 Sept 1888

London, Sept. 21.- Captain Andrews and his boat Dark Secret, from Boston, June 18, for Queenstown, were landed at New York 11th inst. [ie., 11th September] by the Norwegian barque Nor, which had picked them up Aug. 19, in lat. 56 N [*sic* – 46° N], long. 40 W. When taken on board the Nor, Captain Andrews was in a very exhausted state but soon recovered.

### The New York Times

### 12th September 1888

### Picked Up In Mid-ocean

### The Dark Secret and Her Captain Home Again

*Contrary Winds, Unfortunate Accidents, and a Big Sea Serpent Cause Capt. Andrew's Failure*

Early yesterday morning the Norwegian bark Nor dropped anchor off Stapleton, Staten Island, after a two months' voyage from Aarhus, Denmark, and Capt. William A. Andrews, the foolhardy skipper who set out to cross the Atlantic on June 18 last in a little dory called the Dark Secret, came ashore and up to the city. He was picked up in about mid-ocean on Sunday, Aug. 19, by Capt. Bjonness in latitude 46° [N] and west longitude 39° 50' in rather an exhausted condition; but the last month's good living on board the bark had recuperated him, and he looked as healthy as could be yesterday…

He met with very little really bad weather on his two months' trip, but was delayed greatly by contrary winds and hampered by any number of minor accidents. His alcohol stove was filled with water and ruined when he was but a short way out, and he was unable to heat anything the remainder of the voyage. The drag [sea anchor] that he threw overboard while he slept, to keep his boat head on to the seas, broke lose in a gale and a small anchor that he used for a substitute followed its example, so that for over a month he got little or no rest, being afraid to go to sleep with nothing to steady his craft. A little machine that he took along to throw oil over the bow and take the edge off of the oncoming waves broke on its first trial, and it was only the greatest of good fortune that prevented his boat being swamped by the massive rollers that broke over him on several occasions.

Capt. Bjonness said that when he first sighted the dingy little sail of the dory he thought it a boat from some wreck, and hove to wait for it to come up. When he found out who its navigator was he invited him to dinner, which was just ready. Andrews went on board with, as Capt. Bjonness graphically expressed it, the waistband of his trousers seven inches too wide for him, and would have fallen to the deck had not one of the sailors supported him.

His cheeks were sunken, his hair and beard long and matted, his hands roughened like graters with the salt water, his oilskins ragged and torn, and two big holes in the sides of his sea boots, made by continually rubbing against the thwarts. He first spoke as if he intended to go on with his trip, but the bounteous warm dinner changed his mind and so nicely filled up the seven-inch hiatus that he became the bark's passenger without much ado.

The Dark Secret was hoisted on board and its bottom was found to be completely covered with barnacles and sea grass. It lay yesterday athwartships on the poop deck, with its spars in the [*Nor's*] long boat. It is more of a whaleboat than a dory, with a 6-inch keel projecting from the garboard strake and an iron shoe attached to that. It is about 15 feet long, 5 feet wide, and 2 ½ feet deep, and almost entirely decked over. It seemed little damaged by the knocking about it had received. Capt. Andrews gave as his reasons for stopping when but half way through his voyage that he was short of water and pork and worn out from want of sleep, but one of the crew of the "Nor", a stalwart, blonde-bearded, blue-eyed Norwegian, named Jans Carlsen, told a rather different story.

"Cjaptain Andjrews," said he, "cjame willingjly onj boarjd, because hej wasj frightjened byj the seaj serpjent." The rest of his tale, with the redundancy of Norwegian orthography eliminated, is to this effect: "Captain Andrews told me that at 10 o'clock in the morning of Wednesday, Aug. 15, four days before we sighted him, as he was in latitude 45° 10' and west longitude 41° 20', merely drifting along, he saw less than a hundred yards to leeward the head and neck of an enormous brown sea serpent, projected at an angle of 10 degrees above the water and going at the rate of three knots an hour. The sea was perfectly smooth, and through it the monster swished, leaving a long wake of tumbling foam behind.

The portion of him visible was about six feet, but it was impossible to estimate his entire length. The snake kept his eyes straight ahead of him and the little boat and its trembling occupant escaped his notice, but the 15 minutes during which his snakeship kept in sight were by long odds the worst in Capt. Andrew's experience, and he made up his mind that, come what would, he would board the next vessel he met, and he accordingly came back with us."

[Another solo voyager, Howard Blackburn, also reported seeing a "sea-serpent", during his 1901 transatlantic passage in the Great Republic – see **The Legendary Howard Blackburn**, below.]

## TRANSATLANTIC RACE

Capt. Andrews made a second single-handed attempt on the Atlantic three years later in 1891, in a slightly bigger boat named the *Mermaid*, 15ft long and sloop-rigged. Another American sailor, Josiah W. (Si) Lawlor, upon hearing about Andrews' project, decided to compete against him with his own 15ft boat *Sea Serpent*, spritsail-rigged and with a bowsprit. (Lawlor must almost certainly have named his boat *Sea Serpent* in mock imitation of his nemesis Andrews' reported encounter with a 'sea serpent' in *Dark Secret* in 1888.) Andrews and Lawlor set out from Boston on the same day, 21 June 1891. Andrews expected to complete the crossing in 50 days. After the boat capsized on 21 August, he and his little craft were picked up the next day by a passing steamship, the *Ebruz*, bound for Antwerp. He had been at sea for two months and was just 600 miles short of his destination. Lawlor and his *Sea Serpent*, meanwhile, had arrived at Coverack, on the Lizard peninsula in Cornwall, on 5 August after a voyage of 45 days.

## SAPOLIO

The plucky Capt. Andrews made yet another solo attempt on the Atlantic in a small boat in the summer of 1892. His 14ft 6ins *Sapolio* (named for a brand of soap made by his sponsor) was a fold-up boat with canvas deck. He set sail from Atlantic City, New Jersey, on 21 July 1892. By 20 August he was at the Azores where he eventually received a warm welcome and made repairs to his boat. (His first contact there, a coastguard, threatened him with a rifle.) Departing from the Azores on 29 July, Capt. Andrews reached the coast of southwest Spain on 24 September after a solo transatlantic voyage of 65 days in the then smallest boat ever to make the voyage. The voyage was later described by Andrews in his book *Columbus Outdone* (1893). (In the same summer, Si Lawlor, in his 14ft 6ins *Christopher Columbus*, raced for a second time against Andrews to make the fastest transatlantic passage in a small boat. Lawlor, who set out well before Andrews, was never heard from again, presumed lost at sea.)

## PHANTOM SHIP

Capt. Andrews made three more attempts to cross the Atlantic in small boats. On 24 August 1898 he embarked in his 13ft *Phantom Ship*, but after a stormy 27 days, both he and his boat were picked up by a passing ship as Andrews abandoned the crossing.

*25 Aug 1898*

**Across the Atlantic in a Thirteen-foot Boat.-**

> On Wednesday [17th August] Captain William Andrews started from Atlantic City (New Jersey) for London in a small sailing boat, called the Phantom Ship, and expects to arrive in 60 days. His boat, which is painted blue, is 13 feet 5 inches long, 5 feet 4 inches beam, and 22 inches deep, and has a lead keel weighing 350 lb. The boat is so constructed that it can be folded up to facilitate conveyance when ashore. Its sails measure 15 square yards. The water supply is carried in bottles, and Andrews has on board food enough to last him for three months. He is making the voyage quite alone, and has already accomplished four similar trips successfully. [In fact although Capt. Andrews had already *attempted* four trans-Atlantic voyages, he only completed two successfully, the first, in 1878, with his brother Asa.]

*17 Sept 1898*

**Maritime Intelligence**

**Miscellaneous**

> Rotterdam, Sept. 15.- Captain Morgan, of the steamer Robert Adamson, from Galveston, reports that on Aug. 20, in lat. 38 23 N, long. 69 12 W, he passed an open boat under sail, steering east. The occupant stated that he was going to Paris, and was all right and required

nothing. Captain Morgan supposes [believes] that the occupant was Captain Andrews with his boat the Phantom Ship, which left Atlantic City for Europe a few days previous.

### 25 Oct 1898
**Maritime Intelligence**

St. Pierre, Miq. [St. Pierre & Miquelon islands, off Newfoundland], Oct. 8.- The master, Grandais, of the Josephine, from Port de Bouc [near Marseilles, France], reports that during the voyage he encountered a skiff, the occupant of which asked him in what latitude he was. He had left New York 35 days previously, and was going to Paris, and did not need anything.

Assuming the 'skiff' encountered by the *Josephine*, was the *Phantom Ship*, the date of their meeting must have been around 21 September, five weeks into Capt. Andrews' voyage which he abandoned shortly after.

On 13 June the following year, he departed on his sixth Atlantic voyage, bound for the Azores, in the 12ft-long fold-up craft *Doree* (which was actually the same *Phantom Ship* from his 1898 attempted crossing, but shortened in length). Two weeks after departing from New York he was spoken by an eastward-bound steamship, the *Bremerhaven*:

### 15 July 1899

Antwerp, July 14.- The Bermerhaven (s), arrived to-day from New York, reports:- On July 1, in lat. 40 12 N, long. 63 30 W, about 482 miles from New York, spoke the small boat Doree, Anderson [*sic*], which left New York June 17, bound for London. The wind was light from the SW, with smooth waters, so that the Doree was making a fair wind of it.

Andrews might have been "making a fair wind of it", but he had only averaged about 35 miles a day since leaving New York when he was spoken by the *Bremerhaven*. A few weeks later he was forced to abandon that voyage, too. He was picked up by another eastward-bound steamship, the *Holbein,* which landed him at Liverpool. His boat was left adrift.

### 17 July 1899

London, July 17.- Captain Andrew [*sic*], who attempted to cross the Atlantic in a 12 ft canvas boat, was picked up in an exhausted state, about 700 miles out from Land, by the Holbein (s), which arrived in the Mersey [Liverpool] yesterday from New York. His boat was left adrift at sea.

After a few years ashore back home in the United States, Capt. Andrews embarked upon his seventh and final transatlantic escapade. In the summer of 1901 he sailed from Atlantic City bound for Spain with his new wife aboard, in a 20ft-long dory, the *Flying Dutchman*. Apart from speaking a westbound steamship, the *Durango*, about a week into the voyage, which reported that Mrs Andrews was ill, the indomitable Capt. Andrews was never heard from again.

## THE LEGENDARY HOWARD BLACKBURN

### 30 June 1903

**Alone on the Atlantic**.- A telegram from Halifax (N.S.) says that Captain Blackburn* has again set out to cross the Atlantic to France in a 16-foot open dory. One of his legs is badly swollen. Captain Blackburn says that he will keep close to the Nova Scotia coast as long as he can, if the weather keeps clear, in case he should require medical assistance. If not, he will keep a southerly course. He is confident of success, having crossed the Atlantic twice before. If successful, Captain Blackburn will cruise in the Mediterranean.

* Howard Blackburn was born 17 February 1879 near Port Medway, Nova Scotia. He started his seafaring life on a square-rigger to Madeira in 1872, but his fame and renown around the Yankee and Canadian maritime fishing ports came from a voyage he made on a Gloucester, Massachusetts halibut fishing schooner, the *Grace L. Fears*, in the winter of 1883. Fishing in their dory on the Burgeo Bank off the south coast of Newfoundland in January that year, Blackburn and his shipmate Tom Welch, a Newfoundlander, became separated from the *Fears* when a gale sprang up that turned into a violent storm.

For four days Blackburn rowed in the stormy icy seas and blizzard conditions to reach land. Welch died from exposure on the third day. Blackburn made landfall late on the fourth day, on the south coast of Newfoundland where he stayed the night in a deserted fishermen's hut. Two days later, rowing along the coast with the dead body of Tom Welch still in the stern of the dory, Blackburn reached the impoverished fishing settlement of Little River, 25 miles east of the town of Burgeo. There, at their small cabin, the Lishman family tended to Blackburn who was severely frostbitten and weakened by exposure and hunger. No-one really expected him to survive – except Blackburn himself.

And he did survive – but at a cost: after gangrene set in during the two months he was in the Lishman's cabin, Blackburn lost all the fingers of both his hands, half of each thumb, two toes from his left foot and three toes and the heel of his right foot. After he returned to Gloucester, where he set up a cigar and tobacco store, Blackburn had to have his remaining toes amputated. His hands were stumps with minimal vestiges of thumbs by which he learned to manipulate things.

The story of Howard Blackburn's survival as a castaway dory fisherman in January 1883 made him a legend amongst the deep-sea fishing communities of the northeast states and maritime Canada. After a failed expedition in 1897–98 to the Klondike to prospect for gold in Alaska, Blackburn set out on a new adventure in 1899 to sail the Atlantic alone. He commissioned a small Gloucester sloop to be built, 30ft-long and displacing just under 5 tons, which he called the *Great Western*. Blackburn sailed her solo across the Atlantic, departing from Gloucester, Massachusetts on Sunday 18 June and docking at Gloucester, England on 18 August after a passage of 62 days.

Two years later, Blackburn crossed the Atlantic again on a solo voyage in his 25ft-long sloop *Great Republic*. From Gloucester he completed the voyage to Lisbon, Portugal between 9 June and 18 July 1901. The 39-day nonstop passage across the Atlantic by a single-hander was a record that stood until 1939 when Francis Clark sailed his 30ft *Girl Kathleen* single-handed from New York to England in 33 days. Blackburn sent the *Great Republic* back by steamship. He arrived back in Gloucester on 19 August 1901.

During the voyage in his *Great Republic* Blackburn witnessed a curious but not altogether singular phenomenon:

"July 1, 4 P.M. While sitting on the wheelbox steering, boat making about three miles an hour, suddenly I saw something just abaft the starboard beam lashing the water into foam. I stood up and saw what looked like a coil of very large rope. I hove the wheel down and trimmed the sheets in sharp by the wind. The boat would not fetch it on that tack, but passed within 35 or 40 feet to the leeward of it.

As I draw near I could see that it looked like a large snake, but had a tail more like an eel. It was fully 12 to 15 feet in length. It was holding in its mouth either a small turtle or a good-sized fish, with which it was lashing the water into foam. Its head moved so rapidly from side to side that I could not tell its shape, but am inclined to think it resembled that of a serpent. The tail and parts of the body that I could see plainly appeared to be smooth and of a light lead color…It must have been a baby sea-serpent." (from Joseph Garland's biography of Howard Blackburn, *Lone Voyager*)

This was interesting not just because Blackburn saw a 'sea-serpent'. It was interesting because it was not a singular event: Capt. William Andrews had reported seeing a sea serpent during his failed attempt to cross the Atlantic in his small *Dark Secret* in the summer of 1888. Capt. Andrews' beast was very similar in appearance to what Blackburn witnessed in the *Great Republic*. (see **Small Boat Voyagers: The Indomitable Capt. Andrews**)

Blackburn's next attempt on the Atlantic was in a traditional sailing dory that he commissioned to be built at Swampscott, Massachusetts. He named this boat the *Atlantic*. It was just 16ft 9ins and decked over for most of its length. This was the boat, and the voyage, to which the 'telegram from Halifax', above, referred. Blackburn intended to sail the *Atlantic* to Le Havre and then down through the inland waterways of France to the Mediterranean. From Gibraltar he planned to sail back across the Atlantic via Madeira and the Caribbean, and then up the Mississippi to St. Louis, Missouri. At St. Louis he aimed to 'place himself and his boat at the disposal of the Louisiana Purchase Exposition'. (*Lone Voyager*)

Blackburn set off from Gloucester on 7 June 1903. After a month of keeping close to the Nova Scotia coast, storms, high seas, cold and, not least, arthritis in his legs forced him to abandon the attempt. On 8 July the little *Atlantic* arrived at Louisburg on Cape Breton Island from where Blackburn wrote home, 'I did my best, but luck has been against me from the start. A polar bear could not stand such hardships much longer'. (*Lone Voyager*) Back home at Gloucester he settled into running his saloon bar business although not without certain adventures and complications arising from the Prohibition years in the United Sates) and enjoying life as a local legend.

Capt. Howard Blackburn died on 4 November 1932, aged 73 years – minus all of the digits lost to his legendary survival in an open dory in the winter of 1883, but with his stature intact as a legendary seaman and sailor, and lone voyager in small boats in the closing years of the 19th century.

## Almost – But Not Quite…

## 30 Aug 1886

### Maritime Intelligence

Ocean.- London, Aug. 30.- The tug Red Rose, captain Martin, while cruising in the Channel, spoke the barque Mary Graham, off Portland, bound from Quebec for Newcastle, which gave her the following report:-

"On Aug. 11, two men named Anderson and Christensen*, who sailed in a small boat, the Ocean, from Norway, on a voyage to Newfoundland some time back, were taken on board in lat. 49 20 N, long 46 W, with boat and everything belonging to them. The cause for their not finishing the voyage was that they were low spirited after losing most of their clothes and provisions, and all the life tanks but one leaking. On Aug. 5, in a heavy gale from WNW, the boat was turned over and left full of water for 30 hours, the sea being too high to get her bailed out."

*In the spring of 1886 H.P.M. Anderson and C.C. Christensen left Christiana in Oslo, Norway, to sail a 19ft-long open boat, the *Ocean*, across the Atlantic against the prevailing westerly winds and weather, for Newfoundland. Stopping on the way at the Edinburgh port of Leith and then Glasgow, their last landfall was at the northernmost point of mainland Ireland, the Lloyd's Signal Station at Malin Head, which reported their passing.

After sailing something over 2,000 miles, the two men abandoned their voyage after their small vessel capsized in a gale around 350 miles short of their destination.

## *HOMEWARD BOUND*: CAPE TOWN TO ENGLAND IN 250 DAYS

### 8 Dec 1886

**Maritime Intelligence**

Homeward Bound (cutter).- London, Dec. 8.- It is feared from information to hand by the Union Company's steamer Pretoria, Captain H. Owen, which arrived at Plymouth yesterday, that the small cutter named the Homeward Bound, from Natal for England, has been capsized in the Bay of Biscay. The Homeward Bound arrived at St. Helena on Aug. 20, then 30 days out from Cape Town. The crew were in good health, and the little craft proceeded on her voyage three days later. She passed Ascension [Island] on Sept. 2 and wished to be reported all well. The crew then anticipated reaching London before the end of September.* Nothing has been seen or heard of the little cutter since.

The Pretoria, however, reported that the Union Company's steamship Mexican, which arrived at the Cape a few days before the Pretoria sailed, passed a small craft bottom up in the Bay of Biscay, and this is believed to be the Homeward Bound.

### *23 Dec 1886*

**Maritime Intelligence**

Homeward Bound.- Baltimore, Dec. 22.- A steamer which has arrived here reports having spoken on the 15th inst., 300 miles south of the Azores, a small boat called the Homeward Bound, with a crew of only two men, bound from the Cape for England. Both of the occupants of the boat were well.

* The little cutter *Homeward Bound* took 30 days to sail from Cape Town to St. Helena. From their next point of contact at Ascension Island the crew expected to reach London in less than a month, although the distance from Ascension to England was considerably more than twice the distance from Cape Town to St. Helena. The steamship *Mexican* would have sighted the small capsized boat in the Bay of Biscay in late October or early November. However, the steamship at Baltimore encountered the *Homeward Bound* on 15 December, indicating that the capsized boat in the Bay of Biscay was not the *Homeward Bound*.

In fact, the *Homeward Bound*, with just two crew and commanded by Capt. Nelson, put in to Sao Miguel, Azores, towards the end of December 1886 and departed on 3 January 1887. On 7 February 1887, in lat. 43 N, long. 10 W, off the northwest coast of Spain, the Castle Line steamship *Garth Castle* on her voyage to England spoke the *Homeward Bound* and, at Plymouth, reported her 201 days out from "Cape of Good Hope to England…all well".

On 28 March 1887 *Homeward Bound* finally arrived at Dover. *Lloyd's List* reported on that date: "The small Norwegian sailing boat Homeward Bound, 10 months [*sic* – 8.3 months] from Cape Town, has put into Dover Harbour".

## ROWING THE ATLANTIC

### 29 July 1896
**Maritime Intelligence**

**Miscellaneous**

Swansea, July 28.- The master of the Eugen, from Halifax (N.S.), arrived here, reports:- On July 24, in lat. 49 35 N, long 14 41 W, passed the small open boat Fox*, from New York for Havre, with two men on board rowing across the Atlantic. They were supplied with provisions, and hoped to reach the Land's End in 10 or 12 days.

### *1 Aug 1896*
**Rowing Across the Atlantic**

A telegram received to-day from Scilly states:- "The eighteen feet rowing boat Fox arrived here at 11 a.m. from New York, having on board Messrs. Harbo and Samuelson, 55 days passage, in good health but rather exhausted, having rowed the whole distance. They spoke the Norwegian barque Sito [*sic* – Cito], July 15, in lat. 47 10 N, long. 31 20 W, and Norwegian barque Eugenie, July 24, 400 miles west of Scilly, the masters of which examined the boat and certified that no other propelling power than the oars were in the boat.

### *8 Aug 1896*
**Row Across the Atlantic**

Paris, Aug. 7

A rowing boat of about six metres long, named the Fox, manned by two Norwegians, George D. Ulon [*sic* – Harbo], 31 years of age, and Frank D. Samuelson, 36, reached Havre this morning from New York. According to the information given by the two daring navigators, they left New York on June 6, and consequently crossed the Atlantic in 62 days. They had taken seven pairs of oars, and they each rowed alternately three hours at a spell. On the 7th, 8th and 9th of July, they encountered very rough weather, and on the 10th the sea ran so high that it capsized the boat. The intrepid travelers declare that it was only with great effort that they succeeded in righting it.

On July 15 they had been without any sort of food or drink for 12 hours, when they fell in with the Norwegian sailing vessel, the Cito, which furnished them with provisions. As they are completely penniless, they intend to exhibit themselves with their boat, first at Havre, and then at Rouen and Paris. They hope in this way to obtain enough money to pay their passage back to New York.

* George Harbo (1864–1908) and Frank Samuelson (1870–1946) emigrated from Norway to the United States in the 1870s. They each settled on the New Jersey shore where they met and subsequently worked together harvesting clams. Harbo proposed that they do something to make a name for themselves – such as rowing the Atlantic in a small boat. (Both were accomplished in using surf boats in their clamming business. Samuelson had also been a sailor in the merchant marine before he went to the United States.)

They put the idea to the owner of the *Police Gazette*, an Irish-American emigrant, boxing promoter and entrepreneur named Richard K. Fox, who supported the project financially. Harbo and Samuelson named their boat the *Fox* in honour of their supporter. The *Fox* was built by a local New Jersey boatbuilder named William Seaman and his Seaman Sea Skiffs enterprise. It was a surf boat 18ft 4ins long, 5ft wide and double-ended. It had watertight compartments and rails along the keel to right the boat if it capsized.

Harbo and Samuelson set out on their epic row across the Atlantic from the Battery in New York City on Saturday 6 June 1896. They took turns rowing and covered an average of around 50 miles a day, although their best day's row was 135 miles on 11 July. On 10 July the boat capsized in heavy seas. Although Harbo and Samuelson righted her quite quickly, they lost some provisions. On 15 July they met (and had dinner aboard) the Norwegian barque *Cito* which gave them water and provisions. They met another Norwegian barque, the *Eugen*, on 24 July. A week later they made landfall at the Isles of Scilly off Land's End, the southwestern-most point of England. Proceeding up the English Channel and along the south coast of England, they arrived at the French port of Le Havre on Friday 7 August.

Harbo and Samuelson's 3,250 miles transatlantic row from New York to the Isles of Scilly took just 55 days. It was not only the first crossing of the Atlantic by rowing power alone; the time taken remains a record for rowing the Atlantic from west to east, which, considering the sophisticated technology used today to built such boats, is a remarkable accomplishment. A comparison of selected west to east Atlantic crossings by rowers in more recent times is shown below (duration rounded up to the nearest day).

| 1980 | Gerard d'Aboville | Cape Cod – Brest | 2,735 miles | 72 days |
|------|-------------------|------------------|-------------|---------|
| 1987 | Tom McClean | Newfoundland – Scilly | 1,732 miles | 55 days |
| 1987 | Don Allum | Newfoundland – Ireland | 1,720 miles | 76 days |
| 2002 | Emmanuel Coindre | Cape Cod – Ushant | 4,545 miles | 87 days |
| 2004 | Emmanuel Coindre | Cape Cod – Ushant | 3,387 miles | 63 days |
| | Anne QuemereCape | Cod – Ushant | 4,065 miles | 87 days |
| 2005 | G. Groeneveld | New Jersey – Bishop's Rock | n/a | 61 days |
| | R. Hoeve | | | |
| | J. Koomen | | | |
| 2006 | B. Vickers | New Jersey – Bishop's Rock | 3,290 miles | 71 days |
| | D. Le Valley | | | |
| | G. Spooner | | | |
| | J. Hanssen | | | |

The modern-day record of a west to east Atlantic row of 60 days 16 hours 19 mins, was set by the Dutch trio of Groeneveld, Hoeve and Koomen in 2005 – but it was still five days longer than the crossing by Harbo and Samuelson in their 18-ft long surf boat the *Fox* in the summer of 1896.

## Capt. Joshua Slocum

### 30 Sept 1896

**Maritime Intelligence**

**Miscellaneous**

London, Sept. 30.- Our Melbourne correspondent telegraphs that the 13-ton yacht Spray, the only occupant of which was Captain Slocum*, has arrived at Newcastle (N.S.W.). Captain Slocum left Boston in April, 1895, and sailed for Gibraltar and thence to South America and through the Straits of Magellan.

* Joshua Slocum was the first and most famous man to sail single-handed around the world. He left Boston, Massachusetts on the morning of 24 April 1895 at the helm of his gaff-rigged sloop *Spray*, and returned on 27 June 1898 'after the cruise of more than forty-six thousand miles round the world, during an absence of three years and two months, with two days over for coming up'. (From *Sailing Alone Around the World*, by Captain Joshua Slocum.) His return home was recorded as:

*29 June 1898*

**Maritime Intelligence**

**Miscellaneous**

Newport, Rhode Island, June 28.- The 12-ton 39-feet yawl Spray arrived here yesterday, completing Captain Slocum's record voyage unaccompanied round the world. He left Boston on April 24, 1895.

Slocum was born at North Mountain, Nova Scotia, overlooking the Bay of Fundy, on 20 February 1844 and he later became a naturalised American citizen. On 14 November 1909 at the age of 65, he sailed from Martha's Vineyard bound for the Caribbean and South America, single-handed once again at the helm of the *Spray*. He was never heard from again, presumed lost at sea.

## The Unknown *Flying Dutchman* Sailor

### 18 July 1893

**Miscellaneous**

New York, July 7.- Corono (s), arrived here yesterday from Bremen, reports 4th, 1 p.m., stopped the engine for a small boat under sail, named the Flying Dutchman, with one man in it.* Supplied him with some water and petroleum, also with a piece of canvas for a sea anchor, as he had lost his sea anchor in a gale some days ago. He was on the voyage to Amsterdam; his position at the time was lat. 42 N, long. 63 W.

*21 July 1893*

**Ships Spoken**

Flying Dutchman, Shelburne [Nova Scotia] to Amsterdam, all well, July 5, 160 miles SE by E of Shelburne 16 days, reported from New York.

*7 Aug 1893*

**Miscellaneous**

London, Aug. 7.- Steamer Schiehallion, arrived at Dartmouth Saturday, reports, July 25, in lat. 41 34 N, long. 52 32 W, passed the small flat-bottomed boat Flying Dutchman, with one man in it, about 620 miles out from Shelborne (N.S.), bound for Amsterdam. The Schiehallion supplied him with provisions.

*18 Aug 1893*

**Ships Spoken**

Flying Dutchman boat, Shelburne (N.S.) to England, July 29, lat. 43 N, long. 47 W, by L'Oriflamme (s), at Philadelphia.

* After the report by the *L'Oriflamme* at Philadelphia, nothing more was heard about this lone small boat voyager. The man had set out from Shelburne, on the southeast coast of Nova Scotia, around 20 June 1893. Judging by the reports of ships that came across him, his progress was slow. His boat, described as 'flat-bottomed', was probably not suited to anything more than relatively kindly sea conditions, especially not for a long voyage, and certainly not for the potentially boisterous North Atlantic even in summer.

Two hurricanes (No. 3 and No. 5 of the 1893 hurricane season) curved up and out into the North Atlantic in the second half of August and early September into the approximate area the *Flying Dutchman* would probably have been. It is reasonable to assume that this single-handed sailor and his small boat were ultimately overwhelmed by violent weather, either from hurricane or storm force winds, or, simply by any severe gale they might have encountered. There was no record of the boat and its occupant reaching the other side of the Atlantic.

## Ludwig Eisenbraun and *Columbia II*

6 Oct 1903

**Maritime Intelligence**

**Miscellaneous**

Liverpool, Oct. 6.- Captain of Gulf Transport liner Ikbal, which arrived Galveston from Liverpool, Sept. 20, reports as follows:- Spoke on Sept. 10, in lat 39 62 [N], long 54 05 [W], the 20-foot decked boat Columbia II (cutter rigged), Captain Isen Brown [sic – Eisenbraun], 14 days out from Halifax, N.S, bound Marseilles, via Western Islands [Azores]. Captain Brown reports being capsized on Sunday, 6th inst., but managed to right his boat; rudder and sails damaged, which he repaired, but he lost his watch, the only timepiece aboard, and asked if we could replace it. The chief officer gave him a watch set to Greenwich time, and, requiring neither water nor provisions, he proceeded east with a fair wind and fine weather.*

**19 Oct 1903**

**Maritime Intelligence**

**Miscellaneous**

London, Oct 19.- The Etruria (s) brings intelligence that British steamer Greenbrier, from Manchester for Kingston (Ja.), spoke the small sailing boat Columbia II, from Boston for Marseilles, in lat 37 21 N, long 42 45 W, and supplied Capt. Brown [sic] with provisions.

* Ludwig Eisenbraun, captain of the "20-foot decked boat Columbia II (cutter rigged)", above, gave an interview to *Wide World Magazine* after completing his transatlantic voyage. In the published article (September 1904, pages 463–468)), he gave his reason and the background for making the voyage:

"The sailing-boat which you have just seen was built, not for me, but for a wealthy Portuguese gentleman living in Boston, who, one fine day, thought it would be a grand feat to make a trip across the Atlantic to Europe in a small craft. Accordingly he set off on board the Columbia II, which had been specially constructed for the cruise. After sailing for some time, however, he came to the conclusion that it would be much more comfortable – and much more safe – to pay his visit to Europe in the ordinary way, on a big liner. The sea was apt to become rough, and at such times the tiny boat had a nasty habit of shipping water, and he feared that he would never get any sleep – unless it were the sleep that knows no waking. So he put about and was back in Boston in a little more than twenty-four hours after starting out. He declared that to have persevered in his undertaking would have been certain death…

For the next fortnight the papers referred to it in interviews and articles, and it formed the chief topic of conversation at the nautical club of which both the Portuguese gentleman and myself are members. One evening, when I happened to be present in the club-room, the owner of the Columbia II made his usual statement that the voyage to Europe in so small a boat was impossible. He defied anyone to do it, he said. Feeling sufficiently experienced in the handling of small yachts in rough weather to prove that he was in the wrong, I accepted his challenge. The Columbia II changed hands, and I commenced my preparations for the long voyage across the Atlantic."

Eisenbraun, German-born but a naturalised American citizen aged 35, set off from Boston "exactly at ten o'clock in the morning on August 11th, 1903 in the presence of more than twenty thousand people, the majority of whom, I have no doubt, never expected to see me again". Before starting the transatlantic passage, Capt. Eisenbraun put in to Halifax, Nova Scotia for 24 hours to reprovision his fresh water supply. Fifty-six days later *Columbia II* arrived at Madeira on 20 October 1903. From there Capt. Eisenbraun sailed to Gibraltar and then made his way along the Spanish coast, touching at Malaga on 28 November, Almunécar on 8 December, Cartagena on 28 December, Barcelona on 19 January 1904 and Port Vendres near the French border on 12 February. On 12 March 1904 he reached his original intended destination of Marseilles.

Eisenbraun related how, on 5 September in mid-Atlantic, *Columbia II* was capsized by a sudden squall, sending its lone occupant tumbling into the water although Capt. Eisenbraun soon righted his little craft and continued steadfastly on his way. His 'most thrilling adventure', happened "one beautiful moonlight night", when he was awoken by the thump of his boat bumping into a whale "sleeping on the surface of the water". The whale flicked his tail and disappeared into the depths. "I made a note of the exact spot where this exciting incident occurred – 13° 40' longitude [W], 34° 50' latitude [N]", which was just to the northeast of Madeira and presumably on his passage from there to Gibraltar.

Capt. Eisenbraun claimed that the 56 days he was "on the water" was "a record, if I am not mistaken". In this, however, he was mistaken: Josiah Lawlor had made a solo crossing in his 15ft *Sea Serpent*, from Boston to England in 45 days in 1891; and Howard Blackburn had sailed his 25ft *Great Republic* from Gloucester, Massachusetts to Lisbon in 39 days in 1901. Still, Capt. Eisenbraun's single-handed crossing of the Atlantic in 56 days in *Columbia II* in 1903 was the third fastest time to that date. Like others who had gone before him, he encountered "gale after gale, tempest after tempest", such that "I sometimes feared I should have to abandon my attempt and go aboard the first steamer I happened to meet".

Capt. Eisenbraun met only "two English steamers" during the crossing [*Etruria* and *Greenbrier*], "both of which kindly offered to take me on board or assist me in any other way in their power". The plucky lone voyager accepted assistance only in the form of "some provisions" from the *Greenbrier* and a watch from the *Etruria* to replace the one he had lost. As for the travails of the voyage, he felt well compensated for them by his arrivals at ports along the way towards his final destination of Marseilles: "The reception that I received there [Madeira] well repaid me for the hardships I had undergone on my solitary journey. The people were most enthusiastic, as, indeed, they were in all the other ports at which I afterwards touched, and many were the calls upon my time".

## EXPLORATION AND EXPEDITIONS

The 19th century also spawned a great enthusiasm for explorers to venture to the farthest points of the Earth: first to the Arctic towards the North Pole, and later to Antarctica and the South Pole. Arctic and Antarctic expeditions sometimes returned with valuable new information about those hostile regions. More often than not, however, they resulted in tragic loss of life and sometimes little or no trace of their fate. The ones who returned alive, and those who went to their rescue, are the sources for their narratives here.

## NARRATIVES

## CAPTAIN HALL'S *POLARIS* ARCTIC EXPEDITION

# 13 May 1873
### Casualties – Foreign

Washington, 10th May.- The Government has received news from the American Arctic Expedition*. Captain Tyson reports that the ship Polaris reached lat. 82.16 N, in Oct., 1871. Captain Hall had died of apoplexy. The ship left her winter quarters on the 12th Aug., 1872. She broke away, leaving part of her crew in the ice-fields on the 15th Oct. They were found on floating ice, and picked up last Apl., by the *Tigress*, after undergoing great suffering. It is supposed [thought] that the *Polaris* is safe.

## THE AMERICAN ARCTIC EXPEDITION

(From the *Times* of 12th May 1873)

New York, 11th May.- A steamer has arrived at Robert's bay, Newfoundland, bringing twelve men, two women, and five children, belonging to Captain Hall's Arctic exploring ship *Polaris*, which left this port in June, 1871. They were picked up in an open boat forty miles from the Labrador coast, in latitude 55° 30' N. The *Polaris* went through Smith's sound in the summer of 1871 to latitude 82° 16' N. Captain Hall made a sledge journey to the supposed open Polar sea of Dr. Kane, and found it to be a strait fifteen miles wide, but apparently open water beyond. Captain Hall died in November, 1871, it is said of apoplexy.

In August, 1872, the ship being beset and under heavy pressure, in latitude 77° 35' N, commenced landing provisions, when the ice broke up, and those at work on it were carried away. They drifted southward on the ice for one hundred and ninety six days. The ice, originally five miles in circumference, was gradually reduced to a few rods [1 rod = 5 meters/16.5 ft]. They then took to the only remaining boat. The *Polaris* had not been seen since the separation. She had thirteen of her crew left, under Captain Boddington [*sic*], and plenty of provisions, but no boats. It is suspected that the rescued party are deserters, and doubts are expressed respecting the manner of Captain Hall's death.

*26 June 1873*

**The United States Polar Expedition**

New York, 24th June.- The United States steamer *Juniata* has sailed in search of the *Polaris*.

*12 Sept 1873*

**American Arctic Expedition**

New York, 11th Sept.- The *Polaris* has been abandoned and sunk; the remainder of the crew are believed to be safe.

## 13 Sept 1873

**American Arctic Expedition**

St. John's, 11th Sept.- The *Juniata* has arrived here, and reports that the camp of the crew of the *Polaris* was discovered by the *Tigress* on the 14th Aug. at Littleton island, where the ship was deserted. Manuscript records of the expedition up to a period of six weeks before the discovery, were secured. The *Tigress* is still in search of the Buddington party.

* The American Arctic Expedition of 1871–73 was led by Charles Francis Hall (1821–1871), a New Englander who had made two polar expeditions before in 1860–63 and 1864–69. Hall embarked on his first two expeditions to look for evidence of the fate of Sir John Franklin's expedition to the Arctic in 1845–47, in search of the Northwest Passage, in the two ships *Erebus* and *Terror*. Franklin died in June 1847 and it was presumed, although without material evidence, that the rest of the expedition members had also died. Although Hall found artefacts from Franklin's expedition, he found nothing about the actual fate of the expedition members. However, he gained experience of conditions in the high Arctic as well as making invaluable contacts amongst the native Inuit people.

Hall's third Arctic expedition was supported by a US Government grant of $50,000 (augmented by another $50,000 to refurbish and outfit the expedition vessel, *Polaris*) and aimed to reach the North Pole in the *Polaris*. In 1865 Hall had stated his ambition, writing: "I never will be satisfied in voyaging and travelling in the Arctic regions until I shall reach that spot of this great and glorious orb of God's creation where there is no North, no East, no West. Of course that mundane point is the one nearly under [the pole star] Polaris".

The expedition party left New York on 29 June 1871 comprising 25 officers, crew and scientists, including Capt. Sidney Budington as sailing master, George Tyson, assistant navigator, and Dr. Emil Bessels, head of the scientific staff. Hall also brought an Inuit interpreter and hunter named Ebierbing with his wife and child, whom he had met and befriended on his earlier expeditions. Later in the voyage they picked up a Greenland Inuit hunter and interpreter, Hans Hendrik, plus his wife and three children.

On 2 September 1871 the expedition reached its northernmost point, at lat. 82° 29' N. A week or so later they settled in to spend the winter at a place that Hall named Thank God Harbour on the shore of northwest Greenland. On 10 October Hall set out with a sledging party to attempt to beat Sir William Parry's record for reaching the highest northern latitude [82° 45' N], in 1827. He returned to the ship two weeks later without success. That same day, after drinking a cup of coffee on the ship, Hall became ill. Over the following two weeks he was treated by the expedition doctor Emil Bessels. Finally, at 3.25 a.m. on 8 November 1871, Hall died apparently of 'apoplexy' (meaning a heart attack, stroke or some similar malady). On 10 November he was buried on shore in the semi-frozen Greenland tundra. Buddington took command of the expedition.

By around July 1872 the expedition had abandoned its aim of reaching the North Pole and was headed south for home. However, on 15 October 1872, the *Polaris* ran aground on a shallow iceberg and began taking in water. Some of the crew, including (fortunately, as it turned out) all the Inuit, took to the surrounding ice. The floe they were on drifted away from the *Polaris*, stranding the men on the ice as castaways. The Inuit built an igloo shelter and they had almost a tonne of food. For the next six months the castaways drifted south, moving from floe to floe and kept alive by seals killed by the skilled Inuit hunters. On 30 April 1873 they were rescued by the sealing vessel *Tigress* off the Newfoundland coast.

The *Polaris*, in the meantime, with 14 men on board, had run short of coal. She was run aground by Buddington on 16 October 1872 at Etah on the northwest coast of Greenland. (Located at 78° 19' N, Etah was once the most northerly populated settlement in the world, before the harsh climate drove even the resident Inuit population south.) The Inuit helped the men survive the winter. In the spring of 1873 the men built two small boats from wood salvaged from the wrecked *Polaris* and set sail southwards on 3 June. In July 1873 they were picked up by a Scottish whaling ship, the *Ravenscraig*, and returned home via Scotland.

Hall's failed American Arctic Expedition had been riven by tensions and strife amongst the crew since it set out from New York in June 1871. The most evident friction was between the scientific members of the crew led by Bessels, and those focused primarily on geographic exploration, led by Hall. The Sailing Master, Sydney Budington, who took over command after Hall's death, was also at odds with Bessels, amongst others.

The official Board of Inquiry, conducted after the return of the *Polaris* crew to the United States, concluded on 26 December 1873 that Hall 'died from natural causes, viz. apoplexy', according to the Surgeon-Generals of the US Army and Navy who had attended part of the Inquiry proceedings, particularly the examination of Dr Bessels. It was nevertheless rumoured that Commander Hall had been murdered by poison administered by another crew member, probably to the coffee Hall drank when he returned from his sledging trip north of Thank God Harbour.

That suspicion was substantiated in part in August 1968 when his biographer, Chauncey C. Loomis, a Dartmouth College professor, exhumed Hall's well-preserved body from the Greenland permafrost. A colleague, Frank Paddock, performed an autopsy on Hall's body *in situ*. It found within Hall's corpse 'toxic amounts' of arsenic accumulated in the last two weeks of his life. It was, however, impossible to ascertain precisely how the poison had come to be in Hall's body and whether, in view of 'apoplexy' being another possible cause of death, if it was by a murderer's hand.

## LIEUT. BOVE'S ITALIAN "ANTARCTIC" EXPEDITION

### 15 Aug 1882

**The Italian Antarctic Expedition***

Buenos Ayres, July 15.- Intelligence received here announces the wreck, at Cape Horn, of the vessel with Lieutenant Bove and the members of the Italian Antarctic expedition on board. Lieutenant Bove and his companions were saved by the English cutter Allen Goden.

### *22 Aug 1882*

**The Italian Antarctic Expedition**

Genoa, Aug. 17.- A telegram sent by the Governor of Magellan to the Minister of Marine at Buenos Ayres, dated July 4, states as follows:- "I have the honour to inform you that last night, the English cutter Allen Goden anchored in this roadstead, having on board 16 sailors of crew, besides two persons, belonging to the Antarctic expedition of the Argentine steamer San Jose, wrecked at Cape Horn. Captain Printer reports that on May 28 he anchored in Hogget Bay [*sic* – Slogget Bay], Tierra del Fuego, and that on May 31, after a gale lasting three days, with heavy sea from SE, the vessel began to make water, and, one of the chains having enlarged the leak, he was compelled to run her ashore. The San Jose left Punta Arenas May 1, bound to Tierra del Fuego, under the command of Lieutenant Bove." There are no further details of the disaster and no loss of life is mentioned.

* In truth this was not an 'Italian' Antarctic expedition, nor did it ever even reach continental Antarctica. Lieutenant Giacomo Bové (born 23 April 1852) was an officer in the Royal Italian Navy. He had participated in Erik Nordenskjöld's *Vega* expedition of 1878–80 through the Northeast Passage, from north of Norway and Russia to the Bering Strait, linking the Atlantic and the Pacific, before conceiving the idea to explore and survey parts of Antarctica. Support and funds for such an endeavour were not forthcoming in Italy, so he went to Argentina to propose the idea to the Argentine Geographic Institute. General Roca, president of Argentina, assigned two corvettes to the expedition to explore southern

Patagonia and Tierra del Fuego, in a first phase, and Graham's Land on the Antarctic continent itself, in a second phase.

After completing the survey of part of the coast of Staten Island in Patagonia, the expedition transferred to the schooner *San José* at Punta Arenas, the main town on the Magellan Straits. After sailing south towards the port of Ushuaia and the Beagle Channel, the expedition had to be abandoned under the circumstances reported above, namely, that the *San José* was wrecked at Slogget Bay on the southeastern coast of Tierra del Fuego, about 125 km (80 miles) from Ushuaia. There appears to have been no loss of life as a result of the wreck.

Bové later participated in an expedition to central Africa (Congo), in 1885–86, from which he contracted a severe and debilitating illness. He took his own life on 9 August 1887, aged just 35 years. A small museum in his honour was established at his home village of Maranza, in Piedmont, northern Italy.

## S.A. ANDRÉE'S BALLOON EXPEDITION TO THE NORTH POLE

### 12 July 1897

**Maritime Intelligence**

**Miscellaneous**

> Manchester, July 12, 12 30 p.m.- Ragnhild (s), arrived here today from Finland, has on board four carrier pigeons, stamped "North Pole Expedition," two bearing "numbers 65 and 106," but no messages attached. They alighted on the steamer in an exhausted condition in the North Sea.*

* The 'North Pole Expedition' mentioned here referred to Salomon August (S.A.) Andrée's balloon expedition to the North Pole in the summer of 1897. Andrée (1854–1897) was a Swedish physicist, engineer, pioneer balloonist and Arctic explorer. He proposed to reach the North Pole by hydrogen balloon from Svaldbard (Spitzbergen), flying over Russia or Canada *en route*. His first attempt in the summer of 1896 failed, thwarted by northerly winds against him at his base camp on the Svaldbard island of Danskoya.

Returning to Danskoya the following year, Andrée and his two expedition companions, Nils Strindberg and Knut Fraenkel, took flight in their balloon, named *Ören (Eagle)*, on 11 July in favourable conditions. One of their means of communication with the outside world was by homing pigeons supplied to his expedition by the Swedish newspaper *Aftonbladet*, of Stockholm. Four of the pigeons landed on the *Ragnhild*, according to the report above, with no messages attached to them. Another account noted, however, that only one pigeon was ever retrieved, and that by 'a Norwegian steamer'. The pigeon, reportedly the third released by Andrée from his balloon, apparently carried a message saying:- 'All well on board' at midday, 13 July, in lat. 82° N, long. 15 05° E.

Whilst it might have been 'all well' that day, the very next day the balloon was forced to a gentle landing on the pack ice and the three men obliged to disembark from it, far from reaching their objective of flying over the North Pole. On 22 July the trio of explorers began the long trek over the ice southeast towards Franz Josef Land, an archipelago of islands to the east of Svaldbard. On 4 August adverse winds forced them to change course and head southwest towards Sjuoyane (Seven Islands) in Svaldbard. After little more than a month, on 12th September, Andrée decided they would have to winter on the ice and let the floe carry them with the current south towards the island of Kvitoya between Svaldbard and Franz Josef Land. Early in October, as the floe began to break up against the shore of Kvitoya, the three explorers moved onto the island itself.

Andrée's last diary entry was from 2 October 1897. The three men were presumed to have perished shortly thereafter, but their disappearance and whereabouts remained a mystery for 33 years. The Norwegian *Braatvag* Expedition voyaged to Svaldbard in the summer of 1930 to explore the archipelago aboard their sealing vessel, the *Braatvag*. On 5 August that year they landed at Kvitoya and there, by chance, found the remains of the 1897 expedition's camp and the skeletons of S.A. Andrée and Nils Strindberg (identified by their names on remnants of their clothing). On 5 September that year a party of journalists and sailors who had chartered a sloop (the *Isbjorn*) from Tromso, Norway to liaise with the *Braatvag* Expedition, found Knut Fraenkel's remains some distance from the campsite.

The remains of the three explorers were returned to Sweden where they were cremated before a forensic examination could be undertaken to determine the cause of their death. In his 1952 book *De döda på Vitön* (*The Dead on Kvitoya*), Dr. Ernst Tryde posited the most commonly accepted cause of the men's demise (amongst many other suggestions), namely, trichinosis from eating undercooked or raw polar bear meat. In 2010, however, a research scientist at the Swedish medical university Karolinska Institutet, Dr. Bea Uusma Schyffert, concluded from the nature of damage to their clothing that the three men had actually been attacked and killed by polar bears.

## Scott's *Discovery* Expedition to the Antarctic

The British National Antarctic Expedition of 1901–1904, commanded by Robert Falcon Scott (1868–1912) on the *Discovery*, was the first official British exploratory expedition to Antarctica since the three voyages of James Ross in 1839–1843 in HMS *Erebus* and HMS *Terror*. Scott's third officer in charge of stores and provisions on the *Discovery* was Ernest Shackleton, who had to return home early from the expedition because of poor health. Shackleton went on to lead the 1914–1917 Imperial Trans-Antarctic Expedition in the *Endurance* which was crushed in the Antarctic ice. He famously led the rescue of his entire party to safety, with no lives lost.

## 15 Aug 1901

**The British Antarctic Expedition.-**

**The Discovery at Madeira.-**

> Funchal, Aug. 15.- The British Antarctic ship Discovery* has arrived here on her way to the Cape [of Good Hope] and Australia. Both officers and crew are in excellent health and spirits, and Captain Scott, the commander, declares the vessel to be a splendid sea-boat. During the voyage here the routine of the scientific work was settled, and the special sounding gear has been successfully tested.

> * The *Discovery*, built in Dundee and of 1,570 tons displacement, arrived on the Antarctic

coast on 8 January 1902. By the following year it had become trapped in ice at McMurdo

Sound. In August 1903 a relief expedition comprising two vessels, the *Morning* and the *Terra Nova* (both ex-whaling ships from Dundee), set out from Dundee to sail to Antarctica and try to free *Discovery* from the ice. The start for the *Terra Nova* was inauspicious.

### 22 Aug [Saturday] 1903

**Suicide of an Antarctic Relief Ship's Sailor**.- Amid great enthusiasm the Antarctic relief ship Terra Nova left Dundee yesterday. The vessel was anchored in the river owing to the prejudice against sailing on Friday, which still lingers amongst whalers. Last night, after the crew had been mustered and assigned quarters, a seaman named Ryan, belonging to Dundee, jumped overboard. Ropes and buoys were thrown to him, but he cried, "I am all right." The men then sprang into a boat alongside and tried to pass an oar, which he refused to take. Another boat was launched, but before Ryan could be reached the tide had swept him away and he was drowned.

The *Terra Nova* and *Morning* reached Antarctica in January 1904 but could not get close enough to the *Discovery* to free her from the ice. In mid-February, however, the ice around *Discovery* broke up and she was able to set sail for home via New Zealand, returning to Portsmouth on 10 September 1904. One of the successes of the expedition was that Scott and his team reached the furthest southerly position then attained of 82° 17' S, on 30 December 1902.

By contrast, Scott's *Terra Nova* Expedition of 1910–1913, ended in tragedy. His five-man party aimed to be the first expedition to reach the South Pole. When they arrived there on 17 January 1912 they found that the Norwegian explorer Roald Amundsen (1872–1928) had beaten them to it five weeks before, on 14 December 1911, prompting Scott's remark, "Great God! This is an awful place." The five men, including Scott, perished on the return trek. The manner of one of the men's death, that of Lawrence Oates, became famous by Scott's account that he left the party's tent saying, "I am just going outside and I may be some time". The last entry in Scott's diary was dated 29 March 1912.

# 5  Accidental Loss of Life

Loss of life was a routine occurrence at sea. Storm damage might include sails being torn to shreds, spars and deck fittings broken up, boats or crew members washed overboard or water getting into the holds and jeopardising the stability of the ship. Sailors working aloft fell to their death, either to the deck of the ship or overboard where they drowned as there was rarely any hope of rescuing them. The accidental loss of a seaman by a fall from aloft was recorded in the log but otherwise rarely embellished upon.

## May 17 1883

**Miscellaneous**

Queenstown, May 15. – The Astoria, ship, from Astoria (Or.) Dec 30 [1882], arrived here, reports:- Crossed the Equator in the Pacific Jan 25 in long. 117 09 W. Had light variable winds in the South Pacific, passed Cape Horn March 3. Had violent gales from March 5 to 10, varying from SW to NW. March 10, Joseph Houser (seaman) fell from the mizentopmast rigging to deck of after-house, and was instantly killed. He was buried at sea. Crossed the Equator in the Atlantic April 5, in long. 23 40 W.

The master of the vessel would have conducted a simple burial service, the weighted and shrouded body of the dead sailor was tipped into the sea and the routine of the ship recommenced immediately. A melancholic gloom would have prevailed for some time over the ship's crew, but the ship had to be sailed and navigated – and that was that.

Men were often washed overboard by huge seas crashing on board ships in stormy weather. In such conditions it was useless, and usually a danger to the ship as well, to turn around or launch a small boat to search for the unfortunate sailors who would more than likely, and mercifully, die a quick death by drowning.

The full-rigged steel ship *Pampa*, originally built for the famous F. Laeisz (Flying P) Line of Hamburg in 1891, but sold to Finnish owners in 1913, once suffered a truly dreadful incident of men washed overboard. In the winter of 1919–20 the *Pampa* was on a voyage from the Finnish port of Kotka with a cargo of timber for Algoa Bay in South Africa. One night in the North Atlantic in January 1920 the entire watch of seamen and the watchkeeping mate

– probably nine or ten men in total – were washed overboard by a single massive sea that boarded the ship during a storm. The only man left on deck was the helmsman at the wheel, his cries for help drowned out by the noise of the storm. In the morning when the watch below came up they found the helmsman alone and exhausted by his ordeal: the rest of the crew had all disappeared, swept away and drowned by a single swipe of the sea's fury.

Shipwreck and other accidents, together with disease, were by far the biggest causes of death to merchant seamen in the second half of the 19th century. A report published in *Lloyd's List* on 12 May 1871 analysed the mortality of seamen in the British merchant service in 1870.

## MORTALITY IN THE MERCHANT SERVICE

A return has been lately issued, showing the number, ages, ratings, and causes of death of seamen reported to the Board of Trade as having died in the British Merchant Service during the year 1870.

The deaths amounted in all to 4,523, of which 2,946 are ascribed to wrecks and other accidents, 13 to murder and homicide, 21 to suicide, 205 to unknown causes, and the rest [1,338] to fevers and other diseases. The following list will convey some idea of the waste of life:-

In 1870, of British seamen, we lost 355 mates, 2 midshipmen, 16 quartermasters, 140 boatswains, 1,766 able seamen, 417 ordinary seamen, 362 apprentices and boys, 16 surgeons, 314 cooks and stewards, 130 carpenters, 35 sailmakers, 47 minor capacities, 70 engineers, 116 firemen, 4 stowaways, and 733 'unknown.'

That the large majority of these were men in the prime of life is shown by the following list of their ages – 901 [20% of the total] were under 21 years old, 1,821 [40%] were from 21 to 30, 724 [16%] were from 31 to 40, 328 [7%] were from 41 to 50, 91 [2%] were 51 to 60, and 6 [0.1%] were over 60. The ages of the remaining 652 are returned as unknown.

4,523 British merchant seamen were lost in 1870, 4,832 in 1869, and 5,237 in 1868; so that last year's return presents a favourable contrast to its immediate predecessors.

Mortality rates declined towards the end of the century. The table below shows the mortality for seamen employed in British ships between 1895 and 1898.

### British Shipping Deaths by Casualties

| | 1895 | 1896 | 1897 | 1898 |
|---|---|---|---|---|
| **Number of Men Employed** | | | | |
| **Total** | 217,794 | 218,224 | 219,235 | 218,016 |
| *Sail* | 58,537 | 56,095 | 53,269 | 49,858 |
| *Steam* | 159,257 | 162,129 | 165,966 | 168,158 |
| **Number Drowned by Wreck & Casualty** | | | | |
| **Total** | 990 | 783 | 700 | 590 |
| *Sail* | 671 | 414 | 371 | 260 |
| *Steam* | 319 | 369 | 329 | 330 |
| **Total Deaths from Drowning Accidents Aboard & Ashore** | | | | |
| **(Sail + Steam)** | 1,862 | 1,634 | 1,525 | 1,423 |

Source: *Lloyd's List*

The figures show that the number of seamen employed in steam by the end of the century was three times the number employed in sail for all British-registered ships.

The mortality rate for deaths by drowning and shipwreck, for sail and steam combined, was 0.45 in 1895, 0.35 in 1896, 0.32 in 1897 and 0.27 by 1898.

For sail alone it was 1.15 in 1895, 0.74 in 1896, 0.70 in 1897 and 0.52 in 1898. By comparison, the mortality rate for steam in those years was much lower: 0.20 in 1895, 0.23 in 1896, 0.20 in 1897 and 0.20 in 1898.

The main causes of death in 1898 were as follows:

| **Total All Causes** | **2,492** |
|---|---|
| **Of which from:** | |
| Disease (ashore and afloat) | 1,069 |
| Wrecks and casualties | 590 |
| Drowning where vessel not damaged/casualty | 543 |
| Accident (other than drowning in ship's service) | 252 |
| Homicide, suicide (aboard) or accident ashore | 38 |

*Source: Lloyd's List*

## NARRATIVES

## 2 Oct 1871

### Casualties – Home

Portland, 2nd Sept.- The Aasvoer, Stanbesen, from Figueira [Portugal] to Haugesund [Norway], with salt, put into these roads to-day, and reports having been pooped, Ushant bearing NW, distant 48 miles, when the master and one man were washed overboard and drowned.

## 7 Feb 1877

### Casualties – Foreign

New York, 27th Jan.- The Lightning (Brit. ship), Watson, from San Francisco to Manilla, was spoken, 22nd Jan., in lat. 36 N lon. 125 W, and reported that, on the first day out, the topping lift* broke, the boom knocked a man overboard, who was drowned, another man was killed on deck, and the second mate had his leg broken.

* On a full-rigged ship such as the *Lightning* (above), the topping lift, sometimes called the boom topping lift, is a rope that holds up the boom of the spanker, the fore-and-aft sail on the mast closest to the stern of the ship (which, on a three-masted ship, would be the mizzen mast). If that rope broke, the boom would not only drop but might also swing around, potentially causing great harm to anyone in its immediate vicinity – or, as in this case, knocking a man overboard.

## 18 March 1878

### Casualties – Home

Sunderland, 16th Mar., 12.1 p.m.- The master (Paulsen) of the Swedish barque Sverne arrived here yesterday morning from Soon, with timber, reports that on the 19th, during a heavy gale from WNW, he lost a seaman overboard who was drowned, and on the 11th, when in lat. 56 N long. 3 E, a seaman named Soren Solerdsen fell from mainyard to deck, and was killed.

## 6 Feb 1878

**Casualties – Home**

Crookhaven [near Mizen Head, Co. Cork, southwest Ireland], 5th Feb., 11 a.m.- Report of the ship Rokeby Hall, Captain Clark, from Iquique, spoken off here, yesterday, bound to Queenstown for orders:- "On 11th Nov. [1877], lat. 47 S lon. 84 W, carpenter fell overboard and the boat sent after him. After being away an hour and a half, had got nearly back to the ship, when the breaking top of a wave swamped her. Sent another boat, as quick as possible, to rescue them, and she returned after being away also an hour and a half, but only found the lifejackets supplied to those in first boat, and with them the lifebuoy which had been thrown to the carpenter.

The names of those drowned were: J.W. Spence, 2nd mate, Peter Conway, carpenter, Walter Paton, A.B., Matthew Ryan, A.B., Benjamin Stevens, A.B., and William Phillip Eddy, apprentice. Wind ESE, moderate.

## 3 May 1878

**Casualties, Etc.**

The "Rodell Bay" – The narration of a most unusual and eventful voyage deserves more than the accustomed notice. The case to which we refer is the ship *Rodell Bay*, belonging to the 'Bay' line of Messrs. Hatfield, Cameron & Co., Buchanan-street, which left Portland, Oregon, in October last [1877], bound for Queenstown for orders.

This vessel, shortly after leaving port, had the misfortune to lose, by death, her captain, and a fortnight thereafter the mate, who, in a fit of insanity, jumped overboard. To add to the calamitous state of affairs, the ship was practically without officers responsible for the management of the vessel, the second mate having deserted on the eve of leaving port.

Under these untoward circumstances, the responsibility of bringing the ship home was undertaken by the boatswain, Mr. Charles Sweetser, a native of Belfast, Maine, and it is a pleasing duty to record that he navigated the ship with skill and judgment, and brought her safely into harbour after a good average passage. To mark the appreciation of his valuable services, the underwriters on ship, cargo and freight, representing £50,000, have unanimously voted to him a handsome gratuity, which no one will doubt has been deservedly earned.

## 3 Jan 1879

**Casualties – Foreign**

Rouen-Dec 30: The Murton (s), from Swansea, lost overboard her master, Bevan, on the passage. The following particulars are furnished by the mate, Davies:- "On Tuesday, Dec. 24, at 8 P.M., the Longships Light [one mile off Land's End, the most westerly point of mainland England] being SSW, distant about 10 miles, the maintrysail was taken in and made fast, the wind SE, fresh, weather cloudy. I went below at 8 20 P.M., leaving the captain and second mate on the bridge. At 9 30, when about half a mile from Longships, he gave orders to haul the log in and jib down, after which the foretrysail. The second mate and Wilson were on the forward deck hauling the head of sail down, after which they saw the captain get on top of railings that are round the bridge to cast adrift the lashing that was passed round the boom and through the clew of the sail, when, in the act of doing so, the topping lift carried away, the boom fell down, and either he fell or was struck overboard.

The second mate immediately ran on the bridge, thinking the boom had fallen on him. When he got there he could see nothing of him. He shouted to Wilson to look on the lee side, but nothing could be seen. He then ran aft, calling out "Dead slow" to engineer down the engine-room. By this time the man at the wheel (David Rees) heard a moaning noise underneath the ship's quarter. He holloaed out, "Man overboard," which noise awoke the Steward and myself. We both jumped out of our bunks. The steward ran to the after part of the cabin.

By this time I had got to the cabin-door, where I was met by Wilson, who said, "Where is the captain?" I said, "I don't know." "Then he is overboard." I ran on the bridge and immediately got the ship round and back to the place, as I thought, breaking adrift the lifebuoys for the men who were looking out for him, but could neither see nor hear anything of him. We stopped there about an hour, and then were compelled to steer back underneath the land. The wind being SE strong, with nasty cross sea, and very dark, it was impossible for us to launch a boat; had we done so she must have been smashed instantly. David Rees saw him sink underneath in [the] ship's wake. That was the last that was seen of him. We steered up and down the coast until morning, when we came to in St. Ive's Bay, the wind having increased to strong gale."

## 27 Aug 1879

**Casualties – Home**

Plymouth, Aug. 25.- The Russian three-masted brigantine Elsa, Ahlquist (mate), from Kotka for Garston, arrived off the Start, reports that on Aug. 20, the second officer fell from the topsailyard on deck, and was killed on the spot; and that on the 21st, at 10 p.m., wind SW, fresh, heavy sea, Start Point bearing W ½ N, distant 10 miles, the master was washed overboard and drowned.

## 15 Jan 1881

Report of the ship Thermopylae*, Matheson, from Sydney (N.S.W.), in the river:- "Left Sydney on the 14th October [1880], and encountered adverse winds until rounding the south end of New Zealand on the 24th. From thence to Cape Horn south-westerly winds and very boisterous weather was experienced. Passed Cape Horn Nov. 16, and from then to 40 S, moderate westerly winds and weather prevailed. Got SE trades in 19 S, which were moderate and easterly.

Crossed the equator in 27 W. On Dec. 13 caught NE trades in 7 W, which were carried to 27 N. Came into east of Azores. Passed St. Mary's [Santa Maria, Azores] on 28th Dec., and thence to Channel easterly and north-easterly winds. Made Scilly on the 7th inst.; worked up Channel to St. Catherine's, where the wind favoured, and passed Deal on the 12th.

On the night of Oct. 24, in a SW gale, Mr Innes, first mate, and A. Collingridge, apprentice, were lost overboard by a boat's davit breaking away with a sea while trying to secure the boat."

\* The *Thermopylae* was a famous 19 century tea clipper and great rival of the *Cutty Sark*.

## 25 Feb 1882

**Casualties, Etc.**

Master of Ella Constance (s), arrived at Newport, Wales, 23 Feb. 1882, died of shock on receiving telegram from wife that a daughter, 17, had died.- His death was "attributed to the shock occasioned by the melancholy news."

## 25 July 1882

**Miscellaneous**

The barque Adriatic, of Alloa, arrived here yesterday from Quebec and the master (Gilmore) reports that during the voyage, on Wednesday last, a seaman named Robt. Nicol, son of Wm. Nicol, a pilot residing in Armfield, Newhaven, while engaged on the foretopgallantyard of the vessel, accidentally fell overboard. No sooner was the accident observed than ropes and lifebuoys were thrown to the unfortunate man. After swimming about for some time, Nicol managed to lay hold of a buoy, but unfortunately let go his grasp and sunk just as a boat from the Adriatic was reaching him. Nicol was 22 years of age and married. (*Leith, July 23.*)

## 8 Dec 1882

**Casualties, Etc.**

Ben Nevis.- Melbourne, Oct. 26.- The Ben Nevis, from London, at Port Chalmers, was pooped by a sea on Aug. 30, in lat. 42 S, long. 62 E, while running before a hurricane, which swept away poop rail, bulwarks, compass, and everything movable on deck. One of the crew also was washed overboard.\*

Garnock.- Melbourne, Oct. 26.- The Garnock, from London, at Brisbane, reports:- "On Aug 14, in lat. 44 S, long. 21 E, while running before the wind under maintopsail and foresail, was pooped by a sea, which washed two of the men away, carried away the wheel and wheel-box, stove in the cabin skylight and after hatch, flooded the cabin, and carried away the fore-cabin companion."\*

### 12 Dec 1882

**Casualties, Etc.**

Loch Torridon.- Falmouth, Dec. 11, 5 28 p.m.- Arrived to-day, Loch Torridon, Cummings, late Pinder, Calcutta for London (general cargo). Captain [Pinder], second mate, also three men washed overboard and drowned on Oct. 9, during heavy WNW gale in lat. 36 S, long. 127 E [*sic* – 27 E]. Vessel shipping heavy sea, staving boats, bridge, compass, etc., and washing everything movable from off the deck. (Vessel in charge of 1st mate, Cuimmings.)\*

\* The first two incidents, above, happened in the stormy seas of the Roaring Forties in the Southern Indian Ocean. The third, by the famous four-masted barque *Loch Torridon*, happened at lat. 36 S, long 27 E (not "127 E"), off South Africa as she was coming down from Calcutta to round the Cape of Good Hope. Capt. Pinder made a mistake while wearing his ship round in a strong gale. The ship was not going fast enough to avoid being pooped by a heavy sea which swept Capt. Pinder, the second mate, the helmsman, the sailmaker and an apprentice overboard. The mate, Cummings, who was also almost swept away and was only saved by his leg being caught in the main-brace rope, took command of the *Loch Torridon* and brought her home to Falmouth.

## 2 Sept 1886

**Maritime Intelligence**

Mary Graham. Shields, Sept. 1.- The Mary Graham, barque, of Maryport, from Quebec for Tyne, with timber, reports on 13th ult. [August] encountered a severe gale and shipped heavy seas. During the prevalence of the gale the boatswain and an able seaman were washed overboard, and in spite of all endeavours to save them they were drowned. Shortly after this occurrence another sea swept the decks and carried away a large plank, but by the next sea it was sent on board again and struck the master (Captain Barton) such a severe blow on the forehead that he was killed upon the spot. Two of the seamen were also injured. During the storm the vessel suffered severely, her cabin being wrecked, her boats swept away, and her after hatches and part of the deck cargo were also carried overboard.

## 3 Sept 1886

**Miscellaneous**

Falmouth, Sept. 2.- The ship Sophocles, Smith, from Sydney, arrived at the Lizard Aug. 31, reports:- "Left Sydney May 18, and had rather unfavourable winds rounding New Zealand. On the 11th June experienced a very heavy gale from SSW, with a high sea; bar. 28 40. At 2 p.m., while running before it, shipped a sea on the starboard quarter, carrying away wheel, binnacle, compass, smashing skylight, etc.; J. Skinner, A.B., was killed; Mr. Poppy, chief mate, was severely hurt; Mr. Sears, passenger, lost his left arm, and other two of the crew were slightly hurt.

The same night, at 6 p.m., while lying hove to, the tiller carried away, and while trying to secure the rudder by means of chain strops round the rudder head and tackles on them, the master's fingers on the right hand were fractured, necessitating amputation. Passed Cape Horn on June 27, and crossed the Equator Aug. 1, in long. 26 30 W."

## 2 Oct 1886

**Maritime Intelligence**

Rebecca.- Melbourne, Aug. 21.- The barque Rebecca, from Port Augusta for Tonga, was thrown on her beam ends 400 miles from the island, remaining 36 hours in that position. The captain went mad and jumped overboard a few days later...

## 12 Jan 1887

**Miscellaneous**

London, Jan. 12.- The *Melbourne*, ship, arrived at Melbourne Nov. 25 from London, reports that in lat. 23 N, long. 21 30 W, a seaman fell overboard, and Mr. Vale, chief officer, Mr. Coates, fourth officer, and Robert Lewis, A.B., were drowned in effecting rescue. The seaman who fell overboard was saved.

## 19 July 1888

**Maritime Intelligence**

Dunedin.- London, July 18.- The ship Dunedin, Roberts, from Omara (N.Z.), arrived in the river to-day, reports that on May 13, in lat. 51 50 S, long. 101 20 W, experienced a strong gale from NE, with heavy sea; ship under lower fore and main topsails and foretopstaysail, and close hauled on the port tack. While the watch were clearing the starboard fore braces*, a sea broke on board and washed N.J. Bonningh (boatswain), and Hans B. Nilsen (A.B.) overboard. A rope was thrown to Nilsen, and Mr. Murray, chief officer, got hold of the boatswain, but another sea coming he had to let go his hold, and nothing more was seen of the men. Starboard topgallant bulwarks were washed away, and forecastle ladder, capstan bars, two pigs, and sundry other things washed overboard.

* The braces on a square-rigged ship were ropes leading from either ends of a yardarm to the ship's side, or to an adjacent mast, by which the yards were hauled to any required position. The equivalent on a standard Bermuda-rigged yacht would be the sheets, used to trim the vessel's sails. In this case the starboard fore braces were the braces leading from the starboard end of the yards on the foremast, the mast closest to the bow of the vessel.

## 21 March 1892

**Maritime Intelligence**

Nornen.- Christiania, March 17.- The Victoria (s), Svendsen, which arrived here to-day from Sunderland, fell in with the brig Nornen, Olsen, from Norway for England, with ice, on the morning of March 14, about 190 miles WSW of the Norwegian coast. The brig had lost bulwarks and on March 12 had shipped a sea, which smashed wheel and wheelhouse. The master, Olsen, was found dead and the mate unconscious under the fragments. The latter [the mate] was taken on board the Victoria, which put her own first mate on board the brig, with orders to steer back to Norway. It blew a gale in the night of the 15th, and the vessels became separated, so that the fate of the brig is not known.

### 30 March 1892

**Maritime Intelligence**

Nornen.- Krageroe [southeast coast of Norway], March 24.- The brig Nornen, of Sandefjord [just northeast of Krageroe], bound for England, with ice, which was fallen in with on March 17, damaged and with no one to navigate her on board, by the Victoria (s), arrived here safely this morning in charge of that steamer's mate.

## 20 May 1893

**Maritime Intelligence**

Lord Templeton.- Queenstown, May 20, 10 22 a.m.- Lord Templeton, Captain Hawthorn, from London, cargo chalk, for Philadelphia, reports that on May 1, in lat. 44 39 N, long. 45 19 W, in a hurricane from SE and NNW, stove main hatch, lost sails, lowermaintopsail yards, and received sundry other damages; also lost first mate, boatswain, and seven seamen.*

* The *Lord Templetown* (the correct spelling of her name) was one the largest three-masted barques in the world at this time (2,152 grt). She carried a big crew numbering 34

men (and, on this voyage, six passengers). The vessel was 17 days out from London when she encountered hurricane force winds in mid-Atlantic. Sixteen men were working on the main lower topsail yard when it came down after the iron truss holding it to the mast was carried away. Eight men fell overboard and were drowned, another man was killed and four others were severely injured. Considering the circumstances, Capt. Hawthorn decided to put back and eventually arrived at Queenstown, Ireland from where the *Lord Templetown* was towed to Belfast for repairs.

## 18 May 1894

### Three Sailors Drowned

Queenstown, May 17.- The Liverpool ship M.E. Watson (Captain Mitchell), owned by Messrs. Gracie, Beazley & Co., has arrived here from San Francisco, which port she left on Dec. 27 [1893]. On Feb. 18 she experienced terrific weather in the vicinity of 50 deg. South latitude and 100 deg. West longitude. Heavy seas broke on board, and three of the crew were washed overboard. They were bracing the foreyard, and to keep clear of the seas about the deck had got on the rail, when a tremendous wave struck them. Owing to the storm no effort to rescue them could be made, and the men were drowned. Their names are Bearfield, A.B., Cox, A.B., and Cannochy, a boy. The ship has not sustained any damage.

## 29 Dec 1897

### Accidents on a Ship - Seven Sailors Killed

### New York, Dec. 28

A despatch from Bermuda states that the British ship Vanloo, 1,537 tons, of Yarmouth, Nova Scotia, bound from Cardiff to St. John, New Brunswick, has put in there, and reports that a serious accident occurred on board during the voyage. On Dec. 20, while a number of men were aloft, the foreyard parted suddenly and fell to the deck in splinters, carrying down nine sailors with it. Three of them were killed outright. Three others jumped into the sea and were drowned. The bodies were not recovered. A terrible hurricane was experienced the previous day, and a sailor was killed by falling from aloft.

## *President Félix Faure* Loses 15 Men in Indian Ocean Cyclone

## 2 March 1898

### Maritime Intelligence

### Weather and Navigation

Adelaide, Feb. 28.- The barque President Felix Faure, which has arrived here from Barry [south Wales], reports that during a severe gale on Feb. 2 she lost 12 seamen, the second mate, and three apprentices, who were swept overboard by a heavy sea breaking on the deck.

### *Poverty Bay Herald* (New Zealand newspaper)

### *16ᵗʰ March 1898*

### Terrible Disaster At Sea

## Fifteen Sailors Swept Overboard
### Adelaide, March 8

It is not an infrequent occurrence for one hand to be lost from a vessel during a voyage from one side of the world to the other; but on her arrival on Monday at Port Adelaide the French barque President Felix Faure reported the loss of 15 men at one fell swoop. It appears that the voyage had passed without incident until February 2, when she was in [lat.] 43 deg. 10 min. south, and [long.] 67 deg. east, and was running before a strong westerly gale and heavy sea. At 3.30 p.m. a sea broke on board from each side, completely filling the decks, and for a time the vessel was staggering under the weight of the water, which caused a considerable list to port.

After a time the water cleared away, but it was found that the following members of the crew had been washed off:- Jean M. Caradec, August Le Goasduff, Ives Marie Crefell, R.A.G. Sonnett, P. Marie Palodec, Matthieu Pepperder, Jean C. Scournec, Eugene Domaldin, Francis M. Lennandais, F. Marie Marshand, Jean M. Kerboat, Louis M. Andre, and Jean M. Robert.*

The suddenness of the catastrophe, together with the fact that the vessel was running before a heavy sea, prevented the lowering of a boat, even if it were possible or prudent to bring the vessel into the wind, and consequently the course was kept, and the vessel continued her trip, but with the loss of 12 able seamen, the second mate, and two apprentices.

The vessel was built in Havre in 1896, and is a fine specimen of the French four-master. Her solid iron bulwarks are so high that a medium-sized man can just look over them comfortably, and it is evident that when a big sea was shipped it would find no speedy exit, and would run about the deck like water in a bath. Looking at her to-day, with all her yards and rigging in place and her deck gear in good order, it was hard to realise what a pandemonium she must have been on the 2nd of last February, when 15 of her crew were in an instant swept into a raging sea, and lost from sight. When asked how the calamity occurred, her master, Captain Felix Smart Frossard readily narrated all he knew.

The captain, who is fair of face, small of stature, and courteous in the extreme, had received the reporter with a sad smile of welcome, but his brow was clouded with care, for naturally he has been greatly upset by the event. "It was about half-past 3 in the afternoon," he said, "that the accident took place. All hands were on the deck, and the barque was bowling along at the rate of over a dozen knots an hour. Suddenly a sea broke on board from each side, and the vessel staggered under the shock. It took some time for the water to run off, and it was not until the deck was nearly cleared that we discovered that any of the men had disappeared, yet 15 were lost. We had not, when the water was swirling on deck, noticed them go overboard, and by the time we realised what had happened the ship must have been ten miles further on.

When we looked astern there were, of course, no traces of those who had gone; but even if it had been of any use, and there had been any chance by going back of saving life, it would have been utterly impossible in such a gale of wind and in such a heavy sea for the vessel to round to [into the wind and stop]. All we could do was to continue on our course. We were going with a north-west wind, and there were billows running high from the south-west, which explains how the sea broke in on both sides. It took us till half-past five to get

Le « Président Félix-Faure » pendant un cyclone dans l'océan Indien. — (Voir l'article, page 208.)

the deck ship-shape. During the voyage the water had broken on board before, but we had never had so much on deck as that.

   We had to continue our voyage with really only nine men, and had a very trying time before we got here. Two of the men who were swept about in the swirling water had a very narrow escape, and they attribute their preservation to the fact that they fought themselves free of their companions, who had grabbed at one another when the seas rushed on board. One was found in the mizzen rigging and the other on the deckhouse aft. All the victims of the disaster were young, the oldest being 34 and the youngest the cabin boy, Andre, only 16. They were all unmarried. France draws her supply of sailors almost entirely from the coast of Brittany and the shores of the Mediterranean, and 12 of the lost sailors were Bretons. Two were born in Paris, and one hailed from the south of France."

*Although just 13 names are listed here, the newspaper reported 'the loss of 12 able seamen, the second mate, and two apprentices', totalling 15 men (the list probably did not include the two young apprentices). Capt. Frossard confirmed that 15 were lost. With just nine men left to work the ship, the number lost overboard was more than an entire watch. (The crew would have been divided into two watches of an equal number of men. One watch worked on deck while the others were off duty below. Watches rotated alternately every four hours. Both watches could be called on deck, however, to handle a serious problem such as dealing with heavy weather, as was the case here.)

The single loss of that many men at one time was 'one of the worst crew losses at sea known even in the Cape Horn trade' (from *The Bounty Ships of France*, by Alan Villiers and Henri Picard). The *Faure* arrived at Adelaide at the end of February 1898, two weeks after the catastrophe and 131 days out from Barry, south Wales.

During a voyage from New Caledonia to Le Havre with a cargo of nickel ore, the *Président Félix Faure* was wrecked on 13 March 1908, on Antipodes Island in the desolate Antipodes archipelago some 550 miles southeast of New Zealand. All her crew of 22 men survived the wreck. For almost two months they lived mainly on provisions stored at the New Zealand government depot (54 cases of biscuits), and on seabirds. They were rescued by HMS *Pegasus* on 12 May 1908 and landed at Lyttelton, New Zealand three days later.

   Capt. Noël, master of the wrecked ship, described the shipwreck as 'just like any wreck that any sailor might experience in perhaps any part of the world, only for the weather. Oh, that is terrible down there! Rain, fog and wind, rain, fog and wind all day and every day. We were wet all the time. That was, perhaps, the worst part of it. The island seems to never have good weather. The sun seldom shines brightly there, and there seems to be hardly any warmth to its rays'. (*The Star* newspaper, 16 May 1908)

## 21 Dec 1898

### Two Apprentices Drowned

Queenstown, Dec. 20.- Captain Davies, of the four-masted vessel Euphrates, arrived here from San Francisco. He reports that on the 5th inst., in lat. 34 N, long. 32 40 W, Newman Muriel Wright, of Leeds, and Alfred Dyer Simonet, of Jersey [Channel Islands], apprentices, each aged 17 years, fell from the upper maintopsailyard into the sea during a heavy southerly gale, and were drowned. No effort could be made to save them.

## 18 April 1899

**Maritime Intelligence**

**Miscellaneous**

London, April 18.- A Dalziel's telegram, dated Philadelphia, April 17, states:- The British steamer Vigria (?) has arrived. The officer in command reports the captain (James Wasson) fell overboard on Nov. 21 [1898], when near the Bahamas, and was seized and killed by sharks.

## 18 July 1899

**Fatal Accident On Board Ship**

**A Man's Head Torn Off**

A terrible accident occurred at the South Dock, Sunderland, on Saturday, on board the German steamer Martha Sauber, which had just arrived from Hamburg. The vessel was being moored under No. 31 drop, and for this purpose a wire rope was attached to the quay, connected with a steam winch on board the vessel. A seaman named Albert Robert Steinke was standing by this winch, when his shirt sleeve, which, it is supposed [believed], was loose, was caught by the rope, and before he could free himself he was pulled between the rope and the barrel of the winch, and the rope had passed across his neck and entirely torn the head from the body. The deceased was 26 years of age, and a German. At the inquest, on the same day, a verdict of Accidental death was returned, the jury being of the opinion that nobody was to blame.

## 1 Aug 1899

**Second Mate Drowned At Sea**

Messrs. Thompson, Anderson & Co., of Fenwick-street, Liverpool, have received a letter from Captain Murdoch, of their ship Sierra Lucena, dated St. Helena, July 3, in which he states that on June 15 last while the vessel was in lat. 34 21 S, long. 28 11 E, and during a heavy gale, when the crew were shortening sail, the second officer, Mr. Alexander Duncan, was knocked off the yard. Ropes and lifebuoys were thrown overboard, the helm put hard down, etc., but the unfortunate man was not seen to rise. It was impossible to launch a boat, owing to the high sea. Mr. Duncan was only in his twenty-first year.

## 3 May 1901

**Maritime Intelligence**

Lyndhurst.- New York, April 24.- British ship Lyndhurst, Taylor, from Hiogo [Japan], arrived here yesterday, reports:- "Was 22 days on the coast [of Japan] with a succession of heavy gales from NW to SE, with high seas, in which carried away headstays and upper foretopsailyard. Nov. 4 [1900] Captain Beatty, of Belfast, died of heart disease. Dec. 17 [1900], Captain Walters took charge of ship in Straits of Sunda. April 6 [1901], Captain Walters died suddenly of apoplexy.*

*To paraphrase Oscar Wilde (1854–1900) in *The Importance of Being Earnest*: 'To lose one captain may be regarded as a misfortune; to lose two looks like carelessness'. Taylor, in command of the vessel when she arrived at New York, was probably the first mate.

## 16 May 1903

**Sad Fate of a Seaman**.- On the arrival of the West African liner Akabo in the Mersey on Tuesday, Captain Morgan reported that one of the crew had been lost overboard, and he is believed to have been devoured by sharks. While lying at Fercados [Forcados, now in Nigeria] two men were told off to paint the sides of the steamer, and carried out their task by means of a surfboat. J. McWally, a native of Liverpool, was called from the boat by the boatswain to attend to some other duties on the ship, and instead of regaining the vessel's deck by means of a ladder which was available, he climbed up a rope hanging over the ship's side, which he had seen the agile natives freely make use of to reach the deck. When almost at the top of the rope he missed his hold, and fell clear of the surfboat into the water. He must have been seized by one of the many sharks that are known to abound in these waters, as he did not rise again.

# 6  Mutiny, Murder and Mayhem

**M**utiny, whilst not a routine occurrence in 19th century ships, did happen quite regularly. A mutinous crew (sometimes alternatively described in reports as "refractory" or "disaffected") might for some reason, simply refuse to carry out duties, or even to start a voyage, often because they thought the ship was unseaworthy. Paul Stevenson, in his 1898 book *By Way of Cape Horn*, defined mutiny as: 'All that a seaman is ordered to do is duty; all that he refuses to do is mutiny'.

Mutiny at sea occasionally resulted in mutinous crew members injuring, disabling or even killing the ship's officers, including the captain, or other crew members. Although mutinous crew members had a right to their say in court, more often than not they ended up convicted of the offence and sentenced to a jail term or some other punishment such as hard labour, or both.

Most 19th century ships had diverse nationalities amongst their crews – typically including British, Irish, American, Swedish, Norwegian, German and other Europeans. Ethnically mixed crews, however, of northern and southern Europeans in particular, perhaps combined with harsh treatment by a mate or the master, were commonly perceived to be sources of tension aboard a mutinous ship. The infamous mutinies aboard the *Lennie*, in October 1875, and the *Caswell*, in January the following year, were at least potentially caused by the volatile combination of a mixed crew of northern and southern European sailors.

## NARRATIVES

### 23 Nov 1869

**New York, 10th Nov.**

> The *Margt. Cander*, Blackett, was returning from the Gilbert islands [now the Republic of Kiribati], with about 300 coolies on board, for the Tahitian Cotton Company, when the coolies mutinied and murdered the master and two officers. The mate escaped to the hold, placed a keg of powder under the main hatch, and, having called the coolies round it, blew them nearly all up. The rest of them jumped overboard or were killed by the mate and remaining men, and the vessel was taken safely to Tahiti previous to 16th Oct.

*The New York Times*
*10th November 1869*
**Tahiti: A Fearful Scene on a Coolie Ship – The Slaves Mutiny and Kill the Captain and Two Officers – They are Blown to Pieces with Powder by the Second Mate.**

San Francisco, Nov. 9.- Tahiti advices to Oct. 16 have been received…The Tahiti Cotton Company, about six months ago, sent the bark *Margaret Cander*, Captain Blackett, to the Gilbert Islands for a cargo of coolies. The Captain succeeded in securing about 300, and, during the return voyage, they mutinied, and killed the Captain and two officers, horribly mutilating their bodies.

The mate escaped to the hold of the vessel. There he placed a keg of powder under the main hatch, and having arranged a fuse, called the coolies, when the savages crowded around the hatchway. The fuse was then fired, killing nearly all on board. The rest jumped overboard, or fell victims to the mate and remaining men. The vessel was brought safely to Tahiti.

## 23 Aug 1871

**Casualties – Foreign**

Shanghai, 30th June.- The *Kiangsi* has brought into port the master and part of the crew of the Nuuanu, whom she had picked up near the lightship. The Malay portion of the crew had mutinied, killed the mate, and severely wounded the master. The Malays then appear to have set fire to the vessel and jumped overboard. The master ran the ship in close to the Saddles*, and she was then abandoned, on fire.

*The Saddles, or Saddle Islands, were a group of islands off the mouth of the Yangtze River estuary near Shanghai, named for the saddle shape of their mountain peaks. The name is no longer in use; the islands are now called Shengsi Liedao.

## 1 Jan 1872

**Casualties – Home**

Deal, 30th Dec.- Six of the crew of the Weymouth, from London to Shanghai, which arrived in the Downs last evening, have been landed, refractory*.

*In this context, "refractory" here means mutinous.

## 7 Feb 1872

**Casualties – Foreign**

New York, 25th Jan.- The Warren Hallett (Am. Barq.), Wilson, from Boston to the Cape de Verds Cape Verde Islands], put into Provincetown [Cape Cod], 23rd Jan., in consequence of a mutiny among the crew, during which one man was killed and another fatally injured.*

*The distinction, if any, between "killed" and "fatally injured" here is unclear…!

## 31 March 1874

**Casualties – Foreign**

Valparaiso, 30th Jan.- The Adriana Lucia (barq.), from Totoralillo*, 20 days out, was spoken, 14th Jan., in lat. 38 S lon. 89 W, by the *Maria Trinidad*, arrived at Lota*. The master of the

*Adriana Lucia* stated that with the exception of the cook, the steward, and two boys, all the crew had been killed or had jumped overboard, during a mutiny, on the 7th Jan.

*Totoralillo is south and Lota north of Valparaiso, on the coast of Chile.

## 27 Oct 1874

**Casualties – Foreign**

Calcutta, 2nd Oct.- The crew of the Natmoo (schr.), M'Dermott, from Maulmain* to Mauritius, are reported, during the passage of the vessel down the Bay of Bengal, to have mutinied, killed the mate, and severely wounded the master, and then to have scuttled the vessel. The master, with his wife and family, together with the crew, were picked up and brought into this port by the Moorhill (brq.)-

(Another account says, that after the mutiny, the crew, except the gunner and cook were taken off the *Natmoo* by the *Moorhill* on 19 September; that the two vessels came into collision and that the master of the *Natmoo* returned on board his vessel with part of the crew of the *Moorhill* to see what could be done, but that he afterwards went back to the *Moorhill*, leaving the gunner and a few other men on board the *Natmoo*.)

*Maulmain, or Moulmein, a seaport to the east of Rangoon in Burma (Myanmar) across the Gulf of Mattaban, is now called Mawlamyaing. The city was the first capital of British Burma between 1826 and 1852. Burma was part of the British Raj and administered as a province of British India from 1886 until 1 April 1837 at which time it became a separately administered British territory. It gained its independence as a republic on 4 January 1948.

Moulmein appears in the opening lines of the poem *Mandalay*, by Rudyard Kipling (1865 –1936):

> *By the old Moulmein pagoda, lookin' lazy at the sea*
> *There's a Burma girl a-settin, and I know she thinks of me;*
> *For the wind is in the palm-trees, and the temple-bells they say:*
> *Come you back, you British soldier; come you back to Mandalay!*

The city is now the third largest in Burma, with a population of around 300,000.

## THE *JEFFERSON BORDEN*

## 4 May 1875

**Casualties – Home**

Plymouth, 3rd May, 3.40 p.m.- The master of the fishing lugger *Secret*, of Worthing, reports boarding the American schooner Jefferson Borden, from New Orleans to London, when she was 25 miles off the Eddystone [Lighthouse]. Master reports that three of the crew murdered the chief mate, and threw him overboard. Then they threw the second mate overboard, and he was drowned. They were then about to murder the captain, but he armed himself with two revolvers and shot them down. One of the men is severely wounded, the other two slightly, and they are in irons. A Norwegian barque was in company, and had a portion of the crew on board the American to assist her to London. This was reported to have occurred ten days ago.

Porthleven, 1st May.- The *Presto* (fishing lugger), Thomas, of this port, when on the fishing ground yesterday, six miles south of the Wolf [Lighthouse], boarded the 3-masted schooner Jefferson Borden, of Boston, U.S., from New Orleans to London. The master reported having had a mutiny amongst his crew, and that the first and second mates had been killed, two sailors wounded and put in irons, one sailor wounded and chained to a pump, and another in a dying state, the vessel being worked by three hands and captain, whose wife is also on board.

*The Illustrated London News*

### 15th May 1875
### Mutiny and Murder at Sea

A terrible affray on board an American merchant vessel, crossing the Atlantic from New Orleans to London, was made known last week. The vessel was the three-masted schooner Jefferson Borden, of 561 tons, belonging to Boston, and chiefly owned by Mr. G. Town of that port, and by Mr. C. Toft. She was commanded by Captain William Manson Patterson, also a part owner, whose brother, Croydon Prask Patterson, was chief officer or mate, and his cousin, Charles Patterson, was second mate. The steward, whose name was Aitken, four seamen, and a French boy from Calais, were the other persons on board. [In fact, there was one other person on board: Mrs. Patterson, the captain's wife.]

The Jefferson Borden sailed from New Orleans on March 5, with a cargo of oilcake for Messrs. Simmonds, Hunt and Co., Mark-Lane, London…The crew were divided into two watches during the voyage. One of them was an American; another, though he came from London, called himself a Frenchman; a third was a Russian Finn. Their names are given as William Smith, Clew [John Glew], and [George] Miller; the fourth seaman was called Jacob Wheeler. The captain states that Miller, the Russian, behaved very insolently to himself and the other officers from the day of their sailing. On the eighth day, as he threatened them, they put him in irons; but, having been forty-eight hours in confinement, he promised to do better, and signed the official log to that effect. The rest of the crew signed a declaration that if Miller tried to make any fresh disturbance they would inform against him.

Everything went on well until April 20, when, about midnight, Miller came into the captain's room and told him that Clew had fallen and broken his leg, and he wanted the captain to go forward and assist him. Captain Patterson went to the cabin door and called to the second mate, but received no answer. It would be the watch of the second mate, and he should have been on deck to answer the call. Miller came from behind the hawse and asked why he did not go forward, remarking, "For God's sake help the man; he is dying." He had something in his hand, and Captain Patterson, feeling that something was wrong, stepped into the cabin, and would not go forward. Miller then asked the steward, Aitken, to go forward, but the captain desired him not to go.

When daylight came the captain saw the three men forward. They refused to come forward, or to give information as to what had become of the mate. Captain Patterson now told them that if they still declined he should use force. He gave them one more chance, and then fired with his double-barrelled gun. This did not appear to frighten them, so the captain fired his revolver. The men then threw iron and bottles at him. The ship at this time was at the mercy of the waves; the wheel was lashed and the ship merely drifted; it had to be pumped, but the men gave no help.

At night they tried to get the boat out, but she was too heavy for them. The captain then got forward and managed to close the forecastle door, and thus shut them in. They still refused to give in, and he shot at them through the window until they did so. This was about twelve o'clock on the second day. He again asked what they had done with the mate. Miller then said he had killed the mate. He added that Smith and Clew had helped him to throw the mate overboard. The captain asked where the second mate was; and Smith said he had also killed him, and, with Clew's assistance, had thrown him overboard.

The captain then took them out of the forecastle and put irons on them. They were confined for a time in the forecastle, but at night-time were separated. Miller and Smith were made to assist at the pumps in irons, but Clew was too much hurt. The captain dressed their wounds, as they were all wounded.

Eight days after this he fell in with a Norwegian barque, the Brevig, under Captain Larsen, from which he got one sailor to help bring the ship into port. The fishing-lugger Secret, of Worthing, next met the Jefferson Borden, near the Eddystone Lighthouse. The mutineers were still in irons. The captain had much difficulty in working his ship. A pilot came on board off Beachy Head, and the vessel arrived, on Thursday week, at the London Docks, when the captain made a report to the American Consul. The men were removed to the London Hospital, where they are now, in custody of the police.

The Magistrate at Bow-street, Sir Thomas Henry, heard the captain's evidence last Saturday, when Mr. Frigout, of the United States Consulate, was present. Sir Thomas Henry granted a warrant to bring up the men when sufficiently recovered to answer the charge; but said that, this being an offence on the high seas and on board an American ship, the case could not be tried in this country. The case came under the Extradition Acts and Treaties, and the demand for the extradition of the three prisoners would have to be made to the Minister of State.*

*The three mutineers – George Miller, John Glew and William Smith (the latter also "otherwise called Ephraim Clark") – were duly extradited to the United States. On 31 August 1875 they were arraigned before the District Court of Boston, Massachusetts to be tried for the murder of the first mate of the *Jefferson Borden*, Croydon Prask Patterson, on 20 April 1875 while the vessel was on the high seas. (The mutineers were not charged with the murder of the second mate, Charles Patterson.)

The trial began on 21 September and concluded on 30 September. On 1 October the jury announced their verdict: George Miller and William Smith were found guilty, and John Glew not guilty. (Glew, however, subsequently pleaded guilty to another indictment, for mutiny on the high seas for which he was sentenced to ten years with hard labour in the Massachusetts state prison.)

On 4 October, Mr. Justice Clifford, Associate-Justice of the US Supreme Court passed sentence on both Miller and Smith: that, on 14 January 1876, 'between the hours of eleven o'clock in the forenoon and one o'clock in the afternoon', they be 'hanged by the neck until [they] be dead', concluding for each of them, And may God have mercy on your soul!

## THE *LENNIE* MUTINY

## 12 Nov 1875
### Bottle Picked Up

Nantes, 11th Nov.- A bottle was picked up, 8th Nov., on the coast of Nienl [?], containing a paper on which was written in English – 'Send assistance and police, the crew having killed the master, mate, and boatswain. We left Antwerp for New York on the 23rd Oct., and the mutiny occurred on the 31st. Name of vessel LENNIE*, of Yarmouth, Captain Hatfield.' The *Lennie* was at that time not far from the island of Oleron [southwest Atlantic coast of France], and a French vessel was at once sent in search of her. A telegram, dated Rochelle, 10th Nov., 9.42 a.m., announces that a Government steamer had discovered the *Lennie*, of Yarmouth, N.S., and found a boy and five men on board, four of them being supposed [thought] to be accomplices [in the mutiny]. Six of the crew (Greeks) had escaped in a boat the previous evening. It was thought that the vessel would be taken to the island of Aix.

### 13 Nov 1875
### Casualties – Foreign

Nantes, 12th Nov.- With reference to the LENNIE, of Yarmouth, from Antwerp to New York, in ballast, reported yesterday as having been captured after a mutiny during which the master (Hatfield), etc., had been killed, another account states that the *Lennie* arrived in the roads of La Flotte (Ile de Ré) on the evening of the 6th Nov., and her movements creating suspicion, the captain of the *Travailleur* ordered the master to present himself. In answer to this summons a man, who stated that he was a Belgian [the steward, named Constant van Hoydonck], immediately came forward, and was conducted to St. Martin [the main port of Ile de Ré], where he stated that the master of the *Lennie*, having ordered the crew to reduce sail, was murdered by them, together with the mate and boatswain. As the cook knew something of navigation, the mutineers ordered him to conduct the vessel to Gibraltar, but he was compelled to put into La Flotte, on account of heavy weather. On the 10th Nov., the *Lennie* was still anchored about three or four miles NNE of La Flotte.

### 16 Nov 1875
### Casualties – Foreign

La Rochelle, 13th Nov.- The Lennie, of Yarmouth, N.S., from Antwerp to the United States, is now anchored off the military port of Rochefort. The master, mate, and boatswain had been murdered by six of the crew (Greeks), who, upon the vessel being driven towards the shore by bad weather, left her in one of the boats and landed at Sables, where they have been arrested; and the ship has sustained no damage.

### 19 Nov 1875
### Casualties – Foreign

Paris, 17th Nov.- The seamen charged with mutiny and murder on board the Lennie, have been sent from Rochefort to Nantes, and, after examination before the Consul, will be sent to England.

*The *Lennie* was in the Bay of Biscay on 31 October 1875, a few hundred miles off the French coast, when 11 of her crew mutinied. At that time the *Lennie* was described as a full-rigged ship of 950 tons (she would later be converted to a barque rig). She had a 16- (or possibly 15-) strong crew of multiple nationalities – notably, British and northern Europeans mixed with ethnic Turks and Greeks.

Around dawn on 31 October 1875, in response to the captain's berating of the deck crew's incompetence in putting the ship about, the mutineers stabbed and shot to death the captain, the first mate and the second mate. They spared the Belgian steward, named Constant von Hoydonck. The mutineers knew no navigation but believed that von Hoydonck did, and that he could pilot the vessel to Greece where they planned to jump ship. Von Hoydonck, however, steered north, towards the English Channel.

On 4 November the ship arrived and anchored off the Ile de Ré, an island just off the west coast of France near La Rochelle. Von Hoydonck and the Dutch cabin boy wrote notes in French and English requesting help, which they placed in half a dozen bottles and threw overboard. As the above report shows, one bottle was picked up, whereupon a French gunboat, the *Travailleur*, came to their rescue.

The 11 mutineers, six of whom had gone ashore, were all rounded up, arrested and taken to England where they were tried for their crime at the Old Bailey criminal court in London. Four men were acquitted. Three Greeks and a Turk were sentenced to death by hanging. Their execution took place at Newgate Prison at 8 a.m. on 23 May 1876 (the only quadruple execution in Newgate's history). The court awarded steward von Hoydonck, the hero of the incident, a reward of £50 for his contribution to saving the *Lennie* and effectively bringing the mutinous murderers to justice.

## THE *CASWELL* MUTINY

### 10 May 1876

**Casualties – Home**

London, 9th May.- Advices from Rio [de] Janeiro report the murder, by mutineers, of all the officers of the Caswell [barque], of Swansea, bound to Queenstown, the vessel being in lat. 1 S, long. 33 W.

### *13 May 1876*
**Casualties - Home**

Queenstown.-[By tel.] – The Caswell has been sighted off Bantry Bay [southwest Ireland].

### *15 May 1876*
**The Mutiny on Board The Caswell\* (barq.)**

Queenstown, 13th May, 7 40 a.m.- The Caswell (barq.), is just arriving in tow of the gunboat *Goshawk*, which was despatched last evening to her assistance.

Queenstown, 13th May, 10 a.m.- Report of Jas. [James] Carrick, able seaman in charge of Caswell [barq.]:-

The crew on leaving Antofagasta [Chile] consisted of captain, mate, 2nd mate, steward, three Greek seamen, two Italian seamen, two English seamen, carpenter, and two boys. Jan. 4th the Greeks and Italians mutinied, and murdered captain, mate, 2nd mate and steward. Carrick, who knows some navigation, took charge, as the foreign seamen wanted to take vessel to Greece.

About a month after, when off the coast of Brazil, the boys overheard a plot between the Greeks and Italians to murder the remaining Englishmen on board. Carrick and carpenter succeeded in overcoming one Greek, whom they put in irons, but were compelled to kill the other two Greeks, one of whom was ringleader of the mutiny, in self-defence. The two Italians then left the vessel in one of the boats, taking with them a letter from Carrick to deliver on shore.

The vessel was brought to this port by Carrick, an English seaman, carpenter, and two boys, and a little English boy who swam from the *Legaal* (Fr. barq.), to the Caswell when on the equator.

The following telegram was received 13th May by the Secretary to the Admiralty from the Rear-Admiral commanding at Queenstown: Goshawk arrived this morning with Caswell (barq.) in tow. Three Greeks and two Maltese, part of crew, on 4th Jan. last, rose and murdered the captain, 1st and 2nd mates, and steward. The Maltese left the ship in neighbourhood of River Plate [Buenos Aires]. Subsequently, English portion of crew overpowered the Greeks, two of whom were killed, and the other made prisoner, who is now on board. The *Caswell* has been handed over to civil power.

## 19 May 1876
### Casualties – Home

Queenstown, 18th May, 2 p.m.- The Caswell has sailed for Bristol.

## *The Illustrated London News*

## 27th May 1876
### The Mutiny of the Caswell

The Caswell is an iron barque of 499 tons, belonging to Swansea, built last year at Dumbarton. She was commanded by Captain George Edward Best, of London; the chief mate was William Wilson, the second mate was John Allan McLean. Having gone out from Glasgow to Buenos Ayres in the autumn [the *Caswell* left Glasgow on 1st July 1875], and thence on to Valparaiso, she began her homeward voyage on Jan. 1, with a cargo of nitre [nitrate], for Queenstown and Falmouth.

There were on board the captain and two officers named [ie., the two mates]; the steward, William Griffiths, a man of colour; Peter Macgregor, the carpenter; James Carrick and John Dunne, ordinary seamen; two apprentice boys, named Ferguson and Macdonald; and five foreigners – namely, three Greeks and two Maltese. The Greeks were George Peno, called "Big George", a very strong man and great ruffian; and two brothers, Nicholas and Christos Bombos, or Bambos, but the latter has another name. The Maltese were Gaspar Petrolio [sic] and his brother Giuseppe.

George Peno seems to have persuaded the other foreigners to kill the English officers and take possession of the ship. They had only been two or three days at sea when they murdered Captain Best, Wilson, McLean, and Griffiths, attacking each man unawares. The surviving Englishmen or Scotchmen were compelled for a time to submit to their commands. But the mutineers soon disagreed amongst themselves. The Maltese left the ship and went ashore in South America, having left their families there.

After they were gone, our three countrymen, James Carrick, John Dunne, and Peter Macgregor, determined to master the three Greeks, or to kill them, and bring the vessel safe

SKETCHES OF THE CASWELL MUTINY.

home. On the night of March 11, when Peno was keeping watch, Macgregor knocked him down and killed him with a hatchet. The noise aroused the other two Greeks, but Carrick and Macgregor ran to meet them in the cabin. Macgregor attacked Nicholas, who fired, but missed. Next moment the adze in the Scotchman's hand knocked away the revolver, but, missing the Greek's head, it sunk into the side of the ship. Macgregor and Nicholas seized the weapon and fought for its possession. The struggle was a desperate one, for one or the other man must die; but the strength of Macgregor told; he threw down the Greek, and killed him with the hatchet on the cabin floor.

Christos Bambos and Carrick had been meantime fighting desperately: Carrick with a hatchet against the other with a knife. Carrick wounded his opponent in several places, and would have killed him had not Macgregor despatched his man in time, when he turned on Christos Bambos, struck down his arms, and they both pinioned him. They then looked after his wounds. He was bleeding a great deal, and they did all they could to stanch the outflow; they sewed his back up with a packing-needle and thread, and the wound healed. They put him in irons and lashed him to the main hatch, and there Christos Bambos remained until he was given into the hands of the police, on Saturday week, at Queenstown.

As soon as Carrick and Macgregor had overcome the murderers, the question arose what should be done with the ship. Carrick was a chance seaman, taken on board; knew nothing of the owners of the vessel, and was close to Rio Janeiro. But he said the owners would be robbed, and probably justice defeated, by bringing the vessel in there or any other port so far from home, and therefore he determined to sail her to Queenstown – a two months' sail.

He worked out his resolution with extraordinary courage and ability. He scarcely ever left the wheel; he worked like a hero, attending to the navigation of the ship, and watching and attending his prisoner. When he reached Queenstown he was much bent and worn by his dreadful exertions. By parentage he is an Irishman, but by birth this brave young man is Scotch. Macgregor, the carpenter, worked with equal fortitude and perseverance on the two months' voyage home; and under him Carrick's orders were always carried out.

The ship made fair time, and the easterly winds drove her to the Irish coast, where, on Friday week, the 12th inst. [May], she was met by a pilot-boat from Queenstown. Carrick hailed her and got one man on board, saying, in reply to questions, that his crew was sick. This showed the forethought and fidelity of the man. Had it been known that he was so short of hands salvage might have been demanded. But it was found they could not work the ship up to Queenstown, and some hours afterwards they fell in with the pilot-boat again. Carrick then got three men on board; but in order to prevent them making a claim for salvage he drew up a paper, which he made them sign, in which they bound themselves to accept a certain sum for their services.

The gun-boat Goshawk, commanded by Lieutenant Bagge, R.N., was sent, however, to take charge of the Caswell and tow her into Queenstown Harbour. Mr. Mercer, sub-inspector of police, and a body of constabulary went on board the Caswell, next day, and took charge of the prisoner, Christos Bambos, who was sitting on the main hatch, hand-cuffed and guarded by marines. The prisoner was brought before Mr. Starkie, the magistrate at Queenstown, who remanded him until the Monday. He was then again remanded, and has been under further examination at Queenstown several days this week.

This prisoner, Christos Bambos, is a young good-looking man of twenty-seven, with closely cut whiskers, ending in an imperial; he has handsome Grecian features. He was dressed in a red shirt and cap, light trousers, and heavy sea-boots. He speaks Italian fluently, and did not appear to care about his position. One of his companions, killed in the final conflict, boasted of having killed two captains before.

Carrick, Macgregor (the carpenter), and Dunne are young men, twenty-five or thirty years of age. Carrick is a very intelligent man, with great firmness and determination. The log – in which the entire history of the affair is narrated – has been kept by him in a neat and regular way. Each day's reckoning is kept with the same care, and both the writing and figures are very well executed.

The Caswell was brought on from Queenstown to Bristol, where she would be unladen, and would thence be taken to Swansea. She has been inspected at Bristol by a multitude of curious visitors. The cabin of the vessel bore traces of a severe struggle. There were three bullet holes in the state room, where Nicholas fired from the bunk when he and Bambos were surprised by the Englishmen. The glass is broken, and there is a deep indentation on the partition frame of the berth, caused by a blow of the hatchet.

*The mutiny on the *Caswell*, and counter-attack and repossession of the ship by the non-mutinous crew, occurred on her maiden voyage. That was from Glasgow to South America: first to Buenos Aires, where she remained six weeks and then, when she could not find a cargo in the Argentinean capital, around Cape Horn to Valparaiso on the coast of Chile. Not finding a cargo there either, she moved further up the coast to the port of Antofagasta. There she loaded a cargo of saltpetre (sodium nitrate) and sailed for home, back round the Horn, on 1 January 1876.

The crew of the *Caswell* on her homeward – and soon to be mutinous, and murderous – voyage was divided between British and southern European seamen. The Britishers were: Captain George (Bully) Best, from London; William Wilson, first mate, and Allan McLean, second mate, both from Glasgow; another Scot, Peter MacGregor, carpenter, from Dumbartonshire; two young Scottish apprentices, Charles McDonald and Walter Ferguson; Emmanuel Griffiths, a black steward from Wales; James Carrick, able seaman, from Liverpool; John Dunne, able seaman, from Bristol; and Michael Rourke, able seaman, from Ireland. Rook Agineau from Germany was the ship's cook. The last two, however, left the ship before the mutiny: Rourke jumped ship at Valparaiso and Agineau deserted at Antofagasta. Neither was ever heard from again.

The southern European crew members were: Nicholas Morellos, able seaman, Turkish or Greek; George Peno (Big George), able seaman, Turkish or Greek; the brothers Giuseppe and Gaspari Pistoria, able seamen, Sicilian; and Christos Bombos, able seaman, Greek. The Pistoria brothers said they were from Malta but were actually from Sicily; at that time it was easier to get a job on a ship as a Maltese than as a Sicilian!

The mutiny as reported above took place when the *Caswell* was just four days out from Antofagasta, on 4 January 1876, at latitude 24° S, longitude 74° W (according to James Carrick). The mutiny itself became well-known at the time, featuring in *The Illustrated London News* magazine, as much for the mayhem of murders committed during the incident as for the fact of the mutiny itself.

The manner in which the murders aboard the *Caswell* were committed was particularly gruesome. The first man to be killed was the captain. Able seaman George Peno, Big George, the most fearsome of the mutineers, was apparently provoked for some reason by Capt. Best. He ripped out the captain's guts and bowels with his knife. The *Caswell*'s carpenter, Peter MacGregor, later testified, "I saw Big George jump down from the rail to where the captain was standing, and with his left hand on the captain's breast, he gave two cuts in the captain's stomach, one down and one across, and his entrails came out." Another mutineer, the 'Maltese' Giuseppe Pistoria, then shot the captain twice (or possibly three times) in the head. At least one of the other non-British crew members then stabbed Capt. Best several times as he lay dying on the deck.

The 18 year-old black steward, Emmanuel Griffiths, met an even gorier fate. Giuseppe Pistoria shot him three times in the face. Big George then cut his heart out of his chest. Peter MacGregor later testified, "I saw his heart on the deck, and afterwards one of the boys threw it overboard." One of the two apprentices, Charles McDonald, testified that Big George seized the steward by the hair and, with his other hand, "nearly cut him in two" with his knife. The second mate was stabbed and shot a number of times as he tried to get away from the mutineers. The corpses of the four men – the captain, two mates and the steward – were tied by a rope to an anchor and thrown overboard.

After the mutiny the Greek/Turkish/Maltese contingent of the crew took command of the *Caswell*. Nominally in charge were Big George and Nicholas Morellos. The two Pistoria brothers and Christos Bombos, however, seemed to ally themselves to some degree with the British seamen, and to Carrick and Dunne in particular. Apart from those two, the surviving British crew members were the carpenter Peter MacGregor and the two apprentices McDonald and Ferguson.

The mutineers eventually decided to sail the *Caswell* back around the Horn towards Buenos Aires. This was mainly because the two Pistoria brothers wanted to get off there: Gaspari Pistoria's wife and family lived in Buenos Aires. Some time on or around 19 February 1876, when the ship was about 30 miles off the River Plate estuary leading up to Buenos Aires, the Pistorias took their leave of the *Caswell* in a small boat.

From that point Nicholas Morellos apparently took command of the *Caswell* as self-appointed captain (although Big George Peno seems to have thought that he, in fact, was in command), and all three Greeks – Morellos, Bombos and Big George – kept themselves away from the Britishers.

About three weeks after the departure of the Pistoria brothers, near the equator, the British seamen Carrick and Dunne and carpenter MacGregor counter-attacked to retake possession of the *Caswell*. They killed Big George and Nicholas Morellos and injured Christos Bombos who was put in irons for the duration of the voyage home.

Carrick now took command of the *Caswell* and headed for Queenstown (now called Cobh, the port for Cork in southern Ireland). However, a curious incident took place, soon after the counter-attack. As the ship was slipping across the equator, a sail appeared nearby. Carrick headed towards the other vessel; he wanted to get a check on the accuracy of the *Caswell*'s chronometer which was necessary for accurate navigation. The ship was a French barque, *Le Genile*, of Dunkirk. On board was a young English boy who claimed he was being mistreated on the French ship and asked to be transferred to the *Caswell*. Carrick refused the boy's request but next day, with the two ships still close together, the boy jumped off the French ship and swam across to the *Caswell* where he was hoisted aboard. (If they were experiencing typical doldrums weather, with little or no wind, the two ships were probably practically becalmed on a flat sea.)

The *Caswell* reached Queenstown on 13 May 1876. A British gunboat, the *Goshawk*, met the ship off the Head of Kinsale, put a crew on board and towed the *Caswell* into Queenstown. There, Christos Bombos was arrested and taken to Cork County Gaol. He was tried, found guilty of murder in the circumstances of the mutiny on the high seas aboard the *Caswell* on 4 January that year, and sentenced to death by hanging. In response, Bombos declared that he was innocent, and that he had "held one of the mates against the rail [of the ship]…from fear and compulsion of George, who threatened my life with a knife."

Just after 8 o'clock on the morning of Friday, 25 August 1876, Christos Bombos was executed at Cork County Gaol, along with another man, Thomas Crowe, aged 63 from Tipperary, who had been convicted of murder.

The hero of the *Caswell* mutiny, James Carrick, went back to South America to be employed in shipping operations around the coast of Patagonia. There was a worldwide search for the Pistoria brothers that lasted several years, but they were not found – at least, not during that search period. In January 1879, however, three years after the mutiny, Carrick happened to be at a café in Montevideo, Uruguay, when he spotted a man whom he believed to be Giuseppe Pistoria. The man, who was calling himself Francesco Moschara (which was, in fact, his real name), was soon arrested and deported to England, accompanied by Carrick.

Moschara and Carrick arrived at Liverpool on 20 March 1879, and Moschara was handed over to the Irish authorities a few weeks later. He was tried and convicted in July that year of the murder of William Wilson, first mate of the *Caswell*, in the circumstances of the mutiny on board the ship in January 1876, and executed by hanging on Monday, 25 August 1879 at Cork County Gaol – three years to the day that Christos Bombos was hanged at the same jail for his part in the mutiny on the *Caswell*.

The *Caswell* sailed for another 23 years after the mutiny but was lost in 1899 during a voyage from Newcastle, New South Wales, to Guayaquil on the coast of Ecuador. After departing Newcastle on 18 February that year with a cargo of coal, she was not heard from again, presumed lost with all hands during her voyage across the Pacific.

The mutiny on the *Caswell* bears striking similarities with the *Lennie* mutiny of 31 October 1875, most notably the volatility of an ethnically mixed crew of 'Britishers' and southern Europeans – ethnic Turks, Greeks and 'Maltese'.

## 2 Oct 1876

### Casualties – Home

Gravesend, 29th Sept.- The master, Hill, of the Western Chief, arrived in the River from Yokohama, reports that on the 13th Sept., about midnight, one of the crew, a Malay, stabbed two of the seamen. One of the wounded men died almost immediately, the other is recovering. The Malay jumped overboard.

## 7 Nov 1879

### Casualties – Foreign

Macassar*, Aug. 8.- Gem.- Information has been received that Mr. F. Cadell, an Australian trader, when on a voyage from Ambon* to the Kei Islands*, in his schooner, the Gem, fitted with auxiliary steam power, has been murdered by the crew, who afterwards sunk the vessel. One of the boats, with a portion of the crew, has arrived at Amboyna*. The remainder of them have shaped their course for the Kei Islands.

*Macassar is the largest city on the Indonesian island of Sulawesi. Between 1971–1991 its formal name was Ujung Pandang, but the two names are used interchangeably. The town of Ambon on Ambon Island (also called Amboyna), and the Kei Islands are in the Maluku (Moluccas) group of islands in southeastern Indonesia.

## THE *FREEMAN CLARK*: "A BLOODY TRAGEDY"

## 20 June 1882

### Casualties, Etc.

Freeman Clark, ship, arrived at New York from Calcutta. The Chinese cook and steward, on May 27, killed Captain Dwight in his state room, and attacked the mate, who, however, escaped them. The crew were aroused, attacked the murderers, and killed both, throwing their bodies overboard. The Chinese, it is said, were incensed at being deprived of opium. (*Philadelphia, June 18*)

*The New York Times*

*18th June 1882*
### A Bloody Tragedy At Sea

### Two Chinamen Kill Their Captain and Are Slain

A Brutal Murder on the Freeman Clarke – Capt. Dwight's Body Terribly Mutilated – An Attempt to Kill the Mate – The Assassins' Fate

The ship Freeman Clarke arrived yesterday morning from Calcutta after a voyage of 126 days, during the latter part of which a horrible tragedy was enacted on board, in which three lives were lost. Early on the morning of May 27, as the vessel was proceeding under full sail and with beautiful weather, two Malay Chinese, belonging to the crew, arose, and after murdering Capt. James S. Dwight, one of them assaulted the mate. After this they were disabled, and while the second officer and the carpenter were in the cabin, members of the crew dispatched the two Chinamen and threw their bodies overboard…

The Freeman Clarke sailed from Calcutta with a valuable East Indian cargo about the middle of last February. Among the crew were two Malay Chinamen, Ah Cung and Ah Gee, who had shipped as cook and steward respectively some time previous in New York. The cook was the younger of the two and was always spoken of as "the boy." Both wore pigtails and were dressed like the average Chinese sea-cook. They had obtained a slight smattering of English, but when excited they would resort to their native dialect. Capt. Dwight saw that they were treacherous and had no confidence in them. When the vessel sailed from Calcutta he cut off the opium supply of the two Chinamen. They had been indulging quite freely in this drug while at that port, but they made no strong objection to the order of the Captain, and did not show any ill will toward him at the time…

All went well on board while sailing down the Indian Ocean and around [the Cape of] Good Hope. No one imagined that the cook and steward were hatching any plot. The latter had a stateroom in the cabin, while the berth of the former was in the galley. On the morning of Saturday, May 27, at 4 o'clock, the mate's watch went below and the second mate took command of the deck. An hour later the men in the starboard watch were about to wash down the decks, when two of them saw that something strange was going on in the mate's state-room and called the attention of Thomas Lowery, the second mate, to the fact. The latter rushed toward the cabin. In the mate's room stood the cook, with a hatchet in one hand and a carving-knife in the other. The mate, whose face was smeared with blood, was shouting "Murder!" and holding the elbow of the cook, who was trying to strike him with the hatchet.

One of the sailors rushed into the state-room to assist the mate, while the second officer hurried into the cabin. There a horrible sight presented itself. On the deck of the after cabin Capt. Dwight was seen kneeling, while blood streamed down his person from gashes in his head. He was speechless but still alive. The second mate rushed up the after companionway and cried out to the man at the wheel, "They have murdered the Captain!" Then running along the poop to the main deck the officer says he saw the two Malay fiends, each armed with a hatchet and a carving-knife running amuck about the ship and slashing at everyone who came near them.

In a pair of beckets above the Captain's berth was a sword, which the second officer went and got, and with it attacked the steward, cutting him at first only slightly. Finally he struck the Chinaman on the shoulder and caused him to fall upon his knees. Before he could regain his feet a man named Andrew Jansen came up with a capstan-bar and felled him to the deck. In the meantime H. W. Jolsen, the carpenter, had knocked the cook down with one of the handles of the fore pump and had then gone to the Captain's assistance. He found Dwight alone and sitting on the deck. He was covered with blood, and in answer to the carpenter's inquiries, was merely able to groan out a few incoherent words.

The carpenter procured water and washed the Captain's face, in order to get at the wounds which he hoped to stanch. There were 11 knife cuts in Capt. Dwight's head, and three more wounds which had evidently been made by the back of a hatchet. The medicine chest was opened and efforts were made to revive the wounded man, but he died in two hours.

Mr. William Williams, the mate, was stunned by a blow from the hatchet of the cook, and after he had recovered consciousness it was found that both of the Chinamen were dead. How they had received the fatal wounds no one could learn precisely, but there was no doubt that, after they had been partially stunned, the infuriated crew had set upon them and finished with knives and capstan-bars…

Mr. Williams says that he awoke to find the cook standing over him. He had already received one blow from the rascal's hatchet, and, but for a struggle in which a dangerous blow was parried, the Chinaman would have taken his life.

The mate tells of a strange premonition of his death which Capt. Dwight seemed to have had on the evening before the murder. The mate was in command of the deck, and was smoking a cigar when the Captain came up. "You seem quite happy," the latter remarked. "Why shouldn't I be," said the mate, "I am nearly home, where I shall meet my wife. You know we were only married on my last voyage. But you are going to meet your father and mother, and you ought to be cheerful, too." "I know I had," said the Captain, "but somehow I can't. It's because I can't get rid of the notion that I shall never live to reach New York.".…

The *Freeman Clark* was lost, on fire, off the coast of South Africa in 1883:

*14 Aug 1883*
**Casualties, Etc.**

Freeman Clark.- Cape Town, July 24.- The ship Freeman Clark, 1,336 tons, from Calcutta for New York, with a cargo of jute, was abandoned off St. Francis Bay [near Port Elizabeth] on the 18th inst. After encountering a heavy gale for some days, she was discovered to be on fire. In a few hours the crew had to take to the boats. One boat containing the mate and eight men (two having died from exposure) has been picked up by a tug sent in search. The other boat, containing the captain and seven men, is still missing*.

*They were never heard from again, presumed lost.

## 29 Jan 1885
**Miscellaneous**

Plymouth, Jan 29, 9 50 a.m.- Barque, presumed American, 10 days out from Cardiff, anchored off Yealm in a critical position. Captain found dead. Government tug and lifeboat in attendance. Further particulars will follow immediately ascertained. Wind S, blowing strong, with rain thickening.

*30 Jan 1885*
**Terrible Scene On Board Ship**

Information reached Plymouth late on Wednesday evening that a ship had been wrecked in Wembury Bay [on the south Devon coast], and the lifeboat crew were at once called and the lifeboat was launched, and proceeded immediately to the scene of the supposed wreck. As the boat remained away the whole night considerable anxiety was felt as to its safety, but the crew returned yesterday morning and brought news of the murder of the captain, which had been committed by one of the crew on board the barque Wellington, of Windsor, Nova Scotia, the registered owner of which is Mr. A. Armstrong, of Liverpool.

The barque, it appears, narrowly escaped being wrecked, but was eventually got up the River Yealm, where she now lies. The crew have reported that the captain, whose dead body is still on board the ship, was killed on Monday morning by one of the crew in self-defence, the captain having, it is alleged, drunk himself into a state of madness, and then hunted the officers and men all over the ship with a loaded revolver, which he fired in all directions, seriously wounding Adolph Hesse, the carpenter, and another sailor named Martin Nest.

The Wellington is a large barque of 1,000 tons register, and she carried 16 hands, all told, including two mates, a boatswain, cook, and carpenter. She left [Le] Havre on Tuesday week with a cargo of empty petroleum barrels and copper ore for New York. The crew was a mixed one, consisting of Englishmen, Americans, Germans, and Scandinavians, and the captain, whose name was Charles Armstrong, was a brother of the registered owner. Before leaving France the captain received a present of two casks of spirits, and from the time the ship left port the men say that he was drinking heavily, that he behaved in the most eccentric and reckless manner, and showed decided indications of delirium tremens.

On Sunday night he called each watch aft, told the men he intended putting some of them in irons, and asked them what objection they had to make to it. The crew noticed that his manner was changed, and that he was wild; and, anxious not to provoke him, they made no reply to his question. Then he called upon the two mates to assist him, and followed this up by placing the boatswain in irons and fastening him to a stanchion. Then the steward was served in a similar manner, and there being no more irons on board he put the carpenter down the lazarette.

The crew assert that they had done nothing to justify this action on the captain's part, but he seemed to have worked himself into the belief that the liquor which was sent on board for him had been poisoned, that the steward and boatswain knew of this, and had entered into a conspiracy to take his life. The officers obeyed the captain's orders, fearing that if they refused to assist him in putting the men in irons he would shoot them with his revolver which he carried in his pocket. Although the night was bitterly cold and squally the boatswain, steward, and carpenter were kept under arrest for four hours, after which the captain liberated them.

So far as can be ascertained, Captain Armstrong seems to have regarded one of the crew, an American named Jones, as his friend, and as early as 2 o'clock on Monday morning he sent for Jones to come and sit with him. The man went aft and met the captain on the poop. The latter was staring wildly, and told Jones that he must come into the cabin and sit with him. The seaman without replying backed towards the deck, the captain following him closely, and looking, to use Jones's expression, as "if the devil was in him."

When Jones reached the hatch the captain turned round, and passing under the poop, entered the room where the boatswain and carpenter slept together. The carpenter was sleeping in the lower bunk, and the captain, drawing his revolver, shot the sleeping man in the throat, the bullet imbedding itself between the windpipe and the large vessels. The other men were roused by the report of the pistol, and from this time in the darkness of the night the scene was a terrible one.

Captain Armstrong, rushing from the room where he had wounded the carpenter, met the steward running along the passageway, and discharged one of the barrels of his revolver at him, the bullet narrowly missing the man's head and lodging itself in the pantry door. Armstrong then came from under the poop, and meeting the mates outside fired at them, but again missed his aim. He then rushed forward and literally hunted his officers and crew about the deck with his loaded revolver, firing at the men whenever he got a chance. Some of the foreigners hid themselves, and others of the crew seeing that the captain was mad grasped knives, marlingspikes, handspikes, or other weapons, and waiting behind the deck-house, capstan, and other obstacles, tried to disable him as he rushed wildly about discharging bullets whenever he saw a man without any shelter.

Having emptied the seven chambers of his weapon, Armstrong returned to his cabin and reloaded, and then again came on the deck, firing at his crew and officers whenever an opportunity presented itself. At length a seaman named Martin Nest happened to be standing on the quarter-deck as the captain, pistol in hand, rushed round the gangway. Nest at once sprang into the main rigging and reached the third rattling. The captain, walking beneath the unfortunate sailor, exclaimed, "Now I have got you," and while the other members of the crew looked on to render assistance, the captain took deliberate aim at Nest and shot him in the eye, and though the bullet lodged in the man's head, strangely enough he was not killed and is living still.

Armstrong again emptied the barrels of his revolver, again loaded them, and again discharged them with the exception of one barrel. He then went into his cabin and on to the poop, and as he once more descended to the deck, several of the crew made a rush, and in the mêlée the captain, who was a big powerful man, received a blow on the head from a marlingspike which smashed in his skull. As he fell he was secured and placed in irons, and then laid in a bunk. Here it required two men to hold him, and he was continually cursing and swearing, and saying if they would only let him get up he would shoot the whole crew. After lingering for several hours in this condition, Captain Armstrong died on Monday night.

As soon as the captain was secured on the Monday morning the chief mate, who is named Charles L. Patterson, decided to go about and make for Plymouth, the ship then being about 400 miles to the westward of Scilly. He made the Eddystone Light [Eddystone Lighthouse in the English Channel, 13 miles southwest of Plymouth] on Wednesday evening, and the weather becoming thick lost his bearings, and ultimately had to anchor in a dangerous position in Wembury Bay. It was then that the lifeboat went from Plymouth to their assistance, with the results stated, the ship after considerable difficulty, being got safely into smooth water.

## 4 Feb 1886

### Maritime Intelligence

Frank N. Thayer*.- St. Helena, Jan. 18.- On Jan. 11 a boat arrived here containing Captain Clark, wife and child, and 14 men, part of the crew of the American ship Frank N. Thayer, of Boston, from Manila for New York, with a cargo of hemp. Captain Clark reports that on Jan. 2, in lat. 25 S, long. 0 20 W, about midnight, two of the crew, natives of Manila, mutinied, killing the two mates, carpenter, and two men, and severely wounding the captain and four others, finally setting fire to the vessel after barricading the cabin and forecastle doors to secure the remainder of the crew.

On the 4th the captain and crew succeeded in breaking their way out, and all efforts were then made to put the fire out, but without success. The two mutineers in the meantime jumped overboard after being wounded. The boat was then got out and provisioned, all hands getting in, and on the 5th they made sail for this place. The boat has been sold by auction for 20l [£20].

*The Frank N. Thayer was a 1,600-ton full-rigged ship. Her master, Capt. Robert K. Clarke, signed on the two Singaporean seamen in Manila to make up the necessary number of crew, which totalled 21 including himself. His wife and child were also on board. The two Singaporeans had only sailed aboard steamships and had never been in sail before and knew nothing about what to do on a sailing ship. The rest of the crew regarded them with contempt; the officers assigned them the most menial tasks. No-one considered that they would cause trouble – except for the ship's Chinese cook, Ah Say, who seemed to understand immediately that the two men were dangerous.

Ah Say proved to be right. In the early hours of Sunday 3 January 1886, just after the midnight change of watch on a balmy South Atlantic night, the *Frank N. Thayer* was bowling along at up to 10 knots in the southeast trades, heading towards the island of St. Helena, 700 miles to the northwest. The two mates had sat together for a smoke on the afterdeck. The two Singaporeans came up to them and attacked them with knives. The second mate died soon after the attack and the first mate died around 4 a.m. One of the villains seriously wounded the captain as he came up from his cabin when the dying second mate called him. The murdering mutineers then killed the helmsman, the carpenter and a seaman who had hid in a sail locker, pitching them all overboard. The remaining crew members eventually managed to make an assault on the Singaporeans, but at the cost of four wounded and a fifth man dead.

Once Capt. Clarke's wife had patched him up, the crew went in search of the two murderers. When they were found Capt. Clarke shot one of the men in the chest, and he leapt overboard. The other disappeared into the hold where he set fire to the cargo of hemp. After the smoke and heat drove him out onto the deck spluttering and coughing, he, too, was shot and jumped overboard. Soon the blazing flames from the cargo took over the whole ship. The crew prepared and provisioned a lifeboat in which to abandon ship. The *Frank N. Thayer* went down ablaze and sank just before sunset on Monday 4 January. Capt. Clarke and the other survivors of the murderous mayhem of the past two days immediately set sail in the lifeboat for St. Helena where they arrived a week later.

## 20 Oct 1887

### Maritime Intelligence

Johannes.- Copenhagen, Oct. 19, 7 p.m.- The Johannes, Russian schooner, of Haynasch, has been towed in here by the Danish steamer Morso. The carpenter had yesterday morning murdered the captain and five hands and thrown their bodies overboard, and wounded the mate. He was overmanned by the Morso's crew and has been imprisoned.

## 31 Oct 1890

### Mutiny At Sea

The last mail from Ceylon brings news of a mutiny on board the four-masted sailing ship Eusemere*, from Cardiff to Colombo with coals, consigned to the P. and O. Company. She had a captain, four officers, some apprentices, and a mixed crew of British and Scandinavians. During the voyage the captain saw fit to reduce [ie., demote] the boatswain, and the English sailors espoused the cause of the latter. After being 28 days at sea more than half the crew refused to work the sails, and the English showed a very mutinous spirit.

Finding all efforts to get these men to work were in vain, the captain, who was supported by the officers, apprentices, and Scandinavians, decided to remove the food from the forecastle. The ringleaders of the mutineers resisted, and the chief officer, in order to frighten the men, fired a shot from a revolver, which wounded one of them [William Thomas]. The mutineers then surrendered; their knives were taken from them, and the leaders were put in irons. The men then agreed to work, and after a week's incarceration the leaders also agreed to resume their duty. At Colombo they were charged with mutiny, but the proceedings had not terminated when the mail left. [The 17 mutineers were convicted and sentenced to imprisonment.]

*The *Eusemere* was a big steel barque of 2,512 tons, built at the yard of R. Williamson & Son at Workington, Cumbria, on the northwest coast of England. She was one of six four-masted steel barques built there known as the Six Sisters (the other five being *Andelana, Pendragon Castle, Caradoc, Vortigern* and *Conishead*). *Eusemere* was 303.7ft long, 42.2ft in breadth and 24.5ft deep.

Her first owners were Fisher & Sprott of Liverpool, and her first master Capt. Sprott. She was launched in June 1890. The mutiny recorded above happened on her first voyage of 82 days, from Cardiff to Colombo, with a cargo of coal. In 1896 she was sold to a Hamburg shipping company, Reederei B. Wencke & Söhne, and renamed *Pindos*. On 10 February 1912, under that name but with a different owner, she was wrecked off Coverack on the Lizard Peninsula, Cornwall during a southeast gale.

## 7 Oct 1892

### Miscellaneous

Christiansund.- Oct. 6, 1 45 p.m.- Captain Larsen, Norwegian barque Thorbeck VI., reports that mate of barque William Hales, of New York, with some of crew, had been on board his vessel, 4 N latitude, stating that his captain and captain's wife had been murdered by Chinese cook at sea. Murderer threw himself overboard, and was drowned. Ship continued her voyage to Cape Town.

## 6 April 1896

### Maritime Intelligence

Lyman D. Foster.- Shanghai, March 19.- Captain Dryer, master of the schooner Lyman D. Foster, which arrived at Shanghai on March 19, was killed on Feb. 25 by the cook, who became crazy.

## 17 April 1896

### Mutiny on the High Seas

At the Liverpool Police Court yesterday before Mr. Kinghorn, deputy stipendiary, two coloured sailors, named Henry Shaw and John Primus, were brought up, on remand, charged with having refused to obey the commands of their superior officers, and with having assaulted the first and second mates of the British ship Wiscombe Park, of the crew of which they were members. The proceedings were taken under the 225th Section of the Merchant Shipping Act of 1894. Mr. Cripps appeared for the prosecution.

It was stated by several witnesses that when the Wiscombe Park was on a voyage from Newcastle (New South Wales) to Valparaiso, the coloured seamen became insubordinate, and used insulting language to the officers of the ship. The crew were divided into a white and black watch*, and the two prisoners, acting as ringleaders, incited the members of the coloured watch to become insolent. The prisoners on several occasions challenged the officers to fight. On Jan. 31 last a dispute arose on the deck of the vessel, and it was alleged that the prisoner Primus threatened the second mate with a knife, and that Shaw attempted to strike the first officer with a knife. In self-defence, the first officer fired a revolver at the men, and the captain of the ship asked them to quietly submit to being put in irons.

The prisoners questioned the witnesses, with the apparent object of showing that the crew had been bullied by the officers. Shaw admitted having drawn a knife, but alleged that it was done under extreme provocation, and in a moment of desperation. Mr. Kinghorn expressed the opinion that the officers of the ship had only done what was necessary for the safety of the ship, and sent each of the prisoners to jail for 16 weeks, 10 weeks for disobedience, and 6 weeks for assault.

*The most interesting thing about this incident was not the violence of the sailors' behaviour (common enough on sailing ships of those times) but that the crew were divided into the ship's two watches by race: one 'white watch' and one 'black watch'.

The usual practice of picking watches in sailing ships was for the deckhand crew (including apprentices) to line up on deck in front of the first and second mates on sailing day. Each mate then picked a man for his respective watch, the first mate choosing first for his *port watch*, followed by the second mate for his *starboard watch*, and so on alternately until all the crew had been assigned to one or the other watch. The only members of the crew excluded from standing in a watch (meaning that they only worked during the day or when all hands were needed on deck for a particular task) were the sailmaker, carpenter, cook and steward (often one man serving as both, cook-steward) and, if there was one, a cook-steward's assistant. The captain was nominally head of the starboard watch, but that watch was actually kept by the second mate.

Whether in the case of the *Wiscome Park*, above, this usual procedure was kept to or not, is not known. It seems more likely that the two watches were simply assigned according to the race of the crew members, rather than by an alternate selection process. However it occurred, it was quite unusual.

Paul Eve Stevenson, in *By Way of Cape Horn*, wrote during his voyage from New York to San Francisco on the *Hosea Higgins*: "To-day Mr. Rarx [second mate] told me of a novel and very successful way of manning a vessel with what is known as a checker-board crew. Two forecastles are necessary, or one with a dividing bulkhead, all the men of one watch being white and the others black. If they were together in one forecastle, violent hostilities would continuosly prevail; but if separated, they will work against and try to outdo each other; so that, with a little judicious flattery or word of encouragement, such work as the making and shortening of sail, tacking and wearing, will be done with incredible alacrity."

## THE *OLIVE PECKER* AND THE *HERBERT FULLER*

### 19 Aug 1897

**Mutiny At Sea**

Boston, Aug. 18.- News has reached here that the captain and mate of the schooner Olive Pecker, bound from Boston to Buenos Ayres, have been murdered by the crew*, who afterwards burned the vessel and escaped, it is believed, to Bahia [Brazil]. The Olive Pecker belonged to the owners of the barquentine Herbert Fuller**, whose captain and second mate, as well as the former's wife, were murdered *en route* for Buenos Ayres [in 1896].

## 25 Aug 1897
### Tragedy At Sea

Boston (Massachusetts), Aug. 24.- Fresh light is thrown upon the terrible tragedy perpetrated on the schooner Olive Pecker, of this port, while on a voyage to South America, by the confession of Anderson, the steward, made by him to the United States Consul at Buenos Ayres, where he and five of the crew are now detained as prisoners. The schooner sailed from Rockland, Maine, on June 21, with a cargo of lumber for Buenos Ayres. It appears from Anderson's statement that the crew complained to Captain Whitman of the quality of the food, and that the captain put the blame upon the steward, whereupon he and the captain quarreled.

Early in August Anderson crept to the captain's room at midnight, and struck at the captain with a cleaver, inflicting a horrible wound. A second blow split his skull open. Sanders, the mate, heard the captain scream when the first blow was struck, and as he entered the cabin to ascertain the cause, Anderson felled him so quickly with the cleaver that he never even groaned. The steward then set fire to the cabin, and the vessel was soon in flames, and was destroyed. The crew left in boats. They were at that time ignorant of the murders, but suspected Anderson had made away with the captain and mate when they saw the two officers were missing.

*The *Olive Pecker* was a three-masted schooner of 832 tons built at Belfast, Maine in 1889. On 20 June 1897 she sailed from Boston, Massachusetts, under the command of her part-owner Capt. J.W. Whitman, with a cargo of pine and spruce lumber. Her crew comprised: William Wallace Saunders, mate; William Thornburgh, 'engineer of a donkey engine'; John Andersen (or Anderson), cook; and the four ordinary seamen Martin Barstad (of Norway), John Lind (Sweden), Juan de Dios Burial (Spain), and Andrew March (Newfoundland).

On 6 August, about 100–150 miles off the northeast coast of Brazil, between 9 and 10 a.m., the cook John Andersen shot and killed Capt. Whitman and mate William Saunders. A few hours later Andersen persuaded the rest of the crew to help him throw the dead men's bodies overboard. He then poured oil over the deck cargo of lumber and set the ship alight. The crew got away in a small boat, reaching the coast of Brazil a day and a half later. Andersen and Lind reached the port of Bahia, on the northeast coast of Brazil, where they shipped on vessels going to Pensacola, Florida, and Spain, respectively.

The other four seamen, however, informed the Brazilian authorities of the events on board the *Olive Pecker* and of the whereabouts of the murderer, John Andersen, who was subsequently arrested at Bahia. He and the four other seamen were consigned to the charge of the United States Consul who sent the five men back to the United States on board the US warship *Lancaster* in September 1897. The men were landed at the *Lancaster*'s first port of call, Hampton Roads, Virginia, where they were turned over to a US Marshall and jailed at Norfolk, Virginia on 7th November. In the indictment of Andersen *vs.* United States, of 9th May 1898, Andersen was convicted of the murder of mate William Saunders and sentenced to death, his execution fixed for 26 August 1898.

\*\*According to the *Halifax Herald* newspaper dated 22 July 1896, the *Herbert Fuller*, a barquentine of 670 tons, from Harrington, Maine, sailed from Boston on 8 July 1896 with a cargo of lumber for Rosario, Argentina. In the early hours of Tuesday 14 July 1896, the vessel's captain, Charles J. Nash, his wife, and second mate August W. Blandberg, of Finland, were hacked to death by an axe allegedly wielded by the first mate, Thomas Brane, from the West Indian island of St. Kitts. Brane took command of the vessel until 20 July when the steward, Jonathan Spencer, and the only passenger aboard, Lester Monks, arrested Brane and navigated the ship to Halifax, Nova Scotia. They towed a boat astern that contained the three corpses of the murder victims.

The *Herald* began its extensive coverage of the *Herbert Fuller* incident with the headline *A Carnival Of Murder On The High Seas*. It followed that up for days afterwards with graphic accounts by other crew members, including the 'alleged' murderer, Brane, and the passenger, Monks, and sketches of the victims, crew members and the vessel at anchor in Halifax harbour. A New Zealand newspaper, the *Marlborough Express*, published the following story about the incident, with its own interpretation of the sequence of events, on 26 September 1896:

## MUTINY AND MURDER

### CAPTAIN, WIFE AND MATE KILLED

The wooden barquentine, Herbert Fuller, of Machais, Maine, has arrived at Halifax, Nova Scotia, with a terrible tale of murder. The barquentine sailed from Boston on July 8, for South America. The crew sulked from the start, refused to obey the orders of the officers, and complained about the quality of the food and anything else which was unsatisfactory to them. The feeling of insubordination reached a climax on July 11. During the night the crew armed themselves with axes, and crept down to cabins occupied by the master, Captain Nash, and his wife, and assailed them. All three were almost chopped to pieces, and their injuries were of such a serious and horrible nature that death in each case must have been instantaneous. None of the victims made an outcry when attacked, and the officer who was on watch states that he heard nothing.

The tragedy was first discovered when the watch was changed. The officer on duty went to call the second mate and found him dead. The first mate, the ship's carpenter, and the steward then armed themselves, and forced the crew to bring the ship to Halifax, where all were arrested.

### MAD MURDERER ON THE *PRINS CARL*

## 18 May 1900

**Maritime Intelligence**

Prins Carl (s).- Copenhagen, May 17.- The following telegram has been received here from Koping, Sweden:- As the steamer Koping passed the steamer Prins Carl last night at 11 o'clock, a man\* sprung up on the deck of the latter, and shouted, "If any one comes near, I will shoot."

At the same moment it was seen that a woman shrieking for help, was hanging over the ship's side. The man escaped in a boat. The Prins Carl was then boarded, and it was found that 12 men on board of her had been shot down. The remainder of the people on board were locked in. One of the wounded persons died to-day. The murderer is being pursued.

*The man who committed the murders on the Swedish ferry *Prins Carl* on the night of 16/17 May 1900 was John Filip Nordlund. Born on 23 March 1875, at Säter, about 175 km northwest of Stockholm, Nordlund was a career criminal: between 1891 and 1900 he spent two long periods in prison for cattle rustling and theft. Released from Långholmen Prison in Stockholm on 20 April 1900, he conceived a plan to board the *Prins Carl* to kill as many people on her as possible, steal as much as he could from his victims, and then burn the vessel as he escaped. He killed four people outright, including the captain, Olof Rönngren, and wounded nine (of which eight survived), before escaping in one of the vessel's lifeboats.

When Nordlund was captured the following day, he announced to the police that his killing spree was his 'revenge on humanity', and that he would gladly have killed more people on the train he was about to board at the time of his arrest. In prison Nordlund remained unrepentant about the killings on the *Prins Carl*. He was sentenced to death and executed by beheading with an axe, on 10 December 1900, at Västerås County Jail.

Nordlund's execution was the third that year in Sweden. In the following ten years there was a series of reprieves from carrying out the death penalty in Sweden until Johan Alfred Ander, a convicted murderer, was executed at Långholmen Prison on 23 November 1910 – the only person in Sweden ever to be executed by the guillotine. (Capital punishment in Sweden was abolished on 30 June 1921 for crimes committed in peacetime, and from 1st January 1976 for crimes committed at any time.)

## 14 March 1901

**Miscellaneous**

London, March 13.- The master of the Clyde (s), arrived at Southampton, reports:- On Feb. 26 spoke the barque Lorton, becalmed. In reply to a signal "Wish to communicate," [we] stopped and sent away a boat, when the captain of the Lorton handed a written statement as follows:- Lat 18 30 N, long 29 29 W, Veleri Giovanni, A.B., murdered Victor Baileff, A.B., by stabbing him in six different places with a knife, and stated that the prisoner was being brought home in irons.*

### *12 April 1901*

**Alleged Murder At Sea.**- Valeri Giovanni, an Italian seaman, was charged before the Falmouth magistrates yesterday with the murder of Victor Baileff, of Jersey, on board the Liverpool barque Lorton on the high seas on Feb. 15. The vessel left Caleta Buena, South America [Chile], with a cargo of nitrate on Dec. 7 [1900]. Giovanni was the only Italian on board, most of the crew being British. He appeared to be quiet. A little time before the murder, however, he fought with Baileff, who had the best of matters.

On the morning of Feb. 15 Giovanni, it was stated, attacked Baileff with a big galley knife, stabbing him savagely in eight places. He then ran among the cargo, and was soon followed by the captain, armed with a revolver. All hands searched the ship for a quarter of an hour, but could find no trace of the man, when suddenly he came out of the hatch and made a rush for the deck, where he was secured after a desperate struggle. He was then handcuffed and chained and lodged in the donkey-engine room, where he was confined during the rest of the voyage.

As the vessel was in the Tropics it was necessary to commit the body to the deep before night. In the presence of the whole crew the Captain had it placed in front of Giovanni, and then said to him, "See what you have done?" The man did not seem a bit disturbed, and only muttered "Revenge."

*Giovanni, aged 31, was tried at Bodmin, Cornwall, on 17 June 1901, before Mr. Justice Wills, for the murder of Victor Baileff. He was convicted and sentenced to death. The execution, by hanging on 9 July 1901, was the penultimate to take place at Bodmin Gaol.

## 2 Sept 1901

**Maritime Intelligence**

Volant.- Yarmouth, Sept 2, 10 58 a.m.- Volant, schooner, of Goole, from Teignmouth for Keadby, cargo china clay, towed into harbour; captain, his son, and mate severely injured by one of the crew, a Russian, who early this morning attacked them with a hatchet. All taken to hospital, lying in critical state. The Russian afterwards jumped overboard and was drowned.

## 18 Aug 1902

**Maritime Intelligence**

Mihermanos (s).- Manila, Aug. 17.- The native crew of the steamer Mihermanos mutinied in the port of Virac [Catanduanes Island, northeast Philippines] on Thursday, Aug. 14, murdered the chief engineer and wounded the captain, the mate, the second engineer and one passenger, all of Spanish nationality. The constabulary went out to rescue the officers and fired into the crew, killing three. Twenty-five of the remainder surrendered. Five jumped overboard and are believed to have drowned. During the fight the steamer ran aground, but she was afterwards floated.

### THE *LEICESTER CASTLE* MUTINY

## 5 Dec 1902

Queenstown: arrived, 5 Dec, Leicester Castle*, Peattie, San Francisco (wheat) (ordered Manchester [Ship] Canal)

Mutiny At Sea.- Queenstown, Dec 5., 11 42 a.m.- Leicester Castle, arrived from San Francisco, reports that three mutineers shot second mate, Nixon, who died, also wounded Captain Peattie. They left the ship same night, Sept. 2, on a raft, about 300 miles north of Pitcairn Island.

*International Herald Tribune*

*5 December 1902*

**London: A most thrilling story of mutiny and murder at sea is told by the "St. James's Gazette."**

The British ship, the Leicester Castle, belonging to Messrs. Joyce & Co., of Liverpool, arrived at Queenstown yesterday [Dec. 4], and her master, Captain Peattie, told the tale of how three American seamen mutinied on September 2 last, shot the second officer dead and then left the ship on a raft, the captain himself being also shot at and receiving five wounds, though fortunately without serious effect.

## *6 Dec 1902*

## Mutiny On A British Ship

## The Captain's Story

A Queenstown correspondent telegraphs that the British sailing ship Leicester Castle, 2,009 tons, with wheat from San Francisco, yesterday arrived at that port for orders. Her master, Captain Peattie, reported that during the voyage three American sailors mutinied, murdered the second officer, wounded the captain, and to avoid capture made a raft during the night and put off from the ship. The captain's statement is as follows:

"On the night of September 2, a very fine night, though dark with a light easterly wind, we were making 3½ knots under all sail. The second officer had charge of the deck, and I was lying reading before going to sleep, when a man named Ernest Sears, able seaman, American, shipped at San Francisco, came to my room door and asked me to come out, as a man had fallen from the foreyard and broken his leg. I immediately did as requested, and going into the cabin, lighted the lamp so that I could have the table to lay the injured man on.

I then went to the cabin door on the port side, where Sears was standing, and asked him where the wounded man was. He replied, 'Just outside,' and I told him to tell the second mate to bring him into the cabin and put him on the table. Suddenly W.A. Hobbs, able seaman, also an American, shipped at San Francisco, stepped into the cabin by the starboard door, got between me and my room door, and, crying out 'Now then, captain,' fired at me with a revolver. A bullet hit me on the left breast immediately over the heart. I attempted to close with him, and managed to hit him once, but he fired again, hitting me on the muscle of the arm, and then using some heavy club, began to batter in my head.

This brought me to the deck, where the villain fired two more shots at me, which lodged in my armpit and inflicted a bad grazing wound on the forearm. He then recommenced striking at my head with his club. Just then Mr. Nixon, the second mate, hearing the noise, came to the port door of the fore cabin, when Hobbs fired at him, and he fell instantly, the bullet having evidently pierced his heart. The steward and another man [named Dunning] now came on the scene, but by this time my assailants had vanished. I was in a bad state, as I had five wounds from the revolver bullets, and my scalp was severely cut.

I was, moreover, so weak from loss of blood that the mate took charge of the ship. He called the hands aft, where they kept the poop [ie., remained on the poop deck, aft], hoping to catch the mutineers when daylight came; but, greatly to the surprise of all of us, about an hour after midnight, a raft, with three men on it, was observed in the darkness floating past the starboard side. The men on it were Hobbs, the actual murderer; Sears, who lured me out of my room; and another man, shipped at San Francisco, also an American, named James Turner. The mate hove the vessel to, and waited until daylight when, no trace of the raft being seen, the ship was kept on her course.

I have not the slightest doubt that the frail raft, which was made of only a few planks and three cork cylinders taken from the forward life-boat, went to pieces that night, and the three men were drowned. My wounds were dressed by R.J. Brennan, able seaman, who had had some experience of ambulance work in South Africa. After one day's rest I was able to resume my duty, though I suffered considerably and do so yet, as the bullets are somewhere in my body, though the wounds have healed well.

There can be no doubt that it was a pure case of piracy. The intention was to kill me and get into my room, and so obtain the firearms and other weapons there, especially a large Colt revolver which was taken from Hobbs when he joined. If they had succeeded in this they would have murdered everyone who did not join them. Mr. Nixon, the officer killed, was buried the day after his death. We were some 300 miles north of Pitcairn Islands when it all happened, and the revolver used by Hobbs had been stolen from Mr. Nixon.'

*The *Leicester Castle* was a 2,067-ton ship, built at Southampton in 1882 for J. Coupland. On 26 July 1902, then owned by Joyce & Co., she left San Francisco for Queenstown, Ireland, with a cargo of wheat. She was crewed by a typically mixed complement of American, Irish and Dutch sailors under the command of Capt. R. D. Peattie. After the three American mutineers got away from the ship on a raft, Capt. Peattie had 'not the slightest doubt' that they would soon drown. The following report suggested at least the possibility that they might have survived to reach Pitcairn Island 300 miles away:

### *Daily Mail*

### 13 December 1902

### Mysterious Signals on Pitcairn Island

Intelligence reached Queenstown from San Francisco last night that the British ship Howth had arrived at San Francisco and reported that when off Pitcairn Island on September 25 fire signals were observed burning on the elevated parts of the island. The captain believed they were intended to indicate that the islanders had castaways whom they wanted removed. The Howth was manoeuvred to get near the island in order to send a boat ashore, but baffling [adverse] winds prevented this course.

On the arrival of the Howth at San Francisco the captain heard of the mutiny on the Leicester Castle and that the mutineers left on a raft. He believes that the three men reached the island, hence the display of fire signals from that place to have them taken off. The mutiny took place on the night of September 2, the Leicester Castle then being 300 miles north of Pitcairn.

## THE STRANGE CASE OF THE MUTINY ON THE *VERONICA*

## 24 Jan 1903

### Maritime Intelligence

Veronica.- Lisbon, Jan. 19.- The barque Veronica, of St. John (N.B.), was abandoned on fire Dec. 20 [1902], when the master with four men, and the second mate, also with four men, left in the boat. Nothing further is known of the former, but the latter reached Cajucira [*sic* – Cajueiro] Island [northeast coast Brazil], Dec 25, and the men were taken off and brought here by the steamer Brunswick…The first mate and a seaman had previously died.

*31 Jan 1903*

**Alleged Mutiny and Murder at Sea**

The four men who were arrested by the Liverpool police on board the steamship Brunswick last night from Montevideo, were brought up at the Liverpool Police Court yesterday, before the stipendiary magistrate, Mr. W.J. Stewart, and formally charged with the wilful murder of Captain Shaw, the chief officer, the second officer, and four members of the crew of the British barque Veronica, on the high seas between Dec. 7 and 20 last. The names of the prisoners are: William Smith, 31, a Hollander; and Gustav Rau, 28, Henry Flohr, 19, and Otto Monson, 19, all of German nationality. Rau and Flohr speak English, but the others do not. They are all described as able seamen.

The arrest of the prisoners, and the charge preferred against them is based upon the statement of a Virginian negro, Moses Thomas. His story, in brief, is that the accused murdered Captain Shaw and the other members of the crew of the Veronica, and that being unable to take the ship into any port they set fire to her. They then provisioned the lifeboat, left the burning vessel, taking Thomas with them, and finally landed on the island of Teutoia [*sic* – Cajueiro], off the coast of Brazil. From this island they were taken off by the Brunswick, owned by Messrs. Hugh Evans & Co., of Liverpool. To Captain Browne, who commanded the Brunswick, Thomas, on the voyage home, made a communication, which resulted in the arrest of the men…[Thomas's "communication" was that the prisoners' version of events was an invention of Gustav Rau, to cover up their crime.]

Detective Inspector Duckworth said he arrested the prisoners on Thursday morning on the arrival of the steamship Brunswick at the Queen's Dock. He brought them to the detective office, and later in the day charged Rau and Flohr with wilfully murdering the captain, the chief officer, the second officer, and four other members of the crew of the British barque Veronica, on the high seas, on Dec. 7 and other dates…*

*The trial of Otto Monson (18), Henry Flohr (19), Gustav Rau (29) and William Smith (30) for the murder of the captain, officers and four of the crew of the British barque *Veronica* off the northeast coast of Brazil in December 1902 was conducted from 31 January until 14 May 1903. (In fact, they were only officially charged with the murder of Capt. Shaw; charges against the other men killed on the *Veronica* were held in reserve if the accused were acquitted of killing the captain.) The testimony given by the accused men was lengthy and deliberately conflicting and confused, to try to obfuscate and undermine the case against them. Just before the conclusion of the trial, on 12 May, however, 'Mr. Tobin, the King's counsel who led for the prosecution, in a few plain words brought the whole story vividly before the jury:'

"In the middle of October last (he said) the British ship Veronica left Ship Island [near Biloxi, Mississippi] for Montevideo, with a crew of 12 men on board. On Dec. 21 the Veronica was burnt on the high seas and abandoned, and it was alleged that before she was abandoned no fewer than seven of the crew met their death from violence. Of the remaining five three were in the dock, and the other two would give evidence. [Flohr "turned King's evidence" during the trial, so charges against him were dismissed. The cook, Moses Thomas, who was not amongst the accused, also gave evidence for the prosecution.]

The Veronica's crew consisted of captain [Alexander Shaw], first and second mate [Alexander McLeod and Fred Abrahamsson, respectively], cook [Moses Thomas], and eight hands. They were of different nationalities. Two of them, the prisoners Rau and Monson, were Germans; the prisoner Smith was Dutch; Flohr, who would give evidence, was a German; Johanssen, one of the murdered men, was a Swede; one was an Irishman [Paddy Doran], another came from Prince Edward Island [both Capt. Shaw and first mate McLeod were from Prince Edward Island], and another was a Hindoo coolie [Alec Bravo, probably from the West Indies]. The cook was a black man. It was significant, if the case for the Crown was true, that four of the five survivors of the crew were of the same nationality [*sic* – northern Europeans].

For the first fortnight of the voyage all went well. Then disaffection broke out, ending in mutiny and murder. The prisoners agreed to murder the officers and to get rid of those of the crew whom they could not trust – that was to say, those of a different nationality. Flohr, their fellow-countryman, was asked to join in the plot, but refused. Rau, who appeared to be the ringleader, then gave Flohr the choice of joining them or going overboard himself. Flohr then agreed to join them. It was arranged that the crew should be murdered in the chief mate's watch between midnight and 4 a.m. The chief mate's watch consisted of himself, Smith, Flohr, a sailor called Paddy, and Johanssen. Paddy was on the look-out on the forecastle head and Johanssen at the wheel. Smith and Flohr were on deck.

About 3 a.m. Rau told Flohr to kill Paddy, but Flohr hung back. Rau then went forward and asked Paddy if he could see the North Star – a natural question, as the ship was nearing the equator. Paddy bent down and looked under the foresail. As he was bending forward Rau hit him twice on the head with an iron belaying pin. Paddy fell senseless, and was thrown into the port locker under the forecastle head. The chief mate, McLeod, then came forward, and Rau hit him twice on the head with his belaying pin, and Smith and Rau proceeded to throw his body overboard. Then Rau and Smith, each with a revolver, went aft to deal with the captain and the second mate. Flohr remained watching the port locker. Monson was watching the foredeck house (the forecastle), where the sailors Julius Parson and Alec Bravo, a coolie, were. Two shots were heard, and the second mate came running forward crying out that he had been shot.

Flohr was then told to kill Johanssen with a belaying pin. Instead of striking him with an iron one, he took a wooden one and hit him with it. Johanssen ran forward and took refuge in the forecastle. Flohr took the wheel. The captain then came out and was shot twice by Rau. Meanwhile Parson, who had been trying to escape, was struck with a belaying pin and killed, and his body was thrown overboard. The cook had barricaded himself in his cabin, but was persuaded to come out, and was then threatened by Rau with a revolver. He pleaded for his life, and was ordered into the galley to make coffee.

After this the captain and second mate were barricaded in the navigation room. The portholes were boarded over and the skylight roped down. The captain and second mate were kept there for some days practically without food or water.

Then Rau, who wanted instruments for the navigation of the ship, opened the skylight and called for the captain. The second mate came and said the captain was too ill, but Rau insisted, and the captain came. He begged for a drink of water, which was given him by Smith and Flohr. He gave Flohr the instruments he wanted.

A few days later it was determined to kill the captain. Rau, Smith, and Monson stood on the poop armed with revolvers and Flohr with a belaying pin. The second mate was ordered out. He came out and ran along the starboard side of the ship. Smith shot him in the shoulder and the mate ran over the ship's side. Rau put the ship about and shot at him till he sank. The captain was next ordered out, but he did not come. The coolie, Alec Bravo, was sent down with an axe to fetch him out. The captain came out with his hands before his face and was shot dead by Rau. He fell down the companion-way, and his dead body was thrown overboard. The sailor Paddy had been killed by Rau on the first day.

Rau then made up a story to the effect that the ship had caught fire, and that the crew had been obliged to take to the boats. The survivors were made to repeat this story twice daily, Rau standing over them with a revolver. Johanssen and Bravo proved bad learners, so they were shot and thrown overboard. Rau then proceeded to set the ship on fire, and the five survivors took to the forward lifeboat, which they had launched, and which was plentifully stocked with provisions. Rau, who had learned navigation in the German navy, steered the boat, and after five days land was sighted, the north-east coast of Brazil. Rau immediately ordered his companions to throw all the provisions overboard and their caps as well.

They made land on Cazneira [sic – Cajueiro] Island, a point of call for a line of Liverpool steamers. They landed on Christmas morning, and within a few days a Liverpool ship, the Brunswick, called, and Rau and the cook went on board, and told their tale to the captain, and the men were taken on board. The cook asked to be kept apart from the others, and later made a communication to the captain.

When the Brunswick arrived at Lisbon the Consul was consulted, and the prisoners and Flohr were not allowed to come ashore. On arriving at Liverpool Smith made a statement which revealed a new and entirely inconsistent story, throwing all the blame upon the cook. A few hours after they had been in prison Flohr quite voluntarily made a statement, which corroborated the cook's statement in all material particulars, which was the more surprising as Flohr had no notion of what the cook had said. Under these circumstances the Crown had thought it their duty to withdraw the charge against Flohr, and he would appear to give evidence in support of the charge against the prisoners…

## 15 May 1903
### The Veronica Tragedy

…Mr. Justice Lawrence summed up to the jury. He said they had to decide whether the three prisoners acted in concert with the intention of putting an end to the deceased men. Dealing with the [defendants'] suggestion that the officers were guilty of cruelty, it would not justify the men in killing the officers. Cruelty might arouse a strong feeling against the officers, but it would not justify violence. As to the statement [by the defence] that the cook had told one of the prisoners that the officers intended to throw the men overboard, his lordship said he could not understand how it could have been thought possible that three officers could throw nine men overboard.

Moreover, if the men could have been thrown overboard, how could the ship have been navigated by the three officers, who would be the only men remaining? It seemed a marvellous [ie., incredulous] story, and the jury would form their own opinion about it. His lordship went on to allude to Smith's injuries, and pointed to Flohr's evidence as showing that they had been inflicted not by the first mate, as Smith now contended, but by Rau, who had evidently mistaken him for the first mate. Touching upon the allegations made against the cook, his lordship asked whether the jury thought it likely that men who were skilled sailors would allow a man, presumably without any knowledge of seamanship, to take control. The judge added, in reply to one of the jurors, that all they had to concern themselves with was the death of the captain.

The jury retired to consider their verdict at a quarter to nine o' clock, and after an absence of 12 minutes found all three prisoners Guilty. They recommended Monsson to mercy on account of his youth and previous good character.

The Judge, addressing the prisoners, said they had been found guilty, on evidence which had satisfied everybody who had heard it, of wilful murder…His lordship then passed sentence of death. The prisoners received the sentence with composure; but, whilst Rau and Smith walked steadily out of the dock, Monsson was seen to falter for a moment, and press his hands nervously to his brow. Then, gathering himself together with a slight effort, he too stepped briskly below.

## 22 May 1903

The Veronica Mutineers.- The execution of Otto Ernst Theodore Monsson, Gustav Rau, and William Smith has been fixed for Tuesday, June 2, at Walton Prison.

## 2 June 1903

The Veronica Mutiny.- Execution of Two Murderers.- The two condemned sailors of the barque Veronica – Rau and Smith [Monsson had successfully appealed his sentence, commuted to life imprisonment] – sentenced to death at the last Liverpool Assizes for murder and mutiny on the high seas, were executed in Walton Gaol this morning. After conviction the condemned men maintained the same stolid demeanour which characterised them at the trial. They slept well, ate heartily, smoked with enjoyment, and joked with the warders. They seemed in no wise depressed by their coming fate…

…When [William] Billington [the hangman], who was assisted by his brother [John Billington], entered the cells, Rau and Smith submitted quietly to the pinioning process, and afterwards walked firmly to the scaffold, where they stood side by side. Before the drop fell Rau said in a deliberate voice, "I am innocent of the death of these men." The execution was promptly carried out, death being instantaneous.

## POST SCRIPT

## 30 March 1903
### Bottle Picked Up

London, March 30.- A sealed bottle has been picked up in the estuary of the Malltraeth River, in Anglesey [Wales], in which the following was written on paper, with lead pencil:- "Good-bye all. Ship sinking.- Captain Veronica."*

*This was most probably a hoax message written because of the widespread news and notoriety at the time of the mutiny and murders on board the Veronica.

## A Sailmaker's Revenge

**25 Nov 1903**

**Maritime Intelligence**

**Miscellaneous**

San Francisco, Nov 24.- Three sailors are dead, and the first officer of the German ship Octavia is dying. After rounding Cape Horn the sailmaker induced three of the crew to join him in a raid on some whisky, which was part of the cargo. A drunken fight ensued, the three sailors severely beating the sailmaker. Subsequently he induced the same men to join another raid on the whisky, but it is alleged that he caused them to drink carbolic acid. The three died and were buried at sea. The first officer is supposed [believed] also to have drunk some of the poison.

# 7 Sickness, Disease and Malnutrition (...and Suicide)

Disease and malnutrition sometimes weakened crews so much that they limped into port with barely enough manpower to sail the ship. Shortage of provisions on a particularly prolonged voyage might cause malnutrition. Death from starvation because of a shortage of provisions was rare, but it did happen.

## 7 Nov 1903

**Maritime Intelligence**

Alice.- Baltimore, Oct 30.- The French barque Alice, from Rangoon for Bristol, was spoken Oct 19, in lat 31 N, long 37 W, short of provisions, by the Lord Iveagh (s), which supplied her with medicine and sufficient provisions to take her into port. The Alice had been delayed by bad weather. One man had died from want of food, and two others of the crew were ill.

More often sailing ship crews simply endured the hunger of an unvaried and limited diet of salt pork and beef, pea soup, hard ship's biscuits ("hard tack"), and very little in the way of anything even remotely resembling an indulgence that landlubbers took for granted. "Fever", or "Java fever" (the latter most likely malaria, treated with quinine), was a much more common malaise, especially in tropical ports in Africa, Asia or the Caribbean. Whole crews, including the captain, were sometimes struck by "fever" of one kind or another (usually cholera, yellow fever or malaria, but rarely identified in that particular).

On the barquentine *Evadne*, from St. John's, Newfoundland for Pernambuco (Recife) on the northeast coast of Brazil, in April 1901, sickness killed off Capt. Landry, the mate, the cook and three others of the crew during the voyage. Most of the others amongst the crew were sick when the vessel reached port which, under the circumstances, was a triumph of adversity over the odds.

The ship's captain was also the ship's doctor. His medicine chest and manual for curing illness were as rudimentary as his knowledge and the paltry selection of medications available to him. With the dearth of such medical treatment available, death by 'fever' was as likely a way for a 19th century sailor to die as any other peril he faced during a lifetime of voyaging.

The lofty position of ship's master was a lonely one. His responsibilities were heavy and he could not share those charges against him, or any personal problems he might have, with anyone else on board his ship. Sometimes the strain and pressures of that responsibility and isolation, from the rest of the crew could get the better of him, affecting his mind. Suicide and mental illness were sometimes the result.

## NARRATIVES

## 1 Feb 1870

### Casualties – Home

Liverpool, 31ˢᵗ Jan.- The *Juanita*, Doyle, from Rosario [Argentina], arrived here, spoke, on the 17ᵗʰ Jan., in lat. 49 N, lon. 14 W, the Florence Pope, from Lagos to this port, with part of crew dead * and most of the sails blown away; weather fine at the time.

### *2 Feb 1870*

### Casualties – Home

Liverpool, 31ˢᵗ Jan.- The Florence Pope, from Lagos to this port, which was spoken by the *Juanita*, had only the master and three of the crew left, the rest having died. She was apparently making no headway, and there were no signs of any sails being bent [set]; she appeared to be very deep.

*The *Florence Pope*, having come from Lagos on the coast of West Africa, probably had malaria, yellow fever or some other tropical disease on board that killed the majority of her crew.

## 28 June 1870

### Casualties – Foreign

St. Helena, 29ᵗʰ May.- The *Marianna*, of Chittagong [now in Bangladesh], which was spoken, 8ᵗʰ Apl., in lat. 9 S, lon. 69 E, with several of her crew dead, etc., by the *Tweed*, arrived here, was bound from Aden to Chittagong, with pilgrims. Her master and 20 men were dead, and about 15 were sick. She was supplied with medicine and provisions.

## 14 Sept 1870

### Casualties – Home

Dover, 12ᵗʰ Sept.- The *Dee*, Shakles, from Shields to Cadiz, has put in with master deranged.

## 24 May 1872

### Casualties, Etc.

The master (Gibson) of the *Clarence*, arrived in the River from Melbourne, reports:- "In lat. 40 N, lon. 33 W, boarded the Imatra (ship), of Finland, Fellcke, from Guanape to Falmouth or Queenstown, for orders, which reported:- 'Left Guanape Dec. 13 [1871]. On Feb. 24 [1872] one man was found to be suffering from scurvy*. Owing to the want of fresh provisions, and constant wet round Cape Horn, only six men, all told, were left to work the vessel on [by] the 27ᵗʰ Mar., one man being dead. On the 14ᵗʰ Apl. only four men were left, and another seaman died.

On the 6th May, when only two men were left, fell in with the *Mary Scott*, Bulman, from Cochin to London, which vessel sent two men on board to assist in working the *Imatra*. On receipt of the above intelligence, the surgeon of the *Clarence* went on board the *Imatra*, which was afterwards supplied with two extra hands who volunteered for the duty, and with a quantity of fresh and preserved meat, lemon juice, potatoes, magnesia, etc. etc. When last seen on the 9th May, the *Imatra* was hull down astern, having made sail to topgallant sails.

*Scurvy is a disease caused by a deficiency of vitamin C found in fresh fruits and vegetables, and particularly in citrus fruits. Sailors often suffered, and even died from the affliction, because of a lack of fresh provisions on long voyages.

Eating citrus fruits was known before the 19th century to be a remedy to prevent scurvy. The first person to prove the efficacy of citrus against scurvy was James Lind (1716–1794), a Scottish surgeon in the Royal Navy in 1747. The Royal Navy began issuing regular doses of lime juice to its sailors during the Napoleonic Wars (1803–1815) to prevent scurvy. After that the practice became widespread amongst other navies and in merchant ships (although lemon juice is, in fact, a more effective anti-scorbutic than lime). The deleterious effects of an insufficiency of lime juice on board were all too evident on the German brig *Marie* in 1894.

## 13 Oct 1894

**Maritime Intelligence**

Marie.- Brake [northwest Germany, near Bremen], Oct. 8.- From evidence given before the Marine Court here to-day it appears that the brig Marie, of Elsfleth [between Bremen and Brake], Wempe, which arrived at Bremen Sept. 27 from Havre, left Punta Arenas [Straits of Magellan, in Chilean part of Patagonia] April 8, and had reached Falmouth on Aug. 26, after a voyage of 140 days. Nearly all the crew fell ill during the homeward voyage, with symptoms of scurvy. The captain took to his bed on July 8 and died on July 16. The water casks were filled in Punta Arenas, and water was again taken in Cocos Bay [probably Trinidad]. All of the crew who drank this water in an unboiled state were more or less ill, and the only two men who escaped illness had only taken the water when boiled. There was not a sufficient supply of lime juice on board.

## 15 June 1872

**Casualties – Home**

Plymouth, 13th June.- The *Messenger*, Adams, arrived here from Rio Negro [Argentina], reports having fallen in, on the 12th Apl., in lat. 37 S, lon. 42 W, with the Racine (Fr. Barq.), from Buenos Ayres (also arrived here to-day), with master (Dusautoy) dead, and the vessel having no one on board who could navigate. The mate of the *Messenger* (Stowbridge) took charge of her.

## 26 May 1873

New York, 9th May.- The *Lord Baltimore*, which arrived here yesterday from Rio [de] Janeiro, reports having spoken the Amazon, Clark, from Rio [de] Janeiro to Baltimore, 26th Apl., in lat. 17 N, lon. 59 W, with all on board sick with yellow fever*, and master, one seaman, and boy dead.

*Yellow fever was rampant at the time in South American ports such as Rio and Pernambuco (Recife) in Brazil, and Buenos Aires in Argentina. It and other highly contagious tropical diseases were common in ports on the West Coast of Africa, in the Caribbean and in Southeast Asia. Sometimes almost the entire crews of ships coming from those areas were struck down by fever, leaving just a few hands to work the ship.

## 8 Oct 1872

**Casualties – Foreign**

New York, 24th Sept.- The Tropic Bird (schr.), from San Domingo to Boston, with part of the crew dead and remainder sick, was fallen in with, 17th Sept., by the *Universe*, Jones, arrived at Savannah from Liverpool, which placed two men on board the schooner. The vessel was in charge of a coloured seaman.

## 25 Nov 1873

**Casualties – Foreign**

Lisbon, 23rd Nov.- The River Eden (barq.), has been abandoned near Bahia. The master committed suicide after setting fire to the vessel; remainder of crew on board the *Lusitania* (s). [The *River Eden*, Bowden, sailed from Gravesend, 17th Sept., for Valparaiso.]

*1 Dec 1873*

**Casualties – Home**

Liverpool, 28th Nov.- The crew of the River Eden, Bowden, from London to Valparaiso, with a general cargo, have been landed here. They report that the master became insane, and on the 14th, in lat. 16 N, lon. 27 W, he set fire to the vessel and wounded two of the crew, who then abandoned the vessel, the master refusing to accompany them. The boat was shortly afterwards picked up by the *Juanita*, from Shields to Bahia, which sent three men on the burning vessel, who brought off the master, but in the evening he jumped overboard and was drowned. The *River Eden* blew up soon after the master left her. The crew were transferred to the *Oroya* (s), on the 25th, and landed at Bahia, whence they were brought on the *Lusitania* (s).

## 3 Sept 1874

**Casualties – Home**

Swansea, 1st Sept.- The Socrates (Greek brig), from the coast of Africa, was towed into the roads this morning, with only one or two men fit for duty, the remainder of the crew being disabled by scurvy. She left on her homeward passage in April last. One of the crew is in custody on the charge of murdering the master on the vessel's outward voyage from Liverpool.

## 19 Aug 1875

**Casualties – Foreign**

San Francisco, 17th Aug.- The Bremen has arrived. Twelve deaths from scurvy; balance of crew very sick; captain and officers well. (The crew were all Africans.)

New York, 18th Aug.- The Bremen (ship), of and from Liverpool, arrived at San Francisco yesterday, with everybody on board more or less helpless with scurvy. Thirteen persons had died on the voyage and three yesterday within sight of the port.

## 5 Sept 1876

**Casualties – Foreign**

New York, 23rd Aug.- The Joaquina (Span, schr.) was abandoned at sea 17th Aug., in lat. 48 N, lon. 32 W. The captain, Palan, one sailor and a passenger were taken off by the *Frisia* (s), at New York. The rest of the crew were reported to have died of starvation.

## 15 Feb 1877

**Casualties – Foreign**

Stanley, F.I. [Falkland Islands], 2nd Jan.- The Crown Prince, Cochran, from Punta de Lobos, with guano, put in here, 5th Dec. [1876], with crew poisoned by putrid pork.* Five men died within the first three or four days, and the remainder, with scarcely an exception, have suffered severely, some being still in danger…

*The staple meat fed to sailing ship crews was salted beef (sometimes thought more likely to be horsemeat) and salted pork packed in wooden casks. Virtually inedible to landlubbers, and hated by seafarers, it nevertheless sustained sailors for months on end with rarely any ill effects apart from loathing and disgust.

## 5 June 1877

**Casualties – Foreign**

Cape Town, 19th June:- The Nyverheid (brig.), Holst, arrived here from Calcutta, reports having spoken, May 24, in lat. 30 S, lon. 38 E, the Retriever (schooner), from Mauritius for this place [Cape Town], 60 days out, in distress. The master of the Retriever sent a boat to the Nyverheid, and reported that he had lost one man overboard. He (Captain Hinsch) and his crew, with the exception of the mate, were all sick. His chronometer had run down, and the water and provisions were exhausted. The brig supplied them with as much water and provisions as she could spare, and parted company, after setting the chronometer and giving them the course for Natal [Port Natal, now Durban, South Africa], from which port they were then 340 miles off.

When the Retriever had left Mauritius it was found that two sailors had stowed themselves away, a circumstance which proved to be of great assistance, for they, with the mate, were the only ones who had kept free from the fever, and those three alone had worked the ship. The day after leaving them the Nyverheid experienced a heavy Westerly gale, lasting for six days.

## 9 July 1877

**Casualties – Home**

Falmouth, 6th July.- The Catherine (Dan. Schr.) has arrived here from Benin [West Africa] with several hands sick with scurvy, and reports that the master (Sonne) died from the same disease a week ago.

The Norwegian ship Juno, from Maulmain [Burma], arrived last evening with master (Sorensen) sick; he has since died.

Two men sick with scurvy and ague* have been landed from the Ocean Monarch, of Guernsey, from Mauritius, and taken to the Sailors' Home Hospital. The mate and cook died at sea from the same complaint.

*'Ague' was any fever accompanied by paroxysms of chills, sweating and shivering; it was most closely associated with malaria. Yellow fever and malaria were other common tropical diseases contracted by seamen in equatorial or subtropical ports.

## 28 July 1877

**Casualties – Home**

Falmouth, 26th July.- The Brilliant, Cape Hayti [Cap Haitien, Haiti], arrived here to-day with a quarantine flag flying. On being boarded by the authorities, it was found that one of the crew had died yesterday of fever, and that all the others were sick of the same disease.

## 16 Aug 1877

**Casualties – Home**

Falmouth, 9th Aug.- The Poseidon (brgtne.), from Bonny, W.C.A. [West Coast Africa], for Havre, with palm oil, put in to-day, with three of the crew dead from fever. All the others, excepting the master (Lund) have suffered from the same disease, but are now recovering. For nearly 60 days only the master and one man were able to work the vessel.

## 25 Feb 1878

**Casualties – Foreign**

Marseilles, 22nd Feb.- The Ville de Frontignan, Roux, which sailed hence, 12th June [1877], for Noumea [New Caledonia], arrived at her destination 12th Feb., 184 days out. After passing the Cape of Good Hope she encountered very heavy weather. Off St. Paul [island in southern Indian Ocean] a sea carried away part of her after deckhouse, washing away two seamen and a large quantity of provisions. After this time and up to Tasmania the weather experienced was terrific, and 13,000 tiles [part of her cargo] had to be thrown overboard. Off Tasmania she was supplied with provisions and water by an English vessel. The crew of the *Ville de Frontignan* were sick with scurvy.*

*That the *Ville de Frontignan* crew were sick with scurvy was not surprising: the voyage was very long (half a year), persistent bad weather would have weakened the crew, a large quantity of provisions had been washed overboard halfway through the voyage, and she would have had few if any fresh provisions (apart from those provided by the English vessel) to keep the dreaded scurvy at bay.

## 2 July 1878

**Casualties – Foreign**

Bombay, 7th June.- Captain Macgregor, of the ship Shakespeare, died on 1st June of typhoid fever, and Captain Malcolm, of the ship Lennox, on 3rd June, of heat apoplexy. The heat, says a Calcutta paper, on Saturday and Sunday last, 1st and 2nd June, though the temperature has often been exceeded, was the most oppressive that has been felt in Calcutta for some years, as there was not a breath of air stirring.

We regret to add that it has also been attended with most fatal results in the shape of deaths from heat apoplexy, the deaths of no less than four ship captains on Sunday night having been reported at Bankshall*. These are Captain J.S. Cox, of the Duke of Sutherland (s); Captain Casey, of the Great Victoria; Captain R. Sidey, of the Paladin; and Captain Grosell, of the St. Mirren.

*The old colonial Bankshall, in Calcutta, was where Customs duties were collected and other official administrative offices were located.

## 6 Sept 1878

### Casualties – Foreign

Havre, 4th Sept.- A telegram from San Francisco, received at Bordeaux, confirms the news of the loss near Raiatea, Society Islands, of the Nouveau St. Michel, Etcheverry, which left Bordeaux 14th Mar., for Tahiti, and adds the following particulars:- "About half the cargo has been saved; the crew are also saved, but the master has committed suicide."

## 11 March 1879

### Casualties – Home

Queenstown, March 9, 5 30 p.m.- Catherine. – Captain Mordey, of the barque Ottercaps, reports as follows:- "March 2, in lat. 44 N, long. 18 W, at 10 a.m., observed a vessel to windward, which appeared to be unmanageable, and with signals of distress flying. She proved to be the brigantine Catherine, of Liverpool, from West Coast Africa to Channel for orders, laden with palm oil. She bore down upon us, when we ascertained that the captain and mate were dead, and crew were sick, and wanted assistance.

We backed the mainyard and got a boat out with much difficulty, owing to a high beam sea running and sent second officer on board with four hands to know what was wanted. Found only one man on board who was able to work, and he came on board of us leaving one of our men in charge, and stated as follows:- That they buried one man that morning, one was lying at the point of death, and another very ill, and the captain died a fortnight before. He also stated that he had had no rest for four days, that the vessel was out 82 days, and was short of water, provisions, and sails. He also reported that they had spoken several ships, none of which would give them any assistance.

When we first saw the vessel she was making a west course, and it is believed that they did not know where they were. Supplied her with one good topgallantsail, one good royal, one royal staysail, one bolt of No. 3 canvas, 5 skeins of twine, needles, marlinespike, etc., bucket, 150 lbs beef and pork, 10 tins preserved meat, 28 lbs sugar, 2 bottles lime juice, 30 gallons of water, and sent James Reed, second mate, R. Hall, A.B., and A. Bayley, A.B., on board her to navigate her to port. Her sails were in bad order, mainboom and gaff and topsailyard gone. We then took our own boat on board, not without damage, and proceeded on our passage. From the time of leaving the Catherine we experienced fine weather."

## *22 March 1879*

### Casualties – Foreign

Brest*, March 18.- Catherine, schooner, of Liverpool, 199 tons, from Benin [West Coast Africa] for Plymouth (palm oil), which put in here yesterday, had lost, through cold and want of food, her master and three out of the five men that composed her crew. Of the remaining two men, one was in a state of complete exhaustion from illness and the other suffering from sore cheek and an infection of the eyes, when the vessel was fallen in with, on March 2, by the Ottercaps, from Iquique for Plymouth, which put on board an officer and two men and some provisions. The Catherine was compelled to put in here owing to loss of sails, broken gaff, disabled pumps, and want of food and water.

*The *Catherine* was some 650 miles southwest of the Brest Peninsula, around 450 miles northeast of the Azores, when she was assisted by the *Ottercaps* on 2nd March. In her dilapidated and undermanned condition she took two weeks to sail to Brest, arriving there on 17 March, at an average speed of just around 2 knots – less than 50 miles a day.

## 1 Aug 1881

**Casualties – Foreign**

Stavanger [Norway], July 22.- Cito – According to a telegram received here, the Cito, galeas*, of this port, is reported to have been fallen in with by a steamer and taken in to a small island called St. Thomas**, near Lagos. The master, Anderson, the second mate, and one man were dead, and the rest of the crew were sick. [This vessel sailed from Hamburg, March 28, for Brass River [West Africa].]

## 5 Aug 1881

**Casualties – Foreign**

Lisbon, July 30.- Cito – A letter received this morning per mail steamer "Zaire", from Captain Martins, of the Coelho, Portuguese schooner, dated St. Thomas July 2, reports as follows:- "On June 27, in lat. 00 58 N, long. 5 58 E, saw a vessel bearing ESE with sails set and flags flying for assistance, and which appeared to be abandoned. Kept by her until the next morning, and then boarded her, together with mate and three sailors. She was found to be the Cito, Norwegian schooner, Andersen, from Brass River** for London (palm oil). Her captain and five men were found to be in a very miserable state of health.

St. Thome** being the nearest port, Captain Martins, of the Coelho, determined to take the Cito there, and for this purpose left his chief officer and three men on board. On the 29th she was moored in the Bay of Fernao Dias, and on the following day was taken up the river. Captain Andersen, of the Cito, died on the 1st inst."

*A *galeas* was a kind of small sailing vessel from Baltic, Scandinavian and North Sea countries, from the 1600s to the early 20th century. The Scandinavian version was rigged as a ketch, or sometimes a schooner, as with the *Cito* (above). The term *galeas* derived from the Dutch *galliot*.

**St. Thomas, or St. Thome, is the island of Sao Tomé in the Gulf of Guinea, off the coast of Gabon in West Africa. Fernao Dias Bay is at the north of the island. Brass River is in the Niger Delta, near today's Port Harcourt in southern Nigeria. At that time the area today known as Nigeria was a region of separate tribal kingdoms. In 1901 they were consolidated as a British Protectorate territory and gained independence as the Republic of Nigeria on 1 October 1960.

Palm oil was the most common commodity brought out of Brass River in those years. Malaria, yellow fever and other tropical diseases prevalent all along that coast could and frequently did decimate the crews of vessels trading out of there.

## 3 Sept 1881

**Casualties**

Liverpool, Sept. 1.- Aberdeen.- According to advices brought by the Arizona (s), from New York, the barque Aberdeen has arrived at Key West, after having a narrow escape. She was going from Santa Cruz, Cuba, to New York, when the whole of her crew were stricken with fever. Two days after leaving Santa Cruz she struck an unknown shoal, where she remained for the two following days. Shortly after this, fever attacked one of the crew, and gradually spread until the whole of the men were down with it.

When the pilots boarded the Aberdeen they found her drifting at the mercy of the winds. The only man on deck was the captain, who had for the three previous days been continually at the wheel. He, too, had been attacked by the malady, and was in a pitiable state when the pilots took charge. The captain, whose name is Conk, stuck to his post, so much so that he fell exhausted on the deck when she was boarded.

## 30 Oct 1882

**Casualties, Etc.**

Marie Anne, French brig, from Santo Domingo for Havre, has been towed in here by the Spanish steamer Bellver, with three men aboard. All the remainder of the crew and the captain died at sea of yellow fever. The ship and cargo have been libelled*. (Norfolk, Va., by Cable.)

*'Libelled', in this old maritime sense of the law, means that a third party – in this case, the salvor (the Spanish steamship *Bellver*) of the incapacitated French brig – has put in a deposition for claim to the ship and her cargo.

## 8 Aug 1883

**Casualties, Etc.**

Berna.- Stockholm, Aug. 4.- According to a letter received at Gefle [Gävle, on southeast coast of Sweden] by the owner of the Berna, barque, of this port, Nyberg, the master's son died of yellow fever, June 23, while the vessel was at Vera Cruz [Mexico]. The master, his wife, and three of the crew took the fever at the same time, and the three men died, but the master and his wife recovered. After taking in ballast, the Berna sailed from Vera Cruz for Tabasco to load mahogany on the coast, but during the passage several others of the crew sickened, until there were only three remaining in tolerably good health. The vessel, therefore, had to put into Mississippi quarantine station. The mate and four men were taken to the lazarette [quarantine station] in New Orleans, and the mate died there July 12. When the letter was sent off the others were improving, and it was hoped they would recover.

## 30 July 1884

**Maritime Intelligence**

Moltke.- Bremen, July 28.- According to a communication from the German Consulate at Batavia, the German merchant vessel Moltke has been fallen in with at sea by fishermen, drifting helpless, and has been taken in to Cheribon. The crew were sick with the so-called Priok fever*; the master, first mate, and two sailors died.

*'Priok fever' (named after Tanjung Priok, the port area of Batavia – Jakarta – on Java, in Indonesia) was also called 'Java fever', and was almost certainly malaria.

## 9 Sept 1885

**Maritime Intelligence**

**Miscellaneous**

Glasgow, Sept. 8.- The barque Annie Goudey, Sanders, which arrived at Port Glasgow yesterday, left Mobile with timber on July 26 last. Throughout the entire voyage fever and ague prevailed, everyone on board, with the exception of the captain, being seized with illness. For a considerable time only the captain, steward, and one seaman were available for the management of the vessel. On Aug. 3 an able seaman named Jules Schossler was killed by falling from the yard to the deck, and as the vessel was entering the harbour yesterday a seaman named Jens Olsen died from fever. The remainder of the crew are recovering.

## 16 Nov 1885

**Maritime Intelligence**

Eastward.- Key West, Nov. 4.- Captain Morris, of the British barque Moss Glen, from [Le] Havre, reports having found brig Eastward, of Greenock, from New York for Porto Allegre [southern Brazil], hove to, with signals of distress flying. Part of her crew boarded the Moss Glen, reporting that Captain Sabeston, of the Eastward, had hung himself on Oct. 15, and that the mate was incapable of navigating the vessel. Captain Morris put his mate on board the Eastward to take her to her destination.

## THE *MACEDON* ATROCITIES

## 7 Feb 1888

**Maritime Intelligence**

Macedon.- St. John, N.B., Jan. 23.- Ship Macedon, of Digby [Nova Scotia], had bad weather on the voyage from Philadelphia for Hiogo [Japan]. Captain Jones, writing under date of Dec. 23 [1887], says:- "On Sept. 8, while in the Indian Ocean, a typhoon was encountered, and the vessel was thrown on her beam ends, with her yards in the water. She lay there for three hours, and her main hatch was under water the whole time. When the vessel was righted it was found that considerable damage had been done. During the voyage five of the crew died from various causes and the remainder were stricken with scurvy."

*The Times*

*21 February 1888*

**The Macedon Atrocities**

A naval Court at Hiogo has investigated what are called the Macedon atrocities. This vessel sailed from Philadelphia to Japan, and on arrival at Hiogo it was found that every one of the 13 seamen had been attacked with scurvy, and that five had died from the disease or from accidents caused by compelling them to work when rendered unfit by illness. Charges of cruelty against the mate and boatswain were made, and they are now on trial for manslaughter, charged with triceing up a man suffering from scurvy to the mast, forcing another when ill to work aloft, whence he fell, receiving injuries from which he died, and dragging a third along the deck on several occasions, more especially on the day of his death.

The Court found the charges of cruelty proved against the mate and boatswain. The evidence revealed shocking inhumanity to members of the crew while prostrate with scurvy, and neglect of the statutory precautions respecting the distribution of lime juice.

## 21 May 1888

**Maritime Intelligence**

Felix.- Elsfleth [just south of Bremerhaven, northern Germany], May 17.- The Felix, of this port, which was discharging her cargo in the Zambesi River [southeast Africa], has had her crew attacked with climatic fever* and a large portion of them have died, including the master (Monnich) and mate (Wurthmann).

*'Climatic fever' could have been any of a number of deadly tropical diseases, including malaria, yellow fever or dengue fever.

## 24 June 1890

**Maritime Intelligence**

**Miscellaneous**

New York, June 23.- The German barque J.C. Warns has arrived here from Macassar [Makassar, now Ujung Pandang, Sulawesi, Indonesia], in [the] charge of the second mate, her captain and first mate having died from beriberi* during the voyage. The crew are all affected with the disease and will be sent to hospital.

*Beriberi, caused by a deficiency of vitamin $B_1$ in the diet, was especially prevalent in Asia where polished white rice was a staple food. The work of the Dutch physician and pathologist Christian Eijkman (1858 – 1930), who determined the cause of the disease, led to the discovery of vitamins, for which he and the English biochemist Sir Frederick Hopkins (1861 – 1947) were jointly awarded the Nobel Prize for Physiology or Medicine in 1929.

## 26 March 1891

**Maritime Intelligence**

Humboldt.- Plymouth, March 25, 11 13 p.m.- Captain Woolward, of the steamer Don, from Barbadoes, arrived at Plymouth March 25, reports:- March 20 sighted a disabled vessel, with main and mizen masts and foretopsail yards gone. Bore down, and discovered her to be the German barque Humboldt, of Brake, with urgent signal flying. Sent a boat, in charge of second officer, who boarded her, and found captain, mate, and five men, survivors of his crew, all scurvy-stricken and helpless. At their request they were taken on board the Don, and the vessel abandoned. The Humboldt was on a voyage from Altata (Mexico) to Falmouth for orders, and was 192 days out; she was abandoned in lat. 36 18 N, long. 36 20 W, leaking badly.

Another account says that on March 11 the Humboldt experienced a terrific gale, and was thrown on her beam ends, and the mainmast had to be cut away, being followed overboard by the mizenmast and foretopmast and yards. The boats were crushed, and everything on deck was washed away.*

*The mishaps that disabled the *Humboldt* were exceptionally severe: at the time she was abandoned just southwest of the Azores she had been "192 days out" - six and a half months at sea - on a voyage from the small port of Altata on the west coast of Mexico, bound for the German North Sea port of Brake. It was no wonder that the remaining seven men of the crew – the 'survivors' - were stricken by scurvy. No mention was made of how many crew had died by the time the *Don* came across her; it is quite possible, even likely, that more had actually died than survived.

## 21 March 1892

**Yellow Fever***

**Buenos Ayres, March 20**

Upwards of 200 ocean vessels have been infected with yellow fever, including those in the ports of Brazil, whose crews are either dead or have fled. Every vessel touching at Rio [de] Janeiro and Santos carries away the germs of the disease, and the case appears urgently to demand united action on the part of Maritime Powers, with a view to the adoption of methods to arrest the spread of the plague.

A correspondent writes:- "According to intelligence just received from Santos, there are in that port 71 vessels abandoned by their crews. In some cases the captains have died of yellow fever, as well as most of the sailors; in others everyone on board has fallen a victim to the epidemic."

## *2 April 1892*
**Miscellaneous**

Hull, April 1.- Information has reached Hull of the death of the master, Payne, of the barque George Booth, of this port, and four of the crew. The George Booth had only just arrived at Rio [de] Janeiro, when the crew were stricken down with yellow fever, and the captain and four men died on March 1.

*The mortality rate of yellow fever was up to 85% before a South African/Swiss virologist, Max Theiler (1899-1972), developed a vaccine for the disease (the 17-D vaccine), with his colleague Hugh Smith, in 1937, for which he was awarded the Nobel Prize for Physiology or Medicine in 1951.

## 10 Jan 1893

**Miscellaneous**

Madrid, Jan. 8.- A telegram from Alicante states that the master, Kennedy, of the schooner Dora, which arrived at Alicante from Newfoundland about a month ago, was found dead in his berth in circumstances which led to the belief that he had been poisoned by creosote, a bottle of which substance was found under his pillow.*

*Was this a case of murder? Or suicide? Probably the latter.

## 15 Feb 1893

Maritime Intelligence

Syren (tug).- New York, Feb. 14.- The captain of the barque Knudsvig, from Belize for Goole, which was itself abandoned in a sinking condition, reports that on the 6th inst., in lat. 30 N, long. 75 W, he spoke the 200 ton screw steamer Syren, 129 days out from London for Bermuda. The crew had undergone terrible suffering. The vessel had not been long out when the water became impure and, one after another, the men sickened until all were helpless. The steamer drifted for six days at the mercy of the seas. No one was at the helm, and no lights were carried.

During this time the Syren collided at midnight with a barque, name unknown, and one of her boats was smashed. On the following day the captain, having somewhat recovered, came on deck and attempted to take an observation, but just as he was getting the sun's altitude the vessel lurched and he fell, losing his sextant, which was the only one on board. Both provisions and water gave out.

The men had not the remotest notion of their bearings [ie., their position], the vessel became covered with barnacles, and all hope had been given up, when they fell in with the Knudsvig. The latter supplied them with provisions and water, and informed them of their position and the date. The Syren then bore away on her course.

## 24 Oct 1893

### Maritime Intelligence

Quattro Fratelli.- Plymouth, Oct. 23.- The barque Quattro Fratelli, of Spezzia [La Spezia, Italy], from Stockholm, with deals [wood planks], for Marseilles, put in here this morning and reported that her captain, G.B. Bancalari, jumped overboard and was drowned at 5 o'clock yesterday morning, off the Eddystone [Eddystone Lighthouse in the English Channel, 13 miles southwest of Plymouth]. The barque left Stockholm on July 25, and had experienced constant adverse winds.

The captain left a letter for the mate declaring that he was resolved to commit suicide on account of the length of the voyage, and instructing the mate to make the nearest port and send to the managing owner, Signor Dell'Urso, at Genoa, for another master.

## 24 Sept 1894

### Maritime Intelligence

Queen of Scots.- Deal, Sept. 22, 12 50 p.m.- Ship Queen of Scots, of Liverpool, from Bombay for Amsterdam, anchored in the Downs at 7 this morning, with the whole of the crew suffering more or less from scurvy. Four deaths occurred during the voyage, viz., David Thompson, June 1, said to be from heart disease; James Reilly, Sept. 1; William Findlay, 20th; John Wood, 21st; last three from scurvy and weakness. First mate, boatswain and three A.B.s off duty from same cause. Medical officer in attendance, Wood, will be buried at Deal this afternoon, others were buried at sea.

## 1 June 1895

### Suicide of a Captain at Sea

### Melbourne, May 31

The ship Aberfoyle, from Frederikstad to Melbourne, with timber, has arrived here and reports that the captain, during an attack of delirium tremens, committed suicide by drinking carbolic acid after he had been placed in irons. The chief mate was washed overboard early in the voyage. The Aberfoyle, flying distress signals, was sighted on the West Australian coast by the steamer Tagliaferro, whose mate then took charge of her and brought her to Melbourne.

## 25 Nov 1896

### Maritime Intelligence

Smidt.- Galveston, Texas, Nov. 24.- The British steamer Holywell has arrived here with the survivors of the crew of the German barque Smidt, of Bremen. The latter was sighted on the 9th inst., in a dismasted condition, leaking and flying signals of distress. The Smidt, which was loaded with saltpetre, was caught in a hurricane on Oct. 24. Everything on the deck was washed away by the sea, the provisions were soaked, and the fresh water on board became impregnated with the saltpetre. When the ship was discovered the crew were starving, and the captain and two sailors had already died of exhaustion.*

*The carpenter also died.

## 6 May 1897

### Maritime Intelligence

Traveller.- Port Louis, Mauritius, May 6, 11 10 a.m.- Traveller, British ship, wrecked at Rodrigues, February 4; hull and materials a total loss; part of cargo saved, 300 tons. First officer, 14 crew and captain died at sea, fever.

### *10 July 1897*
### Sufferings of the Survivors [of the *Traveller*]

### Liverpool, July 9

Probably one of the most remarkable tales of shipwreck and adventure narrated within recent years was told yesterday to Reuter's Liverpool representative by Mrs. Andrew Christie, widow of Captain Christie, of the wrecked ship Traveller. Mrs. Christie, who belonged to [ie, was from] Liverpool, has just arrived here after undergoing perils and hardships in company with the other survivors of the crew that were almost beyond human endurance.

From Mrs. Christie's statement it appears that the ship Traveller with a cargo of sugar was going from Java to Delaware Breakwater, and almost as soon as the vessel left, river fever of the usual Java type broke out, and this was spread day after day until everyone on board the ship was affected with the malady, including Mrs. Christie herself and even her baby boy about 11 months old.

Death after death took place, and the victims one after another were buried at sea. One of the men, a Dutchman, while delirious with the fever, jumped into the sea and ended his life. The chief officer of the ship died on Dec. 14, and on the 28th Mrs. Christie's husband, Captain Christie, also succumbed. This cast a terrible gloom over the ship. Some of the men gained a little strength, but others died, until the death roll at last amounted to 11. This left 10 men to man the ship, with the second mate, Mr. Ritch, a Liverpool man, in charge.

Mr. Ritch decided to make for Mauritius to obtain assistance. Later on, at a time when he had but two men and himself to work the ship he approached Rodrigues Island [350 miles east of Mauritius]. With wonderful skill they brought up their ship off the island, and then dropped anchor. They thought that they could get assistance and medicine here, and that all danger was passed. The treatment they received, however, Mrs. Christie described as the most remarkable and inhuman, and was rendered doubly so in view of the prostrate condition of the survivors. Rodrigues Island is inhabited mostly by French Creoles. The Governor and doctor, however, are white, and although French, could speak English.

The pilot of the place came off in his boat, but when he heard of the sickness, which was explained to him as the usual Java kind, he would not board the Traveller, but returned to the shore, and the report was spread that the vessel had yellow fever on board. The helpless people waited hour after hour for assistance, but none came, and, fearing that their vessel would go ashore any minute, Mr. Ritch decided to take his crew on shore.

A boat was launched, and Mr. Ritch and the two convalescent seamen lowered Mrs. Christie, her baby, and the other sick members of the crew into it. As they approached the shore the Governor and a number of others rushed down to the water's edge and threatened to shoot the shipwrecked people if they landed. Mr. Ritch asked if they were Christians to treat people in such a manner. His men, he said, had not the strength to pull back to the ship, and if they got there they would all very likely be drowned. Mr. Ritch asked them to give him assistance to take his vessel out of its dangerous position, and to give succour and medicine for his sick crew.

These appeals met with no response, and for fear of being fired on, the poor people had to row back to their ship. Here they arrived more dead than alive, and only got on board the Traveller again with the utmost difficulty. The last of their number had scarcely quitted the small boat when it was carried away and lost. No assistance was sent to the ship either in the shape of a doctor or of hands to man the vessel, and that night the Traveller was carried on to the reefs and wrecked. Fortunately she did not go to pieces then, or every soul on board would have been in all probability lost.

Feeling that something must now be done, the Rodrigues people sent a boat next morning with the pilot, and this boat took off Mrs. Christie and her child. Mr. Ritch launched the ship's lifeboat, but as his crew had not strength to man it some blacks were sent from the shore. All of the shipwrecked people were taken to a sand island where there were no inhabitants, and were kept there for 22 days. They lived in huts made of leaves, and for about three weeks had nothing but leaves to lie down on. So fearful were the Rodrigues people of contact with the shipwrecked crew that the food they sent was conveyed from one small boat to another and then put on the beach. Some blacks, however, were sent to the island to cook for the unfortunate people.

The doctor came off in about a fortnight, but remained in the small boat many yards from the beach, and examined the shipwrecked crew through a pair of binocular glasses. The morning after the wreck, as Mr. Ritch and his companions were being conveyed to the island, one of them, a Scotchman, died, and the authorities made the blacks take him back to where the ship was ashore to bury him in the sea. Another sailor, named Pilgrim, died on the Sand Island, and Mr. Ritch had himself to dig a hole and bury the body.

On the twenty-second day it became patent to those on Rodrigues Island that, as the monsoon was setting in, and it was likely that the island would be covered by the sea, its occupants were in great danger. They were therefore moved to Rodrigues, but their number had now been reduced to eight of the crew and Mrs. Christie and her child. On Rodrigues Island they remained two months, and during that time were well treated. After this they went to Mauritius and there met with all possible attention and kindness. Six of the crew were brought from Mauritius in the Warwick Castle, as well as Mrs. Christie and her baby.

The Rodrigues Islanders allowed the cargo salved to be landed and therefore their aversion to the shipwrecked people could not be explained. Mrs. Christie spoke in the highest terms of Mr. Ritch, Mr. Sargitt, the steward, and the others for their kindness to each other, and to her and her child. Captain Christie belonged to Walls, Shetland, and was 37 years of age.

## 28 July 1897

### Maritime Intelligence

Avenger.- Mauritius, June 29.- The ship Avenger, Barry, from London for Melbourne, put in here on June 26, having been struck by two tremendous seas on the 13th, which swept the deck abaft the mainmast, gutted the cabin and washed overboard the mate, a seaman, and an apprentice.*

*A Board of Trade Inquiry into the loss of the three seamen was held in May 1898. "The inquiry turned chiefly on the mental condition of the master, he having taken little or no part in the navigation of the vessel." The *Avenger* was taking a load of 2,400 tons of general cargo to Melbourne, outbound from London on 1 April 1897. Since the master was rarely on deck, the navigation of the vessel was left to the chief officer Mr. Harry Lindsell. (It was stated in the inquiry that on at least one of the few occasions the captain – who was unnamed - came up on deck he "was said to be under the impression that they were in the English Channel when really [they were] off the Cape [of Good Hope]."

On 13 June the vessel was in lat. 40 S, long. 50 E, "running her easting down" in the southern Indian Ocean, when she came into heavy weather. Around 9 o'clock in the morning a heavy sea washed one seaman, Pringle, overboard. Around 9 o'clock the same evening, another sea washed overboard from the poop and drowned the first mate, Lindsell, and an apprentice by the name of Scobie. (Two others washed overboard by the same sea managed to get back on board.) "The vessel was almost dismantled by the storm."

After putting into Mauritius for repairs the *Avenger* finally sailed for Melbourne "where the captain was taken to an asylum." He was later transported back to London on the *Avenger* as a passenger. The inquiry stated that "the master had voluntarily determined to give up his certificate to the Board of Trade, as, owing to the state of his health, he did not intend to go to sea again."

## 5 Oct 1898

### Maritime Intelligence

Sichem.- Barbadoes (by Cable received Oct. 4).- Norwegian barque Sichem picked up on Sept. 3, in lat. 6 N, long. 26 W. Captain, first officer, second officer, and three of crew dead. No person on board capable of navigating the ship. Brought in here by first officer of Italian barque Speme.

### *12 Oct 1898*
### Maritime Intelligence

Sichem.- Hamburg, Oct. 10.- The steamer Itauri, of the Kosmos Line, on her outward passage, on Sept. 5, in lat. 5 15 N, long. 28 30 W, fell in with the barque Sichem, of Tvedestrand [southeast Norway], from Florida for Buenos Ayres, with wood, 84 days out, and in need of medical aid. The Itauri sent her third mate and four men on board with potatoes, lime-juice, etc., and found that the barque's master, both mates, and three of the crew had died during the voyage of berri-berri. On Oct. [sic – Sept.] 3 a mate and two seamen had been taken on board from the barque Speme, of and for Genoa from Iquique, 4½ months out. Including the Italians the Sichem had eight men on board,* and it was decided to make for Barbadoes.

*The *Sichem* had apparently taken just over 80 days to get from Florida to the position of lat. 6 N, long. 26 W (just a little more than halfway to her destination of Buenos Aires) where the *Speme* put men on board to assist her. The vessel might well have been becalmed for weeks in the virtually windless doldrums of those equatorial regions, causing her to run short of provisions. Six of the *Sichem*'s men had died, including her master, Capt. Loversen. That left just five of her original crew to work the ship, which would have been very difficult without the assistance of the three Italian sailors taken on from the *Speme*.

## 24 July 1900

### Maritime Intelligence

Ville de Rouen.- St. Vincent, C.V. [Cape Verde Islands], July 13.- The steamer Julia Park, Cowie, from Buenos Ayres, reports that on July 8, in lat. 2 40 N, long. 26 38 W, she spoke the French barque Ville de Rouen, of Rouen, from Barry [south Wales] for Port Pirie [South Australia]. The mate of that vessel reported that Captain Lamusse had committed suicide that day, and the mate intended to take the vessel to Montevideo to get another captain there. All was well on board, and no unpleasantness.

## 28 Aug 1900

Kathinka.- Stanley, F.I. [Falkland Islands], July 28.- The German barque Kathinka, Schutte, from Salina Cruz [Pacific coast of Mexico] for Falmouth, put in here on July 26. One of the crew had been washed overboard, four have died from beri-beri, and all the rest, with exception of the captain, are sick with the same disease.

## 6 Nov 1900

### Maritime Intelligence

Shenandoah.- San Francisco, Oct. 22.- Ship Shenandoah, from Sydney, which arrived here Oct. 20, reports that Captain Harvey, while under mental derangement, disappeared during the night of Aug. 21. It is supposed [believed] that he committed suicide by jumping overboard.

## 11 Feb 1901

### Maritime Intelligence

Laura (s).- Halifax, Feb. 11.- The British steamer Laura, which had been 25 days out from Hamburg, put in here yesterday short of coal, after a tempestuous voyage. Captain Andrew Adair was in command. The strain of the voyage had overtaxed his nerves, and he took an overdose of laudanum after reaching port, from the effects of which he died. The steamer proceeds to New York in charge of the first officer.

## "Thrilling Tale of the Sea"

# 18 May 1901

### Maritime Intelligence

Planet.- London, May 17.- Capt. Wall, of the Crown Point (s), arrived in the river from Philadelphia, reports that at 9 15 a.m., on 14th inst., in lat. 49 30 N, long. 13 W, he met the German barque Planet, flying signals of distress. He sent his chief officer on board for information, who reported that the chief mate had died about a week previously, and the master and second mate were sick and helpless. Fresh provisions were wanted, and a navigator to take the ship to Queenstown or Falmouth. A supply of fresh provisions was given, also some medical comforts, and the second officer of the Crown Point, Mr. Bryant, was put on board the Planet to take her to port.

### *The Sphere*

### *15 March 1902*

### A Thrilling Tale of the Sea

One of the weirdest tales of the sea has just been recounted in the Admiralty Court before Mr. Justice Barnes and the Trinity Masters, the tale, therefore, being as true as it is strange. The events here recorded took place last year [1901], but they only became publicly known when Mr. Justice Barnes awarded, as a result of the friendly action referred to, the sum of £642 15s. to Mr. Hedley Bryant out of the salvage of the German barque, *Planet*. Mr. Bryant was second officer on board the *Crown Point* of Liverpool, a steamship of 5,219 tons gross register. At about 8.30 a.m. on May 14 last the vessel was on a voyage from Philadelphia to London with a general cargo, including cattle, and a crew of thirty-seven hands, when she sighted the German barque, *Planet*, in lat. 49° 36' N and long. 13° 30' W.

## SIGNALS OF DISTRESS

"The barque," says Mr. Bryant, "was flying signals meaning 'Can you take me in tow?' This was an unusual request, and we bore down on her. When within hailing distance we discovered that she was German, and with considerable difficulty gathered the information that there was sickness on board. We learned that the chief mate was already dead, the captain was insane and dying, and the second officer was very seriously ill. Captain Wall of the *Crown Point* sent the chief officer, Mr. Walter Lord, to investigate, and that plucky officer went on board the stricken ship.

On his return he reported that the crew were suffering from scurvy, and he gave such a bad account that the captain decided to take the barque in tow. Accordingly I was sent on board to take charge of her, for none of the crew understood navigation. After paying out sixty fathoms of chain the tow commenced. Captain Wall sent all the fresh provisions he could spare and towed me for about two hours. There was a very choppy sea on, and at the end of that time the wire parted under the strain. The captain came back in the steamer and told me to make the best of my way to Queenstown [Ireland] or Falmouth.

# A THRILLING TALE OF THE SEA.

How the 2nd officer of the steamer, "Crown Point," brought the scurvy-stricken barque, "Planet," into Queenstown Harbour after navigating her for fourteen days, during which time the captain

and the 2nd mate died. The whole of the crew were down with scurvy, the barque having been 166 days out from Mexico drifting about the Atlantic until sighted by the "Crown Point"

DRAWN BY C. J. DE LACY FROM A SKETCH BY H. BRYANT

THE STEAMER, "CROWN POINT," ATTEMPTING TO TOW THE DISTRESSED GERMAN BARQUE, "PLANET"

## LEFT ALONE ON THE VESSEL

"When the steamer disappeared the loneliness was terrible. I wanted someone to talk to. The whole thing seemed like a bad dream, but it soon became real enough and I had plenty to think about. The first thing to be done was to get the broken wire and chain on board, but the crew were too weak to heave it in so I slipped [ie., cut and lost] forty-five fathoms of chain and made sail. When this was done I proceeded to explore the ship. I opened the door of the cabin which had been occupied by the mate, who died about eight days before, and the dead man's dog flew savagely at my legs. He could not bite me as I was wearing sea-boots, and the sailmaker, my interpreter, said, 'It was much better that he did not bite you proper, because he has been two veeks already mad.' I also thought it was much better, and I wanted to destroy the poor brute, but the crew were all so fond of him that I let him live, and he recovered in a week."

Later on the dog seems to have been a great companion to Mr. Bryant, for on May 22 his daily diary records, "Dog all right again – am writing this to occupy my mind – dog looking at me." Mr. Bryant found the captain in a wild state of delirium and the second mate was gasping for breath in his room. He was unable to take any food.

"The crew were in an awful state from the terrible disease [scurvy]. Their teeth were loose, their tongues swollen, and they breathed with difficulty. The medicines on the ship were in bottles bearing German labels, and I was afraid to use them, but I found some castor oil, with which I felt safe and of which I made good use. I had also brought some stimulants and a lot of lime juice, which I administered. The crew were so weak that my presence was continually necessary on deck, and I never had more than an hour and a half's sleep at a time. The rats ran over me and the ravings of the dying captain awoke me. On Thursday I sat up with him through the night. There was not the slightest hope, and he died at four o'clock on Friday morning."

## A SHARK ALONGSIDE

Mr. Bryant says that the funeral scene made a vivid impression upon him. It took place in a flat calm which lasted for three days. The vessel was enveloped in dense fog. Right aft the men were grouped together. Amidships stood the solitary mate of the *Crown Point* reading some prayers, for the German whom he had asked to do this was too shy. While the preparations were being made Mr. Bryant observed a shark's fin skimming through the calm water. He says in his log that he did not point this out to the crew – they were already depressed enough. During the funeral the man at the forecastle head was blowing the foghorn in accordance with the Board of Trade regulations.

"The ship," says Mr. Bryant, "had been nearly six months on the voyage. The winds had been light, and her bottom was covered with grass and barnacles, as it was two years since she had seen the inside of a dry dock. The crew had no idea of sanitation and the stench of the ship below was unbearable. On the Monday following the mate's death we had the first fair wind, which served to land us at Queenstown on Tuesday morning, May 28, and the first thing I saw on making the land just off Kinsale was a Lowestoft fishing boat."*

* Second Officer Frederick Hedley Bryant was *from* Lowestoft. By the time of this narrative he had already been promoted "to the command of one of the best vessels in his employer's fleet."

The *Planet* had been 166 days out from Mazatlan, on the Pacific coast of Mexico, when the *Crown Prince* encountered the scurvy-ridden barque drifting about 150 miles southwest of Ireland.

## 11 March 1902

### Maritime Intelligence

H.C. Richards*.- Christiania, March 6.- The owner of the Norwegian barque H.C. Richards, which arrived at Barbadoes on Feb 21 from Madagascar, has received information that all the crew have been stricken with beri-beri. The captain, Olsen Baggerod, and two sailors died on the voyage, and the rest of the crew are now in hospital in Barbadoes.

*The *H.C. Richards* lost an apprentice on her very first voyage to Australia, in 1897/98, as reported by *The Mercury*, of Hobart, Tasmania, on 28th January 1898:

### Arrival of the Barque H.C. Richards

### Loss of an Apprentice

At 9.30 a.m. yesterday a barque, which turned out to be the H.C. Richards, a Norwegian vessel of 766 tons, was sighted off Cape Frederick Henry, and reached port at 2.45 p.m., coming up with a strong sea breeze. The H.C. Richards is 119 days out from Sundsvall [Sweden] with a cargo of 1,000,000 ft. of Baltic deals [planks] and T. and G. [tongue and groove] pine, being the eighth annual shipment consigned to Mr. Fred H. Crisp, and is of the very best quality. With the exception of the loss of a young fellow named Carl Jorgensen, a Norwegian, aged 18, the voyage of the H.C. Richards was uneventful.

The mishap occurred in the North Sea on November 10 [1897], at 10 p.m., whilst the vessel was running before a strong gale and high sea. Deceased had been sent out for'ard by the mate to attend to one of the sails, and while thus engaged he was struck by a heavy sea and lost his hold. The night was very dark and squally, and it was raining, and although the young fellow was heard calling for help he could not be seen, and the weather being so tempestuous nothing could be done to rescue him. This was his first voyage.

# 8  Fire!

Fire on board any ship at sea was a particularly dangerous event. It was especially so for wooden ships or those carrying combustible cargoes such as coal, which was very difficult to extinguish, or petroleum, which was carried in casks and termed case oil. The burning of the wooden emigrant ship *Cospatrick* in November 1874, off the Cape of Good Hope, resulted in the loss of 473 lives amongst its 476 passengers and crew. It was one of the worst maritime casualties of all time until the sinking of the *Titanic* in 1912 with the loss of over 1,500 lives. The *Cospatrick* catastrophe became notorious, too, at the time, for 'cannibalism': in order to survive some of the crew amongst the survivors ate the livers and drank the blood of the dead in one of the two boats that escaped the burning ship.

## NARRATIVES

### 20 July 1870

**Casualties – Foreign**

Falmouth, 18th July.- The *Ellida*, Schweder, from Buenos Ayres, arrived here, reports that the Carolina (Ital. brig), from Genoa to Buenos Ayres, with passengers, was burnt in the evening of the 26th May, in lat. 23 N, lon. 37 W. The *Carolina* had caught fire at 9 p.m., and the ship's boats (3) at once left her, but heavily laden and without oars. The *Ellida* came up with the wreck at 4 a.m., and rescued 13 persons from the rigging, and another vessel took off the remaining 6 or 7. During the night three or four ships were observed to windward. The 13 people taken on board the *Ellida* were soon transferred to a French ship bound to Callao [Peru], but intending probably to call at Monte Video. The fate of the rest of the crew and passengers (about 130) is unknown.*

*There are no further reports of the destruction of this Italian brig, the *Carolina*, by fire in the mid-Atlantic about 700 miles northwest of the Cape Verde Islands. It is highly likely that most, if not all of the passengers were Italian emigrants bound for Argentina. It is equally probable that all those 130 or so crew and passengers left on the vessel perished.

## 1 Nov 1872
**Casualties – Foreign**

New York, [no date].- The Missouri (s), hence to Nassau and Havana, was burnt during a gale off Abaco, Bahama islands; 12 persons were saved and 80 perished, including all the officers and 25 passengers.*

*One of the passengers who died in the *Missouri* disaster was Lewis Cleveland, brother of Grover Cleveland, the only non-consecutive two-term president of the United States (1885-1889; 1893-1897).

## 6 March 1875
**Casualties – Foreign**

Aden, 5th Mar., 11.20 a.m.- The Aracan (Brit. ship), bound to Bombay, with coal*, has been burnt at sea; master and 8 of the crew landed here.

### 18 March 1875
**Casualties – Foreign**

Cochin [now Kochi; southwest India], 17th Mar., 3.15 p.m.- The Aracan's gig has arrived, containing mate and four seamen, all well.

### 24 March 1875
**Casualties – Foreign**

Aden, 8th Mar.- The Aracan was abandoned in lat. 3 N lon. 67 E. She had been on fire several days before the hatches were blown off, and the flames burst out. The 1st and 2nd officers [mates], with ten men, in two boats, are missing. The master and eight men, in one boat, were picked up by the *City of Poonah* (s) and landed here.

### 13 April 1875
**Casualties – Home**

Liverpool, 11th Apl., 1.20 p.m.- The *Rinaldo* (s), from Bombay, brings part of the crew of the Aracan, from Shields to Bombay, abandoned on fire in the China seas [*sic* – actually in the Indian Ocean] on the 17th Feb.

### 28 April 1875
**Casualties – Foreign**

Calcutta, 3rd Apl.- The *City of Manchester* (s), Hardie, arrived here from Liverpool, has brought a boat's crew of 5 men (mate in charge Webster) belonging to the Aracan, Leslie, which was burnt at sea. The men were picked up, 20th Mar., in lat. 10 N lon. 63 E.

*The *Aracan* carried a cargo of coal, a very common but notoriously dangerous cargo for being prone to spontaneous combustion. The usual practice when that happened was for the crew to haul the coal out of the hatches onto the deck, to get to the centre of the combustion and extinguish it either by throwing the burning coal overboard or by drenching it with seawater. For whatever reason the crew of the *Aracan* were unable to extinguish the burning coal, and the ensuing fire caused the destruction – and abandonment - of the vessel around 400 miles due west of the Maldive Islands to the southwest of India.

The *Aracan* boat picked up by the *City of Manchester*, with mate Webster and four men, had drifted (or been navigated deliberately by the mate) over three weeks around 450 miles northwest into a busy shipping lane between Aden and Indian ports. It seems that the only other castaways picked up were the master and eight men. The boat with the second mate and four men appears to have been lost.

## 25 Aug 1881

### Casualties – Foreign

Oriflamme.- The following particulars of the destruction by fire of the English ship Oriflamme, on a voyage from London for San Francisco, are communicated by the owners from information obtained from the ship's log:-

"Sunday, June 5, 1881, lat. 18 06 S, long. 92 12 W*, at noon. At 1'30 a.m., I (captain) was called suddenly by the chief mate telling me that the ship was on fire. Got out immediately, found smoke issuing from the after hatch, also lower cabin full of smoke. Opened the after hatch to ascertain where the fire was, the bales in the fore part of the hatch in a blaze, and also flames in the lower hold. Turned the hands up, battened down all the hatches, covered up all ventilators, and every place where air could get at the fire. Cut holes in the deck, passed the hose down to play on the fire, and all buckets were put in requisition…

At 8 a.m. a vessel hove in sight to windward; hove to wait for his coming down; hoisted signal of distress at the same time, all the water we could possibly get being poured down into the hold in a continuous stream…

At 10 30 all the between decks from the mainmast to the after hatch gave way. The fall of the smouldering bales caused the flames to burst out with increased fury, every exertion made to get the fire under. At length succeeded in getting the flames under, although the fire was evidently spreading in the lower hold…At noon spoke the Italian barque St. Andrea, bound for San Pedro Bay. She promised to keep company with us provided we would keep the ship on course, so as not to detain him, as he was on time charter, which would be cancelled on July 15, 1881…

All hands agreed, without a dissenting voice, to stick by the ship to the last, and all worked with a will to save the ship. Indeed, I cannot speak too highly of the conduct of both officers and men, not one man or boy on board manifesting the slightest disposition to murmur or shrink from his duty. At 1 p.m. kept the ship away on her course, and made sail in company with the barque; pumps and buckets keeping a continuous stream of water pouring on the fire, but to little advantage, the heat increasing every moment, and smoke issuing from all parts of the ship, and the cabin being now full of smoke…

At 4 p.m. the spirit-room caught fire, and blazed up furiously. Finding that there was no possibility of saving the ship, sent the men on board the barque, with the exception of the first mate, carpenter, boatswain, and myself, one A.B. being in charge of the boat alongside.

At 5 20 p.m. the ship was in a perfect blaze from the main hatch aft, the flames spreading very fast, the main deck giving way abaft the mainmast, all the lower hold one mass of fire, and flames bursting through the deck. Seeing no hope of saving the ship, or possibility of doing anything more, we abandoned her and went on board the barque at 7 p.m. The captain of the barque remained hove to until 8 p.m., by which time the ship was in one mass of flames below and aloft…

At 10 p.m., all three masts went by the board; 11 p.m., a heavy explosion took place on board the ship, after which she suddenly disappeared. I suppose she must have gone down at that time."

*The *Oriflamme* was in the Pacific some 1,200 miles off the coast of northern Chile when she burned and foundered.

## 1 Feb 1882

**Casualties, Etc.**

Milton, British ship, from Shields for San Francisco, was burnt in the Pacific Ocean on Dec. 22 [1881]. The crew (23 in number) took to three boats. The second officer, with five men, was picked up in a starving condition on Jan. 15 by the ship Cochin, which has arrived at San Francisco. The fate of the other boats is unknown. (*Philadelphia, Jan. 30*)

## 14 Feb 1882

**Casualties, Etc.**

Milton, McArthur, from Newcastle [NSW] [New South Wales] for San Francisco, with a cargo of coal, took fire Dec. 22, and was abandoned. Capt McArthur, his wife and two children, and five men were in the first boat, the first officer and seven men in the second, and the second officer and six men in the third. The men in the third boat were picked up Jan. 15 in a starving condition twenty-three days after they left the wreck, in lat. 22 N, lon. 123 W, by ship Cochin, at San Francisco Jan 29 from Dundee. Nothing has been heard of the other two boats, and it is feared they were lost. The boats were separated the day following the Milton's abandonment. (*New York, Jan. 31*)

## 27 Feb 1882

**Casualties, Etc.**

Milton.- The captain of the steamer New Berne has reported the picking up, off the coast of Lower [Baja] California, of two seamen, two children, and the wife of the captain of a vessel unnamed. They were famishing, and one child and one seaman died just after the rescue. It is believed they were some of the survivors of the British ship Milton, Captain McArthur, which was abandoned, on fire, at Christmas, in lat. 3 N, long. 110 W. (*New York, Feb. 24*)

## 8 March 1882

**Casualties, Etc.**

Milton.- The officers and a part of the crew picked up some days ago by the steamer New Berne, on the coast of southern California, prove to be Captain McArthur, of ship Milton, abandoned nearly two months ago on fire. The survivors had been 16 days without food or water. (*New York, Feb. 24*)

## 1 April 1882

**Casualties, Etc.**

Golden City (s), from New Orleans for Cincinnati, on approaching Memphis about daylight this morning caught fire. She was headed for the wharf and was moored within four minutes;

but the line parted before many persons could get ashore, and the swift current swept the steamboat in one mass of flames down the river [the Mississippi]. She had 40 passengers and a crew of 60 on board. About 20, mostly women and children, were drowned or burnt to death. All the officers but the second engineer escaped. The burning steamboat set fire to a tug and also to some coal barges at the wharf.

[Later.]- The Golden City, after floating several miles, sank on the Tennessee shore. According to the latest report 23 lives were lost. The fire was caused by the bottom of a watchman's lantern dropping among some jute in the cargo on deck. (*Philadelphia, March 30.*)

## 15 April 1882

**Casualties, Etc.**

Novara.- On March 13, in lat. 14 N, long. 114 W, the ship Novara, from Shields for San Francisco, was destroyed by fire. Eight days later, in lat. 2 N, long. 110 W, the Republic rescued a boat containing five of the crew, including the second officer (Richards). The other two boats, with the remainder of the crew, 35 in number, outsailed the one that was saved, and when last seen was steering north-east. (*New York, April 13.*)

## 26 April 1882
**Casualties, Etc.**

Novara, from Shields for San Francisco, has been burnt at sea; 18 persons saved; one boat missing.

Novara.- A despatch from Wilmington [California] says:- Ship Republic, from Liverpool, reports on March 21, in lat. 2 40 N, lon. 110 W, she picked up a boat belonging to the ship Novara, of Yarmouth (N.S.), from Shields, with coal for San Francisco. The boat contained F.J. Richards, second officer of the Novara, and four men, who reported that on March 13, in lat. 14 N, lon. 114 W, they left the Novara on fire fore and aft, and she burned to the water's edge before losing sight of her. (*San Francisco, April 12.*)

## 8 May 1882
**Casualties, Etc.**

Novara.- A telegram from Captain Corning, late of the ship Novara, from Newcastle for San Francisco, burned at sea, announces his arrival at Valparaiso April 24.*

*It wasn't clear if Capt. Corning and some of his crew were rescued at sea and landed at Valparaiso, or whether they spent the six weeks in a ship's boat from the burning of the *Novara* till arriving at Valparaiso as castaways.

## 17 April 1882

**Casualties, Etc.**

Norval*, burnt at sea; part of crew saved, Honolulu. (*San Francisco, by Cable.*)

## 18 April 1882
**Casualties, Etc.**

Norval.- Owners of the Norval have following cable message from San Francisco:- "Vessel burnt 4th March, in lat. 13 N, long. 120 W; crew landed at Honolulu, except master's boat with seven men, but most probably they will turn up soon." (*Greenock, April 17, 12 25 p.m.*)

*2 May 1882*
**Casualties, Etc.**

Norval, British ship, Halliday, from Hull.- When 114 days out, there was a suspicion of fire, and the next morning 8 feet of water was pumped into the vessel, and pumped out the next day. The same evening, however, an explosion occurred, blowing off hatches and opening decks, and the next morning (Mar 4) she was abandoned in lat. 13 N, long. 120 W. Two boats with the master and second and third mates and 19 of the crew arrived at Hawaii, Mar 24. The remaining boat with the chief officer and seven men has not yet been reported.

*17 May 1882*
**Casualties, Etc.**

Norval, ship, of Greenock, from Hull for San Francisco, abandoned on fire, March 4, as already reported. The captain and part [of] crew of this vessel have arrived at Honolulu, their names are as follows:- Halliday master, Thomas mate, Hendry apprentice, acting 3rd mate, Bradley boatswain, McInnes carpenter, Harpley steward, Kelley cook, Gibbons sailmaker, Brain and Bennett apprentices, Furminger, Bornemann, Grant, Petterson, Oestermann, White, Barwick, Andersen, Ahern and de Souza able seamen, Trey ordinary seaman.

The following are the names of the men in the boat not yet heard of:- Anderson 1st mate, Biggam apprentice, Hurlburt, Martin, Larker, Gustavsen and Wallenius able seamen, and Pearce ordinary seaman. (*Honolulu*, April 10.)

*29 June 1882*
**Casualties, Etc.**

Norval.- The Duke of Connaught, arrived at Liverpool from Astoria [Oregon], reports having picked up, on March 6, in lat. 12 N, long. 123 W, the missing boat of the burnt ship Norval, of Greenock, containing the first mate and seven seamen. She subsequently, when in the South Pacific, fell in with the Indiana, American ship, from Oregon for France, and transferred three men to that vessel, bringing the mate and four seamen on to Liverpool. (*Liverpool*, June 27.)

*The *Norval* was a 1,427-ton iron clipper ship, built in 1873. She left Hull on 28 October 1881, under the command of Capt. G. Halliday, with a cargo of coal for San Francisco. The *City of Lahore* spoke her on 6 January 1882, off Cape Horn, in lat. 56 S, long. 64 W. Six weeks later, at the end of February 1882, the *Norval's* cargo of coal caught fire. Despite the efforts of the crew to extinguish the fire by 4 March she was blazing from end to end. Her crew abandoned ship in two boats. At that time the vessel was around 2,400 miles east-southeast of the Hawaiian Islands. Capt. Halliday's boat, with himself and 21 crew members in it, took three weeks to cover that distance, arriving at Honolulu on 24 March.

The first mate and seven other crew members who escaped from the abandoned *Norval* in the second boat were picked up by the *Duke of Connaught* just two days after leaving the blazing ship. It was another three months, however, before the *Duke of Connaught*, and the other rescue ship, the *Indiana*, arrived back in northern Europe, confirming that the eight men were saved, as indicated by the 29 June report from Liverpool, above.

## 20 May 1885

**Maritime Intelligence**

Juno.- Port Nolloth [northwest coast of South Africa], April 21.- The Swedish ship Juno, 1,284 tons, from Bergen for Melbourne (timber), took fire April 8, in lat. 38 S, long. 12 E,* and the crew attempted to land about 40 miles north of this place on the 17th. In doing so 18 out of 22 were lost. The rest came on to-day, and will leave for Cape Town by the mail steamer Namaqua either this afternoon or early to-morrow. The captain was drowned in landing. Owner's son, named Busch, was one of the saved. The men were under impression that this was Simon's Bay.

Juno.- Cape Town, April 29.- The Norwegian ship Juno, which was burnt at sea, belonged to Bergen, and was bound from Laurvig** for Melbourne, with deals, Kjeller master. The fire was first discovered on April 8, in lat. 38 S, long. 11 E, and seven hours afterwards the ship was in a blaze. In lowering the boats, the first one was swamped. The crew, 22 in number, got into the longboat. They suffered great privations, and nine days after leaving the ship sighted land at a point about 20 miles below the Orange River. They attempted to land through the breakers, but the boat was smashed to pieces, and of the 22 men only four escaped. These men arrived at Port Nolloth in an exhausted condition on April 21.

*The *Juno* caught fire in the South Atlantic about 400 miles southwest of Cape Town. The 22 crew in the longboat sailed approximately 600 miles to land on the coast near Port Nolloth, some 300 miles north of Cape Town in Namaqualand, near the mouth of the Orange River. The boatload of survivors would have been carried up that coast by the Benguela Current, a cold water current flowing up from southern waters and along the southwest coast of Africa.

**Laurvig is the pre-1889 spelling of the town of Larvik on the southeast coast of Norway, just south of Oslo. The Norwegian adventurer, writer and ethnologist Thor Heyerdahl was born at Larvik on 6th October 1914.

## MISSISSIPPI STEAMBOAT DISASTER

## 26 Dec 1888

**Maritime Intelligence**

John H. Hanna (s).- New York, Dec. 25.- The John H. Hanna (s) was destroyed by fire last night on the Mississippi, at Palaquemines, Louisiana. Thirty of the passengers were burnt to death, and a number of others jumped overboard and were drowned. The crew and passengers numbered in all 100, and it is believed that only about a dozen were saved.

*27 Dec 1888*

**Burning of a Mississippi Steamboat**

**New York, Dec. 26**

The first reports of the burning of the Mississippi steamer prove to have been somewhat exaggerated, saying that there were 100 persons on board, nearly all of whom perished. It is now thought that the loss of life will not exceed 20. The accounts of the disaster are full of horrible details. The steamer was near Plaquemine, about 100 miles above New Orleans, when the fire was discovered. It was then about midnight, and most of the passengers were asleep.

The fire was discovered by a negro boatman, who gave the alarm. The steamer was laden with cotton, which was in a very dry condition, and the flames spread with fearful rapidity. They sprang from bale to bale like flashes of lightning, and shot up through the cabin and over the sides, enveloping the entire boat. The alarm had been sounded at the first sight of the fire, the whistle being blown and the bells rung, but within three minutes from its discovery the vessel was one sheet of flame from stem to stern.

The scene that ensued was terrible in the extreme. Men yelled and ran about the decks like maniacs; others, screaming at the top of their voices, threw themselves into the river. The chief clerk, Mr. Powell, went to every door, and made certain that the passengers and hands were awake, and urged them to hurry to the front of the boat before they were cut off. They did so, but were thrown into confusion by the darkness of the night, the blinding smoke, and their own fright. The smoke was so thick and suffocating from the high piles of burning cotton that a number of persons, in trying to force their way to the bow, were overcome by it, and fell suffocated on the deck, where they probably died before the flames reached them or the boat sank.

In the meantime the crew were fighting the flames as best they could, but without success. The steam pumps were worked, but had little effect on the fire. The flames soon reached the engine-room, bursting the steam pipes, and releasing great volumes of steam, that severely scalded several of the men, who were driven from the room. The engineer and his assistants clung to the sides of the boat. The pilot had headed the steamer for shore as soon as the alarm sounded. As she had a full head of steam on at the time she was into the bank in two or three minutes. Then the pilot jumped out over the bales of cotton, and, springing into the river, swam ashore.

The captain, crew, and passengers had fought their way to the front of the boat, getting scorched faces and bruised limbs. The majority of them sprang from the boat when she was about 10 yards from the shore, and the moment she touched the rest leaped into the mud or water. The steamer rested for a moment aground and then swung around, drifting down stream and burning until she finally sank.

Although the crew had escaped from the burning boat they were not all saved. Both the captain and Bob Smith, the famous pilot of another burned steamer, met their deaths after getting ashore. They sprang into the mud on the bank, and becoming fast [ie., stuck in the mud] were slowly roasted to death by the intense heat from the burning boat. They buried their faces and hands into the soft mud to protect themselves, and appealed to the people on shore to come to their assistance. This, however, was impossible. The captain was finally protected from the fire by means of a box, and was dragged ashore with ropes. It was too late, however; he had suffered too serious injuries, and although he received medical care at once, he died before he reached Plaquemine. Bob Smith had figured in several steamboat accidents, and to his courage in sticking to his post on his own burning steamer to the last moment was due the saving of many lives on that vessel.

After the chief clerk had aroused every person on the vessel he returned to the bow, but his escape there was cut off. As a last resort he sprang into the water, and although he could not swim, managed in some way to get on to a floating bale of cotton, but two deck hands jumped on to the bale also and turned it over. Powell fell into the water and was drowned. His body was found in the river 20 miles below Plaquemine this morning. John Crofton, the carpenter, was in the upper portion of the boat struggling to get near the bow. The flames were twisting and sweeping all about him and soon enveloped him. He fell and was burned to death before the eyes of the people, who were not able to render him any help.

Others met with their death while forcing their way to the bow of the boat, being overcome by the smoke, or were burned to death while fast in the mud, or drowned. The boat was about 15 yards from the shore when the intense heat compelled almost all the crew to spring from her. Some reached the shore, and tried to climb the steep, muddy, and slippery levee, but were caught by the flames before they could do so. Others clung to bales of cotton in the river, but in many instances the bales floated against the burning vessel, and the occupants were either roasted to death or compelled to let go, drop into the water, and drown.

## COMPADRE SURVIVORS: 103 DAYS ON AUCKLAND ISLAND

### 3 July 1891

**Maritime Intelligence**

Compadre.- Invercargill [South Island, New Zealand], July 7.- Compadre burnt at sea March 19. Crew saved, and landed here.

### *7 July 1891*

**Maritime Intelligence**

Compadre.- Auckland, July 7.- A schooner has arrived here from the Auckland Islands, having on board the crew of the barque Compadre*, bound from Calcutta for Chilli [Chile]; the latter vessel caught fire at sea, whereupon she was headed for Bluff Harbour, in the province of Otago. Before she could reach port, however, she was overtaken by a storm, and the decks were swept by heavy seas. The fire at last burst through the ship, which was water-logged and sinking, but being blown on to the rocks the crew succeeded in reaching shore, where they remained for 103 days, undergoing great privations and sufferings. One of the seamen was lost in the bush; the others were eventually rescued by a sailing vessel.

*The *Compadre* was an 800-ton iron barque, registered at Liverpool. It left Calcutta on 22 January 1891 with a cargo of baled jute bags for the port of Talcahuano, Chile. On 16 March the captain of the vessel, Capt. David Jones, discovered that a fire had broken out in the after hold. Attempts to extinguish the fire were unsuccessful. The vessel headed for the nearest safe haven, the port of Bluff, on the south coast of South Island, New Zealand.

Early on the 19 March, however, the ship was fighting stormy conditions within sight of the north coast of the Auckland Islands, 280 miles south of Bluff. Water in the holds was increasing. The ship was sinking. To save themselves the crew steered the ship onto the rocks where she was wrecked. All the crew made it to the safety of the land. The one crew member who did not survive, the Norwegian Peter Nelson, A.B., was lost in the bush, presumed to have died of exposure although his body was never found.

The *Compadre*'s crew survived mainly on provisions left at the government food depots located in various parts of the island specifically for shipwrecked castaways, supplemented by catching sheep, goats and pigs that roamed wild. At the end of June, after 103 days on the Aucklands, the remaining fifteen crew members were rescued by the sealing vessel *Janet Ramsay* (Capt. Woods) which landed them at Bluff early in July 1891.

## 28 Nov 1891

**Maritime Intelligence**

Rappahannock.- Valparaiso (by Cable received Nov. 28).- Rappahannock reported to have been totally lost by fire, all on board saved and landed at Juan Fernandez*.

## *18 Dec 1891*

**Maritime Intelligence**

Rappahannock.- San Francisco, Nov. 30.- Rappahannock ship, Liverpool for this port, was burned to the water's edge on the night of Nov. 4 while anchored in Cumberland Bay, in the northern part of the island of Juan Fernandez. The captain, his wife, and crew, took to the boats and were picked up by Chilian despatch boat Hulnell, and taken to Valparaiso.

*The archipelago of the Juan Fernandez Islands lies some 400 miles off the coast of Chile, almost due west of Valparaiso. Cumberland Bay is the population centre of the islands. Juan Fernandez is best known as the place where a Scottish mariner, Alexander Selkirk (1676-1721), was marooned for over four years (from October 1704 to February 1709) and reputedly inspired the idea for the novel *Robinson Crusoe* by Daniel Defoe (1660-1731) which he wrote in 1719/20.

The islands belong to Chile and commemorate both Robinson Cruse and Selkirk. In 1966 the Chilean government renamed the island previously known as Isla Más a Tierra ("Island Closest to Land") as Robinson Crusoe Island, and the other main island, Isla Más Afuera ("Island Furthest Away"), as Alejandro [Alexander] Selkirk Island. The population of the islands – about 630 – resides on Robinson Crusoe Island, mostly in the capital town of San Juan Bautista on Cumberland Bay. The archipelago was an occasional refuge for vessels rounding Cape Horn into the Pacific, to take on fresh water and provisions, and to make any necessary repairs.

## 21 Jan 1892

**Miscellaneous**

London, Jan. 21.- The master of the Imperial Prince (s), from New York, at Portland [Weymouth, Dorset], reports as follows:- "When in lat. 48 02 N, long 18 58 W, observed unusually heavy clouds of smoke and a very large flame twice, as from a great explosion, which proved to be a burning ship, then bearing N by ½ E, distant about six miles, weather at the time blowing a heavy NNW gale, with terrific rain and hail squalls, at hurricane force, and a very high sea running, which had been for the previous 40 hours. I had stormsails taken in, and as soon as opportunity offered, hauled to and steered for the burning ship to render assistance if possible. It was 11 30 a.m. when I hauled to, and about 1 30 p.m. [on the] 16th inst. when I bore away again.

We steamed five miles during the two hours, but about one hour after hauled to a very heavy squall came on, and when it cleared nothing more was to be seen of the burning mass.

I steamed about an hour after losing sight of her, and then decided that any of the crew, whether they were on board or had been successful in getting away, must have perished, as no boats were to be seen. I think but few ships' lifeboats would have floated long in such a sea."

## 22 Jan 1892
### Miscellaneous

London, Jan. 22.- The captain of the Egyptian Monarch (s), from New York, arrived in the river, reports:- "On Jan. 16, at 1 a.m., lat. 48 25 N, long. 19 W, sighted a vessel on fire, apparently wooden, of American build, and from the furious manner in which she was burning, concluded she was loaded with petroleum; bore down to her and found her to be in flames fore and aft; all the masts were gone and only the bowsprit was standing, upon which were two men. It was blowing a heavy gale from NW at the time, with a very heavy sea.

The steamer rounded to, cleared away port lifeboat already to attempt a rescue, but in a few minutes after first reaching the burning vessel the bowsprit fell, carrying with it the men on it, who were not seen again. Lay to until daylight the next morning in hopes of sighting and being able to pick up some of the boats, but none were seen, and as there was a tremendous sea running at the time it is doubtful if any boats could have lived."

## 23 Jan 1892
### Miscellaneous

London, Jan. 23.- A Dalziel's cablegram from New York, dated Jan. 23, states as follows:- There is much speculation in shipping circles here over the probable identity of the vessel reported from London as having been burned in mid-ocean. The weight of opinion inclines to the belief that the ship is the Anna Camp, a Norwegian vessel, which sailed on Dec. 12 [1891] and was in the vicinity of the reported disaster at that time.

# 5 April 1893

### Maritime Intelligence

King James.- San Francisco (by Cable received April 4).- King James abandoned, on fire, March 31, 200 miles off this port. First mate, 15 men landed Point Conception; captain [and] 17 men missing.

King James.- San Francisco, April 4.- News has been received here of the loss of the barque King James, bound from Newcastle (N.S.W.) for this port, which was burned at sea some 200 miles west of her destination. The crew used every effort to save the vessel, and fought the fire – which was first detected on March 19 – for 11 days. On the 30th the vessel blew up, but fortunately the wrecked hull still remained afloat for some time. The crew then took to the boats, which had already been equipped with water and provisions in anticipation of it becoming necessary to abandon the vessel.

In one of the boats were the mate, two of the apprentices, and 13 men, and in the other the captain, his son, the two other apprentices, and the remaining 13 men of the crew. The two boats sailed in company until the 1st inst., when they became separated in a gale. The mate's boat reached the Californian coast, near Point Conception, yesterday. The other boat has not yet arrived.

*7 April 1893*
**Maritime Intelligence**

King James.- San Francisco, April 5.- A steamer has arrived here with the captain and three men of the barque King James, which was burned at sea 200 miles west of this port. They are the only survivors of the 17 men who embarked in one of the boats when the King James blew up.* The boat capsized after leaving the barque, and four men were drowned, while the remainder, including the captain's son, perished from exhaustion.

*Although the *King James'* captain did not know it at the time, the second boat – the mate's boat – had arrived safely at Point Conception (just northwest of Los Angeles), apparently with all its castaways intact. The captain's boat, by contrast, had lost thirteen men, including his son, from drowning and exposure.

## 15 Oct 1895

**Maritime Intelligence**

Parthia.- Valparaiso, Oct. 14, 7 5 p.m.- United States ship Parthia, Oct. 1, totally lost by fire at sea. Part of crew saved and landed here. Captain, first officer and 19 of the crew missing, having left in boats and not since heard of.*

*23 Oct 1895*
**Maritime Intelligence**

Parthia.- London, Oct. 23.- A Central News telegram from New York states:- The *New York Herald*'s correspondent at Valparaiso telegraphs that a cutter has arrived at that port with 19 men, which proves to be the missing boat belonging to the Parthia, wrecked some time ago.

*23 Nov 1895*
**Maritime Intelligence**

Parthia.- Valparaiso, Oct. 16.- The captain of the British barque Sabrina, which arrived at this port from Talcahuano on Sunday, reports that at 6 a.m. on the 13th ult. he picked up one of the boats belonging to the North American ship Parthia, Liverpool to San Francisco, with coal, containing seven of the crew, including the second mate, of that vessel.

The mate reported that in lat. 37 S the ship took fire and the crew had to abandon her and take to the three boats. In the first were the captain and 11 men, in the second the first mate with eight men, and in the third the second mate with eight of the crew [30 in total], and this latter was picked up by the barque Sabrina.

*25 Nov 1895*
**Maritime Intelligence**

Parthia.- Valparaiso, Oct. 15.- Captain Boyer, of the barque Sabrina, reports that the American ship Parthia, previously reported, was burnt in about lat. 40 S, long. 85 W, and the crew left her on Oct. 1. It was 13 days after that the Sabrina picked up the mate's boat, eight of the men of which had been without water. One man had died of thirst, and another is not expected to recover.

*It is difficult to discern from these conflicting reports exactly how many of the burned *Parthia*'s crew were rescued. The British barque *Sabrina* certainly rescued the first mate's boat containing nine men, one of whom died and another of whom was "not expected to recover." The *New York Herald* report is suspiciously defective in that none of the *Parthia's* boats left "with 19 men" in it. Such were the vagaries of reporting maritime casualties at great distances in the 19th century.

At 3,500 tons (gross), 260ft long, 44ft deep and 28ft wide, the *Parthia* was one of the biggest wooden three-masted full-rigged ships ever built. She was the last vessel constructed by the Houghton Bros. yard at Bath, Maine, and launched in January 1891. Houghton operated the *Parthia* on the East Coast to California run around the Horn. She made four complete voyages before burning off the coast of Chile during her fifth voyage where her crew abandoned her on 1 October 1895.

# 9 Ice!

**M**any merchant ships that sailed in high northern or southern latitudes encountered ice in one form or another: bergs, growlers (small blocks of ice) or pack ice. Collisions with ice could and did cause serious, even catastrophic damage, especially to wooden-hulls which were more vulnerable to holing than iron ships. A head-on collision with an iceberg could snap a vessel's jibboom or bowsprit and bring down parts of her forward rigging. A vessel holed by ice near her bows might survive by packing the hole from inside the vessel. Others undoubtedly just sank without trace.

Icebergs in the western North Atlantic were a danger as far south as 45°N, especially in the blindness of thick fog off Newfoundland and the approaches to the St. Lawrence Seaway for ships heading to Montreal or Quebec or other East Coast American ports. Equally, Antarctic 'bergs that drifted up into the Southern Ocean shipping lanes, especially in the Southern Hemisphere summer, were a hazard to vessels sailing around Cape Horn into the South Atlantic or Pacific, or around the Cape of Good Hope towards or from Australia, New Zealand and the Far East.

Voyages back to Europe via Cape Horn from Australasian ports took ships down into the southern latitudes between 40° – 60° S (the 'Roaring Forties' and 'Furious Fifties') of the South Pacific. Lookouts had to keep a keen eye, and ear, to stay out of the way of stray Antarctic ice in those southern seas, too. A ship bowling along at ten or twelve knots in the boisterous westerly winds of those desolate regions could easily, and quickly, be sent to the bottom by a small berg struck without warning in the dead of night or, which amounted to the same thing, in thick fog.

Ships coming round Cape Horn in either winter or summer regularly reported vast areas of ice fields in the South Atlantic. Ice islands many hundreds of feet high and miles in length, as well as smaller bergs and 'growlers' of small pieces of ice were a constant threat to vessels sailing in those seas. One well known incident was the embayment of the 1,771-ton steel full-rigged ship *Monkbarns* in Antarctic ice to the south of Cape Horn for 63 days in the southern hemisphere winter of 1906 while on passage 'round the Horn from Hamburg to San Francisco (she took 206 days). Her master, Capt. Charles Robinson, died while the *Monkbarns* remained trapped in the ice field.

# Ice!

Winter pack ice in the North Atlantic, as well as around the Baltic Sea and Scandinavia, and in the higher latitudes of the North Pacific, could grip a vessel, crush it and leave its crew to a bitterly cold and deadly fate. Whaling and sealing ships most regularly sailed amongst those treacherous icy regions.

## NARRATIVES

## 12 June 1875

**Casualties - Foreign**

Philadelphia, 10th June.- The *State of Georgia* (s), which has arrived at New York, picked up, 5th June, a boat containing five men belonging to the *Vicksburg* (s)*, Bennett. The *Vicksburg* left Quebec 27th May, with 28 passengers and 60 crew. Encountering ice, she was stove in and foundered on the 1st June. The boat which has been picked up, and two others, containing about 40 persons, were successfully launched, but parted company at night.

The men picked up are James Crawley (boatswain's mate), of London; Thomas O'Brien, Liverpool; Patrick Grogan, John Williams, and Jonas Vilkenan. They say that Captain Bennett, with 40 others, went down with the steamer. The rescued men suffered severely from exposure but are doing well.

New York, 10th June.- The *State of Georgia* (s), which arrived here to-day, picked up a boat containing five seamen of the *Vicksburg* (s), from Quebec to Liverpool, that vessel having sunk, 1st June, through being stove in by ice, the night before, 120 miles SE of St. John's, Nfld. The *Vicksburg* had a crew of 60 men, 8 saloon passengers, including 3 women, and 20 steerage passengers, including 4 women. Another boat got away with the first mate and 30 persons, and a third boat with the second mate and 9 hands. These have not yet been heard of. The master and all the rest on board went down with the vessel. The rescued men saw no women in the boats.

## 15 June 1875

## The Loss of the 'Vicksburg' (s)

Philadelphia, 13th June.- A fishing vessel brought into St. John's, Newfoundland, nine of the crew and three passengers of the Vicksburg, who were picked up after being 32 hours in the boat. The names of the passengers are Joseph Penningham, Richard Corbett, Bryan M'Shane, and of the crew, Parker Greenwood, James Callahan, John Ryan, James Dolan, William Jones, James Walker, John Curtin, John Redmon, and Martin Lee.

M'Shane says the ship was in the ice on May 31, and at 11 at night the sides were stove in. Steam pumps were worked all night, but all hope was abandoned at five in the morning. Five boats were launched with plenty of provisions. The ship sank at half-past 6. There was no chance of escape for those left on board. The first officer's boat was upset and lost after leaving the ship. Government steamers have been sent from Halifax and St. John's to search for the missing boats.

## 20 July 1875

## Casualties – Foreign

New York, 7th July.- The master (Steen) of the *Nord Cap*, which arrived at Quebec, 3rd July, from London, reports:- "About a fortnight ago, in lat. 47 N, picked up boat No. 5, of the

Vicksburg (s); it was floating bottom up and contained two life preservers, a life belt, and a cask of water."

*On 27 May 1875 the Dominion Line steamship *Vicksburg*, of 2,484 tons, left Quebec for Liverpool. Four days later, attempting to get through an ice field southeast of Newfoundland, she was holed by the ice and her engine room flooded. On 1 June Captain Bennett ordered the ship to be abandoned and her boats launched. One boat occupied by the first mate and others capsized immediately and everyone drowned. Another boat with five crew was picked up by the steamship *State of Georgia* and landed at New York. A fishing boat picked up a third and its twelve occupants who were taken to the port of St. John's, Newfoundland.

Around half the complement of crew and passengers survived the sinking of the *Vicksburg*; the other half, including Capt. Bennett, drowned.

The *Vicksburg* went down just a few hundred miles north of where RMS *Titanic* was sunk by an iceberg and foundered, with the loss of over 1,500 people, on the night of 14/15 April 1912.

## 4 Oct 1878

**Casualties – Home**

London, 3rd Oct.- The *Waikato* (ship), Worster, arrived in the River from Canterbury, N.Z., reports:- "On the passage from New Zealand to the Horn, experienced contrary winds nearly the whole way. When off the Horn, were blown to the SE by north-easterly gales; and on the 25th July, in lat. 56.50 S, lon. 58.27 W, fell in with a number of icebergs and a great deal of pack ice.* We were for two days and nights embayed in the latter, and had great difficulty in getting clear of it. The barque *Cicero*, ship *Ellerslie*, and another ship in company with us."

## 9 Oct 1878

**Casualties – Home**

London, 8th Oct.- The *Gauntlet*, Lucas, arrived in the River from Brisbane, reports that on the 31st July, in lat. 57 S, lon. 59 W, she passed three icebergs,* length about 24 miles, and height from 300 to 400 feet.

*These two ships were at approximately the same location 250–300 miles east of Cape Horn, at approximately the same time, and were almost certainly within the same ice field, at the height of the Southern Hemisphere winter.

## 30 Jan 1879

**Casualties – Foreign**

Valparaiso, Dec. 14 [1878].- Thalia – The barquentine Nushka, of Swansea, Welsh, arrived yesterday from Buenos Ayres, and brought the crew of the barque Thalia, of Belfast, from Glasgow for Honolulu (general cargo), which was damaged by ice and abandoned south of Cape Horn on the 18th ult. The boat containing the master and nine men was picked up by the Nushka in lat. 58 S, long. 60 W. Another boat, with eight hands, is still missing.

*1 Feb 1879*

**Casualties – Home**

Belfast, Jan. 30.- Thalia, barque, Glasgow to Honolulu.- A letter, dated Valparaiso, Dec. 17 [1878], received from Captain White of the Thalia, barque, states:- "We sailed into ice on Nov. 16, about 2 a.m. When I was called by the second mate I was told there was ice all around. When I came on deck the vessel was in the ice and unmanageable. We were in the ice about two hours when the first hole was made in the ship. There were six holes at least, and the ship making water fast.

After getting the boats clear and provisioned, I made all possible efforts to get the ship out of the ice by using the boats' oars shoving the ice. We remained in ice till 6 p.m. of the 17th; at times we could see no clear water from the masthead. After getting into clear water the ship was unmanageable, having lost her rudder and bowsprit. She began to make a great deal more water. We were pumping the whole night.

At 9.30 a.m. on the 18th we lowered the chief mate's boat and got her clear from the ship; afterwards lowered the lifeboat with the remainder. I had occasion to return for fresh water; the chief mate sailed away then. The water was up to the 'tween decks in the hold, and her scupper holes level with the water. She sank about 20 minutes to 12. I then sailed. The boats were both good ones and well provisioned. We were picked up on Nov. 20 by the Nushka, of Swansea, Captain Welch, and landed at Valparaiso on Dec. 13." The Captain further states that he is in doubt as to the safety of the chief mate's boat with 8 lives.*

*Nothing more was ever heard from them, presumed lost at sea.

## 23 May 1882

**Casualties, Etc.**

Western Belle, ship, from Greenock, ran into an iceberg on May 1, crushing her bows. She sunk in 20 minutes, and the captain and 13 sailors, their boat being swamped, were drowned. A second boat, with the mate and six sailors, who were all frozen badly, was picked up next day, and the men landed at Quebec by the schooner President, from Antwerp, May 19. (*Philadelphia, May 20.*)

Western Belle struck an iceberg, in lat. 45 N, lon. 47 W, and sank May 1. Thirteen of the crew lost; remainder landed here; master drowned. (*Quebec*, by Cable.)

*17 June 1884*

**Casualties, Etc.**

Alumina.- The barque Sir John Franklin, of Copenhagen, bound from Ivigtut [Ivittuut]*, Greenland, for the Continent, with cryolite*, came to anchor in Peterhead Bay on Sunday afternoon. She reported that on May 1 the brig Alumina, of Philadelphia, bound from Oporto for Ivigtut, in ballast, was crushed by ice when near her port of destination, and that the crew 11 in number, escaped in the boats, and reached land after great difficulty, being tossed about in a stormy sea amid huge bergs of ice.

She further reported that the brig Elna, of Copenhagen, Larsen, which left Copenhagen in April for Ivigtut, via Newcastle, with coals, had also been crushed to pieces amongst the ice, and that her crew of 10 men were drowned.

*Ivittuut, on the southwest tip of Greenland, was the site of a cryolite mine between 1865 and 1987 when mining operations there were abandoned. Cryolite was used in the industrial processing of aluminium ore.

## 27 April 1885

### Maritime Intelligence

Maranee, St. John's, N.F. [Newfoundland] (by Cable) – The Maranee, Bowden, from Figueira [Portugal] for St. John's, has been cut through by ice and sunk.

### *8 May 1885*

Maritime Intelligence

Maranee, New York, April 28.- The British barque Maranee, Bowden, from Figueira Jan. 1 for Newfoundland, was abandoned in an ice floe in lat. 46 30 N, long. 45 54 W. Captain Bowden and two of the crew arrived at St. John's (N.F.) on night of April 26, in brig Seretha, from Cadiz and Lisbon.

The Seretha discovered them perishing amid an ice floe in lat. 46 30 N, long. 45 54 W. They had been 18 days exposed to rain, sleet, and snow, without cover and with scanty provisions. When picked up all they had left was a little bread, which was floating about in the bottom of the boat. Their vessel sank on the 5th April, having been crushed in the ice. The first officer and the remainder of the crew are supposed [believed] to have sunk in the longboat shortly after leaving the vessel. Loud screeches were heard by the survivors shortly after the ship's company parted.

## 31 July 1890

### Maritime Intelligence

Speranza.- Quebec, July 31.- The barque Askoy, Captain Halvorson, from Hamburg, arrived on Tuesday night with Captain Anderson, the mate, and four of the crew of the Norwegian barque Speranza. The latter left Liverpool on May 22 for Shediac (N.B. [New Brunswick]), and off the Newfoundland banks ran into an iceberg during a fog. Her bows were crushed in and the vessel began to sink at once. The pumps were put to work, but were ineffectual, and the crew took to the boats. One of these, with the second mate and three of the crew, has not been heard of, and is supposed [believed] to have been lost.

### *1 Aug 1890*

### Maritime Intelligence

Speranza.- Quebec, Aug. 1.- The British barque Foynland has arrived at Bay Verde (N.B.) with the remainder of the crew [ie., those believed to have been lost] of the wrecked barque Speranza.

### Miscellaneous

Halifax, Aug 1.- Four Norwegian sailors, who have landed at Northport, report that their ship struck an iceberg and sank. They were subsequently in an open boat for 10 days without provisions, and suffered terribly. The fate of the six other men belonging to the crew [ie., those in fact rescued by the *Askoy*] is unknown.

## Antarctic Ice in South Atlantic 1892/93 "as far as the eye could see"

Throughout the latter half of 1892 and well into 1893, numerous ships arriving in British and European ports coming from around Cape Horn or the Cape of Good Hope reported an unusually high density of icebergs and ice fields in the area of the South Atlantic just northeast of Cape Horn and to the east and northeast of the Falkland Islands. Apart from the extraordinary quantity, the ice was encountered well to the north of the usual northern extremity of Antarctic ice in the South Atlantic. Some of the icebergs sighted were ten miles or more long and 1,000 feet or more high. All ships reported ice of various kinds and size "as far as the eye could see," or words to that effect.

On 20th January 1893 the ship *Loch Torridon* (Capt. Pattman), in the vicinity of Cape Horn, "passed a berg three miles long, lifting its peak 1,500 feet above the sea!" (from Felix Riesenberg's *Cape Horn*). The *Strathdon* reported an ice island as much as forty miles long (**12 July 1892**).

> On 7th June 1893, the master of the 1,600 ton ship *Marion Inglis*, arrived at Hamburg from Iquique, reported: "…This enormous barrier of icebergs extends, to my knowledge, 140 miles NW to SE, and is right in the track of homeward-bound vessels round Cape Horn. It will be most dangerous to shipping for months if not years to come, and cannot be too widely known. Shipmasters from the Pacific side of the globe should be warned not to go to the eastward of long. 52 30 W until north of lat. 49 S."

The *Marion Inglis*'s master meant by this warning that since Antarctic ice fields that year had drifted as far north as lat. 49° S, ships should not turn east, to catch the southeast trade winds, until well to the northeast of the Falkland Islands, so as to avoid the ice or at least minimise their risk of collision with it.

## 12 July 1892

### Maritime Intelligence

### Weather and Navigation

> London, July 9.- Strathdon, from Sydney, arrived in the river, reports:- "On May 6 thick foggy weather set in. On 18th, in lat. 45 S, long. 35 W, the fog lifted, showing enormous icebergs in every direction. The mists came on again, and only by tacking and running the ship was saved from colliding with the bergs; one immense berg of quite 1,000 feet high was just cleared. The same afternoon the ship was literally surrounded by immense bergs; the only opening visible scarcely appeared wide enough for the ship. She, however, passed through it safely, almost touching the bergs each side of her with the yards.
>
> Got into clear water, and the weather clearing up showed an immense field of pack ice, along which we sailed 20 miles to the SSW, and hove to all night. The next day, wind NW, strong, saw an immense ice island upwards of 800 or 1,000 feet high, stretching along our lee as far as could be seen. Sailed 40 miles along it* and then tacked and got into a clear space and hove to for the night. At daylight, May 20, were clear of the pack ice and also clear of the [ice] island, although upwards of 70 bergs were in sight. At dark again hove to for the night. On May 21, made sail at daylight, about 30 icebergs in sight and more scattered. The last ice was passed on May 22, in lat. 42 S, long. 30 W."

*NB: This enormous ice island was at least 40 miles long and "upwards of 800 or 1,000 feet high."

## 17 Aug 1892

### Escape from Icebergs

The following is an extract from the log of the ship North, of London, owned by Messrs. Tyser and Co., J.J. Fisher, master:- "Left Astoria (Oregon) on April 7, 1892, with a full cargo of flour, bound to Sligo [Ireland]. All went well, nothing particular occurring, only changes of wind and weather, until the morning of June 11. Ship under reefed sails with a fresh NW wind and thick rain. 7 a.m. wind changed to south and cleared. Passed two icebergs, many more visible ahead. At noon, lat. 44 23 S, long. 36 56 W, was sailing parallel to an impenetrable ice barrier composed of bergs of every conceivable size and shape, ranging in height from 20 to 200 feet and upwards, meeting at frequent intervals great quantities of broken ice.

At 5 p.m. put ship under easy sail, and steered NE by E, the only clear passage visible from aloft. 10 30 p.m., dangerous to proceed further; ship surrounded with large icebergs and an impenetrable barrier to leeward. Immense quantities of broken ice low in the water of a dark colour and difficult to distinguish. Tacked ship and stood to the westward until 3 30 a.m. of the 12th, and again tacked and stood ENE, squally, with snow showers. At daylight found the ship embayed in a very dangerous position, this main body of ice trending NE and SW, curving in a deep semicircle to the eastward; ship surrounded by outlying bergs and broken ice. Tacked and made all sail. Fortunately the wind changed to east, which enabled us to reach out into open water, or the consequence might have been serious. A heavy sea settled in from the southward, and broke with tremendous force against the icebergs, sending the spray up to a great height.

I attribute the safety of the ship to the change of wind. As it was it was impossible to beat out without colliding with bergs. We had some marvelous escapes passing between large pieces of ice. 8 30 a.m., from the masthead could see no end to the barrier, or a passage to the eastward, only thousands of bergs packed closely together forming a formidable breakwater over 50 miles long.

Kept ship away SW, water comparatively free of broken ice, passing to leeward or windward of large bergs as wind would permit. 3 30 p.m. arrived abreast of the SW end of the barrier, having sailed 45 miles. From aloft could see the ice extending for miles to the NW until lost in space, an unbroken array of perpendicular cliffs. 5 p.m., darkness coming on, took a grateful farewell of Iceland. I can only compare it in appearance to a large island of volcanic origin. June 13, at 2 30 a.m., passed a very large iceberg, having seen it at a distance of 18 miles. At daylight no ice in sight. Kept away due north, thermometer rising fast."

## 4 Oct 1892

### Miscellaneous

Liverpool, Oct. 3.- The master of the barque Gladys, arrived at Hamburg from Iquique, reports:- "On June 8, in lat. 36 11 S, long. 87 W, the upper maintopsail was carried away and the yard came down, breaking in three pieces, and splitting maintopgallant mast. On

June 18, in lat. 55 S, long 77 W, had heavy SW storm, accompanied with high sea, which washed away everything movable fore and aft. The foresail blew away, and the truss of the maintopgallant yard carried away the yard, doing considerable damage to the mast, and the sail was lost entirely. The lower maintopsail also blew away on July 1, in lat. 43 S, 33 W. The vessel was completely embayed by large icebergs, and had to lay ship to [ie., stop the ship sailing] for the night.

Sailed amongst large icebergs and small detached pieces, with thick fog, up to July 4, ship lying to during night for safety. Lat. 39 30 S, long. 31 49 W, at 4 p.m. of the date last mentioned, while passing to the westward of a large iceberg, saw signs of human beings having been on it; and on the NW side a beaten track was on the berg, and it also appeared as if there had been a shelter formed in the side of the cleft on top of the ice. Also saw what appeared to be five dead human beings lying in different places, one lying outside the place of shelter and one halfway up the path. There were no signs of life, and as the place was densely packed with icebergs, and night coming on, it was not prudent to stop."

## 8 Dec 1892

### Weather and Navigation

London, Dec. 8.- The captain of the Galgate from San Francisco, which arrived off Dover yesterday, reports having met with numerous ice islands and icebergs in the South Atlantic. On the 28th Sept., in lat. 49 S, long. 42 W, she sighted an ice island two miles long and 250 feet high. The next day passed within two miles of another ice island of similar length, and apparently of great height. On the 1st Oct., in lat. 48 S, long. 35 W, sailed between two stupendous ice islands, three miles apart. The next day and day following sailed through an archipelago of icebergs from 350 to 3,000 feet long, and from 200 to 300 feet high.

On the 5th and 6th October, between lat. 41 36 S, long. 28 06 W, and lat. 41 07 S, and long. 27 23 W, sailed through at least 400 large icebergs, many of which were of a dark brown colour, although the majority were pure white; at one time 26 bergs were counted from the ship's deck. When passing through this ice the temperature of the ocean appeared but little affected, even when the ship was within a cable's length* of the bergs, and the air was generally only two degrees above the temperature of the sea, which for many days was of a pale green colour.

*A cable, in nautical measurement, is 1/10th of a nautical mile of 6,076ft, and therefore 608ft.

## 22 April 1893

### Weather and Navigation

London, April 21.- Lindores Abbey, at Galway, reports as follows:- Feb. 8, lat. 51 S, long. 49 W, passed several large icebergs. Feb. 9, lat. 49 S, long. 45 W, also passed a great number of very large icebergs. The night being very clear we were able to steer clear of them and carry all sail. Counted 61 large bergs, from 1 p.m. to 4 p.m., as many as 20 large and number of small ones being in sight at once. We sailed about 180 miles through them and could see them as far as the eye could reach on each side. At 8 p.m. got clear of the ice having passed above 24 hours steering through it, going 7½ knots an hour.

## 23 May 1893

**Weather and Navigation**

Queenstown, May 22.- Master of the barque Aldergrove, from Lyttelton [New Zealand], arrived here, reports:- On March 14, lat. 51 2 S, long. 30 10 W, sighted several icebergs*. March 15, lat. 30 36 S [*sic* - must be **50** 36 S], long. 48 8 W, passed 99 icebergs from daylight till noon, with a great amount of small ice.

March 16, lat. 49 10 S, long. 46 36 W, had strong gale and high confused sea, during which small floe ice continually rubbed alongside. At 2 p.m., had foreuppertopsail split. At 4 30 p.m. sailed into a clear space of about six miles long by four across, but could see no clear passage safe to enter. At 8 p.m. had a fierce gale with terrific hail squalls. At 2 a.m. wore ship to clear ice. While wearing, a terrific squall struck the ship, throwing her over until her upper deadeyes were under water, but ship righted when squall passed. At 3 a.m., sighted a large iceberg, close on the beam. At 3 20 a.m. a squall struck the ship, and the jib and mizenstaysail were blown away. At 4 30 a.m., daylight breaking, ship just cleared another iceberg by about half her own length, and we squared away and endeavoured to keep clear of ice until there was light enough to see a passage. At 11 a.m. passed the last iceberg.

Some of the icebergs were like islands, being at least three or four miles in length and about 200 feet high. Some were huge square blocks, others all shapes and forms.

## 24 May 1893

**Weather and Navigation**

Queenstown, May 23, 11 35 a.m.- Stronza, arrived here, reports:- On Feb. 9, in lat. 50 S, long. 46 W, passed miles of large icebergs, some of them five miles long and 300 feet high.

Dynomene, arrived here, reports:- On March 13, lat. 52 S, long. 50 W, passed large quantities of drift ice, and on two following days to lat. 50 S, and long. 46 W, was surrounded by icebergs of great size, which extended as far as could be seen from the royal yards [ie., the highest points of the ship].

* Ten years after those ice-ridden years, in 1903/04, the same phenomenon of a large quantity of icebergs was reported from the area to the east and northeast of the Falkland Islands, with reference, moreover, to the earlier conditions, in the following commentary.

## 21 Nov 1903

Ice Reported Eastward of Falkland Islands.- Recent reports show that during the months of July and August numerous icebergs have been seen between the parallels of 47 and 54 S, latitude, and the meridians of 46 and 55 W, longitude. It is now nearly 10 years since ice was reported in this locality in any considerable quantity, but during the years 1892 and 1893 large masses of ice were continuously met with hereabouts, and it seems not impossible that icebergs may be encountered more frequently than usual to the eastward and northeastward of the Falkland Islands during the next year or two.

## *Torrens'* Collision with Iceberg

# 11 March 1899

### Maritime Intelligence

Torrens*.- Adelaide, Feb. 8.- The ship Torrens, Angel, from London, reports that at 9 p.m. of Jan. 11, in lat. 46 S, long. 50 E, during thick weather, she ran into an iceberg. Her bowsprit was driven through the knight-heads and broken in three pieces, and foretopmast carried away, and the stem was crushed in, leaving the wood ends open. A good deal of water entered the forepeak and a considerable quantity got below, but the cargo is not supposed [thought] to have sustained much damage.

*The *Torrens'* collision with the iceberg occurred near the Crozet Islands, in the southern Indian Ocean, approximately 1,600 miles southeast of South Africa, as the ship was "running her easting down" towards Australia. The master of the ship at that time was Capt. Falkland Angel, a son of Capt. H.R. Angel for whom the *Torrens* was built and who was the vessel's first master and owner. One of the *Torrens'* apprentices wrote an account of the incident, to explain later rumours in Adelaide that she had actually struck Penguin Island in the Crozets rather than an iceberg:

"At 9 p.m., when running with a strong breeze on the port quarter, in misty weather, we suddenly sighted the westernmost of the Crozet Isles right ahead. We just had time to clear it, and the Old Man [captain] ordered the topgallant sails to be taken off her and the mainsail hauled up. He then went below to look at the chart. After a few minutes, he came up again and gave the mate the course. This course was set to take us to the westward of the Penguin Rock, but the mate, thinking that the Old Man meant to go to the eastward and that he had not allowed enough, altered the course a point more to the east when the skipper had gone below again, with the consequence that we struck the rock.

Luckily there was deep water right alongside, it rises straight up out of the water, and as the look-out reported 'Ice right ahead,' the man at the wheel at once put his helm down without waiting for orders, so that when we struck [the ice] we were already coming up into the wind and only struck a glancing blow. It carried away our bowsprit and fore topmast and smashed a hole in the bows, but we were able to keep her afloat. At the enquiry, we all blandly swore that it was an iceberg that we hit. On the morning after the accident, whilst I was at the wheel, the Old Man pointed astern and told one of the passengers, 'That's what we hit,' and there was no ice in sight, only the Crozet Islands."

The *Torrens* was one of the fastest passenger clipper ships in the Australian trade: in 1887 she made the sailing ship record of 64 days for the voyage from Plymouth in England to Adelaide in South Australia. In 1890/91 the *Torrens* was dismasted in a squall off the coast of Brazil. She was towed into and repaired at Pernambuco (Recife) which lengthened her passage time from London to Adelaide to a rather tardy 179 days. On her subsequent two voyages, from 2 November 1891 till 15 October 1893, the chief officer (mate) of the *Torrens* was the author Joseph Conrad. Capt. H.R. Angel sold her to Italians in 1906. *Torrens* was broken up at Genoa in 1910 after the second time her new owners had run her aground.

## THE *ISLANDER* HOLED BY ICE - KLONDIKERS DROWNED

## 19 Aug 1901

### Maritime Intelligence

Islander (s).*- Victoria, B.C. [British Columbia], Aug. 19.- The Skagway steamer Islander, belonging to the Canadian Pacific Alaskan Line, struck an iceberg near Juneau, Alaska, at 20 minutes to 2 in the morning of Friday last [16 Aug], and foundered in 20 minutes. Sixty-five of the passengers and crew were drowned, including the captain. The steamer was less than a mile from the shore at the time and the water was perfectly calm. A number of bodies have already been recovered. One hundred and seven of the passengers and crew were saved, and have been brought to Victoria by the steamship Queen last night.

Among those reported lost are the wife, daughter, and niece of Mr. Ross, governor of the Yukon Territory, who were returning home after visiting Dawson City; Mr. Andrew Keating and his two sons, lately arrived from England; Dr. John Duncan, Victoria; and Mr. Douglas, a wholesale merchant of Vancouver.

A returning miner strapped $8,000 in gold round his waist. The weight of the money made the life preserver topple over and he was drowned. A million dollars in treasure went down with the ship.

## *10 Sept 1901*

### The Islander Disaster

Mr. F.G. Hinde Bowker, formerly Yukon manager of the British American Corporation, who was one of the passengers on the ill-fated Skagway steamer Islander, which foundered near Juneau, Alaska, has sent home to his relatives at Saffron Walden, Essex, a very graphic account of the disaster. Mr. Bowker, in describing how he left the sinking vessel, says that on seeing a raft on which were eight or ten people, "I slipped down the rope and on to the raft. By this time the bow was sinking, and the stern was up in the air, with the propeller out of the water. Then the stern began to sink. I was hanging on to the outer edge of the raft, and, like some of the others, was struck on the head by the side of the steamer as it glanced by, but was not badly hurt. I took a good hold of the raft and drew a deep breath, and down I went. We were sucked a long way down as the steamer sank. Then the air in the cabin was apparently released, for I was tossed up to the surface quicker than I went down. The only damage I sustained were some bruises in the ribs and on the chest, and a mouthful or two of the cold salt water. As we were sucked down I saw the propeller above me, and when I came up there were only two of our party left, a Chinaman and myself.

I can give an emphatic denial to the story that the captain committed suicide or in any other way wilfully allowed himself to drown. Every man, the strongest of us, was having his work cut out to keep body and soul together. The captain was among those we could hear talking and shouting around us, but could not see owing to the dense fog. He jumped off the bridge as the steamer was going down – at least, that is what I am told. Anyway, I heard others talking to him in the water, and could catch some of the conversation. A minute later some one called out that the captain had gone too, the impression conveyed being that he was unable to longer cling to the wreckage. I did not see the captain at any time after 10 o'clock, when he was in excellent spirits.

There were many Klondikers [gold prospectors] aboard the boat who were coming down after several years' experience in the north. The steamer had $275,000 on board. It was nearly all lost. One man named Hart was probably the heaviest loser; he had $35,000 [in gold dust] in two sacks, and it all went to the bottom."

*The 1,519-ton *Islander* was a steel-hulled steamship operated by the Canadian Pacific Steam Navigation Company between Victoria, British Columbia, and Alaska. She was particularly favoured by prospectors and investors travelling to and from the Klondike gold fields. The vessel left Skagway, Alaska for Victoria on 14 August 1901 with a full complement of crew and passengers, and gold bullion to the value of some $6 million. In the early morning of 15 August shortly after 2 a.m. she struck an iceberg which holed her on her port side bow. She sank within twenty minutes. Sixteen crew including the *Islander*'s master, Captain H.B. Foot, and 23 passengers drowned in the tragedy.

The finding of the Court of Inquiry into the wreck of the *Islander* and loss of 40 persons, on 23 December 1901, included the observation that, "We think that Pilot Le Blanc is open to censure for his action in keeping the ship [at] full speed – at the rate of nearly fourteen knots an hour – after having seen floating ice some ten minutes before the accident." The master and officers of the vessel were exonerated from any suggestion of "intemperance" on their behalf.

# 10  Earthquakes, Seaquakes and Volcanoes

Anjer, at the western extremity of the Indonesian island of Java, was an important coastal village for sailing ships of the 19th century. The village looked out over the Sunda Strait, the narrow channel separating the islands of Java and Sumatra. For ships coming from or returning westward to America or Europe the Sunda Strait was the gateway to ports around the South China Sea, Indonesia, the Philippines and further north to China and Japan. The lighthouse and signal station at Anjer were strategically positioned for such vessels to identify themselves and be reported. Out in the middle of the Sunda Strait was the island of Krakatoa.

The eruption of Krakatoa in August 1883 did not, in itself, cause great damage to deep sea merchant sailing ships, but it did destroy the village and lighthouse at Anjer and caused great loss of life and physical damage to the surrounding area, including Indonesia's main port then called Batavia (Jakarta today). Shipping was affected because that greatest volcanic eruption of modern times changed the physical nature of the Sunda Strait, with new, uncharted islands and rocks, not to mention the loss of Anjer's important lighthouse and signalling station.

Ships occasionally directly felt, and reported such extreme acts of nature. A strong earthquake that shook the coast of northern Chile and southern Peru on 9 May 1877 generated a tidal wave (tsunami) which caused damage to many of the dozens of vessels loading nitrate and guano at Iquique and Pabellón de Pica. (Basil Lubbock gives a vivid description of it in his book *The Nitrate Clippers*.) Undersea earthquakes – seaquakes - could be felt by ships at sea as tremors that shook their timbers or iron plates and no doubt rattled the nerves of crew members, too, who often thought their ship had struck a reef.

The mid-Atlantic Ridge, a range of undersea mountains zipping down the centre of the North and South Atlantic, is a tectonically active slash in the Earth's oceanic crust. The Ridge is the 'divergent-plate boundary' that separates the tectonic plates on either side of it: the African Plate to the east and the South American Plate to the west, in the South Atlantic; and the Eurasian Plate to the east and North American Plate to the west, in the North Atlantic.

Magma erupting from beneath the Earth's crust all along the Ridge causes the African and Eurasian plates to separate – or diverge – from the South American and North American plates by about 5 cm a year in the process of seafloor spreading. Seismic events (undersea earthquakes and volcanic eruptions) along the Ridge are directly related to the tectonic divergence of those plates.

Most ships that reported seaquakes in the Atlantic Ocean were either directly over the mid-Atlantic Ridge or very near to it. Several reported 'quakes near the Azores, the Western Isles as they were also called, jutting straight up from the Ridge, and might even have caused the mysterious abandonment by her crew of the 'ghost ship' the *Mary Celeste* in December 1872.

Reports of seaquakes diminished towards the end of the 19th century as the number of deep sea sailing ships diminished while the number of steamships increased. Sailing ships, being slower than steamships, noticed phenomena such as seaquakes that bigger and faster (and noisier) steamships did not.

## NARRATIVES

## 22 Feb 1870

### A Submerged Volcano

The *New Commercial Advertiser* of 4th Feb. says:- "The captain of the ship *Shirley*, which arrived at San Francisco yesterday, from Manila, reports that he saw a submerged volcano ten miles North East of Smith's Island*. Volumes of smoke were apparently rising from the water, and no land was visible."

*The *Shirley* would have been passing south of Japan and what was called Smith Island on old maps as she headed out to cross the North Pacific. The island is part of an arc of actively volcanic islands stretching south of Tokyo Bay to the Marianas (Guam). The names of these islands attest to their vulcanism: Iwo Jima (Sulphur Island, in Japanese), and the Volcano Islands, with several individual islands called Volcano Island.

## 25 May 1870

### Casualties – Foreign

The *Leicester*, Rowe, arrived at Plymouth from San Francisco, reports that on the 16th May the vessel trembled fore and aft, as if she were passing over a wreck. As the vibration lasted longer than the ship was going her length, and no marks were found on her bow, the motion is supposed [thought] to have been caused by a subterranean eruption*.

*On the 16th May, eight or nine days before arriving in Plymouth, the ship would have been in the vicinity of the Azores, an area of regular undersea seismic activity - seaquakes – originating from the mid-Atlantic Ridge.

## 5 Dec 1871

### Casualties – Foreign

Melbourne, 25th Sept.- The Victory, Brown, arrived here from Calcutta, reports that on the 19th Aug., in lat. 5 S, lon. 99 E*, an earthquake occurred. The shock lasted about 30 or 40 seconds, and the ship shook all over, as if grating hard over ground.

*This position is just off the southeast coast of Sumatra, over the Java Trench, a seismically active area of earthquakes and seaquakes. The epicentre of the 26th December 2004 Great Sumatra-Andaman earthquake was just to the northwest of the ship's position. The tsunami generated by that 9.2 magnitude earthquake – or seaquake - claimed 187,000 lives, with 43,000 listed as missing.

## 17 Jan 1872

### Casualties – Foreign

New York, 5th Jan.- The Niagara, Bormann, arrived here from Iquique [northern Chile], was very much shaken by the shock of an earthquake, on the 5th Oct. [1871], in lat. 29 S, lon. 72 W.*

*This position is just off the coast of northern Chile, between Iquique and Valparaiso. The west coast of South America is one of the most seismically active regions of the world, along the boundary of two tectonic plates; the Peru–Chile Trench is the most conspicuous seafloor feature of that plate boundary. The Nazca Plate of the Pacific Ocean seafloor is slipping under the continental South American Plate by a process called subduction at a rate of approximately 10cm/yr.

Seismic activity – including earthquakes (or seaquakes) – is generated most commonly along such tectonic plate boundaries. More than half of the subduction process along the west coast of South America occurs off the coast of Chile. (An 8.8 magnitude quake of 27 February 2010, about 250 miles south of Valparaiso, near the city of Concepción, was one of the most powerful earthquakes since 1900.)

## 14 March 1872

### Casualties – Foreign

New York, 28th Feb.- The Elizabeth, Gronlund, which arrived at Galveston 20th Feb., from Cardiff, experienced two severe shocks of earthquake*, between Cuba and the former port, about the 13th Feb. It was thought the vessel had struck, but, on sounding, no bottom was found at 60 fathoms.

*The Gulf of Mexico between Cuba and the port of Galveston, Texas, is a shallow basin of water. The ocean floor there is a fairly stable tectonic plate, quite far from any plate boundaries, and earthquakes are rare. However, on 10th September 2006 a magnitude 6.0 "mid-plate" earthquake was recorded along the so-called Cuba fracture zone and centred approximately 375 miles northwest of Cuba, roughly midway between Cuba and the southern Louisiana coast and very near the track the *Elizabeth* would have taken along her passage towards Galveston.

## 3 April 1872

### Casualties – Foreign

New York, 21st Mar.- The Derby, Goff, arrived at San Francisco, from Manilla, encountered, during the whole passage, a succession of heavy gales, varying from NE to WSW and SE.
On the 28th Jan., in lat. 20 N, lon. 121 E, she experienced a shock of earthquake*.

*The earthquake occurred just north of the Philippine island of Luzon, a seismically active area along the so-called "Ring of Fire", the boundary between the huge Pacific tectonic plate and other contiguous plates, arcing around almost the entire Pacific Ocean.

## 3 Dec 1872

**Casualties – Foreign**

New York, 21st Nov.- The Magnet, Frobisher, which arrived at Philadelphia, 18th Nov., experienced the shock of an earthquake on the 3rd Aug., in lat. 42 N, lon. 88 W*.

*The position of latitude 42° N, longitude 88° W is near…Chicago, Illinois! The real position of the vessel – and the earthquake (seaquake) - must have been latitude 42° **South**, at longitude 88° W, approximately 600 miles off the coast of Chile, due west of Chiloe Island, in the Pacific, a seismically active region of the seafloor.

## 9 May 1873

**Casualties – Foreign**

Cuxhaven, 5th May.- The Wiria (s), Wallstein, arrived here from Leghorn [Livorno, Italy], reports…that on the 25th Apl., in lat. 48 N, lon. 10 W, she experienced an earthquake, the barometer sinking to 27.30.*

*The site of this quake – just over the continental shelf due west of the Brest peninsula in Brittany – is not a seismically active area. If this was an earthquake (or seaquake), it was a very unusual one. The relationship, if any, between earthquakes and barometric pressure, as recorded above, is not clear.

## 17 June 1873

**Casualties – Foreign**

Melbourne, 22nd Apl.- The *Buston Vale*, Anderson, arrived here from Mauritius, experienced the shock of an earthquake, lasting about a minute, 8th Mar., in lat. 40 S, lon. 78 E*.

*This was near St. Paul and Amsterdam Islands in the southern Indian Ocean, more or less directly over the boundary between two tectonic plates, the African Plate and the southern part of the Eurasian Plate.

## 29 Aug 1873

**Casualties – Foreign**

Valparaiso, 12th July.- Several vessels arriving here report having experienced the shock of an earthquake, 7th July*, in which they shook as if they had struck a reef.

*The earthquake of 7 July 1873 was felt in various Chilean towns and cities, including the main port of Valparaiso. On 16 August 1906 an earthquake struck Valparaiso that killed around 3,000 people, seriously injured some 20,000 more, and caused the destruction of most of the buildings in the city.

## 1 July 1875

**Casualties, Etc.**

The Red Deer, Ugler, arrived in the River from Kurrachee [Karachi, Pakistan], reports that, on the 6th Mar., she encountered a cyclone in lat. 17 S lon. 79 E, during which she lost sails and sustained considerable damage to bulwarks and gear about the decks. 28th Apl., in lat. 9 S lon. 14 W, from 5.30 p.m. to 8.30 p.m., about 35 shocks of earthquake* were felt, several of them being heavy ones, which shook the vessel all over, and made everything rattle, one shock in particular lasted several seconds.

*The *Red Deer* was just south of Ascension Island, over the seismically active mid-Atlantic Ridge, when she experienced the tremors of this undersea earthquake, or seaquake.

## 5 July 1875

### Casualties – Foreign

New York, 21st June.- The *Hamilton*, Ross, which arrived here, yesterday, from Manilla, reports that on the 4th June, in lat. 19 N, lon. 58 W, she felt the shock, and heard the noise of an earthquake*, lasting about 10 minutes and commencing in smooth water; she pitched bows under during the disturbance.

*The *Hamilton* was just to the east of the Puerto Rico trench, around 250 miles off the Leeward Islands of the West Indies, at the time she experienced this quake. The Puerto Rico trench, the deepest point of the Atlantic Ocean, marks the boundary between two tectonic plates, with regular seismic activity related to it.

## 18 Aug 1875

### Casualties – Home

Liverpool – Aug.- The Fearnought, Graham, arrived here from Rangoon, reports:- "Experienced two shocks of earthquake*, on the 29th June, in lat. 2 S lon. 21 W, and another shock on the 20th, in lat. 1 S lon. 22 W."

### *23 Aug 1875*

### Casualties – Foreign

Queenstown, 21st Aug., 11.30 a.m.- The barque Yanikale, arrived here, reports:- "June 19th, 7 p.m., lat. 1 S lon. 23 W, experienced a sudden shock*, when the ship shook and trembled as if she had struck on a reef, and the crew ran on deck, remarking that ship was on shore; the noise lasted three minutes; at 7.33 p.m. a similar shock lasting one minute; at 8 p.m. another lasting ten seconds; and at 5 a.m. the following day, another shock lasting ten seconds.

*These two ships were within about 60 miles of each other on the 19 and 20 June, at lat. 1° S of the equator and in long. 22° and 23° W respectively. The location of both ships was around 300 miles to the southeast of the St. Peter and St. Paul Rocks, off the northeast coast of Brazil, and directly over one of the most seismically active zones of the mid-Atlantic Ridge. Each ship reported multiple shocks of seaquakes at approximately the same time. The *Fearnought* additionally experienced another tremor on the 29 June in almost the same location. (Being in the calms of the equatorial doldrums, she probably would have been drifting very slowly.)

Paul Eve Stevenson, in his book *By Way of Cape Horn* (J.P. Lippincott Company, 1898), wrote, when near the St. Paul's Rocks on his voyage from New York to San Francisco in the *Hosea Higgins* in the mid-1890s: "The Atlantic Ocean near the equator, between the [longitude] meridians of 18° and 23°, is subject to frequent and violent earthquakes, which have the effect upon a vessel like that of being dragged over a reef, or that of a heavy chain-cable being suddenly run out through the hawse-pipes."

## 24 Jan 1876

### Casualties, Etc.

The Devon, Hicks, arrived in the River, from Tuticorin, reports:- "17th Dec., at 6.30 p.m., in lat. 25 N lon. 22.10 W, felt the effects of a submarine volcano*. The ship vibrated as if she was passing over a shoal, and a noise was heard at the same time as if a heavy cask was being rolled over the lower deck. The watch below came on deck, thinking the ship had struck. The vibration and noise lasted about four minutes. Found the ship making no water."

*The Devon was about 375 miles off the coast of northwest Africa, between the Canary Islands and Cape Verde Islands, at the time it experienced the effects of the "submarine volcano". The floor of the Atlantic Ocean in that area is a generally flat abyssal plain, the Cape Verde Plain, usually a tranquil ocean floor environment. Several volcanic structures have been identified, however, rising from the seafloor just to the southwest of the Canary Islands (the Saharan Seamounts). Something like them, in an active volcanic phase, might have been the source of what the Devon experienced.

## 3 Feb 1877

### Casualties – Foreign

Mauritius, 5th Jan.- The Patrie, Eymery, arrived here from Monte Video, reports that on the 19th Dec. [1876], in lat. 33 S lon. 56 E*, she felt the shock of an earthquake.

*At this location the Patrie was sailing over a ridge of fracture zones on the Indian Ocean seafloor between the Crozet Islands to the south and Mauritius and Madagascar to the north.

## 6 Nov 1877

### Casualties – Home

Queenstown, 4th Nov., 6 p.m.- Report of ship Governor, Tilley:- "4th Aug., left Huanillos*, having had to ship both [anchor] chains, one at 45 and the other at 50 fathoms; light airs and calm. On the 5th, Pabellon de Pica* bearing ENE, offshore about 15 miles, felt a smart earthquake shock**. Had light trades and cloudy weather to lat. 30 South, thence to Cape Horn, moderate westerly winds. Sighted Cape Horn 27th Aug.

Thence to lat. 35 South had strong westerly winds, from thence to lat. 23 S long. 23 W, fresh northerly winds, fresh SE trades to lat. 1 N. Crossed the Equator 28th Sept., in long. 24 W. Had light easterly wind through the Western islands [Azores], thence to the [English] Channel strong SW wind. Carried away lower mizen topsail yard and mizen topgallant yard and split sails. Sighted Fastnet at 6 p.m. on the 3rd inst."

*Huanillos was a nitrate loading 'port' – actually more just an anchorage – between Iquique to the north and Tocopilla and Antofagasta to the south, on the north coast of Chile. Pabellón de Pica was another regular destination along this coast for sailing ships picking up cargoes of nitrate.

**Earthquakes occurred quite regularly along and just offshore of the north coast of Chile. Some, including tsunami (tidal wives) generated by them, did significant damage at the nitrate loading ports, most of which were open and unprotected anchorages and therefore vulnerable to fluctuating weather and sea conditions.

## 5 March 1878

**Submarine Volcanoes**

West Cowes, I.W. [Isle of Wight], 3rd Mar.- The master of the *D. McB. Park*, arrived here from Batavia, reports as follows:- "29th Jan., at 7 a.m., in lat. 4.20 N lon. 21.45 W,* saw several submarine volcanoes throwing large columns of water about 100 feet into the air, while the sea was in great commotion, as it is where there is a very strong under current, the weather at the time being very cloudy, with rain, and nearly calm. The sound was as a distant thunder."

*The vessel was at the time directly over the Mid-Atlantic Ridge in the Atlantic Ocean, just over the equator and very near the St. Peter and St. Paul Rocks. The seafloor there is crisscrossed with fractures and seamounts from the high incidence of seismic and volcanic activity associated with such undersea features.

## 12 Sept 1878

**Casualties – Home**

Falmouth, 10th Sept.- The Arequipa, Dixon, arrived here from Iquique, reports that in lat. 32 S, lon. 80 W, she experienced a heavy S gale which blew away fore, lower and upper maintopsail. On the 21st Aug., in lat. 33 S, lon 37 W, the shock of an earthquake* was felt, lasting a minute and a half, during which time the vessel had a trembling motion.

*The *Arequipa* at that time was around 800 miles off the coast of southern Brazil. The seafloor in that area is characterised by a so-called *aseismic ridge* known as the Rio Grande Rise. Volcanic hotspots below the Earth's crust, and seismic activity, both phenomena related to an aseismic ridge, are probably the source of the undersea earthquake that shook the *Arequipa*.

## 9 Nov 1878

**Casualties, Etc.**

London, 8th Nov. The *Star of Persia*, Mahood, arrived in the River from Calcutta, reports:- "15th Sept., arrived off Cape Agulhas [South Africa]. Had very heavy gales from WSW every three or four days since passing Madagascar. 11th Oct., at 5.40 a.m. (ship's time), lat. 2 53 N, lon. 21 37 W, felt the effects of an earthquake or submarine volcano*, which lasted about three minutes, and made the ship tremble fore and aft as if grounding on a gravelly bottom."

*The ship's position at the time, directly over the mid-Atlantic Ridge halfway between northeast Brazil and the West African coast, was one of the most common regions of the Atlantic for undersea earthquakes (seaquakes) to be experienced.

## 11 Feb 1879

**Casualties, Etc.**

Report of the American barque Jonathan Bourne, Doane, from Huon Islands [New Caledonia] for orders (guano):- "Left the islands Oct. 30 [1878]; passed Cape Horn Dec.

10, and the Equator Jan 10. Nov. 12, when about 200 miles east of the north end of New Zealand, felt two shocks of a submarine earthquake."*

*The location of this undersea earthquake (seaquake), to the north of New Zealand, is directly over the boundary between two tectonic ocean plates: the Indian-Australian plate and the Pacific plate. The subduction zone along this boundary causes regular seismic (and volcanic) activity. The rate of movement of the two plates relative to one another, as the Pacific plate slides under the Indian-Australian plate, is 7cm a year.

## 19 Feb 1879

**Submarine Earthquake**

The Venezuela, Kroncke, arrived at Havana from Huanillos, reports that on Jan. 19, between 3 p.m. and 5 p.m., in lat. 14 N, long. 67 W, she experienced two shocks of a submarine earthquake.* From that date until the 23rd, when she sighted Jamaica, stormy weather and cross seas were experienced.

*The *Venezuela* experienced this seaquake in the Caribbean, approximately halfway between Puerto Rico and Venezuela, near the subduction zone boundary (where one tectonic plate slides underneath its neighbouring plate) of the oceanic Caribbean and continental North Andes tectonic plates. Tectonic plate boundaries are one of the main sources of earthquakes around the world. A US Geological Survey "Map of Seismicity of the Earth 1900 – 2007: Caribbean Plate and Vicinity" identifies a low magnitude seaquake at virtually the same location as that reported by the *Venezuela*.

## 28 April 1880

**Casualties, Etc.**

Report of the Eastern Star, Davis, from Port Natal, in the river:- "Left Port Natal Feb. 11. Passed Cape of Good Hope on the 19th, and St. Helena March 1, SE trade wind very light. On March 6, at 3 p.m., lat 9 10 S, long. 11 59 W, a severe shock* was felt through the vessel, causing the doors, etc., in the cabin to rattle, and a loud rumbling through the hold, so severe as to wake the chief officer who was asleep below, the sea at the time and for several seconds in a complete boil..."

*The *Eastern Star* was about 120 miles southeast of Ascension Is., in the South Atlantic, right over the spine of the seismically active Mid-Atlantic Ridge at the time she experienced this undersea "shock".

## 28 Nov 1881

**Casualties – Foreign**

New York, Nov. 14.- Cherokee, Mallett, arrived here Nov. 12 from London, reports:- "...Oct. 6, lat. 51 35 N, long. 31 36 W, had two shocks of earthquake*, at 5 50 p.m., the first being heavy and the second light, about five seconds between them..."

*The *Cherokee* was directly over the seismically active Mid-Atlantic Ridge, halfway between Ireland and Newfoundland, when she experienced this undersea earthquake.

## 14 Jan 1882

**Casualties, Etc.**

**Miscellaneous**

A smart shock of earthquake* occurred at Iquique on Nov. 13 [1881], and the master of the German barque Shakespeare, from Liverpool, reports that he felt it when about eight miles to the westward of Punta Gruesa, with such severity that he imagined that the vessel had struck on a rock, until the lead showed that he was in deep water. (*Valparaiso, Nov. 26*)

*Earthquakes were reported regularly by ships at or near Iquique and off the north coast of Chile.

## 27 Feb 1882

**Casualties, Etc.**

Report of the Grasmere, Kewley, from San Francisco, at Queenstown:- "Jan. 7, when on the line [the equator], long. 21 W, a volcanic shock was felt*; at first vessel was supposed [thought] to have struck on a reef, afterwards another heavy shock, and then four lighter ones were experienced. Jan. 8 had another smart shock." (Queenstown, Feb. 21)

*The *Grasmere* was on the equator in the Atlantic Ocean at long. 21 W. She would have been right over the Romanche Fracture Zone which cuts diagonally across the mid-Atlantic Ridge, between the volcanic islands of Ascension, 650 miles to the southeast, and St. Peter & St. Paul Rocks, 250 miles or so to the west – a very active area of tectonic, seismic and undersea volcanic activity.

## 27 May 1882

**Miscellaneous**

The Hermes, German barque, arrived at Falmouth, reports that on May 7, at 2 20 p.m. she experienced a pretty strong earthquake*, which lasted nearly a minute and a half. It was travelling from SW to NW.)

*The *Hermes*, commanded by Capt. Grube, was on a voyage from Manila to Falmouth with a cargo of sugar when she experienced this earthquake (seaquake). On 9 May, just two days after the earthquake, she was spoken by a vessel, the *Kong Sverre*, at lat. 31 N, long. 36 W, approximately 700 miles south-southwest of the Azores. On the day of the earthquake, therefore, the *Hermes* would have been just to the east of the central spine of the Mid-Atlantic Ridge, the undersea mountain range characterised seismically by its lively tectonic activity, and running the length of the North and South Atlantic. *Hermes* arrived in Falmouth 25 May.

## 8 Sept 1885

**Maritime Intelligence**

**Miscellaneous**

New York, Aug. 27.- The Norwegian barque Jorsalfarer, from Acapulco for Victoria [British Columbia], which put into San Francisco Aug. 18, reports:- "Sailed from Acapulco July 9, and first day out had three severe shocks of earthquake*, with thunder and lightning. On the same day the captain was taken sick with intermittent fever and then the crew, one after another, until all hands except the first mate and two men were sick. For three weeks the vessel had to run her own course with the wheel lashed. On Aug. 5 signaled the steamer Arabic (British), from San Francisco for Yokohama, which hove to and supplied us with medicines and provisions."

*The west coast of Mexico lies along a fault zone separating two tectonic plates, the Cocos Plate and the North American Plate, where earthquakes and seismic and volcanic activity are regularly recorded.

## Sunk by a Seaquake?

## 8 Feb 1888

### Maritime Intelligence

Gaetano Cicconardi.- Rio Grande [southern Brazil], Feb. 6, 3 10 p.m.- Gaetano Cicconardi, Italian schooner, from Buenos Ayres for the Channel, foundered at sea in lat. 19 S; part of crew picked up by the Renown and landed here; others were picked up by another vessel.

### 13 Feb 1888

### Maritime Intelligence

Gaetano Cicconardi.- Buenos Ayres, Feb. 11, 10 10 a.m.- Italian barque Gaetano Cicconardi abandoned in a sinking condition, in lat. 19 S, long. 37 W; crew saved. Part of crew picked up by the British barque Swansea and landed here. Part of crew landed Rio Grande by British schooner Renown.

### 14 March 1888

### Maritime Intelligence

Gaetano Cicconardi.- Rio Grande, Feb. 11.- British schooner Renown, Mackenzie, arrived on the 4th inst., at this port and landed the chief officer, steward and three sailors of the Italian barque Gaetano Cicconardi, from Buenos Ayres, with cargo of maize, for Falmouth, which vessel was abandoned in lat. 19 13 S, long. 37 15 W, in a sinking condition, and part of the crew taken off by the Renown. The remainder of the crew consisting of the captain, boatswain, and four sailors, were taken off by the barque Swansea, from Windsor [Nova Scotia] for Buenos Ayres.

The captain of the Gaetano Ciconardi reported to Captain Mackenzie, of the Renown, that whilst running before a gale they suddenly experienced a shock, resembling that of a seaquake*, causing the vessel to spring a leak, and which gradually increased until they were obliged to leave her.

*The *Gaetano Cicconardi* was abandoned just off the coast of Brazil, to the northeast of Rio de Janeiro. The seafloor there is not particularly characteristic of seismic or tectonic activity that would generate a seaquake, though there are various seamounts in the region that might suggest the possibility that the vessel experienced some kind of undersea quake. It is equally, or even more possible, however, that the vessel struck some large piece of debris floating just beneath the surface, such as a derelict ship's hull, which would be all but invisible in the stormy conditions prevailing at the time.

## 21 July 1888
**Maritime Intelligence**

**Miscellaneous**

Malta, July 14.- The East Anglia (s), McDowell, from Odessa, reports that on July 11, at 8 50 p.m., Cape Matapan* bearing E. ¼ S [ie., a few degrees south of due east] 46 miles, weather quite calm, the vessel lifted three times as if passing over a shoal or other body, or else from the effects of some volcanic disturbance. The nearest land was 22 miles distant, and no shoals are known of in the neighbourhood.

The Greek steamer Mari Vagliano, Lichiardopulo, from Taganrog [Russian port on Sea of Azov], also reports that on July 11, at 8 30 p.m., Cape Matapan being distant about 19 miles, bearing E. by N., she felt the shock of a submarine earthquake, which lasted about half a minute and caused the vessel to roll as if passing over a shoal.

### *31 July 1888*
**Maritime Intelligence**

**Miscellaneous**

Hamburg, July 28.- The master, Beyer, of the Bakuin (s), arrived here from Batoum [Batumi, on the Black Sea coast of Georgia], reports:- "On July 11, at 9 p.m., Cape Matapan bearing NW by W, eight sea miles distant, felt the vessel tremble strongly for about a minute and a-half, as if she was running over something, supposed [believed] owing to a submarine earthquake."

*Cape Matapan, or Akra Tainaro, on the Peloponnisos peninsula, the southernmost point of the Greek mainland, is located in a highly active seismic area along the edge of what is called, in plate tectonics, a convergent plate boundary (that is, where one tectonic plate is sliding underneath an adjacent plate). A great number of earthquakes, and at least one exceeding 8.0 magnitude, have been recorded in this area of southwest Greece, including a powerful one on 9 September 1888, just two months after the quake reported by these three vessels off Cape Matapan on the evening of 11 July 1888. (See **14 March 1893** for report of another seaquake in this same area.)

## 20 July 1889
**Maritime Intelligence**

**Weather and Navigation**

Antwerp, July 17.- The Volador, Davies, from Magdalena, River Plate (May 19), arrived here, reports:- "Left port with a pleasant whole-sail breeze [ie, with all sails set] from the westward...On the 21st [June], in lat. 23 35 N, long. 40 W, felt the vessel tremble all over, with a rumbling noise, as if a heavy cask had been rolled upon deck. This lasted for about 15 seconds. Came to the conclusion that it must have been an earth (or sea) quake*, as nothing could be seen but clear water..."

*The *Volador* was just to the east of the centre of the Mid-Atlantic Ridge at the time, an area of constant seismic activity, particularly along fracture zones running east and west from the Ridge.

## 26 Nov 1891

**Miscellaneous**

Liverpool, Nov. 26.- The Pacific Mail Company's steamship China reports that she was struck by a wave, supposed [believed] to be result of the earthquake* in the vicinity of Japan.

## *7 Dec 1891*

**Miscellaneous**

London, Dec. 7.- Advices from New York state that the Hesper, barque, on a voyage from San Francisco, reports that when about 75 miles off the Japanese coast, she passed over what was believed to be a submarine volcano. Water flooded the deck, and the water was so hot that the pitch and oakum in the deck seams of the vessel were melted.

*The Mino-Owari earthquake in Japan struck at 6:38 a.m. on 28 October 1891. Its epicentre was at Motosu, in Gifu Prefecture, on the island of Honshu, near the city of Nagoya. It was estimated to have registered at least 8.0 on the Richter scale and caused 7,273 deaths and over 17,000 other casualties. The earthquake was one of the most powerful in the recorded seismic history of the world. The two reports here might be related by the seismic and volcanic activity that the two vessels experienced approximately in the same area and at the same time as the Mino-Owari earthquake.

## 12 Jan 1894

**Miscellaneous**

Liverpool, Jan. 11, 3 10 p.m.- Crown of India reports, on Nov. 1, at 1 15 a.m., in lat. 17 10 N, long. 27 33 W*, weather fine and clear, experienced severe earthquake shock, lasting from 50 to 60 seconds, making ship vibrate from stem to stern, and apparently feeling as if dragging heavily over reef of rocks, etc.

*The vessel's position was just to the west of the Cape Verde Islands, over the Mid-Atlantic Ridge where earthquakes (seaquakes) occur from a high degree of seismic and tectonic activity related to the Ridge.

## 23 Jan 1894

**Miscellaneous**

Liverpool, Jan. 22.- Polestar, arrived at Queenstown, reports:- Oct. 25, lat. 38 52 S, long. 92 28 W, ship was felt to lift forward and then a grating sound was heard, which seemed to travel the whole length of the keel. The shock lasted about two minutes. There was no sign of anything on the water. The pumps were sounded, ship making no water. Supposed [thought] to have been a derelict.*

*Around 850 miles off the coast of Chile, the *Polestar* might have raked over the remains of a derelict vessel drifting just below the surface. Ships regularly reported striking such derelicts which littered the main trade routes of the oceans. The *Polestar* reported sighting nothing in the water, however, and might in fact have felt the tremor of an undersea earthquake: she was right over the seismically active boundary between two tectonic plates, the Nazca Plate to the north and the Antarctica Plate to the south.

## 1 Feb 1897

**Maritime Intelligence**

**Weather and Navigation**

Falmouth, Feb 1, 11 15 a.m.- Newfield, Captain Sharpe, arrived here to-day from Iquique, reports:- On Dec. 27 [1896], 10 45 a.m., lat. 2 N, long. 26 W, felt two sharp shocks of earthquake\*, lasting about ten seconds and some time between each shock.

\*The *Newfield* was around 220 miles northeast of the St. Peter and St. Paul's Rocks at the time, just to the north of the equator between West Africa and northeast Brazil and directly over the seismically active mid-Atlantic Ridge.

## 17 May 1897

**Maritime Intelligence**

**Weather and Navigation**

London, May 17.- Master of barque Zoe, arrived at Queenstown, reports:- At 6 15 a.m. on May 6, in lat. 43 40 N, long. 28 40 W, experienced a very heavy shock of earth or sea quake\*, which lasted for about 30 seconds, causing the ship to tremble all over, as if grating against a hard bottom. The state of the weather at the time was calm and light easterly wind, with a gloomy, overcast sky, and a heavy swell from the north-east.

\*The *Zoe* was around 300 miles due north of the Azores at the time she experienced this 'quake, right over the Mid-Atlantic Ridge where tectonic and seismic activity is a natural and common occurrence.

## 3 March 1903

**Maritime Intelligence**

Barossa.- Melbourne, Jan. 28.- The barque Barossa, which arrived at Sydney on the 22$^{nd}$ inst., from Eureka [northern California], reports that when in the vicinity of Lord Howe Island\* she felt a shock of earthquake. On the following day the barque collided with a whale, cutting the monster in two. The impact dented a plate on the bows of the vessel.

\*Lord Howe Island, in the Tasman Sea between New Zealand and Australia, lies along a seismically active fracture zone related to the 'Ring of Fire' tectonic plates around the Pacific Ocean. Experiencing the shock of an undersea earthquake there and, the following day, colliding with a whale and cutting it in two must rank amongst the most unusual coincidences in the annals of deep-sea commercial sailing voyages.

### KRAKATOA

## 24 May 1883

**Volcanic Eruption in the Straits of Sunda**

Batavia, May 21, 5 P.M.:- There has been a strong volcanic eruption at Krakatoa Island\*, Sunda Straits.

*4 July 1883*
## Volcanic Eruption In The Java Seas

Lloyd's Agents at Batavia have furnished the following particulars of the volcanic eruption at Krakatan [Krakatoa] Island, which was briefly reported by telegraph on May 23. During Sunday (May 20) and Monday (May 21), the eruption was very heavily felt at Batavia, also more or less on Tuesday (May 22), but the shocks have since ceased, although the mountain is apparently still vomiting fire and smoke. The following report is from Anjer, dated May 23, 3 47 a.m.:-

On Sunday morning last, from 6 to 10 o'clock, there was a tremendous eruption with continual shaking and heavy rain of ashes. On Sunday evening and Monday morning it was continued…Captain Ross reports from Anjer that on May 22 he was sailing near Java's first point [Anjer], and tried to get Prinsen Island in sight, but found that it was surrounded by clouds. Then he steered for Krakatan, but found it to be the same there. The captain observed that the lower island or mountain situated on the north side of Krakatan was totally surrounded by smoke, and from time to time flames arose with loud report…

The master of the steamer Conrad, which arrived at Batavia on May 24, reports having passed Krakatan on the north side the previous night, and met with heavy rains of ashes, covering the decks, etc. with about 1½ inches of ashes. He also had to cut his way through about 1½ metres of pumice stone, which occasioned a delay of about five hours…

*28 Aug 1883*
## Volcanic Eruptions In Java

Batavia, Aug. 27.- Terrific detonations from the volcanic island of Krakatoa were heard last night, and were audible as far as Soerakarta [central Java city over 500 km away], showers of ashes reaching as far as Cheribon [central Java port around 325 km away]. The flashes from the volcano are clearly visible from here. Serang is now in total darkness; stones have fallen at that place. Batavia is also nearly in darkness. All the gaslights were extinguished during the night.

It is impossible to communicate with Anjer, and it is feared that some calamity has happened there. Several bridges between Anjer and Serang have been destroyed, and a village near the former place has been washed away, the rivers having overflowed through the rush of the sea inland.

*31 Aug 1883*
## Volcanic Eruption In Java

Batavia, Aug. 28, noon.- All quiet. Sky clear. Communication with Serang restored. Telegraph inspector reports while trying to repair line at Anjer early on morning of 27th saw high column of sea approaching with roaring noise [tsunami], and fled inland. Knows nothing further of fate of Anjer, but believes all lost.

Aug. 29, 10 a.m.- Sky continues clear. Temperature fell 10 degrees on 27th; now normal. Native huts all along beach washed away. Birds roosted during ash rain, and cocks crowed as it cleared away. Fish dizzy…

Aug. 29, 11 a.m.- Anjer, Tjeringen, Telokbutong, destroyed.

Aug. 29, 11 20 a.m.- Lighthouses [in] Sunda Straits have disappeared.

Aug. 29, noon.- Where once mount Krakatau stood the sea now plays.

Aug. 29, 12 30 p.m.- Aspect of Sunda Straits much changed. Navigation dangerous…

## 1 Sept 1883

### Volcanic Eruption In Java

In consequence of the Board of Trade having received through the Colonial Office the following telegram from the Governor of the Straits Settlements, relative to the volcanic eruptions in the Sunda Straits:- "Government telegram from Batavia. Volcanic eruptions, Sunda Straits. Charts quite unreliable; lights destroyed" – they have requested the Foreign Office, Colonial Office, India Office, and Admiralty at once to telegraph to the Governors, Consuls, and other officers at Ceylon, the Cape of Good Hope, Suez, Port Said, St. Vincent [Cape Verde Islands], the Brazils, and Aden, to warn all vessels which may be approaching the Straits of Sunda.

Batavia, Aug. 29, 6 30 P.M.

Sixteen volcanoes have appeared between the site where Krakatoa stood and Sibisie Island. The Soengepan volcano has split into five. A portion of the Residency of Bantam is an ashy desert. The cattle are without food, and the population in despair.

Aug. 30, 1 15 P.M.

Sunda [Straits] is a position dangerous to navigation. Islands disappeared, new ones arisen. Coast line altered. Lighthouses destroyed. Government taking measures to obtain new soundings.

Aug. 30, 4 P.M.

Dead bodies are now being recovered. In the district of Tanara 704 have already been buried, in the coast village of Kramat 300, mostly Chinese, and in the district of Serang 40.

Aug. 30, 5 30 P.M.

Tjeringen, Telokbetong, together with the lighthouses situate there and at Anjer, have been completely destroyed. Krakatoa has entirely disappeared. Sixteen islets have risen, and a complete change has taken place in the formation of the Sunda Straits. The Nederland Company's steamer Wilhelmina, which went ashore at Priok [Tanjung Priok, the port of Batavia (Jakarta)], has been got off undamaged.

The Hague, Aug. 30

An official despatch of to-day's date received from the Governor of the Dutch East Indies announces that the eruption of Krakatoa on the 26th inst. destroyed a great part of Northern Bantam, and deprived the inhabitants of their means of subsistence. The population were flying from the country in despair. On the 27th August a tidal wave [tsunami] from 12 to 30 metres in height swept the coast of Merak as far as Tuiringin. The towns of Anjer, Merak, and Tuiringin were overwhelmed, together with all the Government buildings; and the lighthouses at Virdepunt, in Java, and Vlakkehoek, in Sumatra, were likewise destroyed. Five European and several native functionaries at Anjer and Tuiringin have perished.

The aspect of the Straits of Sunda has undergone a complete transformation. The Island of Krakatoa has disappeared. Sixteen volcanic craters visible between Krakatoa and Sibisie. The full extent of the disaster has not yet been ascertained.

*3 Sept 1883*
**Batavia, Aug. 31, 3 30 P.M.**

There is no news from the Sumatra coast. The Destruction of Telok-Betong was reported by the captain of the steamship Governeur-Generaal Loudon, belonging to Batavia, who was at sea at the height of the eruption and steamed to Anjer to give the alarm, but found that place destroyed. His ship had a layer of ashes 18 inches thick on her deck. In some places masses of floating pumicestone 7 feet in depth were passed. In the district of Tjiringin the loss of life is estimated at 10,000. Some estimates place the total loss of life in the Straits through the eruption at over 30,000.

*4 Oct 1883*
**The Volcanic Eruption In Java**

The following is an extract from a letter from Captain Strachan, of the steamer Anerley, dated Mauritius, Sept. 10, and addressed to Messrs. Watts, Ward and Co. The Anerley had arrived at Mauritius, from Singapore:-

"On Aug. 27, for some 24 hours previous, we had been having some queer looking weather, but at 10 a.m. that morning, it was so dark we had to light all the lights. It commenced raining ashes and pomice stone, and our barometer was rising and falling 5-10ths of an inch within a minute. I bore up and ran back for the North Watcher Island, and came to under the lee of it. Towards night the wind had died out and the ashes stopped, but it was black as night.

At 3 a.m. on the 28th proceeded, and as we neared Sunda Strait we were steaming through a sea of pumice stone and debris of all sorts. A storm or tidal wave had swept the coast, carrying everything before it. Anjer and its lighthouse were gone, a small portion of the foundation only standing. The whole coast, right to Java head, had been swept, and it was hard to distinguish the points as we came along, and harder to believe it was the coast of Java – such a change from what it used to be. The lighthouse keeper asked for news, which we gave him. He said he had had fearful weather, and promised to report us as early as possible. We had some of the ashes as far as 100 miles clear of Java Head."

*The volcanic eruption of the island of Krakatoa in the Sunda Strait, between the Indonesian islands of Java and Sumatra, on 26-27 August 1883, was the loudest and one of the most violent explosions ever recorded in human history. It was heard as far away as Perth, Western Australia (3,100 km away), and Rodriguez Island, near Mauritius (approximately 5,000 km away). The official death toll of the eruptions and subsequent tsunamis (tidal waves) was 36,417 but possibly in fact much greater.

As the main gateway for sailing ships passing to and from the Indian Ocean and the South China Sea, the Sunda Strait, and the town and lighthouse at Anjer, were well known to deep-sea sailors of the 19th century on voyages between Europe and China Sea ports. The town of Anjer, 15 km south of Merak in West Java, and the lighthouse there were destroyed by a tsunami as a result of the Krakatoa eruption. In 1885 King Willem III of the Netherlands built a new, 40m tall lighthouse at Anjer as a memorial to all those killed by the eruption.

# 11  Whaling, Whales and Fishermen

For fishing and whaling men of the 19th century, staying alive was as risky a business as making a living - more so probably for fishermen. Fishing luggers, smacks and dories were much smaller than deep-sea vessels against the multitude of hazards they faced upon the sea: collisions with bigger vessels that never stopped; storms that wiped out whole fleets of boats around the North Sea and Iceland in particular; fog, cold and more storms for the dory fishermen on the Grand Banks off Newfoundland; and accidental loss of life at any time.

Whaling by the later years of the 19th century was in decline. The recovery of crude oil from the ground rather than tried out from the blubber of whales had commenced on a large scale from the first oil well drilled in the United States at Titusville, Pennsylvania in 1858 by Edwin L. Drake, after which whale oil became increasingly redundant. Moreover, the whale population had been decimated by the Yankee and other whaling fleets of the world. But whalers (and sealers) still embarked on hazardous voyages in the ice-strewn Arctic Ocean and along the serrated coastline of the Aleutian Islands of Alaska. Ice in the Bering Sea, north of the Aleutians, gripped many whaling ships and sent them and their crews to the bottom.

The whales themselves did sometimes sink the ships of their pursuers. The sinking of the *Essex* by a sperm whale in November 1820 inspired Herman Melville's *Moby Dick*. (The subsequent story of cannibalism and hardships endured by the *Essex* castaways itself became a well known narrative in the annals of whaling). In August 1851, around the same time that *Moby Dick* was published, the *Ann Alexander* was attacked and sunk by a sperm whale in the Pacific near where the *Essex* had sunk almost thirty years before. (Herman Melville, upon hearing about the *Ann Alexander* incident, remarked to a friend, "It is really and truly a surprising coincidence…I have no doubt it *is* Moby Dick. Ye Gods, what a commentator is this *Ann Alexander* whale…I wonder if my evil art has raised the monster." (from *The Melville Log: A Documentary Life of Herman Melville, 1819-1891*, 2 Vols., by Jay Leda)

The Norwegian whaling captain Svend Foyn (1809 – 1894), from Tonsberg, invented and, in 1870, patented the explosive harpoon gun. In addition he introduced mechanised and steam-powered whaling ships to increase the efficiency of catching and processing whales. Those instruments of cetacean mass destruction were by themselves almost wholly responsible for the holocaust perpetrated against the remaining whale populations of the world over the next 100 years. (Human greed completed the equation.)

But Foyn himself did not always have it all his own way with the leviathan.

## 17 June 1890

**Maritime Intelligence**

Gratia (s).- Christiania, June 14.- According to a telegram from the master of Svend Foyn's whaling steamer Gratia, this vessel was struck, eight miles outside Soroen [islands just off the northwest coast of Norway, near Bodö], by a wounded whale, causing her to sink immediately in 150 fathoms water; crew saved.

## NARRATIVES

## 5 July 1884

**Maritime Intelligence**

Chieftain (s).- Dundee, July 5.- Information was received here yesterday from the British Consul at Reykjavik, Iceland, that a boat belonging to the Dundee whaler Chieftain had been picked up by a fishing vessel off the north coast of the island. The boat contained one man, the sole survivor of a crew of five. He was in a helpless state owing to starvation and exposure. The Chieftain, while whale hunting off Greenland, during a fog, lost four boats, only one of which reached Iceland, containing the captain and five men.

### 9 July 1884
**Maritime Intelligence**

Chieftain (s).- Dundee, July 8.- A telegram received here reports the arrival of the steamer Kara at Lerwick [Shetland Islands], bringing the intelligence that a boat belonging to the whaler Chieftain, of Dundee, had been picked up in Greenland by a Norwegian whaler on June 2. The crew of five men had suffered severely, having been five days without food. No hopes are entertained of the safety of the crew of the remaining boat.

### 17 July 1884
**Greenland Whale Fishery**

The whaler Chieftain, of Dundee, had arrived at Dundee after her disastrous voyage to the Greenland seal and whale fishery. Four boats, while out whale-hunting, were lost in a fog, and only one succeeded in finding the ship. Three others attempted to sail for Iceland, but only one reached that island with her crew. A second boat was picked up with only one man alive, and the remaining boat has never been heard of. The Chieftain brings only three whales. The weather in Greenland is reported to have been exceptionally foggy this season, only 14 clear days having been experienced.

## 8 Aug 1885

**Maritime Intelligence**

Napoleon.- New York, Aug. 7.- Intelligence received here states that the whaling barque Napoleon, of New Bedford, has been crushed by ice in the Arctic regions; 22 of the crew were lost.

*30 Sept 1887*
**A Tale of the Sea**

The White Star steamer Germanic, arrived at Queenstown from New York, brings intelligence of the rescue of a seaman, named James B. Vincent, the only survivor of a crew of 18, of the whaling barque Napoleon, lost in Behring [Bering] Sea in 1885. He tells a terrible tale of suffering.

Eighteen members of the crew were in the ice for 30 days, and during this time his 17 companions died from starvation and exposure. He was picked up by some Esquimaux [Eskimos], and lived two years among them, until reached by the whaling barque Hunter off Cape Behring, which vessel subsequently transferred him to the Revenue cutter Rush, which conveyed him to Victoria, British Columbia.

*Te Aroha News* [**New Zealand weekly newspaper**]
*26 November 1887*
**Wrecked In the Arctic Sea**

**The Story of the Rescue**

**The Sole Survivor of Eighteen Whalers Brought Back to His Kindred**

The story of J.B. Vincent, the sole survivor of the whaling ship Napoleon, will remain one of the most thrilling and eventful of any that has ever been told of the Siberian coast. The Napoleon left San Francisco in the early part of the year 1885. Her crew comprised thirty-six men, all told. After leaving San Francisco she proceeded to the Sandwich Islands [Hawaii], and thence to the Behring Sea, where she arrived in April of that year.

On the 5th of May the Napoleon was crushed in the ice, which came upon her in such fearful masses and so unexpectedly that the crew were only able to divide themselves into gangs of nine each, and, without securing any food whatever, to leave the ship and trust themselves to the tender mercies of an Arctic sea. Ninety hours after the wreck the boats of the second and fourth mates were picked up by the barque Fleetwing, and of the eighteen men who were thus rescued, five died immediately after their rescue from cold and exposure. All of the boats remained together about twenty-four hours after the wreck, but were finally separated by the winds and currents.

The boats of the first and third mates met again after the gale had subsided, and their occupants were found alive. Five days after the wreck these boats drifted in the open sea, nine of the crew succumbing to the exposure, and finally landed upon the ice which skirted the coast. The survivors remained upon the ice for twenty-six days, and on the thirty-sixth day after the wreck, on June 10, 1885, a landing was made about sixty-two miles southwest of Cape Navarin, on the Siberian coast. The next day five of the survivors died from starvation and frost, and the rest remained at the landing for a month afterward.

In March Anton Lawrence, the boatsteerer [harpooner], died, and one day after the first mate, Wilson Rogers, also died. After these the cooper, William Wallace, succumbed, and Vincent was left alone.

Vincent arrived in San Francisco after his two years of forced exile, having been rescued by the United States revenue cutter Bear. His story is an interesting one. His recital of the manner in which his comrades dropped away one by one, crazed by their agonising sufferings, taxes the sensibilities of the most indifferent. It is a repetition of the experiences with which every reader of Arctic travel is familiar. The one bright feature of his story is the humanity of the Indians [ie., local indigenous people], who, as far as they were able, succoured the living and in every instance buried the dead decently and with honours.

Vincent owes his life to the fact that he was a man of extraordinary endurance and great vitality. He is of stalwart build and not over 28 years of age. He became one of the natives and was able, by his skill as a marksman, to make himself useful to them and they became greatly attached to him.

Rogers, the mate, was violently insane for eight days before he died, and his companions were compelled to secure him to escape violence from his frantic exertions. For over a year Vincent remained with the natives, seeing no chance of a rescue, but early in January, 1887, he saw an opportunity of communicating with the outside world, and carried a message on a piece of wood and gave it to a deer man [indigenous] to deliver it to the first whaler that could be sighted, and in June last the man was able to deliver this billet to the Captain of the whaler Hunter, off Behring Cape, of which Captain Crogan was master. The Indian was not intelligent, but the board was quickly interpreted to mean that J.B. Vincent, a survivor of the whaler Napoleon, was alive, and living about ten miles southwest of Cape Navarin.

A copy of the message was given to every whaler, and it came at last into the hands of the Commander of the Bear, who lost no time in clearing for the point named, and happily rescued him.

The experiences of Vincent, as related by him, are most harrowing. During the twenty-six days that they were upon the ice after being wrecked, the entire party of eighteen men had only two seals, which they killed and attempted to eat raw, but their stomachs refused to assimilate the unwonted food and it could not be retained, and for the entire thirty-six days their want of nourishment caused the most intense agony. The vitality of Vincent may be guessed from the fact that for eleven days not a morsel of food passed his lips.

When at last the crew reached the land they found the natives, or deer men, most anxious to assist them; but one by one the crew passed away, and finally but he remained. The experiences from the time when Vincent was rescued by the natives until the happy and fortunate rescue by the Bear was a routine of fishing and hunting – a mere existence. His sufferings after this time were not great, though his deprivations required considerable stoicism to endure. The natives were invariably kind and repaid the efforts which he made for their common good by every kindness and sympathy which they, in their simple way, could possibly offer.

Vincent expresses the heartiest gratitude to them. He describes them as brave and strong and the women as chaste and affectionate to their young. Their habits are simple and temperate, and their manner of living an advance upon those natives of the higher latitudes of the Alaskan coast.

## 6 March 1877

### Missing Smacks

Yarmouth [Great Yarmouth, Norfolk], 5th Mar.- The following is a list of the fishing smacks* of this port, supposed [believed] to have foundered in the North Sea, with all hands, during the gale of 13th Jan. last:- The Contest, Rupicola, Bonny Boys, Twins, Harmony,

Garibaldi, Peep o' Day, Chanticleer, Moselle, Two Sisters, I'll Try, Vane, Plutus, Edith, Sir Roger Tichborne, Guide, Prima Donna, and Rachael; in all 18 smacks, with the total crews numbering 110 men.

*In addition to the eighteen fishing smacks from Great Yarmouth lost in the gales, a further seven from nearby Lowestoft foundered. A fund was established to assist the widows and orphans of the many fishermen from the smacks that were consequently lost at sea.

## 15 Nov 1878

### Casualties – Home

Yarmouth, 13th Nov.- The Oliveleaf (smack), of this port, was assisted into harbour to-day, having encountered the late gale, been severely damaged and lost three hands. A heavy sea struck the vessel and washed four of the crew overboard. Three of them – named Williamson (the master), Davis, and Barber – were drowned; the other (Easter) was saved, but his leg was broken.

## 21 June 1882

### Casualties, Etc.

Brilliant Star.- By the arrival here of the Danish mail steamer Arcturus, from Iceland, yesterday, intelligence has been received of the loss of several vessels, with their crews, on the coast. The Arcturus brought 19 shipwrecked seamen, forming the crews of the barquentine Brilliant Star, of Fleetwood, the Danish schooner Charlotte, and the French fishing vessels Notre Dame du Perpetual Secours, and Ane Marie. The latter vessel, it appears, was in collision with another French fishing smack, named the Marie Eugenie, on the 28th April last, both vessels receiving considerable damage. The Ane Marie was assisted into Reykjavik, where she was condemned. Only three of her crew came by the Arcturus, the remainder being sent home in other vessels.

The Notre Dame, which belonged to Paimpol [port in Brittany, northern France], was prosecuting the cod fishing on the coast, and during a heavy gale drove ashore near Reykjavik, and became a total loss. The Charlotte was on a voyage from Copenhagen to Flato, West Coast of Iceland, and on the 24th of last month, during a violent snowstorm, she went ashore on a reef of rocks, both vessel and cargo, which consisted of general merchandise, being lost. The crew of six men were saved.

The Brilliant Star, it seems, was a vessel of 200 tons register, commanded by Captain Thomas Rohdes, and owned by the Fleetwood Shipping Company (Limited), of Liverpool. The vessel was bound for Iceland, with a cargo of salt from Liverpool. On the night of the 21st April last a heavy sea drove the vessel ashore on the rocks at a place called Beravik, and in seven minutes after she capsized. The crew, seven in number, managed to save themselves by clinging to the keel of the vessel, where they remained for about four hours, by which time the tide had receded, thus enabling them to get ashore by scrambling over the rocks.

The weather at this time was intensely cold, the barometer [sic – thermometer] registering from 12 to 15 deg. of frost [ie., 12-15° F below freezing]. Soon after getting on shore Michael John Boyle, the mate, belonging to Dublin, succumbed to exhaustion and exposure to the cold and snow. The men were all more or less frost-bitten.

YARMOUTH FISHING SMACKS IN THE NORTH SEA

The Danish schooner Bella, Captain Torjesen, belonging to Faroe [the Faroe Islands], was lost on 25th last month at Stalbjergbuk, west coast of Iceland, the crew numbering 20 being drowned. The Danish fishing smack Lovenorn was also wrecked at the same time and place, and in this case the crew of 12 hands perished. Most of the bodies were found by the Icelanders washed ashore on the beach. In some instances the corpses were unrecognisable. Both vessels were afterwards found floating bottom up. The Danish fore-and-aft schooner Sigtruder, Captain Jensen, which left Copenhagen for Reykjavik in April last, has never been heard of… (*Leith, June 18.*)

## 23 May 1885

**Miscellaneous**

Stornoway [Isle of Lewis, Outer Hebrides, Scotland], May 22.- The fishing boat William and Helen, Steuart skipper, arrived here from Wick [northeast Scotland] to-day to prosecute the herring fishing. The skipper reports the drowning of three of his crew while off Cape Wrath [northwest Scotland] yesterday. A sea struck the boat and washed overboard Angus Corner, Wm. Bain, Kenneth Nicholson, and Alexander Nicholson; the latter got hold of the sheet [rope from the sail], and he was washed on board again, but the other three were drowned.

## 10 Sept 1887

**Maritime Intelligence**

Lillian Baxter.- Queenstown, Sept. 9.- The captain of the Cunard Line steamer Umbria, which arrived here this evening from New York, reports having rescued 13 men of the crew of the fishing vessel Lillian Baxter, of Gloucester, Massachusetts, which was completely dismasted and thrown on her beam-ends during a violent hurricane two days previously. One man, named Ronald Perch, was washed overboard and drowned. The suffering of the 13 men on the dismasted craft for two days was very great. Every attention was paid to the rescued men on board the Umbria, and they proceeded in her to Liverpool. The crew of the Umbria set fire to the wreck.

### *29 Oct 1887*

**Rescue at Sea.-** The President of the United States [Grover Cleveland] has intimated to the Hon. C.T. Russell, the American Consul in Liverpool, his intention of presenting to the Cunard commander, Captain M.P. Mickan, of the Umbria, a gold watch, for the eminent services which he and his crew rendered on the occasion when the crew, numbering 13, of the American schooner Lillian Baxter, were rescued.

## 12 Sept 1887

**Weather and Navigation**

St. John's, N.F., Sept. 9.- A furious hurricane swept over the Newfoundland Fishing Banks [the Grand Banks] on the 3rd inst., doing great damage to the fishing fleets, nearly every vessel sustaining losses, and many lives being lost. The schooner Ocean Pride has been found a floating wreck, all her crew being discovered lying dead in the cabin. The French fleet suffered very severely from the effects of the tempest. Another heavy storm passed over the banks yesterday.

## 16 May 1892

### Miscellaneous

London, May 16.- Information yesterday reached Skibereen [Co. Cork, Ireland] of the total loss of a fishing lugger off Castletownshend [Co. Cork, south coast Ireland], the boat having been cut in two by an Atlantic liner. A portion of the boat has been washed ashore at Tolhead, as also have the hats of her crew. The lugger was struck by the liner during a dense fog, and it is feared that all the crew have perished.

## 7 Nov 1892

### Maritime Intelligence

Helen Mar.- San Francisco (by cable received Nov. 7).- Whaling barque Helen Mar totally lost Oct. 6, lat. 71 N, long. 169 W. Part of crew saved.

Helen Mar.- San Francisco, Nov. 7.- Steam whaler Belum, arrived here from the Arctic Ocean, reports the destruction of the whaling barque Helen Mar, and the loss of 35 hands, five only of the crew being saved. The vessel while manoeuvering to secure a whale was carried by the current between two icebergs and crushed. She sank immediately, most of those on board being either drowned or crushed to death. The five survivors clung to a portion of the mainmast which remained above water, and were rescued by a passing vessel. The commander of the barque, Captain Thaxter, was among those who perished.

## 7 May 1895

### Maritime Intelligence

George R. White (s).*- Glasgow, May 6.- A telegram from New York, May 5, states that the steamer Atki arrived at Port Townsend, Washington, May 4, with eight survivors of the crew of the comparatively new steamer George R. White, which on the 14th ult. was wrecked on the coast of Alaska. So suddenly was the vessel driven on to the rocks that it was impossible to even lower the boats. The crew took to the rigging, and 17 men were either washed away or frozen to death.

*The 56 ton sealing schooner *George R. White* left Seattle, Washington, on 14 July 1894, under the command of Capt. J.L. Wheeler and bound for a year's hunting expedition in the Bering Sea and Arctic Ocean. She was hunting for sea otters just off the southwest coast of Alaska around Easter 1895 when, on that Easter Sunday (14 April that year), she encountered a fierce northeast gale, with blinding snow and sub-zero temperatures.

The storm tore the schooner's sails to shreds, disabled her steering gear and reduced her virtually to a drifting wreck at the mercy of the seas. Around midnight the *George R. White* struck a reef. She was soon smashed to bits. Her crew of 28 were thrown into the icy sea three miles off the shore of Tugidak Island, just off the southern coast of Kodiak Island.

On 4 May 1895 the *San Francisco Call* newspaper reported on the plight of the castaways:-

"Some of them in their desperation clutched onto the floating debris and others were drowned. About twenty were fortunate enough to reach the beach through a gale-whipped sea and snowstorm almost dead, with their clothes frozen to their bodies. Without food or shelter they passed a miserable night and at daybreak on the beach they found ten corpses.

The survivors themselves were too exhausted to bury the dead. The most they could was to drag their bodies up on the shore away from the ravenous animals of the sea. Clad in light garments, with no fire or shelter, subsisting on shellfish and suffering from intense cold, three or four more men died.

On the third day after the wreck some native hunters chanced to pass by, and from them fresh meat and a supply of matches to start a fire were obtained. By that time only eleven out of the original twenty-eight had survived. Many of them were badly frozen, their limbs frostbitten so severely that they must suffer surgical operations to save their lives. One man is said to have lost the use of both legs and arms. Scarcely one of the survivors will get through the ordeal without being maimed for life."

There was another victim of the Easter storm that year off the southeast coast of Alaska with even greater loss of life, though the number of the vessel's crew lost in the storm was diversely reported:

## 10 May 1895

### Maritime Intelligence

Walter A. Earle.- London, May 10.- A Central News telegram, dated Vancouver, Weds [7 May], states that the sealing vessels arriving at Victoria [Vancouver Island] report the loss of the schooner Walter A. Earle, which was capsized in a gale last easter. She had a crew of 32 on board, all of whom were drowned.

**From** *The Brooklyn Daily Eagle*

### *22 August 1895*
### All On Board Lost

### Sinking of the Sealing Schooner Walter Earle

Seattle, Wash., Aug. 22.- The steam schooner Excelsior has arrived from Alaska bringing the first definite news of the wreck of the sealing schooner Walter Earle of Victoria, which was capsized April 21, with the loss of every man on board, including Captain Magnesen and a crew of seven white men and eleven Indians. She was found bottom up and the dead Indians were in the forecastle. The crew outside had tried to manage the helpless vessel, but were swept into the sea by the fury of the storm and sunk without the least chance to save themselves.

The *New York Times* of 9th May 1895 reported that the *Walter A. Earle* was wrecked off Cape St. Elias, near the Alaskan mainland about 200 miles southeast of Anchorage and 300 miles to the northeast of Kodiak Island, with the loss of 23 men "part of whom were Indians."

## 25 Sept 1895

### Maritime Intelligence

### Miscellaneous

Greenock, Sept. 25, 10 25 a.m.- Allan [Line] steamer State of Nebraska, arrived here from New York, has on board a French sailor, who was picked up adrift in a boat on 17th inst., in lat. 43 55 N, long. 57 47 W. Another man and he had been fishing on the [Grand] Banks and were driven away from schooner George, of St. Pierre*, during a heavy gale. His companion succumbed a day or two before he was rescued.

*Cod fishermen in their dories fishing on the Grand Banks off Newfoundland quite often got lost from their mother ship, either because of bad weather or fog, and were lost at sea. This man, from the French islands of St. Pierre & Miquelon off Newfoundland, was very fortunate to be rescued.

## 14 Dec 1896

**Maritime Intelligence**

**Miscellaneous**

London, Dec. 14.- There is now little doubt that the ten fishing smacks still missing from La Rochelle foundered in the gale on the 6th inst., and were lost with all hands. The missing crew altogether numbered 60.

## 28 March 1898

**Disaster At The Seal Fisheries.– 48 Lives Lost**

St. John's (Newfoundland), March 27.- The sailing steamer Greenland arrived last night at the fishing settlement of Cape de Verds [Newfoundland], having on board 25 dead bodies of men who had formed part of her crew. She had left 23 more dead on the ice. From the story told by the survivors it appears that on the 21st inst., when about 30 miles off Cape Bonavista, the steamer sighted a large number of seals, and three parties were sent out in different directions across the ice-field to kill the animals and haul the carcases aboard. A sudden storm came on, however, and the ice-field broke up. The steamer, beset by the ice, was unable to reach the men, who drifted on the floes.

Snow fell heavily all that night and next day, and the cold was intense. The unfortunate sealers, cut off from their vessel by impassable lanes of water, wandered about until they were exhausted, and then lay down to die. At length, when the storm began to abate, those on board the Greenland made every effort to rescue their comrades by boats, but only six were found alive, and even they were in the last stage of exhaustion. Twenty-five dead bodies were picked up, but twenty-three more could not be found. Many of the survivors are terribly frost-bitten. The Greenland is expected to come round to St. John's tonight. The disaster has caused a terrible shock to the community, being the worst that has ever befallen the seal industry.

## 7 April 1898

**Whalers Imprisoned in the Ice*** – Vancouver (British Columbia), April 5.- An officer, named Tilton, connected with the British steam whaler Belvedere, has arrived here, after undergoing terrible suffering. He reports that the whalers Orca, Belvedere, Rosario, and a barque, whose name he did not know, are icebound off Point Barrow, Alaska, and that the crews are starving, and almost frozen to death. The vessels have been imprisoned in the ice since October [1897]. The American steamer Bear has been vainly trying to rescue them. Tilton states that when the ice breaks the vessels will be ground to splinters. A party to go to the relief of the distressed crews is being formed.

*In 1897 eight whaling ships became trapped in the Arctic ice off Point Barrow, the northernmost point of Alaska. Early in November that year the owners of the ships and the San Francisco Chamber of Commerce persuaded United States President McKinley to organise a relief expedition to save the 265 whaling men on the ships who would otherwise surely die of starvation and cold in the frigid rigours of an Arctic winter. McKinley commanded the United States Treasury Dept. to undertake the rescue mission. It later came to be known as the Point Barrow Overland Relief Expedition. The vessel chosen to transport the rescuers to Alaska was the US Revenue Service cutter *Bear*, one of three vessels involved in the expedition to rescue the seven survivors of the Greely Arctic Expedition of 1881–1884 in northern Greenland. (The Revenue Service was the forerunner of the United States Coast Guard.)

The expedition was led by First Lieut. David H. Jarvis. Second in command was Second Lieut. E.P. Bertholf. Dr. S.J. Call, a ship's doctor with past experience on Revenue cutters in Alaska was the third member. An enlisted man, F. Koltchoff, accompanied the expedition part of the way. The *Bear* was commanded by Capt. Francis Tuttle who, in November 1897, had only just returned to Seattle from a season with the *Bear* in Alaskan waters when he was ordered to head north again immediately on the rescue mission.

Tuttle had been instructed by Secretary of the Treasury Lyman J. Gage to sail as far north along the west coast of Alaska as the ice permitted and at that point land the rescue party of Jarvis, Bertholf and Call. The three men were to make their way overland to Point Barrow, collecting herds of reindeer along the way to provide sustenance for the stranded and starving whaling men on their icebound vessels. In the event, heavy ice in the Bering Sea meant that the *Bear* could only reach as far north as Cape Vancouver, about 700 miles south of where Secretary Gage had expected them to get (Norton Sound) and where the three men went ashore on 15 December 1897. The *Bear* steamed away south. The small rescue party, with four sleds pulled by huskies and including a Russian and Eskimo guides, faced a 1,500 mile overland trek to Point Barrow in the darkness of an Arctic winter, temperatures hovering around -50° C, treacherous terrain of frozen tundra, ice and mountain passes, and blasted by frequent blizzards.

On 30 December 1897 Jarvis reached the small settlement of St. Michael, around 200 miles northwest of Cape Vancouver, where they acquired fresh huskies. Two days later they came upon a man sent by the whalers to try to get help for them, the third mate of the *Belvedere*, Mr. Tilton, who made it back to Vancouver with the report of his comrades' plight. Jarvis meanwhile trekked on with the assistance of Eskimo guides. On 19 January 1898 he arrived at the home of the Eskimo known as Charlie Artisarlook who provided fresh reindeer. On 24 January, at Teller Reindeer Station, the station superintendent, a missionary named W.T. Lopp, provided the party with 301 reindeer and agreed to accompany them north, together with six Eskimo deer herders. The expeditionary team left Teller Station on 3 February with a herd of 438 animals and 18 deer-drawn sleds.

After another 800 miles Jarvis reached the icebound whale ship *Belvedere* and a clutch of starving men near the Sea Horse Islands. The next day, 27 March, his team finally arrived at Point Barrow with their remaining herd of 382 reindeer (the rest having died on the way). Lopp and the remaining rescue expedition members arrived on 30 March.

At Point Barrow the stranded whaling men were living in cramped and grimy barracks, suffering from scurvy, hunger, abysmal living conditions and with the likelihood of imminent death shrouding their misery (although in fact only three men had died since their stranding). Fresh reindeer meat, together with the discipline and moral support of the rescue party, and Jarvis in particular, brought the men through the winter. Capt. Tuttle and the *Bear* reached Point Barrow on 28 July 1898.

The surviving whalers (only one more had died since the Expedition reached Point Barrow) and Overland Expedition members arrived back in Seattle on the *Bear* on 13 September 1898. In 1899, somewhat belatedly (the Spanish–American War being waged in 1898), President McKinley proposed, and Congress approved the awarding of Congressional Gold Medals of Honor to the three protagonists of the Point Barrow Overland Expedition, Jarvis, Bertholf and Call, who were presented with their medals in 1902. A disbursement of $2,500 was also awarded to be divided amongst missionary Lopp, the Eskimo Charlie Artisarlook and other indigenous reindeer herders who had assisted with the Expedition.

## 22 Jan 1900

### Sad Fatality to a Fisherman

The dangers of winter fleeting in the fishing trade was exemplified by the facts elicited at an inquiry at the Board of Trade Offices, Grimsby, into the death of Alfred Howes, a native of Yarmouth, lately serving on the Grimsby steam trawler Aberdeen, owned by Messrs Hagerup and Doughty. On the 10th inst., the small boat was sent to the cutter [ie., the trawler] to "board" the fish, the boat being in [the] charge of the boatswain, with whom was the deceased, who was third hand, and also the deck hand. When the boat approached the cutter the heavy seas caused the trawler to roll violently, with the result that the Aberdeen's boat was capsized, and the occupants thrown into the water.

The deck hand held on to the painter [bow rope], and was pulled on board the cutter, which also rescued the boatswain. Howes was clad in oilskins and sea boots, but was a good swimmer, and he floated away. The poor fellow, it is stated, remained on the surface of the water for half an hour, but attempts to rescue were of no avail, and he was drowned. The lifebuoys which were in the boat at the time were of no use in such an accident. Howes was 24 years of age.

## 15 June 1900

### Maritime Intelligence

### Miscellaneous

Halifax (N.S.), June 5.- Norwegian barque Leif, from London, in ballast, arrived at Yarmouth to-day and reports that on May 28 she sighted a dory bearing signals of distress. She picked it up and found two men insensible and almost dead from exposure. After careful treatment they revived and said they were members of the crew of the French fishing barque* "Reune," of St. Malo, and had been adrift eight days without food or water. They were removed to the Marine Hospital and are now in a precarious condition.

*The word "barque" here is probably just the French word for "boat", rather than *barque* in the English sense of that kind of rigged vessel. North Atlantic fishing vessels under sail around this time were almost invariably schooners, especially those from the Portuguese fishing fleets that spent six months or so every year on the Grand Banks off Newfoundland fishing for cod. The *Reune,* from the Breton fishing port of St. Malo, was probably either the traditional St. Malo barquentine, or a *goëlette* (schooner), both used by the French for cod fishing around the North Atlantic at that time. It was not uncommon for fishermen in dories on the foggy Grand Banks to become lost from their mother ships and either never be found or, in this fortunate case, be picked up by another vessel.

## 9 Oct 1900

### The Recent Hurricane In Canada –

### Forty-six Fishermen Drowned

Halifax (N.S.), Oct. 9.- The latest reports state that all the New Brunswick fishermen who were missing in the recent storm on the coast of Prince Edward Island last month have surely perished. The death roll now numbers 46. It is regarded as the most terrible disaster of the kind on record as far as the maritime provinces of Canada are concerned. The men were all French Canadians.

### *10 Oct 1900*

### Miscellaneous

St. John's [Newfoundland], Oct. 9.- Seventeen French fishing vessels, with crews aggregating 200 men, are still missing from St. Pierre [the French islands of St. Pierre & Miquelon south of Newfoundland] since the gale of Sept. 12. Casualties in other French vessels swell the list to over 300. The casualties among Newfoundland crews add another hundred to the list.**

*The storm that devastated the fishing fleets off the east coast of Canada was the remnant of the Category 4 hurricane that struck Galveston, Texas, earlier in September that year. The hurricane tracked up through the Midwestern US states, across the Canadian maritime provinces and into the wastes of the North Atlantic. It caused an estimated 8,000 deaths around Galveston, making it one of the greatest natural disasters ever in the United States.

**A later report (20 October) on the number of deaths caused by the storm in the Newfoundland fishing industry stated: "Serious disaster has visited a number of Newfoundland fishing harbours, west side of Placentia Bay alone losing 355 men."

### WHALING BARQUE *KATHLEEN* SUNK...BY A WHALE

## 15 April 1902

### Maritime Intelligence

Kathleen.- Pernambuco [Recife, Brazil], March 29.- The 30 of the crew of the American whaler Kathleen, which was lost off Barbadoes, were picked up by the steamer Borderer, of Liverpool, which put them into their own boats just off this place. Another boat with nine men was not fallen in with by the Borderer. The Kathleen was whaling and had a whale alongside, when another whale charged the ship, causing her to keel over and eventually capsize.*

*The whaler *Kathleen* was originally built in 1847 as a barque-rigged commercial sailing vessel at Philadelphia. She was converted to a whaler in 1851 when she was bought by James

H. Slocum of New Bedford. By the early 1900s the *Kathleen* was owned and operated by Joseph and William R. Wing, out of New Bedford.

Her last whaling voyage began when she sailed out of New Bedford on 22nd October 1901 under the command of Capt. Thomas H. Jenkins. *Kathleen* carried a complement of 28 officers and men, and included Mrs. Jenkins, the captain's wife. Stormy weather hit almost immediately and lasted three weeks ("the worst weather I have ever had on leaving home," from Capt. Jenkins' own narrative, *Bark Kathleen Sunk By a Whale*, H.S. Hutchinson & Co., New Bedford, 1902). After getting down to the Cape Verde Islands and shipping more men there, the *Kathleen* headed southwest. She arrived on the "12-40" grounds (the whaling grounds located around about 12° N latitude, 40° W longitude), some 1,000 miles or so off the north coast of Brazil, in mid-March 1902. By that time there were 38 men on board, including Capt. Jenkins, and Mrs. Jenkins, totalling 39 souls altogether.

On 17th March – "one of the finest whaling days I have ever seen, smooth water and a clear sky," according to Capt. Jenkins – the *Kathleen* got near a pod of sperm whales. The four whaleboats were lowered to give chase. The mate, Mr. Nichols, struck a whale first. After Capt. Jenkins got the dead whale fast alongside the ship, he went up the mast to look out for the other three boats which had disappeared from sight. Sitting high up on the crosstrees, Capt. Jenkins saw a large whale about five hundred feet off, heading directly for the *Kathleen*. Mate Nichols tried to get fast to the whale but failed. The captain observed:

"Instead of the whale going down or going to windward as they most always do, he kept coming directly for the ship, only much faster than he was coming before he was darted at [by Nichols]. When he got within thirty feet of the ship he saw or heard something and tried to go under the ship but he was so near and was coming so fast he did not have room enough to get clear of her. He struck the ship forward of the mizzen rigging and about five or six feet under water. It shook the ship considerably when he struck her, then he tried to come up and he raised the stern up some two or three feet so when she came down her counters [stern] made a big splash. The whale came up on the other side of the ship and laid there and rolled, did not seem to know what to do." (*Bark Kathleen Sunk By a Whale*)

Capt. Jenkins' first priority was to find his other three boats and their crews; the cooper had told him he did not think the whale had damaged the ship. In fact, the *Kathleen*'s wooden hull had been sprung by the whale's blow to her. Water was pouring in and Capt. Jenkins prepared to abandon ship. The men got casks of bread and water. Mrs. Jenkins, in the captain's cabin and unaware of the calamity, "got a jacket and an old shawl," but not before she brought the ship's parrot on deck! Twenty-one people got into the one boat available and pushed off. Five minutes later the *Kathleen* rolled over and sank.

By late in the evening of that day the captain had rounded up the other three boats. "They were very much surprised to hear that the Kathleen was gone. I gave them some bread and water and divided the men up again, so three boats had ten men each and one boat nine men. I told them all to keep in sight of me and that I would keep a lantern burning all night. We then started for the island of Barbados, distant 1,060 miles. It was a beautiful moonlight night with a smooth sea." (*Bark Kathleen Sunk By a Whale*)

On the morning of the day after the whale sunk the *Kathleen*, 18th March, the steamship *Borderer*, of Glasgow, commanded by Capt. Dalton, picked up three of the *Kathleen*'s boats, rescuing a total of 29 of her castaways. Capt. Dalton later explained that he was running three or four degrees to the east of his usual course towards his destination, the port of Pernambuco (Recife) on the northeast coast of Brazil, to try to avoid contrary currents that had headed him so often in the past. It was only because of that quirk of fate that the *Borderer* came upon the Kathleen's boats. The castaways were landed nine days later at Pernambuco.

The remaining crew of the *Kathleen* in the fourth boat also spent another nine days at sea before they reached land, albeit in somewhat less comfortable conditions than their shipmates on the *Borderer*. "The other boat containing one of the mates and 9 seamen landed safely at the Barbados after being in the boat 9 days with but 5 gallons of water and a little ship bread." (from *Bark Kathleen Sunk By a Whale*)

# 12 Shipwrecks, Collisions and Castaways (...and Cannibalism)

S hips came to grief in many different ways which determined, in turn, the fate of sailors (and passengers) whose lives were either lost or castaway by such incidents. Storms and hurricanes, reefs and rocky coasts, collisions, pirates and plain bad luck wrecked ships. Sometimes the fates were cruel and all lives lost. But other times survivors managed, through perseverance, good fortune, and pluck, to endure their hardships as castaways, whether it was on the high seas or in hostile and harrowing conditions on land.

Seamen whose ships sunk beneath them and were not drowned escaped in small boats or makeshift rafts in the hope of being rescued. Some were picked up by passing ships. Others reached land, often after enduring the privations of a long voyage in a small open boat over great distances. Some – probably most - drifted away and were never heard from again. And some, occasionally, were thought to be lost forever, only to turn up months later at a distant port on the other side of the world to which their rescue ship was sailing and where the survivors were landed.

Ships that wrecked on reefs or coasts or islands spewed out their human cargo to make the best of whatever fate befell them - if they survived. Castaways might spend many months awaiting rescue on isolated islands such as the Aucklands, to the south of New Zealand, or along hostile coasts such as the Straits of Magellan in Patagonia, at the end of the South American continent. They survived by scavenging from the land and shore, and by the hope of rescue, which arrived, eventually, for a fortunate few.

## NARRATIVES

### 5 July 1869

**Seychelles, 10th June.**

A full rigged American ship of 900 tons, bound from Calcutta to Mauritius, with grain, is reported to have opened out [planks sprung and leaking] 37 days from Calcutta, and foundered; master's name unknown, name of chief mate Brown. Nine lascars have arrived at one of these islands in a small boat after 37 days exposure, 6 men out of 15 having died.

No news of the other boat, containing the master and remainder of the crew, all lascars.

The men landed are ignorant of the master's name as he took command on the day they sailed. The vessel's name is supposed [thought] to have been Jelly Whitney or J. B. Woodney.

### 27 Sept 1869

**Mauritius, 27ᵗʰ Aug.**

The J.P. Whitney * (Amer.) (Off No. 9,587), Ober, from Calcutta to this port, foundered, 9ᵗʰ Apl. in lat. 15 S, lon. 72 E. The master, mate, and 8 men were brought here on the 10ᵗʰ Aug. Second mate and rest of crew drowned…

*This must certainly have been the American vessel in the 5 July report above "supposed [thought] to have been Jelly Whitney or J. B. Woodney". There seemed to have been two boatloads of castaways: the first, with nine surviving men (lascars) that reached Seychelles "after 37 days exposure", the second mate presumably being one of the six who died in that boat; the second containing the master, Capt. Ober, first mate Brown and eight others who were picked up at sea and brought to Mauritius, arriving there on 8 August. The news that "Second mate and rest of crew drowned" presumably referred to the boat that arrived at one of the Seychelles islands without the other boat at Mauritius knowing about it.

## 8 Jan 1870

**Shields, 7ᵗʰ Jan.**

The Black Swan (s), Knowles, arrived in the Tyne to-day, from London, with both bows stove and fore compartment full of water. She reports that about 6 a.m., to-day, when 10 miles off Flamborough Head, she was in collision with a large laden screw steamer, apparently bound to the Continent, which vessel is supposed [believed] to have gone down almost immediately, with all hands, as she was struck amidships, and the *Black Swan* put out her boats, without being able to discover a vestige of the vessel or crew.

### Grimsby, 8ᵗʰ Jan 1870

A seaman, picked up at sea and landed here by a smack [fishing boat], reports that the St. Bede (s), of and from Newcastle, for Spain, with coke and iron, was run into and sunk by a light steamer, going North, off Flamboro' Head, yesterday. The steamer lay to for half an hour, but rendered no assistance. The seaman believed he was the only person saved.*

*The official Inquiry into this incident found the *Black Swan* "entirely at fault" for causing the collision with the *St. Bede*; however, it absolved the *Black Swan*'s master, officers and crew of "wilful neglect" and decided there was "no ground for any culpable charge" against them.

## 17 Feb 1870

**Casualties – Foreign**

Valparaiso, 3ʳᵈ Jan.- The *Siam* (Fr. Barq.), Leguen, from Payta [or Paita, northwestern Peru], put in here 2ⁿᵈ Jan., to land seven men of the crew of the *Mary* (Amer. ship), from Callao to Queenstown, which foundered in lat. 25 S, lon. 94 W. They were picked up in the open sea, and three days were spent searching for the other boats but without success.

*24 Feb 1870*

**Casualties – Foreign**

New York, 11th Feb.- The master, Hayward, of the *Mary* (ship), of Boston, from Callao to Queenstown, with the cargo ex [from the vessel] *Washington Libby*, reports that the vessel sprung a leak during heavy weather 11th Dec. [1869], and foundered 13th. A boat with the master and part of the crew was fallen in with by the *Iona*, from Guanape islands [off north coast of Peru] to Payta, which vessel took them to the latter place, 31st Dec. The remainder of the crew were in the lifeboat, which was picked up by a French barque [the *Siam* of the first report].

# 5 April 1871

**Casualties – Home**

Tralee*, 3rd Apl.- The Eliza (smack), from Kilrush* to Berehaven*, which was lost in Brandon Bay*, was wrecked there in the night of 14th Mar.. The dead bodies of the crew, and some potatoes and wreckage were washed ashore and taken charge of by the police.

*6 April 1871*

**Casualties – Home**

Tralee, 3rd Apl.- The wreck of the Eliza (smack), from Kilrush to Berehaven, has been sold; also the potatoes.

*All these places are along the southwest coast of Ireland.

# 11 July 1871

**Casualties – Home**

Southampton, 9th July.- A telegram from Bredasdorp [southern Western Cape province, South Africa], dated 19th May, reports the Souvenance (Fr., ship), from Pondicherry [India], to Martinique, a complete wreck; above [ie., more than] 150 bodies had been washed ashore.

**Casualties – Foreign**

Cape-Town, 5th June.- The Souvenance (Fr. vessel), has been lost about Quoin point, and nothing is known beyond the washing up of the bodies of her passengers and coolies.

*29 July 1871*

**Casualties – Foreign**

Bredasdorp, 25th May.- The wreck of a large ship has been found on the beach W of L'Agulhas [Cape Agulhas], near the Quoin Point. Judging from the contracts found on the dead bodies of the 134 coolies, the vessel must be the Souvenance, Bruneteau, from Karikal and Pondicherry to Martinique.*

*The loss of life from a wrecked ship transporting 'coolies' – indentured labourers – was usually very considerable, given the numbers involved. The coast around Quoin Point, just to the west of Cape Agulhas, the southernmost point of Africa, was littered with the remains of ships wrecked there.

# 13 July 1871

### Casualties – Foreign

Bombay, 13th June.- The Mahomudi (bugla*), Nacoda**, from Mangalore to the Persian Gulf, encountered a typhoon about the 5th May, lasting for 10 days, after which the vessel foundered. Nineteen men clung to one of the water tanks, and 15 of the crew to the other, and the remainder to the fragments of wreck. Shortly afterwards the 15 men parted company and 12 of them died. After being 36 days on the wreck, the remaining three were picked up by a cotia***, near Goa, and were landed here, yesterday. The 19 men who had been hanging on to the other tank were picked up and landed at Aden.

*A 'bugla', or baggala, was a traditional two-masted deep-sea dhow sailed in the Persian Gulf and Gulf of Oman.

**Admiral Smyth's *Sailor's Word-Book* defines *nakhoda* (variously spelled in English) as: "An Arab sea-captain." So the name "Nacoda" was just that: the 'captain' of the *Mahomudy* rather than the man's actual name.

***cotia: The maritime author Alan Villiers wrote in *Sons of Sinbad* that "The Indian kotia is very like the Arab baggala."

# 17 Oct 1871

### Casualties – Foreign

Saigon, 16th Oct., 9.16 a.m.- The Taeping* (clipper), from Amoy to New York, with tea, was abandoned, 22nd Sept., on Lodd Reef. Master and 11 men here; two officers and 13 men not yet; HM Gnbt [HM Gunboat] *Teaser* search [for] mates and cargo.

### *18 Oct 1871*

### Casualties – Foreign

Batavia [Jakarta], 16th Oct., 8 p.m.- The Taeping (ship) was abandoned on Ladd Reef, 22nd Sept.; the crew left in three boats; one arrived here; two uncertain.

### *18 Nov 1871*

### Casualties – Foreign

Saigon, 15th Oct.- The Taeping, Gissing, from Amoy to New York, was anchored on Ladd's Reef, about 250 miles east of this place. When the crew left the vessel she was in such a position as to leave hope that some of the cargo might be saved. The master, carpenter, steward, and nine men arrived here to-day in a native boat; two officers and nine men are still on their way to this place in boats. HM Gbt. *Teazer*, which left here to-day, was informed by the master of the *Taeping* of the casualty to his vessel, and the commander of the gunboat has intimated to the British Consul that she is gone in search of the missing part of the crew, and that she will also try to save cargo.

### *20 Nov 1871*

### Casualties – Foreign

Batavia, 18th Nov.- The chief officer and eight men from the Taeping, from Amoy to New York, on Ladd's Reef, arrived here yesterday.

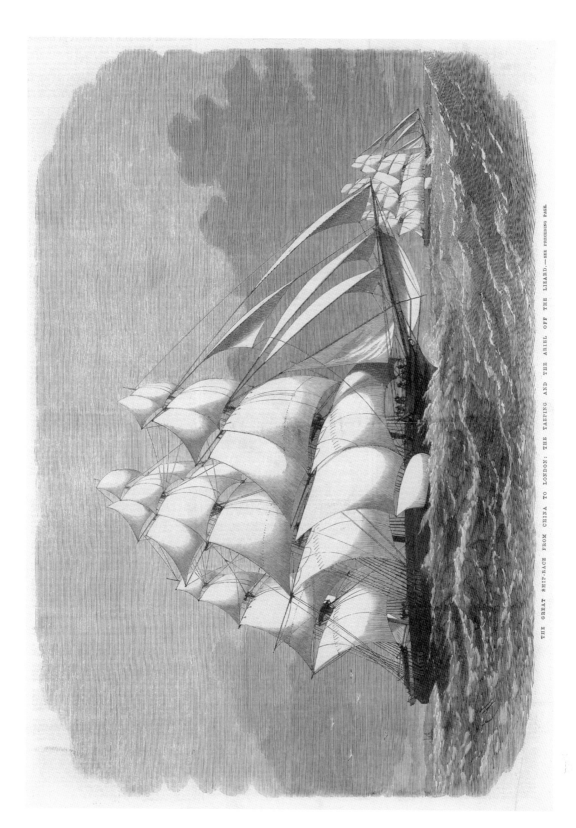

THE GREAT SHIP-RACE FROM CHINA TO LONDON: THE TAEPING AND THE ARIEL OFF THE LIZARD.—SEE PRECEDING PAGE.

## 5 Dec 1871
### Casualties – Foreign

Saigon, 30th Oct.- HM Gunboat *Teazer* has proceeded to the wreck of the Taeping, Gissing, from Amoy to New York, which was stranded on Ladd's Reef, 22nd Sept., and reports having found her in a broken up condition, so that nothing could be saved.

## 1 Jan 1872
### Casualties – Foreign

Batavia, 24th Nov. [1871].- The first mate, McLachlan, and seven men of the Taeping, who were landed here, 17th Nov., left in their boat 18 hours after the disaster, and were picked up by the *Omer & Julie*, Sabatier, five days afterwards; they report that the vessel was broken up when they passed the spot in the *Omer & Julie*, the reef being surrounded with chests of tea.

The *Veronica*, from Whampoa to London, which put in here with crew mutinous, proceeded under command of the above-mentioned Mr. McLachlan, who has been appointed master, with the sanction of the agents here, in place of the late master, Stratford, who has been suspended.

Saigon, 11th Nov.- The missing boat of the Taeping, Gissing, from Amoy to New York, wrecked on Ladd's Reef, was picked up by the *Serica* (since passed St. Helena); it contained the second mate and four men, who have been landed at Anjer [at west end of Java on the Sunda Strait].

*\*Taeping* was a famous tea clipper and rival of *Cutty Sark*, *Serica*, *Ariel* and *Fiery Cross*, amongst other clippers. She was launched at Robert Steele's shipyard at Greenock on 24 December 1863, the same year three other tea clippers were launched at Steele's yard: *Serica*, *Young Lochinvar* and *Ariel*. *Taeping* was similar in size to other tea clippers: 767 tons, 183ft 7ins long, 31ft 1ins wide and 19ft 9ins deep. These sleek ships raced to bring the new season's tea crop from China to London in the fastest time. Vessels that loaded around the same time in Chinese ports such as Foochow (Fuzhou) and Amoy (Xiamen) for London sometimes finished within a few hours of each other after a voyage of some 15,700 miles from the other side of the world. In the famous race of 1866, *Taeping*, *Serica* and *Ariel* all arrived in the Thames within six hours of each other, on the same tide, 99 days out from the Pagoda Anchorage on the Min River with tea from Foochow.

On her fateful final voyage, *Taeping* arrived at Amoy on 30 August 1871 and sailed for New York on 8 September. Ladd's Reef, where *Taeping* was wrecked two weeks after her departure from Amoy, is in the Spratly Islands, in the South China Sea between the Philippines and the southeast coast of Vietnam. As the reports above indicate, all the *Taeping*'s crew members in three separate boats eventually reached land, and no lives were lost.

The *Serica* was wrecked soon after *Taeping*, in December 1872, on the Parcel Islands, to the north of the Spratlys in the South China Sea.

## 24 March 1873

### Reported Loss of the Serica*

From the *Hong Kong Daily Press* of 8th Feb., 1873.

We have been favoured with the particulars of the loss of the above vessel, which have been received from Capt. Hageman, of the Johann Smidt, arrived at Saigon from Touron:-

'Two days before my departure from Touron [Tourane, the French colonial name for Da Nang in then Indo-China/Vietnam] I was told by an Annamite [Indo-Chinese person] that there was a European on shore in the house of the first Mandarin [official or magistrate]. I went there and found a man who said that he was a sailor, and gave his name. He had been boatswain on board the British ship *Serica*. The *Serica* had left Hong Kong on a Saturday morning, bound to Monte Video [Montevideo, Uruguay], and already, the following evening, between 7 and 8 o'clock, struck on a reef, which, as the captain afterwards said, was the North shoal of the Paracels. It being very stormy, masts, boats and deck houses were swept away by the sea; the crew made a raft, provided themselves with some provisions, and left the ship.

The crew consisted of 28 hands. The captain died after four days, and eight men died a few days later. On the eighth day, water and all provisions were finished. On the ninth day the raft was smashed on a rock, whereby the remaining crew, except one of them, were drowned. The surviving man found some rain water, and lived on shells found on this rock. On the sixth day he was saved by a fisherman, and brought on shore to a French missionary, who provided him with food, and with whom he stayed for 6 days.

He then was handed over to a mandarin, and was sent to Touron in a palanquin [like a rickshaw], where he arrived on the evening of the 20th Jan., after a journey of 3 weeks. He speaks very favourably of the treatment he received on the journey and in Touron. He lived there with a Mandarin, received clothing, food, and was provided with everything. He told me that the government intended to send him to Hong Kong in a native craft or steamer, which was to leave shortly. He, however, showed me a letter written by a French missionary, and addressed to a brother in Saigon. The letter was dated Khanhoa [port town in Vietnam], and stated the bearer was a wrecked sailor who had suffered a great deal.'

*The *Serica* was one of the most famous amongst the tea clippers that raced every year to bring the new tea crop from China to London (and New York). She was built in 1863 at Robert Steele's yard at Greenock, on the Clyde, and was 708 tons. *Serica* won her very first tea race, from Foochow to London, beating her closest rival, *Fiery Cross*, by five days.

## 15 Nov 1871

### Casualties – Foreign

Shanghai, 14th Nov.- [By Telegraph] – The Corypheus, from Foo-chow-foo [Fuzhou, China] to Melbourne, has been lost in lat. 12 S, lon. 160 E; mate and part of crew arrived here.

### *18 Dec*

### Casualties – Foreign

New York, 5th Dec.- The Corypheus (barq.), of Melbourne, has been totally lost, together with her cargo, at Ailee in Marshall's Archipelago*. The master (Roe) and three of the crew reached Rockhampton, Queensland, after being in a boat for 47 days.

*Daily Southern Cross* (**Auckland newspaper**)

## 27th October 1871

Brisbane, Oct. 18: Captain Rae and three men have just arrived at Rockhampton in a whaleboat, forty-seven days out. He reports the loss of the barque 'Corypheus' nearly seven weeks ago, at Ailee, in Marshall's Archipelago; the vessel was becalmed and sucked ashore by the current. The crew, in two boats, made for Sandy Cape [just north of Brisbane]; they parted company four days after.

The men suffered great privations, catching water in the boat sails, and subsisting on provisions damaged by sea water. The boat did not sight a single vessel. No tidings of the other boat. The 'Corypheus' bilged [ie., struck] on a reef, and the ship and cargo are completely lost. Five of the crew elected to remain on the island.

## 23 Oct 1872

### Casualties, Etc.

Information has been received from the Admiralty that HMS *Barrosa* has returned to China from her cruise among the South Sea islands, bringing with her the five men left in Ailu island from the *Corypheus*, from Foo-chow-foo to Melbourne, which was wrecked on that island last year.

*The ship was wrecked at Ailu Island – or on one of the Ailu Islands – in the Marshall Islands group, to the northeast of New Guinea. Her location was therefore in latitude 12° *North*, not *South*, at longitude 160° E. (Lat. 12° S, long. 160° E is at the southeastern end of the Solomon Islands, just off the coast of New Guinea.) The distance from Ailu to Rockhampton, on the coast of Queensland, is approximately 1,300 miles, which the whaleboat and four men covered in 47 days, an average of 28 miles/day.

There was a letter of request for a government boat to rescue the five castaways who remained on Ailu, but officials claimed it was too far away and out of their jurisdiction to do so. (The men were taken off the island the following year by a British naval vessel, HMS *Barrosa*, as revealed by the 23 October 1872 report above.) The other boat containing the remaining crew members was, in the absence of any news of her, presumably lost at sea.

## 25 March 1873

### Casualties – Foreign

Monte Video [Montevideo, Uruguay], 27th Feb. [Lisbon, 23rd Mar., 1.45 p.m.] The *Tropic* has brought part of the crew of the British barque James W. Elwell*, from Porthcawl to Valparaiso, burnt off Cape Pillar, Pacific

## 2 April 1873

### Casualties – Home

Southampton, 1st Apl., 10.15 a.m.- The Jas. W. Elwell (barq.), from Cardiff to Valparaiso, was abandoned on fire, 6th Dec. [1872], in lat. 53 S, 200 miles from Cape Horn, and sunk soon afterwards. The master, the stewardess, and a sailor, were picked up in the Straits of Magellan, after being ten weeks in a boat, by the Tropic (s), which arrived at Monte Video,

25th Feb. The remainder of the crew, 12 in number, had died of cold and hunger. When the vessel was abandoned the crew secured only ten days provisions.

*The Canadian barque *James W. Elwell*, of 550 tons, sailed from Porthcawl, between Cardiff and Swansea in Wales, on 15 September 1872, bound for the Chilean port of Valparaiso carrying a cargo of Welsh coal. She was under the command of Captain John Wren, with a crew of 15. It was to be a voyage scarred by mishap and tragedy but ending in salvation. The first mate died from a gangrenous foot, caused by a spar that fell on it. The cook also died, after he was cut by a knife that slipped and gashed his leg when the ship lurched suddenly. Both men were buried at sea.

On 1 December, after the vessel had rounded Cape Horn and was about 160 miles off Cape Pillar at the Pacific entrance to the Straits of Magellan, during a gale, the cargo of coal caught fire. The crew fought the fire before abandoning ship on 5 December. The twelve men and a woman gathered in one boat to make for the Straits of Magellan. Their provisions in the boat were: five bags of hard bread (ship's biscuit), twenty-four 4lb tins of preserved meats, two hams, three cheeses and a box of lime juice. As they worked their way along the shore of the Straits, one by one the crew died from hunger, exposure and exhaustion. Throughout their ordeal the stewardess, Sarah Farington, wife of the dead cook, encouraged the men to have hope that they would be rescued, despite her own injuries and the appalling circumstances in which they found themselves.

A report in the Liverpool "*Daily Courier*" newspaper of 14 April 1873 noted: "It was now [early January 1873] proposed by some of the crew that they should supply their intense craving for food by eating the dead bodies of their shipmates. This Captain Wren prevented by putting to sea from the place and endeavouring to get to the northward, but on getting to the open sea they were blown to southeastward to a harbour about 30 miles distant from where they started, the weather being very bad, almost continually raining, the nights piercing cold, with no shelter and but little fire and scarcely any food."

On the shores of Tierra del Fuego ('Land of Fire') they scavenged mussels and whatever else they could find to eat from the rocks and scrub of that hostile and, at the time, largely uninhabited region of Patagonia, most of which made them ill with nausea and cramp. During that time five seamen died. On about 22 January the remaining castaways set off round the coast to the southeast, hoping to get to 'Sandy Point' (Punta Arenas), the main town in the Straits of Magellan. On 25 January another seaman died, followed by the carpenter three weeks later on 12 February.

Seventy-one days after abandoning the *James W. Elwell*, the last three surviving crew members - Captain Wren, stewardess Sarah and the sailor James Wilson, who was by then unconscious and near death - put back out to sea in the small boat, with hopes that they would be sighted by a ship passing through the Straits. Meanwhile, the White Star liner SS *Tropic* (2,122 tons), commanded by Captain Henry Parsells, was making its return voyage on its regular run between Liverpool and Valparaiso. Captain Parsells was taking a different course from the Pacific through the Straits of Magellan than his usual route round the Horn, to the south, and up into the Atlantic towards home. By that twist of fate in Capt. Parsell's change of routine the *Tropic* came across the small boat with the three survivors of the *James*

*W. Elwell.* Within an hour they were hoisted to safety on board, thus ending their epic ordeal of misadventures and tribulations as castaways in the 'Land of Fire'.

## 21 Oct 1873

### Casualties – Foreign

Hong Kong, 30th Aug.- The R.J. Robertson (Ger. Schr.), Hernsheim, which sailed from Foochow-foo [Fuzhou, China], 3rd July, for Adelaide, with tea, but encountered a hurricane when a few days out, and had to cut away her masts. On the 11th Aug., as the vessel was driving on to a reef, the anchors were let go, and the next day the remainder of the crew (3 men having been lost overboard) landed on an island. On the 13th the [anchor] chains parted, and the vessel drove over the reef and broke up. The crew left the island on the 19th Aug. in a junk, arriving at Keelung [north coast of Taiwan] on the 21st and came on here in a steamer.

### *24 Jan 1874*
### Casualties, etc.

A letter has been received by the Admiralty from the commander of HMS *Curlew*, dated 19th Nov. [1873], stating that on his visit to the Loochoo islands* he learned that a German ship had been wrecked, in July last [1873], on the island of Typinsan, in the Meico Lima group, and that a woman, 5 seamen, and 2 Chinese were saved. On the 14th Nov., Commander Church proceeded to Typinsan, which he reached the following day, and the *Curlew*'s cutter having been sent ashore returned after obtaining confirmation of the wreck of a ship there in July. She was a tea ship, flying German colours, and had been dismasted and driven ashore. It was stated that two of the sailors had died after landing, and that the survivors left in August, for China, in a junk given them. The ship's boat was seen. It was painted white with a black top, but there was nothing to indicate the name of the wrecked vessel.

### *30 Jan 1874*
### Casualties – Foreign

Hamburg, 27th Jan.- The vessel reported in Lloyd's List of 24th Jan. as having been lost in July last on Typinsan, one of the Meico-Lima group, is supposed [believed] to have been the R.J. Robertson (schr.), Hernsheim, from Foo-chow-foo to Adelaide, before reported.

*The Ryukyo Islands (also sometimes called the Nansei Islands), arching southwest between the southernmost Japanese island of Kyushu and Taiwan, were known as the Loochoo Islands in English from about 1830 until the mid-20th century. They were named as either Loochoo, or Luchu, or Lewchew in English, based on the Chinese pronunciation of the Chinese characters for Ryukyu (*Liúqiú* in Mandarin Chinese).

Typinsan is the old German name for the island called Miyako-jima (or Miyakojima), in Okinawa Prefecture, located around 300 km south of Okinawa Island. On old maps it is shown to be located amongst the Meico Lima, or Meaco-sima group of islands. The German name was based on the old Chinese name for the island Tai-pin-shan ('large flat mountain').

On 2 July 1873 the German schooner *R.J. Robertson* was wrecked on a reef near the village of Ueno on "Typinsan" (Miyako-jima) during a typhoon on its voyage from the Chinese tea port then known as Foo-chow-foo (now Fuzhou) to Adelaide, under the command of Capt.

Edward Hernsheim. The inhabitants of the village rescued eight of the crew of the ship and took care of them for a month or so. The survivors (including one woman) then set off in a junk, making their first landfall at the Taiwan port of Keelung on their way back to Germany.

The first German Emperor, Wilhelm I, thanked the villagers for rescuing the crew of the ship by commemorating a stone monument to them on the island in 1876. Around 1932 Capt. Hernsheim published an account of the incident titled "Der Untergang des Deutschen Schooners R.J. Robertson und die Aufnahme der Schiffbruchigen auf der Insel Typinsan". In 1995, as a result of the historical connection between Miyako-jima and Germany, a German Cultural Village was built at Ueno. The village includes a replica of the German medieval Marksburg Castle at Braubach, on the Rhine, as well as parts of the Berlin Wall dismantled in 1989.

## 27 Dec 1873

### Casualties – Foreign

HMS *Basilisk*, on the Australian station, had fallen in with the Peri (schr.), waterlogged, and rescued from her fourteen natives of the Solomon Islands. These men were the only survivors of eighty natives who had captured the schooner; they had been drifting about for some months.

## 19 May 1875

### Casualties, Etc.

The *Souvenir*, arrived at Antwerp, from Philadelphia, reports that on the 22$^{nd}$ Apl., in lat. 37 N lon. 58 W, she fell in with the Cora. Linn (barq.), of Antwerp, from Doboy [assumed to be Doboy Sound, Georgia, United States] to Troon [Scotland], with timber, dismasted and waterlogged, and with seven of her crew clinging to the wreck, over which the sea was breaking. The first mate and four seamen jumped into the water and were picked up by a boat from the *Souvenir*. The cook and one seaman, being delirious, had to be left. The mate reported that the master and four men had been washed off the wreck and drowned.

## 9 July 1875

### Casualties – Foreign

New York, 25$^{th}$ June.- The Egeria (cargo launch) was sunk by the Laura McLellan (barq.), the master (Harris) of the latter, and his wife and seven children being drowned.

## 28 July 1875

### Casualties – Foreign

St. Helena – [Madeira, 26$^{th}$ July] – The Stuart Hahnemann (ship), from Bombay to Liverpool, capsized and sank during a squall on the night of 14$^{th}$ Apl. The vessel was then ten days out from Bombay. A boat with the crew was picked up on the 27$^{th}$ Apl., by the *Blandina* (Austr. Barq.), which landed the men here on the 5$^{th}$ July. The rest of the crew, 38 in number, are supposed [thought] to have been lost.

Another account:- The *Blandina*, of Fiume, from Akyab**, called at St. Helena, 5$^{th}$ July, and landed nine men whom she had picked up in a boat on the 27$^{th}$ Apl., in lat. 63 N lon 89 E*. They were part of the crew of the ship Stuart Hahnemann, from Bombay to Liverpool, which vessel capsized at midnight on the 14th Apl., in lat. 22 N*, longitude not observed. Frazer, boatswain, one of the survivors, states that, notwithstanding every effort made to right the ship after she was thrown on her beam ends, she kept gradually falling over, and eventually capsized.

The masts were standing after the vessel sunk. One lifeboat was observed bottom upwards. The survivors, on righting her, found a monkey alive tied to the thwarts [seats]. They searched the next day for other survivors, but found none until 10 at night they fell in with a boy named Thomas Crumby, floating alive on two planks. They also found six cocoanuts, and lived thirteen days upon the monkey and the cocoanuts. They also caught two flying fish. The master of the vessel (van Norden), his wife, three mates, and 33 of the crew perished.

*None of the longitude and latitude coordinates in this report makes sense. On a course from Bombay to Liverpool, down the Arabian Sea and Indian Ocean, to head around the Cape of Good Hope into the South Atlantic, the *Stuart Hahnemann* would have been on a more or less southerly course, keeping close-hauled with the southwesterly monsoon winds of that time of year on her starboard side. That would suggest her position when she capsized and sank after ten days sailing was around 2° N latitude and 70° E longitude, just to the west of the Maldive Islands, rather than "lat 22 N" somewhere to the northwest of Bombay between the coasts of Oman and Pakistan.

It is quite possible that the southwest monsoon pushed the *Stuart Hahnemann* survivors 600 miles or so east in fourteen days (around 40 miles a day) to as far as 89° E longitude, where the *Blandina* claimed to have picked them up, but at a more plausible 3° N of the equator, certainly not "63° N" - which is approximately the latitude of Siberia!

**The *Blandina* had sailed from Akyab, a port town on the coast of Burma now called Sittwe. The British named it Akyab in 1825, during the first Anglo-Burmese War, after the name of the town's old pagoda, called Ahkyaib-daw, near which the British troops were garrisoned. Akyab was an important rice export port when the British ruled Burma. Sailing from Akyab, the *Blandina* would have encountered the *Stuart Hahnemann* survivors right on her outbound track – at about lat. 3° N, long. 89° E, some 500 miles to the southeast of Sri Lanka.

## 21 April 1876

### Casualties – Home

Queenstown, 20th Apr, 5p.m.: Report of Capt Cedic, of the late French ship Victorine, from Pabellón de Pica [Peru] (Dec 7 [1875]), with guano, for Nantes:-

"Jan 9 [1876], experienced very heavy weather from NW, with very heavy sea around Cape Horn. In lat. 53 S, lon. 85 W, on Jan 14th and 15th, experienced a heavy hurricane from SW to W, with heavy seas. On the 21st, experienced another hurricane from NE, and found ship making much water. On the 22nd vessel had 4 ft of water in hold, set four pumps to work, and jettisoned about 150 tons cargo to try and find leak, but the water still gaining on the afternoon of the same day [and] had to abandon the vessel, and when leaving her the water was level with lower deck beams – took to boats myself, and eighteen men being in one boat, and the mate and eighteen men in the other – the same night lost sight of the mate's boat, and did not see her afterwards. On the 29th fell in with the Nova Scotian, from Lobos to Queenstown, which vessel took us on board and landed us at that port to-day."

Queenstown, 20th Apr, 3PM:- "The Nova Scotian, Hatfield [master], arrived here from Lobos, reports that, on the 29th Jan, in lat. 34 S, lon. 35 W, she picked up the master and 18 men, forming part of the crew of the Victorine (ship), of Bordeaux, from Pabellón de Pica to Nantes, which vessel had been abandoned seven days previously, in lat. 45 S, lon. 38 W, in a sinking condition, having sprung a serious leak. The mate and remainder of the crew (18) separated from the master's boat during the night of the abandonment, and what became of them is not known."

## 20 June 1876
### Casualties – Foreign

[Le] Havre, 17th June:- "Intelligence has been received here stating that the second boat of the Victorine, from Pabellón de Pica to Nantes, which vessel was abandoned 22nd Jan., in lat. 45 S lon. 38 W, had been fallen in with by the Blair Drummond, and that the crew, 19 in number, had been landed at Rangoon."*

*It was almost six months after the *Victorine* sank that the fate of the 19 men in her second boat was known. The castaways were picked up by the *Blair Drummond* somewhere in the South Atlantic and landed upon her arrival at Rangoon. News of the men's rescue probably only reached Le Havre when another vessel from Rangoon, or nearby, arrived at the French port and relayed the 'intelligence'.

## 9 Aug 1876
### Casualties – Foreign

New York, 28th July.- Southern Cross (Br. barq.): Mr. Hoar, second mate, and three men of this vessel, in a small boat, were spoken, no date, in the Straits Lemeure [the Le Maire Strait, between Staten Island and the mainland of Tierra del Fuego, just northeast of Cape Horn], by the ship *Santa Clara*, at San Francisco, 27th July. They reported that the *Southern Cross* was anchored in Goose roads, leaking badly, and with only one pump available, and that they were proceeding to Ushmora Mission Station*, Beagle channel, for assistance. They also reported captain ill, and mate in charge. Having been supplied with provisions and ammunition, they proceeded.

*Ushmora was a missionary station near what is now the town of Ushuaia ('Ushmora'), the southernmost town in the world. It lies on the north side of the Beagle Channel separating the mainland of Tierra del Fuego from Navarin Island and other islands in the Cape Horn region. There were half a dozen indigenous Fuegian tribes around the Tierra del Fuego region. Amongst these were the Yaghan, the Haush, the Alacaluf and the Ona.

Ferdinand Magellan (1480?–1521), the Portuguese-born but Spanish-naturalised explorer, in the service of the Spanish King Charles I, was the first European to encounter Fuegian peoples during his expedition voyage around the world from 1519. The encounters and all other aspects of the expedition were recorded by an Italian scholar, Antonio Pigafetta, who sailed with Magellan. (Magellan himself never completed the circumnavigation: he was killed on the Philippine island of Mactan in April 1521.)

Three hundred years later Charles Darwin (1809–1882) sailed as naturalist aboard the *Beagle*, commanded by Capt. Robert Fitzroy, R.N., during the *Beagle's* epic expedition around the world in 1831–1836. Darwin's *Journal* of the voyage was published soon after he returned to England. It included his observations of the Fuegian "cannibals" and "savages" they encountered at the bottom of South America.

Soon after, the first British Anglican missionaries started arriving in the region, to convert the Fuegian tribes to Christianity. The first, the Patagonian Missionary Society (1844), renamed the South American Missionary Society in 1865, established the mission station near Ushuaia in 1869. Other missions followed. But the missionaries also brought diseases that wiped out the indigenous Fuegians. By the 1920s their numbers had fallen from perhaps 4,000–5,000 before the arrival of Europeans to fewer than 100 all told. Subsequently, all the indigenous Fuegians, who had lived in that region probably for thousands of years, became extinct.

## 7 Nov 1876

### Casualties – Foreign

Mauritius, 12th Oct.- The *Eva Joshua* has arrived here from Diego Garcia*, bringing 22 Lascar seamen, who had arrived there on a raft, and reported that the Rohamanee, Holland, from Calcutta to Ceylon, was burnt at sea, 21st May, the master, his two daughters, three passengers and 30 seamen all perishing at the time of the disaster. The 22 men saved drifted to Diego Garcia on the raft, 24th May.

*The atoll of Diego Garcia is the largest island in the Chagos Archipelago, approximately 1,000 miles south-southwest of Sri Lanka (Ceylon) and due south of the Maldive Islands chain. Since 1965 Chagos has been a British Overseas Territory named the British Indian Ocean Territory. In 1971 the United Kingdom and the United States agreed to set up a joint military base on Diego Garcia. In order for the base to be built, the entire indigenous population of around 2,000 people was evicted, controversially, to Mauritius and the Seychelles.

## 28 May 1878

### Casualties – Foreign

San Francisco, 12th May.- The barque *Sonoma*, which arrived here to-day from Liverpool, has on board Charles S. Harriman, second mate, and six sailors of the ship *P.R. Hazeltine*, wrecked some time ago on the coast of Tierra del Fuego. They were picked up in the Straits of Lemaire, 4th Mar., in a very destitute condition, having been subsisting on mussels for 14 days. They report that during their wanderings after leaving the wreck they discovered a cave, which contained fragments of a boat, some oars, articles of clothing, etc., and skeletons of a boat's crew, but nothing by which the castaways could be identified.

## 7 March 1879

### Casualties – Home

Liverpool, March 5.- Frederick.- The crew of the German barque Frederick, from Doboy [Georgia, United States] for Falmouth, for orders, have arrived here and report that their vessel left Doboy about the 16th January, and encountered very heavy weather. She sprang a leak, and although the pumps were worked night and day, the water could not be got out, the vessel finally being waterlogged. The crew for safety took to the rigging, where they remained for five days and nights without food or water.

The master Lau and the carpenter went on deck to secure a sail, when the former was carried overboard by a heavy sea. Another of the crew was also washed into the water by the same wave, but he regained the deck by the aid of a line. The line was thrown to the master, who grasped it, but failing to retain his hold, he was drowned. Subsequently the Italian barque Gaetano S. hove in sight, and with great difficulty rescued them, afterwards landing them at Holyhead.

## 23 Oct 1879

**Casualties – Home**

Falmouth, Oct. 21.- Sylvanus Blanchard – To-day the barque River Logan, Quinn, from Bassein [Burma], arrived here and landed Mr. C. Brodie, the mate, and six of the crew of the American ship Sylvanus Blanchard, 1,200 tons, from Liverpool for Rio, laden with coals. From the time of her leaving Liverpool until she was abandoned (29 days) she experienced heavy weather, and she eventually sprung a leak, which kept increasing, and, after continual pumping the crew were obliged to abandon her, with 6 feet 8 inches water in her hold, on Sept. 20, lat. 13 40 N, long. 25 10 W.

The captain and nine men left in one boat, and those landed here in the second. The boats kept company until dusk, when they parted in the darkness. For two days the vessel was seen from the boat, but she must soon have gone down, as, before leaving, the crew set her on fire to remove her from the track of shipping. The captain steered for Cape de Verds [Cape Verde Islands], and Brodie intended to go to the same islands.

The second day after abandoning their ship they went on board the Wave Queen, of Shoreham, bound from London to the Cape of Good Hope. They were treated kindly, and the master offered to take them on with him and send them on shore as soon as possible, but they preferred proceeding as before [ie., in the boat], and on the next day, in the evening, they spoke the River Logan, the master of which vessel took them aboard and brought them here.

### 13 Nov 1879

**Casualties – Home**

Falmouth, Nov. 12, 6 30 p.m.- The master of the Vale of Nith, arrived here to-day from Saigon, reports that on Sept. 25, in lat. 12 20 N, long. 26 W, he fell in with a boat containing Captain Adams and 9 men belonging to American ship Sylvanus Blanchard, abandoned five days before and previously reported. Took them on board Vale of Nith, and on Oct. 8, in lat. 28 20 N, long. 32 W, transferred 4 men to British barque New Brunswick, from Japan to Falmouth, all well.

### 18 Nov 1879

**Casualties – Home**

Falmouth, Nov. 16, 8 p.m.- Sylvanus Blanchard – The New Brunswick, Frazer, from Kobe (Japan) (rice), has brought in four men of the crew of the Sylvanus Blanchard, previously reported foundered.

## THE *SHENANDOAH*

### 17 Nov 1879

**Casualties – Foreign**

Port Elizabeth [South Africa], Oct. 17.- Shenandoah*.- This vessel, formerly a privateer belonging to the Southern States during the American Civil War, has sunk off the island of Socotra, in the Arabian Gulf. She was purchased by the Sultan of Zanzibar, and after remaining idly at Zanzibar for some years was sent to Bombay, for repairs, but foundered off Socotra, all hands being lost, except one Englishman and a few Lascars.

*The *Shenandoah* was built by Alexander Stephen & Sons at Glasgow and launched as the civilian auxiliary steamer *Sea King* in August 1863. The vessel was of composite construction (iron frame hull and teak wood planking), 1,160 tons, 230ft long by 32.5ft wide by 20.5ft draft, a full-rigged ship with auxiliary steam power. The American Civil War had begun in April 1861 between the Confederate southern states and the Union states of the north. The Confederate Government bought the *Sea King* just after she was launched, to be used to capture and destroy Union merchant ships outside US territorial waters.

In October 1864 the *Sea King* sailed from London, ostensibly on a merchant voyage to Bombay. She stopped at Madeira, however, to be fitted out as a warship under the command of C.S. Navy First Lieutenant (later Commander) James Iredell Waddell. She was recommissioned there as the CSS *Shenandoah* and proceeded to sail towards the South Atlantic, around the Cape of Good Hope and to Melbourne, Australia, where she arrived in January 1865. During her passage she captured, sunk or burned nine US flag merchant vessels in the South Atlantic.

Repairs to and reprovisioning of the *Shenandoah* were carried out in Melbourne, including the addition of some forty 'stowaways' who were commissioned as crew. After three weeks in Melbourne, Waddell took his warship to sea, intending to attack US merchant and whaling ships in the Pacific. As the *Shenandoah* headed towards North Pacific and Arctic waters, in April and May, the Confederacy back in the United States collapsed. Waddell did not receive confirmation of this until early August 1865, from an English ship that had left San Francisco two weeks before, after he had destroyed or, in a few cases, captured Yankee whaling ships in the Bering Sea and was headed towards San Francisco to make an attack on that city.

With confirmed news of the surrender of the Confederacy to the Union forces, Waddell disarmed his ship and headed back to England via Cape Horn. The *Shenandoah* arrived at Liverpool on 5 November 1865. The following day she was handed over to the Royal Navy.

The United States Government took possession of the vessel and sold her to the Sultan of Zanzibar in 1866 who renamed her *El Majidi*. She was beached and damaged by a hurricane that hit Zanzibar in April 1872 but seems to have survived another seven years, until her demise near the island of Socotra, just off Somalia's Cape Guardafui at the head of the Gulf of Aden, apparently en route from Zanzibar to Bombay to be repaired.

### 1 March 1880

Report of Henry Hughes, Master of the abandoned ship Mistress of the Seas, of Greenock:-
"Sailed from Philadelphia Jan. 23, for Bremerhaven, with a cargo of petroleum, and crew of 25 men. Had fine weather until Jan. 29, thence continuation of heavy gales, veering from

SSW to NNW, with nasty cross seas. Everything went on well until Feb. 12, lat. 43 20 N, long. 34 22 W, when we experienced a strong gale, veering from SW to NW, high sea, ship running under two lower topsails, foretopmaststaysail. 7 P.M., blowing a terrific gale from W, with very high sea, shipped a heavy sea on port quarter, washing men away from wheel, carrying away steering apparatus, broke spanker boom, filled cabin, when ship broached to, and three sails were blown away.

Shipped also two heavy seas, smashing all boats, clearing decks, bulwarks, and rails; skylight was washed away, and ship going on her beam-ends, cut away the backstays, when mizentopmast went over the side, fore and main topgallantmasts and topmastheads carried away, when ship righted a little.

After mustering crew, found that Charles Swanson (Swede), Richard Page, of Liverpool, Alfred Norden (Swede), and G. Colgur (Austrian), seamen, were missing. 10 P.M., mainyard went over the side, carried away topsailyard with it. Pumps were set to work with donkey-engine as soon as there was a chance to light the fire. Gale continued for 15 hours, and on Feb. 14 found water gaining on us, there being 16 feet. At 3 P.M. we saw a ship. Hoisted signals of distress, but she could not render assistance before dark. She lay by us all night, and proved to be the American ship Ivy, of Bath (Me.).

At 7 A.M., Feb. 15, weather thick, the German ship Hermann hove in sight. The crew refused to remain by the ship, and, as nothing could be done towards saving her, asked the Hermann to take us on board. Eight men were taken off to her and 13 on board the American ship Ivy, including two officers, carpenter, nine A.B.s, and master. When we abandoned ship there were 21 feet of water in the hold, and vessel a complete wreck. After getting on board the Ivy were supplied with dry clothing, and during 10 days were treated with the greatest kindness by Captain Lowell and his officers."

Report of A.J. Lowell, Master of American ship Ivy, of Bath (Maine), at Havre, from New Orleans:- "Jan. 15, at 5 P.M., sailed from the Passes, and had variable winds and fine weather to Bermuda, thence to the Channel very heavy southerly and westerly gales. Feb. 12, lat. 42 35 N, long. 35 55 W, encountered a terrific gale from SW to W, lasting 18 hours, during which lost second mate (H.F. Deycke, of Sweden) overboard. Shifted cargo, giving the ship a bad list to port. Twisted rudder-head, stove cabin, wheelhouse, poop, and locker doors; washing away most of the stores and everything movable about decks. Several sails were blown from the gaskets, and portions blown away, sprung foretopsailyards, etc.

Feb. 14, blowing a gale at 3 P.M., sighted the British ship Mistress of the Seas, from Philadelphia for Bremerhaven, with signal of distress flying. I immediately hauled to the wind, but could not reach her before dark; laid by until morning (15th), being thick and rainy; sighted her at 8 A.M.; bore down and spoke her. The captain and crew wished to be taken off, as the ship was in a sinking condition, and her boats all stove.

The German ship Hermann was hove to leeward, and sent a boat, which put five seamen on board this ship, then returned to their ship with eight more and did not return. Immediately put out a boat and sent her in charge of the first officer and rescued those remaining, consisting of the captain, first and second officers, carpenter, and four seamen, whose names are as follows:- Henry Hughes, captain, of Wales; Robert Davies, first officer, of Wales; David Leith, second officer, of Scotland; Archie McNeal, carpenter, of Scotland. Seamen: Samuel Armour, of Ireland; Barkley R. Hewitt, of New Jersey (U.S.); L. Manuel, of

Malta; Nels A. Byrke, of Norway; W. Rickett, of England; W. Smith, of England; W.O. Brien, England; Gustaf Frieden, Sweden; W. Ellis, Maine (U.S.).

The above were rescued in lat. 43 10 N, long. 31 22 W. The weather was bad, and sea running high, and for five days after it blew a heavy gale from WNW to WSW, with very large cross-seas. They saved but very little clothing."

## 28 Sept 1881

**Casualties – Home**

Liverpool, Sept. 27, 2 35 p.m.- Acadia*, ship, from San Francisco for Queenstown, wrecked on Ducie's Island, South Pacific, about lat. 28 S, long. 124 46 W, at 8 p.m., June 5. Crew landed at Pitcairn Island June 15.

## 14 Oct 1881

**Casualties – Home**

Falmouth, Oct. 13, 10 40 a.m.- Acadia – The American ship Edward O'Brien, from San Francisco, arrived to-day and landed Captain George and three of the crew of the ship Acadia, of Liverpool, which had been wrecked on Ducie Island. The crew saved themselves in the boats, and sailed 350 miles to Pitcairn's Island, where they remained 15 days, until the Edward O'Brien called off the island.

## 27 Oct 1881

**Casualties – Foreign**

New York, Oct. 14.- Acadia – Montagnais – The Avona, at San Francisco 12th Oct., from Auckland, has on board five of the crew of ship Acadia, before reported wrecked on Ducie Island. The crew reached Pitcairn's Island in a boat, whence these men were taken by the Avona. The Avona also brought the captain and other officers and crew of ship Montagnais, from Hull for Wilmington (Cal.). The coal of the Montagnais took fire Oct. 2, in lat. 37 37 N, long. 141 47 W. The Avona sighted her, and, after lying by her two days, took all hands off.

*The *Acadia*, a three-masted iron ship, was wrecked on Ducie Island, one of the four islands of the Pitcairn group, the others being Henderson, Oeno, and Pitcairn itself (the final refuge of the HMS *Bounty* mutineers). Pitcairn was first discovered by Europeans on 3 July 1767 when Midshipman Robert Pitcairn sighted it from on board the British sloop HMS *Swallow*. It was thus named after him as Pitcairn's Island, or, as it is known today, Pitcairn Island. In 1938 the British government incorporated Ducie, Henderson, Oeno and Pitcairn as the Pitcairn Islands group, today one of Britain's most remote British Overseas Territories.

Ducie is a 1.5 sq mile atoll, fringed by a circular coral reef. The report above estimates Ducie's position as being at "about lat. 28 S"; in fact it is at 24° 40' S. Ducie's longitude – "124 46 W" – is correct as stated. Pitcairn was more or less on the direct route of vessels sailing from the west coast of North America to round Cape Horn into the Atlantic, and was often sighted by them.

After wrecking on Ducie's coral reef, the *Acadia*'s crew took sail in one of the ship's boats and headed for the main island in the group, Pitcairn, 340 miles (540 km) away to the west. They stopped at Henderson, a little more than half way between Ducie and Pitcairn, probably to look for fresh water (which they would not have found, there being none there), and arrived at Pitcairn on 15 June, ten days after they were wrecked.

One of the *Acadia* crew members, a sailmaker from Nantucket named Phillip Coffin (a venerable Nantucket surname), married a Pitcairn girl and settled on the island. Another, Albert Knight, became enamoured of another local girl, 20 year old Maria Young. She, however, was already engaged to a Pitcairn man, of the Christian family (a descendant of Fletcher Christian, the leader of the original *Bounty* mutineers), although she actually married someone else, Charles Edwards. (She later went to Tonga where she died on 13 October 1934.). Knight was taken off Pitcairn by HMS *Sapho* in July 1882 and banished from ever returning. (A law was subsequently passed prohibiting 'strangers' to Pitcairn from settling there.)

In 1990 the expeditionary cruise ship *World Discoverer* recovered the *Acadia*'s anchor off Ducie and presented it to the people of Pitcairn. The anchor now lies at Adamstown, the only settlement at Pitcairn, overlooking the cliffs that lead down to Bounty Bay. At Ducie itself, the largest island in the atoll has been named Acadia and a monument erected there as a memorial to the recovery of the *Acadia*'s anchor.

## 22 Oct 1881

### Casualties – Foreign

Aden, Oct. 21, 7 45 a.m.- Koning der Nederlanden*, Nederland Steamship Co.'s steamer, broke her shaft Oct. 4, in stern bush, and foundered in lat. 5 S, long. 64 E; Wyberton picked up a boat containing 38 persons; six boats, with 175 persons, missing. [The Koning der Nederlanden was bound from Batavia (Jakarta) for Amsterdam.]

Another account: Oct. 20, 9 55 p.m.- Wyberton arrived at Aden on Thursday. On 11th inst. picked up a boat with 38 people, 350 miles W by N of Chagos [Islands, northern Indian Ocean]. Koning der Nederlanden's shaft carried away near stern pipe; she foundered at sea 5th inst., lat. 5 S, long. 64 E; six boats missing, with 175 people. Assistance will be sent to Chagos immediately. Searched all day; no avail. Will take cabin passengers and others to Port Said [Egypt, at Mediterranean entry to Suez Canal].

### 24 Oct 1881

### Casualties – Foreign

Rotterdam, Oct. 21.- Koning der Nederlanden- According to a telegram of yesterday's date from Aden, the Koning der Nederlanden (s), Bruyns, from Batavia for Holland, broke her shaft in the sternpost, Oct. 4, in lat. 5 S, long. 64 E, so that water penetrated into the vessel, in consequence of which she had to be abandoned next day, and afterwards sank. All who were on board got into the boats, which were provisioned for three weeks, and set course for the Chagos Islands.

The Wyberton (s), Blacklin, on Oct. 11, picked up one of the boats, containing the first officer, a portion of the crew, and some passengers, and brought them to Aden yesterday. When this boat was picked up the other boats were not in sight. The first officer expects that they would reach the Chagos Islands. The authorities at Aden have telegraphed to Ceylon to send out a man-of-war to the Chagos Islands. [N.B. The Chagos Islands are situated about 440 sea miles east from the position where the disaster occurred.]

*29 Oct 1881*

**Casualties – Foreign**

The Hague, Oct. 27.- One of the six missing boats of the lost steamer Koning der Nederlanden has been picked up in the Indian Ocean by the steamship Delcomyn and taken to Aden. This is the storekeeper's boat and contained 19 persons.

*9 Nov 1881*

**Casualties – Foreign**

The Hague, Nov. 7.- Twenty-seven passengers of the Koning der Nederlanden have been landed at Dondra, at the southern extremity of Ceylon. One was a woman. One hundred and twenty-nine passengers are still missing. The report of Captain Blacklin, of the steamer Wyberton, says that the ship sank half an hour after the passengers got into the boats. These remained four days together. Then one drifted away till it fell in with the Wyberton. Captain Blacklin searched one day for the other boats. Wanting coals, he proceeded to Aden. The rescued persons were exhausted by exposure to rain and heat.

*15 Nov 1881*

**Casualties – Foreign**

Aden, Nov. 13.- Koning der Nederlanden – The Madura (s), from Batavia, arrived here last night from the Chagos Islands with Captain Bruyns and 38 of the passengers and crew of the Koning der Nederlanden (s), having fallen in with them at the Solomon Islands [*sic*].

The passengers saved are:- Mdme. Kosting Deheus and her daughter, Mdlle. Vanwae-geningh, and MM. Vanossenbruggen, Lageman, Reinking, Heintz, and De Torbal. M. Trap, the boatswain, M. Zeelt, second officer, M. Koch, third engineer, Dr. Fitz, and Seegers, the steward, were also rescued, together with 13 men of the crew and 12 soldiers. Two bags of mails were recovered. The captain of the Madura reports that Her Majesty's gunboat Ready was at Diego Garcia on the 30th ult., and would shortly proceed to the Maldive Islands in search of the remainder of the passengers and crew.

*12 Dec 1881*

**Casualties – Foreign**

Galle [Ceylon/Sri Lanka], Nov. 19.- Koning der Nederlanden, Dutch steamer.- One boat (starboard No. 3), in charge of the boatswain (Keyzer), arrived at Dandaro Bay on the 6th inst., with 26 persons, including one lady. The saved persons arrived here on the 7th, and embarked for Amsterdam on the 15th inst., in the Prins van Oranje.

*The 3,063-ton steamship *Koning der Nederlanden* had left Batavia (Jakarta, in Indonesia) on 24 September 1881, bound for Amsterdam with around 212 passengers and crew. (Indonesia was a Dutch colonial protectorate at the time.) Two weeks later, on 4 October, the vessel was between the Chagos Archipelago and the Seychelles in the Indian Ocean, heading for the Red Sea and the Suez Canal, when her propeller shaft broke. She filled with water and foundered soon after. Four boatloads of passengers and crew, totaling 122 persons, including Captain Bruyns, survived the disaster. Around 90 others, were never found, presumed lost.

## 5 Sept 1882

**Casualties – Foreign**

Modern.- (*St. Denis, Reunion, Aug. 4*) On July 16 a caffre [pejorative term for a black African] went to the seaside to fish, and when passing a creek called Makake Hole, observed a boat on the shingle. He called several fishermen who were in the neighbourhood, and they, on going up to the boat, found a large rope in the water; they got hold of it, and 20 people managed to haul it out after great exertions. There was a piece of rope of the same dimensions attached to the bow of the boat, which leads to the supposition that the boat had been moored, and that the force of the sea had broken her moorings.

Next day the police took possession of the articles found in the boat, and on the 18th, upon searching the beach, two dead bodies were found about 20 yards from the boat. The younger of the two appeared to be about 20 years of age; his skull was crushed. On his breast was tattooed the name "John Temple"; also, on the right fore-arm, a woman enveloped in drapery, which she holds in her right hand; underneath were the words "Young America," and several other devices in blue, red, violet, and black. On the left arm were two compasses crossed, forming a star, with the initials "t, j, h, s, s, t," a woman holding a crown in her left hand, and several other tattooings, in various colours. The first three fingers of the left hand were tattooed at the third joint.

The other body seemed to be that of a man about 45 years old, and was without marks; the right leg and the left arm were gone; round the waist was a leather belt, with a sheath.

The boat is a whale-boat, measuring about 20 feet long, and 6 feet 6 inches wide, with four thwarts; in the lockers on both sides was a quantity of cork in pieces, and the following words were cut upon the thwarts with a knife - "W. William, born Plymouth Bark Modern which burnt at sea June 25, lat. 32 S, long. 64 E." A small piece of plank was found among the shingle, having on it upon one side, "Burnt at sea, lat. 32 S, June 25, 1882, long. 64 E," and on the other side, "Bark Modern Androssan Rt Pringle." – [The Modern, barque, of Ardrossan [Ayrshire, Scotland], Stewart, sailed from Shields March 20, for Batavia [Jakarta, Indonesia], and was spoken May 17, in lat. 16 S, long. 27 W.

## 6 Feb 1883

**Casualties, Etc.**

Canima.- New York, Jan. 22.- The Canima (s), Davies, from St. John's and Halifax, which arrived Jan. 19, reports:- "Jan. 19, 3 a.m., off eastern end of Long Island, collided with brig Mariposa, Haskell, from Perth Amboy [New Jersey] for Boston, with coal. The Canima was struck on the port side near the bows, carrying away foretopmast and chafing side. The Mariposa was sunk almost immediately, carrying down with her the captain and five men – one only escaped.

*The New York Times*

**21st January 1883**

**Seven Lives Lost at Sea**

**The Brigantine Mariposa Sunk in a Collision**

*Struck By the Steamship Canima Near Fisher's Island – Only One Man Saved – A Struggle for Life*

The steam-ship Canima, which arrived Friday evening from Halifax, bore evidence of having been in collision with another vessel. Capt. Davies reported that early that morning when off the end of Long Island he was run into by the brigantine Mariposa, which sank shortly afterward. One of her seamen, a young man named Charles H. Powers, was saved, but the other members of the crew of the lost vessel were all drowned….The crew consisted of Mate Henry Clifford, of Cherry-street, this city; Second Mate John Norton, of Nova Scotia; Seamen Michael Kent and Patrick Donovan, of St. John, New Brunswick; Martin Emerson, of Norway; and young Powers, who is a native of Eastport, Me., and a colored cook whose name was unknown.

At 3 A.M. on Friday the Mariposa had passed through the Sound [ie., Long Island Sound] and was off Fisher's Island, which is near the end of Long Island….Powers, the sole survivor of the Mariposa, says he was awakened by the cry of "All hands on deck!" He sprang from his berth and hurried on deck. The sailors appeared greatly alarmed. On the starboard side a red light appeared and the dark outlines of a steam-ship loomed up very close at hand. In an instant there was a terrific crash and the vessel listed heavily. The topgallantmasts came down from aloft and Powers hurried under shelter of one of the deck-houses. In a moment he emerged and saw the steam-ship backing away with her foretopmast gone and two large holes in her port bow. The brigantine had been struck on her starboard bow, which had been nearly torn from the rest of her hull.

Capt. Haskell ordered the men to launch the boat, which had been lashed on deck. This was hurriedly put over the side. The brigantine was settling rapidly down in the water. She could not remain afloat more than a moment longer, and four of the crew sprang into the boat. They were followed by Capt. Haskell. The Mate, Emerson, the Norwegian, and the cook were still on deck. Their companions begged them to hurry into the boat, as the brigantine was sinking. But the mate hurried down into the cabin, while the two others went forward. It is supposed that they had left money or valuables in their berths which they were anxious to get.

None of the three men returned to the deck again, for at that moment the vessel plunged forward and her bows sank beneath the surface. The stern was about to follow when the boat pushed off. In an instant she was in the midst of a perfect whirlpool which had been caused by the sinking vessel, the masts of which were sinking rapidly. The boat gave a tremendous lurch and capsized. The men were now struggling in the waves. They reached the bottom of the up-turned boat where they clung and looked around to see if the steam-ship was about to send them aid. But that vessel was a long distance off.

They clung for a few moments in silence. Then Powers looked around to see if all were there, but Capt. Haskell was missing, he having been unable to retain his hold. Powers noticed a moment later that another man was missing. He looked around again and found that no one but Donovan and himself were clinging to the overturned boat. The others had relaxed their hold without a word, to denote that they had given up the struggle.

The two survivors cried out for help but received no answer. A piece of wreckage drifted by, and Donovan left the boat and took refuge on it. Powers saw him clinging to it a moment later. Then came a heavy wave, which dashed Powers from the up-turned boat. He made a desperate struggle, and succeeded in regaining his lost position. He looked around, but saw nothing of Donovan. He was now numb from cold and exposure, but he still clung, with a grip of iron, to the boat's keel. The steam-ship was far off and no boat was approaching. Then he lost consciousness....

The brigantine had disappeared, but as the sea was smooth, the officers of the Canima hoped that the crew had taken to their boat and were still safe. A life-boat from the steam-ship was sent in search of them. Twenty-five minutes after the brigantine went down the crew of the life-boat found Powers in an unconscious state still grasping the keel of the upturned boat.

## 23 Feb 1883

### Casualties, Etc.

Adrienne – Shanklin, I.W. [Isle of Wight], Feb. 21. – The Deal lugger Pride of the Sea landed here to-day the captain and crew (eight all told) of the brig Adrienne, of Aberystwith [north Wales], Captain Jones, from New York for Ayr [west coast of Scotland] (oilcake). The captain reports having experienced terrific weather in the Atlantic. On the 9th inst., a heavy sea fell on board, washing away the deck-house, and the mate being within he was washed overboard and drowned. On the 15th inst., when about 200 miles west of Azores, they were sighted by the Marcia (s), from New Orleans bound for Copenhagen, and rescued from their vessel, she being in a foundering state at the time. They saved a few of their effects, and were transferred to the lugger about five miles off St. Catherine's.

Adrienne. – Cowes [Isle of Wight], Feb. 22, 10 50 A.M. – Captain Jones and the survivors of the brig Adrienne, of Aberystwith, from New York for Ayr, with oil-cake, were landed at Shanklin yesterday. The vessel was abandoned on the 15th inst. in lat. 41 53 N, long. 24 56 W. The men were rescued from the vessel by the boat of the steamer Marcia, of London, and transferred to the lugger Pride of the West, of Deal, and sent to their homes by the agent of the Shipwrecked Mariners' Society.*

The master reports that the vessel experienced a hurricane from north-west on the 11th inst., and had after deck-house, bulwarks, stanchions, boats, steering-wheel and all movables on deck carried away. The vessel made much water, and took a strong list to port. As soon as the weather moderated, [they] jettisoned part of cargo. Owing to the condition of the vessel and to the crew being exhausted, hoisted signals of distress and left her in a sinking state. The mate was swept away with the after deck-house and drowned.

*The Shipwrecked Mariners' Society was established in 1839 as a result of the loss of a number of fishing boats and fishermen from Clovelly on the north Devon coast in 1838. From its headquarters in Chichester, West Sussex, the Society today gives over £1 million a year in financial assistance to "merchant seafarers, fishermen and their dependents who are in need." The motto of the Society used to be for many years "There is sorrow on the sea."

## 22 Nov 1883

### Casualties, Etc.

Rocabey.- Fayal [Azores], Nov. 10.- On Nov. 8 the Thomas Dana, American ship, from Liverpool for New York, landed here 21 men, being the boatswain and part of the crew and passengers of the Rocabey, French brig, Touze, from St. Pierre (Miquelon)* for St. Malo, which vessel was sunk by collision with her Oct. 30, in lat. 48 N, long. 15 W. The Rocabey

TO THE RESCUE.

foundered immediately after the collision. The remainder of the crew and passengers, numbering 88 men, perished.

*The French territorial islands of St. Pierre & Miquelon lie just off the south coast of Newfoundland. An interesting point about this report is that, despite the substantial death toll of 88 passengers and crew who perished on the French brig *Rocabey* when it collided with the *Thomas Dana* and sank, virtually no other news of the tragedy appeared in the press. (Reuters wrote a 36 word report about it, "Collision in the Atlantic," datelined Paris, November 21). The passengers on the *Rocabey* were probably mainly poor immigrants from the fishing islands of St. Pierre & Miquelon going to live in France. The loss of life of such people of a low social status, even when it was substantial, was usually reported with only minimal details, as here.

## 1 Dec 1883

### Maritime Intelligence

Oswingo – San Francisco, Nov 13 – The Oswingo, British barque, Kewin (reported by telegraph as having foundered), left Sydney, Aug. 10, for Wilmington [California], and from the very day of leaving encountered heavy weather. On Aug. 24 she experienced a tremendous NW gale, and shipped a sea, which damaged the pumps, leaving only one to work with. Next day a heavy sea carried away bulwarks and stanchions and stove in main hatch, through which large quantities of water got below. The bad weather still continued, and the vessel strained heavily and became leaky.

On Sept. 2, Oparo Island* (in lat. 28 S) was sighted, and on the 4th, the barque had to be abandoned with 10 feet water in hold 16 miles from that island. After the crew had left her the vessel went down. The crew landed on the island, and were kindly treated by the natives, and the 14th were taken on board by the French gunboat Volage, which brought them to Tahiti, with the exception of two who remained on Gambier Island.

*Oparo was the old European name for Rapa (or Rapa Iti) Island, the largest and only inhabited island of the Bass Islands group in French Polynesia, located at lat 27° 35' S, long 144° 20' W. Sometimes called "Rapa Iti" ("Little Rapa") to distinguish it from "Rapa Nui" ("Big Rapa"), the indigenous name for Easter Island, it was first discovered by Europeans when Capt. George Vancouver RN sighted, and named it Oparo, in 1791. Its population today is around 500.

'Gambier Island' is actually a group of islands (the Tuamotu-Gambier Islands) some 350 miles to the northeast of Rapa, on the southeast corner of French Polynesia. The main island, Mangareva, is probably what was meant by 'Gambier Island'. It is well off the track of a ship going directly from Rapa to Tahiti, unless the ship was, possibly like the French gunboat here, making a tour of the islands before heading back to base at Tahiti.

## 2 April 1884

### Casualties, Etc.

Rainier.- Saigon, Feb. 29.- On Jan. 18, the Catalina, barque, from Newcastle (N.S.W.) for Saigon, fell in with a boat containing the mate and five men of the ship Rainier, of Bath (Me.), which vessel had been wrecked, on Jan. 2, on an islet called Ujaae*, one of the

Marshall group, lat. 9 14 N, long. 166 56 E. One man died on board the Catalina, exhausted. There remained on the islet 22 men and one woman. Captain Williams, of the Catalina, put his ship round and tried, although 300 miles away, to make the wreck, but, in the teeth of strong trades [trade winds], could make no progress. The Rainier was laden with 73,000 cases of petroleum. She is a total loss.

### 19 May 1884

Rainier.- Bath, Me.- May 6.- A private telegram received here announces the safe arrival at Yokohama, of Captain Morrison and crew of the ship Rainier, which was wrecked on one of the Marshall Islands in the Pacific Ocean.

*Ujae Atoll, on the western edge of the Marshall Islands, is a 27 mile long atoll of less than 1 sq mile land area and a lagoon area of 72 sq miles. The *Catalina* could not, practically, have gone to the aid of the castaways on Ujae, because the northeast trades would have been blowing dead against her. The *Rainier*'s captain and crew were most likely rescued by a passing ship and landed at Yokohama in Japan, some 900 miles northeast of Ujae.

## 9 April 1884

### Casualties, Etc.

Alba.- Lerwick [Shetland Islands], April 6.- The Danish barque Alba, wrecked at Whalsay, left Copenhagen on March 30, and experienced fine weather till the morning of the 31st, when the wind commenced to blow strongly from the SE. It continued to increase, and on the afternoon of April 1 the vessel was running before the wind under close-reefed sails. About 10 o'clock on the same evening, the night being very dark and the wind very strong, the vessel was running in a heavy sea, when suddenly breakers were seen right ahead, and before anything could be done she struck on the rocks with a fearful crash, and in a couple of minutes the vessel was in pieces. All the crew, 12 in number, were on deck at the time, but only one of the seven passengers who was not below, a Lutheran pastor named Washbeck, who formed one of Baron Nordenskjold's exploration party to the Arctic regions last year.

The captain and eight sailors were standing on the poop deck when the after part of the vessel was carried away by the sea. The foremast fell on the rocks on which the vessel had struck – a reef lying about half a mile from the shore. By this means the mate, two seamen, and one passenger managed to crawl on to the rocks. None of the other passengers were ever seen again. The four survivors spent a terrible night on the reef, over which the sea was continually sweeping, and they were compelled to stretch themselves at full length and cling to the crevices of the rocks with their hands. They were much exhausted when rescued next morning by a boat from the shore.

## 6 Sept 1884

### Maritime Intelligence

Lastingham*.- London, Sept. 6.- A telegram has been received from Wellington announcing the total loss on Jackson's Head, Cook's Strait [separating New Zealand's North Island from South Island], New Zealand, of the ship Lastingham (owned by Mr. John Leslie), which sailed from London for Wellington, with a general cargo and five passengers, on May 29.

*21 Oct 1884*

## Maritime Intelligence

Lastingham.- Melbourne, Sept. 9.- The Lastingham, from London for Wellington, encountered a heavy gale at the entrance to Cook's Straits on the evening of Sept. 1, and was driven on to the rocks at Cape Jackson, the northeast extremity of the Middle Island. The captain, twelve of the crew, and the whole of the passengers (five) were drowned, but 11 of the crew escaped on to the rocks and were taken on to Wellington in a passing schooner. The vessel is a total wreck.

\*The *Lastingham* was a 1,217-ton iron ship, built in 1876, and just a day away from her destination of Wellington in New Zealand when she foundered after striking rocks in Cook Strait during stormy weather. The ship was battered by heavy seas for an hour or so before she slipped off the rocks and sank with the loss of the captain, his wife, all five passengers and ten (or possibly twelve) crew.

# 5 June 1885

## Terrible Sufferings In An Open Boat

The Warren Line steamer Missouri, which has arrived at Liverpool from Boston, was instrumental in saving 20 persons from what would have been a terrible death. The persons in question were the captain and crew of the ship Themis, and the captain's wife and two children. On the steamer's arrival in Liverpool eight of the crew were taken to one of the North End hospitals suffering severely from frostbite. The remainder of the crew were also suffering more or less from the same cause. Six of the survivors were received by the local agent of the Shipwrecked Mariners' Society, and yesterday told a sad tale of their experience in the ice off the Banks of Newfoundland [the Grand Banks].

The Themis was going from Havre to Miramichi [New Brunswick] in ballast, and when off the Banks a thick fog set in. On the following night, about 11 o'clock, the ship was found to be almost surrounded by three immense icebergs. One of these struck the vessel and smashed in her bows. She made much water, and the boats were lowered. One was smashed, but the longboat was got out safely. The captain, his wife and children, and the crew of the Themis left their vessel, and in a few moments afterwards heard a great crash, and surmised, as it was too dark to see, that their ship had been crushed between the three floating monsters. Next morning nothing could be seen of her.

The crew made for clear water, with the hope of falling in with some vessel. Nothing was seen for three days, at the end of which time a steamer hove in sight. The crew waved a shirt on an oar, with a view of attracting the attention of those on board, but the steamer proceeded on her course, and nothing further was seen for three days more, and the sufferings of those in the boat were of the keenest description. They had but a small quantity of water and biscuits when they left their vessel, and had subsisted on a biscuit and a half per day ever since. Even this was at last curtailed, and eventually not a drop of fresh water remained.

Many of the crew had become perfectly helpless through frostbite, and some, to quench their thirst, had drank the salt water. This only increased their sufferings. When they had almost given up hope of ever being rescued a steamer was descried. This was on the seventh day after the abandonment. To the horror of the men this steamer also went away, but they had scarcely time to give way to their disappointment when the Missouri came up.

The Missouri made for the direction in which the boat was, and a white handkerchief waved at the side told them they were seen. The shipwrecked crew had a distress signal up composed of a blanket on an oar. Several of the men had to be hauled on board the Missouri, and those who were able at once made a rush for the fresh water. They had to be restrained by the doctor and crew of the Missouri. The men received every possible attention from the doctor and others on board the rescuing steamer, and yesterday expressed themselves in the highest terms of thankfulness at their treatment. The rescue itself was most timely, as the men aver that if they had been another day exposed in the open boat many would doubtless have succumbed to their sufferings.

The Themis was a vessel of 975 tons register, and was owned in St. John (N.B.). The men were exactly seven nights and six days in the open boat before they were rescued.

## THE *DERRY CASTLE* SURVIVORS (AND OTHERS) AT THE AUCKLAND ISLANDS

## 21 Sept 1887

**Maritime Intelligence**

Derry Castle*.- Melbourne, Sept. 21, 1 30 p.m.- Derry Castle, from Geelong for London, totally wrecked on Auckland Islands March 20; eight persons only saved, and landed here.

### *28 Sept 1887*

**Maritime Intelligence**

Derry Castle.- Melbourne, Sept. 28.- The Derry Castle struck on a rock at 2 a.m. and foundered; not possible to recover anything; officers drowned; one passenger and seven crew saved.

### *15 Nov 1887*

**Maritime Intelligence**

Derry Castle.- Melbourne, Sept. 24.- The Derry Castle, ship, Geelong for London; eight survivors (seven seamen and one passenger) of the wreck of this vessel reached Melbourne in the Awarua ketch [*sic* – the *Awarua* was a schooner] on the 21st inst., and reported that during the night of March 20 she ran at full speed on to the rocks at Enderby Island, Auckland Islands, and went to pieces almost immediately, the officers and 12 of the crew being drowned. The remaining seven and the passenger subsisted for nearly four months in what they could pick up on the islands, until they were taken off.

*The *Derry Castle* was an iron barque of 1,367 tons (gross), 239.8ft long, 36ft beam, and 21.4ft deep. She was built at Glasgow in 1883 by the shipbuilder Dobie Co. and owned by Speight & Co., of Limerick, Ireland. On 12 March 1887 the ship sailed from the port of Geelong, near Melbourne, under the command of Capt. J. Goffe, with a cargo of wheat, bound for Falmouth, England, via Cape Horn. That was the last anyone heard of her for four and a half months. Lloyd's posted her as missing. Like the fate of many other ships, the circumstances of the *Derry Castle*'s demise were assumed to be unknown, and never to be ascertained.

On 21 September, over six months later, however, a small (45 tons) sealing schooner, the *Awarua*, sailed into Hobson's Bay, Melbourne, and landed eight survivors from the wreck of the *Derry Castle* they had lived as castaways on Enderby Island, in the Auckland Islands, 125 miles or so south of New Zealand, for 130 days. The other fifteen crew members had drowned when the ship was wrecked.

So, as improbable as it might have seemed, there *were* witnesses to the final moments of the *Derry Castle*'s life who survived to recount how the ship was wrecked, and to tell the story of their subsequent privation and suffering.

Eight days after leaving Geelong the *Derry Castle* was sailing with a fresh wind behind her, all sails set, at up to 12 knots. She was heading around the south of New Zealand on her course for the Horn and thence towards Falmouth, which she would expect to reach within about four months. Just before 2 a.m. on the night of 20 March 1887, in *dirty* weather, and without the slightest warning of danger, she slammed into submerged rocks off Enderby Island, the northernmost of the Auckland Islands. The ship broke in two and began to sink. The crew and only passenger, James McGhie, swam for their lives. The shore was just 200 yards away. Only eight made it there alive - seven of the crew and McGhie.

The following morning the eight castaways spied the *Derry Castle*'s sailmaker clinging for dear life to the mizzenmast still sticking up from the wreck. He jumped into the sea and almost made it to shore before the heavy surf swept him back out to drown, following in the wake of his 14 fellow crew members drowned already.

On their first morning as Enderby Island castaways, the eight men discovered the corpses of the captain, first mate and a seaman, washed ashore in the seaweed. Sea birds had plucked out their eyes. The grinding roil of the surf had mutilated their bodies. After stripping them of anything useful (such as clothing), the castaways buried the three dead men in a communal grave they dug out with a knife. Afterwards, exploring the island, they found a small hut and food depot for wrecked seamen. A pint bottle of salt was all it contained. Some food from the wreck floated ashore – some tins of herring, some of the cargo of wheat, and a pumpkin – but otherwise their only food was shellfish from the rocks.

Needing fire, for warmth (winter was coming on) and cooking, they used a revolver cartridge that passenger McGhie had in his pocket, to detonate and strike a flame. They roasted grain over the fire they made which they ground and made into a potable drink like coffee. Fortunately, the island was well endowed with springs of fresh water for the castaways to drink. But their real hope of salvation lay on the main island, at the inlet of Port Ross, visible across the water, where they supposed that a New Zealand government provisions depot had been established. (The New Zealand government established provisions depots on the islands in 1867, as a result of the plight of the castaways from the wrecked *General Grant* in 1866 who spent a year and a half on the Aucklands before being rescued [see below].)

After three months the men found an old axe head buried in the sand. This they used as a tool to build a small boat to get them across to Port Ross. Two of the men made the first crossing in the crudely constructed 6 ft long by 2½ ft wide dinghy. After three days they signalled by a smoking fire to their six comrades on Enderby that they had reached safety. The rest of the men and their meagre provisions were transported in several trips to Port Ross where they established a camp by the stores depot. They had been on Enderby Island from 20 March till 18 June.

A month later, on 19 July, the sealer *Awarua* sailed into Port Ross looking for a small boat it had left there some time before. The following morning the *Awarua's* master, Capt. Drew, went ashore where he discovered the eight survivors of the *Derry Castle*. Taking them on board his own vessel, he landed them at Melbourne two months later, on 21 September 1887.

It was later determined that the charts used by Capt. Goffe were out of date – they placed the Auckland Islands 32 miles further south than their actual position. Capt. Goffe was steering a course well to the north of where his charts showed the northernmost extremity of the islands to be. In fact, he was steering straight for Enderby Island, with the ensuing fatal consequences for his ship, and for him and 14 of his crew.

## THE GENERAL GRANT

The *Derry Castle* survivors were by no means the only, nor even the longest-term castaways saved from the Auckland Islands. On 21 November 1867 ten men and one woman were rescued from Auckland Island by the whaling brig *Amherst*. They had been shipwrecked there for almost 18 months, having survived the wreck of their ship the *General Grant* (1,095 tons) in the early hours of 14 May 1866, after leaving Melbourne on 4 May that year, bound for London with a cargo of wool, hides and gold.

Eighty-three people shipped on board the *General Grant* at Melbourne (though another witness at the inquiry testified that the number was 80: "56 passengers, amongst whom were six ladies and about twenty children; the crew consisted of 24 men, all told."). Most perished at the time the ship was wrecked. Four survivors of the wreck were apparently lost at sea when they attempted to sail in a small boat from Auckland Island to New Zealand on 22 January 1867. One survivor, David McLelland, aged 62, died on 3 September of that year after almost sixteen months cast away. The remaining clutch of eleven *General Grant* survivors was rescued by the *Amherst*, commanded by Capt. P. Gilroy, and landed at Bluff, a small seaport on the south coast of the South Island of New Zealand, on 17 January 1868.

## 5 Oct 1887

### Maritime Intelligence

> Dunskeig.- Buenos Ayres, Sept. 2.- A telegram, dated Viedma (south coast of Patagonia), Aug. 31, gives the following particulars respecting the losses of the Dunskeig and Colorado:- The Mercurio (s) anchored here today. She brought the first mate and some of the sailors of the British ship Dunskeig, and the master (James) and seven men of the British barque Colorado.

The Dunskeig, of Glasgow, was on her voyage from London to San Francisco, with a general cargo. On the night of June 23, during a northeast gale, she struck at Cape San Antonio, Staten Island [northeast of Cape Horn], and her stern was immediately submerged. The first and second mates, and the sailors saved themselves in the rigging; the master (Martin) and two boys were washed away. On June 24 the second mate, the boatswain, and a sailor tried to swim ashore, but were all drowned. In the afternoon a raft was constructed, but it broke up in the sea. The same happened to a second raft, and another sailor was drowned.

WRECK OF THE GENERAL GRANT ON THE AUCKLAND ISLANDS.—SEE PAGE 382.

At 4 p.m. the sail was cut away from the foremast, and the men used part of it as a shelter from the wind and rain. At 5 p.m. the mainmast fell into the sea, and four men succeeded in reaching the shore on another raft. One of them died the same night. On June 26 there was a fall of snow, and the steward and a boy died of the cold. At low tide the remainder of the crew got ashore on another raft, but five of them died soon afterwards, and others had their feet frostbitten.

On June 27 they constructed a tent, and on July 2 four men left to try to get round the island to the lighthouse, but they returned next day, the snow preventing them from proceeding. On Aug. 13 a fire was lighted on the point of the Cape, and it was kept up until Aug 19, when the Mercurio (s) came up. The next day she took them on board.

The Colorado, also belonging to Glasgow, was on her way from Hull to Valparaiso, with coals, and on July 5, at 8 p.m., she went ashore at Cape St. Vincent at entrance to Straits of Le Maire, Thetis Bay, Tierra del Fuego. There being seven feet of water in the vessel's hold, she had to be abandoned next day. The officers and crew, 15 men altogether, crossed Lemaire Strait in two boats, with a view to reach San Juan Lighthouse. They landed in Franklin Bay, and on July 29, the master and eight men started by land to find the lighthouse at Point San Juan. They marched for seven days without finding it, and the cook died. On Aug. 16 they arrived at Cape San Antonio, where they remained with the survivors of the Dunskeig's crew until Aug 19. They kept themselves alive with cocoa.

## 29 Oct 1887

**Maritime Intelligence**

**Miscellaneous**

Seaham, Oct. 28.- Captain Hall, of the Vecta, from Yarmouth, reports that at 9 30 p.m. on Oct. 27, Flamborough Head bearing south, distant about one mile, he passed a man on what was supposed [believed] to be some broken bulwark. In passing the man cried out, "Oh, my God!" As it was blowing a strong gale from SW at the time, no assistance could be rendered.

## 11 Dec 1888

**Maritime Intelligence**

**Miscellaneous**

London, Dec. 11.- Steamer City of Richmond, from New York, arrived at Queenstown last evening, and reported the arrival at Philadelphia, on the 29th ult., of the steamer Panama, from Marseilles. Her captain, Chabot, states that on the night of the 26th ult., during a cyclone 100 miles east of Cape Delaware, the signals of a vessel in distress were seen. After considerable difficulty, owing to the mountainous cross sea running, the steamer bore away in the direction of the distress signals, and found that they proceeded from a full-rigged ship under lower topsails, her hull being very deep in the water, and the waves sweeping over her. Captain Chabot distinctly saw the crew, numbering about 25. Some were in the mizen rigging, waving lights, and others were on the after house.

The latter were shouting in English that their ship was sinking, and they begged to be rescued. All efforts to bring the steamer sufficiently close to the ship to rescue the crew proved unavailing. While the steamer was standing by, all the lights and distress signals suddenly disappeared, and nothing of the ship was afterwards seen. Captain Chabot believes that she foundered with all hands.

## 13 April 1889

### Maritime Intelligence

Emelie.- London, Apr. 12.- The Holland (s), Captain Foot, from New York, arrived in the river 12th inst., reports having rescued at sea 11 of the crew of the German barque Emelie, of Geestemunde, bound from Pensacola for Brake, with timber. The vessel was fallen in with on the 7th inst., in lat. 47 58 N, long. 19 22 W, with only main lowermast standing and the crew in the mainrigging, where they had been for 20 hours. A heavy NW gale was blowing, and a high sea was breaking over the wreck.

The steamer lay by the wreck for seven hours, waiting for the sea to moderate. She then lowered her lifeboat, with Mr. Griffiths, the second officer, in charge, which, with great difficulty and risk to life, succeeded in saving the 11 survivors of the crew of the Emelie, which had previously lost three hands, who had been washed overboard and drowned before the lifeboat reached the wreck.

Captain Foot states that the wreck is in a position very dangerous to navigation, and there are large quantities of timber floating about her. The master, Ohling, of the Emelie, reports having experienced a succession of gales, in which the vessel sprung a leak, had boats washed away, and received other damage. The master and crew of the Emelie speak in most grateful terms of the admirable manner in which they were rescued, and also for the great kindness shown to them on board the steamer.

## 1 Nov 1889

### Maritime Intelligence

Arethusa.- Liverpool, Nov. 1, 11 53 a.m.- Arethusa, barque, Shields, July 13, to Valparaiso:- Telegram received by owners from Valparaiso states Arethusa totally lost; part crew have arrived at Falklands Oct. 7. One boat 13 men missing. Latest advices from Falklands Oct. 14. Names of the crew saved are not mentioned.

### *8 Nov 1889*

### Maritime Intelligence

Arethusa.- Stanley, F.I. (by Tel., dated Montevideo, Nov. 7, 12 25 p.m.).- Arethusa, Tyne for Valparaiso, burnt at sea; part of crew saved; captain died in port.

### *26 Nov 1889*

### Maritime Intelligence

Arethusa.- Liverpool, Nov. 25, 3 37 p.m.- Arethusa: Owners state, referring to our report November, we have received following telegram from Valparaiso respecting the missing boat containing 13 of crew of Arethusa, burnt at sea. Part of the crew picked up and landed here; MacLennad, Moody, Roulsby dead.

2 Dec.- Stanley, F.I., Oct. 17.- The Arethusa, of Liverpool, Hamilton, from the Tyne for Valparaiso, was abandoned about 50 miles off the islands [ie., Falklands], her hatches having blown off. After seven days at sea the longboat, with the captain, second mate and

eight men, arrived off this port, and was brought in by the schooner Hornet. These men had suffered terribly; the steward died in the boat, and the captain only lived a few hours after landing. Another boat containing the mate and thirteen hands is missing.

### 9 Jan [1890]

Arethusa.- Glasgow, Jan. 3.- Extract of letter received from Captain McMurty, of Lady Octavia, barque, dated Valparaiso, Nov. 21, 1889:-

"When about 150 miles NNW of Falkland Islands we picked up a boat belonging to barque Arethusa, of Liverpool, which ship had been abandoned on fire 10 days previous. The crew consisted of first mate, boatswain, cook, sailmaker, two boys, and six seamen. The cook was dead in the bottom of the boat, and we committed his body to the deep. The mate was lashed down in the boat, he having been delirious for some days; he never came to his senses and died on the second day. The boy also was only just alive, and he died 28 hours after we received him.

The feet of most of the men were very badly swollen and they were not able to walk, especially the apprentice boy, whose feet were decaying away, and will have to be amputated. He was sent to hospital, also three others, by H.M. Consul. The others are at the Sailors' Home. We received them on Oct. 12 and delivered them to Consul on Nov. 20."

## 12 Nov 1889

### Maritime Intelligence

Flying Venus.- Auckland, N.Z., Nov. 12, 11 25 a.m.:- Flying Venus, from San Francisco for Melbourne (timber), totally lost on Penrhyn Island*. Crew saved.

### 4 Dec 1889

### Maritime Intelligence

Flying Venus.- London, Dec. 4.- Advices received last night at Queenstown from Apia, Samoa, report that on the 4th ult. a small open boat arrived there containing nine men in an exhausted condition. They were part of the crew of the large Liverpool ship Flying Venus, which was wrecked on a coral reef, four miles south of Penrhyn Island, while on a voyage to Melbourne. The remainder of the crew were left on the island, and the British Consul has despatched a schooner to their assistance.

### 10 Jan [1890]

### Maritime Intelligence

Flying Venus.- London, Jan. 9.- A report in the *Scotsman* [newspaper] of the 7th inst. states that the remainder of the crew and passengers of the ship Flying Venus, who were left on the island where the vessel was wrecked, arrived in Auckland on Nov. 15, having been rescued by the steamer Richmond on Oct. 24, after being seven weeks on the island.

*Penrhyn Island, or Atoll, also called Tongareva, amongst other names, is the most northerly island of the northern chain of the Cook Islands in the South Pacific. The reef where the *Flying Venus* was wrecked on 6 September 1889, about three miles off the northeast corner of the island, was subsequently named Flying Venus Reef after the ship.

The British Consul at Apia in Samoa had ordered an inter-island trading schooner, the *Daisy*, to sail to Penrhyn to bring back the shipwrecked crew and passengers of the *Flying*

*Venus*. The steamer *Richmond*, however, which left Apia several days after the *Daisy*, arrived at Penrhyn almost two weeks before the *Daisy* to take off the shipwrecked castaways whom she transported to Auckland. So when the *Daisy* arrived at the island, there was no one for her to rescue. In order to make her voyage worthwhile, her master, Capt. Sopwith, loaded up the *Flying Venus'* cargo of Oregon timber which a local trader, a Mr Woonton, had recovered from the wreck, and brought it back to Apia nine days later.

Mr Woonton was an ex-sea captain, island trader and resident of Penrhyn He apparently acted as a *de facto* magistrate, doctor and general facilitator for the native people of the island well into the 20th century. A descendant, Dr Robert Philip Woonton (b. 5 Feb 1949) was Foreign Minister of the Cook Islands from 1999 - 2004 and Prime Minister from 2002 – 2004. In 2005 he was appointed High Commissioner to New Zealand but was relieved of his position in 2006 on the grounds that he was alleged to have organised a conspiracy to overthrow his successor as Prime Minister, Jim Marurai (elected in December 2004).

There is a preface to the *Flying Venus* incident directly related to it. Some time before the *Flying Venus* struck upon the reefs at Penrhyn, a four-masted vessel, the *Derby Park*, had loaded a cargo of timber from Vancouver, British Columbia, for delivery to Melbourne. En route, the vessel was wrecked on the northern reef of Penrhyn and was a total loss. When the original consignees of the cargo eventually realised that their vessel was lost, they loaded the *Flying Venus* with a second, duplicate order of timber for Melbourne. She, too, however, spilled her load onto the Penrhyn reef near the wreck of her predecessor.

The villagers nearby enjoyed a double stroke of luck: they salvaged the lumber of Oregon pine from both wrecks to use in building their houses, which the renowned circumnavigator Capt. J.C. Voss remarked upon when he stopped at Penrhyn on his voyage round the world on his yacht *Tilikum* in the early 1900s.

## 15 April 1890

**Maritime Intelligence**

Emilie*.- Invercargill [south coast of South Island, New Zealand], Apr. 14.- Emilie, showing Nicaraguan colours, foundered at sea; part of crew landed here; four of crew saved, captain drowned.

### *22 May 1890*

**Maritime Intelligence**

Emilie.- London, May 22.- The Emilie, Nicaraguan barque, from Bluff for Port Pirie, was totally lost off Cape Egmont, New Zealand, March 26; Captain (Small) and seven men drowned; remainder of crew saved.

### *28 May 1890*

**Maritime Intelligence**

Emilie.- Melbourne, April, 19.- Emilie, barque, from Bluff Harbour for Port Pirie, with timber, was thrown on her beam ends and dismasted by a squall in Foveaux Straits. After drifting five days, the vessel went ashore at Red Head, Southport, Stewart Island. The mate and three men who had remained with her escaped ashore, and after some suffering were found and brought to Bluff Harbour. The captain and seven of the crew got into a boat when she was dismasted, but it was swamped immediately and all in it drowned.

*The 729-ton wooden barque *Emilie* was built in 1875 and formerly named the *Arabella*. On 25 March 1890 she sailed from Bluff Harbour on the south coast of South Island, New Zealand, commanded by Capt. G.L. Small. She was loaded with a cargo of timber, bound for Port Pirie in the Spencer Gulf, South Australia. The day after her departure from Bluff she encountered hurricane force winds which caused her to leak and eventually become waterlogged. One boat being launched in the act of abandoning ship was smashed by a falling mast and eight of the nine men in it killed. The other man climbed back on board the ship which had been knocked on her side.

After she righted herself the *Emilie* drifted for five days. On 31 March the ship wrecked at Red Head on Stewart Island, about 16 miles off the south coast of New Zealand and separated from it by the Foveaux Strait. The four sailors who got ashore survived for a week on shellfish and a dead seal. They were rescued by a party of mutton-bird hunters who took them to Bluff, directly across Foveaux Strait, on the tug *Awarua* where they landed on 14 April. The mate, John Brownrigg, died in hospital shortly afterwards. [The *Awarua* had previously saved the survivors of the wreck of the *Derry Castle* at the Auckland Islands in 1887.]

## 3 Dec 1890

### Maritime Intelligence

Rolf.- Soderhamn [Sweden, on Gulf of Bothnia], Nov. 28.- The schooner Rolf, of Landscrona [Landskrona, Sweden], stranded south of Ago during a terrific snowstorm on Nov. 24. The master, mate, and cook arrived in a boat, with hands and feet frozen, at Ago Light (Hudikswall [50 km north of Soderhamn]), after passing 48 hours on a rocky islet. One man of the crew was drowned, and another frozen to death.

## 13 March 1891

### Maritime Intelligence

Bay of Panama.- Plymouth, March 12, 2 16 p.m.- In consequence of communication [with] Falmouth still interrupted, presume you have not details [of] wreck. Bay of Panama*, [from] Calcutta, [for] Dundee, [with] jute; learn vessel wrecked Penare Point, entrance [to] Halford River. Steamers went to her from Falmouth Wednesday morning, found her abandoned and mainmast gone. Captain, his wife, chief, second officer, boatswain, sailmaker, carpenter, steward, and six seamen, also four apprentices drowned.

One of the rescued states vessel 111 days out from Calcutta, two weeks since encountered heavy squalls, snowstorms. At 1 20 p.m. Monday, perfect hurricane, sighted light and thought to be steamer. Burnt blue lights, but Bay of Panama drifted leeward without canvas set. Captain remarked would clear Lizard and drift towards Western Ocean [ie., the open Atlantic], but at 1 30 a.m. Tuesday ship struck rocks heavily, captain being on deck.

She immediately began to fill fore and aft, seas burst hatches, and sweeping over ship many crew thus swept overboard; some took to rigging, and were found there frozen; others on forecastlehead saved by rocket apparatus. Captain's wife and other bodies found on beach. Expected vessel become total wreck.

Bay of Panama.- London, March 13.-...Captain, wife, and 17 crew drowned, including all officers.

*At 2,282 tons the *Bay of Panama* was one of the largest steel sailing vessels of her time. She was built by the Belfast shipbuilder Harland & Wolff in 1883 and measured 294ft long by 42.3ft wide and 24.3ft deep, rigged as a four-masted barque. On 18 November 1890 she left Calcutta with a cargo of 17,000 bales of jute, bound for Dundee, 'the jute capital of Scotland', under the command of Capt. Wright. Three and a half months later, in the western approaches to the English Channel, she encountered very heavy weather.

Near the Lizard, on 10 March 1891, the *Bay of Panama* was struggling against one of the worst blizzards ever known in the west of England and along the Cornish coast, with high seas and bitter cold. (The blizzard was the reason why "communication with Falmouth," in the above report, was disrupted.) The vessel rounded the Lizard peninsula but was driven ashore just past the treacherous group of offshore rocks called The Manacles, to the south of Nare Point, in the early hours of the morning.

For the rest of the night the ship was hammered by the violent weather. Tremendous icy seas washed over the wreck. The captain, his wife, the second mate and six sailors were swept overboard by a single wave and drowned. Six crew members tried to save themselves by clinging to the ship's rigging but froze to death. The bosun, unable to stand the wretched conditions, threw himself out of the rigging to suffer a quick death by drowning in the stormy seas.

The next morning a shepherd who was out tending his sheep came across the wreck on the rocks below. He alerted others who arrived later on the scene to rescue the survivors. Nineteen souls, including Capt. Wright and his wife, were lost in the wreck, out of a complement of 40. The 21 who were rescued were almost frozen corpses. They were brought to the village of St. Keverne to be revived and rested before making their way in a horse-drawn bus to Falmouth. Snowdrifts up to 30 feet high blocked the road: the men had to walk the rest of the way to Falmouth mostly barefoot and protected only by shreds of clothing and blankets. Their desperate trek was endured, according to *The Falmouth Packet* newspaper, with "as much privation" as they suffered in the actual shipwreck.

## 2 Sept 1891

### Maritime Intelligence

Ellen.- Melbourne, July 25.- Ellen, barque, Newcastle for Noumea [New Caledonia], sprang a leak six days after leaving port, which gained on the pumps, until the vessel had to be abandoned on the 12th inst., and sank an hour later. The officers and crew were in the boat for nine days, during which time the captain and steward died from exposure, and two of the sailors were washed overboard. When the boat reached the coast off Seal Rocks Lighthouse* there were only four left, three of whom were drowned by the capsizing of the boat.

*"Seal Rocks Lighthouse" is actually Sugarloaf Point Lighthouse, about 130 miles northeast of Sydney, New South Wales. In 1863 the authorities recommended building a lighthouse near or on Seal Rocks. At first they approved Seal Rocks as the location for the light but, in April 1873, landing on the rocks was deemed too difficult, and the lighthouse was built on the

Sugarloaf Point coast nearby. The light was first lit on 1 December 1875. One of Australia's worst shipwrecks occurred off the coast there, the wreck of the steamship *Catterthun*, on a voyage from Sydney to China in 1895. Fifty lives were lost. See **Great Disasters, 8 Aug 1895**

## 8 Feb 1892

**Maritime Intelligence**

Embiricos (s).- Scilly [Isles], Feb. 6, 12 20 p.m.- Greek str. [steamer] Embiricos, Cardiff for Malta (coals), struck rocks, supposed [believed] White Island, back of St. Martin's, 4 30 this morning, during thick weather, and foundered in deep water; 12 crew, three Maltese seamen passengers landed St. Martin's in their boat; captain, mate, four engineers, boatswain and three Maltese seamen passengers missing.

*10 Feb 1892*

**Maritime Intelligence**

Embiricos (s).- [Le] Havre, Feb. 9.- The steamer Rutland from Swansea, has picked up and landed here three engineers and a Greek seaman belonging to the Greek steamer Embiricos, from Cardiff for Malta, recently lost off Scilly.

*10 Feb 1892*

**The Wreck of the Embiricos.-**

The following is an extract from a letter that has just been received by Messrs. Green, Holland and Sons from Captain Matthews, the master of their steamer Rutland, which arrived at Havre on Monday:-

"I picked up on Sunday, five miles off the Lizard, four men in a small boat, their steamer (the Embiricos, of Andros, Greece) having foundered. They prove to be the first, second, and third engineers and one Greek sailor. The engineers are Englishmen. They had been out in the boat 28 hours with very little clothing and nothing to eat or drink. It was blowing hard and a strong sea running at the time. Their ship had struck on Scilly on the Saturday morning, at 4 30, and foundered in deep water 20 minutes afterwards. The men I picked up were in a very exhausted condition. I brought them on to Havre to the British Consul."

*The Times, 10th February 1892*

**"Loss of the Embiricos"**

The 15 survivors of the Greek steamer Embiricos, which went ashore at St. Martin's, Scilly, in a fog early on Saturday morning, were landed at Penzance yesterday from the steamship Lyonesse.

Since the wreck, stories of the most sensational character, founded, it is alleged, on the statements of members of the crew themselves, have been circulated and have given rise to considerable speculation as to their truth or falsity. The most serious allegation is to the effect that the captain and the other officers of the vessel were murdered by the survivors. The story is told with much circumstantiality; it is being stated that a mutiny broke out some time before the vessel struck, and that it was in the course of the mutiny, indeed whilst the fighting was going on, that the affair occurred. On the other hand, it is said that the bloodshed did not occur until after the accident, when a rush having been made for the boats, knives were drawn and a fight for life ensued, during which the captain and officers were murdered.

From statements made on Monday it was very evident that there were scenes of violence, for the three surviving Maltese alleged that the Greeks, who formed the large majority of the crew, used all endeavours to prevent their entering the boat. When questioned as to whether the knife was not used, they admitted that there was a call to "knives" but this, they say, was only to cut the boat adrift. Another story was that after the boat had been launched some of the men who have been drowned swam in the rear of the boat for some distance, but that they were threatened with a knife, and one who was clinging to the stern was struck across the hands with an iron bar, which caused him immediately to lose his hold and sink.

John Balzan, one of the Maltese survivors, in an interview yesterday afternoon, said the vessel left Cardiff about 11 o'clock on Friday morning. She was a fine steamer, and made good speed during the day. Towards the close of the afternoon, a thick fog came on, and it was accompanied by a heavy sea, navigation became somewhat dangerous, and the engines were eased down to half speed. He and the other Maltese took no night watches, and consequently they went below during the evening.

Early in the morning he was awakened by a violent shock, which almost threw him from his berth. He went up on deck, and found that they had struck on a reef of rocks some little distance from an island. The rock had apparently torn the bottom of the vessel before the foremast, and, the bow being consequently slightly elevated, the water was pouring in and rushing down into the stern, so that the steamer was already beginning to settle down. The captain was on the bridge endeavouring to direct operations, but there was a general scramble on the deck for boats.

He, himself, with a number of Greeks and two of his fellow countrymen got alongside the lifeboat. The Greeks endeavoured to prevent the three Maltese from getting into the boat, but they scrambled in and refused to turn out. On being asked if any knives were used, Balzan replied that there was a call for "knives" and nearly everyone had a knife, but they did not use them, as far as he knew, except to cut the boat off from the stanchions. The lifeboat was lowered, and they began to pull away.

Balzan alleges that the captain and officers and the men were, at the time they left, trying to launch the other boat. There would have been plenty of room in the lifeboat for them, because there were only 15 men in a boat which could hold about 50. When they had pulled some little distance they heard those who had been left on the ship shrieking out for help and imploring them to come back and save them.

Balzan and the other Maltese immediately began to "back water" with the object of putting back to rescue them, but the Greeks turned on them, took the oar away from Balzan, and threatened what they would do with them if he did not do as he was told. Although the boat was only a few yards distant from the vessel, they refused to render any assistance whatever. They did not see the vessel go down, but when the boat had left about ten minutes they could see no light, and they supposed she must have sunk within that time.

When the men landed at St. Martin's it was noticed that they each carried a knife. It was this fact that, in the first place, formed the extraordinary stories which have since floated about. If the bodies of the officers are recovered, all doubts will be set at rest as to the alleged foul play.

## 16 Aug 1892

**The Loss of the Thracian**

A Liverpool correspondent sends the following particulars of the capsizing and foundering of the sailing ship Thracian in the Irish Sea:- "It seems that on Thursday the steam tug Sarah Joliffe, one of Messrs. Joliffe's fleet, left Liverpool for Greenock in order to tow to the Mersey a new large four-masted ship, the Thracian. This ship, which lay in ballast, had been built to the order of Messrs. W. Thompson and Co., of St. John (N.B.), whose Liverpool agents are Messrs. G.T. Soley and Co., of 28, Brunswick-street, Liverpool. She was under the command of Captain Herbert H. Brown, of Helensborough, on the Clyde, and he was accompanied by his wife.

The Sarah Joliffe, under the command of Captain Owen Jones, a native of Amlwch [Wales], took 10 men to act as a temporary crew for the Thracian, and at the Scotch port they were joined by five others, so that when the big vessel started in tow of the tug she had on board 17 persons. A start was made from Port Glasgow on Saturday evening, and good progress seems to have been made until Sunday afternoon, when the vessels were between the Point of Ayr and Belfast Lough. A gale suddenly sprang up, and as the Thracian was light in ballast, the tug could not tow her along in the teeth of the fierce wind and a mountainous sea. All that Captain Jones could do was to stand by the ship, keeping her head to the sea.

A lull in the weather followed, but about half past 11 [p.m.], when the vessels were three miles south of Port Erin [Isle of Man], there was a terrific squall. To the consternation of those on board the tug, the Thracian turned over. The crew on the tug cast adrift the towing hawser to save the Sarah Joliffe, and Captain Jones then bore close to the ship, which was floating bottom upwards. The thick rain obscured the ship, and when the Thracian was next seen she was about 1,000 yards from the tug. She floated for a couple of minutes, and then disappeared.

No trace of anyone in the water could be discovered. The tug cruised about for several hours, but nothing was seen of the ill-fated crew. Towards 6 o'clock [a.m.] Captain Jones, finding that nothing more could be done, steamed to Douglas [Isle of Man], reaching there about 9 o'clock. He at once gave information of the terrible disaster, wired to his owners, and made the statutory declaration to Mr. Holmes, at the Custom House.

Captain Jones, who is experienced in the towing of vessels, says he never saw a similar accident, although he has towed numbers of big ships in worse weather. Messrs. Joliffe telegraphed to him that if nothing more could be done he should bring the tug back to Liverpool, and, acting on instructions, he set out from Douglas about 1 o'clock. The Thracian, a four-masted vessel of 2,000 tons register, was on her way from the Clyde to Birkenhead [Liverpool], where arrangements had been made for her to ship a cargo for San Francisco."

## 10 Feb 1893

**Maritime Intelligence**

Trinacria (s)*.- Corunna [La Coruña, northwest Spain], Feb. 9.- The steamer Trinacria was wrecked at 6 o'clock yesterday morning at Penas Bermellas, between capes Trace and Las Salas, four miles from Camarinas and near Cape Villano. The morning was foggy and the vessel lost her reckoning, and the strong landward current drew the Trinacria on to the rocks, where she was dashed to pieces; 34 of those on board were drowned. The chief engineer and six sailors saved themselves by swimming to the shore. The masts and bulwarks have gone. Several bodies have been cast up on the beach including that of a woman. The shore is littered with debris and cargo which has been washed out of the ship. The authorities have sent boat round to pick up the bodies and bring them to Camerinas and other places for burial.

Trinacria (s).- Corunna, Feb. 9, 6 30 p.m.- Trinacria (s): The name of the saved are John Rust, chief engineer, James Semple, John McGowan, Donald Megillp, Andrew Kalston, Thomas Moore, and John Kelly, seamen.

*The steamship *Trinacria* was built at Glasgow by R. Duncan & Co. and launched in 1871. Its measurements were: 2,100 tons, and 306ft long, 34.4ft wide and 22ft deep. Operated by the Anchor Line, the ship left Greenock on 2 February 1893, under the command of Capt. S. Murray, bound for Gibraltar and Mediterranean ports. She carried four passengers and 37 crew. Three of the passengers were women missionaries going to work at the British garrison in Gibraltar. The fourth was a young girl.

After a stormy passage down the Irish Sea and across the Bay of Biscay, the *Trinacria* arrived off Cape Villano on the northwest Galician coast of Spain in the early hours of 8 February. Visibility was poor and sea conditions dangerous. She struck the rocks heavily and was broken in two by the seas. The four female passengers drowned when the boat they were put into capsized in the rough seas. Only seven crew members survived the wreck: the chief engineer, two seamen and four engine room stokers.

The *Trinacria* was wrecked at the same place where another British vessel, HMS *Serpent* went down on 10 November 1890 (see **Great Disasters**), with much greater loss of life. She carried 276 passengers and crew of which just three survived. Another Anchor Line steamship, the *Roumania*, was wrecked further down the Iberian coast, at Gronho, in Portugal, near the rocky headland of Peniche, about 50 miles north of Lisbon, on 27 October 1892. Of the 122 people on board the *Roumania*, 113 were lost.

## 23 Sept 1893

**Maritime Intelligence**

Alexandre Petion (Haytian war vessel)*.- New York, Sept. 23.- The Dutch steamer Prins Willem, which has arrived here, brings news of the mysterious wreck of the Haytian warship Alexandre Petion, which was built in France. The story as told by Mr. J.S. Durham, formerly United States Minister in Hayti, who was a passenger by the Prins Willem, is as follows:- The Alexandre Petion left Port au Prince on the 6th inst. Bound for San Domingo. She had on board a number of Haytian diplomats of high rank, who were on their way to negotiate a special treaty with the Dominican Republic, including General Moline, special envoy to the government of San Domingo, M. Cohen, formerly Minister to Mexico, and M. de Jean for some time Consul in France.

Suddenly, when off Cape Tiburon, the warship sank like a stone. One sailor on the look-out was thrown beyond the range of the suction caused by the foundering of the vessel, and by the aid of a plank managed to keep afloat until rescued by a passing vessel, which took him to Port au Prince. His mind was evidently weakened by the shock, and he was unable to explain the disaster. The rest of the vessel's company – 80 in number – are supposed [thought] to have been lost.]

*The ship was named after Alexandre Sabès Pétion (1770–1818), first president of the Republic of Haiti (1806–1818). The Port-au-Prince suburb of Pétionville is also named after him.

## 10 Feb 1894

**Miscellaneous**

London, Feb. 10.- A Dalziel's telegram from Vancouver says:- The ship British General, which has just arrived here, brings news from Java of the wreck of a large vessel on a reef off the Warren Hastings Islands*. The British General, while passing the islands on Dec. 4, was boarded by natives, who reported that 10 moons before a large English ship had been wrecked there and all hands drowned. The king of the natives took on board a metal quadrant [navigation instrument, similar to a sextant] for barter. This the officers of the British General bought of him for four plugs of tobacco. It bears the name of W. Weichert, Cardiff, maker. It is believed that the wrecked vessel was the British ship Morayshire, which sailed for this port, with a cargo of raw sugar, and was never afterwards heard of. [Memo.- The Morayshire, from Samarang for Vancouver, was posted missing June 14 last [1893].]

### 3 July 1894

**Maritime Intelligence**

Morayshire.- Sourabaya [Java], May 26.- HMS Pallas arrived here on May 21 from Warren Hastings and North Islands without having ascertained anything with regard to the loss of the Morayshire or the fate of her crew.

*The tiny and remote Micronesian island known as Warren Hastings Island (or Islands) is part of the Palau Islands group: to the north of Papua New Guinea, east of the Moluccas in Indonesia, and to the southeast of the Philippines. On old maps Warren Hastings Island is named "Pulo Mariere or Warren Hastings Island." It is probably the island known today as Merir, on the southwest edge of the Palau group. As for the *Morayshire* and her crew, like so many other lost vessels, nothing more was ever discovered about their ultimate fate.

## 15 Feb 1896

**Maritime Intelligence**

**Miscellaneous**

London, Feb. 15.- A Central News telegram, dated New York, Feb. 14, states:- A despatch from Carabelle, Florida, states that a boat has been washed up on the beach there containing five dead bodies and six others in the last stages of exhaustion. They had been adrift for one week without clothes, food, or water. The survivors were too weak to move when they were discovered.

## 31 Dec 1896

**A Tragedy At Sea.-** Marseilles, Dec. 30.- The tug Salinien has returned here and reported her inability to rescue the survivors of the crew of the Alix, of Marseilles, ashore on the drifting sands off Beaudieu. Five men had been seen clinging to the bridge of the wreck, over which huge waves washed continuously. The Salinien was despatched to the rescue. When she arrived on the scene she found that the vessel had disappeared except for a few feet of funnel, to which two men were clinging. The crew of the tug found it impossible to get within 50 yards of the wreck, and although several rockets were fired at that distance they were all carried away by the wind.

The Salinien was eventually compelled to abandon the poor fellows to their fate, and they were ultimately washed away and drowned before the eyes of a large number of people on shore. The Alix carried a crew of 13 men.

## 12 Feb 1897

### Maritime Intelligence

City of Agra (s).- London, Feb. 12.- Captain Dudding, of the screw steamer Onega, which vessel rescued the survivors of the City of Agra (s), wrecked 3rd inst., six miles east of Villano light,* furnishes the following description of the rescue, by letter dated Gibraltar, 6th inst.:-

"The pilot had scarcely left us on Jan. 28 when it came on to blow from the NW, and after we had passed Scilly the wind freshened to a smart gale. On Jan. 31 the wind changed to the SW, increasing to a hard gale, with heavy rain. On Feb. 1 made the Spanish coast, between Cape Villanos and Sisargas Light; the wind had then increased to a fierce gale accompanied by heavy rains and high seas. The steamer making little progress, it was decided to stay under the land during the night, there being some little shelter from Cape Villano.

The next morning at daylight it was blowing a hurricane and the steamer anchored in Lage Bay. At daylight on Feb. 3, the weather having moderated, steamed out of the bay, and when about three miles to the westward there was evidence of a serious disaster, as wreckage was floating about, and the chief officer called attention to an object about 2 miles off on the steamer's port side. Steamed towards it and dispatched the port pinnace in charge of the second officer, with two seamen.

The object proved to be a lifeboat, bottom up, on which were huddled together, scantily clothed, and some of them nearly dead with cramp from exposure, eight lascars. These were brought on board the steamer, and by careful tending were brought round. Two of the men spoke English fairly well, and stated that they formed part of the crew of the City of Agra, which had stranded about eight hours before, viz., about midnight on the 2nd February. Having ascertained from them that there were on board the steamer when she stranded about 73 persons, Europeans and lascars, men were sent aloft with glasses to get a good look-out for any that might be on the water.

An object being reported on the starboard bow, steamed towards it and picked up another lascar, who was floating on a long wooden case. Then steamed through the wreckage, hoping to discover further survivors, but had nearly given up hope, when attention was called to a voice calling faintly, "Steamer ahoy!" Then saw a man with a lifebelt on clinging to a door, but so exhausted that it was with some difficulty he was got on board. The man was Captain Frame, of the City of Agra. On getting him on board it was feared that he had already succumbed, but after his clothes were taken off he was covered with blankets, and with the assistance afforded by four men rubbing him for over an hour he was brought round. It was, however, not until five hours after that he recovered consciousness. When taken out he had been over ten hours in the water.

The Onega continued searching amongst the wreckage during fours hours for further survivors, but after scanning every piece of wreckage possible it was decided by consultation with the officers that all that was possible had been done to save life, and that there could be no further survivors in the vicinity of the wreckage; the Onega steamed out to sea and proceeded on her voyage. She put into Gibraltar on the 6th inst. to land the shipwrecked men, having had a long and dreary passage on her way out from Cardiff."

*The 3,274-ton steamship *City of Agra* was on a voyage from Liverpool to Calcutta when she struck the rocks near Cabo Villano on the northwest corner of Spain and foundered, during a severe northwest gale on the night of 3 February 1897. Of the 75 persons on board, 34 (including two stowaways) were rescued; 41 perished.

## Post Script

### 27 April 1897
### Ocean Currents

Captain C.A.P. Talbot, British Consul at Corunna, writes from Corunna, under date April 21:- "A curious and interesting case of the body of a person drowned at a shipwreck having been carried an immense distance before being washed ashore has occurred in this district. The steamship City of Agra was wrecked at Arou Bay, about six miles to the eastward of Cape Villano Lighthouse, which is situated at the extreme north-west of this peninsula, about 43° 9' N latitude, and 9° 13' W longitude. The wreck occurred on February 3, and on March 7 the body of the chief steward of that steamer, recognised from the buttons on his coat and papers in his pockets, was found washed ashore at San Sebastian, close to the French frontier, which is situated about 43° 20' N latitude, and 1° 55' W longitude, so that the body must have been carried along the whole north coast of Spain, close upon 400 miles…"]

## 17 July 1897

The Survivors from the Zuleika.- A Plymouth correspondent telegraphs that Captain Bremmer and a portion of the crew of the sailing ship Zuleika*, of Leith [Edinburgh], arrived there yesterday on board the Orient mail steamer Orient, in which they have come from Australia. The Zuleika, whilst bound to Wellington, New Zealand, went ashore on April 15 during a heavy gale in thick weather. The vessel struck at midnight, and within two hours disappeared. Nine of the crew safely reached the shore, but 12 men were swept off the deck and drowned before the eyes of their comrades, who were powerless to render them assistance.

*The *Zuleika* was an iron ship, of 1,100 tons, built in Glasgow in 1875, and owned by T. Law & Co. of Leith. In the early months of 1897 she was making a voyage to New Zealand, commanded by Capt. John Bremmer, to offload her cargo first at Dunedin, on the South Island of New Zealand, and thence to Wellington at the southern end of North Island. On 16 April she was approaching her second port of discharge at the eastern entrance to Cook Strait in dirty weather, near Palliser Bay. As Capt. Bremmer wore ship to avoid the danger of land close by on her port bow, the vessel struck rocks. Seas washing over the ship disabled the lifeboats, making it impossible for the crew to attempt getting ashore in them. They clung first to the rigging and then, in the middle of the night, to the jibboom at the bow of the ship.

"Shortly afterwards the *Zuleika* lurched into the sea, and every man was thrown into the water. Many of the men struck out for the shore. Those unable to swim clung to pieces of wreckage, and several of these were drowned. Others who could swim were stunned by the wreckage, and their dead bodies were washed ashore, battered and bruised almost beyond recognition. All the bodies, with the exception of three, were washed ashore. Those drowned [12] included the mate, seven seamen, cook, steward and two apprentices." (www. divenewzealand.com)

## 23 Aug 1897

**Maritime Intelligence**

Seladon.- Auckland, N.Z., Aug. 21.- A number of men who have just arrived here who formed part of the crew of the Norwegian barque Seladon, which left Newcastle (N.S.W.) for Honolulu over a year ago, and had never been heard of since. They report that their vessel was wrecked on Starbuck, an uninhabited guano island of the Manakiki Group, in the Southern Pacific, in August of last year. After suffering great privations they reached Sophia Island in their boats, and remained with friendly natives there for 10 months before they were rescued by a steamer. The captain, mate and carpenter died. The captain's name was Adolf Jaeger, the mate's Christian Nielsen, and the carpenter's Tollah Olsen.

*Evening Post (New Zealand newspaper), 23 August 1897*

**The  Seladon Disaster**

**Further Particulars**

**Two Thousand Miles In An Open Boat**

*Auckland, 21*[st] *August*

Starbuck Island, where the Norwegian barque Seladon was wrecked, the crew of which has just been rescued after 10 months' stay on Sophia Island, is very vaguely placed on the charts, and it is to this cause probably that so many wrecks have taken place there. There was formerly a guano depot there, and several Auckland vessels visited it, but it is now deserted. The island is low, and is not visible over seven miles away. It lies 5 deg 38 min south of the Equator [ie., lat. 5° 38' S], and is in 155 deg 55 min west longitude [ie., long. 155° 55' W]. It is surrounded by a narrow, steep reef nearly a mile off the shore, and it was evidently on this that the Seladon struck.

According to the chart the wrecked sailors must have made a voyage of about 2,000 miles in the ship's boat before they reached Sophia Island*. After leaving Starbuck Island they steered northwards for some distance, as Malden Island and Christmas Island lie considerably to the north. Then they sailed south and west till they made Sophia Island, which lies in 10 deg 46 min south lat. [lat. 10° 46' S] and 179 deg 31 min east long. [long. 179° 31' E]. Sophia Island lies north of the Fiji Group, and is a small wooded island two to three miles in circuit.

The rescue was made by the Fiji Government despatch steamer Clyde (Captain Cahhaghan) which was returning from a trip to the Ellice Group [Tuvalu islands to the northeast]. In the 10 months' of the castaways' stay on Sophia Island they only sighted one sailing ship, a good way off, and a steamer, which was too far off to see the signal they hoisted on the highest tree...

The inhabitants of Sophia Island – two Rotuma** men (one of whom died during the stay) and four men – shared what provisions they had with the castaways, and for the rest of the time they subsisted on cocoanuts, sea-birds, and turtle, which were not by any means scarce. The Seladon was a wooden barque of 1,102 tons register. She was owned by Mr. G. Gunderson, of Stavanger, Norway, and was built in 1877.

A notable wreck which occurred on Starbuck Island some years ago was that of the British ship Garston [see **Shipwrecks, Collisions and Castaways (…and Cannibalism), 17 Sept 1889**], laden with Newcastle [New South Wales] coal, bound for America. The crew had a terribly severe voyage of six weeks in an open boat to Wallis Island, where they were picked up by the Auckland schooner Olive, and came on to Auckland in the [steamer] Wainui. On the boat's voyage it was alleged some of the men in the captain's boat talked of "casting lots" amongst themselves to furnish food when all the provisions were gone.

*Sophia Island, now called Niulakita, is the southernmost atoll in the Tuvalu islands, previously the Ellice Islands. Its population (by census) in 2002 was 35.

**Rotuma Island is some 275 miles southwest of Sophia.

## 26 Aug 1897

**Maritime Intelligence**

Cheang Hye Teng (s).- Shanghai, Aug. 25.- The steamer Cheang Hye Teng, 1,436 tons, of Penang, whence she had sailed on a voyage to Japan, via Hong Kong, was struck by a typhoon and foundered. One white man and 10 Asiatics out of her crew of 32 reached Shanghai after exposure five days to a tropical sun, without food or water.

Captain Scott shot himself as the vessel went down.

## 2 Feb 1898

**Maritime Intelligence**

Channel Queen (s).*- London, Feb. 2.- News was received at Plymouth yesterday that the steamer Channel Queen, which left there on Monday night (Jan. 31) for Guernsey, Jersey and St. Brieuc, struck Black Rock, 1½ miles north-west of Guernsey, during a dense fog yesterday morning, and afterwards slipped from the rocks and sank. A telegram from the manager of the company at Guernsey gives the names of 13 of the officers and crew who were saved, including Captain Collins, the first and second mates, the stewards and stewardess, and the second engineer.

The authentic list of drowned is as follows:- Crew: Chief engineer, A. Scawn; fireman, F. Fudge; greaser, J. Hawkings; H. Davey, able seaman; cook, Ernest Thompson. Passengers: Mr. Frank Ewell [sic – Cowl], of Plymouth, and a baby. Twelve Breton onion sellers also lost their lives.

*The steamship Channel Queen, of steel construction, schooner-rigged and built in 1895, was operated by the Plymouth, Channel Islands, and Brittany Steamship Co., to transport passengers and freight between Plymouth, the Channel Islands and the north coast of

Brittany. She was certified to carry up to 365 passengers in home waters but, on the night of her departure from Plymouth on 31 January 1898, she carried just 50 passengers, along with a crew of 18, under the command of Capt. E.J. Collings. Just before 5 o'clock on the morning of 1 February, in foggy conditions, the *Channel Queen* was approaching port in Guernsey when she struck submerged rocks near Black Rock in the Little Russell (or Roussel) Channel between the islands of Herm and Guernsey.

The first casualty of the wreck was Mr. Frank Cowl of Plymouth who, despite Capt. Collings' "entreaties" for everyone to get onto the bridge, "persisted in jumping overboard, and endeavoured to swim to a rock, but was drowned in the attempt," according to testimony from the official Court of Inquiry. A total of 21 lives were lost in the wreck of the *Channel Queen*.

## 23 March 1898

### Maritime Intelligence

Helen W. Almy.- San Francisco, March 23.- The steamer Santa Rosa, from San Diego, having reported that early yesterday morning she passed a derelict floating bottom upwards off Point Bonita, a tug was dispatched to the spot, and found that the abandoned vessel was the barque Helen W. Almy, Captain Hogan, which sailed from Golden Gate [San Francisco] on March 20 for several points on the Copper River. She had 13 sailors and 27 men for Klondyke* on board. It is feared that none escaped. The Helen W. Almy is supposed [believed] to have capsized in a sudden squall.

*The Alaskan gold rush in the Klondike began in 1896/97. By 1898 men from all over the world were heading up to the area around the Copper River to try their luck at panning for Klondike gold. The *Helen W. Almy* was a small 250-ton barque that traded in her early years mainly around the Pacific islands. On her final ill-fated voyage she was taking gold prospectors from San Francisco up to Alaska, against the better judgement of her captain, W. J. Hogan, who was concerned about imminent bad weather. When she capsized apparently in a squall off Point Bonita, the headland just outside the entrance to San Francisco Bay, all 40 of her crew and passengers perished, presumed drowned.

## 26 Aug 1898

### Maritime Intelligence

La Coquette.- New York, Aug. 25.- Fishing schooner La Coquette, of Bayonne, was sunk by the Danish steamer Norge, on the 20th inst., on the Grand Banks. The captain and eight men were saved, but 16 of the crew perished. The collision occurred between 3 and 4 in the morning [*sic* - afternoon]. The weather was foggy. La Coquette sank almost immediately. The Norge sustained no damage.

## *26 Aug 1898*
### Collision off Newfoundland

### Loss of Sixteen Lives

In addition to the reports in our "Maritime Intelligence" of the collision between the steamer Norge and the schooner La Coquette, a Reuter's telegram from New York yesterday gives the following particulars:-

"The collision occurred between 3 and 4 in the afternoon, in lat. 46 N, long. 48 W. The weather was foggy, but was not so thick as to require the Norge to reduce speed. The captain says he could see three cable lengths [1,825 ft] off. The wind was fairly brisk from west to south-west, and when a vessel suddenly turned up from the north with her sails full set and stood directly across the bows of the Norge, the bridge bells were rung to stop and then go full speed astern. But it was too late to stop the Norge.

The vessel fell across the steamer's bows, and with a crash was forced over and sunk by the impact. Three of the crew of the La Coquette sprang on board the Norge. The passengers of the steamer, most of whom were lounging about the decks, made a rush when the collision took place, but the alarm was soon quieted on learning that the Norge was uninjured. In the meantime a boat was lowered, and six men and a dog were picked up. The La Coquette sank almost immediately.

The captain asserts that though as a steamer the Norge was obliged to keep out of the way of a sailing vessel, this was an occasion when La Coquette could do more to help herself than the steamer, because the latter was going full speed. La Coquette was under good steerage way, but she never attempted to avoid a collision. The Norge's large hull should have been visible from a long distance.

Those saved were Captain Berre, and seamen Ruellar, Chevelle, Laquec, Defever, Outin, Brouquent, Lemenant, and Guillette.

The captain of the Norge, in a later statement, said the collision occurred in a dense fog off the Banks. He had been on the bridge for 22 hours, the steamer going at half speed, when he heard the schooner's siren and saw that a collision was unavoidable. The Norge, he said, must either have run the schooner down or suffered the fate of the Bourgogne [ie., sunk by a sailing vessel colliding with her]. As the Norge had a large number of passengers on board he preferred to take his chance. He ordered the engines to be put to full speed ahead, and the Norge ran into the bow of the schooner, tearing a hole three feet wide. The sea was choppy, and as the steamer rose and fell the hole in the schooner's side was made larger and larger. The schooner's crew could be seen struggling in the sea, and the suction caused by the settling down of the vessel drew them under. The accident was quite unavoidable. The Norge sustained no damage."

## 19 Oct 1898

### Maritime Intelligence

Safir.- Stavanger [Norway], Oct. 12.- According to a telegram from Charleston (S.C.), the barque Safir, of this port, has been lost (capsized) on the voyage from Pensacola [Florida] for Bahia Blanca [Argentina]. The master, who sent the telegram, must have landed at a different place from the crew, as he adds that he knows nothing definite about the latter.

### *22 Nov 1898*

### Maritime Intelligence

Safir.- St. Michael's [Sao Miguel, Azores], Nov. 8.- The Norwegian barque Gyller, from Belize, reports that on Oct. 3, in lat. 32 22 N, long. 18 49 W,* she picked up the first and second mates, carpenter and a seaman of the Norwegian barque Safir, from Pensacola for Bahia Blanca, which latter vessel had foundered on the previous day.

From the *Hawke's Bay Herald* (New Zealand newspaper)

**28 January 1899**

**Sailors Eaten By Sharks**

Information has been received at Shields [northeast England] of the wreck of the barque Safir, owned in Norway, and the loss of ten of the crew. The ship was bound from Pensacola to Bahia Blanca, laden with timber, and manned by a crew of fifteen hands, when she fell in with a hurricane. Sorely battered, she gradually heeled over, and eventually capsized. As she turned over the men managed to crawl upon the keel, and the seas broke furiously over the upturned hull, ultimately washing the exhausted mariners off the wreck one by one.

By this time large quantities of wreckage, including the ship's boats, came to the surface. Some of the men managed to reach the boats, while others clung to the wreckage. To add to the horrors of the situation, a number of sharks gathered round, and some of the seamen, in endeavouring to reach the floating wreckage, were devoured. Captain Knudson reached the floating deck-house, on which he remained for three days and nights. The sharks followed all the time. After three days' terrible privations he was taken off by a fishing smack from Charleston (S.C.). The other four survivors were landed at St. Michael's, having been rescued by another Norwegian barque.

*The reported position where the Norwegian barque *Gyller* rescued the four crew from the *Safir* - "lat. 32 22 N, long. 18 49 W" – was between the Canary Islands and Madeira. The longitude position, however, must have been an error for "78 49 W" which, at latitude 32 22 N, is just off Charleston, South Carolina.

The *Gyller*, coming up from Belize in Central America, would have been heading northeast along the eastern seaboard of North America, aiming to get a push from the Gulf Stream towards the North Atlantic and her European destination. Moreover, it took the *Gyller* about a month from the date she rescued the *Safir's* men (3 October) to reach and report from the Azores – about the right time it would have taken her to sail there from the real position of the rescued men, just off the coast of South Carolina. And the Charleston fishing boat that rescued the *Safir's* captain would have been near her home port rather than, as the reported location most improbably indicated, on the other side of the Atlantic near the Canary Islands.

## 3 Dec 1898

**The Loss of the Clan Drummond***

As briefly announced in the *Shipping Gazette* yesterday, the steamer Clan Drummond, one of the numerous fleet known as the Clan Line, belonging to Messrs. Cayzer, Irvine and Co., was totally lost on Monday night in the Bay of Biscay, and out of the crew of 58 on board only 22 were saved, the remaining 36 being drowned…Orders have been despatched to Lisbon to send the survivors home. Captain Crockett, who resided at 28, St. Ronan's-drive, Glasgow, leaves a widow and five children. He had taken with him on the voyage his son, a boy of between 12 and 13, who would, he thought, be the better for the holiday…

*14 Dec 1898*
## The Survivors of the Clan Drummond

The survivors of the Clan Drummond, which foundered in the Bay of Biscay with the loss of 37 lives, while on a voyage to South Africa, arrived in the Mersey yesterday morning from Lisbon aboard the Pacific Company's steamer Orcana…The Press Association's Liverpool correspondent, telegraphing later, says:-

"One of the survivors of the Clan Drummond, a Malay, has, through an interpreter, made the following statement:- 'The sea was running almost as high as any building which I can see about me, and the ship was knocked about like a cork. Suddenly one tremendous sea came upon us while we were lying in the trough of the waves. The sea was like the side of a mountain, and fell on the deck with a crash that was terrific. The hatches of the deck were smashed in and the water roared into the hold. Then most of my Malay friends prayed, and many of them in the midst of their cries for protection were swept away into the great waves. The English officers all worked like devils. Some of the Malays who are dead were swamped in their boats, and their shrieks could be heard over the great wind. It was the most terrible weather I have ever known.' "

Another correspondent at Liverpool sends the following:- "It appears that when the Clan Drummond was crossing the Bay of Biscay she encountered fearful storms, and on Monday, Nov. 28, about 1 o'clock in the day, as the vessel was making about 11½ knots, a big sea broke over her, smashing upon the deck with tremendous force. The main hatch was burst open, and about 18 feet of the deck was stove in. With the seas tumbling aboard it was impossible to prevent the ship being swamped, and in a very short time she filled with water and foundered.

The steamer Holbein was in sight at the time, and witnessing the disaster at once bore down to render assistance. One boat was launched from the Clan Drummond, but was smashed against the side, and several lives were lost. What followed in the midst of the raging storm was a mad struggle for life, the Englishmen working with method, but the Lascars, struggling and praying, clinging about the white men and hindering their movements. The Holbein managed to rescue about half the crew, but the remainder either went down with the ship or were drowned among the wreckage. Among these was the captain's son. The chief engineer was drowned in the engine-room, but the second, third, and fourth engineers were saved.

The third and fourth officers [mates] were lost, the end of the former being particularly sad. He was hauled on board the Holbein, but as he was standing on the deck a heavy sea washed him overboard, and he was never seen again. The captain, too, was drowned when within an ace of rescue. He was being hauled by a rope on board the Holbein when he fell back into the sea and was drowned. One account states that the captain was pulled from the rope by several lascars who were struggling to get out of the water, but another account attributes his loosening of the rope to his inability to hold on, his strength having failed through exhaustion. Captain Crockett had been in the service of the Clan Line for 16 years, and for the last nine in command of various steamers. He was appointed captain of the Clan Drummond in 1894.

The Holbein landed the survivors on Dec. 1 at Lisbon, where the British Consul provided for their maintenance until the departure of the Orcana for Liverpool, last Thursday. The saved included six Britishers and 21 lascars. Everyone speaks in the highest praise of the officers and crew of the Holbein for the noble work of rescue they accomplished in a time of considerable danger."

*The Clan Line's steamship *Clan Drummond*, of 2,908 tons, was on a voyage from the Clyde and Liverpool to Delagoa Bay (Port Elizabeth) in South Africa when she was overwhelmed by a Bay of Biscay gale on 28 November 1898. A wave carried away her bridge, and a boat containing 27 men was launched just before the ship sunk. The steamship *Holbein*, nearby, rescued them, but thirty-seven other men, including Capt. Crockett and his young son, drowned in the disaster.

## THE *MORAVIA*: ANOTHER SABLE ISLAND VICTIM

## 1 March 1899

### Maritime Intelligence

Moravia (s).- Gloucester, Massachusetts, Feb. 28.- The schooner Mondego, which has returned here from a fishing trip, reports having sighted the steamer Moravia, formerly belonging to the Hamburg-American Line, on the north-east bar of Sable Island*, broken in two. She had evidently encountered the storm on the 12th and 13th inst. [February]. As the place where she stranded is 12 miles from the shore, and nothing could be seen of the crew for two days after the wreck was sighted, the captain of the Mondego thinks that they must be lost.

Moravia (s).- Halifax, N.S. (by Cable Feb. 28).- Fishing schooner Nannie Bohlen reports:- Was at Sable Island 15th [February]. No sign steamer previously reported wrecked there. Learned from fishing schooner Arbitrator that about 13th steamer broken forward ashore north-east bar Sable Island. Schooner George Heckman saw floating packages rubber balls, bottles, other bale silk and buoy with name "Arabia" or "Moravia". Steamer Newfield leaves in two or three days for Sable Island.

Moravia (s).- New York, Feb. 28.- On the 14th, the Mondego picked up some wreckage and a life preserver, on which were the words "Steamship Moravia". Four days later the Mondego spoke the fishing schooner Arbitrator, which reported that the Moravia was ashore broken in two, at the point mentioned. The Arbitrator had been in the vicinity of North-East Bar a day or two after the violent gales of the 12th and 13th, and having sighted the wreck, had stood by to watch for signs of life. Failing to see any, however, she proceeded on her way to the fishing grounds [the Grand Banks].

The Mondego afterwards met the schooner Hattie Heckman, which had also seen the wreck and had sailed all round, watching for signs of life, but found the Moravia apparently deserted. The Mondego picked up some wreckage several miles off North-West Bar, Sable Island. The wreck when seen by the Arbitrator lay on the bar about eight miles from North-East Bar, with light seas beating against her. The captains of the Arbitrator and Hattie Heckman also regarded the chances of the escape of the crew in such a storm as of the slightest.

### *2 March 1899*

### Maritime Intelligence

Moravia (s).- Boston (by Cable received March 1).- German steamer Moravia wrecked and totally lost ship and cargo at Sable Island. All on board believed to be lost.

331

*4 March 1899*
## Maritime Intelligence

Moravia (s).- Halifax, N.S. (by Cable received March 3).- Government steamer Aberdeen returned with crew Moravia, wrecked Sable Island 12th [February], except second mate, who died. Moravia broken up.

*4 March 1899*
## The Loss of the Moravia
## Story of the Wreck
## Halifax (N.S.), March 3

The Hamburg-American steamer Moravia, whose crew arrived here to-day, experienced terrible weather before striking on Sable Island and becoming a total wreck. Five of the eight boats and everything on deck were washed away. The second officer, who was on the bridge when the steamer struck, is reported to have mistaken the Sable Island Light for that of a fishing boat. He failed to report the light, and the disaster followed. Some of the men were a day in a boat before landing was effected. The second officer died from exposure, and all the crew experienced terrible sufferings. The survivors were landed here this morning by the Government steamer Aberdeen, which was sent to Sable Island in search of the disabled vessel as soon as the wreck was known. They are being well cared for.

The captain says:- "We were bound for Halifax when we struck. We had a rough voyage and had to change our course. It was then discovered that we had only 100 tons of coal left. For several days afterwards we were unable to take an observation [ie., to determine their position]. We struck at 1 30 on the morning of the 12th, at the extreme north-east end of the dry bar, and within two hours the ship began to break up, and the crew were forced to leave at once.

The Moravia's signals were answered by the Sable Island life-saving crew, who launched the lifeboats and took our crew off as fast as possible. The sea was very heavy and the weather bitterly cold. While we were landing, the second officer, Mr. Fransdorf, died from exposure. The ship broke amidships shortly after the crew left, and immediately commenced to settle down into the sands."

A considerable quantity of the cargo has floated ashore and is being picked up by the inhabitants of the island. The Aberdeen also has on board a portion of the cargo, which will be preserved for the owners.

The survivors speak in the highest terms of their treatment on Sable Island and on board the Aberdeen. They are all in good health, and are little the worse for their experience. When landed on the island many of them were suffering from exposure, but the careful treatment they received at the hands of the keeper of the [lifeboat] station soon got them out of danger. They say that the Moravia was disabled when she stranded.

"When the ship parted," says one of the survivors, "the men prepared to launch a boat. This was attended with extreme danger, and the condition of the steamer became such that it was decided to cut the lines from the lifeboat in order that the crew might reach the island and obtain assistance. The minute the lines were cut the crew began a hard battle for their lives. The little craft was swept from the steamer like a cork, and work as we might we found it impossible to approach the shore, and were gradually carried out to sea. We suffered agonies from the extreme cold and heavy snow. The waves swept across the lifeboat and the water was quickly turned to ice, so that the manning of the oars became more and more difficult. The condition of affairs went from bad to worse. All night long the brave fight lasted, and, as the wind abated the boat was gradually brought under control.

While we were in the boat Mr. Fransdorf, the second officer, succumbed to exposure. His comrades were in almost as sad a plight, nearly all of the 21 occupants of the boat being frost-bitten. Finally, however, the boat was beached and the men were taken to the life-saving station, where everything possible was done for their comfort.

The 19 members of the crew who remained on the Moravia were looked after by a life-saving crew from the island. The first lot of seven were rescued at three in the afternoon. The sea was then breaking over the ship, and the men were all aft. The second trip of the lifeboat was made in the afternoon and only six more men were left on board for the night. These were rescued at daylight. On Monday the hull started to settle in the sands, and by nightfall the vessel had completely disappeared. When the Aberdeen left yesterday the wreckage was still coming ashore."

*Sable Island is a 25 mile (40 km) long, 1 mile (1.6 km) wide island some 120 miles due east of Nova Scotia. This apparently innocuous filament of land is the visible part of a much more extensive area of shoals and sandbars stretching along the continental shelf. It lies directly along the way of the busy transatlantic shipping route between North America and northern Europe. Fog, erratic currents, hurricanes and storms have driven at least 350 ships, and probably many more than that, to their doom on what is known as 'the graveyard of the Atlantic'. Ships wrecked on Sable Island often disappear entirely, consumed by the sands for which the island was named ('sable' is French for 'sand'), which was precisely the fate of the Moravia.

The Nova Scotia government first set up a life-saving station on Sable Island in 1801. By 1895 there were five stations. The crew of the first station were the island's first permanent inhabitants. Two lighthouses, one at each end of the island, were erected in 1873.

The Moravia was launched at Glasgow in August 1883 as the 3,739-ton steamship Bengore Head for the Ulster SS Co. She was built of iron, had a speed of 12 knots, and accommodated 100 first class passengers and 1,200 in steerage. In the same year she was launched she was sold to the Hamburg-America Line and renamed the Moravia. Between 1883 and 1899 she criss-crossed the North Atlantic, mainly taking European immigrants from Hamburg and Le Havre (but also from other northern European ports) to New York. In 1898 she was sold to Sloman, an old family shipping company in Hamburg.

On her last voyage she departed Hamburg for Boston on 18 January 1899, under the command of Capt. Fergusen who apparently, on account of low stocks of coal, changed course for Halifax. That diversion put Sable Island directly, and fatefully, in her path. Since there is only mention of the crew being saved, it is presumed that the vessel was not carrying passengers on her final voyage.

## 9 May 1899

**Maritime Intelligence**

Loch Sloy*.- Adelaide, May 9, 1 55 p.m.- Loch Sloy wrecked and totally lost, ship and cargo, April 24, off the coast of Kangaroo Island [South Australia]. Some of the passengers and crew saved; remainder it is feared are lost. The survivors include one passenger and three of the crew.

Loch Sloy.- Adelaide, May 9.- News has just been received here that the barque Loch Sloy was wrecked on Kangaroo Island as long ago as April 24. One passenger and three of the crew were saved, while five passengers and 25 of the crew were drowned. Three of the survivors are still wandering in the bush.

## 10 May 1899

**Maritime Intelligence**

Loch Sloy.- Adelaide, May 9.- The passengers drowned off Kangaroo Island by the wreck of the Loch Sloy are Mr. Robert Logan, Mr. George Lamb, Mr. and Mrs. Leicester and Mrs. Carttidge. The other passenger, Mr. David Kilpatrick, was left in the bush by two sailors four days ago, and was then in a starving condition and helpless. There is practically no hope that he can have survived. The privations suffered by the sailors themselves were frightful.

## 11 May 1899

**Maritime Intelligence**

Loch Sloy.- Adelaide, May 10.- It has now been ascertained that, besides those already mentioned, a passenger named Macdonald was drowned in the wreck of the barque Loch Sloy on Kangaroo Island last month.

## 18 May 1899

**The Otago Witness**

**The Loch Sloy Disaster. Further Particulars.**

**Four Survivors Out of a Total of Thirty-five**

**Adelaide, May 10**

The Loch Sloy's crew and passengers together numbered 35. The names of the four survivors are:- William Mitchell and Duncan M'Millan (able seamen), William John Simpson (apprentice), David Kilpatrick.

William Mitchell gives the following account of the disaster:-

"The Loch Sloy drifted so close to the rocks that she could not run out again, and she struck heavily. An enormous sea was running at the time. Mitchell declares that he never saw anything equal to the sight, even when going round Cape Horn. This is the third time that he has been wrecked. Captain Nicol was a splendid specimen of a Christian seaman. From the time that the ship struck he never moved off the deck, but stuck true to his post to the last. Within 10 minutes from the ship striking all hands were washed overboard.

The two women passengers – Mrs Cartlidge and Mrs Leicester – climbed the masts, and showed no fear. The masts were washed overboard in a few minutes.

The vessel struck at 5 a.m., and at daylight only the bottom part of the ship was left.

Kilpatrick and Simpson, who were both unable to swim, floated ashore on barrels. Mitchell swam ashore, along with M'Millan. The four survivors were thrown on to the rocks within two yards of each other. They saw no sign of other living beings then or afterwards. Mitchell and Simpson were eight days in reaching Cape Borda, and were delirious when found. Both men revived wonderfully after getting a bath and some food."

The Loch Sloy carried seven passengers. No complete list of her crew is available, but letters are lying at the post office at Adelaide for the following persons:- Captain Nicol, Peter Cleland, T.A. Cleland, Kilpatrick, George Dounden, Empson [Simpson], Robert Smith, Robert Dirnie, G.J. Twidle, J. M'Millan, T.H. Leach, R. Mullegan, Hugh M'Bride (ship's carpenter), J.R. Brown (steward), Archie Martin, R.J. Smith, John Buchanan, George Lambie.

One of the launch hands at the semaphore station states that friends of his named A. Finlayson, M'Kinnon, Neill, and A. Robertson were expected by the Loch Sloy.

The cargo was valued at £34,000. It is understood that it was insured in the London offices, where the hull is also insured.

The lighthouse-keeper found the Loch Sloy survivors seven miles from the lighthouse. They were in a terribly exhausted condition, their feet being cut and bleeding, and they had only a few rags of clothing. Since the wreck they had existed on a few limpets and a couple of dead penguins, which they found on the beach.

*The *Loch Sloy* was a 1,280 ton three-masted barque, built at Glasgow by D & W Henderson for the Glasgow Shipping Company (more commonly known as the Loch Line), and launched in August 1877. She was 250 ft long, 38 ft in width, and 22 ft deep. The vessel was on a voyage from Glasgow to Adelaide and Melbourne with general cargo, under the command of Capt. P. Nicol, with seven passengers and *probably* 27 crew, when she struck the rocks off the southwest corner of Kangaroo Island, South Australia, around 5 a.m. on 24th April 1899. The ship's masts and rigging broke and crashed into the sea, drowning the passengers (including the two fearless women) and crew who had been clinging to them for safety.

Only four people reached the distant shore – one passenger, David Kilpatrick, from New York City, two able seamen, William Mitchell and Duncan McMillan, and the 16-year old apprentice William Simpson.

McMillan, the strongest of the four, went to look for help after they had all scaled steep cliffs rising above the surf. He did not return after three days, so the three other survivors left to try to reach Cape Borda lighthouse, to the north, on their own. McMillan did eventually return but, finding the others gone, again left to seek assistance. He reached the house of a Mr. May who sent one of his family to ride out to the lighthouse to organise a search party.

The second lighthouse-keeper found two of the other three survivors – the able seaman Mitchell and the apprentice Simpson – about seven miles from the lighthouse to which they were heading through the bush, around two weeks after the *Loch Sloy* was wrecked. They had had to leave the passenger, Kilpatrick, in the bush, about twenty miles from the lighthouse, as he was in too poor a condition to proceed.

A local newspaper, the *Advertiser*, in an article dated 10th May 1899, recounted their plight: "The apprentice...and...able seaman, having made Mr. Kilpatrick as comfortable as they could under the circumstances, recommenced their painful crawl towards the lighthouse. Their feet were fearfully torn by the rough rocks and the tree stumps, while their only protection was a few rags and a tattered shirt. They were without food, having given all they possessed to their disabled companion [Kilpatrick], but they subsisted on the limpets they found near the seashore, and they gladly devoured the flesh of two dead penguins which they had picked up near a ravine. These birds had been their only sustenance for several days before they were found; and when the keeper met them the melancholy remains of the penguins were still tied round their necks…"

The body of David Kilpatrick was discovered several weeks later. He was buried where he was found. His stone grave serves as a memorial to all the seamen who died in ships wrecked on the coast of Kangaroo Island (over 80 shipwrecks to date).

Kangaroo Island lies just off the entrance to the Gulf of St. Vincent, off the coast of South Australia, about 112 km from Adelaide which is half way up the east side of the Gulf. At 150 km long and with a land area of 4,405 km², it is Australia's third largest island. The *Loch Sloy* was wrecked about 300 metres off Maurpetius Bay on the southwest coast. The Cape Borda lighthouse, constructed in 1858, is on the northwest tip of the island.

Another Loch Line vessel, the *Loch Vennachar*, was wrecked off West Bay, half way up the west coast of Kangaroo Island, in September 1905, with the loss of all 28 hands. The remains of the wreck were not found, however, until 1976, in eight fathoms of water, below 100ft high cliffs. One of those who perished in the *Loch Vennachar* was an apprentice on the ship, T.R. Pearce. He was the son of Tom Pearce who was one of the only two survivors of another famous Loch Line shipwreck, that of the *Loch Ard*. On a voyage from London to Melbourne, the *Loch Ard* was wrecked on the coast of Victoria in July 1878, claiming fifty-one lives (see under **Sole Survivors**, below, **The Wreck of the *Loch Ard***).

## 29 March 1900

**Maritime Intelligence**

Undine.- Hamburg, March 27.- The owners of the ship Undine, of Hamburg, state:- "We have received a telegram from Captain Danneboom, of our ship Undine, of yesterday's date, from Cape Town, according to which the crew, in two boats, abandoned the vessel, in a sinking state, in lat 31 S, long 26 W. The boats were separated from one another by bad weather. The starboard watch, with Captain Danneboom in the boat, were picked up on March 13 by the sailing vessel Oakhurst, bound to Australia, and were landed at Cape Town yesterday. We have telegraphed to Cape Town to-day for their names. As the Undine was abandoned in the track of homeward bound vessels from the West Coast [ie., of South America] and outward bound vessels for Australia, it is to be hoped that the port watch in the second boat has also been saved."*

*11 June 1900*
**Maritime Intelligence**

Undine.- London, 11 June.- The master of Loch Rannoch, arrived at Adelaide, reports having spoken the barque Sita, of Newport [Wales], Glasgow for Brisbane, April 6, lat 42 S, long 42 E, which reported having picked up boat's crew of German ship Undine.*

*The *Undine* was bound from Salina Cruz on the pacific coast of Mexico for Falmouth when, having rounded Cape Horn, she was abandoned by her crew in the middle of the South

Atlantic. One boat with the captain and starboard watch crew members was picked up by the Australia-bound *Oakhurst* and landed at Cape Town. The second boat, with the port watch crew members, was picked up by the *Sita* on her way to Brisbane; it is not known where the castaways were landed, but they might have been taken all the way to Australia.

## 17 July 1900

### Maritime Intelligence

Falconhurst.- Aden, July 14.- Survivors of the Falconhurst, who have reached here, state that the vessel was wrecked on the coast of Madagascar, 80 miles south of Diego Suarez, on June 19. The vessel ran on a reef about a mile from the coast at midnight, and the captain, first and second officers, an apprentice and eight of the crew were lost.* The rest of the crew were shipped to Aden by the Djemnah (s).

### *1 Aug 1900*

### Maritime Intelligence

### The Wreck of the Ship Falconhurst

London, July 31.- The third officer, Mr. Cruce, of the ship Falconhurst, of Swansea, which was lost off Madagascar, who came home in the steamer Oceana, reports that the vessel was wrecked on June 23, on a reef south of Noshe Barracouta Island, in lat. 12 48 S, long. 49 55 E. He adds that Captain Louis, of the schooner Genesta, reports that while on a passage from Vohemar [northeast coast of Madagascar to Diego Suarez [north tip of Madagascar], he passed the ship Falconhurst at 10 a.m. on June 29, on a reef off Noshe Barracouta Island, the ship heading NW by N. When the schooner was about 2 ½ miles away from the ship she signaled, but received no answer. He also says the ship is in 14 metres of water inside the reef, but the sea being so rough it was impossible to go closer.

The captain of the Genesta thinks that if the captain of the Falconhurst had launched a boat it might have capsized, and if so the crew would have been immediately eaten up by sharks, which are in great abundance.

*In fact only one man was lost after the *Falconhurst* wrecked on the northeast coast of Madagascar, the second mate, David John Jones. At the Court of Inquiry from 7–10 September 1900 it was suggested by some of the *Falconhurst*'s crew that second mate Jones committed suicide by jumping overboard from the wrecked ship, because he had been continually harassed and "nagged" by the master, Capt. Peter Lockman, during the passage outward from Barry in south Wales to Diego Suarez on the northern tip of Madagascar. Others, however, claimed that Jones was probably washed overboard by the seas washing over the wrecked vessel. A lifeboat with the third mate and 13 men got ashore in one of the *Falconhurst*'s lifeboats. In the words of the inquiry, "…after four days, during which they suffered privations, they managed to get overland to Diego Suarez."

The captain and ten other crew who were presumed to have lost their lives in the wreck, out of the 26 total crew, were forced to stay on the vessel until the 10 July, the only remaining lifeboat having been smashed and the weather being too bad for them to get ashore. When the weather moderated the master, first mate and nine of the crew rowed in the ship's two small gigs to Androvina Bay, "where they safely landed. They were on the wreck 17 days and had a terrible time."

## 23 July 1900

**The Campania in Collision**

**A Barque Sunk and Eleven Lives Lost**

The Cunard steamer Campania, which left Queenstown for Liverpool early on Saturday morning, ran down and sank a sailing vessel, the Embleton, in St. George's Channel. There was a dense fog at the time. Eleven lives of those on board the sailing vessel were lost. The following account of the disaster has been furnished by the *Times* correspondent at New York, who was a passenger on board the Campania:-

"We had left Queenstown at 2 38 Saturday morning. All day before there had been fog at intervals, and since Friday noon, when we were 207 miles westward from Queenstown we had but crept toward the coast. Friday, at dusk, in a white mist, a schooner had slid past the bows of the Campania and drifted down her side within 100 yards, burning a green light that looked miles away. At Roche's Point it had partly cleared, but Captain Walker would not take his ship near the shore, and the tender came out to us four miles off. It thickened again soon after we were once more under way. At Tuskar Light the fog closed in denser than ever.

Thirty miles to the north-east of Tuskar, well out in St. George's Channel, a phantom ship rose out of sea and fog directly across our bows. No human being on the Campania had seen or heard her. Thirty seconds later the phantom had become a solid sailing vessel into which we crashed. The steel forefoot of the Campania went through her like the clean cut of a sword; she divided just abaft the mainmast; the forward half sank instantly; the stern swung viciously round; hull and masts and yards for a moment tore at the Campania; a lump of wreckage came down on her decks; then the stern of the barque sank also, and the surface of the sea was littered with splintered timbers, boxes, barrels, the whole upper works and lighter cargo and deckhouses and such matters.

Then, nothing. From the instant when the phantom had come into view from the bridge of the Campania till the last vestige of the actual vessel had vanished, some 60 or 80 seconds had elapsed. In those 60 or 80 seconds a barque of 1,200 tons, the Embleton, of and from Liverpool for Wellington, New Zealand, with a full cargo, had gone to the bottom of the Channel, and out of 18 men on board 11 were dead. Whose fault was it?"*

*A subsequent Admiralty Court of Inquiry found the Cunard steamship *Campania* liable for the sinking of the New Zealand-bound *Embleton*, with the loss of 11 of the barque's crew of 18, on account of her excessive speed in restricted visibility (dense fog). The following year, 1901, the *Campania* was the first merchant vessel to be fitted with Marconi wireless telegraphy equipment. In October 1905 a freak wave in the mid-Atlantic struck the *Campania* and washed overboard five steerage passengers. In 1915, in the middle of the First World War, she was converted to launch seaplanes, becoming the first ship ever to do so while under way and the origin of the Fleet Air Arm (the air force of the Royal Navy). On 5 November 1918 the *Campania* sank in the Firth of Forth after dragging her anchors in a gale and colliding with another anchored vessel.

## 12 Nov 1900

**Maritime Intelligence**

City of Monticello (s).- Halifax, Nov. 11.- The steamship City of Monticello foundered at

# Liner in Collision

THE Cunard liner *Campania*, which was some-what overdue, arrived at Liverpool on Saturday evening from New York, and brought tidings of a disastrous collision in the Channel with a barque. The barque sank and eleven lives were lost. It seems that about nine o'clock on Saturday morning the *Campania* was approaching Holyhead at what is described as "dead slow" speed, rendered necessary in consequence of the prevailing fog. When she was twenty-six miles north-west of the Tuscar, she came into contact with what was afterwards found to be the Liverpool iron barque *Embleton*. Prior to the collision not a sound had been heard of any approaching vessel, and owing to the fog none could be seen. Realising from the cries which arose from the sea on either side of the *Campania* that something terrible had happened, Captain Walker, her commander, promptly ordered out his boats. In a very few minutes after the collision two fully manned boats were lowered and soon picked up seven men. These were hoisted on board the *Campania* and were carefully attended to. From the story that the survivors had to tell, it seems that the barque was struck by the *Campania* almost amidships and cut into halves, the fore part sinking on one side of the *Campania* and the after part going down on the other side. Three minutes elapsed between the moment of the impact and the foundering of the barque. Some of the crew of the *Embleton*, who numbered eighteen all told, flung themselves into the water, and managed to keep afloat until picked up by the boats of the *Campania*. A protracted search was made by the crews of the liner's boats for further survivors, but without result. The seven survivors of the barque's crew were W. R. Williamson, chief officer; Passmore, A.B.; Henry G. Manns, second mate; Lorenzo Grinenez, A.B.; Alfred George and William Snow, apprentices. A collection, which realised 691*l.*, was made among the saloon and second-cabin passengers of the *Campania* on behalf of the shipwrecked men and the families of those who were drowned. Our illustration is drawn by A. Cox from materials supplied by an eye-witness.

THE CUNARD LINER "CAMPANIA" RUNNING DOWN THE BARQUE "EMBLETON"

THE COLLISION IN THE IRISH CHANNEL.

midday yesterday, ten miles from Yarmouth [Nova Scotia], while on a trip from St. John for Halifax, via Yarmouth. Thirty-five persons were on board, and only four were saved. The remainder went down with the steamer or perished in attempting to reach the shore in boats. The City of Monticello had a good passage until nearing the Nova Scotian shore, when a tremendous gale was encountered, with a fearful sea. The vessel sprang a leak and in a few minutes became unmanageable and began to sink. Captain Harding, who was in command, launched two of the boats. One of them had seven persons in her, including three women. The men were Captain Smith, of the Battle line steamer Pharsalia; Mr. Murphy, the third officer of the City of Monticello; Mr. Fleming, first officer; and Wilson, a cook, seaman [*sic* - Wilson Cook, quartermaster]. It is not known who were in the second boat.

A minute after the boats got away from the City of Monticello the latter sank with all on board. The second boat capsized and all the occupants perished. The first boat was dashed on to the rocks. Kate Smith, Fleming, and Captain Smith were saved. The shore is strewn with wreckage to-day. Nineteen bodies have been washed ashore, including that of Captain Harding.

## *The New York Times*

## 11 November 1900

## Steamer Founders: 31 Lives Are Lost -

## City of Monticello Goes Down at Bay of Fundy Entrance -
### Engulfed By Heavy Seas -

## A Boat Tries to Reach Shore and is Smashed, but its Occupants Are Saved

Halifax, N.S., Nov. 10.- The worst marine disaster in the long list of steamers wrecked among the rocks and shoals at the entrance to the Bay of Fundy occurred this morning when the side-wheeled steamer City of Monticello, bound from St. John for Yarmouth, was over-whelmed by the mountainous seas only four miles from her destination and engulfed with thirty-one persons. A heavy gale was raging at the time, and there was a tremendous sea.

The place where the Monticello struck is at the mouth of the Bay of Fundy, where the waters of the bay join those of the Atlantic. There are many reefs and shoals at this spot, and the currents are changeable, it being one of the most dangerous places on the coast. The gale last night kicked up a high sea, and at the time the vessel struck the waves were beating upon the rocks and sending spray for hundreds of feet over the land.

The Monticello was on her way from St. John to Yarmouth with a full freight and a fairly large passenger list. Just before she foundered an attempt was made to reach the land in a small boat in charge of the quartermaster, Wilson Cook. It contained Third Officer Fleming, the stewardess, Kate Smith, Second Officer Murphy, and three passengers. This boat was smashed by a huge comber, the occupants being hurled high upon the beach at Pembroke, uninjured. It is believed these are the only survivors...

One of the passengers in this boat was Capt. A.N. Smith of the steamer Pharsalia...Capt. Smith was the first to bring the news of the disaster to Yarmouth from Pembroke, where he landed. He gave the following account of the disaster:- "The steamer Monticello left St. John Friday morning at 11:15. The wind was blowing heavily at the time, but was not so strong as to cause any alarm. The storm became heavier, however, and after the steamer had passed Pelilo Passage it was feared she was doomed. About 11 o'clock, when four miles off Chegogyinx [Chegoggin] Point, it was decided to send the women ashore in the boat, and J.M. Fleming, third officer, Wilson Cook, acting quartermaster, Nehemiah Murphy, second officer, and I volunteered to take them ashore.

The women numbered three: Elsie McDonald, aged sixteen, daughter of Alexander McDonald, of Yarmouth; Kate Smith of Yarmouth, stewardess; and a colored girl whose name I did not know.

The women were gotten into the boat with great difficulty, the volunteers following, and getting the boat away. The wind was blowing on shore at the time, and the boat was carried rapidly toward the land. When the boat got away they were preparing on board to launch another, but I do not think it got away. I think all the rest were lost. The first boat was rapidly driven ashore near Pembroke, and in nearing the land a gigantic wave struck it and threw it upon the shore, smashing it to atoms. I found myself on the beach holding onto the grass."

## 13 April 1901

**Maritime Intelligence**

Hungfei (s).- London, April 13.- A Central News telegram from Hong Kong, April 12, states:- Last night two Chinese vessels, the Hungfei, bound from Wuchow for Hong Kong, and the Sunchow, a passenger boat, bound from Canton for Wuchow, came into collision. Both vessels sank. Seventy Chinese were drowned, whilst only thirteen were rescued. Amongst those saved was a mandarin [high official], who lost much treasure.

## 24 April 1901

**Maritime Intelligence**

Aslan (s)*.- London, April 24. Reuters' Constantinople correspondent, writing on April 19 with reference to the loss of the Mahsusseh Company's steamer Aslan in the Red Sea on April 1, states that altogether between 180 and 200 men were drowned. When three steamers belonging to the same company tried to tow off the Aslan, a large part of the ship's bottom was torn off, and the vessel foundered when she left the reef.

*The 2,540-ton *Aslan*, launched as the *Leopold II* in 1873, was sold in 1874 to the Royal Mail Steam Packet Co. and renamed the *Minho*. When she was sold to Turkey in 1887 she was renamed the *Aslan*. On 1 April 1901 she was transporting Turkish troops through the Red Sea when she struck rocks off the Saudi Arabian port of Yembo (now Yanbu) and sank with the loss of all on board, numbering some 180 troops and crew.

## THE WRECK OF THE *FALKLAND* AT SCILLY ISLES

## 24 June 1901

**Maritime Intelligence**

Falkland*.- Scilly, June 22, 10 30 p.m.- Barque previously reported as wrecked off Bishop's Rock [lighthouse] is the Falkland, of Liverpool, from Tacoma [Washington]. St. Agnes lifeboat just landed with 22 of crew and captain's wife and child; "six" men missing, viz., captain, two mates, and two stewards. Vessel struck at 7 30 p.m. Weather [wind] SSW, strong, with rain squalls.

Falkland.- Scilly, June 22, 10 37 p.m.- Four-masted barque Falkland, from Tacoma for Falmouth, struck rocks, presumed Crim, this evening and shortly foundered. Lifeboats went from [islands of] St. Agnes and St. Mary's; 22 crew, with captain's wife and children, landed by St. Agnes lifeboat; chief mate, steward, and rest of crew missing. St. Mary's lifeboat not returned.

Falkland.- Scilly, June 23, 9 48 a.m.- St. Mary's lifeboat returned last night from scene of wreck without seeing anything of missing crew, viz., Captain Gracie, chief mate Bateson, steward Anderson and three seamen. It blew a gale from SW during the night.

Falkland.- London, June 24.- A telegram from Penzance reports the foundering off the Scilly Isles of the Falkland, barque, of Liverpool, from Tacoma for Falmouth, with grain. On nearing the entrance to the English Channel she encountered the full force of the most severe southerly gale which has been experienced since winter. The vessel made the Scillies, but apparently came in too close, for on altering her tack when off the Bishop Lighthouse she missed stays [ie., in tacking, did not get fully around onto new course] and drifted on to the rocks and sank in deep water.

## 25 June 1901
### The Wreck of the Falkland

The survivors of the crew of the Falkland, wrecked off Scilly on Saturday, Mrs. Gracie, the captain's wife, and his child arrived at Penzance yesterday. All the crew state that Captain Gracie, and the chief officer, Mr. Bateson, were seen doing their duty bravely up to the time the vessel went down. An old man who stayed with them secured a lifebelt and threw himself into the sea, but he slipped through the belt and disappeared.

## THE SECOND MATE'S STORY

The inquest on the body of Gilbert Bateson, 32 years of age, a native of Bentham, Yorkshire, chief officer of the Falkland, was held yesterday at Scilly. Second Officer F. Patey identified the body. The vessel struck on the rock, the witness said, about 6 45 p.m. For 10 minutes after striking the rock the Falkland remained afloat. The captain at once gave the word for the lifeboats to be manned. When the captain gave this last order the witness was standing with the chief officer by the fore braces. Within eight minutes of the vessel striking, the port lifeboat was in the water, but the starboard boat was still in the davits. Witness was in charge of the port lifeboat, into which the captain's wife and child, which was 15 months old, were placed first by the captain himself. When the lifeboat was afloat they got as many more aboard as possible. Owing to the list of the vessel the starboard lifeboat could not be launched. The vessel carried four boats, but two were sufficient for all those aboard. In his [second mate Patey's] boat were over 20 persons; on board the Falkland there were in all 33 persons.

The witness stood by the ship till she foundered. The captain and chief officer were on the poop, and the boat was standing off the port quarter about 40 yards distant. The last he saw of the chief mate was just before the ship plunged. He also saw another man on the ship standing on the quarter rail. The vessel went under very suddenly, and afterwards the boat picked up a man and a boy. The man was in the water only a few minutes, but the boy was immersed for quite half an hour.

For an hour and a half the witness remained near about. He saw what looked like a man on some wreckage some distance north of him, about half a mile away. The weather was hazy, with a big sea tide running towards the rock. He did not endeavour to go to the man's help, as his craft was so heavily laden, and he feared that she would be swamped. He could not tell why the captain and first mate did not leave the ship. He used every endeavour to get them to leave the ship, and stood by with the object of picking up all persons possible. He told the St. Agnes men that he thought a man was on some wreckage. As the other lifeboat was out and likely to pick up any survivors, it was decided to return to port with those survivors they had in safety before making further search.

The foreman of the jury: Did the St. Agnes lifeboat make any signal to the St. Mary's lifeboat?

The witness: I did not see. I saw both the local lifeboats, the St. Mary's boat being two or three miles to leeward. To the best of my knowledge the two local boats did not communicate. We had six oars besides the sea anchor to keep the boat's head to sea, but no sail, so we threw the mast overboard. No signal was flying from the lighthouse.

The witness, continuing, said the crew tried to stay the ship before she struck the rock. She was standing S.E., with the rocks about 100 yards on the lee bow. She missed her stays and got stern way and went on to the rocks. He did not feel justified with so many lives in his charge in going after the man he thought he saw.

*The big iron four-masted barque *Falkland* (3,676 tons, net), of Liverpool, was 135 days out from Tacoma, Washington state on her voyage to Falmouth with a cargo of grain and commanded by Capt. Gracie. On 22 June 1901 and less than a day's sail from her destination, she struck rocks by the Bishop Lighthouse in the Scilly Isles and was wrecked. Soon after the *Falkland* passed close by the lighthouse she tried to tack (change course). The strong tide running prevented her from coming about and she drifted sideways and backwards onto the rocks, striking amidships and sinking in deep water within about ten minutes.

Two lifeboats from the islands of Agnes and St. Mary's came to the rescue. Only the St. Agnes boat found and picked up survivors, the 25 crew and the captain's wife, Mrs. Gracie and her child from second mate Patey's boat. Six persons from the *Falkland* were drowned; Capt. Gracie, first mate Gilbert Bateson, the steward named Anderson, and three seamen.

## 27 Aug 1901

### Maritime Intelligence

Manchester*.- San Francisco, Aug. 15.- Information has been received from the South Pacific of the finding of some wreckage which it is thought may have been connected with the loss of the barque Manchester, from New York for Yokohama, with kerosene, which was posted as missing last June. A native schooner found the wreckage on Bikar Island, one of the most northerly of the Marshall group. Between four and five hundred cases of kerosene were scattered about, with spars and yards.

In the scrub was found the body of a Swede or Norwegian, who had been dead only 48 hours. His certificate showed that he was second officer; it was sent to the German agent at Jaluit. Near by were the marks of the keels of two boats that had been hauled up on the beach and then launched again. In the sand were footprints of a woman and little children.

A number of native birds were found with the bodies punctured and the flesh uneaten, showing that the castaways had sucked the blood to relieve their thirst. They had also partly eaten some turtles.

*The *Manchester* was a four-masted steel barque of 2,850 tons (gross), built at Sunderland by the well-known shipbuilders William Doxford & Sons, and launched in December 1891, for the Galgate Shipping Co. of Liverpool. On or about 21 August 1900 the vessel left New York for Yokohama with a cargo of 124,168 cases (4,515 tons) of kerosene. She was under the command of Capt. N.F. Clemens who was accompanied by his wife and two daughters. The crew numbered 31 in all.

After being spoken near the Cape Verde Islands by another vessel, the French steamship *Olbia*, on 23 September 1900, she was never seen again until the discovery of her wreckage on Bikar Island almost a year after her departure from New York. Since the *Manchester* would have been expected to reach Yokohama by around February 1900 at the latest, Lloyd's posted her missing in June that year.

The wreckage and other indications of her loss at Bikar suggested that the *Manchester* castaways had been on the island for around six months, and that they departed in boats to find water on another island just a few days before the arrival of the trading schooner. The footprints in the sand must have been those of Mrs. Clemens and her two daughters. In any case, the survivors of the wreck were never heard from again and presumed to have died of thirst or starvation – or both.

Bikar Atoll, on the northeast edge of the Marshall Islands in the western Pacific, is just 0.2 sq miles (0.5 km²) in land area surrounding a lagoon of 14 sq miles (37 km²). In 1887 Spain transferred sovereignty over the atoll to the German Empire. Germany had already taken possession of the Marshall Islands in 1844 and established a trading post there at Jaluit Atoll (4.4 sq miles [11.3 km²] land area). The Japanese took over the archipelago at the beginning of World War I. The population of Jaluit today is around 1,650.

## 13 Nov 1901

### Maritime Intelligence

Astree.- Buenos Ayres, Nov. 12, 11 20 p.m.- Telegram received from Tilly Roads, states:- Argentine mail steamer Chaco reports having picked up at Port Cook, Staten Island [northeast of Cape Horn], captain, first officer, second officer, and 21 of the crew of the French ship Astree, bound from Tyne for Valparaiso, abandoned on fire Oct. 8, off Cape St. John [easternmost point of Staten Island]; six of the crew missing, having left in boats and not since heard of. Also reports having picked up first officer [later corrected to boatswain] and two of the crew of British barque Glencaird*, bound from Tyne for San Francisco, totally lost off Port Margaret, Staten Island. Captain, second officer, third officer and rest of the crew drowned. The names of the lost are unknown.

### *10 Dec 1901*

### Maritime Intelligence

Astree.- Buenos Ayres, Nov. 15.- The Government steamer Chaco, which arrived in Tilli Roads (now called Port Comodoro Rivadavia [southern Argentina]) on Nov. 12, telegraphed to this place that she had picked up at Staten Island the captain, first and second officers, and 21 of the crew of the French ship Astree, from the Tyne for Valparaiso, which vessel was abandoned badly on fire on Oct. 8, between Cape Fourneaux and Cape St. John. One of the ship's boats which left her with six men had not been since heard of.

The Chaco also took on board at Staten Island the boatswain and two sailors, the sole survivors of the barque Glencaird, from the Tyne to San Francisco, which vessel, according to their statement, was lost on the rocks near Port Margaret, Staten Island, and the captain and rest of officers and crew perished. These three men, after leaving the wreck, landed near Las Piedras, where they remained some 40 days.

*The *Glencaird* was one of three sister ships built by the well-established Glasgow shipbuilder Russel & Co.; the others were the *Cairniehill* and the *Sir Robert Fernie*. All three were four-masted steel barques launched in 1889. The *Glencaird* was 2,523 tons (gross), and owned from 1893 by C.W. Corsar, of Liverpool. After leaving the Tyne on 16 May 1901 bound for San Francisco, she was wrecked on the coast of Staten Island while trying to pass through the Straits of le Maire on her way to rounding Cape Horn. Her master at the time, Capt. James English, was a 50-year old Irish-born seaman who took his first command at the early age of just 21.

## THE LOSS OF THE *ELINGAMITE*: "FEARFUL SUFFERINGS" OF SURVIVORS

## 17 Nov 1902

### The Wreck of the Elingamite*

### Survivors' Story – Fearful Sufferings

### Wellington [New Zealand], Nov. 17

The stories told by the survivors found on the raft from the Elingamite which was picked up by H.M.S. Penguin leave no doubt of the terrible sufferings experienced by those on board. The raft left the wrecked vessel on Sunday morning with nineteen persons, three of whom were afterwards taken off by one of the boats. With the sixteen remaining the raft was still overloaded, the deck was submerged, and it was impossible to steer. Once the raft passed within a hundred yards of the shore, but, despite the despairing efforts of the people on board, failed to make any headway, and was washed out to sea again. The other raft and some of the boats were more fortunate and reached the land safely.

By the next morning the raft had drifted out of sight of the shore. The only food on board consisted of two apples. On that Monday the sufferings of the castaways were dreadful. Their only food was one apple divided into 16 parts. One passenger died that night from exhaustion, and two more were found dead in the morning. One of these was Mr. A.G. Anderson, a representative of the firm of Messrs. Lyburg, Sessle & Co., of Sheffield. On the Tuesday the weather was fine, but the sea was wrapt in mist. The distress of the sufferers grew in intensity. Reluctantly they cast overboard the bodies of the dead in order to lighten the raft. Notwithstanding all warnings, some drank sea water. During Tuesday night the castaways saw a steamer's light, and shouted. A boat was lowered, and passed within 50 yards of the raft, but missed it in the darkness, and the steamer ultimately steamed away, leaving those on the raft to their suffering. After this a passenger who had been drinking sea water became light-headed and jumped overboard.

On Wednesday morning the twelve survivors ate the second apple and chewed pieces of linen to stay their raging hunger. Before nightfall occurred another tragedy. A passenger became insane, and in spite of the efforts of his companions to restrain him leaped overboard. During the night yet another followed, singing deliriously, as he drifted away, "Oh, death!"

Next morning the survivors, soaked with sea water and blistered by the sun, had abandoned all hope. The stewardess [Miss McQuirk], who was the only woman on the raft, and who had behaved heroically, died that morning, and shortly afterwards the second steward succumbed. Four hours later the warship Penguin came in sight and rescued the eight remaining persons. All of them are progressing satisfactorily. Altogether 149 of the passengers and crew of the Elingamite have been saved. Three bodies were found on the scene of the wreck, eight died on the raft, and one woman died from exposure. One boat which is still missing is supposed [believed] to contain 30 persons. The Penguin and another steamer are still searching for it.

*The 2,585-ton steamship *Elingamite*, under the command of Capt. Ernest Attwood, carried 136 passengers and 58 crew (and a large consignment of gold coins) when she left Sydney on Wednesday, 5 November 1902 on her regular five-day run to Auckland across the Tasman Sea. On Sunday morning, 9 November, the ship was steaming at reduced speed in thick fog when she struck West King Island, the middle island of the Three Kings Islands 35 miles off Cape Reinga, the northernmost tip of New Zealand's North Island. The *Elingamite* sank within 20 minutes.

Two rafts and five lifeboats plus a small dinghy were launched. One of the boats, the first mate's, reached the mainland and raised the alarm about the wreck. The smaller of the two rafts reached Great King Island. Three other boats came ashore at the same West King Island upon which the *Elingamite* wrecked. Early on the morning of Tuesday, 7 November, the *Zealandia*, a steamship en route to Sydney, was diverted to rescue the survivors who had landed on West King and Great King islands. In the late afternoon of Thursday, 9 November HMS *Penguin* found and rescued the eight survivors on the raft which had by then drifted 63 miles to the northeast of the Three Kings and 40 miles from Cape Reinga. The missing lifeboat, the third mate Watson's, with 30 people in it was never found. Of the 195 souls on board the *Elingamite*, 45 died (17 crew and 28 passengers), making it one of the greatest losses of life by shipwreck in New Zealand.

In January 1903 a subsequent Court of Inquiry into the *Elingamite* tragedy found that Capt. Attwood 'was responsible for the loss of the ship'. He was required to pay £50 towards the cost of the inquiry and his master's certificate suspended for a year. However, in 1911 it was discovered by survey that the Three Kings Islands were located incorrectly on Capt. Attwood's chart: they were a mile or so further south and one-third of a mile further east than charted. Based on that evidence, a new Inquiry determined that the *Elingamite* would not have wrecked on the island if the charts had been correct. The charges against Capt. Attwood were dismissed, and he was reimbursed the £50 fine. Capt. Attwood went on to become a ship surveyor at Wellington.

In June 1903 a bottle was found on a beach near Waverley, just north of Wanganui and about 425 miles south of the Three Kings. Inside was a message written by the young stewardess Miss McQuirk. The discovery was reported by the *Colonist* newspaper of Nelson, South Island, in its 19 June 1903 issue:

**Palmerston North, June 18**

Messrs. Symes, of Waverley, recently picked up on the Waverley beach a bottle which contained a message written by the late Miss McQuirk, telling briefly of the wreck of the s.s. *Elingamite*. Miss McQuirk was stewardess on the ill-fated vessel, and perished from exposure.

Another bottle message was picked up almost five years after the tragedy and reported in the Adelaide *Advertiser* newspaper. The message appeared to be from an *Elingamite* engineer in the lifeboat that was never found, although the engineer seemed to be somewhat confused by the rank of the officer in charge of the boat:

*The Advertiser*

**19 September 1907**

**A Message From The Sea - Elingamite Wreck Recalled**

**Auckland, September 18**

A bottle found near Dargaville to-day contained the following message:- "Elingamite wrecked. Second mate mad, boat leaking. No food for eight days. Good-bye.- Fraser, engineer." Police investigations show that Fraser was in the third mate's boat, which has not been heard of since. It disappeared in a fog, when the officer in charge informed the purser that he intended to make the mainland. The only discrepancy is that W.B. Watson, the third mate, appears in the list of missing, and F. Renant, the second mate, in the list of saved.

## SOLE SURVIVORS

## 9 Dec 1869

**Trieste, 4th Dec.**

The *Marino*, Cosulich, arrived here yesterday from Liverpool, reports that at 7 a.m. on that day, when 12 miles SW of Point Salvore*, she picked up a man who was holding on by a piece of plank, who stated that he was Giovanni Dender, one of the crew of the *Milka D.*, which sailed hence for England, 1st Dec., and that during the night of the 2nd the vessel had decks swept, and that whilst she was continually shipping heavy seas he and 5 or 6 others were carried away from the shrouds [rigging], and washed overboard by a sea. He succeeded in clinging to the floating roof of the house on deck. The others also got hold of pieces of plank, but after a few moments he could see nothing of them.

*Point Salvore is the westernmost headland of the Istria peninsula in the northern Adriatic Sea, now Rt Savudrija, in Croatia.

## 15 Oct 1870

**Casualties – Foreign**

New York, 29th Sept.- A fishing schooner, which arrived at Gloucester, U.S., 27th Sept., from Grand bank [the Grand Banks off Newfoundland], reports having spoken on the 21st Sept.

a barque belonging to Yarmouth, N.S. [Nova Scotia], bound hence to London, with loss of sails and rudder head. The barque reported speaking a schooner which had picked up the master of a foundered vessel, lashed to a plank, the master's wife and seven lady passengers having gone down with the vessel. The same barque also saw another vessel dismasted.

## 18 Oct 1870
### Casualties – Foreign

St. John, N.B. [New Brunswick], 26th Sept.- The *N.&E. Gardner*, Journeay, arrived at Halifax, N.S., 22nd Sept., from New York, and reports having been hailed on the previous day by a schooner, bound to La Have, which had on board the master, Putnam, of the *Nancy* (brigant.), from New York to Cape Breton. The master of the brigantine had been picked up from a plank by the schooner, and stated that the *Nancy* was totally lost in the gale of 19th Sept., and that he was the only survivor.

## 21 Oct 1870
### Casualties – Home

Londonderry, 20th Oct., 9 p.m.- The *Enterprise* (s), from Garston to this port, picked up, off Innishowan Head [north coast of Ireland], at 3 p.m. to-day, a boat containing a sailor and the corpse of a girl. The sailor states that he belonged to the Cambria (s)*, of the Anchor Line, which left New York on the 8th Oct., that the Cambria struck on Instrahull Island, at 10 o'clock last night, and that four boats, besides the one he was in, left the vessel. His boat, he says, capsized, and all those in it, excepting himself, were drowned.

## 22 Oct 1870
### Report of the Loss of the Cambria (s)

The 'Times' has received the following telegram:- Dublin, 21st Oct., 2.30 a.m.- The Cambria (s), of the Anchor Line, has been wrecked off the coast of Derry. She had about 170 persons on board, and it is feared all but one may have perished. One man, named Gartlan, from Omagh, has arrived at Londonderry, having been picked up, after drifting on a capsized boat for several hours. Four boats were launched, he says, but he knows nothing of three of them; his own contained 15 persons, and all, except himself, were lost when the boat capsized.

## 24 Oct 1870
### Casualties – Home

Londonderry, 21st Oct.- The man, J. McGartland, who was saved by the *Enterprise* (s), as reported, yesterday, states in his deposition before the Receiver of Wreck, that he was a passenger on board the Cambria (s), and that the steamer experienced fine weather till the 14th and 15th Oct., on which days it blew hard, but moderated about midnight on the latter day, and remained moderated till the night of the 19th, when, between 11 and 12 o'clock, the ship struck heavily and lifted forward.

He then heard orders given to lower the boats, and got into one of them, forward, with eleven or twelve other persons, amongst whom were two seamen and a female; the rope was not let go till a sea which broke on the *Cambria*'s deck fell into the boat and capsized her. When she righted he found all the people who were in her gone, excepting himself and a female, and the latter he found to be dead. He states there were four other boats launched besides the one he was in.

*The West Coast Times* (New Zealand newspaper)

**23rd December 1870**

**Loss of the Cambria and 180 Lives**

One of the saddest events reported by the mail is the loss of the steamer Cambria, of the Anchor Line, on the coast of Ireland, by which about 180 persons were launched into eternity, after a rough voyage, when, in sight of land, they deemed their troubles over.

John McGartland, steerage passenger, picked up from one of the Cambria's boats off Innissowen Head, reports that the Cambria, during a severe hurricane, struck the rocks off Innistrahall, filling and sinking immediately. Her passengers and crew embarked in four boats. The one containing McGartland, fourteen men and one woman, was upset, he alone surviving. No intelligence of the other boats was received...

*The West Coast Times*

**31st December 1870**

**The Loss of the Cambria – Further Particulars**

The Cambria was one of the finest vessels of Messrs Handyside and Henderson's Anchor Line of steamers trading between [the] Clyde and New York; in fact, she was their last new steamer, having only been launched in March last year [1869]. She was an iron screw steamer, of 2,000 tons, and had engines of 400-horse power, but capable of working far above that. She was 342 feet in length, 35 feet beam [wide], and 22 feet depth of hold, and had six bulkheads. The classification at Lloyd's stood A1 in red for twenty years. She was built at Port Glasgow in 1869 by Messrs R. Duncan and Co., and at the time she was wrecked, was commanded, we believe, by Capt. Carnigan [*sic* - Capt. George Carnahan], an able and experienced officer.

The Cambria left New York for Glasgow on Oct. 8, with about 170 people, all told, on board, and was making a very rapid run home when the calamity occurred. If, as it is reported, the vessel was wrecked about ten o'clock on the night of October 19, she must have been caught in one of the terrific squalls which occurred about that time, and driven bodily on Inistrahull island or rock, almost parallel with Malin Head, and opposite Malin Well, one of the extreme points on the Donegal coast.

The man McGarland, the sole survivor, has made following additional statement:-

"On Wednesday night, Oct. 20 [*sic* – Oct. 19th], the weather was very bad. The wind blew furiously, and a heavy rain fell; and, what with the wind and the rain, and the waves which broke over the gunwale, I could see nothing outside the ship. I don't think anyone could see objects at even a short distance. I remained on deck that night till about eleven o'clock. Then I went below.

I had seated myself at my bunk, thinking over old times and my near approach to home, when suddenly there was a horrid crash, and I was sent spinning forward on my face on the floor. I did not lose my senses, although I was a good deal frightened, and, getting to my feet, I hurried up on deck. Here I found passengers running to and fro in great excitement, but I cannot say there was much crying or shouting. I was myself much put about.

I heard the order given, 'Launch the boats,' but I cannot say whose voice it was; and I also heard someone say, 'There is a mighty big hole in the boat.' Our vessel, I now know, had struck the rock of Inistrahull, bow on, but at that time I really saw nothing beyond the boat itself, the night was so dark, and there was so much blinding rain and spray. I did not see the light on Inistrahull. Some time before the wreck I saw two lights, but I do not know the Irish coast, and I cannot tell you where they were.

As I have said, the order was given to lower the boats. There were seven small boats, I think, on board, four of which were lowered. One of them was in the fore-part, the others in the aft-part, or cabin end. I saw the three boats in the cabin in course of being lowered, but I did not see them in the water, and I know nothing whatever as to their fate. When the boat in the steerage end was lowered, I got into it with others. There were in all, to the best of my judgement, ten or eleven of us, all steerage passengers, I think, besides two seamen. No provisions were taken on board; we were near the shore.

Our boat, however, was scarcely launched, when she capsized. When the boat lurched over I got hold of it, but I cannot say what part of it, and when it righted again I managed to scramble in. I never saw a living soul after that. I did not hear a single cry when the boat heeled over, and I never afterwards saw any of my companions. I was very much put about. I must have grasped the boat quite mechanically, and when I got into it again I don't know that I could have told where I was.

I did not see the Cambria go down. The waves carried my boat quickly away from her. When I recovered myself I observed some one lying in the bottom of the boat. I stooped down and found that it was a young woman, lying face downwards. She was dead. I saw that nothing could be done for her, poor thing; and, to tell you the truth, I did not feel able to do much for myself. The oars were tied with small ropes to the boat, and I was not equal to the exertion of recovering them; I just let the boat drift aimlessly along.

The wind and the waves carried me along all morning with my melancholy burden – the poor thing at the bottom of the boat. At half-past two o'clock that afternoon, after fourteen and a half hours' drifting helplessly in the storm, I was picked up by the Enterprise (Captain Gillespie) in Lough Foyle. I was almost insensible at the time. A rope was passed round my body, and I was drawn on deck. I was brought to Londonderry, and have since been almost entirely confined to bed."

*The Cambria, launched on 1 March 1869, was on its twelfth voyage and within a day of arriving at its destination, Glasgow, as it steamed just to the north of Ireland on the dark and stormy night of 19 October 1870. In its path was the small (0.3 km²) island of Inishtrahull, six miles to the northeast of Malin Head, the northernmost point of mainland Ireland. At the time six families lived on the island.

Most reports state that "around 170 persons" lost their lives after the Cambria foundered on the rocks of Inistrahull Island, although some claim that 196 lives were lost. Whatever the exact number it is certain that just one survived – steerage passenger John McGartland – to tell the story of one of the greatest losses of life from a shipwreck in Irish waters.

## 1 Dec 1870

**Casualties – Foreign**

Nassau, N.P. [New Providence island, Bahamas], 12th Nov.- The Victoria (brig), of Barcelona, sailed from Havana about the 6th Oct., with sugar, for Liverpool, and was totally wrecked on the Cay Sal bank*, about 12th Oct. Of the crew of twelve, only one man was saved after being four days on a small rock.

*Cay Sal bank is an atoll in the Bahamas, around 50 km from Cuba. At 5,227 km$^2$, it is one of the largest atolls in the world, though the land area of its 90 small islands and cays around its rim totals just around 15 km$^2$.

## 10 Aug 1871

**Casualties – Foreign**

Sydney, 14 June.- The master (Brodie) of the Lavinia, arrived here, 21st May, from the South Sea Islands, reports that a white woman and child were in [the] charge of the natives at New Britain*, and that at Duke of York Island* he found the bowsprit of a vessel, apparently of about 500 tons, and which had not been long broken. The natives of the latter island informed him that two women and a child had drifted ashore at New Britain, on a raft or canoe.

*New Britain is the largest island in the Bismarck Archipelago of Papua New Guinea. The Duke of York Islands are in the St. George's Channel between the islands of New Britain and New Ireland. The two women and child must have been the only survivors of the wrecked vessel on Duke of York Island.

## 3 Oct 1871

**Casualties – Home**

Brixham, 2nd Oct.- The James Booth (ship), Kelley, of and from Newcastle, for Genoa, foundered, 26th Sept. The carpenter, the only survivor, was picked up on a plank, on the 27th, in lat. 45 N, lon. 8 W, by the *Royal Tar*, Rennels, arrived here from Myteline [main town of the Greek island of Lesbos].

## 3 Oct 1871

**Casualties – Foreign**

Carolinensiel [north German coast], 27th Sept.- According to the statement of a seaman who drove ashore at Bensersiel, on a piece of timber from the Hercules, Kock, stranded on the outer grounds near Spiekeroog [one of the East Frisian Islands, off north German coast], the remainder of the crew, consisting of the master, his son, the mate, one seaman and the cook, were killed by the fall of the masts and rigging.

## 8 Nov 1871

**Casualties – Foreign**

New York, 26th Oct.- [By cable.] – The Shelehof, from San Francisco to Callao, has been abandoned.

*21 Nov 1871*
## Casualties – Foreign

Philadelphia, 6ᵗʰ Nov.- The *Moses Taylor* (s), while bringing the intelligence of the destruction of the whaling fleet*, from Honolulu for San Francisco, discovered the Schelchopp (brig), which had sailed from San Francisco for Callao; she had been drifting about for 109 days, waterlogged, and all the crew were found dead, excepting the captain, who was saved.

*Daily Southern Cross* (Auckland, New Zealand newspaper)

## 8 November 1871

## Fearful Sufferings At Sea.- A Brig Waterlogged, And Loss of Thirteen Souls

By the arrival of the mail steamship Nebraska we have been furnished, by Mr. H. Craig, purser, with the following harrowing account of the sufferings of the crew and passengers of a water-logged brig, and the ultimate loss of thirteen souls from hunger and thirst. The particulars have been supplied by the captain of the brig (the only man saved), who was picked up off the brig by the steamship Moses Taylor on her last voyage from San Francisco to Honolulu. The Nebraska arrived at Honolulu Oct. 21. She had fine weather and smooth sea all the way from New Zealand. At 7 a.m. on October 22, the *Moses Taylor* arrived at Honolulu, having left San Francisco on October 11. She reports as follows:-

At 8.30 on October 19 sighted a sail bearing down, which turned out to be the remains of a water-logged brig. Sent a boat alongside in charge of the second officer, who reported all the bulwarks, except from the foremast forward, gone, and the sea washing all over the deck. Mr. Redstone, now second officer of the Nebraska, went aloft, and found the crosstrees surrounded with canvas, and a quantity of fish in a sack. When on the point of leaving the foretop to descend, he noticed an object crawl out from under some canvas spread over the forecastle. Upon descending, the first words he heard were, "My God, am I saved!"

After calling the crew and searching for any other survivor, they left the wreck for their own ship with, as it proved, the captain of the brig. After receiving every attention and being sufficiently recovered, he related one of the most heartrending cases of hardship and suffering we have ever heard of. He said: "My name is Luder Hopkin, master of the brig Shelchoff, of San Francisco. I left San Francisco on June 23, with a cargo of lumber for Callao, and several passengers for Navigator Islands [Samoa]. Was waterlogged in a hurricane on July 3, lat. 16 N, long. 117 W."

The following was taken from a memorandum found in a sealed phial:-

"Luder Hopkin, master, San Francisco; F. Johnston, mate, Schleswig-Holstein; J. McCarty, 2ⁿᵈ mate, Port Patrick; Phillip Dunn, steward, San Francisco; Levedore Police, seaman; Reborto Secilia, Italy; Mitchell Velago, Calabria, Italy; Andrew Larssen, Sweden; Lona Lewis Hesson, seaman; Hensburg, Germany. Cabin passengers: Ashby Crane, San Francisco; Charles Davis, San Francisco; Charles Kurtz, Tubingen, Germany. New York papers please copy. Bartholomew Clarrell, native of Charleville, Department de Sardensie, France.- Written on board brig Shelchoff, Monday, September 10, 1871. We have suffered hard from hunger and thirst. Crew, passengers, and officers beg to send this to San Francisco, California, and published there in the papers."

In the "Nautical Almanac" were found the following entries: "July – Cyclone; vessel water-logged. September 6 – Andrew Larssen died. September 18 – Lewis Hesson died. September 22 – Bartholomew Clarrell died. September 21 – On the wreck 80 days; 92 days from San Francisco; no rain; nothing to eat. September 30 – We are on the wreck 89 days. Four (4) dead; please put this in the papers. Monday, October 16 – 105 days on the wreck, all hands dead except the captain and one passenger – Crane."

Captain Hopkin reports that a barque passed them sufficiently close for the survivors then alive (eight) to make out a lady on board with a red and white shawl. He made all the signs he could with pieces of canvas waved by all hands from the foretop [top of the foremast], but she took no notice, and squared away. After moving to the foretop they steered the ship with ropes while their strength lasted, and only came down on deck to catch fish that were occasionally washed on board. Crane, the passenger, lived until 24 hours before the Moses Taylor sighted the brig.

Captain Hopkins kept life in by drinking his own urine, and had come down to the forecastle the day before he was taken off for the purpose of finding some bluestone which he knew was there to mix with the ink he had left to make poison, with which to take away his own life if possible. He found himself so weak, however, that he could not get back to the group where the remainder of the fish was. The only water the crew could save was by spreading out pieces of sheepskin to collect the dew at night, and sucking the wool every morning.

When on board the 'Moses Taylor' he would ask if he was really saved. He had dreamt so often of being taken off that he thought that he was still dreaming. Ink and bluestone he had already mixed, and he intended to have taken it after he awoke from the sleep in which he was found by the men of the 'Moses Taylor.'

*When the steamship *Moses Taylor* arrived at Honolulu en route from Australia to San Francisco, she picked up first-hand news of the destruction of 33 American whaling ships trapped in the Arctic Ocean ice near Point Franklin, northwestern Alaska. In May that year the whaling fleet had headed up towards the Arctic grounds to hunt for bowhead whales, passing through the Bering Strait in late June. Unusual weather conditions later that summer caused the Arctic pack ice to close in on the northwest coast of Alaska. Seven ships managed to escape to the south but, by early September, 33 were iced in. Some were crushed by the ice and destroyed. All 1,219 whalers trapped in the ice eventually abandoned their remaining vessels and made it to the safety of the other seven vessels to the south, by escaping from their ships in small boats and crossing 70 miles of open ocean. Before their return voyage to Honolulu the seven rescue whaleships had to dump their catch and most of their whaling gear to make space for their castaway comrades, at an estimated cost of $1.6m. The loss of the 33 ships itself was a costly disaster for the Yankee whaling industry, hastening the process of the industry's decline since the 1850s and ending with its virtual extinction by the end of the 19th century.

## 16 Nov 1872

### Casualties – Home

Harwich [Essex], 14th Nov., 8.30 p.m.- The Australie (barque), Beckman, was struck by a sea yesterday, which washed away longboat, deckhouses, deck cargo, stanchions, etc., killing one of the crew. This morning, the master, the vessel being full of water, launched a boat to go off to the *Johann* (schr.), Ossendorff, from Riga to Bruges, to get assistance, when the master's wife, in trying to get into the boat, was drowned. The boat, on reaching the *Johann*, capsized, and a man who had accompanied the master also drowned. The *Johann* could render no assistance to the *Australie*, owing to the violence of the gale, and bore up for this place, where she landed the master, who reports that he left the barque at 9 a.m., the Shipwash lightship bearing NW about 14 miles distant, and that there were then on board her eleven men and two of his children.

## 16 Feb 1875

### Casualties – Foreign

Sydney, N.S.W., 24th Dec [1874].- HMS *Sandfly*, which has returned here from a cruise amongst the New Hebrides group*, reports that a man came off in a canoe from Basilisk harbour, Tapoua island*, and reported that he was only survivor of the Tortue (cutter), under French colours, bound from Havannah harbour to Vanikoro, at which latter place they were attacked by the natives. The survivor took to a boat with the master, who died at Tapoua island.

*The archipelago of the New Hebrides in the western Pacific, now the Republic of Vanuatu, was colonised by the British and the French in the 18th century. This culminated in an agreement to administer the islands jointly, as an Anglo–French *condominium*, from 1906 until independence in 1980. Tapoua Island, now called Utupua, is an isolated island approximately halfway between Vanuatu and the Solomon Islands to the northwest.

## 7 Dec 1877

### Casualties – Foreign

Lisbon, 6th Dec, 9:55 AM – The Spanish steamer Rivera, from Antwerp, arrived here on the 2nd [Dec.], reports having picked up, in lat. 48 N lon. 5 W, a boat with John MacCarthy, seaman belonging to the British steamer Margaret, bound from Cardiff to Malta, which foundered at sea; remainder of crew supposed [believed] drowned.

### 11 Dec 1877

London, 10th Dec: The following telegram has been received from Lloyd's agents at Lisbon, in reply to a request for further particulars as to the loss of the steamer Margaret. MacCarthy reports "during violent gale night 29 [Nov] Margaret thrown [on] beam ends; sea washed boat and crew overboard; he and 8 others clung [to] boat but companions perished before 2nd [Dec] when rescued by Rivera."

### 12 Dec 1877

Lisbon, 6th Dec: The Rivera (Span. str.), arrived here from Antwerp, has landed a sailor picked up at sea on the 2nd Dec., and supposed [believed] to be the sole survivor of the Margaret (s), of London, from Cardiff to Malta. The said seaman, John MacCarthy, reports as follows:- On 29th Nov., during a violent gale, the Margaret, whilst lying to, was struck by a heavy sea, shifting cargo to port, and throwing vessel on her beam ends. All the crew then got into the lifeboat on deck, and the sea washed it overboard, but in so doing capsized and stove it. On the following morning only nine survivors were clinging to it, when they managed to right and clamber into the boat. One by one the men all died, and the survivor was asleep when the Rivera fell in with him.

## THE WRECK OF THE *LOCH ARD*

## 4 June 1878
**Casualties – Foreign**

Melbourne.- 3rd June, 10.40 a.m.- The Lochard* and Melbourne [*sic*] have been wrecked at Cardies inlet [off the Otway coast, Victoria State, Australia]; two persons only saved. [The Lochard sailed from Gravesend in March, for Melbourne.]

*29 July 1878*
**Casualties – Foreign**

Melbourne, 2nd June.- The Loch Ard, Gibb, from London to this port, struck on the rocks off the Ottway coast, near the Gellibrand river, last night, and sunk.

3rd June.- Only one of the crew and a lady passenger were saved from the Loch Ard.

Later.- The wreck of the Loch Ard has not shifted; only about eight inches of the mainmast are visible. Surveyors consider it impossible to save vessel; wreckage has floated in.

*The clipper ship *Loch Ard* (1,693 tons, 263ft long) departed Gravesend on 2 March 1878 on a regular run to Australia under the command of Capt. George Gibb. Many of the vessel's 17 passengers were young men emigrating to the British colony that Australia then was. Eight were from one Irish family, the Carmichaels (Dr. and Mrs. Carmichael and their four daughters and two sons), who were also emigrating to Australia. Dr. Carmichael was listed as the ship's surgeon. The crew, excluding Dr. Carmichael, numbered 36 men.

After an otherwise uneventful voyage of three months, the *Loch Ard* was sailing southeast along the Victoria coast of southern Australia, approaching Cape Otway, where Capt. Gibb would change course to head northeast towards Melbourne. Adverse weather for about a week had made navigation difficult, and Capt. Gibb could not be sure of the *Loch Ard's* precise position relative to the coast. In the early morning hours of 1st June the ship encountered fog. As the fog lifted in the dim dawn light, Capt. Gibb, to his horror, saw the cliffs and breakers of the Otway coast nearby. He tried to pull away from danger, but the *Loch Ard* struck the rocks at Muttonbird Island. The rigging fell to the deck, killing some people and preventing boats from being launched. Within fifteen minutes the *Loch Ard* had sunk.

Out of the 53 people aboard the *Loch Ard*, only two survived: the nineteen year old apprentice Thomas (Tom) Pearce, who hung on to the hull of an overturned lifeboat before swimming into a narrow cove and beachy shore, and eighteen year old Eveline (Eva) Carmichael, who clung to a piece of wrecked rigging for five hours as she was swept by the sea amongst the flotsam of the wreck into the cove. (Thomas Pearce was one of the sons of Capt. James Pearce who lost his life when his ship the *Gothenburg* was wrecked off the Queensland coast in March 1875: see under **Great Disasters**.)

On shore Pearce heard Eva's cries for help. He swam back out to rescue her. When they were both back on shore, Pearce clambered out of the cove where he and Eva had landed. He climbed the cliff of the cove and went to look for help. Eventually he came upon two men from a sheep station nearby, Glenample Station, who mustered others to rescue the two *Loch Ard* survivors from the cove. Pearce was honoured for his gallant rescue of Eva Carmichael. Both became celebrities as the sole survivors of the wreck of the *Loch Ard*.

Popular opinion in Australia at the time inclined to the romantic notion that the fair maiden Eva and her rescuer, Thomas, should fall in love and be married, but their paths soon diverged. After three months Eva returned to her native Ireland. Pearce left Australia as third mate on the *Loch Sunart*. Coincidentally, he was wrecked (again) in that vessel on the coast of Ireland. He survived and was taken to a village where Eva Carmichael was living with her husband.

Tom Pearce later married a woman related to one of the men who had died on the wrecked *Loch Ard*. He eventually became a master with the Royal Mail Steam Packet Co. and died around 1930. One of his sons, T.R. Pearce, was an apprentice on the ship *Loch Vennachar* when she was wrecked with the loss of all 28 hands on Kangaroo Island off the south coast of Australia in September 1905.

Just off the Great Ocean Road, which winds around the Victoria coast, is the beachy cove where Thomas Pearce climbed ashore to find help for himself and Eva Carmichael. It is now named Loch Ard Gorge, part of Port Campbell National Park, in memory of the loss of the *Loch Ard*, and of the 52 people who perished with her on 1st June 1878.

## 24 April 1879

### Casualties – Home

Liverpool, April 23, 4 30 p.m.- The master of the Humboldt, from Galveston, reports having sighted, on 4th inst., in lat. 36 46 N, long 63 40 W, the wreck of the Gladiolus, of North Shields, from Doboy for Shields (timber laden), drifting on her cargo, and saved one of the crew (Hans Peter Sarsen).

The master, Williams, and the remainder of the crew had been washed overboard.

## *26 April 1879*

### Casualties – Home

Shields, April 24.- Gladiolus.- The following are the names of the crew who were washed overboard and drowned from the ship Gladiolus, of North Shields, on her passage from Doboy to the Tyne:- The master, Williams, of South Shields; mate, Anthony W. Todd, of North Shields; boatswain, William Smith, of Whitby; cook and steward, Henry Gute, of South Shields; A.B. seamen, Michael Murray, of South Shields, Robert Bran, a Swede, John E. Olsen, a Dane; ordinary seamen, A.F. Jensen, Swede, William, Hassena, Finlander, William Thomson, German; carpenter, Andrew Pedersen, a Dane. The only man saved was Hans Peter Larsen, who was taken off the wreck. The Gladiolus was built at Miramichi [New Brunswick] in 1853, is registered 439 tons, and was the property of Mr. William H. Taylor, of Whitby.

## 1 April 1880

### Casualties, Etc.

Lizzie M. Merrill – The barque Vigilant, which arrived at Queenstown yesterday from Valparaiso, landed Captain Beal, the master of the Lizzie M. Merrill, who had been rescued in mid-Atlantic from a plank eight feet long, to which he had been clinging for 80 hours. The Lizzie M. Merrill, which was bound from New York for New Orleans, was struck by a heavy sea, which burst the decks and caused the vessel to founder. All hands were lost with the exception of Captain Beal, who clung to a piece of plank.

## 12 Nov 1884

**Maritime Casualties, Etc.**

Maartje, Grimsby, Nov. 11.- The smack General Wolseley, of this port, has landed the only two survivors of a crew of 15 of the Dutch herring lugger Maartje, of Vlaardingen [near Rotterdam]. On Oct. 28, 100 miles from Spurn, during a tremendous gale, the lugger was struck by a sea which overturned her, imprisoning 11 men in the cabin, where seven of them were quickly drowned. The other four, after about 10 minutes, when the vessel partially righted, got out, when they found that the captain and the three men who had been on deck were gone, that the mast was broken, and the vessel entirely under water except the stem head, to which the four men clung all night. In the morning one was washed away. In the evening one of the men became delirious and commenced to laugh and sing.

Another night passed without help, but next day, when the survivors were at an extreme point of exhaustion, the General Wolseley came to their succour. Although a very high sea still ran, four of Captain Boxter's hands volunteered to man a boat, and, after great exertions, succeeded in getting two of the Dutchmen aboard, but the third, who had been delirious from the previous evening, wanted to go and tell his seven drowned mates below. He was prevented trying to get below, but he refused to get into the boat.

The mate of the Grimsby smack went upon the wreck and tied a rope around the man's waist. An effort was then made to draw him into the boat, but, as he still clung tenaciously to the wreck, the rope was let go for the purpose of trying other means to save him. No sooner, however, did the man find himself released than he laughed wildly, and, letting go his hold, sank beneath the waves.

## 7 Dec 1888

**Maritime Intelligence**

Frank.- Aalesund [Norway], Nov. 28.- The man who was rescued while clinging to a floating spar, off Stadt [peninsula on west coast of Norway], by the schooner Dagny, was so exhausted that it was five days before he could make his deposition. He now declares that his vessel was the Frank, Brunn [master]. A sea struck her and swept away the rigging and deckload and seven of the crew. On the third day the captain shot himself, and the mate jumped into the sea. The sole survivor had nothing during the five days he remained on the wreck but a little vinegar and brandy.

## 10 May 1889

**Maritime Intelligence**

Wandering Minstrel*.- San Francisco, April 22.- The barque Wandering Minstrel, owned in Hong Kong, left Honolulu on Dec. 10, 1887, on a shark fishing expedition amongst the South Sea Islands. On Feb. 3, 1888, while at anchor in Willis [sic – Welles] Harbour, Midway Island, a furious gale came on and drove the vessel ashore, and she soon broke up. A man named Jorgensen, who had formed one of the shipwrecked crew of the schooner General Siegel, was found on the island, having been left there when the rest were taken off. This man, together with the mate Cameron and the Chinese cook, took the largest lifeboat and left the island on Oct. 15. The rest of the crew – except two sailors who had died and one who had been drowned – were taken off on March 17, 1889, by the schooner Norma, which arrived at Honolulu on April 6.

*The 467-ton *Wandering Minstrel*, commanded by Capt. Frederick Dunbar Walker, was on a shark and *bêche-de-mer* (sea cucumber) fishing voyage when it was forced to put in to Honolulu on her passage from Hong Kong after trouble ("approaching mutiny") among the crew. The two mates were discharged and a man named John Cameron was persuaded to sign on, rather reluctantly, as first mate. The ship sailed with a still unruly crew and reached French Frigate Shoals. From there she sailed to Midway Island, 680 miles to the northwest and 1,300 miles from Honolulu, at the furthest extremity of the Hawaiian Islands chain. This was where they found the stranded Danish sailor named Adolph Jorgensen.

Jorgensen had been a crew member of the small fishing schooner *General Siegel*, shipwrecked at Midway in a gale on 16 November 1886. The other crew members sailed off in a small boat that had drifted ashore, but at the last minute they refused to let Jorgensen come with them. According to Jorgensen's account, they even sank a small punt they had used on the island so that he could not get away. The stranded Dane built a little hut (with, apparently, a veranda extension) and lived a kind of Robinson Crusoe existence until the arrival of the *Wandering Minstrel* in January 1888. On 3 February that year the *Wandering Minstrel* broke up in a gale in almost the same place the *General Siegel* had been wrecked.

Eight months later, Cameron, Jorgensen and a Chinese cook from the *Wandering Minstrel* made the voyage in a small boat from Midway to the Marshall Islands, 1,540 miles away to the southwest. Most of the rest of the crew, including Capt. Walker, were taken off the island in March 1889, a little more than a year after the *Wandering Minstrel* was wrecked. The story is told in an autobiographical narrative of John Cameron's life, *John Cameron's Odyssey*, published by Macmillan in 1928.

## LOSS OF HMS *SERPENT* OFF FINISTERRE: ONLY 3 SURVIVE

## 13 Nov 1890

### Maritime Intelligence

Serpent (H.M.S.).*- Madrid, Nov 12.- An official telegram from Corunna [La Coruña, northwest Spain] announces that the British cruiser Serpent has been wrecked off Cape Buey, near the village of Camarinas [Camariñas], on the north-west coast of Spain. The telegram adds that there were 276 persons on board [sic – there were 176], of whom only three were saved, while the bodies of three ladies have been washed ashore.

### *14 Nov 1890*

### Maritime Intelligence

Serpent (H.M.S.).- Madrid, Nov. 13.- A private telegram from Corunna states that only three men were saved from the cruiser Serpent, which came ashore near the village of

Camarinas, and it is feared that all the rest of the crew have been lost. It appears that the vessel struck on the point of Cape Villano known as Punto de Buey, and she must have gone down almost immediately.

Serpent (H.M.S.).- London, Nov. 14.- A further telegram received from Lloyd's Agent at Corunna, timed yesterday afternoon, relative to the loss of H.M.S. Serpent, confirms the report that only three of the crew have been saved, and the survivors are much bruised and lacerated through being hurled against the shore. They are being duly attended to and looked after by the authorities. Twenty-one bodies have been washed on shore and are already buried. From the statements of the survivors the Serpent stranded about 11 o'clock at night. Lloyd's Agent has promised to telegraph any further news that may be received of the disaster, but he is afraid there is no probability of there being further survivors.

*18 Nov 1890*
### The Wreck of H.M.S. Serpent

Her Majesty's ship Tyne leaves Corunna to-day with the three survivors from the Serpent. [Edward] Burton [AB], one of the three [the other two were leading seaman F.G. Gould and Onesiphorus Luxon, AB], has given the following account of the wreck:- "The Serpent, on the evening of Monday, the day of the disaster, was proceeding on her course as usual. We had left Plymouth on Saturday afternoon, and were hoping shortly to round Cape Finisterre. The ship was going about half-speed. The sea was fearful, and the swell of the billows tended to carry the vessel towards the land. The place where the ship struck is in a bay formed by Capes Trece and Villano. It was a very dirty night. It was raining hard, and a thick mist hid the shore from us.

The Serpent passed very close to Cape Trece, but no one on board could see the light on Cape Villano, and the ship headed straight for the middle of the bay. A few minutes later she struck with a frightful shock. Owing to the bad weather the commander was on the bridge. I was on deck myself, as it was my watch. Thirty of the men were close to me. As soon as we felt the vessel strike Captain Ross ordered the boats to be got ready. He was perfectly calm, and at the same time full of energy. By his orders we got out the rocket apparatus, and fired a rope off towards the shore, but it was of no use. The wind and waves were terrific, and the rope fell short.

About three-quarters of an hour passed before the Serpent went down. Meanwhile, all the crew were ordered to the bridge. Gould, Luxon, and I were told off to man one of the boats, Gould being in command. We went off to get the boat ready, but we had scarcely set about it when a huge sea swept all the boats' crews and the boats as well. Captain Ross then shouted out that everybody must do his best to save himself. Gould heard him say this.

Before we set about getting the boats ready, I and several others had put on cork [life] jackets. The Serpent remained all this time as if balanced between the masses of rock. She was not floating. The waves swept over her with awful violence, and soon she was nothing better than a bare hulk. Boats, men, and even the topsides were carried away. Luxon and some of our shipmates who were swept away by the swell succeeded in gaining the rocks, but Luxon was the only man of them who was able to hold out against the force of the seas and to reach the shore, it is true in an almost lifeless condition. A wave carried me away and threw me ashore near to where Luxon was. We looked back and saw a horrible sight, a shapeless mass of men struggling for life and hurled one against the other by the great seas.

Luxon and I, after resting for a bit, made a move, and with great difficulty reached at length the village of Javina. Gould was much longer in the sea than we were. He is a strong swimmer, and fought the waves to the end, being at last thrown up, almost naked, on the beach just by Cape Trece. We all met in the morning in the coastguard hut, where there were also some men who were looking after the cargo of the British steamer Tunbridge, which was wrecked near the same place some months ago.

When day broke we saw that the Serpent had broken in two. The deck was swept absolutely clear, but the six guns remained in their places. The topsides were totally destroyed a few minutes after the Serpent went down. On the following day the bodies of a number of sailors, with cork jackets on, were seen floating on the surface of the water. All were dreadfully disfigured, and some were headless trunks. Most likely they lost all consciousness by being thrown against the rocks. Forty-eight bodies have been buried, among them one believed to be that of Captain Ross, in a lonely spot called Porto do Trigo, quite close to the scene of the wreck. The parish priest of Javina gave shelter and aid to Luxon, who had also met with some grateful charity from some labourers whom he had met near the beach, and who gave him a piece of bread.

Out of the six boats with which the Serpent was fitted not one could be used for saving life. One has been cast up on the shore in a fairly sound condition, but all the rest were smashed. Most of the wreckage reaching the shore is in small fragments, having been dashed to pieces among the rocks."

*The British Navy 3rd class light cruiser HMS *Serpent* was launched at Devonport Dockyard in 1888. She was 1,770 tons, 225ft long, 36ft wide, and 14.5ft deep, and fitted with, "six 6-inch 5-ton breech loading rifled guns". Under the command of Cdr. Harry L. Ross, she left Devonport on 8 November 1890 bound for the West African Station. By Monday 10th November she was off the northwest tip of Spain (Cape Finisterre), steaming at half-speed in stormy conditions. None of the crew on watch could see the light on Cape Villano when she struck the rocks at Punta del Buey around 10.30 p.m.

Of the 176 souls on board, 173 perished when the *Serpent* wrecked; just three survived. The bodies of the dead that were recovered, including that of Cdr. Ross, were buried at what is known today as the English Cemetery at Camariñas.

## 13 Oct 1891

### Maritime Intelligence

Ellen (?).- London, Oct. 13.- Telegram, dated Trieste, Oct. 12, states:- "A story is published here of a Belgian sailing vessel named Ellen (?) having been tossing about the Mediterranean for 12 days through having lost her bearings. Of the 13 sailors on board 12 died of starvation, and the only survivor was rescued by an English steamer."

## 13 Nov 1891

### Maritime Intelligence

William L. Bradley.- Teneriffe, Nov. 12, 3 40 p.m.- Spanish barque Palma de Canarias, arrived Santa Cruz (Palma), reports having picked up captain of the U.S. schooner William L. Bradley, from Charleston for Boston, which capsized during a gale on Oct. 13 in lat. 37 N, long. 62 W. Fate of crew unknown.*

*18 Nov 1891*

**Miscellaneous**

Madrid, Nov. 17.- Intelligence received from the Canary Islands announces the loss of a British vessel and the whole of her crew except one man. The Spanish ship Fama, which has arrived at Santa Cruz de la Palma after encountering a fearful storm on her passage from America, reports having picked up during her voyage an Englishman who was found in mid-ocean clinging to a small piece of wreckage. The man proved to be the captain of an English vessel, the crew of which, believing it to be on the point of sinking, had attempted to take to their boats. Owing, however, to the heavy sea running all were immediately drowned. The captain had remained on board alone, and when the vessel eventually foundered he managed to seize the piece of timber to which he was clinging when rescued.*

*These two incidents might have referred to the same casualty, if some of the details especially of the first report were in error. If not, the rescue of two sole survivors of two separate ships sinking in mid-Atlantic, and their conveyance to the same port – Santa Cruz de la Palma in the Canary Islands – was an extraordinary and possibly even unique coincidence.

## 16 Dec 1891

**Maritime Intelligence**

Prince Soltykoff (s).- Brest, Dec. 16, 10 50 a.m.- [Translation]:- Prince Soltykoff (s) lost near Ushant [Brest Peninsula, Brittany]. Captain only saved.

*17 Dec 1891*

**Maritime Intelligence**

Prince Soltykoff (s).- Brest, Dec. 16.- Prince Soltykoff, English steamer, from Cardiff for St. Nazaire, was wrecked on Sunday night about six miles from Cape Ushant. Captain Flint and 17 of the crew were drowned. According to the narrative of the sole survivor, a man named Kelk, the vessel was struck by an immense wave, capsized and sank immediately. One of the ship's boats, however, remained afloat, and Kelk getting into it was carried by the currents on to the Porsall Rocks*.

*On 16 March 1978 the very large crude carrier *Amoco Cadiz* (233,690 DWT) ran aground on the Porsall Rocks and split in two. Its entire cargo of 1.6m barrels of oil polluted hundreds of miles of French coastline. It was one of the largest oil spills of all time that caused an equally monumental environmental disaster.

## 26 Jan 1893

**Maritime Intelligence**

Lovisa.- New York, Jan. 25.- A telegram from Harbour Grace (Newfoundland) announces the arrival there of two sailors, the sole survivors of the crew of the brigantine Lovisa, from San Domingo [the Dominican Republic] for Havre. They report that the vessel was wrecked in mid-ocean, and that all the other members of the crew were washed overboard and drowned, and that Mr. Ericson, their captain, died from the results of various injuries he received. The two survivors underwent terrible sufferings before being rescued. Besides being nearly frozen to death, they were 15 days with scarcely any food and fire, the last four days without a drop of water.

## 7 Feb 1893
## Maritime Intelligence

Lovisa.- St. John's, N.F., Jan. 25.- Brig Kestrel, which arrived at Harbour Grace to-day from Trapani, brought in two sailors rescued Jan. 15 from Danish brig Lovisa, which sailed from Porta [Puerto] Plata, Dec. 14 for Havre. The Lovisa was wrecked in mid-ocean and all of the crew except two were lost, Captain Eriksen having been killed by falling masts and the others washed overboard. The two survivors had been without food for 15 days. Their rescue was accomplished with great difficulty.

## 13 Oct 1893
## Maritime Intelligence

Star of the Ocean.- Gravesend, Oct. 12, 4 23 p.m.- Steamer City of London, from Brussels, has landed here two of the crew (one dead) of the brigantine Star of the Ocean, of Whitstable [Kent], from Shields for Ramsgate [Kent], cargo of coals, which vessel was run into and sunk at 4 10 this morning, off the North Foreland, by a steamer, name unknown. The survivor, Charles Evans, reports the fate of rest of crew uncertain.

## 10 Nov 1893
## Miscellaneous

North Foreland, Nov. 10, 11 30 a.m.- A body, supposed [thought] to be that of Captain Uden, of the brigantine Star of the Ocean, which was run down by a Belgian mail steamer on 12th ult., was picked up under the Foreland this morning. His features, however, are unrecognisable.

## 10 Dec 1895
## Maritime Intelligence

Principia (s).- Thorshavn [Faroe Islands], Dec. 1.- The Principia (s), of London, has been lost. She left Dundee [Scotland] on Nov. 16, and passed Cape Wrath [northwest Scotland] at 5 a.m. on the 18th. The sea was very heavy with an increasing SSW wind. Set fore and aft sails. Cargo on deck got adrift, but was secured. Smoke was discovered coming from the holds, and suddenly No. 2 hatch blew into the air and flames broke out at 2 30 a.m. on the 19th. The steering gear got out of order, and the vessel rolled heavily. The captain ordered the leeboat [ie., lifeboat on the lee side of the ship] out, but the davits broke and the boat and one man was lost.

The crew then tried to get the weather boat out, but again the davits broke and the second engineer and the boat were lost; two smaller boats on board were burnt. The engines were now stopped for want of steam. Of eight men who were forward six jumped overboard, of whom four were drowned, and two others are supposed [believed] to have perished in the flames.

On the morning of the 19th they got up steam and tried to subdue the fire with the steam pump and buckets, but without success. The steering gear having been put in order, the vessel was steered ENE, with fire increasing. The vessel now drifted before the wind, and at midnight of the 20th she struck on a reef, though no land was to be seen. The foremast went overboard, taking with it the top of the mainmast. The captain sent up rockets [ie., distress signals], and the crew tried to launch a raft they had previously made, but it was washed away with all the men on it, and the ship went down.

The only survivor is a sailor named Heinrich Anders*, of Rostock, who got hold of a plank, and was picked up at noon on the 21st by a boat from Kirkebo, Stromo Island. A passenger, named Harry Jackson, from Dundee, had hold of the same plank, but was washed away. Six bodies have since been found here – those of the captain, passenger, donkeyman, carpenter, steward, and a fireman. A carpet, two bales of skins, and some bundles of "baggins" have washed ashore on Sando [Sandoy Island], probably the place where the vessel struck; also some broken planks, doors., etc.

*The 3,813-ton *Principia* struck rocks and sank in about 35 metres of water off Sandoy Island in the Faroe Islands on the night of 20 November 1895. The sole survivor was a German sailor, Heinrich Anders, who, along with a passenger, Harry Jackson, clung to a plank from the wrecked ship. A story about what happened next told in Faroe is that a farmer went out in his boat to pick up what he thought was driftwood. Upon reaching the piece of wood he discovered Heinrich Anders clinging to it, the passenger having since been washed away. The farmer rescued Anders and salvaged the plank. The German sailor eventually returned to his home town and the farmer converted the plank into a table in his farmhouse.

In July 1936 Heinrich Anders returned to Faroe to visit the people who had rescued him almost 40 years before. To his surprise, he discovered the plank that had saved his life was now a table in the farmer's house. Today that table is in a 900-year-old wooden building, the Roykstovan (smoke room), a traditional Faroese farmhouse in the cultural heritage village of Kirkjubour, the southernmost settlement on the island of Stremoy and one of the most important historical sites in the Faroe Islands.

## 15 Feb 1897

**Maritime Intelligence**

Cyanus (s).*- Paris, Feb. 12.- According to a Brest telegram published in the *Petit Journal*, Nicholson, one of the survivors of the British steamer Cyanus has made a statement to the British Consul at Brest. About 10 o'clock on Thursday evening [11th February] Nicholson says a violent shock forward was felt by all on board, and it was at once realised that the ship had run right on the rocks. The weather was very dull, and there was a thick fog. The entire crew consisting of 21 men were on deck. The minute after she struck the Cyanus went down, leaving no time to lower the boats, and all on board were thrown into the sea.

Nicholson succeeded in clinging to the bottom of a boat which had been lying bottom upwards on the deck of the steamer, and which floated after the ship disappeared. About 8 o'clock yesterday morning, nearly 10 hours after the wreck, Nicholson was picked up in an exhausted condition by a fishing boat, nine miles to the north-east of the Arnen Lighthouse, and landed on the Ile de Sein. Nicholson is entirely ignorant of the fate of the other members of the crew. For some moments after the vessel sank he saw two men swimming near him but they soon disappeared from view, the dense fog which prevailed blotting out all objects more than a yard distant.

*The George Smith & Sons/City Line steamship *Cyanus*, of 1,635 tons, was on a voyage from Bilbao to the Clyde, Glasgow with a cargo of iron ore. On the foggy night of 9 February 1897 she was wrecked and foundered on the rocks near Ile de Sein off Ushant, at the northwest corner of France, the graveyard of so many ships over the centuries. Of the 21 persons on board, the sole survivor of the wreck was seaman Lawrence Nicholson.

## 5 June 1899

**Maritime Intelligence**

Minerva (s).- Gibraltar, June 3, 11 50 a.m.- A report received from British steamer Eddie states:- Passed British steamer Alsatian, off Cape Gatt [southeast coast of Spain], signalled having picked up from a raft June 1, off Cape Palos, captain and second engineer of Italian steamer Minerva, which foundered at sea. Nothing known of the remainder of the crew.

### *7 June 1899*

**Maritime Intelligence**

Minerva (s).- Marseilles, June 5.- The master of the Koordistan (s), from Barry, arrived here to-day, reports:- At 10 15 a.m., June 2, in lat. 37 31 N, 0 52½ W [just south of Cape Palos], sighted a man floating on a hatch and picked him up. He proved to be a man named Antonio Deioch, and reported that he was a seaman on board the Italian steamer Minerva, bound from Greece to England, with mineral oil, with 23 hands all told. The steamer struck on a rock at 5 30 p.m., May 31, and sank in about ten minutes, but he could not say what became of the remainder of the crew. The steamer belonged to Messrs. Raggio, of Genoa, and was of about 3,000 tons burden.

### *9 June 1899*

**Maritime Intelligence**

Minerva (s).- Liverpool, June 9, 10 15 a.m.- Steamer Alsatian landed here this morning master and second engineer of steamer Minerva (late Carmen R.), which vessel foundered June 1. Remainder of crew, 20, were drowned.*

*The *Alsatian* picked up the captain and second engineer of the *Minerva* off a raft, but not all the "remainder of [the] crew, 20, were drowned": one other survivor, the seaman Antonio Deioch was rescued "floating on a hatch" by the steamship *Koordistan*.

## 27 Oct 1899

**Maritime Intelligence**

Zurich (s).- Christiania, Oct. 26.- The *Morgenbladet* [newspaper] publishes the following from Namsos, on the Norwegian coast:- "The steamer Zurich, of London, bound for London, from Archangel [northern Russia], with a cargo of timber, was wrecked in a gale on the morning of the 20th inst. The way to the cabin and stores was blocked by some of her deck cargo which got loose. The crew constructed two rafts, and managed to keep on the forward part of the vessel until the evening of the next day, when the vessel sank.

On one of the rafts were the captain, the three engineers, the second mate, the steward, four coloured men and two dogs. On the other raft were the mate, the boatswain, a stoker, one white and five black sailors. The captain, on the first raft, was picked up by a boat on the 24th inst., near the Vigten [Vikna] Islands; all the rest had perished. The second raft was washed ashore on Oct. 25 with only the corpse of a negro on it."

## 9 Nov 1900

### Maritime Intelligence

City of Vienna (s).- London, Nov 9.- A Penzance [Cornwall] telegram received this morning states that a steamer has found an upturned boat at the entrance of Mount's Bay, with one man on the keel in a state of great exhaustion. It appears that the steamer City of Vienna, of Dublin, left Swansea on Tuesday with coals for Rotterdam; 16 hours out and in tempestuous weather she came into collision with another steamer, name unknown. The City of Vienna was badly damaged, and soon filled. One of the firemen, a German, rushed on deck, and three minutes later the steamer sank.

The German, with two Dutchmen, got into the small boat, which drifted before the gale. But soon a wave capsized the craft. All three scrambled on to the vessel, where they held on for several hours. Ultimately the two Dutchmen fell off and sank. After 27 hours on the boat and being eight miles off Trevose Head*, the sole survivor was rescued by the steamer Garnet, of Dundee.

*Trevose Head is on the north coast of Cornwall, near the then small fishing village of Padstow. The upturned boat and sole survivor of the loss of the *City of Vienna*, a German fireman named Otto Trink, were found "at the entrance of Mount's Bay", the wide bay on the southwest coast of Cornwall from Penzance to the Lizard peninsula. The boat and Otto Trink could not have been discovered, simultaneously, "eight miles off Trevose Head", off the north coast of Cornwall, and "at the entrance of Mount's Bay" off the southwest coast.

One possible explanation is that the vessel was wrecked eight miles off Trevose Head. Trink and the boat might then have been carried by the current around the southwest tip of Cornwall in the 27 hours they were adrift, before being discovered at the mouth of Mount's Bay and Trink landed at Penzance. Another possibility is that Trink was picked up eight miles off *Trewavas* Head, which is on the Lizard peninsula (eastern) side of Mount's Bay. Whatever the circumstances, Trink was certainly the only survivor after the *City of Vienna* sank.

## 29 Dec 1900

### Maritime Intelligence

Primrose Hill.- Holyhead [north Wales], Dec. 28, 6 15 p.m.- Primrose Hill, from Liverpool for Vancouver, with general cargo, drove ashore on high rocky cliff 1½ miles east of South Stack, immediately broke in two, and sunk in five fathoms water. As she broke the four masts fell. Terrible high sea. Only one able seaman, John Petersen, saved. All the remainder of crew, numbering 34, perished.

### *3 Jan 1901*

The Wreck of the Primrose Hill.- As a result of the publication of descriptions of the bodies of the victims of the Primrose Hill disaster, off Holyhead, another of the bodies has been identified. It proves to be that of John C. Crowe, apprentice, whose parents reside at Ramsey, Isle of Man. Twenty bodies have now been recovered, nearly all being washed ashore in a nude state. It is intended to erect a memorial stone over the grave of the twelve unidentified bodies.*…

A very impressive and solemn scene was yesterday witnessed at the Holyhead Public Cemetery, when from 800 to 1,000 persons of all classes congregated to pay a last tribute of respect to the memory of 12 of the crew of the ill-fated Primrose Hill, whose bodies were that day interred. The bodies were encased in plain pitchpine coffins. One coffin bore the inscription:- "J.C. Crowe, died Dec. 28, 1900, aged 16 years"; and another had simply inscribed on it "Joseph Harwood, died Dec. 28, 1900." The remaining ten coffins had no inscription whatever, as the bodies had not been identified.

*A memorial was subsequently erected in Maeshyfryd Cemetery to the memory of the 33 men and boys who died when the four-masted barque *Primrose Hill* wrecked near the South Stack, off Holyhead, north Wales, on 28 December 1900, during a violent storm. Of the 33 who died, 27 bodies were found of which only 12 were identified. Six were never found.

The 2,520-ton *Primrose Hill*, built of iron in 1886, was bound from Liverpool for Vancouver when she encountered hurricane force conditions off the north coast of Wales, just after Christmas 1900. Despite dropping both anchors to keep her off the rocks, the anchors dragged. At around 2 p.m. on 28 December she struck rocks near the South Stack lighthouse. Within five minutes the vessel broke apart and almost her entire crew was drowned. The sole survivor, John Petersen, was on lookout duty at the time. He was apparently hurled onto the land by the sea.

The storm that drove the *Primrose Hill* onto the rocks wreaked havoc throughout the British Isles. In its edition of 30 December 1900, *The New York Times* reported: 'Hurricane Sweeps the British Isles', and included the details of the *Primrose Hill* tragedy:

"The British bark Primrose Hill (Capt. Wilson, from Liverpool, Dec. 23, for Vancouver) went on the rocks three miles off South Stack (not far from Holyhead). She broke in two and went to pieces in a few minutes. One man out of the crew of thirty-five [*sic* – thirty-four] men was saved by a lifeboat [*sic*]. Some time before she struck the Primrose Hill dropped her anchors, but mountainous seas were running. No sooner had the ill-fated ship touched the rocks than the three aftermasts went overboard and she broke in twain, leaving only the foremast standing. Three minutes later this went also. The vessel was soon smashed up. The steamer Hibernia stood by throughout but was powerless to aid. The Holyhead steam lifeboat made three vain attempts to reach the Primrose Hill. The latter's crew were huddled on the poop, when a huge sea dashed over the vessel, washing all away. One sailor was finally hurled against the rocks, sustaining terrible injuries."

The storm also caused the loss of a 1,645-ton Norwegian steamship, the *Fagerheim*, with the loss of all hands. She was wrecked on the Pembrokeshire coast of Wales after sailing from Troon near Glasgow on 26 December:

*15 Jan 1901*

**Maritime Intelligence**

Fagerheim (s).- London, Jan. 15.- A Cardiff correspondent says it is feared that the steamer Fagerheim, Glasgow for St. Nazaire, foundered off Strumble Head, Pembrokeshire, during the gale of Dec. 27. The body of a Scandinavian seaman was washed ashore a few days ago, and other corpses have been observed floating off the Head.

## Post Script

The *Primrose Hill* had an interesting voyage ten years before her demise. After taking a cargo of coal from Dundee to Rio de Janeiro, she sailed in ballast from Rio for Tacoma, Washington, on 20 September 1890, under the command of the same master present at her wreck, Capt. Joseph Wilson. The bosun had contracted smallpox in Rio and remained behind there. Several of the crew had visited him in hospital, against Capt. Wilson's orders. Contagion by them caused smallpox to break out amongst the crew just as the ship was rounding Cape Horn.

One of the few people on board not affected by the disease was the captain's wife, Mrs. Wilson. She took command of the severely undermanned vessel, in typically boisterous Cape Horn weather, and with ice around to look out for. She also had to care for her baby who came down with the disease. Eventually, three months after leaving Rio, Mrs Wilson brought the *Primrose Hill* into Tacoma on 29 December 1890 where the vessel was quarantined. Her heroic endeavour was to keep the vessel on course to her destination, rather than put in at a closer port such as Valparaiso, to seek medical assistance. That courageous dedication to the ship's welfare saved the *Primrose Hill*'s owners a substantial sum of money for which they rewarded Mrs. Wilson in kind.

## 22 Feb 1901

### Maritime Intelligence

Neilly.- London, Feb. 21.- The Press Association's South Shields correspondent telegraphs:- The steamer Northdene, which arrived in the Tyne to-day, had on board a seaman named Henry Smith, who is the sole survivor of the Sunderland schooner Neilly. Smith states that at midnight on Tuesday (Feb. 19), when off Shipwash Sands, a large steamer hove in sight and immediately afterwards crashed into the schooner, cutting her nearly in two. The Neilly began to settle down, and the crew took to the rigging. Smith reached the mainmast, to which he clung, but the others soon fell off from cold and exhaustion, and the last he saw alive was the captain's brother, a youth of 16. Smith held on to the mast for nine hours, when the Northdene came in sight and rescued him. Nothing is known of the colliding schooner.

## 27 May 1901

### Maritime Intelligence

Elise.- Boston, May 26.- Ohio (s) collided during a fog on Thursday night [23 May], south of Cape Sable, with the barque Elise, from Moss [near Oslo, Norway]. The Elise disappeared in the fog, but the Ohio's boat picked up a lad named Paulsen, who believes that the ship sank with 14 on board. His accounts, however, are conflicting. The injury to the Ohio was slight.

## *28 May 1901*

### Maritime Intelligence

Elise.- Boston (by Cable, May 27).- It is reported that the Norwegian barque Elise, formerly United States barque Fortuna, and Ohio (s), belonging to the Wilson Line, have been in collision off Sable Island. Former vessel sank; latter is slightly damaged; no damage to cargo anticipated. Names of the saved: Paoul Paulsen; 14 supposed [believed] lost. The accident happened in a dense fog.*

*The only survivor of the *Elise*, Powell Christian Paulsen, said later that he clambered into the *Elise*'s boat just before the barque sank and all his 14 shipmates were drowned.

## 4 Feb 1902

### Maritime Intelligence

Chanaral*.- London, Feb. 3.- The Press Association's Falmouth correspondent telegraphs that the Chanaral left Nantes on Thursday [30th January] in ballast for Port Talbot [Wales]; terrible weather was experienced, and owing to heavy seas the barque was hove to about 80 miles north-west of Ushant. The vessel rolled so heavily on Friday morning (January 31) that she capsized and in about an hour disappeared. Previous to this three of her boats were smashed, leaving only one which was launched by the chief officer [M. Legrand] and five of the crew; when the boat reached the water she overturned and the five men were washed away, leaving the chief officer clinging to the boat, which he managed after a struggle to right. He was found next morning alone in the boat by the steamer Victoria, of Bergen. The captain [Capt. Loreau] and 15 of the crew of the Chanaral went down in the ship, and five were drowned through the capsizing of the boat.

### *The New York Times*

### 4th February 1902

### French Vessel Lost and Only One Man Out of Crew of Twenty-two Saved

London, Feb. 4.- The first officer of the French ship Chanaral was landed at Falmouth yesterday. He is the sole survivor of the crew of twenty-two men of the vessel, which was capsized off Ushant (off the coast of Brittany).

The Chanaral left Nantes on Jan. 30, and encountered a heavy gale, in which three of her boats were smashed. The same night her ballast shifted and the ship capsized. The mate and five men had in the meanwhile launched the remaining boat, but this was also capsized, and the five men were drowned. The mate clung to the keel and righted the boat. It was afterward overturned several times, but the mate held on to it, and was picked up after being twelve hours in the water. He is in a critical condition.

The Chanaral was owned by A.D. Bordes & Son of Dunkirk*. She was built at Greenock in 1875, and was of 1,388 tons net register. She was 249 feet 4 inches long, had 38 feet 3 inches beam, and was 21 feet 4 inches deep.

*The *Chanaral* was built at Greenock in 1875 as the *Martin Scott* for R.W. Jamieson of Greenock. She was sold to A.D. Bordes & Sons in October 1893 and renamed *Chanaral*.

**A.D. Bordes & Sons was a famous shipping line of the 19th and early 20th centuries. Its founder, Antoine-Dominique (A.D.) Bordes from Gers in northwest France, travelled to Valparaiso, Chile, in 1834. Around 1847, he became partners with Capt. Le Quellec from Bordeaux, in the acquisition of four ships trading between northern Europe (mainly France and the United Kingdom) and Chile: coal outbound from Europe and guano, nitrates and copper back from Chile. After Capt. Le Quellec died in 1868, Bordes became sole owner of the enterprise which he developed into a large fleet of vessels during the 1870s and early 1880s. Bordes retired in 1883 handing over control of the company to his three sons. He died on 28 May 1883.

In 1890 the Bordes sons commissioned the construction of the first five-masted sailing vessel, the 6,200-ton steel barque *France*, to exploit the Chilean nitrate trade. By 1900 Bordes & Sons had a fleet of 38 ships totalling almost 120,000 tons (register), built up partly on the strength of French government subsidies (bounties) for French shipping begun in 1881. By the start of World War I their 46 ships totalling 163,160 tons comprised the largest sailing fleet under the French flag and was the second largest sailing fleet in the world. A.D. Bordes & Sons was dissolved in 1926 as a result of losing almost half its fleet in the war (22 out of 46 vessels), the reduction in demand for Chilean nitrate and changes in the legal status of French shipowners.

## 17 Dec 1902

**Maritime Intelligence**

Marlay (s).*- London, Dec. 17.- The Press Association's Dublin correspondent telegraphs, Dec. 16.- It is feared that the steam collier Marlay foundered in Dublin Bay this morning. The vessel left Liverpool on Monday afternoon, with coals, for Dublin, where she should have arrived the same night, but her passage was greatly delayed owing to the terrible weather she experienced off Holyhead, which caused her to ship a lot of water. When off the Bailey Light at 4 o'clock this morning she appears to have foundered. The only man, so far, known to have survived is a sailor named McGlue. It is stated that at 4 a.m. orders were given to launch the boats, and the lifeboat, which McGlue entered, was carried away by the heavy seas from the Marlay, and owing to the tremendous seas he was unable to get back to the vessel, which he states disappeared within a very short time of his being washed adrift. McGlue was afterwards picked up off Lambay Island by the steam trawler Peter Johnson.

*The little coal collier *Marlay*, of 800 tons, was built in 1890 and owned by the Dublin coal merchants Tedcastle, McCormick & Co. She left Liverpool at 2 p.m. on 15 December 1902 with a cargo of coal for Dublin, commanded by Capt. J. Hamilton with a crew of 15. Off Holyhead, at the northwest corner of Wales, she encountered ferocious weather and began to take on water as she crossed the Irish Sea in the early hours of 16 December.

Around 4 a.m. the *Marlay* was just off the Baily Lighthouse near Howth on the north side of Dublin Bay when Capt. Hamilton gave orders to launch the lifeboats and abandon ship. Able seaman Michael McGlue was getting into the starboard lifeboat just as a large wave pounded into the vessel's port side, washing away the lifeboat with McGlue hanging onto it. He eventually got into the boat, but the heavy weather prevented him from returning to the *Marlay* to pick up other crew members. The collier sank quickly, taking Capt. Hamilton and all the remaining 14 crew with her. McGlue, the sole survivor of the tragedy, was picked up later that morning off Lambay Island to the north of Howth by the steam trawler *Peter Johnson* and brought into Dublin. The sinking of the *Marlay* and loss of all but one of her crew left 11 widows and 49 fatherless children, for which a widows and orphans fund was established.

## (...AND CANNIBALISM)
## THE *EUXINE*

### 11 Sept 1874

**Casualties – Foreign**

St. Helena, 21st Aug.- The master, Murdoch, the first mate, and 21 men of the crew of the Euxine*, from Shields to Aden, which was abandoned on fire, 8th Aug., in lat. 31 S lon. 8 W, arrived here in two boats on the 18th. The second mate with 7 men in a third boat* are still missing. The master reports that on the 1st Aug., in lat. 35 S lon. 13 W, the vessel experienced a terrific gale. Next day a tremendous sea broke over her, carrying away port quarter, boat, etc., washing one man overboard, and shifting cargo. The fire broke out on the 5th. On the 6th a frightful gale from NW. The crew left her on the 8th, but lay by her till next day, when the flames were raging furiously. The boats separated on the evening of the 9th. The second mate's boat was supplied with nautical instruments, provisions, and water.

### *5 Nov 1874*

**Casualties – Foreign**

Batavia [Singapore, 3rd Nov., 4 p.m.] – Five men* from the wreck of the Euxine were picked up in a boat by the Java Packet (ship), and landed here.

*The crew abandoned the *Euxine* on 8 August 1874 in three boats, around 1,100 miles south-southwest of the island of St. Helena in the South Atlantic. The vessel foundered the next day. Two of the *Euxine*'s boats arrived at St. Helena ten days later.

The third boat left the blazing and sinking *Euxine* with the second mate, James Archer, in charge and seven other men on board. The *Java Packet* reported rescuing only five men from that boat, indicating that three men died during their ordeal before the survivors were picked up.

In fact, Archer admitted later by deposition to the Acting British Consul at Batavia (Jakarta) that he and another man, August Muller, had killed and eaten the flesh of a third man in the boat, Francis Shufus, whom they selected to be sacrificed by drawing lots. The rescued men were transported to Singapore, along with their depositions. After consultations with the Singapore Attorney General and the Board of Trade in London, the men were freed; no criminal proceedings were brought against them for killing Francis Shufus. A prosecution was, however, later initiated in Singapore but eventually dropped because no agreement could be reached on whether the appropriate jurisdiction for the case was Singapore or England.

The *Euxine* incident pre-dates a later case of cannibalism by castaways at sea: the sinking of the yacht *Mignonette*, in July 1884, very near where the *Euxine* went down in the South Atlantic ten years before. In the case of the *Mignonette*, however, the consequences both for the killers and for English law were rather more far-reaching.

## THE *MIGNONETTE*

# 6 Sept 1884

**Maritime Intelligence**

Mignonette, yacht*.- Falmouth, Sept. 6, 10 20 a.m.- The Montezuma, from Punta Arenas [Patagonia, Chile], arrived here to-day, brought in Captain Dudley and two men of the yacht Mignonette, from Southampton for Sydney, N.S.W. The Mignonette left Southampton May 19, struck by heavy sea and foundered July 5, in lat. 27 S, long. 10 W. The crew had just time to get into a boat with no water or provisions; 24 days in open boat, 13 feet long. On the 29th July, in lat. 24 S, long. 27 W, the crew were picked up by the Montezuma, after having drifted and sailed 1,000 miles in their own boat. They were landed here to-day.

## *13 Sept 1884*
### The Wreck of the Mignonette

Captain Dudley arrived in London yesterday morning by the mail train, reaching Paddington at 4 o'clock...Captain Dudley was much fatigued by the journey, but went on by cab to Victoria [train] Station, which he left at 10 minutes to 6, reaching Sutton three-quarters of an hour later....Stephens, the mate, and Brooks, seaman, of the Mignonette, reached Southampton yesterday from Falmouth. Stephens was so weak that he had to lean on his mother's arm, but Brooks showed no special sign of illness. Brooks, on being interviewed, generally corroborated the published story of the wreck [of the *Mignonette*].

He says he shipped at £5 10s a month, or 30s over the average, as the voyage was risky in so small a yacht, but he was accustomed to the sea from boyhood, and thought nothing of the danger. He describes the gale of July 5, and the staving in of the boat's side by the tremendous wave. They did not know they were so far from the track of ships. They had two oars in the small boat, but could not row, the weather being so bad. Parker, the boy, often desired to drink the sea water, but Brooks and the others warned him not to do so. His answer always was he must drink something...Parker suffered the most, and seemed at times in such agony of pain they thought he would die. He appeared at times delirious, would be at the bottom [of the boat] trying to sleep, and when he woke up say he wanted to get on board.

On July 20, when Parker's life was taken, except a little piece of turtle skin and a drop of water got in a storm, they had had nothing for eight days. Parker was lying in the bottom of the boat groaning. Brooks, between the captain and Stephens, had spoken for taking the boy's life in the night, but nothing had been said to him. Stephens believed he would never have consented.

Brooks had been at the helm three or four hours, and was lying in the bows when Stephens made signs to him, which he understood to mean that the captain was going to take the boy's life, as he was dying, and if he had not been killed Brooks had no doubt but they would all have died...If the boy had died they would not have had the blood, and thirst more than hunger was their trouble. Brooks said he did not know when it was to happen, as he had his oilskin over his head. He heard the captain speak, and looking up saw the boy was dead, and Brooks fainted. When he recovered the others were drinking the blood, and he cried, "Give me some."...

AS THE MIGNONETTE WENT DOWN.

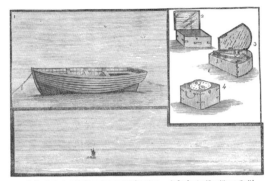

1. The dinghy in which the survivors spent 24 days at sea.   3. Quadrant, with writing on the lid.
2. Lid of chronometer, with the Captain's letter to his wife.   4. Chronometer.

THE LOSS OF THE YACHT MIGNONETTE.

# THE ILLUSTRATED LONDON NEWS

REGISTERED AT THE GENERAL POST-OFFICE FOR TRANSMISSION ABROAD.

No. 2370.—VOL. LXXXV.     SATURDAY, SEPTEMBER 20, 1884.     WITH EXTRA SUPPLEMENT   SIXPENCE.  By Post, 6½D

THE LOSS OF THE YACHT MIGNONETTE.—FROM SKETCHES BY MR. EDWIN STEPHENS, THE MATE.

The way in which they stowed themselves in the dinghy.

Sailing before the wind: How the dinghy was managed during the last nine days.

The following letter, written on the back of the certificate of the chronometer, which was saved from the Mignonette by Captain Dudley, is in his possession...Captain Dudley wrote it while they were in the punt, in the hope that, should they succumb, it might be afterwards found:- "July 6, 1884.- To my dear wife, Dudley, Myrtle-road, Sutton, in Surrey, - Mignonette foundered yesterday. Weather knocked side in. We had five minutes to get in boat, without food or water; 9th, picked up turtle. July 21.- We have been here 17 days; have no food. We are all four living, hoping to get passing ship. If not, we must soon die. Mr. Thompson will put everything right if you go to him, and I am sorry, dear, I ever started on such a trip, but I was doing it for our best. Thought so at the time.

You know, dear, I should so like to be spared. You would find I should lead a Christian life for the remainder of my days. If ever this note reaches your hands you know the last of your Tom and loving husband. I am sorry things are gone against us thus far, but I hope to meet you and all our dear children in heaven. Dear, do love them, for my sake. Dear, bless them and you all. I love you all dearly, you know; but have hopes of being saved. We were about 1,300 miles from Cape Town when the affair happened. Good-bye, and God bless you all, and may He provide for you all.- Your loving husband, Tom Dudley."

## *4 Nov 1884*
## The Mignonette Case

At Exeter yesterday (Monday), Mr. Baron Huddleston, in charging the Grand Jury on a very heavy calendar comprising several cases of murder and other serious charges, gave them particular directions on the case of the master and mate of the Mignonette, charged with the murder of a boy on board their vessel under the painful circumstances so well known. The learned Judge said:-

"The Mignonette, a small yacht of 19 tons, was being sent out to Australia, and the prisoner Dudley, a man of exemplary character, great experience, and courage, applied for and obtained the place of master on board of her. She sailed from Southampton to Sydney on the 19th May, the crew consisting of Dudley (the captain), Stephens (the mate), Brooks (an able-bodied seaman), and Parker (a boy about 17 or 18). They touched at Madeira, crossed the equator, where they fell into very foul weather, and when about 1,600 miles from the Cape of Good Hope, on the 5th of July, in a very severe storm, her starboard quarter was smashed by a huge sea and her side knocked in.

The captain, Dudley, endeavoured to obtain from the cabin some means of sustenance to put on board the boat, which was lowered by the rest, but the Mignonette went down before he was able to obtain more than two 1lb tins of turnips. The three men and a boy were left in the boat without anything to drink, and nothing to eat except the two tins of turnips. On the fourth day they managed to catch a small turtle, upon which they subsisted for a few days, and this was the only food they had up to the 20th day, when the occurrence took place out of which this charge arises.

By the 11th or 12th day the turtle was entirely consumed, and for the next eight days they had nothing to eat. They had no fresh water, and from time to time only succeeded in catching some few drops of rain in their oilskin coats. Their sufferings seem to have been dreadful. On the 18th day, having been seven days without food and five without water, the three men discussed the question as to what was to be done if no succour came, and to have

# THE GRAPHIC
### AN ILLUSTRATED WEEKLY NEWSPAPER

No. 773.—Vol. XXX. ]
Registered as a Newspaper ]

SATURDAY, SEPTEMBER 20, 1884

WITH EXTRA
SUPPLEMENT [

PRICE SIXPENCE
By Post Sixpence Halfpenny

"UNDER FULL SAIL."

A STORM: THE SEA ANCHOR IN USE

## THE CREW OF THE YACHT "MIGNONETTE" IN AN OPEN BOAT AT SEA
FROM SKETCHES BY MR. STEPHENS, MATE OF THE "MIGNONETTE"

considered that one would have to be sacrificed for the purpose of affording food for the rest. The captain suggested that this should be decided by the drawing of lots, but it was not agreed to. Indeed, Brooks seems to have sternly dissented from it, and the boy Parker, who was not then ill, does not seem to have been consulted.

Captain Dudley, in one of his many statements, says that on the day before they killed the boy he proposed to Stephens and Brooks that they should cast lots who should die for the maintenance of the others, but they would not agree to it. Brooks refused, saying that he did not wish to kill anybody, and he did not wish anybody to kill him. Dudley and Stephens talked over the number of their families, and Dudley suggested that they should kill the boy Parker in order that their lives might be saved.

Dudley says:- "If there is no vessel in sight to-morrow morning I think we had better kill the lad. No vessel appearing on the following morning, I made signs to Stephens and Brooks that we had better do it, but they seemed to have no heart to do it, so I went to the boy, who was lying at the bottom of the boat with his arm over his face. I took out my knife – first offering a prayer to God to forgive us for what we were about to do, and for the rash act that our souls might be saved – and I said to the boy, 'Richard, your time is come.' The boy said, 'What, me, Sir?' I said, 'Yes, my boy.' I then put my knife in there (pointing to the side of his neck, opposite to the side over which he had his arm). The blood spurted out, and we caught it in our baler and we drank the blood while it was warm. We then stripped the body, cut it open, and took out his liver and heart, and we ate the liver whilst it was warm. Stephens at that time was in the stern of the boat and Brooks in the bow."

This statement, made by Dudley, is not substantially varied in any of the numerous statements he has made, nor, indeed, is it contradicted by the deposition of Sephens or the evidence of Brooks, who is a witness who will be called before you. Brooks clearly took no part in the death of the boy.

Dudley, Stephens and Brooks fed upon the body of Parker for the next few days. On the 24th day they were picked up by a German barque, the Moctezuma, in a fearful state of prostration, and ultimately brought to Falmouth, whence they were properly committed for trial here...." [The remaining text is an exposition by Judge Huddleston of points of law regarding the case, and the Grand Jury's decision that Dudley and Stephens should stand trial for the murder of the boy Parker.]

*The murder and cannibalisation of Richard Parker, after the sinking of the *Mignonette*, became a landmark case in English criminal law, *R. v Dudley and Stephens* (1884) with regard to whether necessity can ever be justification for murder. In this case, the necessity to kill and eat the corpse of the young boy Parker so that the remaining persons in the boat might survive. After a series of controversial court proceedings, both Dudley and Stephens were convicted of the murder of Parker. They were sentenced to the statutory death penalty but with a recommendation for clemency by Queen Victoria upon the advice of the Home Secretary, Sir William Harcourt. On that advice the death penalty sentence for Dudley and Stephens was commuted to six months imprisonment.

A competition run by *The Sunday Times* newspaper in 1974, asked readers to contribute incidents of extraordinary coincidence. The winner of the competition noted that in Edgar Allan Poe's novella *The Narrative of Arthur Gordon Pym of Nantucket*, published in 1838

(46 years before the *Mignonette* incident), four castaways in a small boat drew lots to decide which of them should be sacrificed to feed the others. That lot fell to the unfortunate man who had suggested the idea in the first place, a sailor by the name of – Richard Parker.

And in Yann Martel's 2001 book *The Life of Pi*, the protagonist Piscine Molitor (Pi) Patel shared the lifeboat in which he took refuge after his ship sank in the Pacific with a Bengal tiger. The tiger was named – Richard Parker.

Donald McCormick's book *Blood on the Sea* (Frederick Muller Ltd., 1962) tells the story of the *Mignonette* incident in great detail. However, this is sometimes more through the creation of a fanciful reconstruction of events than from actual evidence, especially the latter half of the book concerning the later life of Thomas Dudley after he was released from his six month sentence at Holloway Prison and the new life he made for himself and his wife in Australia.

The fantastical element of that sequel story concerns a young girl from the island of Madeira, Otilia Ribeiro. According to McCormick's reconstruction of events, Dudley had rescued Otilia from drowning when the *Mignonette* stopped at Madeira on its fateful voyage. (There was no mention of this in any testimony by Dudley or the other crew members of the *Mignonette*.) Ever grateful to Dudley, Otilia supposedly turned up in Australia to look for him. That part of Dudley's life (including his enthusiasm for smoking opium) was, ostensibly, even more bizarre than his protagonist role in the cannibalisation of Richard Parker, largely owing to the author's creative narrative of Dudley's relationship with the Madeiran girl.

McCormick concluded Dudley's strange life story by noting that Dudley was the first person in Australia to die from bubonic plague in 1900. In reality Dudley probably had a rather mundane life in Australia, the Otilia Ribeiro character and her subsequent relationship with Dudley were almost certainly fictitious in most if not all respects.

A.W. Brian Simpson, in his forensic and scrupulously researched book centred on the Mignonette incident, *Cannibalism and the Common Law* (Penguin, 1986), found no evidence whatsoever of the existence of a young Madeiran girl named Otilia Ribeiro, nor of McCormick's story that Dudley saved her life while the *Mignonette* was at Madeira, prefiguring their later relationship in Australia.

One final note: according to McCormick, during the voyage of the *Mignonette* Captain Dudley was reading a book that cast a shroud of coincidence over the whole affair. The book was Edgar Allan Poe's *The Narrative of Arthur Gordon Pym*.

## THE *TURLEY* INCIDENT

### 24 Dec 1884

#### Cannibalism At Sea

A despatch to the Philadelphia *Press* from Lewes, Del., says:- "The three-masted schooner Helen L. Angel, from Georgetown, S.C., for Baltimore, has brought into port Pilot Marshall Bertrand and Alfred Swanson, a Norwegian, two of the three men who left the pilot boat Turley in a skiff for the purpose of putting Thomas Marshall, another pilot, on board the steamship Pennsylvania, which was bound for Philadelphia. They succeeded in performing this duty, and started back to regain the Turley, which was beating to and fro off the Five Fathom Lightship.

The weather was very thick, and a heavy sea was running, and they never reached their vessel. It was consequently supposed that they had been lost. Several pilot boats were sent in search of them, and one cruised 300 miles off the coast without discovering a trace. Bertrand told the story of their rescue and the horrible cannibalism to which the survivors were compelled to resort.

Soon after leaving the Pennsylvania they found that in the darkness they had lost their bearings. They had no compass on board, and not one of the Delaware lights was visible. Their frail boat became unmanageable, and the wind and sea rose higher every moment. When daylight broke they were drifting rapidly out to sea before the strong north-west gale, and then abandoned all hope, except that they might be carried within sight of some vessel. This was but a forlorn chance, as Bertrand knew that only by some lucky accident would their little craft, which most of the time was in the hollow of the seas, be sighted from the deck of any vessel. All they could do was to keep her as much as possible before the wind.

The weather was bitterly cold, and they had left the Turley in such haste that they had failed to take their thickest clothing or to throw in any water or provisions. Soon the spray, driven by the cutting blasts, froze upon their oilskins, and their stiffened muscles refused to do their duty. One man attended the helm, while the others attempted to keep the boat from swamping by constantly baling her.

All Monday, Monday night, and Tuesday they drifted aimlessly about, suffering the extremes of hunger, thirst, and cold. Towards dusk on Tuesday evening both the Norwegians, who were pilot's apprentices, became delirious, and before Bertrand could control them they had lost the oars and everything else that was loose in the boat. Thus left without any means of handling the skiff, Bertrand can hardly explain how it escaped from filling or capsizing. He says that he occasionally sank into a stupor, in which the ravings of his shipmates, the roar of the wind, and the lashings of the waves were curiously mingled in whatever remained to him of consciousness.

He supposes that it was about midnight of Tuesday when one of the Norwegians, whose name neither himself nor Swanson knew, drew his sailor's knife from his sheath and made several plunges at him, declaring that he would kill him and drink his blood. The deranged man was too feeble to carry out his intention. Exhausted by his long fast, and clad in his icy garments as in a coat of mail, he fell shrieking and gasping across the thwarts at Bertrand's feet. In a few minutes he was dead. The clouds had passed away, the moon had risen, and its beams fell upon the contorted features of the dead sailor, upon whose face the freezing spray quickly formed a film of ice.

To add to the peril of the remaining men, the boat shipped a great deal of water. The baler was among the things the crazy man had thrown overboard, and Bertrand was forced to take off one of his rubber boots to use in its place. Thus he freed the boat from water, but his unprotected foot was frozen. Swanson was so near death as to be incapable of rendering any assistance, and except when he was raving he lay like a log.

When the sun rose on Wednesday morning Bertrand eagerly scanned the horizon in search of a sail, but he saw nothing. As his glance fell upon the corpse of the dead sailor it occurred to him that there might be the means of prolonging life until rescue came.

Horrible as the idea of cannibalism was to him, he realised that nothing else remained between them and death. He roused Swanson, and was happy to discover that his mind had comparatively cleared, and that he understood what was said to him.

The cold had not abated, but the sea had gone down. The day was bright, and Bertrand knew that if they could keep alive until nightfall they would in all likelihood be picked up, as they could not be out of the path of the coasting vessels. Then came the supreme moment. Bertrand indicated to Swanson what he proposed to do, and the latter agreed with him. With the small remnant of strength left them they tore the stiffened oilskins and the underclothing from the dead, and left a portion of the body exposed. Into his breast and shoulders they plunged their knives, and eagerly sucked the blood from the wounds.

They immediately felt refreshed, and the tortures which they experienced were allayed. Pausing for a moment in their work they returned to it, and cut strips of flesh from the corpse. Each devoured a little, though Bertrand says it was with a loathing which only the conviction of self-preservation could enable him to conquer. Then they laid back under the gunwales of their craft, occasionally raising their heads to scan the waters for a sail."

A correspondent of the Philadelphia *Press* found at Lewes (Del.), Marshall Bertrand, the young pilot who was the chief sufferer, still surviving the 60 hours' exposure and the cannibalism. He says:- "Wednesday morning dawned clear, but it was still blowing hard. An hour later I made out a three-masted schooner coming by the wind. We were then 100 miles from the Cape, and about 35 miles from Absecon [near Atlantic City, New Jersey]. I took my mast down, tied my oilskin to it by the sleeves, and waved it with all my might. The schooner came half a mile to windward, but did not see us until it got past. The wind had then moderated.

I wet my hand with sea water, rubbed my lips, and gave the hardest yell I ever gave in my life. They heard me, and the captain put his helm hard up. He ran to leeward, and when he got within hailing distance I heaved the corpse of a man overboard." At this moment Bertrand hesitated for the first time and did not speak freely. "Why did you throw the body overboard?" he was asked. "I didn't want the captain to see it," he replied. "The boat was all bloody. I had kept the man's body up to that time because I meant to eat it that night if it was necessary, and I saw it was fast coming to that."

"The schooner bore down on us," Bertrand continued, "and threw us a rope. Swanson was too weak to take it, so I did, and as the schooner's ladder was down I got aboard without help. Swanson was hauled in over the side. The schooner was the Helen L. Angel, Captain George Tripp, and a guardian angel she proved to us. They treated us as kindly as could be."

## A NEAR THING…

But for the captain's moral rectitude, one (or more) of the castaways from the *Garston*, wrecked on a small Pacific island, might have been fodder for the survival of the others.

## 7 Sept 1889

**Maritime Intelligence**

Garston.- San Francisco (by Cable).- Garston totally wrecked on Starbuck Island*, July 17, part of crew saved.

## 9 Sept 1889
## Maritime Intelligence

Garston.- Sydney, Sept. 9, 12 5 p.m.- Hesper, United States ship, from Puget Sound for Sydney, reports that when passing Humphrey's Island* she was boarded by first officer of Garston, British ship, from Sydney for San Francisco, who reported vessel totally wrecked on Starbuck Island; 20 of crew landed on Humphrey's, where they remain. Captain's boat missing, probably reached another island.

## 12 Sept 1889
## Maritime Intelligence

Garston.- Liverpool, Sept. 11, 6 27 p.m.- Owners state, referring to loss of Garston, on Starbuck Island, following copy of telegram from San Francisco this morning:- "Amongst the saved are Davies, Tangui, Ross, Wahter, Smart, Johnson, Trickey, Petersen, Jonson, Olson, Kelly, Fry, Bird, Clippoe, Garnam, Gribbs, Messenger, Watson, Fairweather, Lawson the cook.

Amongst the missing are: Pye (captain), Bruce, Anderson, Moody, Brenkhorn, Gomer, Muller, Drestwell (? Bracewell), Annesley." We entertain strong hopes, however, of soon hearing of the safety of the nine missing men."

## 17 Sept 1889
## Maritime Intelligence

Garston.- Auckland, N.Z., Sept. 16.- The Wainui (s) arrived here last night, brought the captain and eight of the crew of the Garston, before reported wrecked off Starbuck Island.

## *Otago Witness* (New Zealand newspaper), *19th September 1889*
### Auckland, Sept. 16
### The Wreck of the *Garston*

The *Wainui* from Samoa brings as passengers a portion of the shipwrecked crew of the ship *Garston*, comprising of Captain Pye (the master), Bruce (second mate), Annesley (third mate), and six seamen. The *Garston* was wrecked at Starbuck Island on the 17th July, and the crew, numbering 28, left in two boats. Captain Pye's boat reached Wallis Island, west of Samoa, on August 9th. All the provisions they had were 3lb of salt meat and 20lb of biscuits and the occupants were then in a very weak condition after a 23 days' passage. They had very little water on board, but rain fell frequently, which they saved in their oilskin coats. They sailed 1,600 miles in an open boat. The mate's boat has not been heard of…

On the boat's voyage it was alleged some of the men in the captain's boat talked of "casting lots" amongst themselves to furnish food when all the provisions were gone [ie., to kill one of the men and cannibalise his body for food].

Julian Thomas said that after rowing for 36 hours, Captain Pye determined to make southwards in hopes of striking the Hervey or Cook Islands, or falling in with some vessels bound to San Francisco. An oar was used for a mast, a bed quilt or counterpane (put in the gig by the steward) for a sail. Watches were set and relieved every two hours. One man at the lookout forward, one at the helm. Bruce and Annesley, second and third mates, took their turn with the men; Captain Pye navigated the boat and issued rations. Half a gill of water [1 gill = about ¼ pint] was given to each man.

All shared alike, the captain shared his tobacco with the rest. They stood their two alternate hours of duty and four hours of sleep, or rest, always wet through by the seas which often swamped the boat, always ahungered, always athirst. They bore their lot like men. They had not space to lie down. They were cramped in every movement. The tropical sun beat on them during the day, at night their bones were often racked with cold, yet the warmth of these southern seas saved them.

On the 14th day the mouldy biscuit was all gone, there was nothing but the meat left. On the second day that a tin was opened the meat would be rotten, but it was eaten with avidity. The rain luckily enabled them to fill their beaker. They got weaker and weaker and the devil of despair entered into them. They chewed the leather from their cap linings, the reeds and pith from the captain's sun helmet. They tried to eat their sea boots, but these were far too tough. Twenty days from the wreck the men became desperate, "Only two tins of meat left! Give it us all, and let us have a meal," they said. "No," said the captain. "What if we come and take it?" said one; "there are but two of you." Annesley lay too weak to move at the bottom of the boat, and the captain would only have the second mate Bruce to help him.

But Captain Pye looks a strong, powerful, determined man. "I will throw it overboard first," said he. "You fools! Our only chance is in making this food last as long as possible. If you eat this to-day, what will you do to-morrow?" Then said one of the foreigners, letting out the devil that was in himself and others, "There are plenty of two-legged animals in the boat." Lots must be drawn, and one after the other must become a sacrifice to support the lives of the rest. We all laugh when Mr W.S. Gilbert's ballad of the "Nancy, brig" ** is sung, little reckoning that such experiences have been real ones on the ocean.

Captain Pye now says he would have overturned the boat and sent all hands to Davy Jones' locker before he would agree to such a thing. "I had still my wits about me, and we should all have died together." But he would not cast lots. The skipper might be a sacrifice.

On the 22nd day there was only a pound and a half of meat left, but when near sundown Wallis Island was sighted, the sailmaker calling out "Land!" Another hour and they would have changed their course and missed this, passing it in the night as they did the Samoan Isles. They stood off for a time to avoid the reef, but guided by the full light of the moon the castaways landed on Wallis Island at 4 a.m. on the morning of the 9th, the 23rd day after the wreck of the Garston, after sailing 1,600 miles in an open boat.

*Humphrey's Island is now called Manihiki Atoll in the Cook Islands. Polynesians are thought to have lived on the atoll for at least 3,500 years. Europeans 'discovered' it when the US ship *Good Hope* sighted it on 13 October 1822. Her master, Capt. Patrickson, named it Humphrey Island. Starbuck Island is around 500 miles northeast of Manihiki.

**The Yarn of the* Nancy Bell was a 'Bab Ballad' by W.S. Gilbert, recounting how a crew of mariners from the shipwrecked brig *Nancy Bell* killed and ate each other to survive. The last man – the narrator of the ballad – killed the cook and ate him 'in a week or less', and was then rescued by a passing ship.

## THE *JAMES ALLEN*: CANNIBALISM BY ARCTIC WHALING SURVIVORS

## 18 June 1894

### Maritime Intelligence

James Allen (whaler).- Nanaimo, B.C. [British Columbia] (by Cable).- The steamer Williamette has arrived from Dutch Harbour [Aleutian Islands, Alaska], and brings information of the loss of the whaler James Allen, which was wrecked off Atka Island [one of the Aleutian Islands chain] on May 11. The steamer Dora picked up two of the crew in a starving condition on Bonem Island on June 7, and they report the James Allen ran on a rock near Atka Island, and was so badly damaged that she sank immediately. The captain and mate were in the cabin at the time of the accident and went down with the vessel, but the rest of the crew managed to get away in one of the boats and made for Ounalaska, and are now missing. The United States boat Petrel is searching for them. It is not known what has become of the second mate.

### *3 July 1894*

### Maritime Intelligence

James Allen.- San Francisco, July 3.- A steamer from Sitka, Alaska, brings intelligence of the arrival there of 17 survivors of the crew of the whaler James Allen, which was wrecked off the Western Coast of Alaska. The men had suffered the most terrible privations. Four of the crew were drowned, two died from starvation, and 15 were missing.

### *5 July 1894*

### Maritime Intelligence

James Allen.- San Francisco, June 18.- According to advices received here yesterday the whaling barque James Allen, Huntley, which left here April 14 for the Arctic Ocean, has been lost. The Dora (s), belonging to the Alaska Commercial Company, picked up 20 of the James Allen's crew on Boner Island. They had been living on seal meat for several days, and were nearly starving. They reported that the vessel struck on a reef off Atka Island on June 7 and sank immediately. Only two boats got away, in one of which they were. The other boat, with 15 men, headed away for Oonalaska, and has not yet been heard of. There were 51 hands all told on the barque. The master and mate were asleep and went down with her.

### *The New York Times, 12 July 1894*

### *Fed On Their Dead Comrades*

### A Story of Enforced Cannibalism from the Arctic

Washington, July 11.- A horrible story of enforced cannibalism is contained in a supplemental report made to the Treasury Department by Capt. Healy of the Bear, in connection with the rescue of a portion of the crew of the American schooner James Allen, from Umnak Island [Aleutian Islands chain], on June 14. The vessel left San Francisco April 14, and was wrecked off Amelia [Amlia] Island, Alaska, May 11. There was no time to provision or water the boats, as the vessel sunk within twenty minutes after striking the reefs.

The crew of forty-nine left in five separate boats, and at daybreak the next morning but three boats were in sight. These made for Amelia Island, where they remained a few days and then started for Unalaska, a distance of 270 miles. On the passage one boat was swamped and four men were drowned. Another boat became so leaky that it had to be abandoned. One man died on the way. All the remaining men, twenty-six in number, were crowded into one boat. This boat stopped at Umnak Island, where on the following day three men died from exposure. After several futile attempts, Capt. Huntley, with a crew of six, left for Unalaska, which they reached on June 12, and the Bear, under Capt. Healy, immediately set out for Umnak Island to rescue the remaining men. The situation there and the condition in which he found the men is told by Capt. Healy as follows:

"They were found in a terrible condition. One man, Gideon, had died June 7, and the rest were in a starving condition. Mussels were scarce and the birds wild, so the men said. They had given up all hope of ever being rescued, and were completely demoralized. The body of the man who had died June 7 they had eaten entirely. They had even dug up the body of one of those who had died two weeks previously, and had partially consumed it. The trunk lay just outside of the barabara [a traditional dwelling of indigenous Aleut people], with arms and legs cut off, and portions of the meat were in the pot outside the door. No attempt had been made to hunt or to attract attention from seaward. Not even a mark had been set up on the bluff behind them.

When found they lay around the fire in a hut doing nothing, looking at each other, with the blood of their shipmates on their hands and faces, and bones strewn about them on the floor. Not until the boats had landed and the door of the house been forced open did they know that help was at hand."

## The *Drot* Affair: "Raft of Medusa"

### 24 Aug 1899

**Maritime Intelligence**

Drot.- New York, Aug. 25.- The Norwegian barque Drot, bound from Pascagoula for Buenos Ayres, was wrecked during the recent hurricane on the 11th inst. Of a crew of 15 only one (Necalassas, of Gothenburg) is known to be saved.

### *1 Sept 1899*

**Maritime Intelligence**

Drot.- Baltimore, Aug. 22.- The German steamer Catania reports:- Aug. 20, lat. 30 43 N, long. 75 38 W, rescued from a raft one of the seamen of the Norwegian barque Drot, from Pascagoula for Buenos Ayres, which, on Aug. 11, off the Florida Straits, got into the centre of a hurricane, which wrecked the vessel. The crew consisted of 15 men, eight of whom got on a raft, part of the Drot's deck. In a short time the raft parted, six of the crew on one part and one seaman and the first mate on the other part. They were five days on the raft without food or water. The mate jumped overboard and was drowned. Nothing is known of what became of the others of the crew.*

*The above narrative of the loss of the *Drot* and rescue of the sole survivor of her crew describes only briefly and incompletely a calamity of a much more macabre reckoning. "Nothing is known of what became of the others of the crew". The following newspaper report details exactly what did become of the other men on the other raft, the remaining two of whom were rescued by the British steamship *Woodruff*:-

*Otago Daily Times* (New Zealand newspaper)

**12 October 1899**

**The Barque Drot Tragedy**

**A Terrible Affair – Shipwrecked Sailor Killed and Eaten by His Companions**

A despatch from Charleston (S.C.), dated September 2 says:- "The British steamship Woodruff, from Hamburg, Captain Millburn, arrived here this morning, having on board Morris Anderson and Goodman Thomas [*sic* – Thomasen], two Swedes, who had been seamen on the shipwrecked Norwegian barque Drot. The Drot was caught in the recent hurricane off Florida Straits, and went down in the storm. Of her crew of 17 men, eight clung to a raft consisting of a part of the vessel's deck, while others went down with their ship.

After tossing for a day and a night at the mercy of the waves, the raft split in two pieces. Six men clung to the larger portion, and two remained on the other part. One of these latter was lost [the mate who jumped overboard], while the other one was picked up some days ago by the German steamer Colonia [*sic* – *Catania*] and taken to Baltimore. When the Woodruff sighted the larger part of the raft just before nightfall on Thursday, only two of the six men who had originally clung to it were still alive. These were Anderson and Thomas, and they were in a half-crazed, half-famished condition. While being brought here by the Woodruff they told the terrible story of what had happened on their raft before it was sighted by the British steamer.

The Drot, they said, went down on August 11. It was the next day that their raft split into halves. They had no water and no food, and their only hope of sustenance came from a fishing line and hook that one of the men had with him. He caught many small fish, and these sustained life in the six seamen, but as day followed day and they had no water, the men were crazed with thirst.

The owner of the fishing line lost his mind and jumped into the ocean, crying that he was saved. The five men left then began to fight against hunger as well as thirst. One sickened and died, and before his breath was well out of his body his comrades drank his blood and devoured his flesh. A second man of the company met a similar fate. Thomas and Anderson declare that these men died naturally, but a worse fate remained for the third comrade, a big German.

When they could no longer eat of the two bodies, the three survivors decided that one of their number must die that the others might live. They agreed to cast lots and abide by the decision of chance. Luck was against the big German, and it is asserted that he met his death without a murmur. He even tore the clothing away from his chest that the blow from the knife might reach a vital spot the more readily. He was stabbed to the heart, and his blood was drunk by Anderson and Thomas as it gushed from the wound. They also cut strips of flesh from the body, and devoured it.

When discovered by the Woodruff the raft presented a terrible spectacle. Two crazed men sat beside the three bodies. Thomas was throwing bits of human flesh to the sharks. Two of the dead bodies, half stripped of flesh, were decaying. The men were emaciated, covered with sores and stains of blood, and nearly mad. They told the men of the Woodruff that they had agreed between them to cast lots to see which should kill the other. If the steamer had arrived a few hours later there would have been but one live man on the raft.

Anderson is suffering from the effects of the blow which injured his chest.* I saw Captain Millburn, of the Woodruff, and asked him about the story told by the men of his ship. He did not wish to discuss the matter, but admitted the truth of all the facts that had been given out. He said that the raft presented a spectacle too horrible for words when he found it."

*A *New York Times* report dated 3 September 1899, 'Sailors As Cannibals', revealed that 'Anderson is a raving maniac, and his companion is shockingly mutilated from bites of the crazed man'. Soon after Thomasen and Anderson killed the German, 'Anderson lost his reason and savagely attacked his only companion. Thomasen's breast and face were bitten in several places'.

# 13 Great Disasters

**S**ome shipping casualties ranked well above the magnitude of ordinary collisions, sinkings and shipwrecks. Their losses were counted by the dozens, even hundreds of lives lost in such catastrophic events. A few were not catastrophic in terms of the numbers who died but for the severe impact they left on a community or country. By whatever measure, such disasters were calamitous.

## NARRATIVES

### THE *NORTHFLEET* TRAGEDY

## 24 Jan 1873

### Casualties – Home

Dover, 23ʳᵈ Jan., 8.33 a.m.- The Northfleet* (ship), of and from London, for Hobart Town, with a general cargo, while at anchor off Dungeness at 11 last night, was run into and sunk by a steamer; 30 passengers got into a boat and were brought here.

11.35 a.m.- The steamer by which the Northfleet was sunk is supposed [thought] to have been a Spanish or French vessel. The *Northfleet's* yards are to be seen about two miles off No. 2 Battery. Whitstable divers are expected to be here by next train.

23ʳᵈ Jan., 11.50 a.m.- According to a telegram the coastguard state that 12 persons have been landed at No. 1 Battery; the Northfleet lies between No. 1 and No. 2, and can be seen at low water.

Last night the *Queen* (galley punt), landed here a Captain Swainton of London, coasting pilot, from a two-funnel Spanish steamer, at 8.30; she was schooner-rigged and her description corresponds. The pilot, before leaving, told the captain to stand 3 miles out and course SSW, but instead he put his helm hard aport and went down along shore; steamer was from London, last [port] Antwerp, bound out.

Dover, 23ʳᵈ Jan., 12.55 p.m.- The steamer which ran down the Northfleet was bound down channel [ie., westward]; it is believed she was a Portuguese vessel; a man who is supposed [thought] to have been her pilot, landed here at nine last night.

23rd Jan., 3.30 p.m.- The Northfleet is in 11 fathoms low water; a lugger has saved topgallant sails and a little gear; nothing further can be done without divers.

Dungeness, 23rd Jan.- Mr. Brodrick, pilot of the ship *Corona*, reports that the Northfleet (ship), was in collision, last night, with a screw steamer, and sunk. Emigrants for New Zealand supposed [believed] nearly all perished. The *Corona's* boat put off to the ship, but not a soul seen.

## LOSS OF THE NORTHFLEET

Dover, 23rd Jan., 9.55 a.m.- Twenty-nine of the thirty passengers who saved themselves in a ship's boat are labourers; all are now at the Sailor's Home here. The following is a list of their names:- [list of names, including others saved and landed by various small vessels]

### 27 Jan 1873
**Loss of the Northfleet**
*Message from Her Majesty [Queen Victoria] to the Survivors*

The following telegram from the President of the Board of Trade was received on the 25th Jan., by the Secretary of Lloyd's:-

'I have Her Majesty's commands to convey her heartfelt sympathy to the survivors of the Northfleet. Her Majesty is specially solicitous as to the state of Mrs. Knowles [Mrs. Frederick Knowles, the wife of the Northfleet's master, Capt. Edward Knowles].'

### 31 Jan 1873
**Casualties – Foreign**

Lisbon, 29th Jan., 7.25 p.m.- The Murillo (s), from Antwerp, stopped at Belem [Lisbon], which is unusual, and left suddenly without landing Lisbon cargo; 'was fresh painted starboard bow black and red to water line; had slight indentation near anchor davit [on] port bow.'

[The Spanish Consul in London states, with reference to the above report, that the *Murillo* (s) was painted in London and Antwerp just before starting on her present voyage, and that she received the indentation in her port bow about two years ago whilst entering the port of [Le] Havre.]

### 1 Feb 1873
**Casualties – Foreign**

Lisbon, 30th Jan., 10.20 p.m.- Belem Customs' officials suspended: Murillo steamer illegally despatched for Cadiz.

Cadiz, 30th Jan., 8 p.m.- Northfleet was run down undoubtedly by steamer Murillo, expected here this evening; she was wired to Lisbon to come on immediately to Cadiz if in collision, and did so.

Cadiz, 30th Jan., 8.45 p.m.- Murillo arrived, ascertained to have been ship in collision with Northfleet.

Cadiz, 30th Jan., 10 p.m.- Murillo (s) arrived; positively caused the Northfleet's disaster; no apparent outward damage; authorities take depositions to-morrow, after pratique [health clearance].

LOSS OF THE NORTHFLEET: THE CAPTAIN'S FAREWELL

*The New York Times*

**8th February 1873**

**The Great Disaster - The Loss of the Northfleet**

**Efforts to Save the Female Passengers –**

**Heart-rending Scenes**

The *Pall Mall Gazette* of Jan. 24 says in relation to the disaster in the English Channel, already mentioned by telegraph:

It appears that ninety-seven persons in all have been saved from the Northfleet. The greater number of these came to London last night, having been conveyed free of charge by the South-Eastern and London, Chatham, and Dover Railway Companies. A preliminary enquiry was held yesterday afternoon at the Custom-house, by Mr. G. Bragget, the Collector of Customs at Dover, acting as receiver of wreck on behalf of the Board of Trade, at which the pilot, George Brack, No. 50 Burdett-road, Limehouse [London], gave the following evidence:

## THE COLLISION

The Northfleet proceeded from Gravesend on the 17th inst., at 7 A.M. Witness took charge of her as pilot from that time, and the ship was taken in tow by a steamer, the Middlesex, of London. The ship proceeded all right till she reached Dungeness at about 7½ [7.30] P.M. on the 17th inst. Here the tug was discharged, and the vessel kept beating to windward all the 19th, when the wind having increased to a gale, she proceeded to the Downs for shelter. The roadstead, however, was found so full of ships that the witness thought it prudent to sail to the North Foreland. She continued on her voyage till the morning of the 22nd inst., when she arrived off Folkestone and passed Farleigh Light. She dropped her anchor off Dungeness in the evening.

Nothing occurred till night, when witness was sitting in the saloon, and heard the anchor watch cry out, "Pilot, pilot, come out!" He immediately rushed on deck, and was just able to see a steamer backing out from amidships. He saw that the riding light was burning properly. He instructed the Captain to give orders to set the pump to work, and then conferred with the Captain as to what should be done next. The latter instructed that signals of distress should be burned. All the rockets that were on board the ship were sent up in succession.

During the time there was great confusion among the passengers, and signs of great distress among the women when they saw the ship was sinking. The quarter-boats were lowered, and the Captain, who retained perfect self-possession, ordered that the women and children should at once be got into them. There was a great rush of male passengers toward the boats, and, as far as witness could see, a boat, full of men, was cut away from the ship's davits. Two boats put away full of people. The ship was then rapidly settling down, and witness went into the rigging. He saw a number of persons struggling in the water. On recovering himself, he was just able to see the mizzentop cross-tree out of the water, and swam toward it. He clung to it till he was taken off.

## THE CAPTAIN'S ACTION

The man Thomas Biddiss [alternatively named in other reports as Biddles], says the Dover correspondent of the London *Daily Telegraph*, who was shot by the Captain of the Northfleet, is at the Dover Hospital; and Mr. Grandison, the house surgeon, extracted the bullet from his leg last night. The missile is of lead, and weighs fifty grains. Fortunately the bone of the leg was not injured, and the man is progressing favorably. He has made a rather important statement, to the following effect:

He retired to rest about 10½ [10.30] on the evening of the 22d, and he thinks he had been in bed not more than half an hour when the vessel received a very severe shock. On getting up he ascertained that the vessel had been run into by a steamer; and almost immediately after he received this information, the ship's carpenter, having examined the injured part of the vessel, gave the order for all hands to get on deck as quickly as possible, for the vessel was sinking.

Biddiss went up on deck with the rest, where a scene of great confusion presented itself. The unfortunate emigrants were streaming onto the deck, half-dressed and almost mad with fright. Rockets were fired off, bells were rung, and the usual signals of distress were all quickly given. Biddiss thinks he remembers one gun being fired. The pumps were set to work almost immediately, and nearly everyone on board the vessel worked with hearty good will for about fifteen minutes. Every effort to gain on the water ceased, however, when at the expiration of that time it was discovered that the water had reached the second deck.

Biddiss very much wanted to save something that he had in his chest below, and left the pump to go down for that purpose, when he found that the water had already reached the top of the steps leading down to the deck where his cabin was situated.

The confusion now increased on deck. Some men were rushing about to find their wives and children; some were preparing for the awful catastrophe which they knew must soon happen – unless they received help from the shore, or from a passing vessel – by laying hold of spare spars, ladders, pails [buckets], etc., indeed anything that would float; while others were rushing frantically to the boats.

But amid all was heard the firm voice of Capt. Knowles, who, having seen his wife into one of the boats, stood at the wheel, giving directions for the firing of signals and devising the best means for saving as many lives as possible out of the 400. "The women first," he cried. "I'll blow the man's brains out that dares get into a boat." But this threat came almost too late. Biddiss saw that the boats on either side were filling fast with men, and seeing no reason why he should not make an effort for his life as well as the rest, he jumped into the boat, at the stern in which the captain's wife was sitting under the care of the boatswain, and crouched up at the bow.

Capt. Knowles saw the movement, and, anxious that every opportunity of escape should be given to the frightened women, he ordered him out. Biddiss knew that the vessel would sink almost immediately he got on board again, and that this was the last chance of escape; so he resolutely refused to obey orders. The Captain repeated the order, and threatened to fire if it was not obeyed. The boatswain, who had charge of the Captain's wife, endeavoured to force him out, but it was of no avail. Capt. Knowles motioned to the boatswain to stand clear, and discharged his revolver at Biddiss' head. Biddiss almost felt the ball [bullet] pass over his head.

THE LATE CAPTAIN KNOWLES, OF THE NORTHFLEET.

LOSS OF THE NORTHFLEET: BEACHMEN ON THE LOOK OUT NEAR DUNGENESS.

## THE LOSS OF THE NORTHFLEET.

The terrible disaster in the anchorage off Dungeness on the night of Wednesday, the 22nd ult., when the ship Northfleet, carrying 400 persons, mostly labourers for the railway in Tasmania, was struck and sunk by a foreign steamer, and 320 were drowned, has not ceased to occupy the general mind. Our narrative, published last week, was accompanied with a series of Illustrations—one of the ill-fated vessel; a portrait of Captain Edward Knowles, who died bravely in command; two views of Dungeness; and two representations of this chief incidents—

namely, the ship's boat at the ship's side taking off a party, one of whom was the captain's wife; and the cutter's boat after the ship had sunk, taking off some of the crew from the masts and rigging, which still rose above the water. Several more Illustrations are given in this number of our Journal.

It was observed in our last that various conjectures were entertained respecting the steamer which had come into collision with the Northfleet; and a Spanish steamer, named the Murillo, which had touched at Dover about half-past eight that evening, on her way from Antwerp down the Channel, was mentioned as under this suspicion. The Murillo arrived at

Cadiz on the evening of Thursday, the 30th, having stopped at Belem, the entrance to the port of Lisbon, on the day before, and having them been warned by a telegram to go on to Cadiz without landing her Lisbon cargo. Upon her arrival at Cadiz an official inquiry was commenced at the instance of the British Consul. From the report of Mr. Macpherson, Lloyd's agent at Cadiz, it appears that her starboard bow had been newly painted, black and red, to the water-line, and her port bow showed marks of a slight indentation near the anchor davit. It is stated, however, on behalf of her owners, that the painting was done in London or Antwerp before she started

LOSS OF THE NORTHFLEET: VIEW NEAR DUNGENESS, WITH BEACHMEN WEARING "BACK STAYS."

The Captain, discovering that the first shot had not hit its mark, fired again at the unfortunate man, and this time with effect; for the ball embedded itself in the flesh just above the left knee. Biddiss almost forgot the pain which followed; for the shrieks and cries for help proceeding from the now fast sinking vessel were awful, almost drowning the sound of the alarm-bell, which rang incessantly.

The boat in which Biddiss had escaped but with bare life was still lying alongside; and the poor wretches on the vessel, finding that it was the only available chance of saving their lives, made a rush at the stern to get in, but Capt. Knowles still persevered in endeavouring to save the women. Again the revolver was raised at the first man who entered the boat. The trigger was pulled, but, fortunately for the poor fellow, nicknamed by the crew Billy Ducks, the pistol missed fire. The boat was soon entered by five others; and, before Capt. Knowles could offer any further remonstrance, the ropes were cast off, and the boat was rowed hurriedly away to a tug, which had just steamed up to the spot, and lit up the horrible scene with red lights.

Hardly had the boat, which contained nine persons – namely, the Captain's wife, the boatswain, four laborers, including Biddiss, and three of the ship's crew – got alongside the tug, when, by the gleam of the last rocket in the sky and the lights from the tug, the figurehead of the Northfleet was seen to sink slowly under water. The crowded stern rose up in the air, and with a loud rushing noise, almost disappeared under water, leaving between 300 and 400 people struggling for their lives in the water.

Biddiss says that this was a scene that neither he nor anyone on board the tug will ever forget. The shrieks of the sinking women and the loud cries of the men for help were awful, and must have been heard miles off. Some of those who could not swim were floating on barrels and pails, which they were obliged to leave hold of from sheer exhaustion. Biddiss noticed one friend of his in the water – a married man, who, with his wife and only child, was clinging to a ladder, when a wave came and washed all three off. The woman and child sank, and never rose again. The unfortunate husband managed again to clutch the ladder, but it was out of his power to save his wife and child. Thirty-four people were picked up by the tug, which remained close to the spot the whole night."

*The *Northfleet* was a full-rigged ship of a type known as a Blackwall frigate. She was 951 tons gross, 180ft long, 32.3ft wide, and 20.9ft deep, built in 1863 at Northfleet, near Gravesend in Kent, at a cost of £25,000. On 17 January 1873 she left her berth at the East India Docks in London bound for Hobart Town in Tasmania with around 400 passengers and crew on board, commanded by Capt. Edward Knowles. The *Northfleet* was under charter to Edwin Clark, Punchard, & Co. The company was contracted by the Tasmanian Main Line Railway to provide 350 labourers to work on construction of the Tasmanian railway. Those labourers, along with some wives and children, comprised the *Northfleet*'s complement of passengers. The ship also carried a cargo of around 450 tons of rails and related railway equipment.

At anchor off Dungeness on 22 January, at around 10.30 p.m., the *Northfleet* was struck amidships by a steamer heading west, up Channel. Within an hour after being struck, the *Northfleet* sank with the loss of around 300 lives, including Capt. Knowles. An Australian clipper ship, the *Corona*, was anchored just 300 yards away. However, the sailor on deck watch on the *Corona* was fast asleep; he never raised the alarm about the tragedy occurring so close to his vessel. The *Corona's* master, Capt. Bates, later "assured the chief officer of the Coast Guard that had this man roused either himself or any of his officers, all the passengers and crew of the Northfleet might have been saved".

The Spanish steamship *Murillo*, of 300-ton, was quickly identified as the vessel that had struck and sunk the *Northfleet*. Eight months after she caused the disaster, having fled from the scene of the collision, the *Murillo* was arrested off Dover on 22 September 1873. She was condemned by the Admiralty Court to be sold and her officers "severely censured", not least because of their dereliction of duty to render assistance to the hundreds of unfortunate souls who drowned in one of the worst civil maritime disasters in British waters.

## THE *ATLANTIC*: "AN AWFUL DISASTER"

## 3 April 1873

### Casualties – Home

Liverpool, 2nd Apl., 2.40 p.m.- A telegram to the owners, received from New York, confirms the loss of the Atlantic (s)*. She had on board 762 steerage and 32 saloon passengers, and a crew of 140 – total 934. Out of these, master and from 250 to 300 were saved.

### Casualties – Foreign

New York, 1st Apl., evening.- The Atlantic (s) was putting into Halifax, N.S., short of coal, when she ran ashore. The Cunard and Government steamers had gone to her assistance. She was bound from Liverpool to New York, Williams, master.

### *4 April 1873*

### Casualties – Foreign

Halifax, N.S.- 3rd Apl.- The latest accounts of the loss of the Atlantic state that 560 persons were lost, including 350 women and children; 415 persons were saved, 60 of whom belonged to the crew.

### The Wreck of the 'Atlantic'

### New York, 3rd April

The *Atlantic* is broken in two near the foremast. New York underwriters have despatched a wrecker, with divers, to take charge of and save vessel and cargo, and to make all possible provision for saving and preserving bodies…Three hundred and thirty-six persons saved from the *Atlantic* have been brought to Halifax, and 77 more are on board the steamer *Lady Head*…About half the crew and steerage passengers are lost.

Captain Williams says that on Monday he had 127 tons of coal on board, but, a storm threatening, he determined to run for Halifax. The first intimation of the casualty was the striking of the ship on Mars Island. The vessel remaining fast, the sea swept away all port boats. Rockets were fired at intervals of a minute, but the ship careened to port, rendering the starboard boats useless. The passengers were sent into the rigging, outside the rails, and forward.

Officer Brady [third officer/mate] got a line to the rock, 40 yards distant, and four other lines were subsequently established, about 200 paces distance, between a rock and the shore. 50 persons succeeded in getting to land, but many were drowned in the attempt. Mr.

Brady aroused the islanders at 6 a.m. Three boats shortly afterwards appeared, and took off all the people on the side of the ship and the rock. Officer Frith [first officer/mate] got in the mizen rigging, his rescue being cut off till 3 p.m., when he was saved. Many passengers were frozen to death in the rigging. Among them was the purser. The boilers exploded when the ship rolled over.

## *The New York Times*

## 2nd April 1873

## An Awful Disaster

## Total Wreck of the White Star Steam-Ship Atlantic –

## Over Seven Hundred Lives Lost

Halifax, N.S., April 1.- One of the most terrible disasters that has ever occurred on this coast happened at an early hour this morning, when the White Star ocean steam-ship Atlantic went ashore on Mars Head, at Cape Prospect, during a heavy gale. It is understood that over 700 of the unfortunate passengers were lost out of the thousand who were on board. All of the women and children were drowned.

The news of the awful disaster sent a thrill of horror through the city, and even now excited groups of people stand at street corners discussing the details at hand. Even at this late hour, the details of the disaster are meagre and unsatisfactory. The first intimation we had of the wreck was a rumor that an ocean steamer had gone ashore down the coast, and that several lives had been lost. So vague was the source from whence the report came, that it was not credited for some time. Subsequently, however, more detailed accounts began to arrive, when it was learned that the ill-fated vessel was the steam-ship Atlantic, of the White Star line, Capt. Williams in command.

It was next ascertained that the Atlantic had attempted to make Halifax harbour on her way from Liverpool to New York, in consequence of a shortness of coal. A heavy gale prevailed at the time, so that as she neared the coast, in hopes of sighting the light on Sambro Island, the vessel was resistlessly carried before the wind and by the strong current that always prevails in that locality, right on to shore, causing her to become a total wreck.

Late this evening further and fresher details were obtained. It appears that there were about fifty cabin passengers on board, together with over 900 steerage passengers, so that, with the crew, the total number of souls on boards was over 1,000. During her passage across, the Atlantic encountered very heavy weather, but all was well until yesterday, when it was ascertained that the coal was nearly all gone. About 12 o'clock last night Capt. Williams and his officers believed that they were making straight for Sambro light, but two hours later the vessel struck.

The scene at that moment was a terrible one. The steamer bumped on the rocks two or three times as the heavy waves lifted her, showing that her doom was sealed. Scarcely had the first shock been felt than the passengers rushed from their berths in cabin and steerage on to the main deck, all being terrified and awe-stricken by the perils that surrounded them. An attempt was then made to cut away the boats, and one was soon filled with men and women. It was too late, however, for the steamer suddenly careened leeward, falling over on to her beam ends, and almost immediately sinking, the boat already spoken of being swamped and going down with her.

So close in to shore was the steamer when she struck, that several of the sailors succeeded in swimming ashore with a line after they found themselves thrown into the sea. Fortunately, the fisher men who live on the coast were on the lookout, and they assisted the third officer and his companions in hauling in a rope by means of the halyards they had so bravely carried ashore. By means of this line some 250 men succeeded in getting safe to land, though, shocking to relate, none of the women or children escaped alive, all going down in the raging sea.

The scene of the wreck, as I have already stated, was on Mars Head, the extreme point of Prospect Cape. According to the official charts the Head is laid down as lying in latitude 44° 26' 16" N., longitude 63° 43' 24" W. It is a rocky, peninsular cape, seventy feet high, and forms the western limit of Pennant Bay, the entrance to which is three miles wide and about two miles deep. This little bay is very much encumbered with rocky shoals and irregularly-shaped islands, but it frequently affords shelter to coasting vessels, whose masters are thoroughly acquainted with the passage between them. The land at the head of the bay is moderately high, the highest point, called Hospital Hill, rising fully 250 feet above the level of the sea…

Later.- I have just ascertained that the hull of the wrecked steamer went clear under water when she struck for the fifth and last time. So terrific was the way the vessel struck upon the shore or beach that her bow alone appeared above the surface of the waves. As the majority of the passengers were in their berths or cabins at the time, they were actually drowned between decks, many of them probably being scarcely awake when the waves submerged the ship. We can only imagine the awful scene, for none are here to describe it except, indeed, the third officer, Mr. Brady, who seems wholly unable to give any details. Judging from his statements, the danger was scarcely discovered when all was lost. A few brief moments of terror and dismay, and fully seven hundred men, women, and children found a watery grave…

## THE LOSS OF THE *VILLE DU HAVRE*

## 2 Dec 1873

### Casualties – Home

Cardiff, 1st Dec., 9.25 a.m.- The Ville du Havre (s)*, from New York to Brest and Havre, was run into by the *Loch Earn* (ship)*, of Glasgow, 22nd Nov., and sunk with 226 of her crew and passengers; remainder (87) landed here, this morning, by the *Trimountain* (Amer. ship). [Another telegram.] – The *Trimountain*, from New York, arrived at Cardiff yesterday morning with 87 of the passengers and crew, being the only survivors of the Ville du Havre (s), from New York to Brest, which was sunk through collision with the Loch Earn (Eng. ship), at 2 o'clock on the morning of the 23rd Nov.; 226 lives lost.

Cardiff, 1st Dec., 3.30 p.m.- The passengers and crew of the Ville du Havre (s) supposed [believed] that the Loch Earn might have been expected to arrive at Queenstown, 29th Nov. All persons saved were received on board that vessel, and except three wounded passengers were transferred to the *Trimountain*. The *Loch Earn* was so badly damaged that when the *Trimountain* came up, the passengers and crew, except those wounded, requested to be transferred to the *Trimountain*. The wind being WSW, the *Loch Earn* could not proceed, but wore [ie., "wore ship" – turned around], and was returning.

Cardiff, 1st Dec., 5.24 p.m.- On further enquiry it has been ascertained that the bows of the *Loch Earn* were completely stove in, and that the vessel was only kept afloat by her watertight fore compartment. The master stated that he intended to proceed to Queenstown.

*3 Dec 1873*

## Loss of the Ville du Havre (s)

Capt. Urquhart, of the *Trimountain*, reports as follows: "On the morning of the 22nd Nov., when in lat. 47 N, lon. 35 W, we saw a vessel on the weather bow with her bowsprit gone and sails flying. We hauled up for her, and found she was flying signals of distress. She proved to be the ship *Loch Earn*, of Glasgow, bound from London to New York. We spoke with her, and on coming alongside the captain asked me to take off 50 of the passengers and crew from the *Ville du Havre*, which had been sunk by the *Loch Earn* at 2 o'clock that morning.

I held a consultation with the captain of the *Loch Earn* and the passengers, and we came to the conclusion that it was advisable to transfer the whole of the survivors to my own ship. Accordingly they were transferred as soon as possible, with the exception of two. One of these, a French clergyman, was reported to be deranged, owing to which it was thought prudent to leave him on board the *Loch Earn*; the other was left to take care of him.

After taking them on board the *Trimountain* I consulted with the officers, and we decided to cruise about the spot where the disaster happened. This we continued to do until it was nearly dark, but we were unable to see anything but two casks floating in the water. The search was then given up, and we proceeded on the voyage to Bristol. The *Loch Earn* was very badly damaged in her bows; her bowsprit was clean gone, and there was a great hole; but fortunately the hole was above the water-mark."

*9 Dec 1873*

## Casualties – Home

Plymouth, 7th Dec.- The Loch earn (ship), of Glasgow, Robertson, from London to New York, which was in collision, 22nd Nov., with the Ville du Havre (s), bore up for England, but, drifting to the north, did not make much headway, owing to her being disabled. She was abandoned on the 1st Dec. The master, crew, and the three survivors from the Ville du Havre were transferred to the *British Queen* (barq.), Masters, from Philadelphia to Antwerp, and by her put on board the *Zedora* (pilot cutter), off this port, and landed here last night.

*The New York Times*

*2nd Dec 1873*

## Loss of the Ville du Havre

## The Purser's Story

London, Dec. 1.- The purser of the ill-fated steam-ship Ville du Havre gave the following narrative of the disaster:

"We were seven days out. It was Saturday night. I was sleeping when the collision occurred. Rushing on deck I descried a sailing ship, and three minutes later gained the fearful conviction that the ship was going down by the bow. Thirty or forty passengers

managed to get into the long boat, and life grew strong with them when freed from the sinking ship. But suddenly the mizzenmast fell over the left side of the vessel, killing or wounding nearly all of them. Immediately afterward the mainmast fell on the deck, killing and wounding more. The water was rushing down the windpipe with a fearful velocity.

The vessel was sinking. I jumped overboard with another person, and swam toward the Loch Earn half a mile off. Looking around, I saw the steamer disappear without reeling, going down bow foremost. For a moment a mighty shriek rent the air, the last outbreak of agony. A death-like calm succeeded the noise and tumult. The captain remained on the bridge during the whole scene. He was rescued one hour later."

Six officers out of the fifteen were saved by swimming, except the First Lieutenant, who went in a boat to the Loch Earn. The purser gives a touching narrative of the presence of a French priest, who, amid deathlike calmness on deck, dispensed blessings.

The boats cruised about until 10 o'clock next morning, in hopeless efforts to pick up others. The survivors remained on board the British ship until 3 o'clock P.M., and were then transferred to the American ship Trimountain, commanded by Capt. Urquhart, who gives the following narrative:

"On Saturday morning we saw a vessel with the weather-bow bowsprit gone and sails flowing, which proved to be the Loch Earn, of Glasgow, bound for New York. The Captain asked to transfer the surviving passengers and crew of the steamer Ville du Havre, which sank at 2 o'clock that morning. All except two, one a French priest, and the other, a person who remained to act as nurse, were transferred. It was a pitiful sight to see these human beings huddled together in a small cabin, heart-broken and destitute of clothing, but still thankful for their lives, and grateful for the hospitality received on the Loch Earn. Many were hurt by fragments of the wreck. We cruised till nearly dark, and then proceeded on the voyage to Bristol. Not a vestige of the Ville du Havre – man, woman or child – could be discovered in the neighbourhood of where the collision occurred. There was a rather heavy sea, but little wind when the disaster occurred.

The shock of the collision was fearful. The rapidity in which the steamer went down prevented the launching of more than a whale-boat and the Captain's gig. In twelve minutes after being struck the ship went down. The terror among the passengers paralyzed all efforts to save. Many of the passengers never quitted their state-rooms, whole families meeting their death together.

Among the saved are Miss Nolan, Mary and Annie Hunter, Fanny Beninger, Helen and Madeline Mixter. Mrs. Spafford, of Chicago, lost four children. James Bishop, of New York, floated three hours on a plank. Henry Belknap, of Mount Vernon, near Boston, swam from the wreck and was rescued by the English boat. Mr. Barbancon swam one hour, and Witthaus did the same, and were picked up by the French boat. Mr. Slade, of No. 134 Maiden lane, floated on a plank. Mr. and Mrs. Swift and Mr. Allen, of New Bedford, jumped overboard. Their lives were preserved, but the Swifts lost their daughter.

Fanny Bininger sank with the ship, but floated on the pilot steps, and was picked up by a French boat. She lost her mother. Misses Hunter and Mixter sank with the ship, but floated again, and were picked up by the French and English boats. Mrs. Spafford sank with the ship, but floated again. Near all on the deck perished. The Captain and purser are prostrated. At Cardiff the inhabitants show great kindness to the survivors."

*The *Ville du Havre* was originally built as a 3,950-ton paddle steamer in 1865 and named *Napoleon III*, operated by the French line Cie. Generale Transatlantique between Le Havre and Brest and New York. In 1871–73 she was rebuilt as a 5,065-ton single-screw steamship, her paddle wheel removed and renamed *Ville du Havre*, resuming her transatlantic service early in 1873. She left New York on 15 November 1873 under the command of Capt. Marino Surmonte with 313 passengers and crew bound for Brest and Le Havre.

Early on the morning of Saturday 22 November, a week after her departure from New York, in mid-Atlantic and around 700 miles due east of Newfoundland, the *Ville du Havre* was proceeding under both steam and sail at 12 knots when she collided with the *Loch Earn*. She was a full-rigged three-masted iron ship of 1,200 tons commanded by Capt. Robertson on a voyage from London to New York. The *Ville du Havre* sank within 12 minutes, with the loss of 226 lives. The 87 survivors from the *Ville du Havre* were taken on board the *Loch Earn* and later transferred to the American steamship *Trimountain*. The *Loch Earn* herself was abandoned in a sinking condition on 28 November and her crew picked up by the *British Queen* without further loss of life.

## THE BURNING OF THE *COSPATRICK*

### 28 Dec 1874

**Casualties – Foreign**

St. Helena [Madeira, 25th Dec., 5.40 p.m.] – The Cospatrick, from London to Auckland, N.Z., with passengers, took fire at sea and was totally destroyed, 17th Nov., in lat. 37 S, lon. 12 E; second mate and two of the crew saved; passengers and remainder of crew supposed [believed] to be drowned.

### 29 Dec 1874

St. Helena, 9th Dec.- [By tel. from Madeira].- The Cospatrick burnt 19th Nov.; second officer and two seamen picked up by *British Sceptre* 27th, and landed here 6th Dec.; it is feared that the rest of the crew and passengers were lost.

*The Illustrated London News*

### 2nd January 1875
### Burning of the Emigrant-Ship *Cospatrick* at Sea

"The most terrible catastrophe of the old year was the destruction by fire of the emigrant-ship *Cospatrick*, and the consequent loss of over 450 lives, in the early morning of Nov. 18. The *Cospatrick* was a teak-built sailing ship, of 1,200 tons, constructed at Moulmein, in India [sic – Burma], and classed A1 at Lloyd's until 1883. She was 190 ft. in length, 34 ft. in breadth, and had 23 ft. depth of hold. Purchased by her present owners, Messrs. Shaw, Savill, and Co., of 34, Leadenhall-street, from the late Mr. Duncan Dunbar, she was now making only her second voyage under the flag of that house.

Formerly employed in carrying troops to and from India, and occasionally engaged in the conveyance of coolies, she had also on a previous occasion made a voyage from England to New Zealand with a large party of emigrants. She had been for many years under the command of Captain Elmslie, her late chief officer, who retained his position when the

# THE ILLUSTRATED LONDON NEWS.

REGISTERED AT THE GENERAL POST-OFFICE FOR TRANSMISSION ABROAD.

No. 1849.—VOL. LXVI.　　　SATURDAY, JANUARY 16, 1875.　　　WITH EXTRA SUPPLEMENT { SIXPENCE. By Post, 6½d.

COTTER.　　　MACDONALD.　　　LEWIS.

THE SURVIVORS FROM THE COSPATRICK.

L'INCENDIE DU *COSPATRICK*.

vessel was transferred to her new owners, and who was in chief command on the present voyage.

The *Cospatrick* left Gravesend on Sept. 11 last, carrying 429 emigrants, sent out through the General Agency of New Zealand, and bound for Auckland. There were 177 male adults, 125 women, 58 boys, 53 girls, and 16 infants under twelve months. Her crew was composed of 43 persons – officers, men, and boys, all told. There were also on board four independent passengers, making in all a total of 476 souls.

The fire broke out in latitude 37 deg. South, and longitude 12 deg. East – one account has it west. A telegram from Madeira in the *Daily News* says that at midnight on Nov. 17, when the second officer left the deck, everything was apparently all right, but at half-past twelve he was awoke by the alarm of fire. The captain was on deck immediately, and all hands attempted to get the vessel before the wind, but without success. The flames came up the fore hatch within a quarter of an hour, and in less than half an hour the fire was nearly all along the deck. A special cablegram in the *Daily Telegraph* goes on to say that the flames and smoke were driven aft, setting fire to the boats which were placed in the fore part of the vessel, and thus effectually prevented their use.

The excitement on board now became terrible, and the passengers rushed to the quarter boats, which were on the davits hanging over the side, and crowded into them. It is estimated that about eighty people, most of them women, thus got into the starboard boat, and remained there till the davits bent down over the side and the boat's stern dipped into the sea. Then it capsized, and all its occupants were immediately drowned alongside the vessel. Just afterwards the fore, main, and mizen masts all fell over the side in quick succession, killing many of the emigrants and adding to the terror of the rest.

But the worst had not yet come; for suddenly the stern of the vessel blew out with a loud report under the poop deck, and completed the destruction of the ship. Two boats under the command of Mr. Romaine [chief mate] and Mr. Macdonald [second mate] had meanwhile been filled, and reached some little distance from the *Cospatrick*; but Captain Elmslie, his wife, and Dr. Cadle remained on board the vessel until she went down. When the last moment had come the captain threw his wife overboard, and then leapt into the sea after her. At the same time the doctor jumped overboard with the captain's little boy in his arms, and all were drowned together.

The two boats kept together for a couple of days. They were separated by bad weather. The missing boat contained the chief officer, the ship's butcher, five seamen, and twenty-five passengers. She has not since been heard of, but it is hoped that she may have reached the island of Tristan D'Acunha. In Macdonald's boat thirst soon began to be severely felt. One man fell overboard while steering. Three others died after becoming mad. On Nov. 23 four more died.

The survivors then suffering so intensely from hunger and thirst that they drank the blood and ate the livers of two of the dead.

Other deaths followed; and when, on the 27th, two more of the men died, one was thrown overboard, but nobody had strength enough to lift the other. Ultimately five men were all who were left alive in the boat, and of these two had gone mad. They died soon after being rescued by the ship British Sceptre.

Macdonald, Thomas Lewis, and James Cotter, the three survivors, were most kindly treated on board the *British Sceptre*, which landed them, on Dec. 6, at St. Helena. Thence

THE BURNING OF THE "COSPATRICK" — THE SURVIVORS IN THE BOAT SIGHTING THE SHIP OF RESCUE, "BRITISH SCEPTRE"

DRAWN FROM DETAILS GIVEN TO OUR ARTIST BY MR. C. HENRY MACDONALD, THE SECOND OFFICER

they left in the *Nyanza* for Southampton, touching, *en voyage*, at Madeira, whence the foregoing particulars of the lamentable calamity have been telegraphed to England."

The only three survivors of the total complement of 476 crew and passengers of the *Cospatrick* were: Charles Henry Macdonald, second mate, of Montrose, Scotland; Thomas Lewis, able seaman and quartermaster, from Anglesey, Wales; and Edward Cotter, aged 18, ordinary seaman, "the son of a gardener at Kensington [London], but who was trained in the *Chichester* for sea service."

*More reports of the *Cospatrick* tragedy were published in *The Illustrated London News* of the 9 and 16 January 1875. A book about the event was published in 2006, *Women and Children Last: The Burning of the Emigrant Ship Cospatrick*, by Charles Clark (University of Otago Press).

## The Wreck of the *Gothenburg*

# 5 March 1875

*Casualties – Foreign*

Melbourne, 3rd Mar.- The Gothenburg (s)* has been wrecked on Flinders island, Port Darwin [*sic*]. She had on board 85 passengers, a crew of 35 men, and 3,000 ozs. of gold. Only four men are at present known to be saved. Three boats full of passengers are adrift, and fears are entertained for their safety.

*8 March 1875*

**Casualties – Foreign**

Melbourne, 5th Mar., 12.30 p.m.- The Gothenburg was caught in a cyclone and became a total wreck at Cape Melville. Part of the crew have landed.

*9 March 1875*

**Casualties – Foreign**

Melbourne, 6th Mar.- Up to the present time there are 22 survivors from the Gothenburg (s). Judge Welling [*sic* – Circuit Court judge Justice William Wearing QC] and many women and children were drowned.

*The 501-ton auxiliary steamship *Gothenburg* was built in 1854. Like many steamships of the time, she was also rigged with sails as a three-masted barquentine, combined with her coal-fired steam propulsion. She ran between ports in New Zealand and Australia in the 1860s and subsequently went into service along the Australian coast.

On 17 February 1875 the *Gothenburg* left Port Darwin in the Northern Territory for Adelaide, down south. She was under the experienced command of Capt. James Pearce with a complement of around 90 passengers and 35 crew (the precise number of passengers being uncertain). She also carried a consignment of 3,000 ozs. of gold worth £40,000 at the time, for deposit in an Adelaide bank.

Off the coast of northeast Queensland, just after rounding the Cape York Peninsula, the little steamship was struck by one of the worst cyclones ever to hit Australia. On the evening of 24 February, a week after leaving Darwin and driving southward hard into the storm, the vessel pitched onto the western (inward) side of Old Reef on the Great Barrier Reef, 25 miles off Cape Upstart between the coastal towns of Townsville and Mackay and near the Whitsunday Islands.

(The first report of the incident, dated 5 March 1875, above,, inexplicably and incorrectly said the *Gothenburg* was wrecked on Flinders Island, which is in Bass Strait between the southeast coast of Australia and Tasmania, and nowhere near the place of the actual wreck on the northeast coast of Queensland.)

In the middle of the night of 25 February with the doomed *Gothenburg* broadside onto and battered against the reef, Capt. Pearce lowered the ship's four lifeboats. Many people in them drowned immediately. Some others, survived as the weather moderated over the next two days.

One boat reached nearby Holbourne Island on 26 February where four of the *Gothenburg's* crew had landed the day before. Those 18 survivors were eventually rescued and taken to safety on the mainland. Another four crew in a lifeboat were picked up by a steamer, the *Leichardt*, two days after the *Gothenburg* wrecked.

The only survivors of the wreck of the *Gothenburg* were those 22 people – twelve crew and ten passengers. Approximately 102 others drowned including Captain Pearce and all the officers, all 25 women and children on board, and a number of high-ranking public officials, diplomats and dignitaries. (One of Capt. Pearce's sons, Thomas, became the hero of the *Loch Ard* disaster when that vessel was wrecked off the southeast coast of Australia on 1 June 1878; Thomas rescued the only other survivor, a young Irish girl named Eva Carmichael: see **Shipwrecks, Collisions and Castaways, 4 June 1878**.)

Several weeks after the wreck, divers recovered the 3,000 ozs of gold kept in Capt. Pearce's cabin. During the recovery operation several sharks caught near the wreck were found to have human remains and jewellery in their stomachs.

## LOSS OF THE *SCHILLER* AT SCILLY ISLES

## 10 May 1875

### Casualties – Home

Plymouth, 8th May, 11.15 a.m.- A telegram from Scilly states:- Schiller* went ashore at 10 last night on Retarriers ledges, east of Bishop's lighthouse, dense fog preventing either Scilly lights being seen. 5 passengers and 2 of the crew saved; perhaps others may be on other islands, but doubtful. Has on board 60 first, 80 second, and 50 steerage passengers, and 100 crew. Captain and second mate known to be drowned. Steamer lying broadside on, under water, with mainmast gone. Lifeboats, other boats and steamer have gone to the wreck to search for passengers and crew. Vessel must become a total wreck.

Plymouth – [By Tel.] – The Schiller (s), lost off Scilly, was said to have 266 passengers of whom 26 were to land here; 250 sacks mails, including Australian and New Zealand; and $300,000 for the Continent.

Scilly, 8th May, 11.27 a.m.- The Schiller was wrecked in a dense fog, on Retarriers rocks, about three quarters of a mile east of Bishop lighthouse, in about 4 fathoms water. Crew saved:- Chief Officer; Harry Hillers, seaman; Charles Lemke, stoker; Hans Bolling, stoker; Max Gouldberg, sailor; Henry Wallis, sailor; Hans Peterson Peck, sailor; and one of steerage stewards.

# THE ILLUSTRATED LONDON NEWS.

REGISTERED AT THE GENERAL POST-OFFICE FOR TRANSMISSION ABROAD.

No. 1867.—VOL. LXVI.　　　　SATURDAY, MAY 22, 1875.　　　WITH EXTRA SUPPLEMENT { SIXPENCE. By Post, 6½d.

WRECK OF THE SCHILLER: THE RETARRIER LEDGES AND BISHOP ROCK LIGHTHOUSE, SCILLY ISLES.

Passengers saved:- Ludwig Reiderer, of Wurtemberg; Henry Stern, of New York; Carl Kuhn, of St. Gall (Switzerland); Peste, of Philadelphia, son of Genl. [General?] Peste, of Hanover; Frank O. Schellenberg, of New York; two landed dead. It is possible a few more may be saved. Number on board when wrecked about sixty-five first-class passengers, sixty-four second, hundred and twenty steerage. Had on board English and German mails, $300,000 gold, some silver bars, and a general cargo of cotton, cigars, tobacco, lard. Steamer, lifeboat, and pilots searching for any people who may be floating.

*The Illustrated London News*

**15th May 1875**

**Three Hundred Lives Lost By Shipwreck**

One of the greatest disasters at sea that have been recorded took place, on the Friday night of last week, near the entrance to the British [English] Channel. The fine German mail steam-ship Schiller, which ran from New York to Hamburg, calling at Plymouth and Cherbourg, was totally wrecked on the Retarrier Ledges, near the Bishop Lighthouse, Scilly, and more than three hundred lives were lost, with a great part of the homeward (via San Francisco) Australia and New Zealand mails.

The Schiller was an iron screw-steamer, built at Glasgow, in 1873, by Messrs. Napier and Sons…Her tonnage was 3,421 gross, 2,326 net; her length, 380.5 ft., by 40.1 ft. of breadth, with a depth of 24 ft. 4 in., or, reckoning from her topmost deck, 32 ft. 1 in…The Schiller belonged to the port of Hamburg, and was registered as one of the steamers of the German Transatlantic Steam-Packet Company, the Eagle (Adler) Line…

The Schiller left New York on the 27th ult. [April], but was unable to pass over the bar at Sandy Hook until noon on the following day. She had on board fifty-nine first class passengers, seventy-five second class, 120 in the steerage, and a crew of 101 officers and men, all told, making a total of 355 persons. She also brought the Australian and New Zealand mails, in all 250 bags; specie [gold] to the value of 300,000 dols., for Cherbourg; and a full general cargo.

In the first part of the voyage hard weather was experienced, and during the three days before the disaster it was so thick that no observations could be taken [ie., she could not ascertain her exact position]. On the night of Friday week the fog suddenly increased, and in fifteen minutes it was impossible to see the length of the steamer. Sails were at once taken in, the engines were reduced to half speed, and the number of men on the lookout was increased. Almost immediately afterwards the Schiller struck heavily on the Retarrier Ledges. She made four great lurches, and then settled on the rock…

It was ten o'clock in the evening when the ship struck. A little festive party had been given in honour of the birthday of one of the officers, but the working of the ship was in no way neglected…There was an idea that land was near, and the majority of the male passengers were on deck on the lookout. Nearly all the women and children and a few men were in bed; others were sitting about, talking, smoking, or playing cards and dominoes. There was not the slightest warning of the disaster. The shock appears to have been so slight at first that few were aware the ship was on a rock. The fog was so dense that it was impossible to judge of her position. A cannon was fired half a dozen times, till the powder got wet; and rockets were sent up, without bringing the slightest help. Meanwhile, all those on board crowded on deck. It was a scene of wild terror and dismay…

# THE WRECK OF THE STEAMER SCHILLER.

LANDING OF SOME OF THE RESCUED PASSENGERS AT PENZANCE PIER.

SAVING A MAIL-BAG ON BOARD THE QUEEN OF THE BAY, SCILLY PACKET.

GENERAL VIEW OF BISHOP ROCK LIGHTHOUSE AND THE RETARRIER ROCKS, FROM ST. AGNES LIGHTHOUSE.

The officers and crew succeeded, with great difficulty, in launching the starboard gig. It was instantly filled with men, eager to save themselves, and thrusting back the women and children. The port gig was also got clear, and both boats kept near the ship…The starboard life-boat was launched by an almost superhuman effort, but it capsized. By this time a great many people crowded into the remaining boats, so that it was impossible to clear them. The captain fired his pistol over the men's heads to compel them to keep better order, but in vain. With the greatest difficulty the remaining five boats were swung out from the davits, ready to be launched as soon as the sea subsided. Heavy bodies of water washed over the ship, so that it was impossible to stand on deck…

About midnight the smoke-stack fell over and smashed two of the starboard boats. Two of the port boats were swept away by a heavy sea. Rockets were again thrown up and guns fired. Soon after the fog cleared away, but only for a short time, and the bright, clear light of the Bishop Rock Lighthouse became visible about one o'clock. But dense darkness again came on.

There was a refuge in the deckhouse over the first-class cabins until about two o'clock, when a heavy sea, which ran up to the top of the mainmast, swept away the deckhouse, and a heart-rending cry rent the air. Groans and cries for help and long piercing cries of children were heard for a few seconds above the roar of the waves. Nearly two hundred thus perished.

The captain then gathered for safety some people on the bridge-way, the highest place, in the hope of saving them; but every wave washed some of them overboard. About three o'clock the captain, chief engineers, and doctor, the remaining persons on the bridge, were swept away…The rigging of both masts was now crowded with people. With every lurch the steamer careened over to the starboard side until the yards touched the water, and the cargo began to float about…

About five o'clock the fog cleared a little, and the lighthouse became visible. A shout went up from both masts, but was lost in the roar of the breakers. At six o'clock it was evident that the masts would soon go, and about half-past seven the mainmast went over the side, and, being mostly iron, sank. One of the seamen on it seized hold of a spar and a trunk, which supported him above water. Soon after the foremast fell, with every person on it, and, being also of iron, sank. Some had life-belts on, and others got on pieces of wood and were drifted about with the tide.

The people of the nearest Scilly Isles were meantime becoming aware of the disaster. Two rowing-boats put off from the island of St. Agnes and picked up seven men floating on the tide. Two Sennen fishing-luggers [from Sennen, near Land's End on the Cornish mainland] returning from fishing found three and five men respectively floating by means of life-belts and pieces of wood about a half mile from the wreck…

Two of the Schiller's boats, containing together twenty-six men and one woman, reached Bryer [Bryher] first and then Tresco, the seat of the lord proprietor of the isles, Mr. Dorrien Smith, who kindly took care of them. They had been carried towards Bryer by the force of the current. A few more were rescued by the boats belonging to the islands, which picked them up as they dropped from the mast; or while swimming, after they had been again and again washed from the rocks to which they had endeavoured to cling.

Altogether, during the day, forty-three persons were saved alive, but only one woman, a passenger, named Mrs. Jones, whose husband had got her a place in a boat. The first,

THE WRECK OF THE SCHILLER: FUNERAL PROCESSION AT THE BURIAL OF THE DROWNED, ST. MARY'S, SCILLY ISLES.

second, and fourth officers of the ship were among the saved. Nineteen dead bodies were brought in on the first day, and many of the mailbags from the wreck; others were collected on Sunday and Monday. The Australian and New Zealand letters were delivered through the Post-Office on Wednesday, damp with sea-water.

*The *Schiller* wrecked on the rocks known as the Retarrier Ledges on the southwest perimeter of the Isles of Scilly, because dense fog had prevented her officers from taking astronomical observations to fix the vessel's position for the three days before she struck. It was notable, however, that the officers did not take any soundings whatsoever to ascertain the depth of water, determined by dropping to the bottom the lead line, a pre-measured length of rope weighted with lead. That would at least have told them, by the chart, that they were in shallow water and approaching a dangerous landfall. In the event, the only precaution taken was to slow the ship to half speed. Moreover, in the fog, no one saw the two lighthouses at Scilly – one on the westernmost island of St. Agnes, the other the Bishop's Rock – and nor did they hear the fog bell. In other words, the *Schiller* was sailing virtually deaf, dumb and blind towards her calamitous and fatal destruction.

The number of people concerned with the wreck of the *Schiller*, especially the number of crew, survivors and dead, was variously reported. Some claimed there were 101 crew, some claimed 118. (It is generally agreed that there were 254 passengers, not 266 as communicated in one of the first reports of the wreck, above.) The death toll was at least 310, and possibly as many as 335, making the *Schiller* one of the worst ever civil maritime disasters in British waters. Some reports stated there were 37 survivors, others, 47. However, only one survivor was a woman, and all the children on the ship perished.

## COLLISION OF THE *AVALANCHE* AND THE *FOREST*

# 13 Sept 1877

### Casualties - Home

### Fatal Collision off Portland Between the 'Avalanche' and the 'Forest'*

Portland, 12th Sept., 10.5 a.m.- Avalanche been in collision and foundered off Portland; nearly all passengers and crew drowned. Further particulars when obtained. At present only John Sherrington, third officer, and two seamen found.

Another telegram.- (From John Sherrington, above referred to):- Avalanche foundered; nearly all crew and passengers drowned.

Weymouth, 12th Sept., 11.25 a.m.- Twelve men landed, Avalanche and Forest having been in collision; four dead bodies washed on shore. Will report more fully.

12.45 p.m.- Avalanche, London to New Zealand, foundered off Portland after collision with the Forest (ship), Nova Scotia. Forest also foundered. Third officer and two seamen only saved from *Avalanche*. [The *Forest* was bound from London to Sandy Hook [New York], in ballast.]

Weymouth, 12th Sept., 2.45 p.m.- The third mate and two seamen of the ship Avalanche, Williams, from London to Wellington, New Zealand, and the master (Lockhart), mate, steward, and six seamen of the ship Forest, of Windsor, Nova Scotia, from London to Sandy Hook, in ballast, landed at Portland this morning, both ships having been abandoned about

9.30 last night, 15 miles S by W of Portland, after collision. *Avalanche* sank in about three minutes after being first struck, *Forest* was abandoned about a quarter of an hour after. Five dead bodies washed ashore at Portland. One identified as carpenter of the *Avalanche*, and other four as seamen of the *Forest*. Captain, pilot, and all passengers on board the *Avalanche* must have sunk with the ship.

Weymouth.- [By tel.]- Sherrington, MacCarthy, and Mills are the only three men saved from the ship Avalanche; no passengers saved.

Weymouth, 12th Sept., 3.48 p.m.- ...The following particulars of the disaster have been received by the owners of the *Avalanche*, per telegraph from Weymouth:- 'Collision between Avalanche and Forest, of Windsor, took place 9.15 last night [11th Sept] about 15 miles South by West from Portland. *Avalanche* on port tack, *Forest* on starboard. Latter first struck Avalanche amidships, then twice further aft, causing her to founder in about three minutes from first striking; no time to launch boats.

Second and third mates and some of crew got on board *Forest*; abandoned her in a sinking state quarter of an hour after collision. Third mate and two seamen landed in same boat as master and mate of the *Forest*. Boat in which second mate left picked up bottom up, so fear he is drowned. Carpenter's body washed ashore. Captain, pilot and all passengers must have gone down with ship.'

## *14 September 1877*
## Casualties – Home

## The Collision Between the 'Avalanche' and the 'Forest'

Weymouth, 12th Sept.- The third officer, J.C. Sherrington, one of the survivors of the Avalanche, reports as follows:- "On Tuesday, the 11th Sept., about 9 p.m., the weather being very dark, wind SW, blowing a stiff breeze, the ship being about 15 miles S by W from Portland, under short sail, with both lights burning brightly, sailing by the wind, second mate's watch on deck, Channel pilot in charge, heard the man at the look-out forward report a light, which was followed by the pilot calling out 'Hard up' to the man at the helm, and 'Port your helm' to the stranger [ie., the *Forest*], the meantime taking in spanker, and endeavouring to square cross-jack yard. At this time I was in my bunk; jumped out, and rushed on deck, when I heard second officer say to the chief officer, 'Come on deck, I think there will be another smash.'

The first thing seen was the jibboom of the stranger coming through main rigging, and striking mainmast, breaking jibboom in two. I got as far as quarter hatch, when I felt myself lifted up, and pitched head foremost down the hatch, falling on a number of passengers. A sudden rush of wind indicated that the ship was filling. The stranger had by this time struck the *Avalanche* a second time abaft the mainmast; I sung out to the passengers to get on deck and save themselves if possible; rushed on to the poop and saw the captain standing by the break; caught hold of him, and told him to save himself, as the ship was sinking; let him go when I, as the bows of ship [*Forest*] were coming down a third time, sung out to him to catch hold; this time the Avalanche was struck in the fore part of the mizen rigging. In the rising of the stranger I caught hold of a chain, and was dragged up clear of the *Avalanche*, and as she was going down the fourth time jumped on to the forecastle and went to the port side and saw the *Avalanche* almost gone, her decks being under water.

# THE ILLUSTRATED LONDON NEWS.

REGISTERED AT THE GENERAL POST-OFFICE FOR TRANSMISSION ABROAD.

No. 1993.—VOL. LXXI.　　　SATURDAY, SEPTEMBER 22, 1877.　　　TWO WHOLE SHEETS ) SIXPENCE.
AND SUPPLEMENT ) BY POST, 6½D.

THE COLLISION IN THE CHANNEL: LANDING OF THE SURVIVORS FROM THE AVALANCHE AND FOREST.

The passengers and crew had by this time gone forward, the stern being under water, and after some most heartrending screams she gradually disappeared. Then threw ropes off the forecastle and went aft, when I observed a great deal of confusion amongst the crew. Heard the order given 'Square the foreyard,' when I called out to 'Hold on everything;' then saw 2nd mate of *Avalanche* on quarter-deck, and asked if he saw anyone in command, to which he answered 'No.' Steps were then taken to launch boats, as it was said this ship, which proved to be the *Forest*, was in a sinking state.

After a considerable time got boats over the side, and with much trouble 12 hands got into the long boat. Screaming was then heard proceeding from the anchor, but the sea being so bad, could not approach that part of the ship. A quarter of an hour was expended in getting away, and shortly after this blue lights and a rocket were observed on the poop. Kept the boat's head to wind all night, and at daybreak this morning kept away for Portland light. Hoisted signals, when 2 boats from shore came off, took us on board, and landed us about 10 o'clock."

Captain Lockhart, of the *Forest*, reports:- "On Tuesday the 11th Sept., weather hazy, wind SW, blowing a smart breeze, the ship being about 12 to 15 miles WSW of Portland Bill, under reefed sails, with both lights burning well, having been inspected by me 20 minutes previously, sailing on the wind, heading SSE, and going 3½ knots an hour, the man on the look out and second mate saw a ship's green [ie., starboard] light a short distance on the lee bow, and reported same. I then gave orders to luff ship and keep her close, in order that the stranger [*Avalanche*] should see lights and keep off. The *Forest* seems to have lost her way, and fell off, and in a short period she struck the stranger somewhere amidships. Backed yards to clear the stranger, and in two minutes the other vessel had disappeared.

Gave orders to get out boats and save life, but no persons were seen, and the boats were nearly swamped alongside. Then directed officers to take lamps and see if there was any water in the hold, when they reported it to be up to between deck beams, or nearly there. Finding it was impossible to save vessel, gave orders for all hands to take [to] the boats, and after much difficulty I believe they all got safely into them. Then remained as near as possible with safety, until she was lost sight of, and our boat rode to windward all night until about half-past 8 this morning, the sea during the whole time beating against her, and drifted into the bay. At daylight looked round, but found neither of the other boats in sight.

We hoisted a signal which was seen by persons on shore, and shortly afterwards two boats came off, and transferred us all, viz., 12, in to theirs, and landed us at Portland at about 10 o'clock. After taking to the boats, discerned 3 men that had belonged to the stranger with us, which proved to have been the ship *Avalanche*."

*2 Oct 1877*

## Casualties – Home

Dartmouth, 1st Oct, 12 45 p.m.- The body of a middle-aged female, in night dress, with a wedding ring, was picked up, this morning, at the mouth of the harbour; supposed [believed to be] passenger from the *Avalanche*.

*The *Avalanche* was an iron ship of 1,210 tons, built in 1874, her dimensions being 214ft 6ins long, 36ft wide and 21ft 1ins deep. She was under the command of Capt. Edmund

Williams, bound from London to Wellington, New Zealand on 11 September 1877, carrying 63 emigrants and 34 crew. Off Portland Bill in the English Channel that evening and in charge of a Channel pilot, she was run into by the *Forest*, a 1,488-ton wooden ship of Windsor, Nova Scotia in ballast and bound for Sandy Hook, New York. The *Forest* was under the command of Capt. Ephraim Lockhart, with 21 crew.

The *Avalanche* sank almost immediately after the collision, with the loss of 94 lives: the only three saved were John Sherrington, the third officer, and two seamen. The *Forest* only partly sank; it was later blown up as it was a danger to shipping. Nine members of the *Forest's* crew, Capt. Lockhart and eight other sailors, survived the collision. The total death toll of the collision was 107 lives from the two ships.

## RIGHT OF WAY

The key circumstances prevailing before the two vessels struck each other were (1) the wind was from the southwest; (2) *Forest* was heading approximately southeast, with the wind on her starboard side – i.e. she was on starboard tack; (3) *Avalanche* was heading approximately northwest, with the wind on her port side – i.e. she was on port tack; and (4) the two vessels were heading towards each other on a collision course.

In the circumstances of two sailing vessels on different tacks converging on a collision course, as was happening with the *Forest* and the *Avalanche* at around 9.30 p.m. in the Channel, the vessel on starboard tack (*Forest*) has right of way and is required to *stand on* (keep to her course). The *give way* vessel on port tack (*Avalanche*) is required to keep clear (give way) by taking appropriate action to avoid collision. The *stand on* vessel must, however, "take such action as will best aid to avoid collision" when it becomes clear that the *give way* vessel (*Avalanche*) is not complying with her obligation to do so. In such a situation, the preferred option is for both vessels to turn to starboard away from each other early enough to avoid striking each other, thereby passing each other on their respective port sides.

In this incident the *Avalanche* tried at first to keep out of the *Forest's* way by crossing ahead. *Avalanche's* master, Capt. Williams, finally realised that by this action he would not clear the *Forest* but would collide. He only then took avoidance action by turning to starboard. By that time, however, it was too late.

The *Forest's* Capt. Lockhart's key observation was that his vessel was "sailing on the wind, heading SSE, and going 3½ knots an hour, the man on the look out and second mate saw a ship's green [i.e. starboard] light a short distance on the lee bow, and reported same. I then gave orders to luff ship and keep her close, in order that the stranger [*Avalanche*] should see lights [i.e. his port sidelight] and keep off. The *Forest* seems to have lost her way, and fell off, and in a short period she struck the stranger somewhere amidships".

Capt. Lockhart saw that his vessel had right of way over "the stranger" (*Avalanche*), because his *Forest* was on starboard tack while *Avalanche*, on a collision course with *Forest*, was on port tack. Since *Avalanche* did not seem to be taking action to avoid a collision by turning his vessel to starboard, (which he could easily have done with the southwesterly wind blowing at the time), Capt. Lockhart ordered his helmsman to head more into the wind ("to luff ship and keep her close" to the wind), so that "the stranger" would see her (*Forest's*) port sidelight "and keep off". His intention by turning to starboard into the wind and luffing his sails was that both vessels would pass each other safely on their respective port sides.

But *Forest* did not stay luffed into the wind; she "seems to have lost her way, and fell off". In other words she started to fall (turn) away from the wind and directly towards *Avalanche* – just as *Avalanche* was taking late avoidance action by turning away to starboard and thus presenting her port side to the oncoming *Forest's* bows. As a consequence *Forest* "struck the stranger somewhere amidships" on her port side.

## COURT OF INQUIRY

The Court of Inquiry into the tragedy found the *Avalanche* to blame for the incident, by not heading away from the *Forest* sooner than she did. However, it also reprimanded the *Forest's* master for allowing his vessel to fall off the wind – resulting in her heading more towards the *Avalanche* – before he was certain of what the *Avalanche* was doing. Both acts, but primarily the *Avalanche's*, resulted in the collision between the two vessels. Lockhart was not censured by suspension or cancellation of his certificate only because the Court recognised his 26 years of service as master and his good conduct after the collision.

## THE USS *HURON*

### 27 Nov 1877

**Casualties, Etc.**

**Atlantic Storms**

> Philadelphia, 25th Nov.- Terrific storms have prevailed along the Atlantic coasts since Thursday, causing floods in the Virginias and the Carolinas, washing away bridges, and obstructing railways.
>
> The Huron (United States sloop-of-war)*, from Fortress Monroe to Havana, was wrecked on Saturday morning on the Carolina coast, 50 miles N of Cape Hatteras, in a gale blowing 70 miles an hour. The *Huron* is a total loss, and, of 135 persons on board, only 35 are known to have been saved. Every officer was drowned, except one ensign, two engineers, and a paymaster. A steamer has gone to their assistance from Norfolk.

*The USS *Huron* was wrecked on shoals near Oregon Inlet, just south of Nag's Head and Kitty Hawk, North Carolina, as a result of storm force winds blowing onshore. A total of 110 persons on board the 541-ton sloop-of-war steamer were reported to have lost their lives, although a monument to commemorate the wreck states that "Near this spot, Nov. 24, 1877, the U.S.S. 'Huron' ran ashore with loss of ninety-eight lives". A contemporary newspaper report states that the vessel "had a crew of 149 men and 11 officers". Most reports stated that the only survivors were 30 men and four officers. The boat from a "wrecking steamer", the *D. & J. Baker*, which went to the *Huron's* assistance, was swamped as it attempted to land, and five of its nine men drowned.

## THE *ATACAMA*

### 11 Jan 1878

**Casualties – Foreign**

Havre, 9th Jan.- Advices from Valparaiso dated 4th Dec. [1877] give the following details concerning the loss of the Atacama (s)*, Lambert, from that port to Callao. The Atacama stranded 30th Nov. [1877], at 8 a.m., on rocks 8 leagues from Caldera, where she was entering. She sank three minutes afterwards. Twenty-three persons were saved, including Mr. Kennedy (a passenger), five women, and two children. The steamer had on board about 200 persons in all; more than 150 are said to be drowned.

### *15 Jan 1878*

**Casualties – Foreign**

Caldera, 3rd Dec. [1877].- The Atacama (s), Lamberth, which left Valparaiso 28th Nov. [1877], for Callao, via Coquimbo, Huasco and Carrizal bajo, struck on the Caxa Chica rock, about two miles off the old port of Copiapo, during the night of the 30th Nov. [1877], became a total wreck, and entirely disappeared within five minutes of the time of striking. She had a crew of 67, with 63 passengers, and of these only 26 persons in all were saved. A considerable quantity of deck cargo is floating about and being secured by the natives, who try to hide it.

*The Pacific Steam Navigation Company steamship *Atacama* was on a coastal voyage from the Chilean port of Valparaiso to the Peruvian port of Callao (for Lima), when she struck a rock known as Quiebra Olas ["break waves"] just outside the port of Caldera on 30 November 1877 at about 8 p.m. The master, Capt. Lambirth, "a thoroughly experienced man", together with around 103 other crew and passengers lost their lives.

According to a *New York Times* report of 6 January 1878, "One very bad incident took place. Mr. Kennedy, agent for the Pacific Steam Navigation Company at Chanaral, was returning from Valparaiso on his wedding trip. He managed to fasten a life-belt on his bride, and threw himself with her in the water; but before they could extricate themselves from the floating debris, a spar fell, striking the poor lady on the neck, and causing instant death. The husband afterward reached the shore, and the body of the bride was washed upon the beach".

## LOSS OF HMS *EURYDICE* AND HMS *ATALANTA*

### 26 March 1878

**Casualties, Etc.**

#### Loss of H.M.S. Eurydice

St. Catherine's Point, I.W. [Isle of Wight], 25th Mar., 8.45 a.m. – 24th (night) – HMS Eurydice* capsized in a snow squall off Dunnose [Isle of Wight], about 4 p.m., 24th. The Coastguard report that all hands but two are lost. [HMS *Eurydice* was homeward bound from the West Indies.]

West Cowes [I.W.], 25th Mar., 9 a.m.- HM training ship Eurydice, with about 315 souls on board, capsized yesterday, at 4 p.m., when about two miles off Dunnose head.

THE DISASTER IN THE CHANNEL—H.M.S. "EURYDICE" OFF DUNNOSE, JUST BEFORE THE SQUALL

THE DISASTER IN THE CHANNEL—H.M.S. "EURYDICE" ON HER BEAM-ENDS, JUST AFTER THE SQUALL

## THE LOSS OF H.M.S. "EURYDICE"

SKETCHES FROM THE WEST COAST OF AFRICA—H.M.S. "BOXER" SURROUNDED BY WATERSPOUTS

Two seamen, Cuddiford, A.B., and Fletcher, O.S., have been saved, the remaining 313 are supposed [believed] to be drowned. Three bodies have come ashore, two identified as those of Colonel Ferrier, R.E., and Lieutenant Tabor, R.N.; the third is that of an A.B. The masts of the vessel show above water.

Ventnor, I.W., 25th Mar., 1.45 p.m.- Two Government tugs have been in attendance at the wreck of HMS Eurydice since daylight. No other bodies have been landed up to the present. The 3 bodies landed last night are identified as those of Colonel Ferrier, R.E., passenger from Bermuda; Lieutenant Tabor, R.N.; and Bennett, petty officer.

Cuddiford, one of the survivors, gives the following report of the casualty:- "Left Bermuda 6th Mar., and had fine weather all the passage. Yesterday, weather being fine, the ports were opened, and all sails carried except royals. At about 3.30 p.m. the captain ordered sail to be shortened, and before this could be done, a sudden and furious squall caught the vessel, causing her to heel over and capsize. The only available boat was to leeward, and this was carried away by the force of water."

Cuddiford afterwards found himself overboard, and struck out for the shore. He was fallen in with and picked up by the Emma (schr.), of Padstow, as was also Fletcher, the other survivor, and the three bodies. The two men and the dead bodies were transferred to the Coastguard boat and landed here.

*HMS *Eurydice* was launched at Portsmouth on 20 May 1843. She was a three-masted, wooden, 32-gun frigate of 921 tons. She was 141 ft long (overall length) by 38 ft 10 in beam by 8ft 9in draught (a rather shallow draught for that size vessel, deliberately designed to be able to operate in shallow waters). In the service of the Royal Navy she became renowned for her speed. In 1876–77, at Mr. John White's yard at East Cowes, Isle of Wight, she was converted and refitted for seagoing service as a training ship for which she was commissioned on 7 February 1877. On 13 November that year she sailed from Portsmouth for a tour of duty to the West Indies and Bermuda.

On 6 March 1878 she left Bermuda on her homeward transatlantic passage, with good weather all the way and taking just 18 days to arrive off the Isle of Wight. She carried 368 souls on board, "though this is very much a matter of conjecture, as, besides her own officers and crew, she was bringing home a number of military officers, supernumeraries, and invalids from the West Indies". (*The Times*, 26 March 1878)

The vessel was sailing up the English Channel with all sail set. Her maindeck portholes had been opened to let air in to the main deck mess. Around 3.45 pm when a few miles off Dunnose Head, near Ventnor, Isle of Wight, the *Eurydice*'s commander, Capt. Marcus A.S. Hare, became aware of the sudden approach of bad weather off the land from the northwest. He ordered sail to be taken in. As the crew was shortening sail the furious snow squall struck quickly, heeling the *Eurydice* over. Unfortunately the squall was "too sudden and powerful for the crew to relieve the ship in time". (*The Times*, 26 March 1878)

The *Eurydice* capsized and sank from the press of wind. She sucked under and drowned most of the men on board, although "there is good reason for supposing that the majority succumbed through becoming chilled by the cold". (*The Times*, 26 March 1878)

A 137-ton cargo schooner, the *Emma*, on passage from Poole to Newcastle with a cargo of coal, was also off Dunnose Head when the squall sunk the *Eurydice*. She picked up five of the

*Eurydice*'s crew floating in the water: 1st Lieutenant Francis H. Tabor, Col. Louis J.G. Ferrier, R.E. (Royal Engineers), Petty Officer 1st class George A. Bennett, Able Seaman Benjamin Cuddiford of Plymouth and Ordinary Seaman Sydney Fletcher, aged 19, of Bristol. The first three were dead or died before they reached land. Cuddiford and Fletcher were the only survivors of the sinking of the *Eurydice*.

The official Coroner's jury soon after the disaster found that "from the evidence adduced… no blame whatever can be attached to the captain, officers and men of the ship for its sinking". The death toll of some 366 souls was one of the single worst maritime disasters suffered by the Royal Navy in peacetime.

## HMS *ATALANTA*

The ship that replaced the *Eurydice*, HMS *Atalanta*, was similarly converted as a sail training frigate. She went missing in April 1880 on her return voyage – like the *Eurydice* – from the West Indies and Bermuda. The *Atalanta* had diverted to Bermuda because of yellow fever on board, arriving there on 29 January 1880. She left two days later, expecting to arrive back at Portsmouth in early April. When she was posted overdue, the Admiralty sent out ships to search for her, as well as alerting all shipping across the North Atlantic to look out for her or any possible wreckage, even as far north as Iceland and Greenland.

With no news of the *Atalanta* by May 1880, the Admiralty concluded that she must have foundered, possibly overwhelmed by a ferocious winter storm to the northeast of Bermuda in mid-February.

Around the middle of April 1880 the barque *Swansea Castle*, from Talcahuano, Chile for Falmouth, found wreckage in mid-Atlantic, at lat. 37 N, long. 40 W (northeast of Bermuda), that included "a white life-buoy of conical shape, similar to those used in the Royal Navy", possibly the only evidence of the fate of the *Atalanta* and of the approximately 265 men and 15 officers who perished with her – just like the 366 souls of her sister ship the *Eurydice* two years before.

## THE *SPHINX* TRAGEDY

## 4 April 1878

### Casualties – Foreign

Larnaca [Cyprus], 19th Mar.- The Sphinx (Aust. Lloyd's str.), from Cavalla to Latakia [Syria], with about 3,000 Circassians*, was lost, 5th Mar., off the coast of Cyprus. On that day at 7 a.m. she was doubling the rock [called] "Klito" off Cape St. Andreas, in a strong SE wind, with the intention of going to Famagosta [Cyprus] to await better weather and take provisions for the emigrants. At 3 p.m. a heavy sea washed away 40 refugee Circassians.

Towards sunset she made out Cape Grego, and was about 6 miles from the coast of Famagosta. At 6.45 smoke was seen issuing from the fore hatch, the vessel shipping heavy seas. A little later she grounded on a sand bank. The heavy sea threw her on the coast, and she sprang a leak. There was no working the engines.

Meanwhile the fire increased. During the night attempts were made to extinguish the fire, but without success. 500 emigrants perished, and on the 6th the surviving emigrants

THE MISSING TRAINING-SHIP ATALANTA.

were landed. The master and crew fled from the wreck, as the Circassians threatened to murder them. Two days afterward a French gunboat received on board the master and crew, and next day HMS *Coquette* took on board the first mate. The Circassians robbed the vessel before leaving her of everything portable– plate, linen, furniture, and all the clothing of the officers and men. The vessel is completely destroyed from bow to midships, and the engines are all that it is hoped to save.

*Historically, Circassia (or Cherkessia) was that part of the northwest Caucasus region which is now the southern half of Russia's Krasnodar Territory and most of its Stavropol Territory, along the eastern coast of the Black Sea between the Crimea to the north and Georgia, Armenia and Azerbaijan to the south. After the indigenous Circassians fought a series of wars with Imperial Russia (1763–1864), they were later expelled to parts of the old Ottoman Empire, including Syria, Jordan, Turkey and Lebanon. The shipload of 500 or so Circassians that died in the wreck of the *Sphinx*, above, might have been part of that Circassian diaspora, or possibly Circassian refugees from the 1877–1878 war in the Balkans and the Caucasus between Russia and the Ottomans.

## The *Princess Alice* and *Bywell Castle* Collision: Tragedy on the Thames

### 5 Sept 1878

**Casualties, Etc.**

**Collision on the Thames***

The steamer Princess Alice, belonging to the London Steamboat Company, on her passage from Sheerness and Gravesend [Kent] to London on the evening of 3rd Sept., had arrived off Woolwich at about 8 o'clock when a collision occurred between her and the steamer Bywell Castle, owned by Messrs. Hall Brothers, of Newcastle, which was going down the river in ballast. The *Princess Alice* sunk in a few minutes, and a great number of her passengers were drowned.

The following is an extract from the log of the *Bywell Castle*:- "At 7.45 p.m., in pilot's charge, proceeded at half speed down Gallion's reach. Being about the centre of the reach, observed an excursion steamer coming up Barking reach showing her red and masthead lights, when we ported our helm [ie., turned vessel to starboard (right), to keep out of way of the other vessel] to keep over to Tripcock Point. As the vessels neared, observed that the other steamer had ported [ie., as above], and immediately afterwards saw that she had starboarded [ie., turned left, towards the *Bywell Castle*] and was trying to cross our bows, showing her green light close under our port bow.

Seeing collision inevitable, stopped our engines and reversed full speed, when the two vessels collided, the bow of the *Bywell Castle* cutting into the other steamer, which was crowded with passengers, with a dreadful crash. Took immediate measures for saving life by hauling up over the bows several men of the passengers, throwing ropes ends over all round the ship, throwing over four life buoys, a hold ladder, and several planks, getting out three boats, and keeping the whistle blowing loudly all the time for assistance, which was rendered by several boats from the shore, and a boat from another steamer.

The excursion steamer, which turned out to be the Princess Alice, sunk under our bows.

Succeeded in rescuing a great many passengers, and anchored for the night. About 8.30 p.m., the steamer Duke of Teck came alongside and took off such of the passengers as had not been taken on shore in the boats. The Bywell Castle subsequently returned up the River and brought up off Deptford, with no apparent injury."

*The *Princess Alice* (251 tons), named after Queen Victoria's third daughter, Princess Alice, Grand Duchess of Hesse-Darmstadt, had been an excursion paddle steamship on the Thames since 1866, operated by the London Steamboat Company. On 3 September 1878 she left Swan Pier near London Bridge at 10 a.m. for an excursion to Gravesend and Sheerness downstream in the Thames Estuary. She was licensed to carry 936 passengers. The exact number of crew and passengers she had that day is not known but has been estimated from 750 to 900.

Around 7.45 p.m. that evening the *Princess Alice* was returning from her excursion coming up the Thames from the section of the river called Barking Reach, about a mile below Woolwich. She was rounding a bend in the river marked on the south side by Tripcock Point when, coming up from Gallion's Reach just ahead of her, the collier *Bywell Castle* (1,376 tons) was coming downriver on a voyage from Millwall Docks to Newcastle to pick up a cargo of coal.

Captain Grinsted on the *Princess Alice* turned her to starboard, north and away from the path of the *Bywell Castle*. Captain Harrison of the *Bywell Castle* asked Christopher Dix, the Thames pilot in charge of his vessel, to turn to starboard as well, south towards Tripcock Point. If both vessels had kept to their course changes, they would have stayed clear of each other on opposite sides of the river. Unexpectedly, the *Princess Alice* made another turn, this time to port towards the *Bywell Castle*, putting both vessels on a collision course. The *Bywell Castle* put her engines astern to try and avoid striking the *Princess Alice* but cut into her starboard side, just behind her starboard paddle wheel.

The *Princess Alice* was cut in two by the collision and sank in less than five minutes. Many passengers on her open forward deck were thrown into the water and drowned immediately. Others, below in the saloon, drowned as the ship went down. At that time the water in this part of the Thames was heavily polluted by raw sewage pumped into the river from the nearby Becton North outfall sewer, and by raw effluence from industrial plants at North Greenwich and Silverton, compromising the survival of anyone thrown into the water.

Attempts to rescue survivors of the *Princess Alice* were hampered by the suddenness with which she sank; boats from shore took too long to come to their aid. Moreover, the *Bywell Castle* was in ballast (empty), so she was high in the water. This made it almost impossible for any survivors to get up her sides to safety. The collier had also drifted a distance downstream, away from where the *Princess Alice* had sunk. The boats she launched therefore took quite a long time to get back upstream to any survivors in the water. The *Duke of Teck*, another London Steamboat Company excursion steamer, arrived about ten minutes after the disaster to rescue some survivors.

The first Inquiry into the disaster concluded that the *Princess Alice* was to blame. A second Inquiry, at Millwall, attributed blame to the *Bywell Castle*. A third, at the Admiralty Court, blamed both vessels equally.

In total an estimated 640 people from the *Princess Alice* died that summer evening of 3 September 1878. It was one of the worst peacetime disasters in British maritime history.

THE GREAT DISASTER ON THE THAMES—COLLISION BETWEEN THE "PRINCESS ALICE" AND THE "BYWELL CASTLE," NEAR WOOLWICH.

Included amongst the dead were Captain Grinsted and three of his relatives, and William Towse, general manager of the London Steamship Company, along with his wife, sons and parents. Captain Harrison of the *Bywell Castle* never went to sea again. The collier itself was lost in the Bay of Biscay on a return voyage from the Mediterranean five years later in 1883.

## *Byzantin* Disaster in the Dardanelles

## 20 Dec 1878

### Casualties – Foreign

Galata [Istanbul], 19th Dec., 3.30 p.m.- The Byzantin (str. [steamer], of the Fraissinet Line), Marseilles to Constantinople [Istanbul], and the British steamer Rinaldo, Hull to Constantinople, general cargo, collided near Gallipoli [Gelibolu]; *Byzantin* sank; 150 lives lost; *Rinaldo* slightly damaged.*

### *23 Dec 1878*

Pera [Galata – Istanbul], 20th Dec.- The *Rinaldo* (s), which arrived here last night, had on board 94 passengers saved from the wreck of the *Byzantin* (s). The master states that about 1 o'clock on the afternoon of the 18th, while lying off Lampsaki, in the Dardanelles, with two anchors down, the ship being brought up [ie., anchored] from the force of the gale, and for the purpose of getting a bill of health vised [endorsed], the French steamer *Byzantin*, in attempting to anchor, crossed the bows of the *Rinaldo*, collided with a fearful crash, and then passed along the ship's side, raking her with the anchor.

He, the master of the *Rinaldo*, made signs to the passengers on board the French vessel to jump on board his steamer, but they were so panic stricken that only 90 managed to save themselves in this way. The *Byzantin* then passed under the stern of the *Rinaldo*, and went down stern first in five minutes after the collision. The master of the English steamer did his utmost to save life, but the gale that was blowing at the time rendered these efforts almost futile. Indeed, the boats which had been lowered were blown out of the Dardanelles into the Sea of Marmora. HMS *Flamingo* is going out to recover them. The master of the *Rinaldo* believes that over 200 people were drowned.

### *24 Dec 1878*

### Casualties – Foreign

Constantinople, 19th Dec.- The doctor, a lieutenant, the chief engineer, and eleven of the crew were all that were saved from the *Byzantin* (s). All the other persons that were on board, including 150 passengers, were drowned.

*The 906-ton French steamship *Byzantin* was carrying some 260 persons on her voyage from Marseilles to Constantinople (Istanbul). On 18th December 1878 a storm off Gallipoli in the Dardanelles forced her to attempt to anchor off Lampsaki, near where the British steamship *Rinaldo* (1,660 tons) was already at anchor awaiting health clearance. The stormy conditions swept the *Byzantin* across the bows and along the side of the *Rinaldo*. The collision sank the French vessel within five minutes.

Around 90 persons from the *Byzantin* saved themselves by jumping on board the *Rinaldo*. HMS *Flamingo* recovered the boats launched by the *Rinaldo* which had been swept by the storm into the Sea of Marmara. Another steamship, the *Vindomara*, rescued five *Byzantin* survivors in the Dardanelles strait. A boat with three officers (the doctor, a lieutenant, and the chief engineer) and eleven crew from the *Byzantin* was also recovered. The rest of those on board the *Byzantin*, including about 150 passengers and an unknown number of crew, were drowned when the ship went down.

## The *Oncle Joseph* and the "Damned Ship" *Ortigia*

30 Nov 1880

### Loss of the Steamer "Oncle Joseph"

The steamer "Oncle Joseph", of the Valery Line, from Naples for Genoa, and the Ortigia*, Florio Company's steamer, from Genoa for Leghorn [Livorno] and Naples, were in collision at 3 a.m. on Nov. 24, off Spezzia [La Spezia, near Genoa], when the Oncle Joseph foundered. The Ortigia had left Genoa at 11 30 p.m. on 23rd instant [November], with a crew of 44 men and 36 passengers. The "Oncle Joseph" had about 800 tons merchandise [cargo] and 305 persons, including emigrants and crew, some of the former comprising whole families going out to Buenos Ayres via Marseilles, by the Berlin steamer. The total number of lives saved is said to be 55, of which number 23 belong to the ship, so that the total loss of life may be put down at 250.

The survivors of the crew of the "Oncle Joseph" state that about 3 a.m., when off Spezzia, a tremendous crash was heard and it was found that a large steamer had run into the Oncle Joseph, striking her amidships and cutting her down to the water's edge. The crew and passengers rushed on deck, and some of them succeeded in climbing on to the bows of the Ortigia, but the latter backed astern, and as soon as the vessels parted, the water rushed in through the side of the "Oncle Joseph", and she sank in less than eight minutes, the sea, which was quite smooth at the time, being covered with a struggling mass of human beings.

It is said that only one small boat could be got out by those on board the Ortigia, a few lives being saved by that means. The Ortigia herself sustained serious damage to her cutwater and plates on port bow, and probably owes her safety to her watertight bulkhead. The Captain, Lacombe, of the "Oncle Joseph" is among the drowned. An investigation into the cause of the disaster is to be held.

*The French steamship *Oncle Joseph*, of around 820 tons, was on her way home to Marseilles via Genoa when the Italian steamship *Ortigia*, heading south from Genoa to Livorno and Naples, struck the French ship amidships in the middle of the night. The much bigger *Ortigia* (1,850 tons) was running at full speed and the *Oncle Joseph* sank quickly, taking around 250 passengers and crew, including her master, Capt. Lacombe, to their death.

The *Ortigia* was involved in a number of other collisions over the years resulting in substantial loss of life. The most notable happened 15 years after the *Oncle Joseph* disaster, with the *Maria P* in July 1895.

*22 July 1895*

### Maritime Intelligence

Maria (s).- Genoa, July 21.- A terrible maritime disaster occurred at half-past 1 this morning off the Isola del Tino, at the entrance to the Gulf of Spezzia. Two Italian steamers, the Ortigia and the Maria, came into collision. The Maria sank immediately, and of 178 passengers on board 148 were drowned.

Maria P. (s).- Genoa, July 21, 10 p.m.- Up to the present very few particulars have been received regarding the collision in the Gulf of Spezzia. It has, however, been ascertained that the Maria P. was bound from Naples to this port and carried a crew of 17 hands and 173 passengers, who were to have been transferred on her arrival to-day to the steamer Sud America for conveyance to the River Plate [ie., Buenos Aires]. The Ortigia sailed hence at 9 o'clock last night. The collision appears to have been due either to the prevalence of fog, or to the fact that the night was extremely dark [there was no moon that night], as the look-out men on the Ortigia saw nothing of the ill-fated vessel until it was too late to avoid a catastrophe.

The force of the collision was terrific, the stem of the Ortigia penetrating the starboard side of the Maria P. to a depth of 18 feet. The Maria P. sank in three minutes. Most of the passengers were in their bunks and had no time to save themselves before the vessel foundered. The Ortigia remained in the vicinity until some hours after daylight and succeeded in saving 14 of the crew and 28 passengers. Two sailing vessels are still cruising about near the scene of the collision in hopes of picking up other survivors. The Ortigia has a large rent in her bows four yards long just above the water-line. She returned to Genoa under her own steam.

### 23 July 1895
### The Sinking of an Italian Emigrant Steamer
### Genoa, July 22

Some further particulars can now be given regarding the circumstances attending the collision between the Italian steamers Ortigia and Maria P. The night was dark, the moon being obscured by clouds [*sic* – there was no moon that night], while the sea was rather rough. The captains were both asleep in their cabins, the Ortigia being in charge of the third officer, Signor Revello, while Signor D'Angelo, the second officer, was in command on board the Maria P. The Ortigia was steaming between 11 and 12 knots, and the Maria P. at about 10 knots an hour.

When off the island of Tino, some 12 miles from Spezia, the two vessels were preparing to cross each other's path as prescribed by the rules of the road, when, through some error at present unexplained, the Maria P.'s course was altered, with the result that she stood broadside on across the bows of the Ortigia. The officer in command of the Ortigia, perceiving the danger, ordered the engines to be reversed with all speed, but owing to the close proximity of the vessels it was too late to prevent a collision, and the Ortigia's bow crashed into the side of the Maria P., cutting her half through.

In three minutes the ill-fated vessel had disappeared, together with her 173 passengers, who were all below at the time. The Ortigia promptly lowered all her boats, and succeeded in saving 28 of the passengers and 14 of the crew. The whole of the passengers were Italian emigrants bound for the River Plate and Brazils [Brazil]. The survivors are quite panic-stricken, and are unable to give any account of the actual collision.

Captain Ferrari, of the Maria P., states that he was asleep in his bunk when he was suddenly awakened by a terrific crashing noise, followed by piercing cries of distress. He rushed on deck and found that the Ortigia's engines had been reversed. His own ship was sinking rapidly, and he realised that all would soon be over. He threw himself therefore into the sea, and was picked up afterwards by one of the boats lowered from the Ortigia.

Among the rescued passengers of the Maria P. are a jeweller named Balena and his wife. Their three children, however, were drowned. Signor Balena has given the following account of his experiences:- "I was in my cabin, but had not turned in when the collision occurred. On hearing the crash I seized two of my children in my arms and my wife carried the other. We ran upon deck and then jumped into the sea together. The children, of course, hampered my movements, and in a little time I sank. After many struggles I came to the surface again, but found that the children had disappeared. My wife had caught hold of a piece of wood and by this managed to keep herself afloat. Finally we were saved by one of the boats sent off to our rescue. We have lost everything we had in the world."

The rescued also include a child eight years old, the sole survivor of a family of seven persons. The second officer of the Maria P., named Angelo, was among the drowned. Two of the crew of the steamer who were saved sustained serious injuries. The Ortigia, after remaining until 8 o'clock close to the spot where the Maria P. foundered, returned under easy steam to Genoa. An inquiry, under the direction of the captain of the port, has been opened here into the causes of the collision.

Over the course of her life more than 400 persons lost their lives by the collision of their vessels with the *Ortigia* (none, so far as is known, from the *Ortigia* herself); hardly surprising, therefore, that she has been called "una nave davvero maledetta" ("a truly damned ship").

## THE *CIMBRIA* DISASTER

### 23 Jan 1883

Cimbria (s)*.- Hamburg, Jan. 21, 1 p.m.- The Hamburg steamer Cimbria, for New York, with about 490 passengers and crew, was run into by the English steamer Sultan, and sunk off Borkum [the largest and westernmost of the East Frisian Islands off northwest coast of Germany] in a dense fog on the morning of Jan. 19; 39 persons landed at Cuxhaven; five steamers searching for Cimbria's boats.

Cimbria (s).- Hamburg, Jan. 22, 1 46 p.m.- Cimbria: 95 crew; 380 passengers. The vessel sunk in 90 feet of water at 2 15 a.m., within 15 minutes. Four boats set out; one capsized; three left; one with 39 passengers arrived at Cuxhaven; second with 17 persons picked up and people landed at Bremerhaven; third missing. Captain and all the rest probably drowned. Steamers searching have not returned. The Sultan is here, damaged above the waterline.

*The New York Times*

**22nd January 1883**

**Lost In The North Sea**

**Over Three Hundred Persons Go Down With The Cimbria**

London, Jan. 22.-...A dispatch from Berlin says: "Besides the 39 survivors landed at Cuxhaven and the 17 at the Weser Light-house, another vessel has landed 11, but their names have not yet been ascertained. The number of lives lost is estimated at fully 300. The passengers were mostly emigrants from East Prussia. Among them were six American Indians, who had been on exhibition in Berlin for some time.".…

## *The New York Times*

## 24th January 1883

## The Wreck of the Cimbria

## Only Sixty-Seven Survivors of the Disaster

## All the Boats Launched Accounted For –

## The Sultan's Captain Maintains that He Is Not to Blame

Hamburg, Jan. 23.- According to the statement of another survivor of the disaster to the steam-ship Cimbria, as late as 2 o'clock Friday morning Capt. Hansen received a report that the Cimbria's lights were all burning brightly. The breach made by the collision was so great that the Cimbria immediately laid over with a portion of her deck under water. Upon an attempt to lower the boats one of them capsized. The time elapsing between the crash and the final sinking of the Cimbria was only a quarter of an hour.

The 39 persons brought in by the Theta appear to have been occupants of two boats. One of the boats contained 30 persons, the other only 9. The latter had been tossing about nine hours and was water-logged. All the occupants could do was to keep themselves from being washed away by grasping the thwarts. The other 17 persons saved were brought in by the Diamant. There are also reports of another lot of 11 or 9 persons rescued. Thus all the boats that left the Cimbria are accounted for…

London, Jan. 24.- A Hamburg correspondent narrating incidents which occurred on board the Cimbria after the collision says: "One red Indian brandished his tomahawk before an officer of the steamer and had to be disarmed. The tumult on board was indescribable. One married couple cut their own throats in order that they might die together. The ship's surgeon encouraged those in the rigging to hold fast, telling them that the Sultan would soon rescue them, but several became delirious and let go their hold. The surgeon subsequently leaped into the sea, saying he would 'make an end of it.'"

Another Hamburg dispatch says: "Several persons were killed by the collision itself, owing to the flying about of splinters and planks. A passenger in the shrouds [rigging] begged his neighbours to push him into the sea, he being too much chilled to move himself. They refused to do so, when he let himself fall headlong into the waves. An elderly woman, holding her Bible in her cramped hands and singing loudly funeral hymns, was washed away from the deck. Two girls belonging to the Salvation Singing troupe, having secured life belts, swam about a long time frantically crying, 'Help! Help! Save us!' The people in the rigging replied: 'Come to the rigging; we cannot move.' The girls, half benumbed and no longer able to swim, cried out for the last time: 'We cannot come,' and disappeared beneath the waves."

## *14 March 1883*

## Casualties, Etc.

Cimbria.- Copenhagen, Monday night [12 March] – The Danish salvage steamer Kattegat has returned from the wreck of the Cimbria. The divers report that one large lifeboat is in its place on the deck, where also parts of human remains are found jammed in amongst the gear, while the entrances to the cabins are closed by one compact mass of bodies. It will be next to impossible to save any of the cargo, as three decks would have to be exploded, while the explosions could also have the effect of shattering to pieces the 400 corpses in the hold.

*The 3,037-ton Hamburg-Amerika Line steamship *Cimbria* left Hamburg under the command of Capt. Hansen on 18 January 1883, bound for New York via Le Havre. She carried around 385 passengers and 92 crew, although exact numbers vary according to different reports. In the early morning of Friday 19 January in dense fog off the German East Frisian island of Borkum, the British steamer *Sultan* collided with the *Cimbria* which foundered within 15 minutes.

Lifeboats were launched, two of which with 39 survivors, were picked up by a British barque, the *Theta*, on the morning of Sunday 21 January landing at Cuxhaven on the German mainland. Another, with 17 persons, was picked up by the British ship *Diamant* and landed at the nearby Weser Lighthouse. A fourth boat, with nine survivors, made it to Borkum Island on its own. Approximately 400 people perished in the disaster, including Capt. Hansen, his first officer, and nearly all the 70 or so women and 87 children on board.

## *City of Columbus*: 97 Dead

## 21 Jan 1884

**Casualties, Etc.**

City of Columbus*.- Boston, Jan. 19.- The steamship City of Columbus, bound from this port for Savannah, with 81 passengers, one-third of whom were women and children, and a crew of 45 men, struck on a ledge early yesterday morning off Gay Head, the most westerly point of Martha's Vineyard Island, on the coast of Massachusetts. Of those on board, 104 persons perished, including 55 first-class and 15 steerage passengers, and 34 of the officers and crew. The remaining 22 persons were saved by the revenue steamer Dexter and landed at New Bedford.

When the vessel struck, the passengers rushed on deck, and were nearly all washed overboard. A heavy gale prevailed at the time, and the boats which were launched were consequently swamped, those who were saved being rescued from the rigging. The vessel has now broken up. Among the passengers drowned is M. Iasigi, Turkish Consul-General at Boston.

City of Columbus (s).- Boston (by Cable).- The City of Columbus, United States steamer, which left here Jan. 17 for Savannah, was totally wrecked at Gay Head on the 18th at 4 a.m.; 25 persons only saved; 100 of the crew and passengers drowned.

## *22 Jan 1884*

**Casualties, Etc.**

City of Columbus (s).- Boston, Jan. 21.- The search for the victims of the wreck of the City of Columbus is being actively continued. Ten of the survivors, including the purser, the second assistant engineer, six of the crew, and two passengers, have been found at Gay Head Lighthouse. Further search along the coast has resulted in the discovery of several groups of dead bodies. A corrected list of those on board the vessel shows that there were 81 cabin and steerage passengers and 45 officers, seamen and waiters. Of those, 12 passengers and 17 of the crew were saved.

*The 3,000-ton SS *City of Columbus* was one of two flagship passenger steamships of the Boston and Savannah Steamship Company, operated by the Nickerson Company of Boston. The vessel was employed on a regular run between Boston and Savannah, Georgia. On Thursday 17 January 1884 she left Boston for another voyage to the south, taking 81 passengers to warmer climes, under the command of Capt. Schuyler Wright with a crew of 45 and a pilot on board. Thirty-five of the passengers were women and children. In the early hours of Friday 18 January, the vessel struck rocks just off Gay Head, Martha's Vineyard, in Vineyard Sound. Capt. Wright reversed his vessel off the rock, unaware that her hull had been holed. Once off the rock, water flooded into the vessel where her hull had been breached. The *City of Columbus* sank quickly by the stern in 30–50ft of water, leaving her masts, rigging and smokestack sticking out of the water.

At the break of dawn the wreck was sighted from shore. Three lifeboats of the Gay Head Lifesaving station were launched. One was smashed attempting to reach the wrecked ship. The other two boats rescued 21 survivors. Later in the day, the US revenue cutter *Samuel Dexter* arrived on the scene, homeward bound to Woods Hole, and rescued a further eight people. Just 29 persons were saved from the wreck of the *City of Columbus*. Ninety-seven persons perished including all the women and children, either through drowning or freezing to death as they clung in desperation to the rigging. At the time, it was the greatest loss of life of any peacetime maritime disaster on the coast of New England.

## LOSS OF THE *DANIEL STEINMANN* OFF HALIFAX

### 7 April 1884

**Casualties, Etc.**

Daniel Steinmann (s).*- Halifax, April 4.- The steamer Daniel Steinmann, from Antwerp for New York, via Halifax, struck last night and sunk off Sambro, about 20 miles from here. Nine men only have as yet reached land out of 140 persons on board. From further particulars it has been ascertained that the Daniel Steinmann had 90 passengers and a crew of 34 men on board, of whom only five have been saved, including the captain. She sunk soon after striking on a ledge of rock.

Daniel Steinmann.- Halifax, April 5.- According to the latest intelligence received here regarding the wreck of the Daniel Steinmann (s), the crew numbered 39 men, of whom five were saved, together with the captain and three of the passengers. The names of the latter have not yet been ascertained. All the saved are now on Sambro Island. Communication with the wreck is impossible owing to the heavy sea.

### 9 April 1884

**Casualties, Etc.**

Daniel Steinmann (s).- New York, April 7.- Eleven bodies have been washed ashore from the steamer Daniel Steinmann. They are all terribly mutilated from contact with the rocks, and the features of some are quite unrecognisable. Among them are the corpses of the mate and of three children, two of them girls.

*The 1,790-ton steamship *Daniel Steinmann* left Antwerp in late March 1884 on a voyage to New York via Halifax, under the command of Capt. Van Schoonhoven. She carried 90 passengers, mainly German emigrants, and a crew of 40. On the night of 3 April, having encountered the usual dense fog over the Grand Banks off the coast of Newfoundland, and therefore without an observation for the previous two days to determine the ship's position accurately, Capt. Van Schoonhoven seemed nevertheless confident that he was heading safely into Halifax harbour.

However, around 10 p.m., the ship struck rocks just a few hundred metres from the Sambro Light at the head of the harbour. A heavy sea swept over the vessel and she sank quickly by the stern, taking many passengers on deck to their doom, together with most of the others below in their berths. Only one lifeboat, with five crew members and two passengers, reached the safety of land. Capt. Van Schoonhoven and a boy were rescued from the rigging just above sea level at dawn the next morning. Out of 130 persons on board the *Daniel Steinmann*, 121 perished by drowning; just nine survived the catastrophe.

## THE WRECK OF THE *SYRIA* AT FIJI

### 23 May 1884

**Casualties, Etc.**

> Syria*.- Fiji (by Telegraph from Wellington, N.Z.), date May 21.- The British ship Syria, Calcutta for Suva [Fiji], has been totally wrecked on Sasall Reef; part of crew landed here. It is reported that 70 passengers are supposed [thought] to have been drowned.
>
> Syria.- London, May 22.- The Syria struck on the reefs of Nabula on the 11th May; is a total wreck and has been abandoned. The captain is saved, but many of the coolies, of whom she carried 453, are lost.

### *4 July 1884*
**Casualties, Etc.**

> Syria.- Levuka [Fiji], May 14.- According to a pigeon message received, dated Suva, this morning, the Clyde, Callaghan, has just returned from the wreck of the Syria, from Calcutta for Suva, on Susall Reef, and reports all but three of the Lascar crew missing; also about 60 or 70 of the coolies missing. The vessel broke in two yesterday morning; everything washing out of her; the master was in town with foot rather badly hurt.

*Following the abolition of slavery in 1834, the British colonial powers initiated an indenture system to obtain cheap labour from India for transport to other British colonies. Between 1838 and 1916 the British conveyed 1.2m Indians to British colonies under indenture agreements. In the period 1879–1916, 60,500 Indians were transported to Fiji under the system (which was abolished in 1921), mainly to work in Fiji's sugar plantations.

The Indian labourers, mostly from Madras (Chennai) and Calcutta, were known as *girimtiyas*, from *girmit*, meaning indenture. *Girmit* contracts required Indians to work in Fiji for a specified period, usually a minimum of five years, after which they were free to return to India at their own expense, or after ten years at the expense of the colonial government.

The *Syria* was a 1,010-ton iron ship operated by the Nourse Line, primarily employed to transport indentured Indian workers to British colonies. Before her final voyage to Fiji in

1884, the *Syria* had mainly transported Indian labourers to Trinidad. On 13 March 1884 the ship left Calcutta with 497 indentured labourers bound for Fiji. On Sunday 11 May around 8.30 p.m., the vessel struck the Nasilai Reef, off the southeast coast of Viti Levu, the main island of the Fiji archipelago. Of the six lifeboats launched, only one, with four crew members reached land, at the village of Nasilai, early on the morning of 12 May. An inability to communicate with the villagers resulted in the *Syria* crew members being taken to Levuka, on the island of Ovalau some 12 miles away where a rescue party was organised later in the day.

The rescue operation, initiated and overseen by Dr. William MacGregor, Acting Colonial Secretary and Chief Medical Officer, started on the morning of Tuesday 13 May. When the rescue boats reached her, the *Syria* was lying on her side, her masts and rigging toppled and lying dishevelled about the wreck. Most of the passengers were on or around the reef or trying to swim to land. The rescue boats took over 400 survivors ashore to Nasilai village, but 56 passengers and three Indian lascar crew members died on the wreck. Eleven of the rescued survivors died within two weeks, making the final death toll of 70 one of the worst maritime disasters in Fiji's history.

Today the wreck of the *Syria* is both a poignant reminder for Fijian Indian descendants of the *girmit* era, as well as an historic memorial to the courage of the Nasilai villagers who helped save 439 of the *girmitiyas* on board the ship when she wrecked just a few miles offshore.

## THE *KAPUNDA* DISASTER OFF BRAZIL

### 31 Jan 1887

**Maritime Intelligence**

Kapunda*.- Bahia [northeast Brazil], Jan. 31, 10 15 a.m.- Ulysse, French barque, arrived, having on board the crew of the Kapunda, London for Australia, lost at sea; run down and sunk by a vessel; name unknown; 360 of the crew and passengers drowned.

### *1 Feb 1887*

**Maritime Intelligence**

Kapunda.- Bahia, Jan. 31, 2 20 p.m.- Portion of the crew and passengers of the Kapunda saved; the remainder, "203" in number, lost. She had been in collision with the Ada Melmore, British barque, from Coquimbo [Chilean seaport, about 240 miles north of Santiago] for England (ore), which sustained extensive damage, and bore up for Pernambuco in imminent danger.

Kapunda.- Pernambuco, Jan. 31, 3 20 p.m.- Ada Melmore, British barque, of Belfast, from Coquimbo, and Kapunda, British ship, from Plymouth for Australia, have been in collision; both vessels sank south of Maceio. The former lost two and the latter lost "302" lives. Part of the crew and passengers picked up by the Ulysse, French barque, and landed at Rio; part of crew and passengers landed at Maceio.

Kapunda. Bahia, Jan. 31, 3 50 p.m.- Part of the crew and passengers of the Kapunda picked up and landed here. The names of the crew saved are:- Cottrell, Norman, Meaks, Anderson, Hughes, and Gordon; besides [also], Forbes (and) Maunter who remained on

THE BRITISH EMIGRANT SHIP "KAPUNDA," RUN DOWN AND SUNK OFF THE COAST OF BRAZIL WITH A LOSS OF 298 LIVES

board the Ada Melmore. The following is a list of passengers saved:- Wiggins, Barnes, Daly, Russell, O'Calahan, Sandford, Reece, Broadhurst. All females perished. [Full list of passengers and crew follows.]

## 2 Feb 1887

### Maritime Intelligence

Kapunda. London, Feb. 1.- In reply to a telegram sent from Lloyd's to their agents at Bahia requesting further particulars as to what boats left the Kapunda and the chances of there being any other survivors beyond the 16 already mentioned, the following reply has been received, dated Bahia, Feb. 1, 3 35 p.m.- "Kapunda sunk almost immediately on Jan. 20, at 3 a.m.; impossible to lower boats. No chance of further survivors. A further report states that the Ada Melmore foundered at sea; crew landed at Maceio."

*The Illustrated London News*

### 5th February 1887

### Great Disaster At Sea

### Loss of Two or Three Hundred Lives

A terrible disaster to a British emigrant-ship, bound for Australia, took place on the 20th ult. [January], off the coast of Brazil. The Kapunda, a sailing-vessel, built of iron, 1095 tons register, owned by Messrs. Trinder, Anderson & Co., of London, left London on Dec. 11 [1886], and Plymouth on Dec. 18. She was bound for Fremantle, Western Australia, and had on board four cabin [first class] passengers, 268 steerage passengers, Dr. Bentham (the surgeon in charge), and a crew of forty. She was commanded by Captain John Masson. News came on Monday from Pernambuco that the Ada Melmore, barque, of Belfast, from Coquimbo, and the Kapunda had been in collision, and both vessels had sunk south of Maceio. Part of the crew and passengers of the Kapunda – namely, the first mate (Mr. W. Cottrell), the carpenter, baker, and five seamen, with eight male passengers – were picked up by the Ulysses, French barque, and landed at Rio, and a number of others were landed at Maceio.

The Ada Melmore was an iron barque, of 591 tons, built at Glasgow in 1887, and owned by Messrs. W. Porter & Sons, Belfast. It was not certainly known, up to Wednesday, how many were saved and landed at Maceio, or whether these belonged to the Kapunda or to the Ada Melmore, which was abandoned by her crew in a sinking condition. But the number lost on board the Kapunda must exceed 200, in any case, and may be nearly 300; there are, indeed, 298 missing, which includes all the women and children. It was impossible to lower any of the boats from the Kapunda. The full list of passengers is published in the London daily papers of Wednesday.

## Feb 23 1887

### Maritime Intelligence

Kapunda.- Bahia, Jan. 31.- The ship Kapunda, of London, from London for Fremantle [Western Australia], with a general cargo, and 279 emigrants, on Jan. 20, at 3 30 a.m., in lat. 13 45 S, long. 27 20 W [about 640 miles off the northeast coast of Brazil], was run into by the barque Ada Melmore, Miliken, from Coquimbo for the United Kingdom, with manganese ore. The Kapunda was hit about the fore-rigging, and went down so fast that nothing could be done to provide for the safety of the crew and passengers. The carpenter and an ordinary seaman, with seven emigrants, contrived to jump over on the barque; six others of the crew and passengers found a boat afloat and saved themselves.

The Ada Melmore is stated to have lowered a boat which only picked up the chief mate, William Cotterell. These 16 persons are the only survivors; thus the number of the perished is 303, including all females and children. Those saved remained on board the Ada Melmore until Jan. 25, when the French barque Ulysse, from Marseilles for Mozambique, came up and took 14 of them on board, calling at this port yesterday for the purpose of landing them.

The carpenter Forbes, and the ordinary seaman Maunter, remained on board the colliding barque which was completely stove in forward, having lost her bows down to the forefoot, and had all headgear carried away. The collision bulkhead, although severely strained kept her from sinking, and an attempt was made to bring the ship to Pernambuco. As it appeared very doubtful whether she would keep afloat long enough to be got into any port at hand, everything was made ready for abandoning, and that is the last heard of her up to this moment.- [The Ada Melmore has since been reported by telegraph from Pernambuco as having foundered to the south of Maceio.]

### 3 March 1887
**Maritime Intelligence**

Ada Melmore/Kapunda.- Liverpool, March 2, 7 p.m.- The Orator (s), from Maceio, brings the master, mate, one seaman and apprentice of the Ada Melmore, and carpenter of Kapunda. On Jan. 28 the Ada Melmore's bulkhead gave way, and vessel commenced to fill; crew took to boats and landed at Maceio. After being abandoned vessel was seen to founder.

### 8 March 1887
**Maritime Intelligence**

Ada Melmore- Liverpool, March 7, 1 17 p.m.- The Fedele Primavesi (s), from Pernambuco, brings mate and two seamen of the Ada Melmore, and Stephen Mounter, ordinary seaman of the Kapunda.

*According to the *Board of Trade Wreck Report, 1887*, the collision of the *Kapunda* and the *Ada Melmore* resulted in the loss of 299 lives, all from the *Kapunda* (although other reports insist on 303 lives lost). The Board of Trade Inquiry concluded that "the wrongful act and defaults" of the *Kapunda*'s master, Capt. William Millikin, and the *Ada Melmore*'s chief officer, Nelson Wannell, were responsible for the collision.

## THE *SIR JOHN LAWRENCE*: LOSS OF ALL CREW AND 730 PILGRIMS

## 6 June 1887
**Maritime Intelligence**

Sir John Lawrence.- Calcutta, June 5.- It is now unhappily certain that the Sir John Lawrence was lost in the recent cyclone. It was hoped for a time that she might have weathered the storm, but the fact that one of the steamers sent in search came across a number of bodies, chiefly of native females, and the chest belonging to the captain, has put an end to all hope.

There were 730 passengers on board, most of them native ladies, going to Poori to celebrate the Rath Jattra festival*, at the temple of Juggernauth.

*The Rath Yatra is an important Hindu festival held in the monsoon season, either June or July. Now celebrated all over India (and amongst Hare Krishna communities in the rest of the world), it originated at Puri, in Orissa state.

Juggernauth is the Jagannath Temple at Puri. (*Jagganath* is Sanskrit for Lord of the universe and is the name of one of the incarnations of the Hindu deity Krishna.) The Rath (a chariot or cart) Yatra (a pilgrimage or procession) involves a procession of huge wooden chariots carrying the statues of the deities Jagannath, his brother Baladeva and sister Subhadra through the streets of Puri. Millions of devotees attend the festival each year which is also broadcast live by Indian television. The Jagannath chariots, which are built each year, are the origin of the English word juggernaut. There are other Rath Yatra celebrations in other Indian cities but the event at Puri is the original and most important.

## THE *QUETTA* DISASTER IN THE TORRES STRAIT

### 3 March 1890

**Maritime Intelligence**

Quetta (s).- Brisbane, March 1, 9.10 p.m.- Quetta, British steamer, struck on an unknown rock near Somerset, Torres Straits*, and became a total wreck; she sank almost immediately. It is reported that 200 souls were drowned.

Quetta (s).- Brisbane, March 2.- Queensland Line steamer Quetta, from Brisbane for London, struck on an unknown rock off Cape York, on Friday night, and sank in three minutes. She had 280 souls on board at the time, only 116 of whom are saved, among them being the captain, the second, third, and fourth officers, the purser, and the following saloon passengers:- Miss Nicklin, Messrs. Corsen, Clarke, Renton, and Debney.

Quetta (s).- London, March 1.- Owners have received following telegram from Brisbane, dated March 1, 9.10 p.m.:- Quetta (s) is a total loss; struck alleged unknown rock 9 p.m. yesterday, near Somerset, Torres Straits; sank three minutes afterwards. According to report 100 saved, including captain. We fear loss of life is considerable. Will wire particulars as soon as we receive them.

Quetta (s).- London, March 3.- A telegram dated Brisbane, March 3, 5 16 a.m., states as follows:- Merrie England arrived to-day, Thursday Island, from wreck; reports of 282 souls all told, including about 60 Javanese, 136 saved. Albatross still searching islands. Quetta's side completely torn out.

### 4 March 1890

**Maritime Intelligence**

Quetta (s).- London, March 3.- A telegram dated Brisbane, March 3, states as follows:-

Saloon passengers missing – Mesdames Archer, Lord, Nicklin, Watson, Whish, Corser, Poland; Misses Barrow, Cooksley, Prentice, Ross, Wright (two), Waugh, Tabatt, Lack (two); Messrs. Archer, Nicklin, Watson, Whish, Blackford, Gape, Prentice, Dawsen, Hall; Masters Lord, Corser.

Steerage missing – Mesdames Urotharl and one child, Compeland, Williams, Willett, McGladdery, Coombe, Griffen, Brightman, each of the above with two children; Davidson, with three children; Jackson, with four children; Cross, Green (child), Woodhall, Lewis, Misses Smith, Whitty; Messrs. McGladdery, Alban, Garner (two), Green, Jackson, Binns, Jeffers, Moore, Williams (two), Hurst, Glasgow, Fulton, Marshall, Learl, Reilly.

Deck passengers missing – 14 Javanese. European crew missing – Gray, Poland, Barnicoat, McMurchy, Rose, Henderson, Cudack, Weech, Stamys, McKenzie, Smith, Nash; Mrs. Muncle, Jones, Brooks (last two engaged at Brisbane).

Native crew missing – 33. Inquiring if fully protected salvage; ship was in charge of pilot Keating, who was saved.

Quetta (s).- Brisbane, March 3.- One hundred and fifty-eight persons from the Quetta (s), including the first officer and Miss Lacy, have arrived at Thursday Island. The brother and sister of Mr. Archer, Agent-General for Queensland in London, are reported among those missing.

Quetta (s).- Brisbane, March 4.- When the Quetta struck upon the rock and began to sink, some of the coloured men monopolized one of the boats, while the other boats conveyed the remainder of the survivors to Adolphus Island, three miles distant, whence they were rescued by the Albatross and Merrie England and taken to Thursday Island. Miss Lacy was found after she had been swimming for 20 hours.

## 5 March 1890
### Maritime Intelligence

Quetta (s).- Melbourne, March 4.- An incessant search has been kept up for survivors of the disaster, but all efforts have been fruitless, although several bodies have been found. According to the latest intelligence, the total number of saved is 149, and of lost 133. Quetta (s) sank broadside on, some plates having been torn out by the collision with the rock.

Quetta (s).- Melbourne, March 4.- Some accounts received here of the loss of the Quetta report splendid acts of heroism on the parts of the passengers, but state that the natives on board ruthlessly thrust aside the ladies and children who were trying to enter the boats, and became a frantic and undisciplined mob. The captain and pilot positively assert that the rock on which the vessel struck was not marked on the chart, whereas in some quarters it is declared to be well known as the Mid Rock.

Quetta (s).- Melbourne, March 5.- The opinion expressed by a number of captains and pilots to the effect that the rock upon which the Quetta struck is not marked on the chart is confirmed. The excessive number of fatalities among the ladies on board is attributed to the fact that at the time of the disaster they were sitting under an awning which carried them down with the sinking vessel.

*The Torres Strait separates the northernmost tip of Australia, the Cape York Peninsula, from the southeast coast of New Guinea. Littered with small islands, rocks and reefs, many unmarked to this day and sluiced by unpredictable currents and rips, it is a hazardous place through which to navigate at the best of times. Thursday Island is the main inhabited island in the Strait.

The 3,484-ton steamship *Quetta*, was built at Dumbarton, Scotland, and launched in 1881. On 18 February 1890 she departed Brisbane under the command of Capt. Alfred Saunders, with 293 passengers and crew, bound for London. Her initial course would have been north along the east coast of Australia, passing westwards through the Torres Strait and across the north of Australia towards the Indian Ocean.

The *Quetta* was just coming into the Torres Strait on the evening of 28 February, in the charge of Mr. Keating, a Torres Strait pilot, when she struck an "allegedly" uncharted rock near Mount Adolphus Island at the eastern entrance to the Strait. The rock ripped open most of her port side and she sank within minutes. Some survivors reached the small settlement of Somerset on the York Peninsula while others landed further west at Thursday Island. A total of 160 lives were saved. The loss of life from the *Quetta* – 133 passengers and crew – was the greatest of any Torres Strait shipwreck.

The official report on the wreck of the *Quetta* concluded: "The board are of opinion…there is nothing in the evidence…on which to found a charge of default against Captain Saunders, his officers, or pilot Keating, who are therefore exonerated from all blame.- Marine Board Office, Brisbane, 26 April 1890."

## The Sinking of the *Utopia* at Gibraltar: Over 500 Dead

## 18 March 1891

### Maritime Intelligence

Utopia (s)*.- Gibraltar, March 17, 8 10 p.m.- British steamer Utopia, in coming in, collided with British iron-clad Anson, at anchor; former sank immediately off Ragged Staff; many lives lost; large number people still in rigging; Channel Squadron boats rescuing them; further particulars later; blowing a strong gale; wind SW.

Utopia (s).- Gibraltar, March 17, 9 30 p.m.- The British steamer Utopia, with 700 Italian emigrants on board, bound for New York, foundered in the bay here this evening, during a south-westerly gale, after colliding with another vessel. Some of the passengers have been saved, and others are at present being rescued by the boats belonging to the Channel Squadron. It is feared that many women and children have been drowned.

Utopia (s).- Gibraltar, March 18, 1 a.m.- It is impossible at present to say exactly what is the loss of life through the foundering of the Utopia, but it is believed that over 200 souls have perished. The crew of the steamer are reported to have been saved. It seems that the Utopia was steaming into the bay, when she came into collision with the British ironclad Anson, which was lying at anchor, and went down in a short time. Boats were at once put out from all the vessels of the Channel Squadron, and also from the Swedish man-of-war Freya, which was near at hand, and they were successful in saving many lives. Over 180 of the rescued people are now on board the different men-of-war [warships], and others have been brought ashore, where they have temporarily been housed in the station, the colonial hospital, the Garrison Recreation Rooms, and Sailors' Home.

Utopia (s).- Gibraltar, March 18, 10 a.m.- From the latest accounts it appears that the Utopia sank in five minutes, and it is feared that the loss of life is even greater than at first reported, although it is at present impossible to estimate the exact extent of the catastrophe. Several bodies of men, women, and children have been washed ashore on the Spanish coast. The survivors were rescued by the launches and boats of the [British] fleet, of the Swedish corvette

Freya, and the cable ship Amber, but the work of rescue was most difficult owing to the gale. So furious indeed was the sea that several boats belonging to the fleet were completely wrecked.

## 19 March 1891

### Maritime Intelligence

Utopia (s).- Gibraltar, March 18, 9 20 a.m.- The disaster occurred at 7 o'clock. The ram of the Anson tore a hole 30 feet long in the side of the Utopia near the stern, and the vessel sank within 10 minutes, going down stern first. Her funnel and masts are just above the water. There were 800 passengers all told on board. A heavy south-westerly gale was blowing at the time of the collision, and the tremendous seas washed everything on deck overboard. It was feared that quite two-thirds of the passengers had been drowned. Captain Mackenzie, commander of the Utopia, and the doctor and steward are saved.

Utopia (s).- Gibraltar, March 18, 11 55 a.m.- Ascertained number crew saved 20, including captain, first, third officers, doctor, steward, third engineer. Agents telegraphing names. Saloon lady passenger saved; second officer and Charles G. Davies, Boston, saloon passenger, missing. Vessel got in among ironclads [battleships] and fouled ram Anson, blow amidships; stern sank five minutes, vessel settled 15 minutes.

Utopia (s).- Gibraltar, March 18, 2 55 p.m.- Utopia: Agents inform us total complement, 830 passengers, 50 crew. Saved, 24 crew, 292 passengers; bodies recovered, 50; balance supposed [believed] went down in ship. Divers being employed. Hales' body recovered.

## 21 March 1891

### Maritime Intelligence

Utopia (s).- Gibraltar, March 20, 5 40 p.m.- Utopia: Number saved 344, including 47 crew, 284 Italians, 40 Hungarians, 1 Austrian, 2 saloon passengers; actual number on board before catastrophe 59 crew, 815 emigrants, 3 stowaways, 3 saloon passengers.

## 23 March 1891

### The Wreck of the Utopia (s)

### Gibraltar, March 22, 6 p.m.

Twelve wagons filled with the bodies of victims of the disaster to the Anchor Line steamer Utopia, taken from the wreck by divers, were removed to the North Front Cemetery at noon to-day, and the funeral ceremonies are now taking place. At the meeting of the Board of Health yesterday it was resolved that in future all bodies recovered shall be buried in the Straits [the Straits of Gibraltar]. They will be sewed up in tarpaulin and placed in weighted bags, and thus buried.

The verdict of the coroner's jury, of accidental death, was not reached until nearly midnight last night. In the course of the coroner's investigation, it was brought up in favour of Captain McKeague that he had had 20 years' experience, and had never before had an accident. The Marine Court will assemble tomorrow for the purpose of investigating the cause of the collision. The Utopia is a great obstruction to navigation, and the wreck will be removed as soon as measures can be taken to that end.

A subject that has been discussed with much interest during the last few days has been the fact that the lifeboat did not go out on the night of the wreck. Only six men of the crew turned up, and they were not sufficient to man the boat.

Many more bodies have been washed ashore in Catalan Bay, and also on the coast of Morocco. Altogether nearly 200 bodies have thus far been recovered. The divers continue their operations, and are constantly bringing up bodies of the drowned. The reports show that the struggles of the victims to leave the ship at the time of her sinking were of the most desperate character. The divers have found many bodies with their heads out of the port holes, while the hands of these unfortunates were clutching the screws, and they had evidently been trying to pull themselves through, and were drowned in this position. In many cases the divers have found the bodies of several of the victims clutched together, sometimes to the number of eight, and it has been extremely difficult to disentangle the corpses. The electric light is now thrown all the night through upon the spot where the Utopia lies.

There are now quite 130 bodies buried at the cemetery, and the loss of life is estimated at 564.

*The Utopia was a 2,731-ton steamship built in 1874 and operated by the Anchor Line. Commanded by Capt. John McKeague, she left Naples on 12 March 1891, with a complement of 815 Italian emigrants, three saloon passengers, three stowaways, and 59 crew, total of 880 souls on board – bound for New York. Five days later she was coming into the Bay of Gibraltar during stormy conditions. By the early evening darkness the ship was amongst the British Mediterranean Fleet anchored there. The Utopia struck the underwater ram of the ironclad warship Anson which tore a hole 26ft long by 15ft wide in the Utopia's hull.

The Utopia went down by the stern and sank in about 55ft of water causing the death of 533 people. One saloon passenger, twelve crew and 520 emigrants as well as some others involved in trying to rescue them.

The subsequent coroner's inquiry ruled that the collision was accidental. The Marine Court of Enquiry (cf.: Board of Trade Wreck Report for 'Utopia' and 'Anson (HMS)', 1891) found Captain McKeague guilty of a "grave error in judgement" that caused the tremendous loss of life but took no further action against him. Although it could have suspended or cancelled his master's certificate. The wreck of the Utopia was raised to the surface on 18 July 1891.

## Loss of the *Bokhara* in the South China Sea

### 18 Oct 1892

**Maritime Intelligence**

Bokhara (s)*.- Amoy, Oct. 17, 8 58 p.m.- Bokhara (s) wrecked and totally lost, ship and cargo, at Pescadores. Some of the passengers and crew saved and landed at Swatow [Shantou, Guangdou Prov., China].

Bokhara (s).- London, Oct. 18.- The owners have received the following telegram, giving particulars of cargo supposed [believed] to be on board the Bokhara, dated Shanghai, Oct. 18, 11 30 a.m.:- Specie, $200,000; silk, 1,363 bales; tea, 400 tons for Bombay; general cargo, 225 tons for London; general cargo, 200 tons for France.

Bokhara (s).- London, Oct. 18.- The following additional particulars have been received by owners per telegram, dated Hong Kong, Oct. 18, 1 40 p.m.:- "Chief officer Bokhara reports: Bokhara struck Monday, midnight, 10th Oct., vessel becoming helpless at 10 p.m. Monday owing to heavy seas putting fires out. All deck fittings and boats gone before vessel struck, she sinking immediately.

European and native crew behaved splendidly throughout; 120 of the crew missing, viz:- Captain Sams; second officer Ingles; engineers O'Bryan, Coban, Paton, Hills; boilermaker Houston; winchman Kendall; carpenter Brennan; boatswain Reeves; quartermasters Gaskin, Friend, Hudson, Thiel, Phillip; steward in charge, Ward; stewardess Barstock; stewards Poppi, Wilson, Mitchell, Elliott, Pettit, Chipps, Reading, Briscoe, Garwood, Boxall, and 70 native seamen and firemen."

## The Wreck of the Bokhara (s)

Our "Maritime Intelligence" of yesterday included several telegrams announcing the total wreck of the Peninsular and Oriental Company's steamer Bokhara, on Sand Island, one of the Pescadores Group, while on a voyage from Shanghai for Hong Kong. The commander and majority of the officers and crew were reported as lost. One telegram stated that only 23 persons had been saved, while another correspondent said there were 34 survivors. A telegram received this morning from the Shanghai correspondent of the *Standard* states that about 200 persons were on board at the time of the disaster, and that of those no less than 170, including 20 passengers, were drowned…

The Bokhara was built in 1873 by Messrs. Caird and Co., of Greenock, and was refitted in 1880. She was of 2,970 tons and 3,000-horse power, and of the following dimensions:- Length 361 feet, breadth 39 feet, and depth 29 feet.

The Pescadores are a series of small islands lying to the north-west of Formosa [Taiwan], a large island off the coast of China, but at a considerable distance from the straight track usually pursued by steamers in passing up and down the northern part of the China Sea. Ships generally "hug" the main coast as closely as possible.

The Bokhara was at the time of the disaster engaged in carrying the mails from Shanghai to Hong Kong and Colombo, where she would have joined the main line, and would then have proceeded to Bombay.…

In the course of communications on the subject of the disaster a correspondent writes:- "The course from Shanghai to Hong Kong is one of the most dangerous in that part of the world. It abounds with rocks and islands, which are inadequately lighted. The coast is rough and inhospitable, with powerful currents, and near to the island upon which the Bokhara lies wrecked there is a well-known jungle swarming with tigers and other wild beasts.

At this season of the year the China Seas are raided with typhoons, and one occurring in the particular region where the Bokhara has been wrecked places a passing ship in certain jeopardy. Large numbers of coasting steamers of high tonnage are lost yearly, and one company writes off in advance contingent losses. The Chinese junks go down in scores – incidents common to the coast, and attracting little more than passing notice. The P. and O. commanders, during the run down or up the coast, invariably pass the night on deck, even in the finest weather, so critical is the navigation and strong the currents.

Another element of danger to a shipwrecked crew is in the latent piracy which still exists in Southern China, where, it has been roughly stated, every Chinaman is a born pirate. Less than a year ago a British steamer was seized by a stratagem and looted by pirates, several officers being shot dead, and the passengers locked in the saloon and smothered with stink-pots. Much credit is due and freely acknowledged to the efforts made by Sir Robert Hart, the Chief of the Imperial Chinese Customs Service, for the opening of lighthouses along the coast of China from Hong Kong to Newchang."

Another correspondent says:- "Though nearly 20 years old, the Bokhara, whose loss with her captain and nearly all the crew is one of the saddest calamities at sea reported this year, was a ship of more than ordinary seaworthiness. Like her sister ships, the Hydaspes and Cathay, which now run the winter mails between Genoa, Brindisi, and Alexandria, she was of a class specially adapted for service in rough seas. They were of the build known as flush deck without top hamper to catch the full violence of sudden squalls, and all of them have weathered many a hurricane.

The Bokhara was built by Messrs. Caird and Co., of Greenock, so long ago as 1873, before the introduction of mild steel, of which so many of the finest merchant steamers are now constructed; but her iron ribs and hull were of the toughest workmanship, and she was in such good condition 12 years ago that the owners spent a large sum in fitting her with new boilers. Since she made her first voyage down to the present time the Bokhara has been engaged in the Eastern Service, and had passed through the storms of many winters in the notoriously dangerous China Seas. Her commander, Captain Sams, who is supposed [believed] to have perished at his post when the ship went down, was an officer of much experience, in whose abilities as a seaman the company had every confidence; and he held a commission as lieutenant in the Royal Naval Reserve.

This season the gales in those latitudes have been of exceptional violence, driving ships frequently far out of their course. This does not seem to have been altogether the case with the Bokhara, as she must have kept to the ordinary trade route for at least two-thirds of the 870 miles between Shanghai and Hong Kong. In the dangerous Straits of Formosa, however, the hurricane must have disabled her before she struck, for with such an experienced navigator as Captain Sams nothing but the force of winds against which he found his ship powerless to battle could have driven her so far east as the Pescadores Islands, which are only one degree [60 miles] west of the Island of Formosa. Near them are dreaded banks amid the thundering surf, of which no seaman would risk running his ship during a storm if he could by any means beat up against it. That terrible weather was encountered we learn from the brief telegram in which the sad fate of the Bokhara and her crew is told."

## 19 Oct 1892
### Maritime Intelligence

Bokhara (s).- *Hong Kong*, Oct. 18.- Her Majesty's cruiser Porpoise arrived here to-day with the survivors of the steamer Bokhara, which was lost on Sand Island, in the Pescadores Group, while on the voyage from Shanghai to Hong Kong. The Bokhara, which left Shanghai on the 8th inst., encountered a ferocious gale on the 10th inst. The sea ran mountains high, repeatedly sweeping the decks, and finally extinguishing the engine-room fires. Being thus rendered quite helpless, the Bokhara drifted towards Sand Island, upon which she struck at midnight and sank immediately afterwards.

All on board were lost except two of the passengers, three of the vessel's officers, two of the European and 16 of the native crew. Altogether, 125 persons perished. The survivors, after passing two days on Sand Island, a desert spot, were taken off by the Chinese to Wakung, where they were found by the Douglas Line steamer Thales, which took them on board and subsequently transferred them to the Porpoise.

*There were 148 persons on board the *Bokhara* when she left Shanghai for her return voyage to Hong Kong on 8 October 1892. Of those, 125 lost their lives when the ship was wrecked two days later on Sand Island, one of the Pescadores Islands near the coast of Formosa (Taiwan) in the Straits of Formosa (Taiwan Strait). Just 23 survived. These included Dr James Lawson and a Lt. Markham, two members of a 13-strong Hong Kong cricket team who had played an Interport match against the Shanghai cricket team on 3 October at the Shanghai Cricket Club and were returning to Hong Kong on the *Bokhara*.

## THE *CATTERTHUN* DISASTER

## 8 Aug 1895

### Maritime Intelligence

Catterthun (s)*.- London, Aug. 8.- A Central News telegram states:- Steamer Catterthun, Sydney for China, struck Seal Rocks, between Sydney and Brisbane, 2 this morning. Boat landed Forster [coastal town north of Sugarloaf Point and Seal Rocks] containing Captain Fawkes, Doctor Copeman, second mate Langfear and Mr. Crane. Feared other boats lost.

Catterthun (s).- Newcastle, N.S.W., Aug. 8, 3 15 p.m.- Catterthun (s) wrecked and totally lost, ship and cargo, at Seal Rocks. Full particulars not yet received, but it is feared there has been a serious loss of life.

Catterthun (s).- Sydney, Aug. 8,- A boat's crew of Chinese sailors have landed at Forster, about 100 miles north of Sydney, and report that the steamer Catterthun, from [*sic*] China, was wrecked last night. No further details are yet to hand.

### 9 Aug 1895
### Maritime Intelligence

Catterthun (s).- Sydney, Aug. 8.- British steamer Catterthun struck the Seal Rocks, off Cape Hawk, early this morning, during a heavy gale. The passengers were asleep in their berths at the time. The number of those on board is not definitely known, but is believed to have been 70. Of these 45 were Chinese and three European passengers. The second mate is known to have been saved. The remainder are missing, but it is thought that they are in the ship's boats which may have been blown to seaward.

Catterthun (s).- Sydney, Aug. 8, 10 30 p.m.- A tug has just returned from the scene of the wreck of the Catterthun, and reports that nothing could be seen either of the vessel or of her boats. A heavy sea prevailed, and there is little doubt that 60 persons were drowned. Of these 46 were Chinese. Mr. Langfar, the second officer, who was in charge of the deck when the ship struck, states that the night was dark and cloudy. The shock was terrific, and the vessel foundered in a few minutes. The Chinese passengers made a rush for the boats, causing much confusion. The missing Europeans include three lady passengers and a gentleman from the Cape, the ship's doctor, the chief officer, four engineers, the steward, and the quarter-master.

Catterthun (s).- London, Aug. 9.- The Catterthun, lost off Seal Rocks, carried 11,000 sovereigns and a general cargo.

## 10 Aug 1895

## Maritime Intelligence

Catterthun (s).- London, Aug. 9.- The following telegram has been received from the managing agents of the company at Sydney re: Catterthun (s) – Following are saved: Second mate; passengers Fawkes, Crane, and Copeman; 22 Chinese. Very much fear remainder drowned.

Catterthun (s).- Sydney, Aug. 9.- The steamer which was sent out to search for any survivors of the Catterthun has returned here with a boat belonging to that vessel. It was empty when picked up.

*The *Catterthun* was a 2,179-ton steamship. She was built in 1881 by W. Doxford & Sons of Sunderland for the Eastern & Australian Steamship Co., to be employed on a regular run between ports on the east coast of Australia – Sydney, Melbourne, Adelaide – and China, including Hong Kong. On 2nd August 1895 the ship berthed at Sydney to load cargo and embark passengers for her return voyage to Hong Kong. The cargo included a consignment of ten wooden boxes of almost 9,000 gold sovereigns, part of which was to be consigned to a bank in Darwin, Australia, and part to a group of Hong Kong Chinese merchants.

The *Catterthun* left Sydney bound for Hong Kong on the cold southern hemisphere mid-winter afternoon of 7 August with 81 persons on board, under the command of Captain Neil Shannon. Off the New South Wales coast the ship encountered gales with frequent rain squalls and high seas. In the early hours of 8 August the ship was off Sugarloaf Point. Second officer Alfred Lanfear, on the bridge, could see the beam of Sugarloaf Point Lighthouse.

Several miles off the coast lay Big and Little Seal Rocks, jutting up just a few metres above sea level and directly in the path of *Catterthun*'s course. Lanfear saw breakers over Big Seal Rocks and immediately adjusted the ship's course to clear the danger. However, the new course took the *Catterthun* directly over a reef projecting from Little Seal Rock. She struck the reef and foundered in 30 fathoms within about 45 minutes.

As the stormy seas swept over the sinking ship, Capt. Shannon and first officer William Pinney were washed overboard and drowned. Lifeboats were swamped and their occupants drowned as soon as they were launched. The one lifeboat that did reach safety contained 26 survivors: the second officer, three European passengers and the remaining 22 Chinese. The boat headed north towards the coast. A fishing boat near Charlotte Head took the survivors off and landed them a few hours later at Forster, Cape Hawkes Bay, around nine hours after the *Catterthun* sank. Fifty-five others from the ship had drowned.

A year after the wreck on 20 August 1896, divers recovered seven of the ten boxes of gold sovereigns in the *Catterthun*'s 'specie room', an ironclad storage compartment below the bridge. The seven boxes of sovereigns were worth £7,944. About half of that went towards paying for the salvage operation. The three remaining wooden boxes containing 800 gold coins had disintegrated and the coins were never recovered. Today the wreck of the *Catterthun* lies in around 30 fathoms of water just to the north of the Little Seal Rock reef that ripped her bottom out.

## CHINESE TRANSPORT EXPLOSION: 500 DEAD

### 23 Oct 1895

#### The Explosion On Board a Chinese Transport

Particulars have been received at Shanghai, from Kinchow, of the disaster to the transport [ship] Kung Pai, with troops on board, which occurred on the 14th inst., about 20 miles from that place. An explosion occurred in the powder magazine, setting fire to the vessel. The crew worked hard to extinguish the flames, but made very little headway, an in half an hour a second explosion occurred. The boilers were blown to pieces, fragments being scattered over the vessel from midships to the stern.

The captain and chief officer were wounded by the first explosion, and were put in a boat to be taken to the shore. The soldiers, however, made a rush for the boat, and so many crowded into it that the davits broke, and the boat was smashed to pieces, all the occupants being drowned. The second mate and the first and second engineers and one passenger were killed by the explosion, while of the 700 troops on board 500 perished. The survivors, consisting of the third engineer and 200 soldiers, clung to the stern of the wreck, and, owing to the heavy sea which was running, remained in that perilous position for 17 hours before they could be reached by boats and landed. Twenty-seven wounded men were taken to the Kinchow Hospital. They presented a dreadful appearance.

## DRUMMOND CASTLE WRECKED OFF USHANT

### 18 June 1896

#### Maritime Intelligence

Drummond Castle (s)*.- London, June 17.- The owners have received the following telegrams from the chief lighthouse keeper at Ushant and Mr. Marquardt, one of the surviving passengers:- June 17, 4 10 p.m. – (1) Drummond Castle wrecked about midnight at Ushant, Mr. Marquardt sole survivor at Ushant, two other survivors [at] Ile Molene, six bodies recovered, including officer about 25 years of age, fair moustache, and young girl about six years old, bodies placed in special house. Kindly telegraph instructions for burial. Ship sunk in three minutes. (2) Drummond total loss off Ushant, am probable sole survivor, proceeding London as soon as possible – Marquardt.

Drummond Castle (s).- Brest, June 17.- Last night towards 12 o'clock the Cape Liner Drummond Castle, bound from Cape Town for London, struck on a rock off the island of Molene, which lies between Ushant and the mainland; three minutes after striking the steamer went down. The Maritime Prefecture has received a telegram which has been communicated to the British Consul, stating that 250 persons, including passengers and crew were on board. The latest telegram from Le Conquet, a small port on the Atlantic coast opposite the island of Molene, says that all on board perished except three. Six bodies have been washed ashore on the island of Ushant. The French Admiralty tug Le Laborieux left Brest this evening for the scene of the disaster, to search the sea in the hope that some further survivors may be picked up.

Drummond Castle (s).- Southampton, June 18.- The steamer Hirondelle, from Bordeaux, arrived here early this morning, having passed the spot where the Drummond Castle was

THE CAPE LINER "DRUMMOND CASTLE," WRECKED OFF USHANT, JUNE 16.

lost shortly after the disaster. Master of the Hirondelle states that the weather in the Bay of Biscay was very bad, with a high SW wind, thick, small [light] rain and heavy fog. The Hirondelle made Ushant at 8 yesterday morning, and at that point the sea was very high, and the weather very thick. Nothing whatever was seen of any boats, wreckage, or bodies, but 25 miles further off a lifebelt was noticed floating on the water.

*19 June 1896*

## The Wreck of the Drummond Castle

As soon as the doors of Messrs. Donald Currie and Co.'s offices in Fenchurch-street were thrown open yesterday morning the place was besieged by anxious inquirers after relatives and friends. Sir Donald Currie and the directors of the Castle Mail Packets Company, to which the Drummond Castle belonged, were at the offices at an early hour, together with the staff…

…Apart from numerous private inquiries, the first telegram that reached Messrs. Currie was from Ushant, dated yesterday, 12 30 p.m. It was from the chief lighthouse-keeper there, and was in French, the following being a translation of the message:- Marquardt [sole surviving passenger] states that no boat could be launched. The persons saved and the bodies recovered were all found in the water clinging to life-belts, spars, or pieces of wreckage. The two other survivors are named James Wood and William Godbolt, steersmen. We have no longer any hope of recovering other survivors…

…The British Consul at Brest telegraphed yesterday at 1 25 p.m.:- "Names of two saved (Molene) – Charles Wood, quartermaster, and William James Godbolt, seaman. Both arrived here this morning. Name of survivor (Ushant), Charlie Marquardt…Three only at this hour known to be saved…"

*20 June 1896*

## The Wreck of the Drummond Castle (s)

### Brest, June 19

The interrogation to which the two surviving seamen, Wood and Godbolt, have been subjected by Mr. Hoare, the British Consul, and by the agents of the company has not tended to throw much light on the cause or circumstances of the disaster. The vessel sank so rapidly that there was absolutely no time to realise what was happening on board. At the Admiralty office it is believed that the ship must have been broken up by the explosion of her boilers. This theory would account for her total disappearance.

The first news of the disaster was brought to Molène by two fishermen named Masson and Mathieu, owners of the smack Couronne de Marie, who rescued Wood and Godbolt. They were fishing at 6 o'clock in the morning off Point Stiff, to the north-east of Ushant, when they observed two men in the water clinging to wreckage and making signals of distress and shouting for help. The fishermen immediately went to their assistance, and succeeded in picking them up. They then conveyed them to the island, but as the fishermen did not know a word of English they were unable to understand anything they said beyond grasping the fact that the rescued men were survivors of a shipwreck. It was not until they had been conveyed across to Conquet, and the Commissary of the Maritime District had been communicated with, that the nature and extent of the catastrophe were ascertained.

Three hours after Wood and Godbolt were picked up a number of other boats, which were engaged in lobster fishing about 10 miles west of Molène, came across a number of floating boxes and other wreckage, among which one of the fishermen, named Le Bras, owner of the Augustine, perceived the body of a man, on which, when it had been recovered, was found a gold wedding ring and a silver watch. The watch had stopped at 11 o'clock. Round the body was a lifebelt.

A search among the rocks was then begun, and soon resulted in the discovery of the remains of several other victims, including a number of children. The latter were in their night-dresses. The seventh body recovered was that of a lady wearing a silk dress, in the pocket of which were six sovereigns…When the fishermen returned to Molène with the dead they found that the women, with the assistance of the curé, had launched the lifeboat, but they reported that no trace of any survivors beyond those already rescued could be found…

*The steamship *Drummond Castle* was just over 3,700 tons, 365ft long, 43ft 6ins wide, 31ft 3ins deep, and brig-rigged. She was built at Glasgow and launched in 1881 for D. Currie & Co. of London, whose Castle Mail Packets Co. (a forerunner of the Union-Castle Line) operated the vessel on a regular run taking passengers and freight between South Africa and the United Kingdom. On 28 May 1896 she left Cape Town for her voyage to London, via Las Palmas, in the Canary Islands, which she left at 3 p.m. on 12 June with a complement of 246 persons, comprising 143 passengers and 103 crew. The *Drummond Castle* was under the command of Capt. W.W. Pierce, who had joined the Castle Line as an apprentice in 1868 at the age of 14 and been with the company almost continually.

On the night of 16 June 1896 the vessel was off Ushant, the island off the northwest tip of Brittany, considered the southern point of the western entrance to the English Channel (the Isles of Scilly being the northern point of the gateway). The weather was foggy and visibility restricted. About 11 p.m. and steaming at around 12 knots, the *Drummond Castle* struck the Pierres Vertes rocks off Ile-Molène near Ile Oessant, the island of Ushant, and she sank apparently in less than five minutes. Of the 246 people on board, only three survived: a first class passenger, Mr. Charles Marquardt, and two members of the crew, the quartermaster named Wood and a seaman named Godbolt, all three rescued by local fishermen.

Of the 243 who perished in the *Drummond Castle* disaster, only about 70 bodies were eventually recovered. Many of them were buried on Ile-Molène and at Conquet on the mainland.

The judgement of the Official Inquiry into the loss of the *Drummond Castle* ascribed the cause of the disaster to the combination of two adverse factors: first, the easterly setting current off Ushant taking the vessel further east than Capt. Pierce believed his position to be, and thereby wrecking the ship on the rocks known as the Pierres Vertes off Ile-Molène; and second, Capt. Pierce's sparse use of the leadline to take soundings in order to determine his position. The Inquiry noted in particular that a cast of the lead at around 8 p.m. must have convinced Capt. Pierce that he was in a safe position according to his chart of the Ushant area, and that there was no need to take further soundings as he believed his vessel was heading on a safe course into the English Channel.

The Inquiry concluded that "she was not navigated with proper and seamanlike care, inasmuch as the use of the lead was neglected, and she was going at too great a rate of speed in thick weather in a very dangerous locality. The casualty was primarily owing to there not having been proper allowance made for the easterly current, the effect of which [ie, the shipwreck and loss of some 243 lives] would doubtless have been averted if the master made frequent use of the lead".

## Postscript

### 1 July 1896
### Bottle Picked Up

Haverfordwest [Pembrokeshire coast, southwest Wales], July 1, 11 55 a.m.- Picked up at Littlehaven, St. Bride's Bay, yesterday, bottle containing a slip of paper marked "Drummond Castle off Ushant, struck rocks, filling quickly, no boat, Morris, Fort Salisbury."

The *Drummond Castle*'s passenger list included a Mrs. Morris "from Natal". The "Fort Salisbury" in Mrs. Morris's message, presumably her home town, was founded by Cecil Rhodes as a fort in 1890. It subsequently became Salisbury, the capital town of Rhodesia in its various manifestations and, from 1982, became Harare, capital of the newly-established Zimbabwe.

Mrs. Morris's body was never recovered, or at least never identified. Her last communication, which must have been written in great haste, was committed to the fate of a bottle's drift and eventual discovery for posterity.

## The Loss of the *Salier*: Over 200 Dead

### 11 Dec 1896

### Maritime Intelligence

Salier (s).*- London, Dec. 10.- A telegram from Vigo [Spain] received by Messrs. Keller, Wallis says:- "Salier totally lost on Corunas Corrubedo shoals. So far as known, no lives have been saved."

Salier (s).- Bremen, Dec. 10.- The Salier had 210 passengers on board and a crew of 65 men. The passengers consisted of one German, 113 Russians, 35 Galicians and 61 Spaniards. According to the latest news, the steamer was totally lost off Cape Corrubedo, and it is feared that all on board were drowned.

### 12 Dec 1896

### Maritime Intelligence

Salier (s).- Corunna, Dec. 11.- It has now been ascertained that the number of passengers on board the lost liner Salier was 214, of whom only one was a German. The others consisted of 35 Galicians, 113 Russians, 10 Italians and 55 Spaniards. All these were steerage [passengers], there being no saloon passengers on board. The crew numbered 66 hands, so that the total death toll amounted to 280. The vessel was commanded by Captain Wempe. She had a pilot on board at the time of the disaster, but it is supposed [believed] that her steering gear got disabled in the hurricane, and that the steamer was driven onto the shoals off Cape Jorroveta late on Monday night [7th Dec.]. But little hope is entertained that any of those on board escaped. Up to the present no bodies have been washed ashore.

Salier (s).- Vigo, Dec. 11.- The complete wreck of the Norddeutscher Lloyd steamer Salier, and the supposed loss of all on board, renders it difficult to obtain any trustworthy particulars as to the circumstances of the loss of the vessel. She left Corunna at 4 o'clock in the afternoon of Monday last, the 7th inst., and the same night ran on the rocks off Cape Corrubedo, known as the Corona Reefs, a little to the north of Arosa Bay. Both ship and cargo are a total loss. Some bodies have already been washed ashore, including that of the captain, who has been identified. He was still wearing his watch, which was found to have stopped at 5 30, presumably on Tuesday morning. The precise loss of life is given at 281.

*The Norddeutscher Lloyd steamship *Salier* was built in 1875–76. She was 3,200 tons, 354ft 4ins long, 39ft 7ins wide and 24ft deep, and was mainly employed taking European emigrants from Bremen to New York. However, on 7 December 1896 on her final voyage, the *Salier* left the port of La Coruña (Corunna) in Galicia, northwest Spain, with a diverse complement of European emigrants bound for Buenos Aires. As usual off that coast in the winter months the weather was boisterous. She rounded that jaggedly serrated corner of Spain to head southwest across the Atlantic towards the River Plate at Buenos Aires before her steering apparently became disabled by the stormy seas.

Without steering, the *Salier* would have been at the mercy of the seas along a notoriously treacherous stretch of the Galician coast punctuated by its myriad reefs and rocky headlands. The shoals off Cabo Corrubedo, the headland at the western end of the Arousa Estuary, took the vessel down with all her 281 passengers and crew so that the particulars of the *Salier*'s final hours can only be surmised.

## LOSS OF THE *VILLE DE ST. NAZAIRE* OFF CAPE HATTERAS

## 18 March 1897

### Maritime Intelligence

Ville de St. Nazaire (s).- Paris, March 18.- The *New York Herald*'s Paris edition publishes a telegram from New York, of yesterday's date, stating that the French steamer Ville de St. Nazaire foundered off Cape Hatteras on the 8th instant. Of the 80 persons on board, passengers and crew, only 4 survive. Eight boats were launched, but four were dashed to pieces against the side of the ship. The other four got off successfully, but three of them soon afterwards capsized. In the remaining boat were 35 persons. These passed 7 days with nothing to eat or drink, and when on the 14th inst. the boat was sighted by a sailing ship 31 of the occupants had either died of starvation or had gone mad. The four survivors were brought into New York by the sailing ship. Confirmation of the news has been received at the office of the Compagnie Transatlantique, but the officials were unable to give any information as to the number of victims.

Ville de St. Nazaire (s).- New York, March 18.- The *New York Herald* publishes the following:- The French liner Ville de St. Nazaire, which left here on the 6th inst. for the West Indies, has foundered. She carried eight passengers and a crew of 74 men. The schooner Hilda arrived here yesterday with four out of 38 persons who left in one of four boats which were launched. They state that the other 34 went mad or died of starvation. They drifted for seven days without compass or sail. The Hilda sighted them on Sunday last. There are no tidings of the other boats. The Ville de St. Nazaire was commanded by Captain Jaqueneau.

*19 March 1897*

**Maritime Intelligence**

Ville de St. Nazaire (s).- New York, March 18.- The survivors of the steamer Ville de St. Nazaire are Inspector Berri, Dr. Maire, the ship's doctor, M. Stants, third engineer, and M. Tajardo, a passenger. One of the survivors says that a leak was discovered on March 7, when one day out from New York, but it was not thought to be sufficiently serious to warrant a return to port. On the second day, however, the leak increased and became dangerous. A violent hurricane broke the same night, and rendered the escape of the vessel impossible. Under these circumstances there was no resource but to abandon the vessel. The crew behaved admirably. The missing, who it is feared must have perished, include Captain Jaqueneau, nine passengers, and 68 officers and crew.

*22 March 1897*

**Maritime Intelligence**

Ville de St. Nazaire (s).- New York, March 21.- The steamer Kaiser Wilhelm II, which arrived last evening, reports having spoken the steamer Yanariva, off the Banks of Newfoundland, at midday on the 17th inst. Her signals were not clear, but were believed to mean that she had picked up 16 survivors of the wrecked steamer Ville de St. Nazaire. The Yanariva is from Newport News [Virginia], bound for Glasgow, where she is due on the 31st inst.

*23 March 1897*

**Maritime Intelligence**

Ville de St. Nazaire (s).- New York, March 22.- A steamer from New Orleans which has arrived here has found a lifeboat belonging to the Ville de St. Nazaire containing six dead bodies.

*29 March 1897*

**Maritime Intelligence**

Ville de St. Nazaire (s).- Lizard, March 27, 7 10 p.m.- Steamer Maroa, of Liverpool, Norfolk, Va. for Hamburg, passed 6 p.m. signaled:- Captain, engineer, second mate and one fireman French steamer Ville de St. Nazaire, Compagnie Transatlantique. This signal was preceded by DMS, which it is supposed should have been DMSL, meaning, picked up.

Ville de St. Nazaire (s).- Greenock, March 29, 9 54 a.m.- Steamer Yanariva, Weston master, which arrived at Tail of the Bank [the anchorage off Greenock at the mouth of the River Clyde] yesterday afternoon from Newport News, had on board 15 of crew and one second-class passenger of French steamer Ville de St. Nazaire, which foundered off Cape Hatteras. They were picked up from their boat on 12th inst., in lat. 31 22 N, long. 71 22 W. Other 13 men who had been in the boat succumbed before steamer effected rescue.

*8 April 1897*

**The Loss of the Ville de St. Nazaire**

**The Captain's Report – Paris, April 6**

Captain Jaqueneau, of the Transatlantic Company's steamer Ville de St. Nazaire, arrived in Paris on Saturday from Hamburg, where he had been landed by the British steamer Maroa, by which he had been picked up with three other survivors after six days exposure, without food or water, and has since presented to the company a long report on the loss of the steamer and the events that followed.

Captain Jaqueneau relates that he left New York on the afternoon of the 6<sup>th</sup> March for Port-au-Prince [Haiti], the vessel being perfectly seaworthy. He had on board 600 tons of merchandise, with six cabin passengers, one of whom was retired Captain Berry, of the French navy, inspector of the Transatlantic Company, and six steerage passengers – three men, a woman, and two young children, all of the same family.

"All went well," says the report, "on the first and second days. The holds were dry and the engines worked well, but on the afternoon of the 7<sup>th</sup> the weather looked ugly, with violent squalls and a heavy sea. The steamer rolled considerably, as she was lightly laden, but rose well on the waves with a speed of about eight knots. About 6 in the morning she gave a lurch more violent than the others, and shipped by port and starboard a great quantity of water, a part of which entered the stokehole. The chief engineer went below and found a considerable quantity of water, but not sufficient to reach the fires, as it only washed across the floor of the stoke-room as the steamer rolled. He set the pumps to work, and then came up to inform me that the rolling of the steamer impeded the working of the pumps.

I put her head to the sea, and she then laboured less, but the water continued to rise and reached the engine-room. The coal bunkers and cargo holds were still dry, and it became evident that there was a considerable leak under the machinery compartment, but it could not be reached in consequence of the water. I ordered the watertight bulkheads of the engine-room and passages to be closed, but in spite of the pumps and the work of a chain of men with buckets the water reached the furnaces, putting out the fires. How the leak had occurred it was impossible to say. Some of the crew said that they felt a shock when the steamer gave a heavy lurch, as if she had touched on some hard body. I supposed then that we had struck on a sunken wreck, which had made a rent of some length in the bottom of the steamer, under the boiler and engine-rooms. It is well known that floating wreckage is common in those waters.

At daylight on the morning of the 8<sup>th</sup> it was evident that nothing could be done to save the steamer as the compartments were filling, and that it was time to take measures to save the passengers and crew. Captain Berry and the crew were of the same opinion. At 6 in the morning I gave orders to have the boats provisioned, and prepare for the launching of them. This latter operation took a long time, from the state of the sea and the inexperience of the crew, composed principally of blacks, who are generally bad seamen. We at length succeeded in putting out four boats. Four others were crushed by the rolling of the steamer. Two of those launched were large lifeboats; the others were a smaller boat and the whaleboat.

I placed the passengers with the doctor, Captain Berry and 19 of the crew in one of the lifeboats. Captain Berry, to whom I had already pointed out the position of the steamer on a chart as about 75 miles north-east of Cape Hatteras, took the command, and stood off at a short distance to the leeward of the steamer. The second lifeboat took 25 men and went and joined the other with the chief officer. Lieut. de Andreis with nine other persons took the smaller boat. The whaleboat in which I was to embark with eight other persons, including the first lieutenant and the chief engineer, was the last to leave the steamer, which was then settling down with a list to starboard. I might have remained longer on board and only abandoned her at the last extremity, but the other boats were waiting for me to sail in company towards the land.

It was then one in the afternoon. I gave the signal to leave, land being then distant about 60 miles. We kept company all the afternoon, and only lost sight of each other during the night. The two lifeboats were provided with Coston lights and rockets. They made signals which we perceived until about midnight and then saw no more of them, for they sailed faster than our boat. At daybreak on the 9th we were alone. Our provisions had become wetted with sea water, and we scarcely touched them. We continued to steer westward all this day. At about 5 in the evening we thought we could see land ahead. The water had become smooth and had changed colour. We saw a sailing vessel, but at a great distance. We rowed hard to reach land, but a thick fog came on and we could see nothing more.

About 9 in the evening a strong wind from the west sprung up and the sea became rough, and the wind increased. In the morning of the 10th we had lost sight of land, as the wind and the current had driven us out to sea. From that moment some of my companions began to lose courage. The steward was becoming delirious. We were all wet through, and with the fatigue were losing energy. We strove on nevertheless, as I encouraged them from time to time by words and by my example. On the 11th we were all exhausted, and the chief engineer began to rave like the steward. Cold, wet, fatigue and privations were producing their effects. During the morning two of the blacks died, and some hours later we threw them overboard. Those men have no force of resistance or energy.

On the 12th we were still endeavouring to make for land when the weather permitted. The stewardess died in the afternoon, and we threw her overboard at night. The steward raved more and more and could not sit upright. He imagined he could step from the boat on to land, and while I was setting the sails he threw himself overboard before our eyes without our being able to save him. I had already once saved him when he clung on to the gunwale, but this time he had not strength to hold on. The chief engineer had become furious.

When daylight on March 13 appeared, the wind was carrying us westward, but it blew strong and the sea was rough. At 6 in the morning we were changing the set of the sails, but only three of us – myself, Lieutenant Hebért, and a seaman – were able to work. The carpenter was exhausted, and in attempting to help us fell overboard with a lurch of the boat, and as the boat was going fast through the water we were unable to save him.

We were sailing westward when, about 3 in the afternoon, we perceived a steamer coming down on us. We made signals, which were seen, and she stopped and took us on board. It was the Maroa, Captain Adams, of Liverpool. Twenty-four hours later we should have been all dead. Captain Adams, and, indeed, all his officers, treated us most tenderly, and I cannot too strongly recommend him to the French Government for a well-merited reward."

Lieutenant Nicolai, who had the command of the second lifeboat, picked up by the Yanariva, has also arrived at Havre with 15 other survivors, and given an account of their voyage and sufferings. "Until the evening of the first day," he said, "the three other boats remained in sight. We had provisions on board, but I was resolved to ration them out, as it was uncertain how long the voyage would last. When night came on the gale increased. We were sailing before the wind, but the sea drenched us on all sides. I had neither a compass nor a glass. I had only one man whom I could trust, Joseph Chaudiere, a seaman, who remained for three days at the helm, with only drawers and a woolen vest on, the cold being intense.

Neither he nor I thought of eating. From time to time I crept underneath the sails to warm myself, for I had scarcely any clothing on. But I could not sleep. My companions ate but little, and when we were rescued we had still twenty pounds of good biscuit remaining; but we had no water. From the third day some began to lose their reason. The spectacle was a horrible one, as we were suffering terribly from thirst. Some drank sea water; others held out their hands to gather the few drops of rain that fell.

Insanity was at least as fatal to us as the exposure. Some of my companions were subject to strange visions. Our quartermaster, Picard, who was the first to die, on the Thursday, became raving mad. He cried aloud that there were men concealed below, and attempted to smash the boat. He had become so dangerous that we were forced to bind him, but he suffered fearfully from a broken arm when on board the steamer. When he became calmer he was released, but he then drank sea water, became delirious, and jumped overboard. The next day there were seven madmen in the boat. This was the fourth day since we had left the Ville de St. Nazaire, and was the most painful of our voyage.

At about half-past 5 in the morning we perceived a cargo boat at about three miles from us. We all rose up, and thought salvation was at hand. We put a French flag at the end of an oar, and made signals of distress. The steamer came nearer, to within about a mile, stopped a moment, then went on its way and soon disappeared. It required all my energy to overcome the feeling of despair of my companions. 'Cheer up,' I said; 'if they did not come to our assistance it was because they thought we were in no danger, for we must be near land.' It was impossible to distinguish the flag of the steamer.

During the fourth and fifth days we lost 12 of our companions, six from delirium and six from exposure. My cabin boy Adolphe, a young Creole of 13, who had borne up manfully, died of cold. His body had become quite blue. It remained for some time under the gunwale, until it was projected into the sea by a lurch of the boat. The other bodies we threw overboard in the morning. Among the most tragic scenes I witnessed was that of the fireman, Duja. He had a vision that he was a spectator of a ballet in a theatre, and described his impressions with horrible fits of laughter to his companions, kissing his hand to the imaginary dancers. He ended by throwing himself into the sea.

On the afternoon of the sixth day we were sighted and picked up by the Yanariva. One of our number, a passenger named Saint Hilaire, became mad with joy, and jumped overboard."

According to Lieutenant Nicolai, his boat contained four children besides the 25 persons mentioned by Captain Jaqueneau. The total number saved alive is 24 – four by the yacht Hilda, taken to New York; 16 by the Yanariva, landed at Greenock; and four by the Maroa, at Hamburg. No tidings have been yet received of the third boat with ten on board.*

*Of the 79 passengers and crew on board the *Ville de St. Nazaire*, 54 died from delirium or exposure while in the boats while just 25 survived. Twenty six of the 30 died in the first boat containing nine passengers, Alphonse Maire, the ship's doctor, Capt. Jules Berri, Inspector of the Compagnie Transatlantique line and 19 crew, just four being rescued by the schooner *Hilda*. In the second boat, 13 of the 29 died, with 16 saved by the *Yanariva,* including Lieutenant Nicolai; five of the nine persons in the whaleboat died, commanded by the *Ville de St. Nazaire's* Capt. Jaqueneau, with four saved by the *Maroa*; and all ten in the third and smaller boat were never heard from again, presumed lost.

## 565 Die in *La Bourgogne* Disaster off Sable Island

## 6 July 1898

### Maritime Intelligence

La Bourgogne (s).- Halifax (by Cable received July 6).- Allan [Line] steamer Grecian coming up harbour with British ship Cromartyshire in tow. Cromartyshire in collision five Monday morning, 60 miles south Sable Island, with French steamer La Bourgogne, which sank. All lost except purser, three engineers, about 30 crew, and about 170 passengers.*

### *7 July 1898*

### Maritime Intelligence

La Bourgogne.- Halifax, July 6.- The Allan Line steamer Grecian entered the harbour here this morning with the ship Cromartyshire in tow. She brings the news that at 5 o'clock on the morning of the 4th inst., a dense fog prevailing at the time, the Cromartyshire, which was then 60 miles south of Sable Island, collided with the steamship La Bourgogne, belonging to the Compagnie Générale Transatlantique, bound from New York for Havre, with over 800 passengers and crew on board. The French liner sank almost immediately. Of those on board her only 170 passengers and 30 of the crew were saved. Only one woman was rescued. All the La Bourgogne's officers were drowned except the purser and three engineers.

### *9 July 1898*

### The Bourgogne Disaster

### Boston, July 8

Many of the survivors of the Bourgogne arrived here have been interviewed, and fully corroborate the tales of brutality on the part of the crew already published. Among the most remarkable escapes were those of three stokers named Lejulien, Alvany, and François. Although they were warned by other members of the crew not to talk, they have made the following statements:- They were, they say, in the stoke-hold when the engines were stopped by the collision…Five minutes after the crash the water began to come into the boiler-room, and was soon rushing in great volume…The fires were put out, and the engines stopped.

The chief engineer gave orders to close the water-tight doors, and this was done, but even after they had been closed the water came in almost as fast as before. When it was seen that all hope was gone, the chief engineer blew the whistle twice as a signal for all to escape who could. A rush followed, but about 15 men were drowned in the stoke-hold and the engine-room. The three who succeeded in getting out found that all the boats had left. They plunged into the sea, were picked up, and taken on board the Cromartyshire.

A passenger, Fred Nyfeler, asserts that he got into a boat packed with men and women, waiting for the sailors to cut it loose. The crew did not come, and the boat sank with the ship. Nyfeler was the only one of its occupants who was saved. While in the boat he saw the captain on the bridge alone. He was walking up and down and shouting excitedly. Nyfeler declares that he saw one boat leaving the ship containing only sailors, and he further asserts that he saw five women, who were clinging to the rope of a raft, thrust off to death with boat-hooks and with their hands by the French sailors on the raft.

DRAWN BY J. NASH, R.I.

MR. AND MRS. LACASSE.

FROM MATERIALS SUPPLIED BY MR. AND MRS. LACASSE.

THE FOUNDERING OF THE FRENCH LINER "LA BOURGOGNE": THE DESPERATE STRUGGLE FOR LIFE AS THE VESSEL SANK

M. Achard relates how he succeeded in getting his wife and two children into a boat when the ship's funnels fell directly across it, crushing it and knocking all its occupants overboard. The funnel struck M. Achard's wife across the chest, literally tearing the body asunder. M. Achard had with him twenty thousand dollars, which he succeeded in saving. Messrs. Zaiser, Achard, and Liebra all assert that when everyone was surrounding the boats the fourth engineer said, "D--- the passengers! Let them save themselves! We will save ourselves first!" He also said if he had a revolver he would shoot the passengers.

M. Gardot, another passenger, while admitting that individual members of the crew saved their lives at the expense of others after they had once got into the water, declares that down to the time the vessel actually sank, the captain, officers, and crew appeared to be doing their utmost to save all the lives possible. The captain remained on the bridge to the last, gave his orders quite coolly, and succeeded in getting a great deal of work out of the crew.

As soon as the boats were lowered there was a great scramble to get into them, and the frenzied passengers jumped into the water in the hope of reaching them. Most of the crew and passengers who were rescued and taken on board the Cromartyshire afterwards left her in boats, to help in picking up those who were still floating in the water, and were the means of saving a good many. A considerable number of those who were drowned were lost through upsetting of the boats after they had been launched, owing to the mad scramble that occurred. M. Lacasse, whose wife was the only woman saved, says there was really plenty of time to save everybody if the people had only remained cool. He himself saw nothing of the brutality attributed to the sailors, nor did he see any knives flourished.

## *10 Aug 1898*
## Maritime Intelligence
## Miscellaneous

London, Aug. 9.- Master of Londonian (s), arrived in the river, reports:- "July 30, foggy weather, lat. 42 54 N, long. 60 47 W [about 50 miles due south of Sable Island]. 9 30 a.m. fog cleared a little, saw several dead bodies floating, and a lot of wreckage. Stopped ship and put out a boat to investigate. First body brought alongside was that of a man of about 45, supposed [believed to be] an Italian steerage passenger or sailor; found nothing upon him to identify except a red handkerchief marked "V.O." We took off the lifebelt, which was marked "La Bourgogne," and buried the body. The second one brought alongside proved to be that of Richard Jacobs, a first-class passenger, by passenger tickets found on him for himself, wife and child by La Bourgogne; took off the lifebelt, also marked "La Bourgogne," and buried him. The fog set in again and we were obliged to proceed. In all we passed from 15 to 20 bodies, some of them in a very decomposed state." **

## *Bay of Plenty Times* (New Zealand newspaper)
## 24<sup>th</sup> August 1898
## The Bourgogne – Cromartyshire Collision

The following extracts are from the New York Tribune's account of the terrible disaster at the beginning of last month.- The story of the loss of the French mail steamer La Bourgogne, sunk in collision 60 miles south of Sable Island on Monday morning, is a tragedy of the sea with few parallels in history. Not since the ill-fated White Star liner Atlantic ran on the rocks off Prospect, at the entrance to this harbour, in 1873, and sank with 600 passengers (see **Great Disasters**, The *Atlantic*: "An Awful Disaster"), has such a tale of disaster at sea reached this city as was brought by the Allan liner Grecian this morning.

The powerful French liner crashed into the British ship Cromartyshire in a dense fog a few minutes after five o'clock on the morning of July 4th, and of 714 souls on board only 165 all told, escaped. The waves engulfed the big steamship scarcely more than half-an-hour after the collision occurred. Only one woman was saved, Mrs. A.D. Lacasse, of Plainfield, N.J. The Cromartyshire lay to and picked up the passengers and seamen who were rescued, transporting them to the Grecian, which came along a little later, and the Grecian towed the disabled ship into this port.

The Cromartyshire was running at five knots under reduced canvas when her bow struck the French liner in her race through the fog. She struck the La Bourgogne on the starboard bow, and ripped up the starboard side. Captain Deloncle, who was in the saloon, hurried to the bridge. For a moment or two the whole extent of the damage was not realised, and the La Bourgogne still dashed onward. The sailors thought the sailing ship had gone to the bottom, but a few minutes later the waves poured through the bulkheads of the steamer with the roar of a mighty torrent. Then all on board realised the awful nature of the collision, and there was a rush from the cabins and steerage for the deck above.

Christopher Brunon, of New York, said if the sailors had acted properly the majority of the passengers could have been saved. One of the engineers said he did not care whether passengers were saved or not. He was not there to save passengers he said, and was not paid for that kind of work. He was only sorry he had not a revolver to shoot some of them. He would not have anything to do with life saving.

Some of the scenes enacted on board the La Bourgogne just after the collision were terrible to witness. An Italian passenger drew a knife, and made direct at one who, like himself, was endeavouring to reach the boats. Immediately his action was imitated in every direction. Knives were flourished, and used with effect. Christopher Brunon saw a sailor belonging to the La Bourgogne strike a passenger over the head with an oar and kill him.

Strangely enough, Lacasse is the only man of the saloon and cabin passengers who survived, and his wife is the only woman of 200, not only of the first saloon cabin but of the whole ship, who escaped. Mrs. Lacasse was roused from her berth by her husband, who was on deck at the time of the collision. She ran to the upper deck, and one lurch of the steamer threw Lacasse and his wife clear of the deck, and into the water. They sank together but came up. Fortunately they were near a half submerged life raft, on to which the man clambered, dragging his wife after him.

Captain Henderson's wife was on the deck of the Cromartyshire where the La Bourgogne crashed into the ship. Mrs. Henderson had grown nervous in her stateroom, because the weather was bad and the fog so dense that objects on shipboard could scarcely be distinguished 20 ft ahead. She gathered her children about her, and stood near her husband.

Captain Henderson was on the poop [deck] with his third mate, A.C. Stewart. A sailor, Halley, was on the look-out, and the first officer, Killman, was on the forecastle deck. Halley was the first one to see the ocean liner. She was then half a ship's length from the port bow. The Cromartyshire crashed into the side of the La Bourgogne at a point near the engine room, and the La Bourgogne scraped the whole length of the Cromartyshire's port side, and then veered off. The third mate, Stewart, estimated the speed of the liner at between eighteen and nineteen knots an hour, but others put it at seventeen knots.

*The loss of 565 lives from the sinking of the *La Bourgogne* 60 miles south of Sable Island ranks third amongst the greatest maritime disasters off the east coast Maritime Provinces of Canada. On 6 December 1917 at the entrance to Halifax harbour, the cargo ship *Mont-Blanc* collided with the Norwegian ship *Imo*, causing an explosion resulting in the loss of around 2,000 lives in that city. The RMS *Empress of Ireland* sank with the loss of 1,012 lives after colliding with the SS *Storstad* in the St. Lawrence River on 29 May 1914.

**Many vessels from the North American east coast arriving in British and European ports in the summer of 1898 reported sighting floating dead bodies and wreckage from the *La Bourgogne* disaster as their course took them just south of Sable Island before heading out northeast into the North Atlantic. The *Londonian* herself was lost in a gale about 500 miles southwest of Ireland in November 1898; 45 men were saved but 18 drowned.

## *MOHEGAN* WRECKED ON THE MANACLES

### 15 Oct 1898

#### Maritime Intelligence

Mohegan (s)*.- Falmouth, Oct. 15, 7 26 a.m.- Atlantic Transport steamer Mohegan (late Cleopatra), with 59 passengers, 115 crew, foundered after striking Manacles. Great number reported drowned.

Mohegan (s).- London, Oct. 15.- Mohegan (s): The Press Association's Falmouth correspondent telegraphs as follows:- A telephonic message from Porthoustock states that 16 of the crew have been found alive on the rocks and that three dead bodies have been picked up. The funnel and foremasts of the steamer can be seen above the water. About 150 persons are drowned.

### *16 Oct 1898*

#### The Mohegan Disaster

#### Cause of Wreck a Mystery

The wreck of the steamship Mohegan, which was briefly reported in the *Shipping Gazette* [ie., *Lloyd's List*] of Saturday, has proved, as was feared, to be a terrible disaster. The Mohegan (formerly named the Cleopatra), a fine cargo and passenger steamship belonging to the Atlantic Transport Company, left the Thames on Thursday afternoon bound for New York. She carried 53 saloon passengers, and the total number of persons on board is officially stated to have been 156. As this was her return voyage she was light in cargo, and her hull was high out of the water.

On Friday evening the Lizard peninsula came in sight, and just as darkness came on the passengers assembled in the saloon for dinner. Between half-past 6 and 7 o'clock – witnesses vary in their statements as to the precise time – a grating sound was heard, and this was quickly followed by crashing noises, as if the bottom of the ship were being torn out by jagged rocks. From some unaccountable cause the Mohegan had been steered direct on to a ledge of rocks forming part of the Manacles reef.

# The Wreck of the "Mohegan"

On Friday last, October 14, just after dusk, a shipwreck of the first magnitude occurred off the iron-bound Cornish coast. The

THE MANACLE ROCKS
From a Photograph by R. S. C. Pearse

*Mohegan*, a new steamship of 8,500 tons, belonging to the Atlantic Transport Company, went down on the Manacle Rocks, near the Lizard, a group which for the last century has had the most sinister reputation among Cornishmen, and upon which the transport *John* foundered forty years ago with a loss of 200 lives. The loss of the *Mohegan* was only second to that. According to the latest accounts the ship had on board fifty-three passengers, only thirteen of whom have been saved, and a crew of 104, of whom thirty-six are now alive. The total loss of life was therefore 108. No one of the officers has lived to explain the cause of this terrible, this inexplicable, disaster. The ship was ten to fifteen miles north of the course she should have taken; and the one explanation that is put forward—though it fails to account for the course the ship took after passing Start Point, the extreme southerly promontory of Devon—is that the officer on duty, in sighting St. Anthony's Light, mistook it for the Lizard Lights. Under these circumstances, having as he thought cleared the Lizard, he would shape a more northerly course and would infallibly run on to the coast. Another explanation is that he suddenly realised the mistake, for St. Anthony's Light in hardly any way resembles the twin lights of the Lizard, and attempting to clear the Lizard promontory was too far in to do so, and suddenly found himself in the grip of the Manacles. Be this as it may, the one thing that is clear and certain is that the ship on a clear night, with not a very great deal of sea running, rushed on to the rocks at full speed, tore her bottom out, heeled over to starboard, and sank in less than twenty minutes.

What happened after that there is, unhappily, a great deal of tragic evidence to show. The passengers had just sat down to dinner when the shock of impact came. It does not appear to have been a terrifying one. Only one of the passengers, of those saved, a Mr. Hyslop, who was reading in his cabin, confesses to having realised at once what had happened. The others remained at the saloon tables until the steward stumbled down the main stairway with a warning cry to them to be up on deck for the ship had struck. There was a rush and many frightened cries, but even now none of the passengers seems to have recognised the deadliness of the disaster—how should they do when a moment before they had been dining, and a few minutes before had been able to see land and the twinkling lights of the shore?

One lady relates that her companion went down into the cabin to fetch an overcoat, and even after that returned to try and find a jewel case. For some minutes there was a natural and inevitable confusion, and the ship was fast listing over. The deck slanted so far that the crew, struggling with the port lifeboats—all of which, in the absence of any suspicion of danger, were swung inboard—gave up the attempt, and the voice of the captain—Captain Griffiths, commodore of the fleet—and of the chief officer, Mr. Llewellyn Couch, were heard shouting that everyone was to go over to the starboard side. Here again there was difficulty with the boats. According to one passenger, Mr. Pemberton, the stern of the ship was cocking up, and this may account for the fact that only two of the four boats on the starboard side were launched at all. Of these one was launched properly, and twenty-eight people were saved in her. Among them was Mr. Pemberton, his wife, his two children, and their maid. The whole of the family were thus saved. A singular instance of the vagary of chance is that of another family named King, every member of which was lost.

While another terrified crowd was surging and trembling about the second boat on the starboard side, a loud explosion was added to the terrors of the wreck. It was the water getting to the boilers. Instantly every light went out, even to the electric head light on the ship's foremast, and the ship began to settle and sink in the darkness. The ropes of the davits somehow were slackened in the case of the second boat, and she touched the water with thirty people who had scrambled in to her. But the ropes at her bow and stern still held her to the ship, and she soon half filled with water. A woman's voice shrieked out to "cut the rope!" and the rope by the bow was actually cut and the knife passed hand to hand to the stern to cut the rope there also. But the man who tried to do it exclaimed that he could not, and the knife slipped from his hold into the bottom of the boat. Then a wave of the heavy swell that the south-east wind was rolling up the Channel broke on the boat

MAP SHOWING THE SCENE OF THE WRECK

and she capsized. A few people clung on to her. Two women were underneath, their bodies in the water, their heads supported by the seats. A miracle saved both of them, Miss Rodenbusch, an opera singer, and Mrs. Compton Swift, an American lady, who says that during all the terrible hours that elapsed before she was picked up consciousness never left her. How the capsized boat broke away from the sinking ship there is no one who has lived to explain.

On the ship the scenes were no less tragic. There is a heart-rending story told of a little girl who pleaded for help "because she didn't want to die yet." But the crew and the officers seem to have faced danger and death with resolution and without panic. According to Boatswain Cruickshank, the crew and the officers gathered up by the stern, and when nothing more was to be done Chief Officer Couch stripped to his underclothing, and told the men to dive and do the best they could for themselves. They stopped till the ship began to settle and then dived. Chief Officer Couch was the last to leave the ship; what became of the other officers nobody says. The suction of the sinking ship dragged many of these last stragglers back, and most of them returned to the rigging. Mr. Couch, although a fine swimmer, was never seen again. Another man succeeded in swimming to Coverack Cove, two and a half miles away. But one poor fellow who made a desperate bid for life was found out of reach of the waves on the rocky shore with his limbs beaten and battered and life extinguished. Yet another man who could not swim at all, was nevertheless picked out of the rigging alive.

Meanwhile the news of the wreck had reached the villages about the Manacles, and first the Porthoustock lifeboat (James Hill, coxswain), and then the boat from Coverack, and, long afterwards, a tug from Falmouth, put out. The Porthoustock lifeboat was the

THE MANACLE ROCKS, WITH THE BUOY SHOWING THE EXTENT OF THE REEF
From a Photograph by E. R. Housdon

first, and
signalled
scattered
before he
already b
Porthous
people c
seemed,
turned i
Then t
Noble, w
she said,
up from
"surely
came up
two peop
by other
to Port
straight t
a seama
Five m
broke. I
and elev
clung for
was the s
who wer
men wer
were fou
the dead.
but the t
for weeks

89 Italia
lish; and
and 4 to
the portra
Room of t

The C
triumphal
Africa, an
is to be
cable and
to Cape T
bearing t
bows, the
and Ame
Britannia
sailors of
Stripes.

The A
of his wi
other day
I desire t
solation."
preserved
deathbed
the flowe
The othe
and divid

At this point of the coastline the rocks are particularly bold, and the ridge, which juts out for a mile and a half into the sea, can be seen for miles when exposed by receding tides. At the southern extremity of the ridge there is a bell buoy, and the safe passage for vessels lies a good deal to the south of this. But neither this safeguard nor the brilliant lights of St. Anthony at the entrance to Falmouth Harbour and the Lizard availed to keep the Mohegan away from the locality. It was a clear night, although the darkness was intense. There is nothing to explain why the vessel was so far out of her proper course, nor is there likely to be any adequate explanation, as the officers, who alone could furnish one, have perished. It is stated that she ought to have been 10 or 15 miles from the land…

Twenty minutes at the most elapsed between the striking of the vessel on the rocks and her foundering. During that time scenes of pathos occurred on board the sinking ship, although there was an absence of anything like panic. Mothers' agonised entreaties for the safety of children, the heartbreaking separation of members of families, and the severance of comrades were incidents which have burnt themselves into the memory of all who witnessed and have lived to narrate them. For a few minutes after the foundering the sea around the sunken ship was alive with struggling and shrieking people, but gradually the cries died away, and when the last survivors were taken from their perilous positions on the rigging of the submerged vessel the only sounds audible were the roar of the breakers and the rush of the wind.

At about 7 o'clock rockets from the Porthoustock lifeboat station gave the alarm to the district. Some of the crew of the lifeboat live at a distance, but by half-past 7 o'clock the boat was launched. A ship's lifeboat, bottom up with men clinging to it and people inside it gradually suffocating, was the first object to demand their attention. After dragging all but one of those clinging to the boat's bottom into the lifeboat and having to allow one poor fellow to remain, the lifeboat-men turned the boat over and found that the greater portion of those who had sought safety in it were dead. Of the two or three who were still alive, one lady, Mrs. Grandin, was so crushed that she had to be cut out from the boat. Although every care was taken of her she died before the lifeboat got back to Porthoustock.

Two men hanging on to wreckage were next rescued, and then the lifeboat encountered the other ship's boat with 23 persons. The ship's boat was waterlogged, and her passengers in a perilous condition, and they were taken into the lifeboat. Miss Noble, a lady passenger, was found clinging to a plank and was picked up. The lifeboat returned with 26 survivors, and having landed them put out again…Sixteen persons, including one woman, Mrs. Piggott, the assistant stewardess, were found clinging to the rigging [of the *Mohegan*]. Two or three hours were spent in the perilous task of taking these off one by one.

Both the rescued and rescuers alike received attention on reaching the shore. One or two other lifeboats had been called out, but they naturally did not arrive until late. One man named Maule was picked up by a Falmouth lifeboat tug after having been over seven hours in the water…

\*The Official Court of Inquiry into the loss of the *Mohegan* on the Manacles rocks near Falmouth concluded that "the cause of the stranding of the vessel was that a wrong course, W. by N., was steered after passing the Eddystone [Lighthouse] at 4.17 p.m.". The Court found that "every possible effort" was made by the crew, the Coastguard and lifeboat services to save

# THE GRAPHIC

### AN ILLUSTRATED WEEKLY NEWSPAPER

No. 1,508—Vol. LVIII.] 
Registered as a Newspaper]

SATURDAY, OCTOBER 22, 1898

WITH EXTRA DOUBLE-PAGE SUPPLEMENT
"The Wreck of the 'Mohegan'"

[PRICE SIXPENCE
By Post, 6½d.

DRAWN BY W. HATHERELL, R.I.

FROM A SKETCH BY OUR SPECIAL ARTIST, T. S. C. CRAWFORD

A SAD TASK: IDENTIFYING THE DEAD IN THE CHURCH OF ST. KEVERNE

THE WRECK OF THE LINER "MOHEGAN" OFF THE COAST OF CORNWALL

lives. It concluded that the loss of 106 lives, including Capt. Griffiths and all his officers, with only 53 persons saved, was a consequence of the suddenness of the vessel's sinking within 15 minutes which quickly extinguished all her electric lights. Her emergency signalling rockets and oil lamps were largely ineffective or unavailable because of where they were stored on the sinking ship. On such a dark night – it was a new moon that night – the absence of any lights that might have shown the position of the vessel made it difficult for lifeboats from shore to find the wreck and any survivors.

The Court could offer no explanation about why the *Mohegan* was so far off course in the first place: any officers of the vessel who might have provided such information were all drowned.

Many of the victims recovered from the *Mohegan* were buried at the nearby village of Keverne in the parish church of St. Keverne. A stained glass window was made in their memory and placed in the east end of the church. It was unveiled on 19 April 1899, the inscription reading:- *To the glory of God, and in memory of the 106 persons who perished in the wreck of the steamship Mohegan on the Manacles Rocks, October 4, 1898. This window was dedicated by the Atlantic Transport Company, owners of the vessel.*

## LOSS OF THE *STELLA* IN THE CHANNEL ISLANDS: 112 LIVES LOST

## 1 April 1899

### Maritime Intelligence

Stella (s).- London, March 31.- A Press Association telegram states that the London and South-Western Railway Company's passenger boat Stella, running in the Southampton and Channel Islands service, met with a disaster during a fog on Thursday [30th March] afternoon. She ran on the Casquets off Alderney, and foundered in ten minutes, the boilers exploding with a tremendous report. There was no panic and it is believed all the ladies were saved. Two boats containing 40 persons were picked up by the Great Western steamer Lynx, and two containing 37 by the South-Western steamer Vera. Estimates of the loss of life vary between 60 and 100. The major portion of the passengers were from London.*

### *3 April 1899*
### The Stella Disaster

According to an official list issued by the London and South-Western Railway Company last night, 53 of the passengers who were on board the Stella when that vessel foundered on Thursday are still reported missing. Their names have been chiefly obtained through the inquiries of their friends. This number is, of course, exclusive of the members of the crew who were lost in the disaster. Owing to obvious reasons, the South-Western Company find it impossible so far to compile an absolutely complete return of the number and names of the victims. Many of the survivors arrived at Waterloo [Station, London] on Saturday. The thrilling stories they recite bear out the simple and noble tale of heroism which lightened the first news of the disaster.

Several bodies are rumoured to be floating near the scene of the wreck, but up to yester-day afternoon only two had been recovered and identified. They were a boy named Claud Arnold, of the London Polytechnic School, who was on board with his mother, sister, and elder brother, and a commercial traveller named George Westwick, who lived at Catford... Arnold's elder brother owes his life to a remarkable circumstance. A football he held in his hands when the vessel struck the rocks helped him to float in the water. He was drawn into the vortex of the sunken vessel, but the ball brought him to the surface again. He was rescued by one of the vessel's boats, and now lies at Cherbourg in a somewhat critical condition.

Terrible experiences were endured by the passengers who escaped in the boats. Several succumbed to their hardships, and their bodies in some instances were thrown overboard. Many, according to the narrative of one young lady, prayed to die, and then cheered and consoled each other...

### *9 April 1899*
### The Stella Disaster

...Colonel G.W. Dixon, of Sutton, Surrey, was with his wife and son, among the passengers saved from the Stella. Yesterday he made the following statement:- "We left Southampton punctually, and had a very pleasant trip for about two-thirds of the way across. Then we ran into a bank of fog, and the speed was reduced considerably. We continued steaming slowly for some little time, when there was a temporary lift in the fog, and we again went full-speed and, though the fog held, continued to do so. It was remarked by several people that it was unusual to go at such a speed through the fog, and while I was talking to a friend – Mr. Townsend, of Wimbledon, one of the missing – about it, a friend of his, a native of Guernsey, said he had crossed the Channel a good many times, but had never known a steamer to run like that in a fog.

I left them, and was walking about when just at the foot of the bridge I met the captain, who was standing there smoking. I said, 'It is an unfortunate thing this fog,' and he replied, 'Yes, it has spoiled a good run.' We had one or two other words together, and I walked to the front and was standing there leaning over the promenade deck, when I saw rising out of the fog a big rock. I should think it was about 250 yards distant. We were then going right on to it. By an extraordinary manoeuvre we missed the first rock. The helm was then worked, and we went between the big rock and the little one. I hoped we had cleared, but before we could get right through there was a fearful crashing and rending of the bottom of the steamer, and I felt there was nothing to do but to save our lives.

I tore down the canvas covering of the lifebelts and obtained three, which I fastened on my wife, my son, and myself, and then found that the starboard lifeboat was being lowered. I knew that there was no chance of jumping off there either for my wife or myself, and we therefore went to the lower deck. I there found an iron door in the side of the ship and undid one bolt, and a sailor who came along at that moment unbolted the other. As soon as the tackle was undone and the boat clear, I dropped my wife into it. By this time several other ladies had come up and two men. We put the ladies in, and called to some others whom we also put in, as well as some children. As there was no one else left at this part of the deck, we felt it our duty to get in ourselves.

There were then 32 or 33 people in the boat, and I implored the sailors to push off, as the Stella was settling fast, and the decks were awash. Fortunately we had four sailors and Reynolds, the second mate [the only officer of the *Stella* to survive], with us. When we were about 60 or 70 yards from the vessel her bow went up in the air, and she went down with a

THE WRECK OF THE "STELLA" ON THE CASQUET ROCKS ON MARCH 30: THE LAST MOMENT.

DRAWN BY H. C. SEPPINGS WRIGHT, FROM INFORMATION SUPPLIED BY A SURVIVOR.

*Twelve minutes after striking, the vessel sank. When as many passengers as possible had been got off, Captain Reeks cried, "Men, see to yourselves," and throwing up his arms, went down with his ship.*

tremendous roar, due to the crashing of the timbers and the bursting of the deck. Certainly there was no explosion, as some people say.

As the vessel went down I saw the captain and two or three others on the bridge. There were a lot of people about the decks, and as she plunged into the water several of them sprang off. Two men swam out and implored us to take them in. Some of the people in the boat shouted that we could not hold any more, but I caught hold of one, and with assistance dragged him into the boat. He turned out to be Mr. Willis, with whom I had been talking a good part of the morning. A little afterwards another man asked to be taken in, but the sailor said, "We cannot allow anybody else in now. We have got to get over the rocks, and we cannot have her too much loaded." However, we got hold of him, and dragged him in…

We rowed about until 7 o'clock, and saw several people floating in lifebelts, but evidently dead. Reynolds then said that the safest thing to do would be to anchor, and the anchor was got out and dropped. The other boat which accompanied us had no anchor, and was made fast by a rope to our boat. The tide was running very strongly – about eight knots – and suddenly we found that the strain of the two boats was too much for the small anchor, and that we were drifting. Within a minute or two we touched the rocks, and in getting clear we lost our rudder. Reynolds told us that we must pull for our lives and get away, or we should have the boat smashed. We pulled out and eventually got into Alderney Race, which carried us along past Alderney and Cape La Hague, and we were somewhere off Cherbourg before – at about midnight – the tide turned.

Then we began drifting back. Our great fear was that we should drift back on the rocks. At 2 o'clock in the morning we saw two red lights, which Reynolds said were the Alderney lights, and the passengers were naturally very anxious that we should make for these lights. Reynolds, however, said he could not take the responsibility because the fog would probably come on again, and we should then find ourselves among the rocks. The result was that we all took turns at pulling, and by-and-by we saw the lights of the horrid rocks again, and we had the hardest job in the world to keep away from them. Providentially we managed to pull hard enough to keep us just outside the danger zone.

During the whole night my duty was to stand up in the boat and listen for the roar of the breakers and look for lights. When I heard anything the boat was stopped, and Reynolds listened carefully, so that he might know in which direction to pull in order to get away from the danger. I also had to keep my eyes on the other boat to see that we did not lose it, and with the object of assisting them I used a box of matches which I happened to have in my pocket, striking one every now and then to windward. The whole of the passengers in the boat behaved splendidly. The ladies were most courageous. I see it is stated that the ladies prayed for death, but I never heard anything of the sort, neither did anyone else in the boat to whom I have spoken. On the contrary, most of them were most cheerful, talking about ordinary subjects to pass the time away…

Fortunately about 7 o'clock we saw a steamer making in our direction. We hoisted signals of distress by tying handkerchiefs on boat-hooks, and pulled out in the direction we thought we should intercept her. She saw us when about two or three miles away, and turned out to be the Vera…"

*The cross-Channel passenger steamship *Stella* left Southampton for Guernsey and Jersey at 11.25 a.m. on Thursday 30 March 1899, the day before Good Friday that year, with 174 passengers and 43 crew, a total of 217 persons on board. Just before 4 p.m., in fog and travelling at full speed, the *Stella* ran on to Black Rock, one of the Casquets rocks off the island of Alderney, the northernmost of the Channel Islands off the Cherbourg peninsula. The vessel sank quickly and 112 persons, including Capt. Reeks, were drowned.

The subsequent Court of Inquiry concluded that, considering the poor visibility, "The vessel was not navigated with proper and seamanlike care. The cause of the stranding and consequent loss of the vessel [and 112 lives] was that she had not made good the course set, and that the master continued at full speed in thick weather, when he must have known his vessel was in the immediate neighbourhood of the Casquets, without taking any steps to verify his position [i.e. by regular soundings with the lead line]". There was some suggestion by the Court that the *Stella*'s master might have kept up speed to shorten the passage, "for the purpose of competing with the boat from Weymouth", scheduled to arrive at Guernsey around the same time as the *Stella*. Upon that point it advised that "it cannot be too strongly impressed on masters of vessels that the first and infinitely most important consideration should always be safety".

## Wreck of German Training Ship *Gneisenau* at Malaga

## 17 Dec 1900

### Maritime Intelligence

Gneisenau (German training ship)*.- Madrid, Dec. 16.- The German training frigate Gneisenau was wrecked to-day in the harbour at Malaga and sank. According to private despatches 40 lives are reported to have been lost.

### *18 Dec 1900*

### The Loss of the Gneisenau

### Berlin, Dec. 17

A disaster which recalls the foundering of the Eurydice with all hands in sight of Portsmouth Harbour [March 1878] has befallen the German Navy. As reported in our "Maritime Casualty" columns yesterday, the training ship Gneisenau, which had a complement of 460 men, including 49 naval cadets and 230 youths in training for the fleet, was wrecked on Sunday at the mouth of the harbour of Malaga. The sorrow which this calamity has spread throughout the German Empire cannot be measured by the length of the list of the missing. The cadets, very many of whom, it is feared, perished in the waves or were dashed against the rocks, represent the flower of the youth of Germany devoted to the naval career...

The Gneisenau, an armoured corvette, was built at the Imperial shipbuilding yard at Dantzic, and was launched on Dec. 4, 1879. She had a length of about 240 feet, a beam of about 48 feet, and a displacement of 2,856 tons. She was a single screw steamer, with an indicated horse-power of 2,500, and a maximum speed of 13 knots. The Gneisenau formed part of the fleet which appeared before Zanzibar in 1886, under the command of Rear Admiral Knorr, in order, as the *Berliner Neuste Nachrichten* puts it, to "break down the influence which the English exercised over the Sultan [of Zanzibar] to the disadvantage of Germany."

For the last ten years she has been employed as one of the five German training-ships for naval cadets. She started on her last cruise on Sept. 18. After spending some time off the Portuguese and Spanish coasts she conveyed the German Minister to Tangier, and returned to Malaga on the 13th inst. Her crew consisted of 14 officers, 49 cadets, 200 men, and 230 boys, under the command of Captain Kretschmann, who perished in the disaster.

**Madrid, Dec. 16**

The Gneisenau had been at Malaga since Nov. 1, engaged in big-gun practice. At 10 o'clock this morning, while the boys were being inspected, the wind began to blow with great force. The commander gave orders to get steam up as quickly as possible, but, owing to the violence of the sea, the vessel parted from her anchors and was wrecked at the entrance to the harbour. The crew jumped into the sea and endeavoured to save themselves by clinging to spars and wreckage, but before long most of them had disappeared beneath the waves. Captain Kretschmann went down with the ship, which is submerged half-way up the masts.

Heroic efforts were made by a small boat to rescue the drowning sailors, but, when 15 had been taken in, their weight caused the light craft to sink, and 12 perished. The three survivors were saved by ropes which were thrown to them. The harbour staff worked with great energy, and it was due to their efforts that many of the German sailors were saved.

**Madrid, Dec. 17, Evening**

Further details regarding the wreck of the Gneisenau show that the commander of the vessel perished at his post, refusing to be saved. A Spanish sailor named Fons, who got quite close to the frigate, threw a rope to Captain Kretschmann and the latter threw his sword to the Spaniard. The first officer struggled with the waves for an hour, clinging to a piece of wood, but succumbed at last to fatigue.

*The *Gneisenau* was a three-masted topsail sailing schooner with auxiliary engines, employed by the German Navy as a training frigate for young cadets. She sank just off the entrance to Malaga harbour as gale force winds blew her onto the east breakwater of the outer harbour. Although not a 'great disaster' in terms of numbers of dead, the loss of Captain Kretschmann and 41 others was a cause of national mourning in Germany. A memorial to the memory of those who died was later erected at the Old Protestant Cemetery in Malaga.

### CITY OF RIO DE JANEIRO SUNK OFF SAN FRANCISCO

## 23 Feb 1901

**Maritime Intelligence**

City of Rio de Janeiro (s)*.- San Francisco, Feb. 22.- The steamer City of Rio de Janeiro, from Hong Kong and Yokohama, with a number of passengers a valuable cargo, sank outside the Golden Gate this morning. A dense fog prevailed all night and this morning in the bay and outside the heads. The vessel struck on a ledge when entering the Golden Gate and went down in 20 minutes. A portion of the crew and passengers have been already landed from two boats, and a third boat is crossing the bay. The passenger list of the City of Rio de

Janeiro shows that she had 29 cabin passengers and 7 whites, and 58 Japanese and Chinese steerage passengers. The crew numbered 140.

City of Rio de Janeiro (s).- San Francisco, Feb. 22 (Later).- It now appears that the wreck of the City of Rio de Janeiro was attended by serious loss of life. It is impossible at present to give the exact number of the drowned, but none of the reports place the number of victims below, while some estimates are as high as 150. The steerage passengers carried by the steamer are now said to number upwards of 140. So far as known only three ship's boats previously reported got safely away and reached port, but as soon as the first news of the disaster reached here tugs and other craft at once put out to the scene of the wreck. It is stated by survivors that Captain Ward locked himself in his state room and went down with the ship. The pilot Jordan was severely injured.

City of Rio de Janeiro (s).- San Francisco, Feb. 23.- According to the latest details the number of lives lost in the wreck of the liner City of Rio de Janeiro is 122. They were mostly Asiatics. Those who perished included 24 saloon passengers, 19 officers, 36 Chinese belonging to the crew, and 43 Asiatics who were steerage passengers. Seventy-nine persons were saved, including 12 cabin passengers, 11 officers, 15 Asiatic steerage passengers, and 41 Chinese members of the crew.

One of the ship's boats was smashed, owing to the falling of the mizenmast, and many of its occupants were drowned. The captain stood on the deck until surrounded by water, when he went on to the bridge and remained there giving orders till he went down with the ship. One of the rescued passengers reports that he saw Mr. Wildman, the American Consul-General at Hong Kong, and his wife and children drowned.

The cargo of the City of Rio de Janeiro was estimated to be worth $500,000 [worth about $13m in 2010, inflated by the US dollar Consumer Price Index], and it is said that she carried $600,000 [worth about $16m in 2010] in specie [gold] in a chest.

## 25 Feb 1901

### Maritime Intelligence

35 white passengers, 37 Asiatic passengers, 18 white officers and crew, and 14 Asiatic hands were lost in the wreck of the City of Rio de Janeiro. Only three out of 18 women aboard were saved. Not more than 11 bodies have so far been recovered.

## *The Age* (Australian newspaper)

### 25 February 1901

### The Captain's Blunder - He Sinks With His Ship

It appears that the [City of] Rio de Janeiro had a San Francisco pilot, Captain Jordan, on board, and that he warned the captain of the steamer that it would be unsafe to proceed in such a fog. His advice, however, was disregarded by Captain Ward, and immediately after the steamer struck the rock with great force. The pilot, instantly realising the gravity of the situation, shouted, "All hands take to the boats!" A scene of fearful confusion ensued. The Chinese, who comprised the greater portion of the passengers and crew, howled frantically in their terror, whilst the female passengers screamed piteously in an agony of fear. Everybody but the captain and the officers of the steamer scrambled hurriedly to the boats, and some, losing all presence of mind, madly jumped overboard.

In the disorder, Captain Ward showed calmness and courage, and did all that was possible to lessen the consequences of his blunder in disregarding Pilot Jordan's warning.

*On 2 February 1901 the 3,500-ton steam-powered, barquentine-rigged *City of Rio de Janeiro* left Yokohama in Japan for San Francisco via Kobe and Honolulu. Under the command of Capt. William Ward, she carried just over 200 persons: 94 passengers and 107 crew. The ship arrived off the entrance to San Francisco Bay, the Golden Gate, in dense fog in the early hours of 21 February. A San Francisco pilot named Jordan boarded the vessel and advised Capt. Ward not to attempt entering the bay in such restricted visibility. Capt. Ward, for whatever reason, countered that advice by proceeding at slow speed to enter the Golden Gate.

At around 5 a.m., slightly off course to the south and near Fort Point, the *City of Rio de Janeiro* struck rocks and sank within ten minutes. Confused by an already chaotic situation, the mostly Chinese crew did not understand the emergency orders given in English and just three lifeboats were launched. Capt. Ward went down with his ship, along with 121 of his passengers and crew. Just 79 souls, 27 passengers and 52 crew, were saved. Bodies floated ashore for some years after the disaster. In 1903 the remains of Capt. Ward washed ashore, identifiable from a watch chain around his rib cage.

A *New York Times* report dated 22 February 1901 ("The Golden Gate Wreck – Loss of Life in City of Rio de Janeiro Disaster Was 128 - Captain Held Responsible") noted: "R. P. Schwerin, Vice President and General Manager of the Pacific Mail Steamship Company, in discussing the loss of the Rio de Janeiro, said he thought the blame was due to Capt. Ward in bringing his vessel in during a fog. 'Time and again', said Mr. Schwerin, 'we have warned our captains never to leave or enter port during a fog. It is erroneous to think that when a pilot boards a vessel that the Captain has no more responsibility. A pilot is simply a guide for a Captain. The statements made to me by Pilot Jordan indicate that there was a fog hanging around the Heads, and I think that undue haste was shown by the Captain in bringing his vessel in'. "

A later inquiry blamed the disaster on the lack of communication between officers and the Chinese crew of the *City of Rio de Janeiro*, and on Capt. Ward's insistence on proceeding in dense fog.

## A "Working-Class" Disaster off Brittany

### 4 Feb 1902

#### Maritime Intelligence

Jules Jean Baptiste.- London, Feb. 4.- From Calais it is reported that the vessel Jules Jean Baptiste, of St. Brieuc [Brittany], which was bound there with 50 passengers, mostly dock labourers, is several days overdue, and grave fears are entertained that the ship has been lost with all hands.

### 26 Feb 1902

#### Maritime Intelligence

Jules Jean Baptiste.- London, Feb. 26, Advices from Calais report a maritime disaster, involving a loss of nearly 80 lives, including 60 passengers and the crew of the sailing ship

Jules Jean Baptiste, which was due at St. Malo over a month ago. The maritime authorities have now posted the vessel as lost. The passengers were chiefly working-class people.

## *Camorta* Sunk in Bay of Bengal Cyclone: 739 Dead

## 15 May 1902

### Maritime Intelligence

Camorta (s).* - Rangoon, May 14.- The British India Company's steamer Camorta, which was due to arrive here last Tuesday from the Madras coast, has not yet been sighted. It is believed that she was caught in a cyclone which raged fiercely on the 6th inst. in the Bay of Bengal. She carried a crew of 89 all told and had 650 native passengers on board. One of her lifebuoys and a boat boom have been picked up near the Krishna Lightship [off southeast coast India] by another of the British India Company's vessels, which was looking for her. It is feared that the Camorta has foundered.

### *4 June 1902*

### Maritime Intelligence

Camorta (s).- Rangoon, June 4.- The British India Steam Navigation Company's steamer Camorta, which has been missing since early last month, was discovered yesterday 15 fathoms deep with her masts standing six feet above water, and her head [ie., facing] south by west in the track of shipping on Baragua Flats, in the Irawaddy Delta [southern Burma/Myanmar]. A flag has been hoisted indicating the position of the wreck.

*The SS *Camorta*, a 2,119-ton cargo and passenger ship of the British India Steam Navigation Company, took all 739 persons on board to their death when she was sunk by a Bay of Bengal cyclone en route from Madras (Chennai) on the southeast coast of India to Rangoon in May 1902. It was the fourth greatest civilian loss of life from any British-registered merchant ship, exceeded only by RMS *Titanic* in 1912, RMS *Empress of Ireland* in 1914 and RMS *Lusitania* in 1915.

# 14  Odds & Sods & Mollycods (including The Mystery of the Mary Celeste, Not So Friendly Natives, "Celestial Visitors"…and Pirates)

## NARRATIVES

## 2 Oct 1871

**Casualties, Etc.**

The *Elcano*, from New York, arrived at Bristol, reports as follows:- "On Sept. 24, in lat. 49 58 N, lon. 10 56 W, caught a bird, with cloth attached to it, dated 'ship Oriflamme, Sept. 24, lat. 9 40 N, lon. 12 W.'"*

*On the face of it this report makes no sense. First, the dates on which the bird was released and caught – "Sept. 24" – are the same and whilst they *might* have been exactly a year or even several years apart, it seems rather unlikely! Secondly, the location of the bird's release – lat. 9° 40' N, long. 12° W – was in northern Sierra Leone near the border with Guinea in West Africa! On the other hand, there *was* both a sailing ship and a steamship named *Oriflamme* at this time, and one or the other *might* have been up a river in West Africa – the location of lat. 9° 40' N, long. 12° W could be on the Mongo River in northern Sierra Leone where a crew member *might* have attached a piece of cloth to a bird…

The *Elcano's* position, however, at the time it ostensibly captured the bird – at the western approach to the English Channel – was over 3,000 miles from the position of the *Oriflamme* when it tagged the bird – on, apparently, exactly the same date as the *Elcano* captured it!

**N.B.** The English full-rigged ship *Oriflamme* caught fire, was abandoned by her crew and sank at lat. 18° S long. 92° W in the Pacific Ocean off the northern coast of Chile, on a voyage from London to San Francisco on 5 June 1881.

## 17 Oct 1871

**Casualties, Etc.**

The *Elizabeth Brown*, Perriam, arrived at Rio Janeiro, reports that on the 3rd Sept., Cape Frio [just north of Rio de Janeiro] bearing about SW, 30 miles, she caught a Cape pigeon, which had a piece of cloth secured to its neck, on which was written, as far as could be deciphered:- "August 25, 1871.- Barque Bellarat, from London for Auckland, 50 days out, lat. 29, lon. 30 S*. Bill Babot, of Poplar [London]."

*This should be lat. 29 S, long. 30 W, a spot in the mid-South Atlantic about 850 miles southeast of Rio. If so, the bird flew approximately that distance between 25 August when it was caught and the cloth attached to its neck, and 3 September – nine days – at an average of 93 miles per day.

## 10 April 1872

**Casualties – Foreign**

New York, 28th Mar.- Advices by the *Montana* (s), which arrived at San Francisco yesterday, from Australia, etc., report that HMS *Basilisk* had picked up a waterlogged schooner (name defaced), with several dead and fourteen dying Kanacas* on board. The vessel was supposed [thought] to be the Peri, which had disappeared from the Fiji islands about two months previously.

*"Kanaca" – or Kanaka – came to be a common, and then pejorative term for South Pacific islanders, especially those indentured to work in British colonies around the Pacific. Originally, however, it only referred to indigenous Hawaiians, called *kanaka oiwi* or *kanaka maoli* in the Hawaiian language.

## 4 July

**Casualties – Foreign**

Madras, 4th June.- The Streemoothoocomorasawmy* (native barq.) has stranded opposite Messrs. Parry & Co.'s office. In consequence of several bags of rice being in a state of fermentation, it has been decided to blow the vessel up.

*This 23-letter name is possibly the longest single name of any vessel ever reported in *Lloyd's List*!

## 25 Nov 1872

**Casualties – Home**

Boston, Lincs., 22nd Nov.- A terrier dog, white, with yellow head, supposed [believed to be] from some vessel, landed at Sutton, Lincolnshire, on the 19th Nov., from the direction of the German Ocean [North Sea], in a very exhausted state.

## 29 Nov 1872

**Casualties – Home**

Deal, 27th Nov.- The *William Landreth*, arrived in the Downs, from St. Helena, reports that a large bird flew on board, 11th Oct., in lat. 3 S, lon. 16 W, having a calico wrapper attached to the beak and neck, with the following marked thereon:- "Jura, lat. 5 S, lon. 18 W, Oct. 9, 1872."*

*Someone on the *Jura* attached the piece of calico to the bird at a position just to the northwest of Ascension Island. The bird landed on board the *William Landreth* approximately 150 miles to the northeast of where it was 'tagged' two days before.

## 17 April 1873

**Casualties – Foreign**

New York, 2ⁿᵈ Apl.- The *Nabob* (barque), from Boston to Port Elizabeth [South Africa], was spoken, 26ᵗʰ Mar., in lat. 41 N, lon. 68 W, with loss of two men overboard. The master (Featherstone) reported that after leaving port he found that he only had three men on board who had ever been to sea before.*

*It was commonplace for sailing ships to be provided with at least some crew members by *crimps*, men who preyed on whatever rabble happened to be hanging around the docks near the time a ship was due to sail and who tricked or otherwise coerced some of them to sign on a particular vessel. These 'sailors' often had no experience of the sea and were shanghaied at the last minute to sign on as crew members, either through the crimp's trickery, by fraudulent inducement, or because they were dead drunk and had little if any idea of what they were doing – or more usually by some combination of all three factors. It seems the master of the *Nabob* might well have found himself with the majority of his crew from that disreputable but common source of recruitment.

## 30 Oct 1873

**Casualties – Foreign**

Natal [Durban], 26ᵗʰ Aug.- The *Teutonia*, which arrived here 24ᵗʰ Aug., from London, reports that when off Tristan d'Acunha, a cape pigeon flew into the rigging, and a paper was found tied to one of its legs bearing the words "French ship *Pekin*, Captain Ponce, lat. 40 S, lon. 70 E*".

*This position is in the southern Indian Ocean near the island of St. Paul. The bird, a very common and populous species in the Southern Ocean, therefore flew approximately 3,800 miles due west to the vicinity of the island of Tristan da Cunha in the South Atlantic where it was snagged in the *Teutonia*'s rigging.

## 19 Aug 1875

**Casualties – Home**

Portsmouth, 18ᵗʰ Aug., 9 p.m.- H.M.yacht Alberta*, in coming from Osborne [Isle of Wight] to this port, was in collision at 6 o'clock this evening, off Stoke's bay, with the schooner-yacht Mistletoe, which sank immediately. The captain of the *Mistletoe* was killed, and the mate and one lady were drowned. The *Alberta* lost bowsprit and received other damage.

Ryde, I.W., 18ᵗʰ Aug., p.m.- The Alberta, with Her Majesty on board, on passing from Cowes, has sunk the yacht Mistletoe, off Stoke's bay pier; one man badly hurt. Above information received from a pilot boat cruising off the spot. A good deal of wreckage floating.

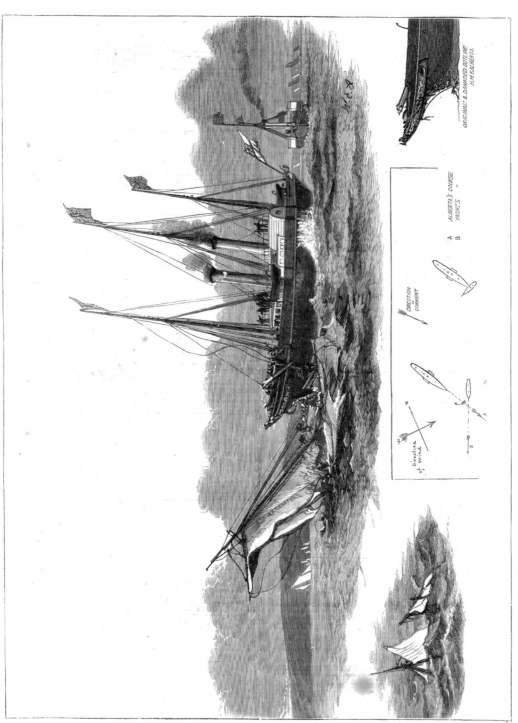

ORIGINAL & DAMAGED OUTLINE
H.M.Y. ALBERTA.

DIRECTION
OF CURRENT

Direction
of Wind

A    ALBERTA'S COURSE
B    YACHT'S    "

POSITION AND COURSE OF THE TWO VESSELS

THE COLLISION IN THE SOLENT—THE "ALBERTA" MEETING THE "MISTLETOE"

*HM yacht *Alberta* was a twin-funnelled paddle steamer commissioned in 1863 for Queen Victoria (1819–1901) and Prince Albert (1819–1861). The vessel was intended to be used for short voyages between their Isle of Wight home, Osborne House, and Portsmouth.

## 12 March 1877

### Casualties – Home

London, 10th Mar.- The *Daylight*, Abrahamsen, from Swan river [Perth, Western Australia], arrived in the River, reports that on the 1st Feb., in lat. 3 N lon. 25 W, she fell in with the Ilva (barq.), of Dundee, from Cadiz to Monte Video, with salt, which vessel was flying a signal of distress. Upon boarding her it was ascertained from the mate (Pyott) that on the previous day the master (Clark), in a fit of drunkenness had shot a boy and fired at the mate and others of the crew, and eventually, upon the crew attempting to secure him, had jumped overboard and was drowned.

By advice of Captain Abrahamsen, all the spirits on board were thrown overboard, and the mate, who held a master's certificate, stated that he felt capable of taking the vessel to Pernambuco, which port he intended to make, being satisfied with the behaviour of the crew. The logbook of the vessel did not contain any entries of insubordination against the men. At noon the vessels parted company, and the *Ilva* when last seen was steering about SSW.

## PITCAIRN ISLAND

## 27 April 1881

### Pitcairn's Island

Queenstown, Apr 26, 3 48 PM.- Captain of Wandering Jew reports having called at Pitcairn's Island, and taken on board one of the natives, who is great grandson to the ringleader of mutineers of the Bounty [Fletcher Christian]*, who escaped to the island.

*On 28 April 1789 Captain's mate Fletcher Christian led a mutiny aboard HMS *Bounty* which had loaded breadfruit at Tahiti for the return voyage to England. The mutiny occurred 30 miles off the island of Tofua near Tonga, 1,300 miles west of Tahiti. Christian set Capt Lt. William Bligh and 18 loyal crew members adrift in the ship's 23ft boat. Bligh and his boatload of crew sailed 3,600 miles to reach the Dutch colony of Timor in Indonesia on 12 June 1789.

Meanwhile, Christian and 18 mutineers, plus another four crew members ordered to stay aboard, sailed the *Bounty* back to Tahiti. In September 1789 Christian left a number of mutineers on Tahiti and immediately sailed to look for 'Pitcairn's Island', the remote refuge necessary to escape from the consequences of their crime of mutiny aboard a Royal Navy ship. He took with him nine other mutineers, eleven Tahitian women, six Tahitian men, and Sarah, a baby born to one of the Tahitian women.

The *Bounty* and its crew arrived at Pitcairn on 15 January 1790, where they settled to form the small community that survives to this day. Christian had two sons and a daughter. One of the sons, Thursday October, is the ancestor of virtually everyone on Pitcairn with the surname of Christian. Pitcairn Island today is a British Overseas Territory with a resident population of approximately 60 people.

PITCAIRN ISLAND

1. Thursday October Christian, Grandson of Fletcher Christian, and Oldest Man in the Island.—2. Map of Pitcairn Island.—3. Pitcairn Island and the Landing Place, Bounty Bay.—
4. H.M.S. "Opal."—5. Mrs. Young (Selwyn), Daughter of Moses Young.—6. Mary Warren.—7. Mr. J. Russell McCoy, Present Magistrate and Chief Ruler.—8. Miss Young, Organist of the Island.—9. Moses Young, Second Oldest Man in the Island.—10. Queen Te-haa-Papa, of Huahine, Society Islands.

A VISIT TO THE PITCAIRN ISLANDERS BY H.M.S. "OPAL"

Commanded by Captain Tapley, the *Wandering Jew* had left San Francisco 29 December 1880 with a cargo of wheat, bound round Cape Horn for Queenstown, Ireland, where she arrived 26 April 1881. Pitcairn, at lat. 20° 04' S, long. 130° 06' W, would have lain along her south-bound route in the South Pacific.

## 5 Nov 1884

### The Pitcairn Islanders

The Jorsalfarer, Norwegian barque, from Portland (Oregon), arrived at Falmouth, reports having touched at Pitcairn Island on the 21st July, when she was boarded by James Russell McCoy, the principal of the place*, who stated there were then on the island 130 inhabitants**, who were all well, and wished their respects to be conveyed to the people of England. They were in want of nothing at present, but would be glad to receive newspapers.

*James Russell McCoy (1845–1924) was the great-grandson of William McCoy (c. 1763–20 April 1798), one of the nine mutineers who arrived at Pitcairn on 15 January 1790 to evade capture by the British authorities for their crime of mutiny on board HMS *Bounty*. William McCoy became an alcoholic. It was said that he died by jumping off a cliff while in a crazed drunken state. However, a Tahitian woman on Pitcairn later claimed that his body washed ashore bound by his hands and feet, suggesting that others had thrown McCoy to his death, possibly because he had become a blight on the community.

The father of James Russell McCoy was Matthew McCoy (1819–1853), who had married Margaret Christian, the granddaughter of Fletcher Christian (1764–1793), leader of the *Bounty* mutineers. James McCoy was Magistrate (effectively the official leader of Pitcairn) four times: 1870–1872; 1878–1879; 1883; and 1886–1889. He was also President of the Council from 1893–1904. In 1884, although McCoy was clearly a *de facto* leader of the Pitcairn community, the magistrate at the time was Benjamin Stanley Young, another descendant of one of the original *Bounty* mutineers.

**The population of Pitcairn reached a maximum of 233 in 1937 (the Census of 1936 counted 200 people) and declined thereafter. The 2008 Census counted 66 permanent residents on Pitcairn, many of them direct descendants of the *Bounty* mutineers. There have been no McCoys on Pitcairn since around the time of Matthew Edward McCoy (1868–1929), most having emigrated and also because the McCoy family produced a high proportion of daughters.

The *Firth of Clyde* called at Pitcairn in 1889, shortly after the islanders were converted to Seventh Day Adventism.

## 13 May 1889

### Pitcairn Island

Report of the barque Firth of Clyde, captain Smith, from San Francisco, arrived at Falmouth 10th May:-

"On 9th February, 28 days out from the Golden Gate, laid to off Adamstown, Pitcairn's Island; and Mr. McCoy, chief magistrate, and five men, came off in their whale boat*. They brought pumpkins, cocoa nuts [coconuts], pineapples, bananas, eggs, and a beautiful bunch of flowers. Mrs. McCoy also sent half a cooked fowle and a piece of pudding made from sweet potatoes and Indian corn, for the captain's dinner. Captain Smith had the greatest difficulty to get them to accept of anything, it being their Sabbath day. They hold the seventh day of the week [Saturday], instead of the first; their reason for doing so is in obedience to the fourth commandment. The only thing Mr. McCoy would accept was some wine for communion purposes and some medicine.

Captain Smith supplied them with all the latest newspapers, both American and English, which were thankfully received. Religious books were eagerly sought after, also the *Christian Herald*. Mr. McCoy held divine service on board, and a number of Moody and Sankey's hymns were sung. There are 117 souls on the island, 45 males and 72 females; 38 of this number are children. They were all in good health. They take a lively interest in the doings of the outer world, and were well posted in American politics – that Harrison had been elected in place of Cleveland**, etc. After remaining for about two hours the islanders took their leave, and the crew bade adieu to one of the brightest spots in this dreary waste of waters."

*To this day Pitcairn islanders launch their longboats to come out to greet or board passing ships to sell their handicrafts for a few hours. The islanders (those English mutineers from the *Bounty,*) were originally Church of England. In 1876 a box of literature about Seventh Day Adventism was sent to the islanders from the United States. A decade later, an American missionary, John I. Tay, arrived on the island to promote Seventh Day Adventism. An entry in Mary McCoy's diary from March 1887 records their conversion:

*The forms and prayers of the Church of England laid aside. During the past week meetings were held to organize our church service on Sabbath.*

**Pitcairners got fairly regular news of the outside world from passing ships in the years before radio telegraphy. Bejamin Harrison defeated Grover Cleveland in the 1888 election to become the 23rd president of the United States from 1889–1893. Cleveland was elected again in 1893 to become the only US president to serve two non-consecutive terms of office.

## SEVENTH DAY ADVENTISM AT PITCAIRN

### 9 Feb 1891

#### Maritime Intelligence

Phoebe Chapman.- London, Feb. 9.- Despatches received at Queenstown on Saturday night from Honolulu contained the intelligence that the missionary barque Phoebe Chapman was lost on the coast of Tahiti, Society Islands, on Nov. 30 [1890], and all hands on board, numbering 16 persons, were drowned. The vessel was bound for Pitcairn Island from Honolulu.

*Review and Herald* (**Seventh Day Adventist newspaper in San Francisco**)

#### 3rd February 1891

#### Is It the "Phoebe Chapman"?

San Francisco, Jan. 29.- Private advices from Tahiti, in the Society Islands, report that wreckage has been discovered, supposed [believed] to be from the missionary schooner "Phoebe Chapman," which left Honolulu over two years ago in charge of Elder J.H. (*sic*

– A.J.) Cudney, of Nebraska, a Second Adventist missionary. The "Chapman" was bound for Pitcairn Island. She carried a crew of six men. All are now given up for lost, and at the General Conference of the Advent society resolutions of condolence with Elder Cudney's wife and children were passed. Another missionary schooner was sent to the South Seas some months ago, and reports that there is no longer any doubt of Cudney's fate.*

*After the Pitcairn Islanders were first introduced to Seventh Day Adventism in 1876 by a box of literature sent there by two American Adventist members, James White and John Loughborough, another missionary, John I. Tay, went to Pitcairn "to carry the message to the islanders". He arrived in October 1886 "and stayed about six weeks". A few years later A.J. (Andrew John) Cudney was chosen to return to Pitcairn as a missionary Elder of the Adventist church to bring the islanders more literature and continue to "carry the message" of Seventh Day Adventism.

Cudney and a crew of five other missionaries on the *Phoebe Chapman* left Honolulu on 31 July 1888 for Tahiti to pick up John Tay, and from there proceeded to Pitcairn. The schooner never reached Tahiti. The assumption by the Adventist church was that 'No doubt they perished in some great storm'. Cudney would have been the first ordained Adventist missionary to Pitcairn. In 1890 John I. Tay finally did arrive at Pitcairn to baptise the islanders officially as Seventh Day Adventists. Pitcairn Islanders have retained their Seventh Day Adventist faith to this day.

The story of how the *Phoebe Chapman* came to be named as such is told by the daughter of Phoebe Chapman herself: *Phoebe was a beautiful, popular young woman in Adventist social circles in Oakland [California]. A man who desired to win her favor informed her that he had named the first Adventist missionary vessel for the South Seas the* Phoebe Chapman. *But Phoebe, with a toss of her pretty head, replied, 'I hope it sinks!' All her life my mother regretted those foolish words, avoiding any mention of that ill-fated ship, which was lost at sea with never a word as to the passengers and crew...* (*Review and Herald*, 28 February 1980).

## 6 Aug 1881

### Casualties, Etc.

The Milne Bank.- The Marana (s), which arrived at Liverpool Aug. 4 from New Orleans, reports:- "On July 27, at about 4 a.m., in lat. 44 16 N, long. 40 20 W, got in what appeared to be shoal water with quantities of sea weed supposed [believed] to be Milne Bank*, searched for unsuccessfully believed in 1868.**"

*Milne Bank refers to the Milne Seamounts, some 800 miles northwest of the Azores, about halfway between the Azores and Newfoundland. The seamounts are at depths of between 3,500 and 22,500 feet, so could hardly be called "shoals". Nevertheless, a vessel called the *Joseph Hume*, on a voyage to Liverpool from Mobil, Alabama reported on 22 August 1827 that she sighted "a sand bank" (the vessel reported sounding in "20 fathoms water, sandy bottom") at lat. 39° N, long. 64° W, between Bermuda and Halifax. That position was near the Kelvin Seamount which is today charted at a depth of over 5,000 ft.

**This is probably a reference to the voyage of HMS *Gannet* in 1868. In July that year, on her homeward voyage from the North American and West Indian Station where she had been based for three years, *Gannet* sailed from Halifax to ascertain the depths and water temperatures of the limits of the Gulf Stream, which flowed over the Milne Seamounts out in the mid-Atlantic. Commander W. Chimmo, R.N. of the *Gannet*, later reported that upon taking a sounding over the "Milne's Bank", they found "no bottom at 2280 fathoms," meaning that the sounding line dropped 2,280 fathoms – 13,680 ft (over two and a half miles) – without reaching the seafloor. This is probably why the *Marana* report says "searched for [Milne Bank] unsuccessfully".

## But what happened to the dog?!

## 21 Aug 1883

**Casualties, Etc.**

Livonia.- Grimsby, Aug. 19.- The Livonia, fishing smack, of this port, left the fish dock on Aug. 18, on the morning's tide, for the fishing grounds, but owing to the light winds anchored in the Humber [River]. The master took the boat by himself to go on board of another vessel at anchor in the Humber, when the dog jumped overboard and swam after the captain. The captain stopped the boat to haul the dog in, but fell overboard and was drowned.

The second hand jumped overboard after the captain was 20 minutes in the water, and was rescued by a boat from another smack in an exhausted state. A boy also fell down in a fit. The vessel returned to port and came into the Royal Dock on the evening's tide, and the boy was conveyed to the hospital. The captain's body has not yet been recovered.

## 7 Nov 1883

**Weather & Navigation**

Gravesend, Nov. 5.- The Ecclefechan, Dow, from Calcutta, in the river, reports:- "…On Aug. 7 passed all day through fields of pumice stone* spread as far as we could see from the masthead, lat. 6 39 S, long. 92 44 E…"

*When it passed through the field of volcanic pumice stone, the *Ecclefechan* was approximately 800 miles to the west of the volcanic island of Krakatoa, off the coast of Sumatra. The volcano first erupted in May 1883, and then, more explosively and destructively, towards the end of August that year (see **Earthquakes, Seaquakes and Volcanoes: Krakatoa**). Pumice might have come from Krakatoa in May or later on during lesser eruptions, drifting to the position of the *Ecclefechan* with the westward flowing current in that region. After the August mega-eruption ships' captains reported fields of pumice stone floating in the vicinity up to several metres deep. To this day pumice is commonly found around the shores of the Sunda Strait, from the regular if less spectacular continuing volcanic activity of the islands.

## 3 Jan 1884

**Casualties, Etc.**

Report of the Callixene, from Calcutta, at Falmouth:- "Dec. 27, at 6 30 p.m., passed a barque on the port tack, compelling us to take the spanker in and keep the ship hanging in the wind to avoid collision, and would not keep away until close aboard. At 7 p.m. on the same day sighted a vessel's light on the port tack, who persisted in standing in, and would not keep away until within hail, compelling us to shorten sail, and throw the yards aback to avoid collision. We hailed her and found her to be a barque of Bremen, 16 days out from Cardiff for Rangoon, steering SW, lat. 46 7 N, long. 17 11 W.

I think it very hard that, after a long passage, and being short of provisions, we should be compelled to shorten sail and lose considerable time on a perfectly clear night to avoid collision with a vessel entirely in the wrong and in utter disregard of all rules."*

*Apart from some other considerations, sailing vessels on the starboard tack – that is, with the wind coming over their starboard side – generally have right of way over sailing vessels on the port tack – that is, with the wind on their port side. A vessel on the port tack must keep clear of a vessel on the starboard tack. The captain's complaint here was that the two vessels he encountered were both on port tack and should have kept clear of his vessel, rather than *him* having to take action to avoid collision, assuming, of course, that he was on starboard tack. The rules of the road are clear, that even a vessel with the right of way has an obligation to take action to avoid collision when the other vessel has not done so – which is what the master of the *Callixene* has done here…twice.

## 29 March 1884

**Casualties, Etc.**

Marie – Nantes, March 27.- The Marie, of this port, Royer, arrived at Bordeaux from Martinique, reports that she left Trois Rivieres Feb. 21, and in the passage touched bottom lightly. The same day, when off Dominica [the next island north of Martinique], she was struck by a large swordfish, causing a leak. The portion of the interior planking which was pierced by the sword was cut away, and the leak stopped, as well as it could be done…

## 12 Aug 1886

**Maritime Intelligence**

Stabbing On Shipboard.- At the Stratford [London] Police Court, on Aug. 11, John Campbell, 30, a seaman of the schooner Mary Ann Mandall, lying off Creek's-mouth, Barking [London], was charged with stabbing Charles Feltham, mate of the vessel, on the 10th inst. The prosecutor [ie., the plaintiff, the mate] stated that on the morning in question the prisoner complained respecting the dinner provided. He quarrelled with him (the mate) about it. He was saucy, and the prosecutor "sauced" him in return. The prisoner threw a plate at him, striking him in the face with it. He subsequently became very violent, and threw a knife at him. A struggle afterwards ensued for the possession of the knife, and while the prosecutor was endeavouring to get it away, the prisoner cut his hand. The prisoner made no defence, and was committed [to jail] for one month with hard labour.

## 18 Oct 1887

**Maritime Intelligence**

Tamaris*.- London, Oct. 18.- According to a telegram received from the Governor of South Australia, dated 22d ult., a dead albatross has been found on the shore at Fremantle [near Perth, Western Australia], and attached to its neck was a piece of tin, on which the following

was written in French:- "Thirteen shipwrecked persons on the Crozet Islands, Aug. 4, 1887."
The vessel to which these shipwrecked persons belonged, according to the Journal du Havre
of Oct. 15, is supposed [believed] to be the Tamaris, bound from Bordeaux for Noumea
[New Caledonia], which vessel was posted as missing on Aug. 31, and the crew of which
was composed of 13 men.

*The isolated and rocky Crozet Islands, 1,200 miles southeast of South Africa, in the
Southern Ocean, lay directly in the path of sailing vessels running their easting down in the
Roaring Forties, as the *Tamaris* was doing on her passage from Bordeaux towards Noumea
on the French island of New Caledonia in the western Pacific. The crew of the *Tamaris*,
shipwrecked on one of the Crozets, attached their message to an albatross on 4 August 1887.
It was found on the dead albatross at Fremantle, Western Australia – 3,000 miles away – six
weeks later around 21 September. Despite the almost miraculous discovery of the *Tamaris*
castaways' message, they themselves were never found.

## 21 March 1889

### Maritime Intelligence

### Weather and Navigation

Falmouth, March 20.- The Caroline, Davies, from Caleta Buena, arrived here, reports:- "In
lat. 19 4 to 27 N, experienced fresh northerly gales for eight days, with high confused sea,
and the wind then gradually veered to the east. On March 9, 10, and 11, in lat. 43 to 44 N,
long. 28 to 25 W, the atmosphere was remarkably clear; during the day the sun, moon, one
or two planets, and several stars of the first magnitude [eg., Sirius, Canopus, Capella, *et al*]*
were visible at the same time. On the 11th they were visible at noon.

Robert Finnick, belonging to Glasgow, died at sea at 3 p.m. on Feb. 21."

*Stars such as these are used to take astro-navigational sights of celestial objects at dawn
and twilight, when they still appear visible while there is just enough daylight for the navigator
to see the horizon (necessary to determine the angle of the object above the horizon) for the
purpose of determining the vessel's position. The brightest planet, Venus, is sometimes visible
during the day in very clear conditions. It is unusual, however, to be able to see even the
brightest stars during the day.

## 15 Dec 1890

### Maritime Intelligence

### Miscellaneous

New York, Dec. 15.- The captain of the Norddeutscher Lloyd steamer Trave, which arrived
here yesterday, reports having experienced a stormy passage. A number of animals intended
for the Central Park menagerie were on board, and they were so terrified by the rolling
of the ship that they became wild. A passenger named Mrs. Oelwing was lost overboard
during the voyage.*

*The Central Park Zoo in New York City was originally just a "menagerie" of exotic animals
donated to it from 1859. It was officially established as a zoo in 1864. The *Trave*, having sailed
from Bremen in Germany, was bringing some "9,000 birds, two tigers, one lion, two hyenas,

six ostriches, one antelope, and one horned sheep" to the zoo, according to a *New York Times* article of 15 December 1890 relating to the incident of Mrs. Oelwing's disappearance.

Mrs Ida Oelwing was described in the article as "a good-looking young German woman of twenty-eight years…conspicuous for her gayety and good humor". The article speculated that, since the sea was calm on the night of her disappearance, "she could not have been washed overboard, and it is supposed that she deliberately jumped to her death".

## 2 May 1891

**An Eleven Thousand Miles Sailing Ship Race.-**

A race from Calcutta to Boston (United States) has just been concluded between two Scotch sailing vessels, and resulted in a somewhat exciting finish. The distance is over 11,000 miles, and the vessels were the Ardencraig*, 2,072 tons, and the Trafalgar*, 1,696 tons, the latter a four-mast vessel. The start was made by the Ardencraig on the 10th December [1890], and the Trafalgar three days later, and 35 days out the Trafalgar overtook the other vessel and spoke her. The Ardencraig reached Boston at 10 o'clock on the morning of the 15th ult. [April], and the Trafalgar was signaled on the evening of the 8th ult., passing the highland Light, and therefore she was held to have won. The Trafalgar was to enter Boston the same evening, and was said to be the first four-masted vessel sailer that ever went into the port.

*The *Ardencraig*, built in 1886, was 277ft 7ins long by 40ft wide and 24ft 9ins deep. She was wrecked on Crim Rocks in the Isles of Scilly, in fog, in January 1911. *Trafalgar* was originally a four-masted iron ship but later converted to a barque, built in Glasgow in 1877, 271ft 5ins long by 39ft 3ins wide by 23ft 4ins deep. She was wrecked off the coast of Brazil in November 1904 during a voyage from Sydney to Falmouth with a cargo of wheat.

In October–December 1893 *Trafalgar* made "a fearful voyage" that left only a young boy (the senior apprentice) to navigate the ship to port.

## *18 Dec 1894*

**Miscellaneous**

Melbourne, Dec. 17.- The barque Trafalgar* has arrived from Batavia after a fearful voyage lasting 48 days. The captain, two officers, and three seamen died of fever on the passage, and several others were prostrated with the disease. A youth of 18 navigated the vessel into port.

*The *Trafalgar* left Batavia (Jakarta) in Indonesia on 30 October 1894, bound for Melbourne. Just before and during the voyage most of the crew, including the captain, succumbed to Java fever (probably malaria). The 18-year-old senior apprentice William Shotton, assisted by the sailmaker, Hugh Kennedy, navigated the ship safely to Melbourne where they arrived on 16–17 December.

Shotton, the boy captain, was the first person to be awarded the Meritorious Service medal, established by Lloyd's in 1893, for his accomplishment. The *Trafalgar* was owned at the time by Andrew Weir Shipping & Trading Co. Ltd., of Glasgow, forerunner of the Bank Line that was established in 1905. Both of their companies trade to this day as an integrated global shipping group.

## 22 Nov 1892

**Maritime Intelligence**

Platina.– Philadelphia, Nov. 21.– The barque Clark, which has arrived here confirms the loss of the barque Platina, with her captain and crew of 13 hands. The Clark left Ivigtuk* on June 6 last in company with the Platina.

## 8 Dec 1892

**Maritime Intelligence**

Platina**.- Philadelphia, Dec. 6.- The arrival at this port yesterday of the barque Serene, after a stormy passage of 30 days from Greenland, revives the hope that the barque Platina, of the Kryolite fleet, may not have foundered. The Esquimaux residents on the Greenland coast reported to the crew of the Serene that a ship manned by Europeans had landed 40 miles up the coast. The Danish Government have been communicated with by Cable, and they have intimated that they will endeavour to discover the identity of the vessel.

## 16 Dec 1892

**Maritime Intelligence**

Platina.- Philadelphia, Dec. 5.- Captain Holmes, of the barque Serene, arrived here from Ivigtut, reports that a few days before he left Ivigtut some Eskimos brought word that a ship manned by Europeans had put in about 40 miles further up the coast. The Eskimos reported that the vessel was barque-rigged and painted green, which corresponds to the colour of the Platina. The Danish Government sent men north to find the belated vessel, but Captain Holmes was compelled to sail before they returned.

*Ivigtuk (Ivittuut) on the southwest tip of Greenland, was the site of a cryolite mine between 1865 and 1987 when mining operations were abandoned. The cryolite was used in the industrial processing of aluminium ore.

**The *Platina*, although described here as "of the Kryolite fleet", was an American whaling barque of 214 tons, 94ft in length, 25ft 3ins wide and 15ft 2ins deep. She was built at Mattapoisett, Massachusetts and launched at New Bedford in 1847. Originally rigged as a ship, she was changed to a barque rig in 1850 and sailed as a whaler for 63 years. Her final whaling voyage ended when she arrived back at New Bedford on 24 August 1910 with 2,050 barrels of sperm oil after a 22-month cruise. In 1911 she was sold to transport lumber and passengers to and from the Cape Verde Islands. After her third voyage to the islands late in 1913, she was "surveyed by government inspectors and condemned as unseaworthy". The old *Platina* was then broken up for her value as firewood ($1,300).

One of *Platina*'s whaling voyages was unique in the annals of whale fishery. In July 1901 she set off under the command of Captain Thomas McKenzie. A man named Amos Smalley was signed on the voyage as "boatsteerer", or harpooner. Smalley had only just returned home from his first voyage in the *Platina* during which he was promoted from steward to harpooner. He was a Native American born in 1877 at Gay Head, Martha's Vineyard, and was in the image of the character of Tashtego, one of three harpooners in Herman Melville's epic whaling novel, *Moby Dick*. Melville says of Tashtego that he was 'an unmixed Indian from Gay

Head…which has long supplied the neighbouring island of Nantucket with many of her most daring harpooners'.

A year out, the *Platina* was on the Western Grounds (whaling grounds south of the Azores) when they spotted a sperm whale's spout about a mile away. Approaching the whale in one of the boats, chief mate Andrew West exclaimed, "That fish is white! He's white all over!" Smalley got his iron (harpoon) into the heart of the whale. After sounding, it rose to the surface soon after, dead.

The 90ft sperm whale taken by the *Platina* that day was the only white sperm whale ever taken by a whaling ship. Smalley narrated his account of the incident in a first person article in *Reader's Digest*, June 1957, titled *I Killed 'Moby Dick'*, for which he was awarded $2,500. Amos Smalley died in 1961.

## 15 Jan 1894

**Miscellaneous**

London, Jan. 15.- The Central News says:- Advices have been received at Plymouth of the arrival at Galveston (Texas) of the Norwegian barque Elsa Anderson, having in tow the hull of an English-built brig, which is supposed [thought] to have burned at sea more than 50 years ago, and which appeared on the surface of the ocean after a submarine disturbance off the Faroe Islands. The hull of this strange derelict was covered with sea shells, but the hold and under-decks contained very little water. In the captain's berth were found several iron bound chests, the contents of which had been reduced to pulp, excepting a leather bag, which required an axe to open it. In it were guineas bearing date 1809, and worth over 1,000l [£1,000]. There were also several watches and a stomacher* of pearls, blackened and rendered valueless by the action of the water. Three skeletons were also found, one of a man nearly seven feet high.

*A stomacher was a long v- or u-shaped panel worn on the front of a woman's gown – or, less commonly, on the front of a man's doublet – mainly for decorative effect, although it could also provide support to the garment. A stomacher was either made as part of the gown or doublet, or tied to it as a separate piece. It was in fashion from the late-1500s until around the mid- to late-1770s.

## HOAX "SOLE SURVIVORS"

## 18 March 1895

**Maritime Intelligence**

"Yeoman".- London, March 18.- A Dalziel's telegram from Marshfield (Oregon), dated March 17, states:- "The schooner Leeds has arrived here, having on board Daniel Clark and Thomas Moore, believed to be the only survivors of the British ship 'Yeoman', bound from Antwerp for Redonda. Clark told a reporter to-day, that while the crew were shortening sail the vessel was struck by a squall and he was swept overboard. A lull followed, during which the ship righted, and Clark was pulled on board. Moore, the ship's cook, had his head split open by being hurled to the deck by a lurch of the vessel, while Captain Ferguson and the mate were swept overboard by a huge wave. Clark cut loose the lifeboat and placed Moore, who was unconscious, in the bottom of the boat, which he succeeded in pushing off just before the vessel sank. The men drifted about in the boat 14 days.

## 22 March 1895
### Maritime Intelligence

British Yeoman.- Liverpool, March 21, 2 49 p.m.- British Yeoman: Following received from owners:- The friends of those on board the British Yeoman having been made very uneasy by the report of the loss of a vessel called the Yeoman, we cabled our Portland and San Francisco friends to investigate the same, and they replied respectively as follows:- "Yeoman.- Report unfounded." "Yeoman.- Newspaper canard."*

*In other words, this was a hoax! A clue to this being a hoax was the supposed destination of the vessel, Redonda, an uninhabited island in the Caribbean near Antigua and Montserrat and the subject of an elaborately fantastic history for over 100 years. Apparently discovered and named Nuestra Señora de la Redonda by Christopher Columbus, the island was claimed by annexation in 1865 by Matthew Dowdy Shiell, a Montserratian merchant, while sailing near the island. Shiell created a mythical Kingdom of Redonda, proclaiming his son, M.P. Shiell, King Felipe 1 of Redonda on his 15th birthday. Shortly afterwards the British declared that Redonda was a dependency of Antigua, which officially it continues to be although still inhabited only by goats and seabirds. (The story might have originated from M.P. Shiell himself, later in life when he became a science fiction writer and might have invented the origins of the kingdom and his kingship of Redonda.)

Ever since that time there has been a succession of fantasy kings of the Kingdom of Redonda, with a history of fanciful appointments to the title. After the death on 27 August 2009 in Canada of King Robert – King Bob the Bald – otherwise known as Robert Williamson (r. 1989–2009), a British yachting writer, Michael Howorth, claimed his right to the title, styling himself King Michael the Grey at a coronation ceremony in Antigua on 11 December 2009.

## 27 May 1895
### Maritime Intelligence

Eva.- Rosario [Argentina], May 2.- The Swedish barque Eva, when about to load a cargo of wheat for Europe, and having only 100 tons of ballast on board*, was caught by a strong gust of wind last night and capsized off the railway moles, and sunk in about 22 feet of water; master and three men drowned.

*A vessel is most vulnerable to this kind of incident when she is about to load her cargo with not much ballast on board to keep her upright, especially if a strong wind strikes her as she lies alongside the loading dock. The Eva was on her first trip to Rosario. Her 16 crew jumped into the water when she capsized. Twelve were picked up but the other four, including her captain, were drowned.

The British ship Blairmore was lying at anchor in San Francisco Bay with 250 tons of stone ballast to keep her upright when a squall struck.

*10 April 1896*

**Maritime Intelligence**

Blairmore.- London, April 10.- A Central News telegram dated New York, April 9, states:- A terrible gale swept the bay of San Francisco to-day. The British ship Blairmore capsized in a sudden squall, and six of her crew were drowned, including Mr. Ludgate, the mate, and Kenny, steward.

## 19 Oct 1896

**A Negro Giantess**.- One of the passengers by the Campania which arrived in the Mersey [Liverpool] from New York on Saturday morning, was a negro giantess from South Carolina.* She stands 7 feet 8 inches high, and is 22 years of age [*sic*]. She created no little excitement amongst the people on the landing-stage.

*This negro giantess was Mme. Abomah, who toured the world in the late 19th century, and into the early years of the 20th century as 'the world's tallest woman'. She was usually identified as around 7ft 6ins tall but might have been closer to 6ft 10ins or so, by careful comparison with other known tall people of the time. She was born in Laurence County, South Carolina. The year of her birth was commonly reported as around 1862 (two years before the abolition of slavery in America), although her age of 22 in the above report suggests that she was born in 1874.

## 7 Nov 1896

**Smothered By Mud**.- At a Limehouse [east London] inquest yesterday it was found that a Wapping waterman [river worker] named Hack, who died on Tuesday evening, had been literally smothered in the mud at the bottom of a dock. He was climbing down a ladder from the steamship Iona to get to a barge, when he fell and disappeared from sight in the soft mud. The bargeman immediately got a hitcher and hooked the poor man out, but he died in a few hours from slow suffocation from the mud which had found its way into his nose, mouth, and windpipe.

## DUEL ON DECK

## 12 Jan 1897

**Maritime Intelligence**

Madeleine (s).- London, Jan. 12.- A Dalziel's telegram from San Francisco, Jan. 11, says:- Advices received here this afternoon state that the French steamer Madeleine has been arrested at Acapulco, in Mexico, pending an inquiry by the French Minister in Mexico into an incident which happened on board that vessel. It appears that the Madeleine sailed from Callao, Peru, and that during the voyage two of the boilers burst, killing seven of the stokers, engineers and crew. On account of this serious event the Madeleine put into Acapulco for repairs, which having been duly made she sailed again for San Francisco.

A day later, however, the Madeleine returned to Acapulco, flying the police flag. The captain reported that the chief engineer and the second officer had quarrelled, that they had fought a duel on deck with pistols, and that the second officer had been killed.

## THE SINKING OF THE BATTLESHIP *MAINE* AT HAVANA

### 16 Feb 1898

**Maritime Intelligence**

Maine (U.S. cruiser)*.- Havana, Feb. 16.- A most terrible explosion occurred about a quarter to 10 last night on board the United States cruiser Maine, which was lying at anchor in the harbour here. The loss of life was very serious, and the vessel suffered most severely, the explosion, besides doing great damage, having set fire to the ship, which was still burning at midnight. All the officers escaped, but it is estimated that over 100 of the crew were killed.

*The Court of Inquiry into the explosion that sunk the United States Navy's 2nd class battleship *Maine* while it was anchored in the harbour at Havana, Cuba, on the night of 15 February 1898, concluded that 'the *Maine* was destroyed by the explosion of a submarine mine', killing 260 men aboard. The sinking of the *Maine* led directly to the start of the Spanish–American War which lasted just over four months from 25 April until 12 August 1898, and ended with decisive victory by the United States. By the Treaty of Paris of 10 December 1898, Spain ceded possessions including Guam, the Philippines and Puerto Rico to the United States. After three years of US military government, Cuba gained independence on 20 May 1902.

### 30 March 1898

**Maritime Intelligence**

Bothnia.- Swansea, March 29.- The steamer Challerton, from Port Nolloth [South Africa], reports that when 250 miles south of Scilly [the Scilly Isles] a carrier pigeon came on board to which the following message was attached:- "Mail steamer La Bretagne, March 27, 8 a.m. An English sailing vessel is succoured by La Bretagne. Delay probable. (signed) Captain Reynaud." On the paper is also written, apparently afterwards:- "Saved the crew of the Bothnia, three men of that crew killed."

## THE VOYAGE OF COUNT RUDOLPF FESTETICS DE TOLNA

### 28 April 1900

**Maritime Intelligence**

Tolna (yacht).- Havre, April 25.- According to information from Suez the steamer Birchtor arrived at that place, having on board Count Festetics* and two of the crew of the yacht Tolna, which was wrecked some time ago in the Indian Ocean. The yacht stranded on Minicoy Island, which belongs to the group of the Maldives. The Count and crew stayed there two months, after which they were taken off by the steamer Birchtor. Before leaving the island, Count Festetics set fire to the Tolna, rather than she should be pillaged by the natives.

*Count Rudolpf Festetics de Tolna was born at Boulogne-sur-Seine (now Boulogne-Billancourt) in the western suburbs of Paris on 17 June 1865, and was related to the Austro-Hungarian aristocratic family of Festetics. In 1890 he met Eila Haggin, a wealthy Californian heiress at a reception in Paris and married her in February 1892 in New York City. The couple returned to San Francisco to live. There the Count began the construction of a schooner yacht to be named *Tolna* (after the name of the count's ancestral castle in Hungary), for a cruise around the world.

The *Tolna* was 88ft long, 24ft 6ins wide, 11ft deep, and 78 tons net. The Count and Countess and crew sailed in her from Sausalito, across the bay from San Francisco, in October 1893 first stopping at Hawaii. They later visited Tahiti and Samoa in 1894, where they were guests of Robert Louis Stevenson staying at Sydney for over six months, they departed on 23 June 1895 for Japan arriving May 1896 via various island groups of the western Pacific. Their most memorable stops were at the Solomon and Admiralty Islands, where they encountered native cannibal tribes about which the Count later wrote extensively.

On 20 April 1898 the Count and the *Tolna* left Singapore without the Countess who was thoroughly tired of living on a boat for five years without the comforts of land life. The Count accused his wife of constant flirtations with certain men they met during the cruise and a year later the Countess filed for divorce. The *Tolna* arrived at Colombo, Ceylon (Sri Lanka) on 16 June 1899. Sailing south, the vessel was wrecked on a reef off Minicoy Island in the Maldives archipelago on 11 February 1900.

For three days the *Tolna* remained relatively dry. On the fourth day she started to fill with water, obliging the Count and his two crew members to go ashore. As he described it: 'As I saw that I could save nothing more and that the natives were beginning to plunder the yacht, I set her afire, pouring kerosene on her. She was burning for three days and then disappeared altogether'. The native lighthouse keepers shut the Count and his crew in the Minicoy's lighthouse for two months before the British steamship *Birchtor* took them off the island.

Count Festetics had salvaged the extensive collection of native artefacts and photographs he had accumulated during his cruise of almost seven years, which he later donated to the National Ethnographic Museum of Budapest. He also wrote two books about the voyage that were published in 1902 and 1903. His life after divorce from his first wife was highly varied, complex and interesting. He died in Paris in 1943.

## 29 Aug 1900

**A Chinaman's Assault.**- Ah Chung, a young Chinese seaman, was charged before Mr. Mead at the Thames Police Court yesterday with assaulting Ak Lung, also a seafaring man of Chinese nationality. When the prosecutor [plaintiff] entered the witness-box some difficulty arose as to the manner in which he should be sworn, he not knowing enough English to explain his religious belief. Eventually Mr. Mead elicited from the would-be witness that he "worshipped the sun."

This was of no assistance to the court in determining the form of oath, so the evidence of the police-constable concerned was taken. Police-constable 5K stated that at 12 o'clock midnight he was on duty in West India Dock-road when the prosecutor told him that Ak Lung had struck him with his fist in the face. The Prisoner: "Belly tlue; me punch him – fist. Belly tlue." Mr. Mead bound the Celestial offender over to keep the peace.

## 10 Aug 1901
**Maritime Intelligence**

Anita S.* - St. Nazaire, Aug. 8.- The following is a copy of the letter from the captain of the Italian brig Anita S., received at sea by the captain of the steamer Sapphire, from Tampa:-

"Dear Sir.- Will you be kind enough to give me some oil, because all is finished. If you can give me some bread and potatoes and some use rises [?]. I come from Teneriffe – 77 days. I am very near foolish [?]. Calm and strong winds from Nord [north], NNE and NE all time, or very calm. Please report me on your arrival to have found at sea one desaspered [desperate] captain. I give you thousand thanks for your kindness.- Your truly friend, Cap. A. De Rosa, of Anita S. Lat 45 40 N, long 11 34 W, about 38 to 400 miles off Belle Isle [Brittany coast]."

*Some time after this encounter with the *Sapphire* to the northwest of Cape Finisterre and within about 380 miles of its destination of Nantes in Brittany, the *Anita S.* turned around to sail over 1,000 miles back to Teneriffe in the Canary Islands. It arrived there on 7 September "with sails damaged and cargo shifted". A French steamer, the *Conseil*, was then chartered to take the *Anita S.*'s cargo of Martinique sugar and convey it to Nantes which left Teneriffe for Nantes on 17 October. Whether or not the *Anita S.*'s captain De Rosa was "very near foolish" on this voyage, he certainly had every reason to be "desaspered".

## A "PLUCKY FRENCH SAILOR"

## 5 Nov 1901
**Maritime Intelligence**

Tourny.- Algiers, Nov. 4.- Off Cape St. Antoine*, last Monday night (Oct. 28), the captain and crew of the French sailing ship Tourny, bound from Valencia for Marseilles, in ballast, abandoned the ship, fearing that she would go down. A fierce storm was raging, the sails had been torn to ribbons, and the ballast had shifted. Only one man refused to leave the ship, a sailor named Denis, who declared that he could navigate her. He was accordingly left on board. Yesterday the Tourny met the steamer Syrian Prince, which towed her into Algiers, where she arrived this afternoon. The plucky sailor remained on board till his ship was safely anchored.

*The Evening Post* (**a New Zealand newspaper**)
**4 January 1902**

A plucky French sailor, named Denis, stands the chance of making a windfall. He was on board a barque [the *Tourny*] which received so severe a buffeting in the Mediterranean that the captain and crew decided to abandon her and boarded a passing vessel. Denis refused to go, and remained on board doomed, so his companions thought, to a watery grave. However, the vessel remained afloat, and some time after was picked up and towed [by the *Syrian Prince*] into Algiers with the lone sailor aboard. Denis intends to claim salvage.

*Cape St. Antoine would have been Cabo de San Antonio, just south of Valencia in the province of Alicante. The distance from there to Algiers was about 200 miles. A New Zealand newspaper, *The Feilding Star*, reported on 24 December 1901 that Denis 'was unable to leave the helm to procure food and suffered great privation', adding that 'his sole companion [was] a dog'.

## 20 Jan 1902

### The Sailmaker and the Shark

Benjamin F. Barker, of Brockton (Mass.), sailmaker's mate, has been recommended by the officers of the United States training-ship Alliance for a medal of honour. When the vessel was at St. Thomas (D.W.I. [from 1666 till 1917 the Danish West Indies – now US Virgin Islands]), the crew were ordered to refrain from swimming, as the harbour was full of sharks. One night three boys stole overboard, taking the ship's dog with them. The dog was seized by a monster shark. Terror-stricken, the three men swam for the ship, but the shark gained upon them. Baker dived over the rail, and, armed only with a dirk [dagger], swam directly towards the approaching shark, and, diving beneath it, thrust his knife into its belly, ripping it open from throat to tail. The shark measured 14 feet 9 inches. The dog had been swallowed whole.

## THE MYSTERY OF THE *MARY CELESTE*

## 16 Dec 1872

### Casualties – Foreign

Gibraltar, 13th Dec., 1.45 p.m.- The Mary Celeste* (Aust. brgtne.), from New York to Genoa, with alcohol, has been found derelict at sea, and brought here by three men of the *Dei Gratia* (Brit. brgtne.).

### *17 Dec 1872*

### Casualties – Foreign

Gibraltar, 14th Dec., 7.25 p.m.- The Mary Celeste (Brit. brigantine), is in the possession of the Admiralty Court.

### *18 March (1873)*

Gibraltar: cleared, Mar 7, Mary Celeste, Blatchford, for Genoa

### *31 March (1873)*

The 'Mary Celeste.'- In the Vice-Admiralty at Gibraltar on the 14th inst., the Hon. the Chief Justice gave judgement in the *Mary Celeste* salvage case, and awarded the sum of £1,700 to the master and crew of the Nova Scotian brigantine *Dei Gratia* for the salvage services rendered by them; the costs of the suit to be paid out of the property salved. The *Mary Celeste* was valued at $5,700, and her cargo at $36,943 – total, $42,643, so that the award may be set down as one-fifth of the total value.

The judge further thought it right to express the disapprobation of the court as to the conduct of the master of the *Dei Gratia* in allowing the first mate, Oliver Deveau, to do away with the vessel which had rendered necessary the analysis of the supposed spots or stains of blood found on the deck of the *Mary Celeste* and on the sword, and his lordship also decided that the costs of the analysis should be charged against the amount awarded to salvors.

*The ghost ship mystery of the abandonment of the *Mary Celeste* remains one of the great unsolved puzzles of maritime lore and legend. She was built in 1861 as the *Amazon*, a 103 ft long, 282-ton brigantine, at Spencer's Island, Nova Scotia. Salvaged after she went ashore in a storm in 1867, she was sold to American owners who renamed her *Mary Celeste* in 1869.

Early in November 1872 the vessel departed New York bound for Genoa, Italy with a cargo of 1,701 barrels of commercial alcohol, to be used to fortify wine. The *Mary Celeste*'s complement comprised the master, Capt. Benjamin Briggs, aged 38, his wife, Sarah, aged 30, and their two-year-old daughter, Sophia Matilda. The crew of seven comprised two Americans, a Dane and four Germans.

On 5 December the British brigantine *Dei Gratia*, under the command of Capt. David Morehouse (who knew Capt. Briggs personally) and having sailed from New York a week after the *Mary Celeste*, came upon a vessel approximately halfway between the Azores and the coast of Portugal. She was under full sail and heading approximately towards Gibraltar, to the southeast. Capt. Morehouse recognised her as the *Mary Celeste*. He observed her erratic zigzag course for two hours, concluding that she was abandoned and drifting. He sent his first mate, Oliver Deveau, along with a few of his men in a small boat to board the *Mary Celeste*.

The boat party discovered that there was no one on board. The last entry in the ship's log was for 24 November when she was approximately 100 miles west of the Azores. The ship's slate showed that she reached just offshore of the Azorean island of St. Mary (Sta. Maria) the next day, 25 November. The *Dei Gratia* boarding party found her compass destroyed and the ship's chronometer, sextant, navigation book and ship's register and documents were missing. The only lifeboat appeared to have been launched without undue panic. A rope, frayed at the end, trailed from her stern. The subsequent Admiralty Court record noted that 'the whole ship was a thoroughly wet mess'.

*Dei Gratia* crew members sailed the *Mary Celeste* to Gibraltar where their salvage claim was heard in the Admiralty Court. A salvage award was made to the *Dei Gratia* crew in March 1873, but the amount was reduced on the suspicion of the Court that there was 'wrongdoing' on the part of some of the crew, although that allegation was never proved.

The *Mary Celeste* sailed for another dozen years under various owners. She was finally wrecked on Rochelois Reef off the coast of Haiti in January 1885.

Numerous, varied and often colourful theories and speculations have been attributed to the disappearance of the crew and passengers of the *Mary Celeste*, their fate and the reasons why they abandoned their vessel in mid-ocean. The violent tremors of a seaquake have even been mooted as a cause.

A number of seaquakes have been experienced by vessels near the Azores and reported to Lloyd's:

## 19 Jan 1875

**Miscellaneous**

The following is an excerpt from a letter from Captain Le Couteur, of the Bonny Mary, arrived at Cadiz from Pernambuco:- "Off the Azores, about 100 miles to the SW of Santa

Maria, on Dec. 22, experienced a heavy shock of an earthquake, when I thought the vessel would have shaken her bottom out. I have never felt anything like it before."

Undersea earthquakes – seaquakes – produce exactly the kind of phenomenon recorded above: a violent shock wave from the sea bottom to the surface that would severely agitate even very large vessels and their crews directly above. Such a violent tremor might have caused the crew of the *Mary Celeste* to abandon their ship, leaving it to sail into the lore of most puzzling mysteries of the sea.

The seismological station at Zurich recorded a strong mid-Atlantic earthquake on 25 November 1872. There was also an 8.1 magnitude earthquake in the Azores itself just one month before. So there was considerable seismic activity in the area the *Mary Celeste* would have been in, and potential cause for her abandonment if a seaquake rattled her timbers – and her crew's nerves. However, with no conclusive evidence about her fate the story of the *Mary Celeste* remains an enduring mystery.

By coincidence, another vessel by the name of *Celeste Marie* was wrecked at almost the same time as her English-named version was abandoned in mid-Atlantic, and reported as follows:

## 7 Dec 1872

**Casualties – Home**

Lowestoft, 5th Dec.- The wreck of the *Celeste Marie*, from Hull to Dieppe, which went ashore at Covehithe [south of Lowestoft on the Suffolk coast], 30th Nov., has been sold for £32.

## NOT SO FRIENDLY NATIVES

## 27 May 1870

**Casualties – Foreign**

Brisbane, 15th Feb.- The Sperwer (cutter), of Sourabaya, Gascoigne, from Melbourne to New Guinea, with rice, sugar, tea, etc., was seized by the natives of Wednesday Spit, about 9th Apl., 1869, and was run ashore by them near Red Point, Prince of Wales Island*. 7 lives lost.

*Prince of Wales Island (called Muralag in the local indigenous language) is the largest island in the Torres Strait between the tip of the Cape York Peninsula, northern Queensland, and the southeast coast of New Guinea. The indigenous people of Muralag and nearby islands are the Kauraregs, who are more closely related to Australian aboriginals than the other Torres Straits islanders in this area.

## 28 Sept 1872

**Casualties – Foreign**

New York, 13th Sept.- Advices from Honolulu state that the crew of the Lavinia (schr.) have been massacred by natives of the Saloman [Solomon] islands.

*4 Dec 1873*

**Casualties – Foreign**

HMS *Beagle*\*, which arrived at Sydney from the Solomon Islands, 11ᵗʰ Sept., had on board the master and 4 of the crew of the Lavinia (schr.), the others having been murdered, and the vessel seized by natives of New Ireland.

\*This was not the HMS *Beagle* of the famed naturalist Charles Darwin's circumnavigation from December 1831 to October 1836. This *Beagle* was a 1-gun British naval schooner based in Sydney from 1872 until 1883.

## 20 Jan 1874

**Casualties – Foreign**

Sydney, 1ˢᵗ Dec. [1873].- The Plato (barq.), of Sunderland, Clarke, which sailed from Newcastle, N.S.W., 29ᵗʰ Apl. [1873], for Hong Kong, with coal, went ashore on a reef outlying from New Caledonia and became a total wreck. The crew reached Port Adams (Malayta\*) in one of the boats, but were all murdered there by the natives, except one man, who has been brought to Brisbane by HMS *Dido*.

\*Malaita Island in the Solomon Islands lies about 600 miles north-northwest of New Caledonia.

## 30 Aug 1876

**Casualties – Foreign**

Glasgow, 28ᵗʰ Aug.- Information has been received by the 'Western Morning News' of the British vessel *Dancing Wave* having been captured by the natives of Florida island, one of the Solomon group [Solomon Islands], and the crew murdered by savages. One man escaped to an adjoining island, from which a barque set sail and found the *Dancing Wave* a complete shamble. Another vessel's crew had been treated in a similar manner. HMS *Sandfly* had been sent to the spot.

*31 Aug 1876*

Casualties – Foreign

Melbourne, 10ᵗʰ July.- The *Dancing Wave* (schr.), Harrison, arrived at Sydney, 4ᵗʰ July, from the Solomon group, under charge of the mate of the *Sydney* (barq.), the master and all the crew of the schooner having been murdered, 22ⁿᵈ April, at Florida island, by the natives, who also plundered the vessel.

A communication from H.M. Consul at Noumea [New Caledonia], dated 17ᵗʰ June, states that he had just heard from Captain Lind, owner of the *Laura Lind*, that he fell in with the Rev. Mr. Inglis, in the missionary vessel *Dayspring*, who reported that an English vessel called the May Queen or Mary Quinn, a labour vessel from Queensland, had run ashore at Tanna, at a place called Vagoos; that the crew fired at the natives, who attacked them in return, burned the vessel, and then killed the crew. Capt. Lind is the person who saved the surviving crew and passengers of the Isabella, lost on Brampton shoals, and he fears there are now more castaways on the same island, belonging to three British vessels, the remains of which he found there.

## 20 Aug 1878

**Casualties – Foreign**

New York, 5<sup>th</sup> Aug.- Advices from Hong Kong state that the master, Williams, of the *Beatrice* (Brit. schr.), which left Guam on the 15<sup>th</sup> June for Yokohama, reported that when at Pulwat Island* he was informed that 12 men who had landed in a boat at Namayonne, had been murdered and eaten by the islanders, and that on going to look for the boat he was told that it had broken up. On his return to Guam Captain Williams was informed by the master of the *Tuitela* (Ger. schr.), which had arrived four days previously, that he had seen the wreck of a vessel of about 1,000 tons burden on Namayonne island, but was warned away from her by the natives.

*Poluwat Island is a 7 km² atoll in the Chuuk (formerly Truk) Islands. Chuuk is part of the Caroline Islands, one of the four island groups comprising the states of the Federated States of Micronesia, to the north of Papua New Guinea.

## 2 June 1886

**Maritime Intelligence**

**Miscellaneous**

Hong Kong, April 28.- The German barque Melusine, Mehlburger, which arrived here April 25, from Penarth [near Cardiff, Wales], reports as follows:- "At daybreak on April 12, with very little breeze, sighted Sansoral Island*. At 7 o'clock we saw five large native boats or canoes put off from the island and steer direct for the ship. Seeing that they were well filled with men, and suspecting that they were not coming for a peaceable purpose, we kept the ship more to the west, and steered away from the island. There was but little breeze at the time.

At 7 30 a breeze from the east sprang up and freshened, so that at 7 45 the ship was going 6¼ knots. Still, however, the boats were gaining on the ship. The three boats which were most astern gave up the chase, but the other two kept on, and were at 9 o'clock about one mile astern. Then the wind freshened more, and a heavy NE sea set in, and as land had now disappeared from sight, these two boats also gave up the chase.

The boats appeared to be about 35 or 40 feet long. They looked like some sort of outrigger craft, with two long masts and lock sails attached to them. Each boat had, as we counted them, from 18 to 20 men. As we had no firearms, what would have become of us if it should have remained calm may easily be judged, for with 15 men we should not have been able to cope with 80 to 100 men. Vessels are therefore warned not to approach too near to these islands." Sansoral is one of the St. Andrews' Islands, which are situated in lat. 5 20 N and long. 132 12 E, and lie a little SE of the Philippines.

*The tiny atoll of Sonsorol (also called Dongosaro) Island is, together with Fanna, one of the two Sonsorol Islands of the Southwest Islands group of what is now the Republic of Palau, Micronesia. The name of St. Andrews' Islands on old maps and in the report above, is now out of date.

Sonsorol State (the islands of Sonsorol, Melieli, Pulo Anna and Fanna) is one of 16 states of the Republic of Palau. At the time of the incident reported by the *Melusine*, Palau was under Spanish administration (1885–1899). It successively came under the following foreign colonial administration: German 1899–1914; Japanese 1914–1945; UN Trusteeship/US Trust Territory 1945–1994. In 1994 Palau became an independent republic.

## 1 Dec 1899

### Maritime Intelligence

### Miscellaneous

Norfolk [Virginia], Nov. 17.- The crew of the steamer Kurdistan report that on the passage from Iquique, when off the Patagonian coast, near Tierra del Fuego, the vessel was caught in a storm and fog and came to anchor. A boat's crew went ashore, and hearing strange noises proceeding from a cavern near their hiding-place, inspected it. A party of savages were in the cave engaged in eating what seemed to be the dismembered body of a human being. The savages attacked them, whereupon they fired upon them, killing one savage. His companion carried the dead body away and devoured it. In the cavern was a Danish flag and much wreckage. On the shore near the cavern lay the wreck of a wooden brig.

## 10 Jan 1900

### Maritime Intelligence

Nukumanu.*- Hamburg, Jan. 6.- With reference to an attack on a ship's crew in New Guinea, the *Rh. West Zeitung* [German newspaper] publishes a letter dated Nov. 13, written by Blaser, a citizen of Ludenscheide, to his parents, stating as follows:-

"The Nukumanu, belonging to Messrs. Forsyth & Co., of this place, left here about four weeks ago for the Admiralty Islands, to trade with the natives. The crew consisted of captain, mate and about 15 black sailors. The captain one day was on deck weighing copra, etc., brought in by the natives, whilst the mate was engaged below. Suddenly the captain was felled from behind by blows with an axe, and the mate on coming up on deck, met the same fate, and then the whole crew were massacred, except three boys who hid themselves, and the vessel was completely plundered.

The natives made a feast on shore, at which they ate their victims. They were then about to burn the vessel, but two days after the massacre the motor launch Angarea, belonging to the same owners, came up to the spot and rescued the vessel and the three boys."

*The *Nukumanu* was a South Seas trading schooner of 59 tons, registered at Sydney and owned by Mr. J.M.C. Forsyth of New Britain, the largest island of the Bismarck Archipelago off the east coast of New Guinea. It was named after Nukumanu Atoll, an isolated atoll to the north of the Solomon Islands but administered as part of New Guinea.

The New Zealand newspaper *The Otago Daily Times* of 22 September 1900 reported that the *Nukumanu* left the New Hebrides (now the Republic of Vanuatu) to trade in the Admiralty Islands, under the command of Capt. Dahte with a crew of 13 or 15 native black sailors and a mate. At Los Negros in the Admiralties, the vessel *was attacked by hordes of savages, and the captain, mate, and crew were stabbed to death.* The natives stripped the *Nukumanu* of everything they could take. Before they could burn her as she lay at anchor, a trader named Moltke arrived on the scene (presumably in the motor launch *Angarea*) and rescued the vessel, noting that *her decks liberally bespattered with the blood of the unfortunate victims.*

The Danish-born explorer, anthropologist and ethnologist Richard Parkinson (1844–1909) mentioned the massacre in his best known work, *Thirty Years In the South Seas – Land and People, Customs and Traditions in the Bismarck Archipelago and on the German Solomon Islands,* first published in German in 1907: *Pálamot people settled years ago at Limondrol on Papitálai. Their chief Kámau was the instigator of the attack on the sailing ship Nukumanu, the crew of which was murdered.*

The *Nukumanu* was taken back to New Britain where she was refitted and subsequently chartered for a new voyage. Outward bound she encountered strong currents in the St. George's Channel between the islands of New Britain and New Ireland, and was wrecked on a reef between the islands of Mioka and Uln and completely destroyed. Her captain and crew got away safely in boats.

## 18 July 1903

**Maritime Intelligence**

**Miscellaneous**

Berlin, July 17.- A telegram from Hamburg to the *Vossische Zeitung* states that according to advices from Matupi [Burma/Myanmar], the captain, named Howard, and the entire crew of a British vessel have been killed by natives of the Admiralty Islands, in the Bismarck Archipelago [off New Guinea]. After seizing arms and ammunition, the natives ran the vessel ashore.

## "CELESTIAL VISITORS"

## 11 Jan 1896

**Maritime Intelligence**

**Miscellaneous**

Liverpool, Jan. 11.- The master of the steamer Loch Etive, from New York, at Cork, reports that on the evening of the 6th inst., the entire heavens became suddenly brilliantly illuminated, and remained so for a few minutes.* At the same time a pretty loud report was heard, and a peculiar sensation experienced by the crew through the Loch Etive trembling. The captain further states that while the illumination lasted the sky and ocean as far as the eye could reach, became such as they would be at noon with a brilliant sun shining and a clear atmosphere. Asked as to whether the phenomenon may not have been the result of an explosion aboard a steamer previously passed bound west, the captain states that immediately after the thought struck him that this might have been so, but he is unable to account for it.

An enquiry was subsequently telegraphed to the Queenstown agents for the steamer, and an interview with the captain was obtained. The captain and his officers, in reply to questions, said they thought what they had witnessed was due to some atmospheric disturbance, and that it was not caused by an explosion on board a steamer. The second officer said he was satisfied it was not an explosion on a steamer.

*The *Loch Etive* probably witnessed the fireball of a meteorite burning through the Earth's atmosphere. In his 1898 book *By Way of Cape Horn,* Paul Stevenson writes: *I remember the* *case of the large British ship* Cawdor, *Captain Jardella, during one of her recent voyages from Swansea to San Francisco. She made a very long passage on this occasion of one hundred and eighty-four days. She had a terrific battering in the Southern Ocean, and reported on arrival that off Cape Horn an enormous meteor plunged into the sea with a stunning explosion, so close as to flood the decks.*

The magazine "Popular Science Monthly", Vol. 54 (1899), reported the incident: "Even more remarkable was the escape of the British ship *Cawdor*, which was given up by the underwriters, but which reached San Francisco November 20, 1897. During a heavy storm, August 20th, a large meteor flashed from the sky and passed between the main and mizzen masts, crashing into the sea with a blinding flash and deafening detonation. For a moment it was thought the ship was on fire, and the air was filled with sulphurous fumes."

Various American newspapers also reported the incident, among them *The Newark* [New Jersey] *Daily Advocate* on 1 December 1897:

**Imperiled By A Meteor**

**Narrow Escape of a British Ship in an Electric Storm**

The British ship Cawdor arrived in San Francisco recently with a story of miraculous escape from a great meteor during an electric storm off Cape Horn. On Aug. 20 a great electric storm prevailed, and after a blinding flash of lightning, when all hands were on deck, a huge meteor flashed through the heavens and plunged into the sea so close to the ship that all on board thought that the vessel was lost. A strong, sulphurous odor hung around the vessel, and the water was churned up so that it swept over the deck. The ship was uninjured, but it was three weeks before she could get around the Horn.

## 17 Nov 1898

**Maritime Intelligence**

Galileo (s).- New York, Oct. 29. Belgian steamer Galileo, arrived here from Rio Janeiro, reports:- On Oct. 20, in lat. 11 57 N, long. 58 26 W [just southwest of Barbados], at 4 30 a.m., a large aerolite [meteorite] fell in the sea close to the ship, the splash from the waves dropping on to the ship's deck. About the same time a flash of lightning struck and split the main deck.

## BALLS OF FIRE

## 16 July 1896

**Maritime Intelligence**

**Weather and Navigation**

San Francisco, July 1.- The British ship Wasdale, arrived here to-day from the Tyne, reports:- On April 21, in lat. 58 S, long. 71 W [southwest of Cape Horn], at 10 30 p.m., our yard arms and mastheads were lit up with balls of fire*, and at 11 30 p.m. we were struck by a furious hurricane, which continued for 20 hours and kept the lee side buried, damaging all our running gear, smashed both side-light screens, damaged starboard poop rail, smashed in side ports and deluged half deck. At noon on the 22nd had to cut away the lower foretopsail to relieve the ship. At this time the sea was breaking frightfully, causing the ship to lurch very heavily and setting the cargo of coke to leeward slightly. After 6 p.m. the gale began to moderate; the lowest reading of both barometer and aneroid was 27.56.

Had a continuance of heavy gales until May 4, lat. 48 S, long. 80 W, then more moderate and variable to May 12, lat. 34 S, long. 97 W, when we had a furious gale and terrible cross sea, which commenced suddenly from a slight breeze and heavy rain at ENE, but shifting rapidly to N and NW.

*This is the phenomenon known by sailors as corposants, or St. Elmo's fire (from St. Erasmus of Formiae, St. Elmo in Italian, the patron saint of Neapolitan sailors). The fire is actually glowing plasma created in electrically-charged environments such as thunderstorms. It manifests particularly at the extremities of pointed objects such as church steeples, and the masts and yardarms of sailing ships.

In chapter 119, *The Candles* of Herman Melville's *Moby Dick*, the *Pequod*'s spars and masts were lit up by St. Elmo's fire during a typhoon:

'Look aloft!' *cried Starbuck.* 'The corpusants! the corpusants!'

*All the yard-arms were tipped with a pallid fire; and touched at each tri-pointed lightning-rod-end with three tapering white flames, each of the three tall masts was silently burning in that sulphurous air, like three gigantic wax tapers before an altar.*

The next ball of fire was related not to a thunderstorm but, apparently, to an earthquake.

## 14 March 1893

**Miscellaneous**

Malta, March 6.- Captain Cotter, of the Brenner (s), from Dedeagath [Turkey], reports that on March 3, 9 30 a.m., when about 30 miles W of Cape Matapan [Akra Tainaro, on the Peloponnisos peninsula, the southernmost point of the Greek mainland], his vessel was struck by a ball of fire, but the decks being flooded at the time she sustained no damage; the ball struck the deck and passed over the stern in thousands of pieces. The ship at the time was trembling violently, and continued to do so for 15 to 20 seconds. The captain is of opinion that there was an earthquake in the locality.*

*The *Brenner* was in the vicinity of the island of Zakynthos (Zante), in an area of regular seismic activity. Zakynthos suffered a major earthquake on 31 January 1893. Aftershocks occurred for some time after the main quake, which is what the *Brenner*, "trembling violently", might well have experienced.

## (...AND PIRATES)

## 31 Aug 1875

**Piracy off Cape de Gatte***

**Gibraltar, 21ˢᵗ Aug.**

Captain H. Yonge, the master of the Pleiades (schr.), of Wildervank, which put in here yesterday afternoon, made the following deposition:-

"On the 16ᵗʰ Aug., while on the voyage from Trieste to Rio Grande [southern Brazil], and when ten miles off Cape de Gatte, a Spanish boat ranged alongside with a crew of seven men, offering to sell fruit and vegetables. The master refused to buy anything, when six of the men, armed with revolvers, swords, and daggers, jumped on board the schooner and threatened to murder the crew if they resisted. The crew of the schooner, six in number, took refuge in the rigging, but the master remained at the wheel, and one of the pirates, presenting a revolver at his breast, demanded the surrender of some of the cargo, or otherwise he threatened to shoot him. The master offered half a barrel of flour of his own stock, and, the crew being ordered down from the rigging, the mate was taking this out of the storeroom, when the pirates broke open the fore-hatch and took out 14 barrels of flour, which he forced the crew to assist in transferring to the falucho**, on which they embarked and made off, rowing straight for the land, but before doing so flung on board the schooner a few bunches of grapes and some potatoes."

*Cape de Gatte (Cabo de Gata) is near Almería in southeast Spain. ** A *falucho*, in Spanish, is a small coastal boat rigged with a triangular lateen sail.

## 10 March 1886

### South Sea Pirates

Hong Kong, Feb. 1.- The German barque Augusta, which arrived here Jan. 30 from Cardiff, had a very narrow escape from falling into the hands of South Sea pirates whilst in the vicinity of the Tupoo Islands*. On Jan. 15 nine armed native canoes were observed approaching the vessel, manned by about 150 savages. The captain having been warned against these islanders when leaving Europe, armed his crew, and, the savages approaching nearer, though warned off, fire was opened upon them, and they were finally driven away, several being killed or wounded.

*These were most likely the islands around Tongatapu, the largest island and administrative centre of the Kingdom of Tonga.

## South China Sea Pirates

## 13 Jan 1870

### Hong Kong, 7th Dec. [1869]

The ship Crofton has been abandoned in a sinking state, near Macao, having been attacked by pirates, who murdered all the Europeans except the master and six men, whom they took as prisoners.

### *17 Jan 1870*

### Hong Kong, 6th Dec. [1869]

The crew of the Crofton, Rook, from Saigon to Yokohama, reported by telegraph as having been abandoned near Macao, are known to have left in boats. The mate and four men have arrived here. The master and six men landed on an island, and were murdered by the natives.

## 6 Aug 1870

### Pillage of the 'Hackmatac'

### Report from H.B.M. Consul at Canton [Guangzhou]

The following copy of a report from H.B.M. Consul at Canton, of the attack and pillage by Chinese pirates, of the English ship 'Hackmatac', has been received from the Board of

Trade:- Nicholas Lehmann, master, late British ship *Hackmatac*, registered No. 36,845, Liverpool, states:-

"Left Bangkok on 14th March, with 3,500 peculs [1 picul = about 60 kg, so about 210 tonnes] of rice, and 20 Chinese passengers; crew consisting of 2 Europeans, 2 Indians, 1 Javanese, and 1 Chinese, bound for Hoi-ho [Haikou], in Hainan [Hainan Island, southern China].

On 3rd May, at 12 noon, making for Hainan Straits, had light wind till 6 p.m., a strong current setting to N.W. from 6 p.m. to 9 p.m., steering S.E. At 9 p.m. kept the ship up to S.E. by E. running about 3 knots; weather dark and cloudy. At 10 30 p.m. ship struck on a reef about 2 miles North of Cape Cami. We backed yards and put an anchor out astern, and threw overboard 200 bags of rice to lighten the ship, but she remained fast.

We waited for high water, which would be about 10 a.m., but pirates came off about 9. The supercargo [ship's officer in charge of cargo] went ashore at 8 a.m. to get assistance, and came back at 9. A boat anchored close to us; she was well armed – men to the number of sixteen came off from her, and boarded us. They first went into my cabin and took out the chronometer and instrument, after which they overhauled [ransacked] the passengers' baggage and took their money and clothes from them. Then they went away.

The supercargo went ashore again but did not return. We tried to get the ship afloat again, but the pirates prevented us. There were about thirty junks on the spot. Another lot of pirates came on board, took our clothes, and then began to knock the ship to pieces. The sails were taken off the yards, and on the pirates attempting to seize us we went overboard into the boat and pulled ashore at Haipak. We walked to the mandarin's house, but he refused assistance, and sent us on further to another mandarin. It was 10 30 a.m. when we left the ship, and we did not reach the mandarin (Hsii-wen-heen) till 10 p.m.

We were lodged for the night, and next day the mandarin went to Haipak himself, but he would not let us leave the house. He came back with the supercargo and one of the passengers, and told us that the ship had been burnt, and also that a Hainan junk was among the number of piratical vessels. He went to Hainan to look for the pirates, and was away for three days; after which he came back, saying their number was too great for him to do anything.

The day after the mandarin told us that the next day we would leave for Canton [about 500 km away]. He gave me and the mate $20 each, and $3 to each of the crew. We left Hsii-wen-heen on the 11th, four men accompanying us. The mate and I had chairs, the crew walking. On the 13th we reached another station, and we went on thus from station to station until the end of May, when we occasionally travelled by water. On the 31st we reached Yunghung, on the 1st June, Samshui, and on the 2nd, at 9 a.m., reached Canton. Went into the city to the Nanhai, and thence to the Consul in the city.

List of articles lost by the master – 2 sextants, 1 chronometer, 1 watch and chain, 2 glasses [binoculars], 2 swords, 15 dollars, clothes, ship's papers.

List of articles stolen from the mate, H. Schneider – 1 octant, papers, clothes."

The attack by a band of south China coast pirates on the British steamship *Greyhound* in October 1885 showed how well organised the brigands were.

## 24 Nov 1885

### Piracy in the China Seas

### The Greyhound

### Hong Kong, Oct. 20

For many years past there has been such an entire absence of piratical attacks on foreign vessels, either steamers or sailing vessels, that foreign merchants in Hong Kong and China and foreign shipowners have fondly assured themselves that the days of piracy on foreign craft, once so common in the China Seas, especially in the southern latitudes, were completely over. This pleasant belief has, however, been rudely shattered by the terrible tragedy which was enacted on board the British steamer Greyhound on Saturday last. It is many years now since anything of the same nature occurred, but the tactics employed by the daring men who committed the piracy on Saturday are exactly similar to those employed by the men who attacked the Canton river steamer Spark in 1874. The story of the attack in the Greyhound is as follows:-

The British steamer Greyhound, of London, 227 tons register, left here on Saturday morning (the 17th inst.) at daylight, for Hoihow [on Hainan Island], with a general cargo and about 120 Chinese passengers and 30 of a crew on board. The steamer was under the command of Captain C.W. Syder, formerly chief officer of the British steamer De Bay, and was officered as follows:- George Sherville, first officer; C.F. Jacobsen, second officer; William Bennett, chief engineer; and George H. Da Silva, second engineer; the rest of the sailors and firemen being Chinese.

All went well with the vessel until she had arrived off the island of Ku Lan (or Tai Lou), about 30 miles SW from the Ladrone Islands and about 70 miles from Hon Kong, the historical hunting ground of the Kwantung [south China coast] pirates. It was then about noon, and those members of the Chinese crew who were not actually at work were engaged on their mid-day meal on the forecastle. The weather was somewhat rough, and the rest of the passengers were down on the 'tween deck, most of them more or less actually affected by *mal de mer*, and a number of men, who afterwards turned out to be pirates, feigning to be so.

### EMERGENCE OF THE PIRATES

The captain and the chief officer were on the bridge, amidships; the second officer and the chief engineer were at the after-part of the ship, on the starboard side, and the second engineer was down below in the engine-room. While the crew were in the respective positions described, some of the passengers, on the pretext that they were sick, came on to the main deck from the main hatch, and no sooner were a number on deck than they came out in their true colours as pirates, and commenced firing at the chief engineer and second officer.

The latter were, of course, taken entirely by surprise, and rushed towards the saloon, amidships, where their cabins and the armoury were. As they ran forward they were fired at by several of the men, and the second officer received no less than seven bullet wounds and the chief engineer two before he reached the forehold, where they took refuge. Immediately the first shot was fired the Captain looked round, and shouted to the man who had fired it; but at once he and the first officer, seeing other men aim at them with their revolvers, realised what was going on, and while the Captain made to get to the chart room, on the bridge, where his revolver was, the chief officer ran down the starboard steps leading to the main deck, thence down the saloon steps into his cabin below, in order to get his revolver. Here Sherville closeted himself, so as to get his revolver loaded.

## MURDER OF THE CAPTAIN

The captain, less fortunate, was at once confronted by three or four of the ruffians who had reached the bridge by the port steps leading from the main deck, and before he could reach the chart room (also on the port side) his assailants had poured a regular volley into him with their revolvers (some of them had two). The captain, as might have been expected, offered a strenuous resistance before he was overpowered, but, unarmed as he was, it was impossible for him to contend with the odds against him. We have not been able to find anyone who saw the whole encounter between the captain and his murderers, but one of the crew saw the captain pinned against the chart-house by one of the pirates, while another drove a long knife into his breast. They then lifted him up and threw him overboard, and fired at him even after he was in the water.

Meanwhile other members of the buccaneering party were engaged in overawing the other members of the crew and the rest of the passengers. The second engineer, hearing the shooting going on, came up on deck to see what was the matter. No sooner had he done so than he received by no means pleasant and pressing attentions from several of the desperadoes, who fired seven or eight shots at him, but luckily failed to hit him. He, also, made a dart for his room, which he succeeded in gaining without injury. Here he locked himself in, but on the pirates politely informing him that if he did not come out they would kill him, and that if he did and looked after the engines, they would not, he thought the wiser plan was to let his arbitrary masters have their own way.

He then came out of his room, and was ordered down into the engine-room, being accompanied by one of the pirates, a tall, muscular man who compelled the trembling lad to obey his orders at the muzzle of a revolver. At the top of the engine-room stairs stood another guardian, also armed with a revolver.

The purser (Cheung San Yu), a fluent speaker of English, was also visited by one of the murderous gang, who quietly asked him to step out of his room. At first the purser seemed disinclined to comply, but a bullet passing dangerously close to his body, he obeyed with some alacrity. Outside, his attendant saluted him in the same agreeable manner four times, but, strange to say, not one of the shots took effect on the object. Seeing what was wanted of him, the purser slipped a valuable jade-stone bangle off his arm, and handed it over to his dangerous attendant, and also promised him all his money. This seemed to satisfy the pirate, and firing ceased so far as the purser was concerned. He and the passengers were, however, advised to retire as quietly and as quickly as possible to the 'tween decks, over which the pirate leader had planted sentries.

In the meantime, those of the crew forward who were not required on duty were also requested to retire aft, and the leaders, through some of the "boys" who had secreted themselves in the cabin, informed the chief officer, who was still closeted in his own room, that if he consented not to hurt them, and gave up the keys of the treasure chest, they would not hurt him. Thinking prudence the better part of valour, the chief officer accepted those terms, and gave up the keys. He was then ordered into the forehold. He was afterwards ordered into the 'tween decks aft, where the second officer and chief engineer were also removed. There they were all battened down, along with the *bona fide* passengers, and left to ruminate over their unhappy fate.

## Pirates in Control

The pirates were now in full and undisputed possession of the ship. Two men with revolvers kept the bridge, and compelled the regular quartermasters to turn the ship about and steer in the direction of Hong Kong. With the greatest nonchalance they now and then scanned the horizon with the captain's binoculars, and once when they saw a passing steamer and some junks they ordered the Greyhound to be steered away from them. Sometimes also, although they did not seem to understand the use of the "telegraph," they would order the engines to be stopped, to go half-speed and so on, apparently for sheer devilment and amusement.

While these two were thus employed on the bridge, the other members of the band, which is estimated to have numbered between 30 and 40, were ransacking the captain and officers' cabins, the saloon, and chart-room, taking everything which was of value and easily portable. Money and jewellery were the most favoured articles. Those drawers which were locked were prised open; the treasure (amounting to $2,000) was carried off, and they had also the audacity to take away the watches, bangles and earrings from the passengers, and even rifle them.

## The Plunder: "A Pretty Fair Haul"

Among the articles taken were a telescope (the stand was left behind), bought only a few days before from Messrs. Gaupp & Co. for $90; five gold watches, three silver watches, four gold chains, four gold rings belonging to the officers, a gold scarf ring, some studs, six breech-loading rifles from the ship's arms-rack, two or three revolvers, two anchor lights, a telescope from the ship, several leather travelling bags, and a quantity of mandarin silk clothes, meant for presents, about 500 pieces of Chinese clothing, and some valuable Chinese medicine. One of the gold watches was enamelled and set in pearl. The only cargo taken was a box of opium. Altogether the property and money taken is valued at $10,000, a pretty fair haul for a band of Chinese pirates.

All these articles were collected together for transhipment, and about dusk, when the steamer had by this time made her way back to within 40 miles of Hong Kong, and was quite near Man-san, one of the Ladrones [Islands], three junks came alongside in answer to the pirates' signals. The plunder was then transferred to the junks.

During the time the booty was being transferred, some of the leading spirits, after having ordered the engine to be stopped, went down into the engine-room, ordered all the steam to be blown off, compelled the firemen to draw the fires, and then removed some of the most necessary parts of the engines, rendering the ship utterly helpless. Among other things they took away the lever of the feed pump, and a number of the brasses, and threw them overboard. They also stove in all the four boats, so that no one could leave the ship.

To complete their devilish work one of them proposed that they should set fire to the ship. Another more merciful, apparently, suggested that as they had got a good deal of plunder and the ship was helpless, they should give the many unfortunate people a chance of being picked up by some passing steamer. Happily, but most unexpectedly, the better counsels prevailed, and no one, so far, has lost their life by this most audacious and desperate attack but the captain. It was noticeable that the pirates took care not to call each other by their proper names, but made use of a vulgar term when addressing each other. Nearly all could speak a little English, and one of the men, who was apparently a leader, spoke English, Portuguese and Chinese.

Two of the pirates, injured by the promiscuous shooting, were taken off by their comrades.

## The Get-Away

All three junks were two-masted, and resembled strongly the ordinary type of salt smugglers. The two with most booty on board left first, and then the junk remaining, the most heavily armed of the three, followed. Before it did so, its occupants coolly informed those on the steamer that if they saw any signs of smoke from the funnel, they would immediately return and fire in to her.

This threat, however, did not deter the second engineer and those under him from at once starting to provide substitutes for the missing parts of the engines and relight the fires. A wooden lever for the feed pump was manufactured within an hour from the time the pirates left, about half-past 8 in the evening, and this was very cleverly rigged up by means of lead ends, and wire ropes and iron bolts, to the engine. We understand that this substitute was provided under the directions of the chief engineer. To whoever it belongs, we give full credit for the very clever and effective manner in which the essential substitutes were provided.

When the chief officer was released, the Greyhound was about four miles W. by N. of the Ladrones, and he could see the three junks standing on the starboard tack, as if they were bound for Macao.

Steam was got up about half-past 12, and the steamer moved ahead again for Hong Kong at 10 minutes to 1, and arrived here about 9 a.m. yesterday. On their arrival the Admiral and the police were at once communicated with, and as soon as might be the injured men were removed to the Government Civil Hospital, where they are now doing well. About 6 o'clock in the evening the British gunboat Midge, with a Chinese detective and interpreter and the two quartermasters who were on duty on the Greyhound while the pirates were in charge on board, went off in search for the pirates. Her movements are uncertain.

## Captain Syder

The murder of Captain Syder is indeed pitiful. He was a young man, having been born in London in 1854, and was about to be married, his bride being expected to arrive here on the 6th of next month. A pathetic incident is told in connection with his death. His little black dog on seeing its master attacked, made a vicious onslaught on its master's murderers, one of whom fired at and hit it three times. All three shots seem to have grazed off the faithful animal's back.

From the above recital, it can easily be seen that the officers, crew and passengers of the Greyhound have had an experience which few people would envy. For over eight hours they were completely overawed by and at the mercy of a band of determined and reckless scoundrels, and it can easily be imagined that, as one of the crew expressed it, "the eight hours looked like a week."

## NORTH AFRICAN PIRATES

In the late-1890s piracy by the tribespeople of the northwest African Mediterranean coast of Morocco, extending into western Algeria, was quite a regular occurrence. The Riff region of mountainous terrain was home to a number of traditional Berber tribes, of which the Bocoya and Kabyle were two (see **Rosita Faro, 27 Aug 1897**). The Bocoya were towards the west along the Moroccan coast while the Kabyle were around and to the east of Algiers.

## 1 Sept 1892

### Maritime Intelligence

Jacob.- Madrid, Aug. 31.- A telegram received here to-day from Palma (Majorca) states that on the 20th inst. a Spanish cutter, called the Jacob, trading between Cape July* and the Rio de Oro*, was boarded and robbed by Moorish Corsairs [ie., pirates], who carried off 11 of the crew as prisoners. The five other men managed to escape in the cutter's boat, and were picked up at sea by the Spanish schooner Venganza. The captain of the latter returned to the place where the cutter had been attacked, and the Jacob was found drifting, having been deserted by the pirates after they had secured [ie., stolen] the 400 bales of wool forming the cargo.

*This is Cabo Juby, an ex-Spanish protectorate between the Spanish Sahara territory on the west coast of Africa and Morocco to the north. Río de Oro was a province in Spanish Sahara. The whole area was the focus of a bitterly contested struggle between the Polisario Front rebel guerrilla group, Morocco and Mauretania which bordered it to the east, after Spain withdrew from the territory in 1975.

## 1 Aug 1894

### Maritime Intelligence

Mayer.- Gibraltar, July 31.- The schooner Mayer, of this port, which sailed hence on the 28th inst., with a cargo of coal and gin for Melilla*, was becalmed when about 20 miles east of Pinon de Gomera, off the coast of Morocco. While there the vessel was boarded by an armed band of Riff Arabs**, who seized the cargo and hauled down the flag. After they had stripped, not only the ship, but the crew bare, they took their departure. Next morning a breeze sprang up, and the Mayer setting all sail returned to Gibraltar, where she arrived to-day.

*Melilla is one of Spain's two autonomous enclaves on the Mediterranean coast of Morocco, the other being Ceuta. ** "Rif Arabs" are Berbers from the Rif Mountains along that northern coastal strip of Morocco.

## 1 May 1895

### Maritime Intelligence

Anna*.- Gibraltar, April 30, 7 25 p.m.- Dutch brigantine Anna towed in here by Hercules.

On April 28, 3 p.m., when off coast of Riff [Morocco] becalmed, was attacked by Moors who fired on the crew. Captain killed, mate seriously wounded. Moors took away provisions, ropes, spare sails, also eight casks of oil cargo.

### 2 May 1895
**Maritime Intelligence**

Anna.- Gibraltar, May 1, 12 10 p.m.- The following information is from crew of Dutch brigantine Anna.- Was boarded by pirates when becalmed six miles off coast, Alkuzemas Bay. Was boarded by one boat containing seven men who, having killed captain and dangerously wounded mate, were followed by seven other boats. Full particulars will be sent by mail.

*The *Anna* was sailing along the Mediterranean coast of Morocco, from Bari in southern Italy to Lorient in Brittany, northwest France, with a cargo of olive oil.

## 6 April 1896
**Maritime Intelligence**

St. Joseph.- Madrid, April 3.- A telegram from Algeciras states that the barque St. Joseph, from Gibraltar, has been seized and robbed by Moors off the Riff coast. The ship was cleared [ie., robbed] of her cargo, and the passengers and crew were left destitute. They reached Gibraltar in a pitiable state.

## 27 Aug 1897
**Maritime Intelligence**

Rosita Faro.- Madrid, Aug. 27.- Intelligence has been received here that the Portuguese barque Rosita Faro has been attacked on the Morocco coast by Becoya Kabyles, who carried off the captain and four of the crew. The vessel was bound from Oran for Gibraltar.

### 4 Sept 1897
**Maritime Intelligence**

Rosita Faro.- Tangier, Sept. 2.- A telegram from the Spanish settlement of Alhucemas* states that the Portuguese barque Rosita Faro, which was recently captured by Bocoya Kabyle, who took prisoners the captain and four of the crew, has again fallen into the hands of the Riffians, who have now made captive the captain's brother. Two sailors liberated by the pirates have arrived here.

*Al Hoceima (Alhucemas) is one of five Moroccan provinces and main port of the Riff region, one of the main tribes being the Bocoya.

## PERSIAN GULF PIRATES

## 17 Dec 1895

**Piracy in the Persian Gulf.- Six Men Murdered**.- Kurrachee [Karachi], Nov. 26.- Another case of piracy is reported from the Persian Gulf. A country craft, Dowlutpursad, Tindal [captain] Hussein, had six of her crew murdered near Bussorah [Basra, Iraq]. The pirates also looted Rs. 5,000 in cash. The craft belongs to Cutch Mandvi, and was bound for

Bussorah to secure a cargo of dates. When within a few hours run of Busreh [Bushehr, Iran] she ran aground, but after getting off, and when about to set sail, she was approached by an Arab dhow manned by armed Bedouins and fired at.

Most of the crew jumped overboard, but were pursued and seized, two being wounded. Four were taken on board, and asked to point out the place where the money was kept. They replied that they had no money, whereupon their throats were deliberately cut. One of the crew who hid himself in a water tank was also discovered while the vessel was being searched for loot. He was asked to point out where the money was hidden, otherwise he would share the same fate as the others. Through fear he consented and took the pirates where the sand ballast was, and told them if they dug through they would find a bundle containing Rs. 5,000. This they did, and on securing the booty made away with it without injuring the informer. The matter has been reported to the authorities.- *Times of India*

# Conclusion

It would have been unusual for a deep-sea sailing ship not to have experienced at least some of the incidents recorded here, and many others too, during a lifetime of voyaging. Many ships and many more sailors ended their voyaging lives as a result of such diverse hazards, and their stories were never told.

Some, however, did get thrown a lifeline of fortune that cast rescue, deliverance and salvation their way. Some, indeed, were hauled back from the edge of the vortex like Ishmael, the sole survivor of the *Pequod's* destruction by 'Moby Dick', and returned from it. And some, the fortunate few, did tell their stories about what they experienced.

R.A. Fletcher in his 1928 book *In the Days of the Tall Ships* wrote about the life of sailing ship men as follows:

> *They were simply small companies of men living on floating specks on a vast ocean. They were sailing in little ships that sometimes were remarkable only for the hardships inflicted on those aboard them; they, or some of them, felt the intensely close communion with nature, as represented by wind and sea, which was inseparable from their waking moments and sometimes was with them in their dreams; they felt, too, the companionship of the stars by night; there was the never ending study of the ever varying clouds by day and the weather indications they give; they saw the fickle and wanton beauty of the always changing sea, and the cold brilliance of the moon and Southern Cross in southern latitudes; they felt the consciousness of the possibility of hidden and sudden peril, even in the finest weather: all these conditions, and many others, helped to make the sailor of the wind-driven ships the self-reliant cheerful man he always was, risking his life more often in a single voyage than most landsmen do from a sense of duty in ten years, and laughing death in the face.*